T0287807

The Sociological Interpretation of Dreams

To my mother

Bernard Lahire

The Sociological Interpretation of Dreams

Translated by
Helen Morrison

polity

First published in French as *L'Interprétation sociologique des rêves* © Éditions La Découverte, Paris, France, 2018
This English edition © Polity Press, 2020

Polity Press
65 Bridge Street
Cambridge CB2 1UR, UK

Polity Press
101 Station Landing
Suite 300
Medford, MA 02155, USA

The translation of this work was supported by the Institut Universitaire de France

ISBN-13: 978-1-5095-3794-5

A catalogue record for this book is available from the British Library.

Library of Congress Cataloging-in-Publication Data
Names: Lahire, Bernard, author.
Title: The sociological interpretation of dreams / Bernard Lahire ;
    translated by Helen Morrison.
Other titles: Interprétation sociologique des rêves. English
Description: Medford : Polity, 2020. | Includes bibliographical references
    and index. | Summary: "A major new account of dreams that rivals Freud's
    classic work"-- Provided by publisher.
Identifiers: LCCN 2019045571 (print) | LCCN 2019045572 (ebook) | ISBN
    9781509537945 (hardback) | ISBN 9781509537952 (epub)
Subjects: LCSH: Dream interpretation. | Dreams--Social aspects. |
    Sociology.
Classification: LCC BF1078 .L3313 2020 (print) | LCC BF1078 (ebook) | DDC
    154.6/3--dc23
LC record available at https://lccn.loc.gov/2019045571
LC ebook record available at https://lccn.loc.gov/2019045572

Typeset in Times New Roman 10 on 11 pt by
Servis Filmsetting Ltd, Stockport, Cheshire
Printed and bound in Great Britain by CPI Group (UK) Ltd, Croydon

For further information on Polity, visit our website: politybooks.com

Contents

Figures

Acknowledgements

This work would not have been possible without the time made available through my delegation to the Institut Universitaire de France and the funding allocated to completing it in the context of a research programme entitled 'Sociology of dreams: oneiric productions between the incorporated past, the circumstances of waking life and the context of nocturnal life' (*Sociologie des rêves: les productions oniriques entre passé incorporé, circonstances de la vie diurne et cadre de la vie nocturne*).

I would like to thank Howard Becker (formerly of the University of Washington), Gary Alan Fine (Northwestern University), Christian Baudelot (ENS Ulm) and Roger Chartier (Collège de France) for their kind support in this research project; Ludwig Crespin (Université de Clermont-Ferrand) for allowing me access to his thesis even before its submission; Perrine Ruby (INSERM) for our discussions prior to the writing of this book; Julien Barnier (Centre Max Weber, CNRS) for his invaluable 'schematic' contribution to the thinking behind this project; and to all the dreamers who, since January 2014, have regularly shared their dreams with me and who have put up with many hours of interviews, thus helping me to test the theoretical and methodological arguments which are discussed in this work. Their stories, both real and dreamed, will be revealed in a second volume.

Finally a special thanks to Nathan for sharing my moments of both enthusiasm and doubt and for his helpful and wise suggestions for some of the titles. Thanks also to Hugues Jallon for his attentive re-reading of the manuscript, for his advice and for his unwavering support.

Introduction:
A Dream for the Social Sciences

A dream is a sausage mill you feed your life into.
(Benjamin Whitmer, *Pike*, p. 168)

Dreams are both extremely appealing and extremely troubling for the sociologist. Their appeal lies in their potential to throw light on an aspect of our experience which generally remains intriguing and yet ultimately unfathomable. For any researcher with a taste for adventure, the prospect of attempting to comprehend the incomprehensible represents an exhilarating scientific challenge.

Yet the curiosity and intellectual excitement provoked by such a phenomenon can quickly give way to anxiety.

Initially this is linked to several characteristics of the object in question. The dream is a mental phenomenon, occurring when subjects are asleep and, consequently, when they are incapable of speaking. It is a product of the imagination but something which the dreamers themselves experience as though they were plunged into the most vivid reality. It is not always remembered on waking and, even when that is the case, is often quickly modified or forgotten, consequently rendering the researcher's task infinitely more difficult than that of getting subjects to talk about their waking activities. Finally, the dream appears strange, incoherent, delirious or incongruous in the eyes of the person who has produced it. The task is therefore theoretically and methodologically extremely challenging for researchers, and the study of dreams can rapidly turn into something of a nightmare.

And that is not all. Like the fairy-tale castle to which we seek to gain access, the dream-object is surrounded by thorns and guarded by a dragon. These thorns, this dragon, which render access to the dream so difficult, represent all the many past attempts to interpret dreams, and especially that associated with psychoanalysis. For a twenty-first-century researcher, it is difficult to dissociate dreams from the name of Sigmund Freud. The extent of Freud's work, with its multiple shifts, whether acknowledged or unspoken, the abundance of commentaries it has inspired, and the schools or trends which have shared its heritage are all enough to dampen the desire for knowledge and to keep the inquisitive at bay.

The social sciences have been notably absent from the history of scholarly study of sleep and dreams. In contrast to the sustained involvement of all forms of psychology, from psychoanalysis to cognitive psychology, or more recently of the neurosciences, from neuropsychiatry to neurobiology, the contribution made by the social sciences in general, and sociology in particular, remains extremely peripheral.

Some people will consider all this as only normal given that dreams are after all an activity which is both universal (everybody dreams), individual (everyone's dreams are unique) and par excellence involuntary. That sociologists, anthropologists or historians can speculate on the way in which the dream has been viewed, approached, interpreted by different eras, societies or groups is hardly surprising. But for them to try to probe into the logic of dream creation, to see it as the result of a process which is linked to the situation of dreamers within the social world is, on the contrary, far from obvious.

It was during a period spent at the University of California at Berkeley in 1997 that, during the course of my reading, I by chance stumbled, to my great interest, on the beginnings of a sociology of dreams.[1] The research programme which followed, the first scientific formulation of which will be read in these pages, took shape over the course of twenty years of reading and research in parallel with other projects. This knowledge of research on the subject of dreams, both past and present, emerging from very different disciplines (psychoanalysis, psychology, neuroscience, linguistics, sociology, anthropology, history, etc.) has enabled me to formulate a new integrative theory which, by taking as a starting point the knowledge gained from the synthetic model of interpretation imposed by Freud in his time, sets out to correct its weaknesses, its shortcomings and its errors by drawing on the many scientific developments which have emerged since the extraordinary feat of understanding represented by his book *The Interpretation of Dreams*, written on the cusp of the nineteenth and twentieth centuries.[2]

If we consider the dream-object as a *problem* which needs to resolved, then we must be able to define all the terms of this problem and to express them in a coherent manner in order to reach a satisfactory solution, both from a theoretical point of view and from one which is compatible with the empirical facts. An involuntary psychic activity occurring during sleep, the dream can also be characterised as a specific form of expression through which the dreamer works on all the various problems preoccupying him or her, with varying degrees of consciousness, during waking life. I will attempt to demonstrate that such a form of symbolic expression can only really be understood by taking into account a number of elements relating to the incorporated past of the dreamer, to the recent circumstances of his or her life, and to the specific context of sleep in which the dream occurs and which is characterised notably by a withdrawal from the flow of ordinary social interactions and demands, by the slackening of the reflexive control of mental activity, and by the establishment of a self-to-self communication which is predominantly visual and largely implicit.

These different elements will be explained in detail and set out in a *general formula for the interpretation of dreams* that will allow us to think in a more dynamic way about the process of dream-making. The dream will be more generally thought of as a specific *form of expression* situated within an expressive continuum (dream, daydream, delirium, hallucination, play, literary creation or artistic expression, etc.) that varies depending on the conditions in which the psychic activity takes place. Practical analogy, which is, along with association through contiguity, one of the elementary forms of human psychic life and a feature of its historic nature, will be placed at the heart of oneiric operations (of symbolisation, condensation, metaphorisation, substitution, etc.) which make the expression of the dream so unique. And, finally, we will show how the dream can be scientifically interpreted provided it is associated with a non-dream state which forms its existential background.

This theory of oneiric expression which has been formulated from within sociology, but which also brings together a whole range of multidisciplinary work, allows the dream to make its entry into the social sciences from a perspective that is both dispositional and contextual. Succeeding in making the dream a focus of study for the social sciences is a way of expanding the field of study of these sciences by allowing access to what, even today, still remains very much a *terra incognita*.

Norbert Elias drew attention to the limits which, without always fully realising it, researchers in the social sciences have long imposed on themselves by studying 'societies' within national limits and by concentrating on adult individuals who are already socially constituted, as though they had never been children. But the list of unexplored domains and dimensions does not end there. For researchers have until now focused their attention almost exclusively on the most collectively organised behaviours of waking individuals, neglecting the fact that approximately one-third of their time is spent asleep and that these periods of sleep are accompanied by dreams.

What do these dreams tell us about the lives of individuals and about the societies in which they live? How are the social experiences of dreamers woven into the fabric of their imaginations, even during those times when the intentional consciousness no longer controls the flow of images? These are the crucial questions that emerge, questions which sociologists have hardly even attempted to answer. When the objects of their investigations fall asleep, sociologists close their eyes.

But a theory of oneiric expression is also, and even more importantly, an opportunity to contribute to the transformation of the social sciences by restoring to them legitimate ambitions which specialisation and a standardised form of professionalism have tended to undervalue. By focusing their attention on such a curious object, and by agreeing to step outside their comfort zones and to embrace multidisciplinary learning, researchers can begin to focus on crucial scientific questions: the fundamental psychic mechanisms peculiar to the historical and linguistic beings represented by socialised human beings; the internalisation of all kinds of social regularities in the form of *incorporated dispositions* or *schema*, ready to find expression at the slightest occasion, even during sleep; the relationship between past and present in human experience; the respective share of conscious and unconscious, of the voluntary and involuntary, of control and absence of control in psychic operations and in human behaviour; and, finally, the freedom and determinism which, today more than ever before, stimulate debate on the 'reasons' for our acts or our thoughts. If the dream is indeed to make its entry into the great house of social sciences, it does so not with the intention of leaving the place unchanged but in order to shake up old habits and to reconfigure the space.

In contrast to what Freud believed (for reasons which will be closely examined), the dream will appear finally as the symbolic arena freed most completely from all the different forms of censorship, whether formal or moral, that lie mercilessly in wait for dreamers the moment they awake. The self-to-self communication in which the dream is expressed, overturning linguistic and narrative conventions, liberating dreamers from any kind of restraint, in a sense represents the most intimate of private diaries, the most unequivocal expression of all forms of freedom of speech. Consequently, for those who are interested in them, dreams thus offer the elements necessary for a deep and subtle understanding of what we are. Studying them essentially enables us to discover *our deep-seated and hidden preoccupations* and to understand what thought processes operate within us beyond the reach of our volition.

In all scientific research, a balance needs to be found between, on the one hand, the formulation of a general theoretical model along with the methods associated with it and, on the other hand, the identification of the socio-historical structures, processes, mechanisms or logics peculiar to specific individuals or groups of individuals within a social reality. In order to achieve such a balance, the results of the research will need to be published in the form of two separate volumes.

Because of its previously unexplored nature, the sociological interpretation of dreams, as a form of expression and as a unique process, initially called for the construction of an integrative and empirically pertinent theory – i.e. one which took into account all the theoretical-empirical knowledge already existent – that would enable the dream (the logics behind its production and not merely its uses and interpretations) to enter the realm of the social sciences. In this phase of the study, the sole purpose of any examples of dreams or of extracts of dreams included is to prove the relevance and the rich potential of the theoretical model or of the methodological tools associated with it. This implies not that such examples are mere illustrations but, rather, that their purpose is to demonstrate the capacity of the model to take on any example whatsoever and to emphasise the way that it is indeed implemented on the basis of predetermined methods. Such is the purpose of this first volume.

A systematic study of the precise corpus of dreams, such as I began to undertake in order to elaborate and support my theoretical and methodological thinking, implies, on the other hand, that the established theoretical model, even though still subject to improvements and transformations, be applied to the understanding of a clearly determined empirical material. It is then the reality being studied and its specificities which predominate. Both the theoretical model and the methodological tools take a back seat in order to turn the spotlight onto this reality which they have made it possible to understand. This will be the purpose of the second volume.

It is important, from my point of view, not to see this division into two volumes as representing any opposition between theory and empirical knowledge, given that theory and empiricism will be present in both volumes. It is simply that they do not occupy the same space within the framework of the scientific task undertaken. If a more specific description of the two phases of research is needed, it would be better to refer to an *experimental phase*, that of putting together an empirically based theoretical-methodological creation (by taking into account any empirical knowledge already accrued in the construction of a synthetic theoretical model), and a *phase of systematic exploration*, theoretically and methodologically orientated, on determined empirical corpora.

1

Advances in the Science of Dreams

> Reading is a terrible infliction, imposed upon all who write. In
> the process everything of one's own drains away. I often cannot
> manage to remember what I have that is new, and yet it is all
> new. The reading stretches ahead interminably, so far as I can see
> at present.
> (Sigmund Freud, letter to Wilhelm Fliess, 5 December 1898, in
> *The Origins of Psychoanalysis*, p. 270).

The poet and mathematician Jacques Roubaud emphasised the importance, in both the arts and the sciences, of turning to tradition in order to
enable genuine innovation to emerge:

> The new things we are to do, he declared, have their roots far back in
> the past. This is a phenomenon which extends far beyond the realm of
> poetry and can be observed in mathematics, in science. At any given
> time, the mathematical community becomes fascinated by certain
> problems, ignoring a whole range of others, which must be returned
> to at a much later stage. We must therefore see the past as a future,
> too. . . . When we try to innovate, can we really be sure that we are
> genuinely doing so? There is no way of knowing. But when I turn
> my attention to the poetry of the past, it is with a view to producing
> something that is different from what I have written previously. As a
> result, I am nevertheless looking to the future.[1]

Caught up in the current mode of thinking, with its emphasis on
rivalries and the latest 'wonder' and its tendency to assume that the most
recently published findings are invariably the correct ones, researchers can
easily end up losing sight of the fact that significant scientific advances
involve both absorbing the lessons from the past and setting their own
search for knowledge within the context of a long history during the
course of which many generations of scholars have learned, little by little,

to differentiate between the certain, the probable, the imaginable and the impossible.

By focusing their attention on key issues and by enthusiastically embracing a wide range of existing knowledge, scholars as diverse as Marx, Durkheim, Weber or Freud have thus succeeded in making genuine progress. Yet, as Erich Fromm pointed out with a certain irony: 'Of course if the social scientist has only trivial questions and does not turn his attention to fundamental problems, his "scientific method" achieves results sufficient for the endless papers which he needs to write in order to promote his academic career.'[2]

The history of scientific progress is composed of periods of specialisation, during which researchers work on specific issues but in a diffuse and uncoordinated manner (in different disciplines and in different sectors within each of those disciplines), and of periods of synthesis, where researchers join forces and discuss ideas which had hitherto been fragmented, translating into a shared language a body of significant results written in a wide range of disciplinary dialects and formulating integrative theories or synthetic models. It is within the context of this second phase that the thinking expressed in this work belongs.

And since any such synthesis requires a shared language, an emphasis on clarity is fundamental. The ability to get to the very core of problems, with the fewest detours possible, is a significant scientific challenge for the social sciences, which sometimes struggle to cast off the affectations of literary rhetoric. In a country such as France, there is all too often a tendency to confuse depth with obscurity or, in another genre, intelligence with lightness of style and verve. The penchant for theoretical mystery or for a quasi-literary style, encouraged by the leading universities, can only be explained by the aristocratic pleasure it brings to readers who feel themselves part of a chosen world in which everybody thinks they understand each other implicitly. We may, however, prefer those writers who eschew fine words and who instead favour an approach which advocates 'of two possible words, always choose the lesser' (Paul Valéry).

When the resolution of problems is favoured over the use of a seductive style, when the priority is to shed light on questions or to ask them more pertinently rather than to showcase writing skills or originality, then it is possible to get straight to the point. Nor does such an approach preclude writing well, but simply, 'Elegance is *not* what we are trying for' (Wittgenstein).

Armed with a knowledge of the history of scientific research, the ambition to solve a wide range of fundamental problems, a multidisciplinary curiosity, a willingness to see very different types of research brought together rather than set in opposition to each other, a scientific belief in the possibility of real progress in knowledge, and a policy of clarity in terms both of reasoning and of writing, every researcher is in a position to make genuine progress.

The dream before Freud

Dreams have long fascinated scholarly circles in the Western world, some-times with unreasonable expectations. Scholars have sought to penetrate the mystery of dreams, starting with those of important figures (kings, chiefs, heroes, etc.), in an attempt to decipher their divine or demonic messages, or else to predict the future either of dreamers or of the world in which they live.[3] From the eleventh century in the West, the dream begins to lose 'its sacred character' and become increasingly 'democratised', according to the words of the historian Jacques Le Goff,[4] with the gradual emergence of an interest in the dreams of more lowly people which begin to be credited with meaning.[5] Then, in the twelfth century, 'dreams, it might be said, begin to acquire a more tangible form and are increasingly linked to the particular nature of the dreamer, to his or her physical exist-ence and personal emotions, to the notion of sleep as a physical reality, just as much as to the influence of angels and of demons.'[6] At the very heart of Christianity, the possibility of a psychological science of dreams begins to emerge, for not only did writers view dreams as psychological phenomena,[7] they also enabled them to be perceived as autobiographical realities.[8] It was not until the seventeenth century, however, and notably with the arrival of Descartes, that dreams began to be associated with the dreaming individual, and in particular with the brain and nervous system, rather than with any supernatural forces. It is this 'physiological and indi-vidualistic paradigm',[9] even when it comes under criticism, which will give rise to a considerable body of scholarly research on the dream over the course of the second half of the nineteenth century and the first half of the twentieth century.

But as early as the second half of the eighteenth century, one writer, Abbé Jérôme Richard, canon of Vézelay, a learned man and member of the Institut de France, to which he was elected in 1795 in the field of zoology, produced the first major scientific study on dreams, following in the footsteps of Descartes' *Treatise of Man* (1633). If he concedes to oneirocriticism[10] that a handful of rare prophets or saints might have had premonitory dreams, his argument is that, in general, dreams have no connection with the future. Often cited as a precursor by the nineteenth-century writers who were seeking to establish a science of dreams and sleep, Abbé Richard was deeply convinced that scientific knowledge could bring men happiness: 'Would it not be contributing to their happiness to teach them the true cause of dreams and how little these concern the future?'[11] Moreover, in his *Théorie des songes*, published in 1766, he launches a scathing attack on the 'prejudices', 'ineptitudes', 'superstitions', 'deceptions' and 'lies' which, since time immemorial, have continued to dominate thinking on the dream. In particular, Artemidorus of Daldis is cited as being someone who has learned from 'fortune-tellers' the 'art of fooling the mob'.[12]

Abbé Richard wondered in particular why God would give us access to our future in dreams which the majority of people are incapable of understanding. His intention was therefore to rid the dream of the 'marvellous' and the 'supernatural' by referring in highly Cartesian terms to the 'fibres of the brain' and the action of 'animal spirits'. By distancing himself in relation to oneirocriticism, Jérôme Richard sought to secularise dreams, relocating them in the human realm. But, most importantly, his ideas pave the way towards an explanation of dreams through the mind of the dreamer who is not always attentive to what he or she produces and who does not constantly control the flow of his or her mental images:

> The chaotic way in which the imagination presented all these images during sleep, and which left such a marked impression on the spirit, becomes the sole focus of attention on waking; astonishment and surprise overwhelm us; while the habit of reflecting on what has happened is enough to convince us that we have shaped these dreams ourselves without realising it, as in the case of the thousands of other natural and essential actions to which we need pay no attention, even though they are no less significant, but which are perceived, moreover, as so entirely natural that nobody would dream of seeking for the marvellous or the divine in them.[13]

Throughout the nineteenth century, gripped by the same feverish quest for scientific knowledge, many scholars undertook to note down either their own dreams, or those of people close to them, in the hope of reaching a better understanding of this essentially nocturnal symbolic production.[14] More systematic and accurate[15] research was conducted by French, Belgian or German writers such as Moreau de la Sarthe, Gotthilf Heinrich von Schubert, Théodore Jouffroy, Antoine Charma, Alfred Maury, Léon d'Hervey de Saint-Denys, Karl Albert Scherner or Joseph Delbœuf,[16] who would precede and prepare the ground for the Freudian approach to the interpretation of dreams.[17] This latter, the most famous, would synthesise the preceding research and would draw upon a number of case studies to set out an original vision based on a theory of the unconscious.[18]

Whatever the originality of his thinking, Freud must be seen in the context of an extended body of earlier research which rendered his own work possible. He sifted through good and bad arguments or concepts, refining the former by giving them new strength and dismissing the latter. He hierarchised and organised the remaining elements into a coherent ensemble, an integrating theoretical model based on a theory of repressed consciousness and censorship. Strictly speaking, not one of his findings can be described as truly original.

Reading the work of his predecessors that constitutes the sources of his theory, no reader can fail to be struck by the extraordinary work of reappropriation undertaken by the father of psychoanalysis. Like all great scholars, Freud clearly invented very little: symbolism, dramatisation, condensation, displacement, visualisation, the secondary role of both internal bodily stimuli and external stimuli during sleep in the creation of dreams, the association of ideas, the unconscious, censorship and the circumvention of censorship, transference or projection, etc. – all of these concepts can be found, at some point, in the work of the various writers who preceded him.

His role is nevertheless by no means insignificant. It is as though Freud found himself faced with a mass of objects of diverse origins, crammed into dusty boxes in a junk room and including various Lego blocks some of which were originally part of the construction of an enormous space-ship, for which the assembly instructions had long since disappeared. His task was therefore 1) to sift any useless objects or irrelevant Lego blocks from those which can be used to construct an object – the spaceship – the finished shape of which he did not initially even know; 2) to clean or repair each piece in order to restore it to its former glory; and 3) to assemble the blocks in such a way that each one was correctly positioned as the construction gradually took shape. Such a metaphor is limited in scope if we consider that at some stage there were indeed assembly instructions and pictures of the spaceship. Yet it enables us to understand both that scholars stumble against aspects of reality which lie outside their own points of view and that they make progress by gradually rejecting blind alleys and by organising, in a more satisfactory way than hitherto, the different elements on which they agree.

For this reason, it is impossible to consider *The Interpretation of Dreams* as *the* book which would completely transform the history of the relationship between man and the dream. Yet this is precisely what Michel Foucault does in describing an abrupt switch from the non-significant to the significant, from the meaningless to the meaningful, from the unintelligible to the intelligible: 'With the *Traumdeutung*',[19] he wrote,

> the dream makes its entry into the field of human meanings. In the oneiric experience the meaning of the behaviour seems to blur. As waking consciousness darkens and flickers out, the dream seems to loosen, and finally to untie the knot of meanings. Dream had been taken as if it were the nonsense of consciousness. We know how Freud turned this proposition around, making the dream the meaning of the unconscious.[20]

All very elegant, very clear and extremely seductive for those who relish dramatic revelations, but this is nevertheless historically and anthropolog-ically inaccurate. When it was first published in 1900, *The Interpretation of Dreams* did not appear as a lightning bolt of knowledge suddenly illumi-nating the dark night of ignorance.

Foucault's Western and intellectualist ethnocentrism – which he shares with many others – allows him loftily to ignore all the shamanic practices of traditional societies, along with those of Mesopotamian, Egyptian or

Greek oneirocritics, as well as the numerous authors whose keys to the meaning of dreams have punctuated the history of humanity. The philosopher's stance is all the more problematic in that Freud himself claimed to be closer to Artemidorus of Daldis (second century AD) than to certain scientists who see dreams simply as disorganised sequences of random images.[21] The arrival of the dream in the field of human meanings quite simply preceded Freud by several thousand years.

Taking a charitable view, it might be argued that Foucault's focus was on the history of human sciences and that, when he refers to the arrival of the dream in the field of human meanings, he is in fact looking at the arrival of the dream as an object of study in the field of human sciences. But, here again, the dream had made its grand entrance more than a century before Freud. Many others before him had, each in their own way, considered that dreams had meaning and that this meaning was in some way connected to the physical, emotional or cultural experience of the dreamer.

And after Freud came many more who would pursue his thinking and put his model to the test. The Freudian conception would thus become the object of scrutiny of other key figures claiming to be associated with psychoanalysis (Otto Rank, Carl Gustav Jung, Alphonse Mæder, Erich Fromm, Thomas M. French, etc.) or other branches of psychology (Joseph Breuer, Théodore Flournoy, Alfred Adler, Eugen Bleuler, etc.). Several decades later it would in particular find itself the object of radical criticism coming from psychology[22] and neuroscience.[23] The message is crystal clear: nothing begins or ends with Freud.

The need for an integrative theory

The Austrian physicist Erwin Schrödinger had a rather radical way of opposing any form of fragmentation of knowledge: 'It seems plain and evident, yet it needs to be said: the isolated knowledge obtained by a group of specialists in a narrow field has in itself no value whatsoever, but only in its synthesis with the rest of knowledge and only in as much as it really contributes to this synthesis something toward answering the demand ... 'who are we?'[24] For him, specialisation was never 'a virtue but an unavoidable evil', and he believed it was necessary to contribute to 'the integrated totality of knowledge'.[25] In all fields of knowledge, a willingness to synthesise learning is the contributory factor in solving the most difficult problems. It is by linking, combining, bringing together the solutions to an assortment of micro-problems, often formulated within different sectors of knowledge, that the greatest problems can finally be resolved.

It was by proceeding in this manner that the British mathematician Andrew Wiles was able to prove the famous 'Fermat's last theorem',[26] considered by many mathematicians to be insoluble. And it was also, albeit in different ways, the method chosen by a mathematician such as Alexander Grothendieck. The latter, who saw the fragmentation of scientific work as a major problem,[27] was not intellectually satisfied unless the problem he was working on led him back to a more general problem. He sought the overarching point of view which enabled each case to be understood as one possible case and only ceased working on the resolution of a problem at the point where he could no longer go back to a more general form of it.

This was exactly what Maurice Halbwachs so rightly observed, long before Wiles's proof or Grothendiek's work: 'A mathematical proof is an analysis only in appearance and after the event. In reality it implies a synthesis, in other words the merging of several propositions which have been established by separate groups of researchers.'[28] This observation applies equally aptly to sociological models for the interpretation of human behaviours:

> In my own experience I have found that, for sociologists, the chance of making a discovery is greater the less specialised and narrow, and the richer and more diverse, is the learned knowledge with which they set out to work. Those who are richly equipped theoretically and empirically can receive many stimuli for scientific investigations by keeping their eyes open to previously unknown connections, to individual observations that are not quite ordinary and are perhaps somewhat unexpected, to ill-fitting concepts that can be corrected, and much more – there is much to be done.[29]

The study of dreams is no exception to this rule, and by linking the constituent elements of dreams studied by very different researchers real progress has already been made and will continue to be made in the future.

From the nineteenth century onwards in particular,[30] and throughout the twentieth century, European scholars began to study dreams scientifically by keeping notebooks of their own dreams,[31] or by relying on other people's accounts of their dreams, by observing certain nocturnal events or by deliberately provoking them, by noting the diurnal events which had preceded dreams, and by analysing the personality traits of dreamers or studying their personal histories, interests and preoccupations. As a result, there are a great number of dream accounts and a considerable amount of information about dreamers, and research certainly does not suffer as a result of any shortage of data.[32] The plentiful examples of dreams in the hundreds of available studies means there is no need to plunge blindly into the reckless production of new data, as though nothing had previously been done. What is most lacking, on the other hand, is a theoretical framework which would enable researchers to know what kind of information is worth collecting, what precautions need to be taken in order to gather it, and what hierarchies and connections need to be set up between the various sources of information in order to give dream reports a scientifically acceptable meaning. What is needed therefore is a well-defined approach which allows the cases of previously published and interpreted dreams to be integrated within the researcher's own investigation.

If, along with Norbert Elias, we refer to 'a unified theoretical framework' to describe the work of synthesis and of general theoretical reformulation carried out by certain researchers which is sometimes based on new data but also, and more importantly, on bringing together in a previously untried way data uncovered by researchers who either do not communicate or who communicate at cross purposes without seeing what their common points might be, then we are obliged to admit that Freudian theory fits this description rather well. In spite of the many attempts to totally discredit psychoanalysis, coming from extremely different sectors of learning,[33] a serious understanding of the history of dream studies leaves no doubt that Freud proposed the first major synthetic and unifying theoretical model of this type.[34] Much criticised, often justifiably and sometimes inappropriately or excessively, the Freudian model of dream interpretation has remained unsurpassed since its first appearance,[35] even if some researchers have made laudable efforts so to do.[36]

If this is indeed the case, it is because Freud made sure he drew on all the research and studies available at the time of writing in order to propose an original synthesis based on a theory of psychic activity. In doing so, he was extending knowledge of human behaviour by focusing on 'symbolic representations being evolved from the previous fund with regard to segments of the universe that were previously unrepresented, or perhaps less clearly and succinctly represented, by social symbols.'[37]

A satisfactory theory of the dream is a theory capable of resolving a series of micro-problems attached to its focus of study, of measuring the relative importance of these in relation to each other, and of finding a way of expressing them in a coherent manner. If, moreover, this theory turns out to be capable of considering objects other than simply the dream-object by making it possible to understand in what sense the dream is merely *a particular case of the possible*, then it becomes an even more powerful general theory. From this perspective, Freud was one of the greatest theoreticians-synthesizers in the history of the study of dreams, combining questions of method (free associations) and very broad theoretical questions (the unconscious, repression, censorship, the different properties of the dream-work, nocturnal perceptions, day residues, etc.) from the starting point of an overarching ambition to throw light on the mysteries of human psychic activity.

Without the perspective offered by wider knowledge, no significant progress would be possible on the subject of dreams. Freud was particularly aware of the importance of knowing 'the first step to take'.[38] For 'all one's interest in a problem is evidently insufficient unless one knows as well of a path of approach that will lead to its solution.'[39] His letters to Wilhelm Fliess (doctor and otolaryngologist) during the period in which he was writing *The Interpretation of Dreams* demonstrate the immense task of resolving problems and of synthesis based on the mobilising guidelines which Freud had adopted in order to produce a coherent and robust general theory. In a letter of 2 March 1899, he wrote: 'The realm of uncertainty is still enormous, problems abound, and I understand theoretically only the smallest fraction of what I do. But every few days light dawns, now here, now there, and I have grown modest and count on long years of work and patient compilation, backed by a few serviceable ideas after the holidays, after our meetings.'[40]

Scientific progress and relativism

Contrary to what might be suggested by a certain relativist vision which tends to see scientific research in terms only of irreconcilable points of view, changing depending on the era and on scientific or extra-scientific contexts, incapable of mutual communication and consequently impossible to link together or to debate, the problems I shall be discussing in this book are problems which have been constantly scrutinised and reformulated and ones to which many generations of researchers throughout history have tried to find answers. And, rather than putting these continuities down to simple cultural invariants or to some kind of *epistemes*, it seems to me that the persistence of problems which represent a stumbling block for researchers stems from the very structure of the object under scrutiny.

When confronted with the reality of the facts, researchers cannot avoid encountering these problems since they are dealing with the properties of the real. They can, depending on their area of interest, their personal scientific culture and the state of scientific research, reformulate the problems; they can even discover other problems that their predecessors had not seen, but they never completely invent the reality of these problems. And when they succeed in solving certain problems, or when they manage to integrate all of them in a coherent theory, they are undoubtedly achieving something that can be called scientific progress.

It seems to me particularly important to reaffirm the potential for scientific progress, given that the relativist mentality currently in vogue has turned it into something of a taboo, a situation which scarcely encourages the desire to achieve significant advances.

> One has sometimes the feeling that sociologists have given up the hope that it is possible to make discoveries in their field as significant and verifiable as discoveries in the field of the natural sciences. Lacking the conviction that it is possible to make such discoveries, they obviously fail to make them. There are many discoveries yet to be made in the field of the human sciences![41]

A relativist or constructivist climate has, in fact, pervaded scholarly communities within the human and social sciences, inhibiting any desire to compare rival research programmes, all of which are consequently regarded as points of view equally worthy of interest even before close examination, and discouraging any search within the history of human and social sciences for any fixed points which might enable invariants to be identified and scientific progress to be made.

In spite of repeated attacks on the notion of 'progress', the history of the 'discovery of the unconscious',[42] like the numerous attempts to analyse oneiric production, show that the scientific study of dreams is indeed making substantial progress, that certain issues are becoming sharper and more precise while others disappear for want of coherence, robustness or failure to concord with available facts.

From this point of view, certain historical or ethnological studies on the dream can prove to be somewhat problematic for researchers seeking to take the science of dreams forward. In fact, both scientific historians and ethnologists often suspend judgement entirely on the veracity of the knowledge of the actors they are studying (scholars from the past just as much as shamans or oneirocritics). The study of the social usages of dream accounts, and of the significance attributed to them in different societies or in periods predating our societies, conveys the impression that, given that each conception of the dream has its own logic and rationale, there are consequently no real advances in knowledge but, instead, only cultural discontinuities in the understanding of the oneiric reality. Yet it would be no insult to say that the Guajiros people (a Native American group living close to the Colombian and Venezuelan border)[43] or oneirocritics such as Artemidorus of Daldis, who was already indicating 'a certain distance between the supernatural and the divine',[44] were wrong to see dreams as premonitions, that the Christian Middle Ages were scientifically wrong to believe that dreams were divine or demonic messages or that certain neurobiologists for a while erroneously believed that dreams only manifested themselves during REM sleep ...

If the human and social sciences simply confined themselves to observing that Artemidorus of Daldis proposed one method of interpreting dreams while Freud proposed a different one based on a theory of the unconscious, they would be subscribing to this relativism.[45] The history of modes of appropriation (types of reaction and of interpretation) of dreams should not preclude the history of scientific progress in the field of dream study. We should be able to say that those who attributed a premonitory function to dreams, who interpreted them as prophecies or who saw them as having divine or demonic origins were wrong, as were those who thought that dreams had no meaning and were merely a random sequence of images, sounds and emotions, or those who believed that dreams were rooted in the traumas of birth, in foetal experiences or in the collective unconscious and those who were convinced that they were provoked exclusively by the stimuli of the immediate surroundings or by internal corporal stimuli during sleep. It should be possible to track the history of opinions and practices linked to the cure of scrofula, to telepathy, astrology, prophecy or premonition, without allowing it to be thought for a single instant that these have any pertinence whatsoever in the light of the known facts.

Yet, in the eyes of some people, such suggestions are undoubtedly already totally sacrilegious and are simply evidence of the ethnocentrism of the researcher today. How can a balance be achieved between the analysis of historically and ethnologically differentiated ways of interpreting or understanding dreams and the scientific knowledge of oneiric facts? The solution to this type of problem seems to me in fact a rather simple one. It involves recognising that we are dealing with two very different objects. The first is *human activity associated with a phenomenon*, the dream account, which is not investigated as such but examined purely from the perspective of how it is used and appropriated, the practices and opinions it gives rise to, etc.; the second, on the other hand, is *the human activity which gives rise to the phenomenon* in question, and therefore the very process of production of the images in the dream and the dream account. In one case, the uses and appropriations of dream accounts are studied through the sociology, anthropology or history of the representations and practices surrounding dreams.[46] In the other, the dream itself is studied in the context of a science of dreams.

Declaring: 'This is what this society or these scholars said about dreams or this is the cultural context to which they belonged', and sometimes trying, subsequently, to link these usages, commentaries and interpretations to the characteristics of a given era or society is a perfectly legitimate approach. But it should not lead to a scientific relativism which renounces any notion of scientific development or progress in the study of oneiric phenomena. Paradoxically, the same relativist researchers can, with some justification, accuse certain researchers within their field of a lack of seriousness while failing to see, from a relativist point of view, that they are developing a discourse different from their own which would be just as relevant and as worthy of interest as the one they are themselves developing. And, similarly, it would be highly surprising if these researchers did not manage to agree on the fact that predicting the future of dreamers by studying their dreams has no scientific relevance whatsoever. Faced with the evidence, it is hard to carry to its conclusion a relativist perspective both as a researcher in competition with other researchers and as a scientist implementing a rational argument based on facts.[47] The relativist point of view is useful in research in order to avoid stifling practices and opinions by labelling them as superstition, erroneous belief or nonsense. But it becomes extremely problematic when it leads to researchers no longer wanting to seek out the truth of the facts and to distinguish true from false. We must therefore find the happy medium between a radical relativism, which denies any progress in the history of knowledge, and a science-based dogmatism, which denies any social influence on the knowledge acquired.

Yet, the researcher seeking to develop an understanding of the true nature of the dream, of how it is actually produced by specific dreamers, cannot behave as though all representations of the dream were more or less the same. He or she must observe that certain interpretive approaches used in the past have been abandoned because of a lack of empirical evidence, while others were confirmed, consolidated and refined. Similarly, they will note the useful action of researchers making regular efforts over time to propose original syntheses of the most reliable evidence afforded by current scientific knowledge.

It could, of course, be pointed out that Western scholars who, from the seventeenth century onwards, no longer credited dreams with any premonitory capacity or established any connection between oneiric productions and spirits, demons, angels, the devil or God are part of a historic process of the secularisation of the world. Gods and demons have been gradually driven out from all domains, including that of dreams. Yet this historical relativism does not prevent the idea that, in the course of this socio-historical process, we now have a clearer and more pertinent view of the reality of the situation, and that it is, as a result, more accurate to say that the dream is a symbolic production related to the life of the dreamer rather than a coded message sent by supernatural entities.

It is, moreover, not as simple as all that to think in terms of 'era' or 'society', for the early stages of our thinking sometimes find their roots in writers from antiquity who were partially at odds with their cultural milieu and who sought, albeit hesitantly, compromise solutions, which other writers, even long afterwards, can still use as a basis for their own work. Hippocrates (460 BC), for example, cleverly distinguished between supernatural dreams, which fall within the realm of magic, and natural dreams, which are a matter for medicine, and consequently nineteenth-century writers working on dreams were able to refer to him, thus stepping into a breach which had already been opened.[48]

Nor is Hippocrates an isolated case. He is by no means the only writer from the ancient world to make a distinction between 'natural dreams' and other kinds of dreams. The Alexandrian doctor Herophilus (third century BC) also distinguished between dreams inspired by a god and dreams which he referred to as 'natural'.

> This tradition, as Vincent Barras so rightly points out, which would certainly not claim to be the only medical approach to dreams in antiquity, stands out, from Hippocrates to Galen, in so far as it makes a clear distinction, in terms of the practical use to which medicine can put dreams, between prophetic or divine dreams and dreams linked to a physical state, which, consequently, are the prerogative of medicine. No history has as yet been written going into the details of the theoretical elaborations and the practical uses to which dreams have been put, from Galen right up to the nineteenth century. Yet it is certain that some elements of this ancient claim still find an echo today with some medical writers, at the crucial moment when the 'science of dreams' is taking shape.[49]

A further scientific step would undoubtedly have to be taken before dream images can be seen as anything other than the simple products of perceptive stimuli, external or internal-corporal – in other words, something depending on the past and present experience of the dreamer. But scientific breakthroughs come about gradually, a small step at a time, and the confidence of scientists in the nineteenth and twentieth centuries draws its strength from the hesitant progress of writers from a distant past.

For its part, scientific realism does not prevent psychologists, anthropologists or sociologists understanding that dreamers can, for cultural reasons, dream of spirits, angels, demons, of the devil or of God, or believe that what they have dreamt has been dictated, in some way or other, by supernatural entities. If scholars are in a position to assert that the dream has, *in reality*, nothing at all to do with entities such as these, which are the products of collective representations, they are at the same time perfectly able to take such beliefs into account when they are interpreting dreams from the past or dreams originating from societies different from our own.

The art of limping: the end of pure speculation

Scholars who have contributed to the development of the science of dreams abandoned the domain of pure speculation either by transforming themselves into the object of study or by closely questioning other people. This involved, on a more or less regular basis, keeping dream notebooks, with or without additional commentary, and conducting various kinds of experiments during sleep in order to record the possible effects of external stimuli on the nature of dreams, etc.

For example, when, in 1861, Karl Albert Scherner, philosopher and psychologist, published *Das Leben des Traums* (The life of dreams), a book which was both much criticised and much quoted by Sigmund Freud in his own work because it emphasised the symbolic aspect of oneiric language, he highlighted from the outset the importance of seeing the dream in terms of empirical material:

> Let us look first of all at how we should not proceed in order to explore the soul if we wish to obtain a decisive result. Results cannot be obtained on the basis only of pure speculation, since the action purely of reason alone, without account being taken of what is observed (thus without regard to the receptivity of the faculty of knowing, which must of necessity be linked to the object of that knowledge), remains forever and eternally only a subjective unilateral movement of the mind, which – however sublime the subject who is thus philosophising may feel themselves, however ingenious, rigorous and refined the thought process being developed – ultimately states only what the free flowing meditation wished to think, in other words without concern for the real psychic object, and precisely that which

the freely chosen foundation of the system and its consequences allowed to be understood of the soul; and not what the psychic object itself ordered to be said on this subject, and which would lead to a sharp, penetrating and exhaustive examination of the subjectivity of the mind.[50]

Sigmund Freud has been much criticised. He has been accused of overzealous interpretation or excessive theoretical generalisation, as well as sometimes lacking methodological rigour in his method of gathering the empirical material on which he based his analyses and in the implementation of his method of interpreting dreams. All this is not unfounded, and, in the interests of science, I shall in the course of this project be continuing the critical process already set in motion by very many others. Yet it is important not to overlook the fact, in my opinion an essential one, that Freud nevertheless conducted himself as a true scientist. He adopted a scientific approach by using the work of all those who had put forward analyses of the process of dreaming or interpretations of specific dreams in order to construct his own original synthesis. And it was as a scientist too that he based his interpretations on the cases of patients who had undergone analysis, or on the individual dreams of people whose life story, medical history and situation at the time of the dream were generally well known to him. In spite of the limits inherent in any operation undertaken by ambitious theorists – and Freud was certainly one of those – all this is a thousand times more useful than the way certain philosophers have referred to dreams.

Thus, the same Karl Albert Scherner completely swamps his undeniable psychological contribution in a philosophical style referred to by Freud as 'pompous gibberish' (and described by one of his own followers as 'mystical confusion' and as 'sumptuous and dazzling meandering').[51] Any informed reader today could observe that Freud's writing, with its quest for conceptual clarity and for acquired and verifiable knowledge, is infinitely closer to prevailing scientific practice than Scherner's rhetoric, mired in metaphysical turns of phrase full of ornate metaphors. Scherner's text, which over the course of a good hundred pages pompously explores philosophical generalities on the dream and on the life of the soul before then embarking on an attempt to untangle dreams, to analyse them, to link them to the experiences of the dreamer's lives and to classify them, is constantly torn between an aristocratic desire for philosophy – 'it is this that has received the supreme dignities of the mind in the human world'[52] – and the scientific desire to produce empirical knowledge. Freud would have needed a great deal of patience to extract the most relevant scientific elements from a prose which borders sometimes on prose poem, sometimes on spiritualist rantings.[53]

It is also the case, for example, of Alfred Schütz, social phenomenologist and pupil of Husserl, who saw the dream – forty-five years after the publication of *The Interpretation of Dreams* – as a 'limited domain of signification' among others, simply repeating in another theoretical language (one referring to 'multiple realities') the idea of the psychologist William James on the different orders of reality: 'All these worlds – the world of dreams, imageries and phantasms, especially the world of art, the world of religious experience, the world of scientific contemplation, the play world of the child, and the world of the insane – are finite provinces of meaning', and, for that reason, each has a 'peculiar cognitive style'.[54] And since the author has no means of taking any further the description of the 'multiple realities' to which he refers, since he has neither any means of accessing reality nor, as a result, empirical material on which to work, he can only stretch out indefinitely this general and very elastic hypothesis of the multiplicity of realities.

Moreover, Schütz believes the problem of going from one 'world' or 'province to the other' can be resolved by referring to 'experiences of shock'. For him, the experience of falling asleep 'as the leap into the world of dreams', the moment the theatre curtain is raised and the audience is projected into the world of the stage, the visual concentration on a painting, the snatching up of the toy by the child in order to enter the world of play, 'Kierkergaard's experience of the "instant" as the leap into the religious sphere', as well as the 'decision of the scientist to replace all emotional participation in the affairs of "this world"' by 'a disinterested, contemplative attitude', are all examples of such experiences of shock.[55]

It is, however, hard to see what the image of the 'shock' – or the added one of the 'instant' taken from Kierkegaard's work – brings to the understanding of all these realities, given that it consists only in pinpointing the moment of transition from one sphere to the other by describing it as a 'shock'. Of the cognitive processes underlying all of these experiences or specific to one 'sphere' or another, or of objective contexts (situations such as that of the sleeper or of the child at play, institutions such as the museum, the laboratory, the church, etc.), nothing will be learned, since the person speaking has not given themselves the means to enable us to understand them. And, rather than studying the sociogenesis of the 'disinterested contemplative attitude' and of the scientific institutions which support it, which would inevitably take it into the domain of the history of social sciences, he turns it into a question of an *individual decision* on the part of the researcher.

But the truth of this type of philosophical discourse on dreams, stripped of any empirical foundation, is in fact provided by the author when he explains the purely verbal operation of transcription that, in spite of everything, allows him to continue to write on subjects with which he is not himself familiar by a strategy of drawing on existing knowledge:[56] 'All this Freud and psychoanalysis have thoroughly studied, and our present intention is restricted to translating some of their results, important for the topic at hand, into our language and to giving them their place within our theory.'[57] The manner in which the philosopher unashamedly dips into empirical theories (painstakingly formulated by scholars synthesising in a critical manner the many results from the empirical research of other scholars and working on their own empirical material) for elements to flesh out 'his own theory' clearly demonstrates the relationship of domination which develops between the plunderer (philosophy) and the plundered (the human sciences). There are grounds for seriously questioning the basis for such 'second-degree sociological theories', as Jean-Claude Passeron[58] terms them, where the only knowledge of the real world comes from what others say in their research, and which take from this research only the theoretical dimension (ignoring the empirical methods and materials used), the only one they have learned to recognise and respect. 'All too often in the science of the mind and of thought processes', wrote Alfred Maury in 1861, 'patient and methodological observation, the only sure path which can lead us to the truth, are replaced by conceptions drawn from preconceived ideas or purely speculative theories; hence the very slow progress made by psychology.'[59]

Another significant example is that of the Swiss philosopher and psychiatrist Ludwig Binswanger. In spite of being a psychiatrist, it was as a philosopher that he wrote the text entitled *Rêve et existence*. And what does he have to say on the subject of the dream? For Binswanger, positive science 'cannot take into account the totality of the world, a world in which we live, we act and we feel, and which is for us no simple object of knowledge. It is only the appreciation, through philosophy, of the spiritual dimension of our experience of the world that can truly open the gates of the dream for us.'[60] The philosopher is leading us into a major regression here. He is suggesting nothing short of abandoning science and looking to religion, to the mysterious or to spirituality, under the pretext that science cannot explain everything. But Binswanger might have asked himself what such excursions out of the realm of science would really produce other than a halt to all knowledge, which would instead be replaced by feelings, beliefs and a certain form of acceptance of the mystery of life.[61] Freud's reaction to this comment is therefore perfectly normal from a scientific point of view: 'Faced with the metaphysical and religious intoxication that he then discovers in Binswanger's work, Freud contrasts . . . his own sobriety as a scientist.'[62]

Knowledge of the real, whether physical, biological or social, requires a combination of theoretical viewpoints, of the resulting methods of accessing reality, and of empirical materials produced according to these methods and interpreted from the relevant theoretical viewpoints. This process, which demands detailed knowledge of all the research undertaken in the relevant field and of how the various elements can be linked and critically reappropriated, as well as a willingness to engage in the production of new empirical materials capable of providing answers to some of the questions raised in the research process, is often a very long one requiring quiet patience rather than the haste of someone making a great deal of commotion without really advancing.

In the conclusion to his famous work entitled *Beyond the Pleasure Principle* (1920), Freud, who was continuing to develop his theoretical model of psychic activity, acknowledges the vast number of questions 'to which at present we have no answers'. However, as a tenacious scientist, he does not despair of this situation:

> We must be patient and await fresh methods and occasions of research. We must be ready, too, to abandon a path that we have followed for a time, if it seems to be leading to no good end. Only believers, who demand that science shall be a substitute for the catechism they have given up, will blame an investigator for developing or even transforming his views. We may take comfort, too, for the slow advances of our scientific knowledge in the words of the poet:

> Was man nicht erfliegen kann, muss man erhinken.

> Die Schrift sagt, es ist keine Sünde zu hinken.[63]

We could not put it better.

On the scientific interpretation of dreams

This book is based on the gamble – a theoretically and empirically founded one – that a scientific interpretation of dreams is possible. This implies, first of all, setting aside the notion that the dream might be merely a random and incoherent flow of images, sounds and sensations which do not stem from any regulatory context and are not subject to any organising process. This conception of the dream has been held by many scholars, sometimes in reaction to ancient beliefs of oneiromancy[64] which attribute coherence to dreams but in the form of some sort of premonitory message.

In *The Interpretation of Dreams* Freud attempted, as others had done, to focus on finding sense rather than nonsense and absurdity, coherence rather than incoherence. It is on this note that the Swiss psychiatrist Eugen Bleuler wrote to him on 13 September 1913: 'Your greatness lies in having turned the non-sense and madness of the dream into something rational.'[65] It is no coincidence that, in his major work, Freud refers to *Oneirocritica* by Artemidorus of Daldis, since he shares with the famous oneirocritic the idea that dreams are not devoid of meaning. Knowing that, in Freud's time, 'most scholarly oneirologists perceived nocturnal visions as gratuitous and random phenomena',[66] it is not difficult to understand why the father of psychoanalysis should take an interest in those who, for the first time in history, had attributed meaning to dreams and established relationships between the state of wakefulness and that of dreaming, even if they did so in the scientifically inadequate sense of a premonition.

Freud was not the first person to give a scientific meaning to dreams. He was, for example, preceded by the French sinologist Léon d'Hervey de Saint-Denys (1822–1892). The latter observed critically in 1867 that a certain Albert Lemoine, the 1855 winner of a competition set up by the Academy of Moral and Political Science on the theory of sleep and dreams, presupposed that the dream was simply an attempt to bring together completely disparate perceptions.[67] Yet, twenty years after the publication of *The Interpretation of Dreams*, the zoologist Yves Delage could still claim in a peremptory manner that 'most of our dreams, let us say ninety-nine out of one hundred, are without any particular significance, and we should expect no more from them than we would obtain from a novel, that distraction from the monotony of real life.'[68] And, since the end of the 1960s, it is from the domain of the neurosciences that doubts about the very possibility of interpreting dreams have sometimes been expressed. For some researchers in this field, the dream would be no more than a 'hotchpotch of all sorts of images and impressions' produced by 'random stimulation of the brain',[69] and therefore no interpretation of dreams would be possible.

Belief in the possibility of a scientific interpretation also implies the conviction that the interpretation is not the mysterious practice it is sometimes imagined to be: subjective, multiple and even infinite. Scientific interpretation is not simply a clever cast of mind and has nothing in common with unsystematic hermeneutics. Whether in a positive sense, for those who favour free interpretation,[70] or in a negative one, for the most dogmatic of scientists, interpretation is often associated, quite wrongly, with literary rather than scientific practice. And, of course, the former reinforce the latter in their conviction that all interpretation is inevitably outside the realm of science.[71]

As an example of this, when a reader with a scientific bent comes upon this interpretation of 'dreams about cars' by the psychoanalyst Tobie Nathan – 'Men often dream about cars, for the dream is the machine in movement. I sometimes even find myself thinking that the car was invented to resemble a dream'[72] – the same reader could justifiably conclude that interpretation is simply a random projection of personal fantasies onto reality. But psychoanalytical interpretations of dreams are not systematically as misguided as this kind of example might suggest. And there are even sound reasons to believe that the vast majority of psychoanalysts seriously consider suggestions of this type as utterly ludicrous and, from both a scientific and a therapeutic perspective, of no use whatsoever.

In spite of the volume of empirical material gathered by psychoanalysts in the context of psychoanalytic therapy or hospital-based therapeutic treatments, denigrators of psychoanalysis continue to claim that 'the psychoanalytical dream theory is not scientific because it is not empirically based.'[73] This exaggeration stems from the belief that any research on dreams based on empirical methods other than those produced by studies of the brain is regarded as literary and non-scientific.[74]

For some of those interested in hermeneutics, dream accounts would be the equivalent for others of literary works – in other words, objects whose infinite richness would resist the most subtle and the most sophisticated attempts at interpretation. In the case of some of these, one can sense the desire to preserve the mystery of the dream in the same way that others sought to sanctify a certain mystery in written texts.[75] For them, science will inevitably lose out in the face of a work of art or a dream, and, when it struts about with all the airs of a big winner, it would be by stifling interpretation, unjustifiably reducing the irreducible, rigidifying the teeming reality, forcing its awful pre-established frameworks onto realities whose mysteries should be joyously welcomed.

We shall see, however, that not only is the dream capable of being interpreted but that it can be interpreted in a scientifically based way – that is to say, within limits fixed by the incorporated past and the context of the present life of the dreamer. And when a number of different interpretations are possible in spite of this restrictive framework formed by the past and present life of the dreamer, we will also see that they can be linked intelligibly in relationship to each other. For it is in the very nature of the dream to condense realities (people, animals, objects, places, situations) which are apparently disparate yet linked by analogy.

A scientific interpretation of dreams also implies a rigorous scientific methodology which allows the data necessary for the interpretative work to be collected. To what kind of data should the researcher have access in order to correctly interpret the dream? How should it be obtained? What measures can be taken to eliminate ill-founded, unjustified interpretations – that is to say, mere surmises which tell us more about the person interpreting than about the dream or the dreamer? These are the questions which psychoanalysts and researchers from other disciplines but with an interest in dreams have continued to ask (themselves), ever since Freud. For even if 'the practising neurologist Freud managed to make his therapeutic activity a research instrument, . . . he lacked a strict methodological discipline, which must have led to his turning individual cases into apodictic conclusions and . . . unjustified generalisations.'[76]

It should not, however, be assumed that researchers who were contemporaries of Freud, even those most genuinely impressed by his model of interpretation, did not express some resistance to these fundamental theoretical, methodological and empirical questions. So, for example, Eugen Bleuler, the great Swiss psychiatrist, was quick to express his frustration in the face of certain interpretations which lacked foundation from an empirical point of view. He wrote to Freud in a letter dated 17 October 1905: 'What I find lacking is the material from which you draw your conclusions. Naturally I imagine it to be absolutely vast.'[77] And, six years later, Bleuler was still surprised at the 'reasons which lead [Freud] to certain hypotheses and particularly to generalisation' (6 October 1911) with reference to his case study of President Schreber's paranoia, and requested 'more proofs' (4 December 1911).[78] Bleuler was perceived as 'ambivalent' by Freud and his entourage, but he was in fact simply pointing out the 'rigour of an ethos closely committed to objectivity'.[79]

For example, a few decades later, in 1964, the American psychoanalysts Thomas Morton French and Erika Fromm, motivated by sound scientific intentions, strove to transform interpretation into a better controlled practice than had hitherto been the case. Their starting point was the acknowledgement that the concepts of psychoanalysis are too often stereotyped (oral eroticism, anal eroticism, phallic eroticism, Oedipus complex, guilt, etc.), and as a result the material collected tended to end up all too quickly caught in the net of a preconceived scheme of interpretation, notably by presupposing experiences (from childhood or more recently) about which not enough was known. It was essential therefore to avoid using theory to forcibly superimpose schemes of interpretation onto empirical material which is either unreliable or clumsily put together. Moreover, this stereotyped use of Freudian or post-Freudian concepts often goes hand in hand with an intuitive, spontaneous interpretation which does not take the time to gather sufficient evidence or which relies only on part of the available evidence. Interpretative plurality, considered by some as inevitable, therefore often results from the fact that the interpreters do not take into account the same elements of proof when formulating their interpretation of the same dream.

French and Fromm do not deny the role of intuition in psychoanalytical interpretation but seek to transfer this intuition from art to science. If it wants to claim to be in any way scientific, interpretation must be verified and controlled by systematic methods. After all, intuition can very easily prove to be false on the grounds that it is distorted by the emotions and conceptions of the psychoanalyst. It can also turn out to have failed to take into account all the available evidence and, as a result, be corrected by a subsequent more precise and exhaustive reference to the material available. French and Fromm were therefore anxious to ensure interpretation involved 'reasoning carefully from more detailed evidence'.[80] In all cases, the mass of information represented by the account of the dream and the associations made on its subject is generally too vast to be understood in its entirety at a single glance, even the most expert one. Scientific interpretation needs to be constructed one step at a time, by gradually incorporating the different elements available to the analyst.

It is important therefore not only to distrust stereotypical models of interpretation but also to be patient enough to take account of all of the various associations obtained in the interpretation process. The wavering attention guided only by the unconscious of the psychoanalyst is not in itself sufficient to trigger in the patient associations on specific points in his or her dreams. Rather than the feeling of immediate intuitive comprehension, it is important to accept the need to take time and to encounter resistance – that is to say, elements which do not correspond to what might have been expected and which instead contradict or jeopardise the proposed interpretation. The process of interpretation is like a gigantic jigsaw puzzle where the different pieces are gradually fitted together to make up the final complete image:

> The analyst should not be content with fragmentary bits of insight. His constant aim should be to understand how different trends and themes in the patient's associations fit together into a single intelligible context. Trying to understand a patient's associations is like trying to piece together a jigsaw puzzle. This kind of fitting together into a single intelligible cognitive structure is our only reliable immediate check on the correctness of our interpretations. Consequently, we should not be complacent but actively puzzled if the pieces do not fit together intelligibly.[81]

In spite of the laudable methodological effort made and clarified here by French and Fromm, it emerges incidentally that, in the purest and undisputed psychoanalytical tradition, the analyst never records the sessions (which only last one hour) and simply takes notes on what the patient says.[82] This point is not, however, simply a technical detail, since any attempt to attain the degree of precision rightly aspired to by the authors would make recording the sessions indispensable. Only by utilising recording methods and a complete transcription of the exchanges, as currently commonly practised by sociologists, is it possible to go back, as many times as necessary, over the little details which, at first sight, appear trivial or important but too rich or too complex to note in detail during the duration of the session itself. Nor is taking notes during the treatment the most efficient way of remaining attentive to what the patient under analysis keeps expressing; it undoubtedly results in missing a great many opportunities to understand better what the patient is saying and to follow it up in order to obtain any further information necessary.

Overall, therefore, the scientific interpretation of dreams requires the interpreter to ensure that everything is in place methodologically to allow him or her to learn more about the dreamer than about the interpreter (his or her interests, the contexts of the interpretation, etc.). If the interpretation were no more than the simple projection onto the dreams in question of whatever the analyst saw in them, it would certainly not be scientific. In order for the dream to be correctly interpreted, the analyst must fill in all the 'gaps' which are characteristic of dreams, not by elements of his or her own making but by those which are obtained carefully, and with the utmost rigour, from the dreamers themselves.

Beyond Freud

Paying homage to Freud means both taking him very seriously, by acknowledging the scale of his accomplishment, and subjecting his work to a critical scrutiny by examining point by point the whole body of theoretical assertions on which his model of dream interpretation is based. 'In psychoanalytic theories', Eugen Bleuler wrote, 'there is both true and false; in the practice of psychoanalysis there is good and bad. On account of what is false, Monsieur Hoche and some others wish to see the whole of psychoanalysis completely rejected; I seek, because of what is true, to keep it and gradually cleanse it of its erroneous elements.'[83] He added that 'Freud's ideas will gain ground, and, if they are stripped of their exaggerations, they will still contain such good things that they will continue to represent for a long time one of the most significant developments in the understanding of the psyche.'[84] A fine example of the most scientifically fruitful type of attitude.

If I were to sum up my own position with regard to the Freudian model, I would say that Freud first of all deserves the credit for having proved that dreams are not simply a matter of a random and uncoordinated sequence of images, sounds and impressions but are in fact productions with a logic of their own and which it is therefore reasonable to seek to interpret. He was also right in linking diurnal experiences from the distant past, diurnal experiences from the immediate past (events of the day before the dream) and nocturnal experiences. Finally, he drew up a largely relevant description of certain of the main formal characteristics of the 'internal language' of the dreamer and of the characteristics of the dream-work (representation-visualisation, symbolisation, use of metaphor, condensation, dramatisation-use of hyperbole-exaggeration).

In many aspects, however, Freudian analysis seems to me to be questionable and often falls a long way short: for example, on the central concept of the dream representing the fulfilment of an unsatisfied wish or desire; on the nature of the unconscious; on the notions of repression, censorship and the ability to get around the censorship within the dream; on illustrative reductionisms,[85] whether infantile, sexual or event-focused; on the ambiguities and ambivalences around the (universal or personal) nature of symbols in dreams; on certain interpretive acrobatics which are detrimental to his approach; on a certain naturalism or biologism and a lack of consideration for the historical and social nature of the mechanisms or complexes on which he focuses; on the unique nature of transference and countertransference in the context of the analysis treatment; on the notion that the dream has a function and is the guardian of sleep; and on a number of other points which will be discussed during the course of this book.

My own attitude in reading Freud and other psychoanalysts and in formulating a sociological model for interpreting dreams is guided by a desire to rid psychoanalysis of certain errors and of certain generalisations, but at the same time to retain what it has taught us. Thinking both for and against Freud, in order to acknowledge the progress he made possible and to enable further developments to take place, is simply a reflection of the normal pattern of all non-dogmatic scientific thinking. By following that path, there is the classic risk, like that incurred by Bleuler in his time, of being 'caught in the crossfire' and of being 'attacked from both sides'.[86] On the one hand are the denigrators of psychoanalysis, whose aim is to be able to classify once and for all the entire work of Freud, along with that of the many writers who were inspired by it, under the label 'pseudo-science' of the history of ideas, and on the other are the most orthodox of Freud worshippers for whom interfering with even the smallest element of the model would constitute a crime of *lèse-majesté*.

Yet scientific practice should not be tainted by the atmosphere of rival camps or clans who essentially clash with each other on the basis of extra-scientific interests. As Bleuler said to Freud in 1911, 'the precepts "Whoever is not for us is against us" and "All or nothing" are, in my view, necessary for religious communities and useful to political parties but not to science.'[87] What matters is the relevance of the problems to be solved and the arguments and the empirical proofs necessary for their resolution.

Dream research has made considerable progress since Freud's day, but this progress has very often been achieved only by separating elements he had tried to bring together in order to make up a coherent theoretical whole. The need to examine closely all the micro-problems that make up Freudian theory, some of which had already been partially resolved by Freud's predecessors, has led to research becoming fragmented and specialised. Cognitivist psychologists have worked on analogical reasoning or on day residues, linguists on the importance of metaphors in dream accounts or on the properties of private or internal language, neuroscientists on cerebral activity during the different phases of sleep, on the question of consciousness and unconscious cognition, etc.

What is needed now is a theory of dreams which is scientifically more accurate, more rigorous and more coherent than that formulated by Freud, a theory which is based on his findings but which also takes account of certain scientific developments which have taken place since then (in linguistics, in cognitive psychology or in neurobiology as well as in sociology). It is just such a theory that I shall be setting out here, a dispositionalist-contextualist theory which allows the dream to be viewed as a specific form of expression (or of symbolic production) within the context of all other forms of human expression.

The theory of dreams which I shall formulate, and which is based on the findings of a sociology on the individual scale, must therefore be considered as a *particular formulation conjugated within a general theory of human practice and expression*. It is, to my mind, simply a way of pinpointing and making more complex both a research programme which deals with human behaviour in general, and human forms of expression in particular, at the intersection of incorporated dispositions and of contexts of action (and of expression).[88] But it is also an attempt to carry out a conceptual synthesis and a critical reappropriation, from the perspective of a dispositionalist-conceptualist sociology, of the very many partial theoretical-empirical results produced by a host of researchers before, and especially after, the first great scientifically ambitious synthesis undertaken by Sigmund Freud. By working, from the starting point of sociology, towards just such a synthesis of the problems and findings coming from a range of extremely varied disciplines, my aim is to go beyond the *acade-mismus* referred to by Norbert Elias, which is the 'projection of academic departmentalization and the rivalries connected with it into the subject matter of departmental research.'[89]

It is not therefore simply a matter of allowing the dream to enter the field of the social sciences or of sociology as they currently exist; it is also to do with transforming the social sciences and forging or adapting their theoretical and methodological tools so as to allow them to take into consideration all the existing knowledge about the oneiric experience, and to know where and how to see the reality of the dream in order to have a chance of understanding it. Without that, the researcher would be left to rely on the scientific routines of his discipline, ill-adapted to the object in question, or would have to make use of an implicit model surreptitiously dominated by already existing theories, and in particular by psychoanalysis, or at least by what scholarly usage has retained of it.

The scientific programme on practices and forms of expression that I have been working on for the last twenty years[90] can only ever yield partial results, depending on the allocated time scale and the data available. But the proliferation of research projects in the form of specific aspects of one or another part of this overall scientific programme gradually enables the initial architecture to be strengthened or modified.

2

The Dream:
An Intrinsically Social
Individual Reality

Studying an object like the dream, which seems as distant as possible from the disciplinary foundations of sociology and, more generally, of the social sciences, is an exciting challenge which enables us to re-examine the question of what sociology is, and what it can do, and to explore further the meaning of the adjective 'social'.

In spite of the multiple blows which have in practice been dealt to the notion of sociology as a science of collectives, many sociologists still believe that the social means the group, the institution or the collective movement, and select their research subjects accordingly. Yet the biographical journey of a particular and even an atypical individual, the individual criminal act, neurosis, emotions or dreams are not in themselves asocial realities which can be detached from the history and from the network of constraints imposed by the social world within which they occur and are understood and dealt with.

Society is not only a formal context within which individuals attend to their individual business and think or feel like isolated and autonomous beings. Such individuals do not exist. Yet it is as such that they are seen by 'the classic systems of philosophy from ancient times up to Kant, to the psychological works of the nineteenth century, Maine de Biran, Jouffroi, Stuart Mill . . . and even of Bergson himself.'[1] Referring to 'mind, judgment, memory, association of ideas, perception, they limit themselves and us to the consciousness of the individual without any connection with the environment or with other men.' Such works seem not to question 'that the mind could develop its faculties and exert its functions in the state of isolation, as it is supposed by them.'[2] Just like any other form of psychic activity and of expression, dreams reveal their mysteries only if, instead of being made into an insular reality locked within the confines of the cranium, they are seen as part of the history of the dreamer and of the network of constraints imposed by his or her experiences.

Can the social be absorbed into the cerebral?

In the 1950s, certain researchers flirted with the hope of being able to pen-etrate the neurobiological substratum of dreams when they believed they could 'localise' oneiric activity during the periods of what is referred to as 'REM' (rapid eye movement)[3] or 'paradoxical'[4] sleep. During these phases (between three and six periods per night, amounting to about 100 minutes in all), researchers recorded a relaxing of muscular tone, rapid ocular move-ments, brain activity similar to that of the waking state, an irregular cardiac rhythm and erections in the case of men. The first experimental studies established that waking people up during the periods of paradoxical sleep resulted in more than 80 per cent of remembered dreams, as opposed to a mere 6 per cent during other sleep periods,[5] and a conclusion was reached, a little hastily, that *REM sleep* or paradoxical sleep corresponded to the dreaming period. As a result, many researchers at the time found them-selves using terms such as 'coupling', 'correspondence', 'isomorphism', 'causality', and many other expressions supporting the claim that it was indeed now possible to identify the neurobiological and neurophysiologi-cal conditions in which dreams took shape and that between these phases of sleep and the dream there was a perfect 'correlation'.

But in the end the hypothesis was not confirmed, and other research projects, as early as the 1960s, suggested the continuous production of dreams all through the night, during phases of non-REM sleep, whether light or deep, as well as in paradoxical sleep, and even while falling asleep (hypnagogic images) or while waking up (hypnopompic images). As David Foulkes sums up:

> dreaming is not limited to REM sleep. It also clearly occurs during much non-REM sleep and during the transition from wakefulness to sleep. Dreaming even has been observed, if generally momentarily, in relaxed wakefulness, when people let their minds 'go' or 'wander' (Foulkes & Scott, 1973; Foulkes & Fleisher, 1975). The occurrence of dreaming in ordinary non-REM sleep, at sleep onset, and in relaxed wakefulness has been repeatedly documented and is now generally accepted.[6]

Such research confirmed that the gap between the probability of recollect-ing dreams was much less significant than had initially been suggested (at least 80 per cent of dreams were remembered in paradoxical sleep and at least 50 per cent during the other phases, even if the recollections tended to be a little less detailed than those produced during the phases of paradoxi-cal sleep).[7] However, all things considered, the existence of memories of dreams in 6 per cent of cases where sleepers are woken up during periods of non-paradoxical sleep should already have steered researchers away from the notion of a complete conformity.

In spite of this, the very powerful desire to link sleep and dreams, and ultimately cerebral activity and psychic activity, explains why well-known researchers (John Allan Hobson, an American neuropsychiatrist, or Michel Jouvet, a French neurobiologist, to mention but two) would, for even a decade after the initial study had been revised, continue to insist that the period of paradoxical sleep *is* the dreaming period. Paradoxical sleep, writes Michel Jouvet in 2016, 'opens us to a consciousness of the dream'.[8] He refers, incorrectly, to 'experimental oneirology' and to the 'modern neurophysiology of the dream',[9] to 'paradoxical sleep considered as the physiological translation of oneiric activity'[10] and to 'four or five periods of paradoxical sleep (which correspond to oneiric activity).'[11]

What explanation can there be for such a denial of reality and the refusal to acknowledge error? Michel Jouvet provides the key himself when he writes: 'The theatre of "Science" is not necessarily a peaceful one where objectivity reigns, and scientists are no different to any other men: since their discoveries are the only capital they have, it is natural that they should defend them . . . with all necessary means.'[12] Only power struggles between scientific disciplines can explain such obstinacy in the face of the evidence of facts which all researchers should acknowledge. After all, a firm belief that psychological research can be guided by studying the mechanisms of the brain is a seductive idea that no one is inclined to give up very easily. If researchers were not blinded by the desire for power, they would simply agree to work only on the various states of sleep or the cerebral activities accompanying oneiric activities and not on dreams themselves or, more precisely, on the accounts that dreamers are capable of giving of them on waking.

The study of neuronal activity during the different phases of sleep and the study of dreams themselves are not dealing with the same subjects and nor do they call for the same theories or methods. Knowledge of the neurobiology of cerebral activity during sleep does not bring with it any knowledge of dreams themselves, of their particular logic, their characteristics and their significance.[13] Nor is there even, as Jouvet points out, on the one hand, an 'objective and experimental' study exploring dreams 'from the outside' on the basis of the hypothesis 'that the mechanisms of dreaming are the same as those of paradoxical sleep, its neurobiological basis', or, on the other hand, a study which 'explores the dream from the "inside", studying the subjective content of dreams by analysing recalled memories of them.'[14] Not only does the dream fail to correspond to particular phases of sleep; in addition, it can only be studied objectively, as a series of associated images and sensations, by the human and social sciences working directly on dream accounts and not just on sleep, which is merely the *condition* in which these images and sensations can appear.

Even if he claims to study the dream as a 'physiological mechanism' and to distance himself from psychoanalysis, Michel Jouvet has, throughout his career as a neurobiologist and with the exception of a few very limited incursions which lack scientific detail, worked more or less exclusively on sleep rather than on dreams. It is as though, in the early 1960s, the researcher had been seized with the somewhat wild ambition of being able to link neurobiological processes and psychological oneiric activity and had never quite managed to escape from its clutches. He calls himself an 'oneirologist', but he has never seriously studied dream accounts or proposed any theory of oneiric production. The failure to respect levels of reality which means that dreams known through dream accounts are of a different nature to what the neurobiologist is in a position to study constitutes a major scientific obstacle.[15] In the absence of respect for the various levels of reality, it would be possible to say to the biologist that the objects of his study can only be understood through atomic physics, given that the cells of the human body are made up of molecules which are themselves made up of atoms.

Similarly, the American neuropsychiatrist Allan Hobson, carried away by his radical criticism of psychoanalysis and his determination to explain dreams through the study of cerebral function in the REM phase of sleep, ignores experimental studies which prove the inadequacy of the formula '*REM sleep = dreaming*'. For him, the prospect of this coupling held the promise of what could finally be considered a scientific study (that is, from the point of view of the neurosciences) of dreams and an escape from approaches deemed too 'literary' and non-scientific. 'Over the centuries and even today, dreams have been looked at subjectively and as experiences whose significance is cryptic, needing to be decoded in some way. A new way of viewing dreams, as transparent, their significance available to the dreamer unaided by prophet or psychoanalyst, derives from the objective studies of modern sleep science and neurobiology.'[16]

Hobson does not hesitate to set out very directly a reductionist certainty which can be detected more discreetly in other researchers and is nevertheless largely contradicted by the facts.

> So strong is the relationship between the form of mental activity in dreaming and the form of brain activity in REM sleep that we may begin to entertain a unified theory of mind and brain, To that end, I use the hybrid term *brain-mind* to signal my conviction that a complete description of either (brain or mind) will be a complete description of the other (mind or brain). At some future time, the two words may well be replaced by one.[17]

The laboratory study of REM sleep and of the dream purported 'to suggest a parallel between a distinctive state of the brain (REM sleep) and a distinctive state of the brain (dreaming).'[18] 'Parallel', 'correspondence', 'concomitant', 'brain-mind isomorphism' between the psychological and physiological domains, or complete assimilation of one by the other, Hobson's reductionism is clearly at the root of most of his arguments.

However, the type of data on which he works keeps Hobson too at some distance from the desired reductionist programme. He himself claims not to be interested in the specific content of dreams (the fact of dreaming of this rather than of that) and concentrates his attention on the formal, structural properties of the dream: 'Instead of looking at dreams as stories, we needed to establish a quantitative inventory of formal dream features: the sensations, movements, emotions, and thought patterns that distinguish dreams from waking mental activity in humans. Then we could attempt to explain the observed differences in terms of the neurophysiological details emerging from the comparison of the REM sleep and the waking states in experimental animals.'[19] However, the comparison with animals seems largely irrelevant since, if the latter do indeed dream, they are incapable of giving any account of their dreams, thus rendering impossible any comparison of the formal, structural qualities of dreams in animals and in humans. Knowing that when human beings dream they experience 'intense feelings (such as anxiety, surprise, fear and elation)', and that these powerfully experienced impressions are undoubtedly due 'to activation . . . of emotional centers, probably of the limbic brain',[20] does not help us to understand why a particular dreamer experienced fear in a dream (rather than joy), why he or she felt fear in such a situation (e.g. a car accident) rather than in any other (e.g. a fire, a bomb exploding or a tsunami), and why he or she dreamt about this type of situation rather than any other kind of situation. Fear is accompanied by chemical and neurophysiological processes, but it is linked to social situations which relate to the dreamer's personal experiences.[21]

If neuroscientists could genuinely study the dream itself, its structure and specific contents, it would mean that, even beyond the question of dreams, all the subjects of psychology, sociology, anthropology or history would be absorbed into the neurosciences, given that everything studied by these sciences is, in fact, made possible by neurobiological or neurophysiological mechanisms. Without a brain or a nervous system, no psychological activity, no language, no culture, no social interaction or collective organisation would be possible.

But speaking of *conditions of possibility* is not the same as speaking of the *identity* of the phenomena or of the possibility of understanding dreams by studying the neurobiological or neurophysiological properties which accompany them and make them possible. Setting out to study dreams by studying the properties of sleep means succumbing to a reductionism which denies any discontinuity between cerebral mechanisms and the socio-psychic dynamics that lead to dreams as they are experienced during sleep, then to the memories of dreams, and finally to dream accounts. In all cases, what we are capable of knowing about dreams ultimately comes down to the memory of dreams and to dream accounts. Dream accounts, which represent the one and only possible access to the content of what has been dreamt during sleep, are a logical hybrid or a compromise between the product of psychic activity in the sleeping state (*experience of the dream*), the recollection of it (*memory of the dream*) and the verbal account made in the waking state, either for the dreamer's own benefit or for someone else, of what had been dreamt during the periods of sleep (*dream account*).

The dispositions and skills constantly at work in our daily practice are rarely studied by the neurosciences. It is not easy to follow the brain activity of someone who is moving around, working, eating, speaking and at the same time doing all sorts of other things, etc. When they want to study certain mental processes, researchers often have to reduce the activity of their subjects considerably, by reducing the complexity of the task they are to undertake or of the problem they are seeking to resolve and by getting them to sit down or lie on a bed (in order to be able to position any recording instruments on the subject's body) or on a table which will slide into a cylinder (in order to conduct MRI[22] scans). It is therefore no coincidence that the focus has tended to be on sleeping persons, who are objectively near perfect subjects for experiments, in spite of the fact that it is difficult to fall asleep on a hard table, wired up to sensors, with no pillow and with no possibility of changing position ...

Working on a level of reality which is that of relationships between human beings, social science researchers generally do not feel the need to raise the question of the cerebral conditions of possibility of the social realities or the social relationships such as they observe them with their own methods. Yet it is indeed the biological and physiological capacities of humans which render possible the kinds of relationships which develop socio-historically in an autonomous way. Humans act thanks to a brain and a nervous system which distinguish them from other living species, notably by allowing them to master a relatively sophisticated language, as well as the potential to incorporate equally complex skills and dispositions. But as the human beings studied, as members of the human species, are endowed at birth (except in exceptional cases) with the same cerebral equipment and the same general capacities, it makes sense for sociologists, anthropologists and historians to concentrate on the specificity of the nature of social relationships and on what differentiates the human beings in question in so far as they have different stories and life patterns.

But are human beings really the same asleep or awake? Clearly their capacity to think, act and feel are not identical. For example, the possibilities for action are limited by periods of muscular atonia and by the absence of waking consciousness allowing control over movements. And the same is true of their linguistic capacities, the perception of a whole range of external stimuli and the possibilities of interaction with others. When it comes to studying dreams, the sociologist must focus on the inextricably linked cerebral, psychological and social states of an individual during sleep. The question of dreams reintroduces into the sociologist's area of investigation the relationship between the cerebral and the social which is inevitably forgotten in the ordinary sociological production focused on waking behaviours. Forced to confront the thorny problem of comparing forms of expression in waking and sleeping modes, the researcher is reminded of the presence of the brain and of the different ways in which it functions depending on the time of day. The expressive possibilities of dreamers are the result of this intertwining of 'conditions'.

For example, the deactivation during sleep of parts of the prefrontal cortex (the dorsolateral), which plays an important role in concentration, the control of representations, the working memory and logical reasoning, could help to explain the sometimes strange or unusual nature of dream accounts.[23] Yet this discovery made by neuroscience has only 'confirmed what psychological analysis revealed' a considerable time ago on the basis of the study of dream accounts. 'Indeed, we were aware, long before the existence of neuro-imaging techniques, that, during sleep, thought is stripped of intentional control and as a result lacks continuity, reflective capacities and memory.'[24] And we shall see that this phenomenon is indissociable from the type of communication situation (with the self) in which the dreamer finds him- or herself.[25] In the same way, Freud and some of his predecessors had emphasised the strong visual dimension of dreams on the evidence of the study of dream accounts, and this realisation was formulated before the emergence of research demonstrating the intense activity of the visual cortex during periods of sleep.

Everybody sleeps and everybody dreams, and it might be said that it is part of the biological and physiological condition of the human being both to dream each time they fall asleep and to be capable of 'recording' their dream in a linguistic form once they wake up again. But if a period of time spent asleep is a necessary element of human biology and physiology, and if the specific mechanisms of the human brain during sleep are universally shared, all dreamers do not have identical forms of social life, their life stories are different and therefore they do not dream of the same things or accord them the same importance; nor do they necessarily feel the same propensity to discuss their dreams, and, when they do talk about them, the skills they draw on in order to narrate them vary considerably. The neurobiological reductionism is no more admissible in terms of dream studies than in any other object of study: human beings dream with given culturally acquired symbolic capacities, with given past and present social experiences, and neuroscience alone will never be able adequately to 'explain' the images, sounds and sensations produced by any one dreamer in any given oneiric production. It is because of this, and not out of mistrust of the principle, that Freud logically resisted any kind of organic reductionism.[26] And it is the same reason that drives the researcher in social sciences to draw up a model suited to the interpretation of dreams.

A few precedents in the social sciences

In the history of the scholarly study of dreams, or more precisely of dream accounts, the social sciences in general, and sociology in particular, have generally played very little part. A handful of brave or reckless researchers are the exception to this rule. Three historians – Jacques Le Goff, Peter

Burke and Jean-Claude Schmitt[27] – opened up avenues of research for a cultural or social history of dreams by compromising to a greater or lesser extent with Freudian theory. Such efforts to venture into the study of a subject as complex and as full of pitfalls as the dream are worth drawing attention to. Nevertheless, the (short) formats of their contributions make it impossible to clarify fully many points which would merit elucidation. Take, for example, the question of the scales of observation utilised, and particularly the need (or not) to shift from an individual scale to a collective scale for a history of dreams and the effects this change of scale might have in practice; the question of the nature (personal or universal) of oneiric symbols; the question of the difference between the obvious content (which appears in the dream) and the latent content (which is supposedly hidden beneath the obvious content); or even the issue of the information needed by historians in order to interpret the dreams of dreamers whose biography is often unknown or incomplete and who can no longer provide the associations Freud deemed necessary for interpretation. But, in more general terms, there is the question of how the different elements of the Freudian conceptual heritage are integrated or not, since this is not systematically addressed by these authors, who sometimes borrow concepts from psychoanalysis (libido, manifest content–latent content, symbolisation, unconscious, censure, etc.) without explanation.

In the same way, the remarkable work by Charlotte Beradt on dreams during the Third Reich, which was originally published in German in 1966,[28] led to a number of psychoanalytical, historical and philosophical commentaries which in turn stimulated discussions sometimes touching on the way the social sciences could turn their attention to dreams. And finally, and perhaps above all, it was the turn of anthropology, which, since the beginning of the 1950s, has successfully initiated a series of studies on the way dream accounts circulate and are shared within the social world (particularly in 'primitive societies' rather than in societies which have more clearly separated private and public life), on variations in dream accounts according to whom these are shared with, or on the way dreams are interpreted differently in different cultures.[29]

Yet, on closer scrutiny, the dream also appears in a number of sociological studies. Firstly, for example, in the few pages summing up a lesson given by Émile Durkheim in 1883–4 at the Lycée de Sens and devoted to the subject of sleep and dreams.[30] Durkheim's succinct remarks, based on the work of Théodore Jouffroy, consisted in pointing out the continuity of the work of association of ideas between a waking and a sleeping state. More detailed, on the other hand, is the contribution of the Durkheimian scholar Maurice Halbwachs, who was intrigued by the dream in relation to his work on the social contexts of memory:[31] the dreamer is removed from the flow of social interactions and his or her oneiric activity cannot be understood without taking into account the properties of what could be referred to as the 'context of the dream'. But, at the very moment when he appears to indicate a possible path towards a sociological analysis of dreams, the sociologist, for whom 'the sleeping man is outside the control of society', places the dream 'outside the field of sociology by conferring on it a status of counterexample'.[32]

It was then the turn of Roger Bastide, who, in an article entitled 'Matériaux pour une sociologie du rêve' (Material for a sociology of dreams), initially published in the *Revue internationale de sociologie* in 1932, wrote that, 'to date, few researchers have sought to develop a systematic sociology of the dream' which would, however, represent 'a new path which might produce some interesting results'.[33] He expressed regret that 'sociology is only interested in the waking individual, as though the sleeping man was a dead man.'[34] He suggested studying dreams throughout the entire life of an individual, or the dreams of immigrants split between two different cultures, and refers to the 'social contexts of our imagination even within sleep',[35] but his very broad approach, dealing with categories of dream and of culture (or of make-believe) in an abstract way, wavering between criticism and a simple acritical reuse of psychoanalytical schemas (notions of the unconscious, of repression, censorship, manifest content and latent content)[36] and drawing on a rather fragile methodology (his studies referring to the black population in Brazil, for example, result in only very brief commentaries which tend to have very vague methodological outlines), struggles to convince the reader. We are therefore a very long way from a satisfactory sociological theory of oneiric production.

At the end of the 1970s, sociologists under the leadership of Jean Duvignaud conducted a new survey of the dreams of French people.[37] The aim was to objectivise 'the oneiric scenario or the dramatisation of dreams within the context of their collective roots' and for that purpose to assemble 'a large number of dreams from across all social levels and all age groups' in order to get away from 'the clinical corpus' generally associated with psychoanalysis. The authors of the study point out the lack of dreams in Freud's work from workers or peasants, shop workers or craftsmen, and stress the importance of including a fuller sample of classes, professions, regions and ages: 'Thus making it possible to glimpse correlations between a wide range of nocturnal experiences and the integration, different in each case, of men and women in their social context.' According to them, 'the comparisons or correlations established between social situations and dreams' appear 'to challenge the homogeneity or the universality of the nocturnal experience'. This study, which could have represented an important first step towards a sociology of dreams, is, however, riddled with methodological weaknesses, theoretical errors and interpretive peculiarities.

Firstly, from a methodological point of view, the reader will never know exactly what method was used to collect the 'two thousand dreams or fragments of dreams gathered from all over France and from across the socio-professional categories of every region, limiting to their appropriate statistical proportion the dreams of "intellectuals"', or if the accounts used were obtained within the context of interviews or written questionnaires, from notes made spontaneously by dreamers (in dream notebooks) or from notes made at the request of sociologists. Of these two thousand dreams (or fragments of dreams) supposedly 'closely examined' by researchers, no genuinely quantitative examination is in evidence; not a single table of data is included, not a single figure cited, not a single statistical correlation made. Moreover, there is no indication of how and in what circumstances the dreamers questioned were selected. In certain cases, the reader is provided only with their profession, in others their age, their sex and a few secondary details, and in yet others more precise elements of past history or of more recent events or preoccupations are included. But there is nothing systematic here either, thus making it virtually impossible to provide an interpretation with any degree of precision of the numerous dreams cited, not one of which is examined in detail. And in some cases there are even thematic analyses (on death, sexuality, hunger, mass media, etc.) without any attempt to link these specifically to dreamers' lives. Thus, when a female dreamer, a 55-year-old employee, uses televised images of flooding in her dream, the authors discuss the link between the dream and the media, whereas any knowledge of oneiric processes[38] would suggest that such images are simply borrowed in order to play out a situation linked to a sense of danger experienced in waking life:

> On the previous day, I had seen pictures of floods in the South-West on television. That night, I dreamt I was in my bed here and that water was pouring in from all directions. Yet there isn't a river anywhere near here. I was trapped in the room and the water level was rising and I couldn't do anything about it. I felt as if I was suffocating, and that's what woke me up.

La Banque des rêves also fails from a theoretical point of view. The authors do not include discussion of any theory or any previous research. They simply reproach Freud for ignoring some 'social classes'. But, as it is set out, the argument about 'class' does not make a great deal of sense. It is true that Freud had access only to people from Viennese bourgeois circles, and indeed only to those who chose to consult a psychoanalyst or who were forced to do so by those close to them because they were suffering from psychological problems of various kinds. This may have led Freud into error regarding the type of family structure of the patients consulting him, and which he assumed was universal, and also when it came to the kinds of problems patients were working out in their dreams. But Freud's theory of dreams is a *general* theory of dreams, which essentially sets out not to explain what people dream according to their social situation but, rather, to understand the general mechanisms which lie behind the creation of dreams. Varying the social or geographical origins of dreamers (the authors refer to 'dreams of countryfolk') is not in itself enough to establish a sociological theory of dreams, since the approach fails to touch on the complex mechanisms which lie behind the production of dreams.

In addition, the links established between the 'manifest' dream themes or scenarios (the authors being critical of the idea that dreams should be linked to non-spoken or implicit elements) and broad social categories are too crude or too loose to be really pertinent. The fact that a turkey farmer dreams that she is counting her turkeys out of fear that they might be stolen, an agricultural worker dreams of people with whom he works, and a domestic worker aged twenty dreams that a school teacher is helping her recite a text and she is troubled because she has not learned it merely tells us that dreamers draw on past or recent experiences for the images which make up their dreams. But without more detailed investigations into the recent events which might have triggered the memory of similar scenes in the past, and into the recurring preoccupations of dreamers, whether lasting or more transitory, dreams cannot really be interpreted. Finally, while their investigation is very much focused on the idea that dreams are especially sensitive to the realities of class, the authors nevertheless sometimes lapse into metaphysical notions of dreams as a space of freedom and of the magical obliteration of social determinations.[39]

Except for the tentative suggestions made by Maurice Halbwachs, the most solid scientific support for the elaboration of a social science of dreams has come from the other side of the Atlantic. Initially, even when they refer to a theoretical corpus which is largely psychological, studies statistically based on dreams enable crude links to be made between the subjects of dreams and the situations experienced by the dreamers. The pioneering work of Mary Whiton Calkins at the end of the nineteenth century,[40] based on 205 personal dreams and 170 dreams of a man (her partner), like those of the psychologist Calvin S. Hall[41] based sometimes on the study of several thousand collected dreams from hundreds of dreamers without any particular pathology, are full of information on the situations, people, places or objects most frequently dreamt about. They provide strong evidence of a certain continuity between diurnal preoccupations or interests and imaginary nocturnal scenes. Focusing on a great many accounts of dreams, they nevertheless neglect any detailed reconstruction of the personal journeys and social characteristics of the dreamers. This neglect was partially redressed when Alan P. Bell and Calvin S. Hall produced a detailed study of the dreams of an incarcerated paedophile[42] or when Hall and Richard E. Lind studied the dreams of Franz Kafka.[43] But, whether statistically based or relying on in-depth case studies, such approaches nevertheless favour the analysis of dream content and neglect the processes which lead to the dream, such as those specific to the 'dream-work' which mean that the dream most often appears to the waking individual as strange, absurd and sometimes barely coherent. Finally, at the end of the 1980s, American sociologists launched an original study rooted in the tradition of symbolic interactionism and were provided with a platform within the American Sociological Association. An edition of the journal *Symbolic Interaction* in 1993 was therefore devoted to the sociology of dreams[44] but was not followed up by any significant number of studies or research projects.[45] Apart from one or two exceptions, these articles focused their attention less on the dream itself and its creation than on the interactions through which dreams are recounted and shared in a social context.

Finally, we should mention a study carried out in 2004 and 2006 by J. F. Hovden involving 266 students from Volda University College in Norway. This study focuses not on dream accounts but on questions concerning memories of recurring dreams. The researcher listed forty categories of dreams (thirty-four of these were taken from a comparative American-Japanese investigation carried out in 1958 with college students) in order to establish what the subjects dreamt of most frequently, asking them to state how often they remembered their dreams, to assess their degree of logical coherence, and to gauge whether their dreams could have been experienced in real life. The results showed that the most frequent dreams were those about falling, school, situations where the dreamer is attacked or chased, and dreams of a sexual nature. If the Norwegian author refers to Bourdieu's theory of practice, he nevertheless still reduces dreams in a positivist way to 'social practices' which can be studied like any other without ever considering the specific nature of oneiric production.[46] Moreover, the idea that recurrent dreams, rather than 'unique dreams', represent the 'the most fruitful object for the sociologist'[47] is based on a narrow concept – and one which could be described as 'sociologistic' – of sociological objects. Hovden thus gives the impression of returning to the old conflict between history as the science of events which do not repeat themselves and sociology as a science of recurring events and relatively stable structures. Even Durkheim, to whom Hovden refers, did not believe that events which occur only once in life – such as suicide for example – are in any way less apt to become the objects of a sociological investigation. Finally, the question remains as to who decides, and on what basis, about the recurrence of a dream. More often than not it is the dreamers themselves who claim that they dream 'the same things' or have 'recurring dreams'. This suggests that the recurrence is linked to the *manifest* scenario of the dream, recognisable to the dreamer. But this recurrence of schemas is more extensive than might be thought, and the dreamer is not necessarily aware of it. It is usually concealed by the apparent diversity of dream images. To access this kind of recurrence nevertheless requires a switch from the declarative to the study of accounts of specific dreams, backed by verbal material on the dream and on the dreamer's past.

Limitations of environmentalist approaches: the ecology of dreams

There are two major ways of approaching dreams in the human and social sciences. Either the focus of study can be on the ways in which dreams are recounted, shared, circulated, dealt with and interpreted by societies, groups or categories of different individuals or it can be orientated towards a science of dreams in the sense of a science of the production and the meaning of dreams which sets out to answer the question of why we dream what we dream and why our dreams take the forms that they do. The *science of oneiric production* can thus be quite clearly distinguished from the *science of the uses made of dreams* (how they are shared, communicated, interpreted).

In the first scenario, scholars focus on practices *around the dream* or *concerning the dream*, but not on *the dream* as such. Their research begins once the dream is over, from the moment when it is possible to observe what individuals do with it or think about it. What do different societies or different groups do with the dreams of their members? Do they encourage the telling and sharing of them, and, if so, in what form and in what conditions? In what circumstances is the dream voiced and to whom? How do accounts of the same dreams vary depending on the people to whom they are recounted (partner, friend, analyst, etc.)?[48] What conceptions do dreamers have of the role of dreams in a particular culture, at a particular era or in a particular group?[49] How do they interpret them or to what uses do they put them?[50]

An implicit division which has gradually arisen as a result of the history of research carried out under different disciplinary banners tends to associate the social sciences with the science of uses and to class the science of production with the psychological sciences (psychoanalysis, cognitive psychology, psychiatry, etc.). The same applies well beyond the question of dreams. While psychology, psychoanalysis or psychiatry all set out to penetrate the logic of various mental illnesses, history, sociology or anthropology focus their attention on the nosographies of diseases and their development, on psychiatric institutions, on the management of people with mental illness, on the way the mentally ill are treated and how others interact with them, etc. The situation could be summed up by saying that, while the sciences of the mind study the vessel (its shape, material, content, the way in which it was made), the social sciences, for their part, take a broader view (the way the vessel is used and shared, the market in which it operates, the institutions which control it and which legislate for it, the meanings which are attributed to it, etc.). By confining researchers in the social sciences to the study of the environment in which the dream occurs, their ambitions risk being reduced to a sort of *ecology of dreams* which agrees not to get involved in the actual process of the production of dreams. This same division rests fundamentally on the conflict between the (psychological) sciences of the individual and the (social) sciences of the collective.[51]

This phenomenon of the separation of goals is particularly noticeable in anthropology, the discipline within the social sciences which has undoubtedly shown the most frequent interest in the subject of dreams.[52] In an article published in 1954, the American anthropologist Erika E. Bourguignon[53] cites the observations made by Dorothy Eggan,[54] who would suggest using accounts of dreams as anthropological material.

Distancing herself with regard to psychoanalysis which explores the psychic dynamic that makes dreamers express their unconscious latent content in a manifest form, Eggan asserted that only the manifest content of dreams should be of interest to the anthropologist because of its obvious cultural dimension; in the dreams studied, she looked for central elements of the Native American Hopi culture she was investigating, using the method that Calvin S. Hall and Robert L. Van de Castle would subsequently adopt – that is to say, by establishing the frequency with which certain categories of objects, people, places, etc., appeared in dream accounts. At the same time, Georges Devereux also supported the idea of the cultural structuring of dreams,[55] and twenty years later David D. Schneider and Sharp Lauriston demonstrated that the most significant elements of dreamers' culture clearly appeared in dreams, so that, for example, the frequent outbursts of aggression between the various groups which make up the Yir Yoront people in Australia and the important figures of the mother's brothers and older brothers appeared in dreams.[56]

But what primarily interested Erika E. Bourguignon was the way in which different cultures see (and sometimes interpret) dreams and the relative importance they give them. It is in this context that she studied dreams among Haitian peasants. And many anthropologists have subsequently pursued a similar kind of focus.[57]

In the same way, with regard to interactionist approaches to the dream in sociology, the favoured direction for research focuses not on studying the production of dreams itself, a process which is inextricably social and psychological, but on the study of interactions *around* the dream. For example, Gary Alan Fine and Laura Fischer Leighton are adamant that dreams form part of a 'public rhetoric' (Freud himself had emphasised the 'secondary elaboration' of the dream as soon as there is transition from the memory of the dream to the account of the dream), that they are 'recurring events' which are part of the social order and that they are 'collectively interpretable'.[58]

In terms of the social production of dreams, the authors seek no further than the old 'reflection theory' by referring to the fact that dreams 'reflect reality' and that the dreamer's cultural values and motivations are 'reflected' in dreams.[59] And the sociological orientation that they tend to favour in the matter of dreams focuses, on the one hand, on the accounts of dreams given in social interactions which conform to certain rules and, on the other hand, on the significance given to dreams and the fundamentally cultural processes used to interpret them.

The research carried out by Robin Wagner-Pacifici and Harold J. Bershady, a very typical example of this type of approach,[60] focuses on the interpretation of a dream in the context of a police murder hunt. The authors begin by pointing out that dreams are no longer interpreted as accounts capable of foretelling future events, but that they are seen as private entities, associated with a specific individual. They cite the case of a dreamer who made a connection between his dream and a crime which had recently been committed in which a woman had been beaten to death very near to where he lived. Encouraged by his wife and friends, the dreamer went to the police to recount his dream in order to assist the investigation. But the close match between the account of the dream and what had actually taken place led to his being charged with murder. The dream was therefore seen by the police not as such but, instead, as a confession in disguise, and, as a result, its different elements were interpreted not as symbols of other things but literally as proofs of the man's involvement in the crime. The metal object in the dream was taken for a description of the crime weapon found at the scene rather than as the symbol of something else. What the authors found interesting in this news story is that the 'same' dream is told or interpreted in very different ways depending on the different people and contexts involved, since the dreamer's mistake was naively to give the police an account of a dream which should only have been confided to a close circle of people who had some degree of intimacy with him.[61]

All the studies which fall within the social ecology of the dream are of course scientifically legitimate, but, to my mind, they fail to represent conclusive evidence that dreams should be seen as entirely social objects. This is nevertheless what many researchers believe, whether implicitly or explicitly. 'Remember', writes the medievalist Jean-Claude Schmitt, 'that the dream exists socially only in so far as it has become an account, something which belongs not only to an individual but to a social group which receives it, passes it on, adapts it according to its own values and to the context of its beliefs.'[62] Dreams are indeed shared, explained, interpreted according to frameworks of belief and collective cultural expectations. But that is not the only reason which enables them to be considered as a social reality. Nor is it the main or prime reason for doing so. The dream is social through and through, both in terms of what lies behind it and in the particularities of its production, as well as in the observable regularities of its content.

Limitations of literal approaches: content analysis of dream accounts

One of the methodological approaches to the study of dreams has involved developing quantitative methods on a relatively substantial corpus of dream accounts. The principle behind most of these studies is a simple one: dream accounts are linguistic productions, which can be studied in the same way as any other linguistic productions, and the linguistic properties (lexical, stylistic, thematic, compositional, or other) of these productions can be examined in relation to certain of the dreamers' main social characteristics (sex, age, era, society in which they live, social or professional milieu, education, etc.). All that is required for recurrences to become apparent (and this already represents a considerable challenge in itself) is access to dream accounts and to any social characteristics of dreamers which may be judged as relevant. Supporters (psychologists for the most part) of these methods can ponder whether it is preferable to obtain accounts of individual dreams written by a large number of dreamers with specific social characteristics (*sets of dreams*) or if it is better to focus on the comparative study of long series of dreams experienced by the same individuals (*series of dreams*), but a quantitative approach to the data is seen by some of them to represent the only pertinent scientific and objective method.

As a result, they give the impression that the main reason for the exclusive use of content analysis lies in a determination to 'do science' by applying quantitative methods. This is typically seen in the scenario of researchers who mimic the methodological standards of the dominant scientific disciplines rather than questioning the relevance of a literal analysis of content in the study of dreams. This kind of attitude is clearly visible in the work of Michael Schredl, a German psychologist with an active interest in the field of sleep and dream studies. Schredl writes: 'Dream content analysis is one of the basic methods applied in psychological dream research (Domhoff, 1996; Hall & Van de Castle, 1966; Schredl, 2008). This method has the advantage that it satisfies the common criteria of science such as replication by another research group, assessment of reliability and validity, and minimizing experimenter bias.'[63] It goes without saying that such a definition of science would disqualify a good deal of the research in the human and social sciences (psychology, sociology, ethnology, history) which are very often non-replicable in the strictest sense. And it is of course psychoanalysis that is primarily targeted by this kind of declaration of scientific war which hides behind the objectivity of science. However, the use of individual case studies is characteristic of many scientific disciplines, including some of the most important of these.[64] We should therefore question the relevance of an approach to dreams which uses quantitative analysis of content in order to grasp their full interest and extent.

The first study based on a corpus of dreams dates back to the end of the nineteenth century. This study did not yet involve the statistical analysis of correlations between the frequency with which certain elements of dream accounts occur and the characteristics of the dreamers themselves, but it is undoubtedly the origin of the so-called *continuity hypothesis*[65] advocated by American researchers (Hall, Van de Castle, Domhoff, etc.). So it was that Mary Whiton Calkins published in the *American Journal of Psychology* the results of her study based on 205 of her own dreams and 170 dreams noted by a man.[66] Aware of the difficulty of recalling dreams and the fact that the task necessitates an immediate attention to the content of the dream, Calkins took the precaution of setting out the conditions in which dreams would be collected. The two dreamers must write them down immediately on waking, and for that purpose paper, a

pen, matches and a candle were carefully laid out. The notes were then
re-read and commentaries were added indicating, where possible, any
connections between the dream and waking life. The dreamer herself was
twenty-eight and noted 205 dreams over the course of fifty-five nights and
the man in question was thirty-two and took notes for forty-six nights
with a total of 170 dreams. In both cases the average number of dreams
per night was around four. In the vast majority of cases, the dreamers (the
female dreamer a little more often than the male dreamer) were able to
establish links between the dream and recent events of waking life, and
Calkins stressed the congruence and continuity between waking life and
the world of dreams.

There are of course marked differences between dreams and descriptions of waking life. Calkins emphasises the comparative feebleness of
both attention and will, the absence of discrimination demonstrated by
dreamers, and a modified perception of reality, but, contrary to the belief
that 'one never dreams of subjects of vital interest to oneself', she shows
that 'the home, the family, the school, profession or business figure in all
our dreams, and yet are of the deepest interest to ourselves' and that 'all
these subjects, however, are connected with persons, places or things of
which we have frequent sense impressions.'[67] It is, she adds, 'the persons,
places and events of recent sense perception or of very vivid imagination'[68]
that make their appearance in dreams. The approach adopted by Calkins
working on a large number of dreams does not, however, completely
break away from the qualitative approach in so far as she is using accounts
made by dreamers to establish links between what is dreamt about and
experiences prior to the dream.

From the end of the 1940s, two American psychologists, Calvin S. Hall
and Robert L. Van de Castle, began to develop a method of analysing the
content of dream accounts which they claimed was quantitative and objective.[69] This involved breaking dreams down into a series of elements, clas-
sifying these elements by using lists of categories (frameworks or contexts,
people, objects, body parts, animals, actions, types of relationship between
people or the kinds of roles they play, the dreamer's emotions, successes
and failures, etc.), noting the frequency of occurrence of each category,
and comparing frequency or ratios with those of a control group. The
researchers assumed, somewhat naively, that, the higher the frequency of
apparition of any particular category, the greater the preoccupation that
was accorded to this category in waking life. In 1972, Hall referred to a
collection of 50,000 dreams from across the entire world.[70]

Following in the footsteps of that earlier work carried out by Hall
and Van de Castle, two other American researchers, Adam Schneider
and G. William Domhoff, backed by the Psychology Department at the
University of California in Santa Cruz, set up the 'DreamBank', which
included almost 22,000 dream accounts from dreamers aged between
seven and seventy-four. In some cases, information is provided on some
important characteristics of the dreamers (blind adults, children, students,

teachers, entomologists, experimental psychologists, etc.), but for the most part only details of age and sex are supplied. The dream accounts are collected in a variety of conditions, ranging from a sleep laboratory to classrooms and including personal dream diaries.

What is to be gained, or indeed lost, from this type of research, carried out on hundreds or thousands of dream accounts? The principal advantage of this research is to confirm that dreamers from the same group, from the same community, the same segment of the population, or sharing the assumptions of the same era tend to share the same images, themes and vocabulary. This holds no particular surprise for the sociologist, but demonstrating proof of this with reference to a domain as singular as that of oneiric production marks a major milestone in thinking and is not without significance. The images of dreams provide sociological evidence of the shared realities and experiences of dreamers – commonality of place, object, institution, activity, event, etc. In spite of the individual particularities stemming from multiple and combined experiences, classes of experiences which are to a large extent shared can be identified when an objective approach is adopted.

This explains why all those who have lived through the same traumatic events can end up having very similar post-traumatic dreams:[71] why dreamers in Germany dreamt of situations which reflected their fear, their feeling of dispossession, of humiliation, etc., in the face of the rising tide of Nazism,[72] why some of the dreams of former members of the Red Brigades locked up in Palmi maximum security jail shared a common matrix, why the dreams of people with a disabled brother or sister[73] or those of prostitutes in Bolivian brothels[74] could have common features, why sports students dream about sport more often than psychology students[75] and why the frequency of sports-related dreams should be strongly correlated with the amount of time spent on sports activities during the day,[76] why students are more likely to dream about music because this occupies a significant role in their lives,[77] why first-year medical students often dream of their alarm clocks not going off, of problems with the transport system, of illegible exam questions, of misreading questions or of handing in a blank answer sheet on the night before their exams,[78] why refugees from Central America to the United States have recurring dreams of scenes where the dreamer is pursued by men seeking to kill them,[79] why Kurdish children living in Iraq and exposed to a high level of traumatic events (with the sense of danger, anxiety about their family's safety, loss of close relatives and memories of horrific events) dream of disturbing atmospheres,[80] or why Palestinian children living in the Gaza Strip dream more frequently about violent scenes than those living in the West Bank.[81] In 2003, summing up much of the empirical literature from within the field of dream research, Michael Schredl and Friedrich Hofmann showed that, even if the nature of continuity varied from one study to another, the so-called continuity hypothesis was broadly confirmed by the facts; they cited continuity between the dream and the significant events in the dreamer's life, the pre-sleep psychological state, the dreamer's personality traits, or certain problems associated with neurosis.[82]

Dream images can moreover be correlated in a more classical way with the social properties of dreamers (age, sex, social or professional milieu, qualifications, family situation, etc.) given that these properties are synthetic indicators, albeit crude ones, of the realities experienced by dreamers or of their internalised dispositions (how they see, believe, think, feel, act). In this way, studies conducted during the 1960s were able to throw light on how dreams were affected by the gender of the person questioned, so that, for example, women dreamt less often of attacking than of being attacked, men dreamt more often of the outside space and women of the indoors and of the family circle, or men dreamt more about other men than women, who dreamt just as much about women as about men, etc.[83]

The analysis of thousands of dreams renders it possible finally to establish important observations about the nature of the experiences which make their appearance in the oneiric world. First of all, when researchers are able to work on long sequences of dreams from one individual, it becomes apparent not only that 'most people are consistent over years or decades in what they dream about', but that 'the most frequent characters, social interactions, and activities in their dreams are continuous with their waking interests and emotional concerns (Domhoff 2003).'[84] Maurice Halbwachs made the same point in 1925 when he observed that simply writing down dreams was enough to show that dreams can

> be classified depending on whether they relate to particular groups of relatives, friends, colleagues, or to certain particularities of our professional life, to specific facts, feelings, activities, education, hobbies, holidays and also to certain specific places which have a defined social significance such as the home, certain local areas or certain streets within a city, certain regions, and finally to specific categories of human beings such as children, the elderly, tradespeople, society people, scholars, etc.[85]

Following on from this, it is clear that 'the people who enter our dreams are the ones with whom we are emotionally involved.'[86] Parents, brothers and sisters, spouses and partners, lovers and mistresses, friends, classmates or work colleagues – all those with whom we interact and with whom tensions or conflicts can surface – feature most frequently. Sometimes well-known or famous people (film stars, politicians, kings and queens, journalists and scholars) also feature, and it can only be supposed that these symbolise certain properties (authority, power, beauty, cruelty, kindness, intelligence, etc.). In the same way, as in the case with people, the incorporation of activities from waking life into dreams is linked to the level of emotional investment in these activities.[87] Finally, dreams speak more about anxiety and conflicts, tensions, doubts, failures and difficult situations than about joys, successes and achievements.[88]

But what is lost by correlating elements taken from dreams with groups or categories is the study of the precise mechanisms which govern the transition from waking life to the dream. Just as certain anthropological studies whose authors think that 'they have related dreams to individual life histories' end up 'relegating them to the status of subjective, "private" non-social experience',[89] research like this, conducted on a large corpus, is implicitly based on the idea that a science of the individual cannot possibly exist. As a result, the statistical viewpoint which is distanced from individual particularities runs the risk – and this is very often what happens – both of neglecting the role of all the incorporated past that implicitly structures dreams without directly featuring in their content and of failing to take into account metaphorical and symbolic transformations or the effects of condensation, substitution, etc., which contribute to producing the dream images. A dream is a meaningful production among others, but it is a production that has certain distinctive features because of the particular conditions in which it takes shape. A dream theory will therefore be incomplete if it simply limits itself to conducting quantitative analyses of content without seeking to find out what lies *behind* the images, the feelings and the words, what constitutes the *backdrop* which gives it structure it and enables it to take shape.

Those researchers who argue in favour of the objective and scientific character of methods analysing content forget that counting the frequency of certain themes or categories of items does not in itself constitute a genuine scientific practice. For that to be the case they would have first to question whether words or images had different meanings depending on the different contexts in which they appeared; they would need to question what it was they were counting, what these elements represented in the eyes of dreamers, the nature of the link between what is being counted and the extra-linguistic reality. Content analysis fails to investigate the nature of the people, objects, places, situations or actions which are dreamt about. Are they known to the dreamer in waking life or not? Do they refer to elements which are real or unreal? What relationship does the dreamer have with these different elements? In the absence of answers to such questions, there is the danger of falling into the trap of a statistical positivism which appears to be scientific but which in fact consists simply in meticulously counting elements of uncertain status and ends up suppressing any general scientific ambition.[90]

Such positivism is clearly demonstrated in the case of those researchers who claim that the meaning of dreams is to be found in the dreams and not in theories about them (viewed as ready-made interpretation grids).[91] Hall even goes so far as to claim, contrary to psychoanalysis, that 'numerous studies convince me that the dreams of a person express directly and explicitly, without the need of interpretation, what is on the dreamer's mind, his or her preoccupations, concerns, anxieties, conflicts, ambiguities, wishes, conceptions of himself or herself and of others and of the world, and much else.'[92] But this demonstrates a lack of understanding both of what constitutes a theory and of the supposedly obvious meaning which emerges simply as a result of familiarity with the oneiric material. As Jacques Montangero so clearly sums up,

> research based on content analysis is conducted in a wholly empirical spirit (Hall and Van de Castle, 1966; Domhoff, 1996; Strauch and Meier, 1996). Such research involves collecting a large number of dream accounts and then looking at which categories of content occur most frequently. This research is carried out outside any precise theoretical framework, without any preliminary hypothesis or, generally speaking, any desire to provide answers to a question.[93]

By reducing dream accounts to their verbal surfaces, by taking words only at their literal value, the analyst thus eliminates any specificities and dismisses any differences between dream accounts, literature, diaries, ordinary conversations, etc. This elimination of the specificities of verbal material is sometimes fully acknowledged and accepted by these researchers.[94] What they fail to take note of are the social frameworks in which these verbal utterances are formed and expressed: the literary game, the context of interaction, the context of sleep and of the recounting of the dream, etc. In all cases (writer, interactant, dreamer, etc.) the schemas of experience or the incorporated dispositions are of central importance and are expressed (or revised). But the conditions in which this occurs radically alter the manner in which they are expressed. And what essentially changes is the nature and the very meaning of the words used.

The main problem with literal readings of dream accounts lies therefore in the fact that these neglect the many discrepancies between the real life of the dreamer and the life portrayed in oneiric productions. Dreams can entail partial or total transformations of reality (the dreamer sees the parental home, but it is much more attractive than in real life, or sees a brother in the dream but as he was as a child), adjustments in comparison with reality (the dreamer sees themselves acting confidently in a situation where they would normally be extremely ill at ease), examples of symbolisation-metaphorisation (seeing the collapse of a bridge as the symbol of the end of a romantic relationship), condensations (the dreamer's mother appears but dressed like his wife, or else the dreamer is convinced it is she but what he actually sees is an animal) or substitutions (the dreamer replaces a place, a person or an object by another which generates an analogical resonance in his or her mind).

How, without any discussion with the dreamer, is it possible to know if the person, place or object in the dream should be taken 'at face value' or if they should be considered as the symbols of other realities? Is the weapon seen in the dream a substitute for a penis, an object symbolising someone's hostility or aggression, or a real weapon, the dreamer having in real life been held up by armed robbers? We know, for example, that post-traumatic dreams can take the form of an almost literal repetition of what happened (the dreamer was involved in a train crash and dreams that he or she is travelling in a train which derails and ends up lying across the tracks just as happened in real life), but that they can also be metaphorical (instead of dreams about train crashes, there are scenes involving hurricanes, fires or tsunamis which are equally terrifying and reproduce the same type of situation involving the sudden loss of all control over events).[95] What does the researcher really discover when he or she observes recurrences in the elements which make up dreams, and what does that enable him or her to say about dreams and about the processes governing their creation?

Applied to literature, a strictly literal reading would, for example, prevent us from understanding that the monstrous insect of Kafka's *Metamorphosis* is the despicable, repulsive being he perceived himself to be in the eyes of his family. It would not go beyond discussion of the themes of insects or animals. In this way, such a reading does manage to attain a certain coherence in terms of the verbal material used which is always in some way connected to the life of the dreamer, to their personal preoccupations, cultural milieu, period in which they are living, etc. But what is totally lacking is the complex link between what dreamers experience and have experienced and what they dream about – in other words, the interplay of transformations between what they have experienced in life and what happens in the dream. In their study of Franz Kafka's dreams, Calvin S. Hall and Richard E. Lind explain that their work is based on the hypothesis that 'frequency of occurrence of a given category in a series of dreams is a direct index of the intensity of the dreamer's preoccupation with that category.'[96] But should a person who dreams frequently of animals necessarily be considered to be preoccupied by animals in real life? The naivety of the hypothesis becomes apparent when we manage to establish, through the interview with the dreamer, whether the animal in the dream is a literal or a symbolic creature.

Bell and Hall were themselves already conscious of the limitations of their analysis of a corpus composed of the dream accounts made by a paedophile called Norman, noting that an 'omitted element' could, however, be very important in the life of the dreamer.[97] In this instance this is the case with Norman's father (who is the cause of his son's paedophilic behaviour, having regularly forced him as a child to practise fellatio on him), whose absence from the dreams should have led the authors to conclude that he was of little importance in Norman's life. But in fact he is present in the dreams usually in the form of animals which symbolise danger, power and sometimes impulsiveness (Norman dreams, for example, that a bull is attempting to have sex with him; in other dreams, the father might take the form of a bear, a dragon, an elephant, a fox or a bucking horse).[98]

But, in the purest formalist or structuralist tradition, the researchers are of the opinion that there is no need to know what happens outside the dream in order to understand it. 'For a large majority of dreams', wrote Calvin S. Hall and Vernon J. Nordby, 'a simple analysis of the dreamer's interactions with people, animals and objects can tell us a great deal about the dreamer. No other information is necessary except the dreams themselves.'[99] And, in the same way, Domhoff describes his use of content analysis of dreams in this manner: 'It does not make use of free associations, amplifications, autobiographical statements, or any other information from outside the dream reports themselves.'[100] The text, nothing but the text, said Barthes;[101] the dream account and only the dream account, declare those content analysts working on dreams.[102] What researchers fail to see here is the whole operation of oneiric transposition of waking experience both past and present. By remaining on the surface of the images put into words in dream accounts, they do not question which schemas of experience might lie behind the dream images and assume that these images are immediately transparent.

The historian Peter Burke was therefore justified in asking, with reference to seventeenth-century dream accounts, if dreams featuring kings were literally about kings or if they were metaphorical ways of dreaming about other powerful people, and notably about father figures, as psychoanalysts would perhaps be inclined to think. But, of course, dreaming of a 'king' when you live under a monarchy does not have the same significance as dreaming of a 'king' in the context of a democracy. And, in the same way, dreaming of a 'king' when you frequent the king does not have the same sense as dreaming of a 'king' when he is merely a distant figure. In the present case, not being in a position to interrogate the dreamers, Peter Burke is reduced to making conjectures while leaning towards the hypothesis of the literal significance of the presence of the king.

> We find eight dreams of kings (one of James I, six of Charles I, and one of Charles II). It is of course common for psychoanalysts to claim, following Freud, that a king in a dream symbolizes the father of the dreamer. However, like a literal-minded historian, I am convinced that in the sample, at least on one level and on some occasions, 'the king' meant the king. After all, Laud, who dreamed of the king most (four times) frequently saw and spoke to Charles I. Ashmole dreamed of the king three times in 1645–6, in other words at the height of Civil War. Josselin dreamed of the deposition of Charles II. On the other hand, Sewall, far away in America, was the only one of the four not to dream of a king at all.
>
> The point about kings is a special case of a more general contrast between the seventeenth century and the twentieth. Calvin Hall found that only 1 per cent of the dreams he collected were of what he called 'famous or prominent public figures'.[103]

Only a precise knowledge of the dreamer's situation at the time of the dream would enable someone to know if the king in the dream did indeed refer to the king, but also if it perhaps referred to the father too, to the immediate hierarchical superior or to any other authority figure with whom the dreamer might have come into contact in waking life. For, as Burke rightly observes: 'It may be that these seventeenth-century dreamers were making use of political events and figures to symbolize private anxieties. We have returned to the problem of distinguishing manifest from latent content, the problem whether 'the king' in Laud's dreams really meant Charles I or not.'[104]

Douglas Hofstadter and Emmanuel Sander perfectly analysed the role of metaphors, analogies and the various allegories which are permanently woven into our existences to the extent that nobody would dream of saying that someone had made a literary comment because he said in a speech that 'you cannot judge a book by its cover' or of claiming that an individual seemed especially interested in animals because he had talked about 'a frog who wished to be as big as an ox' and about somebody 'crying wolf'. The possibility that words can say something other than what they seem to be saying because they are being used in a metaphorical way should be a warning to all content analysts:

> the mental categories associated with proverbs have meanings that on the surface are extremely different. This means that such categories are very broad, and that they bring together situations whose common gist is located only at a high level of abstraction. The French proverb 'Qui vole un œuf vole un bœuf' has a relatively little-known counterpart in English: 'He who will steal an egg will steal an ox.' There is also a proverb in Arabic that says 'He who will steal an egg will steal a camel.' Someone might argue that these two proverbs express very different ideas, a camel and an ox being rather different beasts. Of course this takes things at a ridiculously literal level. In hearing either proverb, we are meant to understand something far more general than the notion that a male human being who has stolen an egg will one day also steal either an ox or a camel. We are supposed to infer, through our natural tendency to generalize outwards, that any person, male or female, who steals something smallish stands a good chance of going on and committing more serious acts of thievery later on. . . . In that case, the proverb's meaning becomes roughly, *'Small acts are a prelude to larger acts'*.[105]

Yet the same applies to the metaphorical images found in dreams, and it is therefore essential to identify the schemas which make up the very fabric of dream scenarios[106] rather than engaging in literal readings which go no deeper than the linguistic surface.

Finally, one last problem with the content analysis of dream accounts lies in the fact that such an approach tends to break dreams down into categories of people, places, objects, situations, etc., and consequently ends up failing to grasp the more general or broader meaning of the dream. Just as a house cannot be reduced to the sum of its components (rubble or stone, cement, woodwork, tiles, metallic parts, etc.), the account of a dream is not simply the sum of its linguistic components. As in the well-known saying, the whole is greater than the sum of the parts. The different components which make up dreams are fixed within a unique *combination* and cannot be separated from the *narratives* to which they belong.[107]

If the results furnished by content analysis cannot be swept brusquely aside and do indeed form a base on which any theory of dreams should clearly be established, the absence of any theoretical framework allowing the organisation of research, the determination of which data should be collected in order to be able to interpret dreams in a pertinent manner, the understanding of the exact nature of each type of evidence, and how these should be linked together is an indication that we are a long way from the general theoretical model which the current state of research on dreams demands. It is, however, clear, on the other hand, that, away from these large-scale studies, some well-constructed and well-analysed cases, for which all relevant data have been gathered, could indeed be capable of forming a solid base on which to elaborate a theory and a synthetic method which would include the various points of view and the results of the existing state of knowledge.[108]

Rather than trying to define the content and the meaning of dreams with inadequate means, it would be more productive to study, by means of quantitative investigations, socially differentiated relationships to the dream according to the social characteristics of dreamers. Even if we know that everybody dreams each night, we could then ask ourselves to what extent the propensity to remember dreams is subject to social variation? Who has written down their dreams at some point? Who describes their dreams to other people? And, within their circle, who are they are most likely to discuss them with? Who are the readers and users of dream books? Who believes dreams can be premonitory or thinks that they have no real meaning? Even if questions such as these might not lead to progress being made in the field of dream interpretation, they will nevertheless be useful in establishing the social barriers to the objectivisation of dreams.

In what sense are dreams a social issue?

Dreaming as a solitary, purely mental activity, associated with sleep and apparently unsolicited by any individual or social framework, does not at first sight appear to lend itself to sociological investigation. In what sense then is the dream a profoundly social matter? In order to answer this question, we must first of all define what is meant by *social*.

Defining the social

Traditionally in the context of sociology, the term 'social' has long been used to refer to anything relating either to society as a whole (as distinct from nature) or to collective entities such as institutions, communities or groups, collective movements, or categories of individuals with shared characteristics. In contexts such as these, 'collective' is a strict equivalent of 'social', and 'individual' refers to anything outside the 'social' and notably to the 'psychological'.

Yet this division between what might be seen as social and what could be considered as psychological falls apart as soon as we begin to speculate about what goes into the making of any individual from within a given society or group, or how he or she became this relatively unique person endowed with particular ways of seeing, feeling and acting. If a so-called social reality is always associated with the collective, it does not always take the form of a collective. Thus, objects made by individuals in a given society – everyday objects, tools, machines, architecture and public spaces, works of art, clothing, etc. – are thoroughly social, just as each individual is thoroughly social in the sense that he or she is the product of socialising processes associated with the groups or institutions frequented over the course of a lifetime.

If the social implies an element of the collective yet cannot be simply reduced to that, how can a more satisfactory definition be reached? It might be said, for example, that, whenever relationships between individuals are at stake, there is some kind of social reality to be studied. This reality goes beyond the will and the control of each particular individual and can be studied as such, in its own right. Yet this initial formulation is decidedly inadequate if all possible misunderstandings are to be avoided. Taken in a narrow sense, it could imply that only inter-individual relationships are sociological objects, which would logically lead to two types of exclusion.

Exit first of all societies, communities, classes or groups. For what links, for example, the members of the same social class are not the direct interactions between them but similar positions within a social division of labour and within lifestyles and conditions. In the same way, what objectively links different social classes to each other has little to do with relationships between their respective members; rather, it concerns the relations they maintain within this social division of labour and within certain lifestyles and conditions. Even if they have very few opportunities to interact, in the sense of 'meeting each other', the shareholders and employees of a multinational company, or Brazilian coffee pickers and European coffee drinkers, are no less interdependent, mutually relying on each other in what they are and do.

Exit next anchorites and other hermits shut away from the world, the shipwrecked Robinson Crusoe alone on his island, along with the mental activity of an individual lost in daydreams or deep in sleep. Is it not possible for a lone individual, temporarily or more durably cut off from interaction with others, to be a sociological object? In fact, these solitary individuals have reality themselves as thinking, feeling and acting individuals only because they have a *past involving socialising relationships of interdependence*. They are social beings because what they feel, think and do is based on the whole history of their relationships with other people. The behaviour, the feelings and the representations of the anchorite monk, of Robinson Crusoe (without Man Friday) or of the sleeper who are not involved in any interaction with others are no less *social* than those of individuals who integrate with others, interact, work together, demonstrate together, or enjoy the same entertainment. The whole range of perceptions, thoughts, feelings or gestures of these isolated individuals is structured by their past socialising experiences which have sedimented within them in the form of dispositions (or schemas) and skills. Without these past socialising experiences, without these disposition and skills, these individuals would not have structured their personalities, their thinking, their feelings and their behaviours; they would never have been able to interact with others and possibly would not even have survived.

It is moreover impossible to think about the relationships of interdependence which have contributed to making individuals who they are without immediately noting the central role of language. Human beings only see, feel, think and act in so far as they are capable of symbolising, describing and communicating with the help of elements of language (oral, written, gestural, iconic, etc.), which have meaning only because of the existence of the communities of human beings which constitute society. Existing relationships of interdependence, the history of past relationships of interdependence and linguistic practices, which form an integral part of the psychological development of each human being, are inextricably linked. The mental representations or the psychic activity of unique individuals, even when they find themselves alone or isolated, are fundamentally social in the sense that they presuppose the groups or institutions (and their history) to which those individuals have belonged, along with their particular linguistic history (different types of language), which would have no meaning outside of the group. The very fact that the dreamer, whether sleeping or waking, can mentally conjure up narrative sequences of actions independent of what is actually happening in the world is proof of the fundamentally social character of both dreams and daydreams. For it is thanks to language's capacity to structure – that tool which links human beings together and is adapted to all the different kinds of relationships they have – that such mental representations are possible.

The social cannot therefore be reduced either to collectives (to society, to social groups, to social categories, to institutions or to social movements), which are realities captured on a macro-sociological scale, or to direct and visible interactions between individuals, which are specific moments or events among all the social realities captured on the micro-sociological scale. It implies relationships of interdependence between collective entities as well as between individuals, and it can manifest even when no collective seems immediately present or when no direct interaction is in place to regulate or to structure individual action or thought. Sociology can just as easily study the configurations (or structures) which

form groups of individuals or individuals in relationships of interdependence as it can each individual as an intersection point of all the past and
present relationships of interdependence which transform that individual
into this relatively unique dreaming, thinking, feeling and acting being.

By understanding the social as a series of internal and external constraints, by demonstrating that each individual is the product of his or her
past social experiences and that he or she always acts in specific contexts
of action, we are better able to understand individual particularities from
a sociological point of view, and especially the most intimate psychic
activities of individuals. The time when the social sciences could exclude
the individual from any analysis and concentrate simply on the study of
'trends', of 'milieus', of 'groups' or of 'institutions' is now long gone. As
an involuntary, psychic activity occurring during sleep, the dream can thus
be recognised as a form of expression which can be understood only at the
intersection of the past and present social experiences of the dreamer.

A dispositionalist and contextualist programme for dreams

A sound knowledge of the history of scholarly studies on the dream (for
the most part psychoanalytical, psychological, psychiatric and neuroscientific, but also to a lesser degree historical, anthropological, linguistic or
sociological) enables the researcher gradually to get a sense of all the elements of the *problem* which needs to be resolved today.

First of all, many studies demonstrate that the dream is by no means
a 'spontaneous and random' phenomenon and therefore devoid of any
significance, but that it can be linked to the dreamer's life, to his or her
preoccupations, tensions and conflicts, desires and fears, etc. This association between waking experiences and nocturnal dreaming has been noted
since the earliest Greek and Latin observations on the dream. Lucretius
(first century BC), for example, wrote in his *De rerum natura*:

> Now, whatever activity is the object of our closest interest and attach-
> ment, or whatever business has occupied much of our time in the
> past and has received our mind's special attention – this is usually the
> subject of our dreams. Lawyers dream that they are pleading cases
> and drafting contracts; generals that they are fighting battles; mari-
> ners that they are continuing to wage war with the winds; and I that
> I am tackling my task of constantly investigating the nature of things
> and expounding my discoveries in my native tongue. The position is
> usually the same when other pursuits and arts occupy people's minds
> with delusions in their dreams.[109]

And, again, Artemidorus of Daldis, in his interpretation of dreams, takes
into account the personality and the current situation of the dreamer at
the time of his dream.[110] The continuity hypothesis supported by certain
researchers today was therefore formulated a very long time ago.[111]

The question nevertheless remains to determine 1) what is meant by the 'life' or the 'past experience' of the dreamer and 2) what kind of methodological steps need to be put in place in order to reconstruct this 'past experience' and relate it to the person's dreams.[112] From the standpoint of a dispositionalist sociology, links must be woven between the schemas of experiences incorporated by the dreamer in the course of his or her socialisation and oneiric themes, between the existential situation and the oneric situation, and between elements of the sociological biography and oneiric scenarios. The most powerfully structuring elements of the dreamers' lives must be analysed in order to understand the nature of the themes explored in the dreams.

Dreams can therefore be seen as *the condensed forms of social experiences involuntarily shaped by the dreamer during sleep* and meriting sociological analysis. In a certain sense, all dreams are autobiographical. That does not imply that the dream is simply the transcription, in the form of a dream account, of the 'dreamer's life'. But if all dreams can be considered autobiographical, it is because they are always the expression of the questions that the existential situation of the dreamer has led him or her to ask. Unlike literature, even in its most closely autobiographical form, each dream does not represent a response to the dreams of other dreamers but is directly linked to the dreamer's own schemas of experience. Within the context of the theory of fields, there is no oneiric field, just as there is no dream capital to conquer or to redefine, no competition or clashes between dreamers, no accumulated oneiric past which dreamers could appropriate, etc.

Thus, a good number of studies have established the importance of events occurring on the day preceding the dream or in the few days beforehand. Some of the dream images are thus taken from very recent scenes in the dreamer's life (interactions experienced or observed, something recently read, a film or show seen, etc.).[113] Freud gave numerous examples of such scenes, of poems or novels read, or plays recently watched which furnish the dreamer with the materials, the contexts or the scenarios of his or her dream. But we need to understand the exact status of these elements taken from recent waking life and to grasp how this recent past is connected to elements of a more distant past in the dreamer's life (for example, the period of childhood in a Freudian perspective) or, better still, with elements of the incorporated past which have taken shape in the forms of schemas (of emotion, of action, of representation, of perception, of appreciation, etc.), sometimes seen by psychology in terms of 'personality structure' and which dispositionalist sociology understands in terms of an individual heritage of dispositions and schemas.

Moreover, the psychological and structural properties of dream activity have been widely described, analysed and endorsed by very different writers.[114] Among these we find reference to the absence of planning, reflexivity and control of the narrative that sleep occasions and which contributes to the impression of incoherence, the implicit nature of private language, the importance of images, of symbolisation and of a visual use of metaphor,[115] and the presence of what Freud called condensation, which can result in images from different sources being brought together to evoke situations, places, objects or people that are different but analogous in one respect or another, or the tendency for emotional exaggeration or for the dramatisation of situations (when, for example, a dreamer visualises the death of someone against whom he simply holds a grudge). In the course of this book we will be looking in more detail at each of these aspects.

Finally, another series of problems, this time of a methodological nature, emerges from the scholarly literature. These centre on the conditions in which information about dreams is collected along with any relevant information about the life of the dreamer which need to be taken into consideration in order to interpret the dreams correctly. Focusing his attention on the construction of a model for the interpretation of dreams and the theorisation of psychic activity, Freud paid little attention to these methodological aspects, which are nevertheless crucial in the context of a scientific study. The dreams interpreted by Freud could have been noted down immediately on waking or recounted several days, several weeks or several months later. Information about the dreamer's life could be based on an acquaintance with the dreamer acquired after several days, weeks or months of psychoanalytic therapy, on self-understanding in the case of interpretation of one's own dreams, or on an indirect knowledge of the dreamer acquired from those close to him or her. Similarly, the technique of free association of ideas (or of impressions) in relation to the elements of the dream and the duration of each session of analysis are not always defined very precisely and vary from one psychoanalyst to another.

On all these points, dispositionalist-contextualist sociology, which looks at practices at the intersection of incorporated dispositions and the contexts in which they are deployed,[116] can therefore provide ways to set out problems, methodological approaches and answers of its own. In this context, dreams can only be understood by focusing attention on three major elements which will be combined in a general formula for the interpretation of dreams and which will be discussed in more detail in the course of this book:

1. the most frequently recurring elements of the dreamer's inherited stock of incorporated dispositions and of his or her existential situation that can be discovered by studying his or her *sociological biography* (a diachronic study of the main categories of socialising experiences encountered by the individual in question): this process of reconstruction requires numerous hours of interviews with living dreamers or the study of archival documents in the case of dreamers now deceased;[117]
2. the immediate circumstances of diurnal life (usually dating from the day before the dream) which have provoked the dream in question by reviving certain incorporated schemas and certain elements of the

existential situation: these elements can only be obtained through interviews with the dreamer;[118]
3. the specific context of the oneiric expression, characterised notably
   by the withdrawal of ordinary social interactions and the absence of
   demands from any external entourage, the weakening of the capacity
   for narrative control, the fact that lights are often turned out and movement ceases, the relative silence, the need to express oneself predominantly in images, and particularly the use, totally ignored by Freud
   and psychoanalysis, of an 'internal language' or a 'private' one which
   accounts for the presence of the many implicit or unspoken elements,
   given that the dreamer is not subject to any audience and is expressing
   themselves for their own purposes in an elliptical manner.[119]

All these properties associated with *the context of sleep* show, contrary to
what some writers claim, that dreams are not spontaneous, free productions expressed outside of any specific context but instead respond to very
precise logics which are indissociable from the constraints imposed by the
context of sleep.[120]

From the specific point of view I am advancing, a dream cannot
therefore be correctly interpreted if the dream account is not in some way
linked to the incorporated dispositions of the dreamer, some of which
may date back to early infancy, to the state of the existential situation he
or she is facing at the time of the dream (the nature of the problems to be
faced, the preoccupations or obsessions he or she may have), to contextual
elements from the immediate past which trigger the dream (for example,
on the day preceding the dream) and to the context of sleep within which
the animated images of the dream take shape.

The intellectual position I am adopting here is first of all based on an
extended period of personal research and, in particular, on a longstanding
theoretical deliberation regarding the individual scale of sociology,[121]
on the elaboration of a method capable of constructing sociological
portraits of specific individuals,[122] and on a clearly defined method of
sociological biography.[123] It is also based on the evidence obtained from
critical examination of the relationships between psychoanalysis and the
social sciences.[124] Finally, it stems from a body of empirical research and
theoretical considerations on implicit language,[125] daydreams,[126] private
diaries and autobiographies.[127]

In a previous study, I had the opportunity to show how Kafka's literary
work could be understood by linking his sociological biography, which
enables us to understand the social processes structuring his personality,
his particular dispositions and the series of recurring problems he had to
deal with in his life, the precise circumstances behind each of his works
and the literary contexts in which he was exercising his creative role (the
literary microcosm of Prague, the German-language literary world and,
beyond these, the international literary scene).[128] The main difference
between the 'dream' and 'literary creation', two symbolic productions

which Freud liked to compare, lies in the fact that symbolic productions which occur during sleep occur in individuals who, on the one hand, do not control the flow of their consciousness in the same way as in certain waking situations and, on the other hand, are not constrained by a social context equivalent to a literary context.

The dream can therefore be analysed as a *visual narrative unintentionally implemented during sleep*. Like other forms of expression with which it has sometimes been compared (children's games, daydreams, literary creation, informal oral accounts, the reading of fictional texts, etc.),[129] it takes place at the point of intersection between the incorporated experiences of the dreamer and that dreamer's context of expression. It is therefore a matter both of identifying which schemas of experience are involved and which events or circumstances have triggered them and of conducting a detailed analysis of the effects imposed by the context of sleep on these transposed experiences.

The many social determinants of dreams

For all the reasons referred to, Maurice Halbwachs was wrong to claim that it is 'not in memory but in the dream that the mind is most removed from society' and that, 'if purely individual psychology looks for an area where consciousness is isolated and turned upon itself, it is in nocturnal life, and only there, that it will most be found.'[130] The dreamer is certainly cut off from the surrounding social world but remains intensely focused on the problems he or she faces in this world. Because he struggled to understand how the social world penetrated the dream, and because he never fully grasped the logics behind the processes of analogy which secretly organise the dream images, Halbwachs sometimes even saw these as random images to which the sociologist was particularly ill-equipped to respond: 'Almost completely detached from the system of social representations, its images are nothing more than raw materials, capable of entering into all sorts of combinations. They establish only random relations among each other – relations based on the disordered play of corporal modifications.'[131] Halbwachs did, however, make some pertinent objections when, in a self-correcting about-turn, he wrote:

> We said in the previous chapter that, when he dreams, man ceases to be in contact with the society of his fellow creatures. Are we not going too far in this, and, even in sleep, do not some of the beliefs and conventions of the groups in the midst of which he lives still impose themselves on him? Undoubtedly there must be many common notions between the dream and the waking state. If there was no communication between these two worlds, if the mind did not have the same means of understanding what it perceives in both of them, in the dream he would be reduced to the kind of conscious activity attributed to certain animals, and perhaps to small children, and

would not give objects, people and situations similar names or accord them the same meanings as when he encountered them in waking life, and he would not be capable of recounting his dreams.[132]

Even when a socialised individual is 'momentarily and partially freed' from the influence of the group, it is still possible to 'verify also to what extent it is exerted deep down and conditions our entire psychic life, since, even in the isolation of the dream, it is still present, fainter and fragmented, but still perfectly recognisable.'[133] Halbwachs saw a proof of 'the action of society' in the fact that 'we do not create men and objects from scratch any more than we do the situations which appear in dreams' and that 'they are borrowed from our experience of waking life, in other words, in the state of isolation in which sleep places us, we see again what has caught our gaze or modified our senses when we were in contact with our fellow creatures.'[134] And, even when we dream of 'completely unexpected events' or of 'strange and monstrous figures', we are still capable of 'realising it on waking' and of 'interpreting them with the help of notions common to those within our group'.[135]

In order to condense the argument which will be developed throughout this book, the dream could be said to be a social reality:

1. because dreaming implies sociologically constituted symbolic capacities and, in particular, the capacity to narrate, and form visual metaphors for, feelings, situations, relationships and sequences of socially significant actions;
2. because dreams are primarily concerned with the problems and preoccupations of the waking lives of socialised individuals;
3. because these problems and preoccupations reveal the schemas or dispositions (types of attitude, ways of acting, of seeing, of feeling) socially constituted long ago in the course of various social experiences;
4. because these problems or preoccupations and these dispositions have been reactivated by situations experienced in the course of social life in the waking state (scenes of interaction experienced or seen, words overheard, books or other texts read, films or shows seen, etc.);
5. and, finally, because dreams can only be accessed through dream accounts involving language skills which are socially constituted and unevenly distributed among dreamers.

Finally, even if it is impossible to deny the fundamentally individual character of the dream, the latter can moreover, like any other social reality, be looked at in the context of two very different scales: on an individual scale, taking into account the singular nature of both the dream and the dreamer, or on a group scale, with the focus on the shared properties of dreams and on categories or groups of dreamers.

I shall be focusing here primarily on the dream on the individual scale, but this will by no means prevent me – indeed, quite the opposite is true – from investigating the issue of the social nature of dreams on the collective scale. On the individual scale, it is possible to reconstruct *recurring schemas of experience*, a single dreamer clearly bringing with them a vast number of schemas of experience all of which are the products of the history of his or her social experiences. On the group or category scale, it is possible, by eliminating the specificities, to reconstruct *categories of relatively similar schemas of experience* linked to *relatively similar categories of conditions of existence or coexistence*. For any one particular dreamer, the probability of dreaming of certain situations is greater or smaller depending on the conditions of his or her existence or coexistence and, consequently, depending on the categories of schemas of experience which encompass his or her own experiences.

A general formula for the interpretation of dreams

The different elements involved in the process of creating dreams which have been referred to above, and which will be examined in more detail in the course of this book, can be summed up in a general formula for the interpretation of dreams. Such a formula follows on from a general formula for the study of practices which has already been set out, and which needs to be clarified and expanded in order to be adapted to the dream object.

The general formula for interpreting practices

The simplest formula designed to understand why individuals act as they act, think as they think, feel as they feel, can be summed up as follows:

Disposition <—> Context of action => Practice

or, alternatively:

Incorporated past <—> Context of present action => Practice

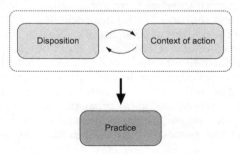

Figure 1 General formula for interpreting practice

This formula sums up the aim of research which focuses on practices at the point of intersection of incorporated dispositions and abilities (resulting from varying amounts of time spent in socialising contexts in the past) and the always specific context of the action in which these are deployed. For example, a pupil's behaviour in the classroom depends at the same time on past family experience and on the nature of the educational context in which that pupil is acting. It could be said that practices are always 'compromise formations' (in the Freudian sense) between a structuring incorporated past and a restrictive present context. Yet this compromise is in no sense a 'disguise' in response to the censorship. Instead it is the very expression of the *historic nature of the human being*, who has a past (and the incorporated memory of all that past) and is constantly confronted with present situations which are to a greater or lesser extent consistent with that past. When practices are forms of expression, they can be described as being based both on the incorporated past and on the conditions of expression, as much cerebral as structural or moral, which are subject to variation (the brain does not function in quite the same fashion according to whether the person is asleep or awake. The structural demands vary according to the type of verbal exchange or the context of the utterance, and particularly depending on the degree of formality of the situation in which the utterance occurs. Moral constraints vary in the same way).

This formula has the advantage of being equally applicable to a micro-sociological scale (individual actions within the context of the interaction) and to a more macro-sociological scale (practices on the scale of a group, of a sphere of action or of a more general social formation) and of encompassing all possible social formations. It operates therefore on a fundamental anthropological level: human beings are a species whose cerebral elasticity renders them capable of learning throughout their existence, and these human beings act in social frameworks which vary considerably and are more or less organised (institutionalised). But all the terms of the formula – dispositions and abilities formed within contexts and in the course of specific modalities of socialisation, contexts of action, types of practice – are historically variable.

In all known human societies there are groups, collective forms of life and of activity, and individuals who are socialised and act within these groups or within these forms of collective life. In all human societies, links exist between dispositions and abilities (the result of relatively long-lasting frequentation of different forms of social life) and 'contexts of action', the nature of which varies according to the type of society and even within a given society. The 'universality' of such links is therefore not without connection to the natural, biological capacities of the human being and, in particular, to their mnemonic capacities and to the kind of brain and nervous system they possess which distinguishes humans from other animals.

A simplified[136] formula of this kind first of all suggests that any attempt to explain purely by context alone (pragmatic contextualism of the situation, contextualism of the framework of interaction, contextualism of the field, the institution, the organisation or system of action) or purely on the basis of the incorporated properties of the actors (essentialism of theories of character or of personality, mechanistic dispositionalism, etc.) is reductive. If the analysis of contexts of action allowed us to infer actors' behaviour, sociology would be a *science of contexts*. And if, conversely, analysis of dispositions and abilities allowed us to predict the behaviour of actors without regard to the context of the action, sociology would be a *science of incorporated properties*.

The conflict between a contextualist explanation and one made exclusively on the basis of dispositions is not confined to sociology. This same tension occurs in the psychoanalytical analysis of dreams, hindering an understanding of the dynamics and the complexity of the dream. For example, neglecting the manifest content of the dream which draws on images or recent scenes experienced by the dreamer, and seeing this as simply the basis of a latent concealed content linked to the childhood of the dreamer, is typical of the unilateral dispositionalist tendency. As a psychoanalyst himself, Thomas Morton French sought to rectify the strong tendency of psychoanalysis to bring every single element of the dream back to elements of the childhood past by ignoring the significance of the present situation, and particularly of current problems, as the trigger for dreams: 'Let us inquire now as to what the dream has done with present reality. What is conspicuous here is the phenomenon of transference. The patient reacts to a present situation with reactions appropriate rather to a childhood situation.'[137] In order to understand the 'cognitive structure' of the dream, we need first to try to understand the dream as a response to the emotional situation at the time of the dream, before investigating which other analogous situations from the past it might be linked to.

Conversely, doing as content analysts do, and focusing only on dream accounts and on what links these to the immediate circumstances, means yielding to a contextualism and a presentism which makes it impossible to understand why one set of images is selected rather than another. For present contexts hold the attention of the dreamers only in so far as they echo past experiences incorporated by the dreamer in the form of schemes, schemas or dispositions. Rather than focusing only on the 'topicality theme', it would be better, as René Allendy so pertinently writes, 'to seize on the point where the current impression intersects with the background tendencies.'[138]

To take an example concerning the analysis of post-traumatic dreams, we see how this tension continues to resurface:

There are currently two theories of traumatic pathology: on the one hand, traumatic neurosis and, on the other, post-traumatic stress syndrome. In very simple terms, I would suggest that with regard to stress, it is accepted that its intensity and suddenness provide an adequate explanation of the nature of the illness. However, with traumatic neurosis we take account of the impact of the trauma but we consider it in relation to the subject's level of tolerance and view the whole experience in the context of the individual's life.[139]

The powerful nature of the effects of trauma can lead us to forget that, however powerful it may be, it takes on different meanings or produces different effects depending on the past experience of the person who has undergone it. A balanced interpretation implies taking into account both the traumatised individual's incorporated past (does the trauma in question echo traumatic situations previously experienced?) *and* the nature and intensity of the trauma.

Researchers can then focus on one particular aspect of the formula, seeking to throw light on the modalities of socialisation and the incorporation of dispositions, looking at the particular form taken by the accumulated stock of dispositions and abilities in relation to the effects of socialisation to which the actors have been subject, showing how particular dispositions are triggered in practice in any specific set of circumstances, revealing the logic behind a group, an institution, a field, a world or a given context of interaction, drawing up the sociogenesis of these contexts of action, studying the structural relations of interdependence between the different spheres of action or the individual transitions from one sphere of action to another, etc. In this way it is possible, depending on the chosen objectives and the problems identified for resolution, to get to the heart of the mental processes and behaviours of individuals, as in the case of a dream study, just as we can contribute to the analysis of the broadest and most plurisecular social structures without ever ceasing to be a sociologist, and without losing sight of the overall formula which, in the last analysis, enables us to explain practices in as much depth as possible.

A general formula adapted to dreams

In order to be able to study a very specific type of 'practice' such as dreams, the simplified formula nevertheless needs to be adapted by introducing a number of stages and some supplementary elements: the first stage (wakefulness *pre*-dream) is the one in which, before the dream and still in a wakeful state, the internal stimuli are formed that will then play a role during the second stage – that is to say, the one in which the images and sensations of the dream itself appear (sleep period); the third and final stage (*post*-dream wakefulness) is the period of *recollection* and of the *dream account* in a waking state.[140]

In order to clarify in verbal terms these three periods and the dynamics between them, it might be said that, during the hours or days preceding the sleep period, a particular context (an event, an interaction seen or experienced, something read or seen, etc.) triggered elements of the dreamer's incorporated past (their current existential situation and incorporated

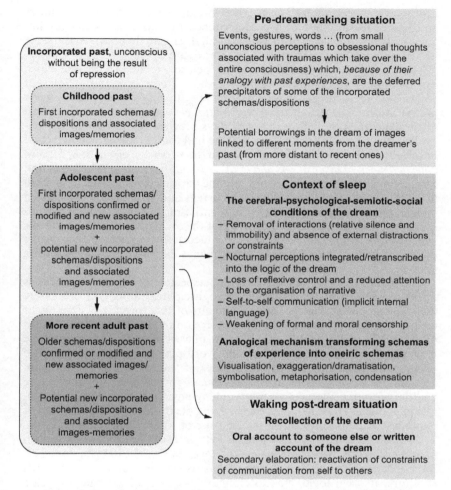

Pre-dream waking situation

Events, gestures, words … (from small unconscious perceptions to obsessional thoughts associated with traumas which take over the entire consciousness) which, *because of their analogy with past experiences*, are the deferred precipitators of some of the incorporated schemas/dispositions

↓

Potential borrowings in the dream of images linked to different moments from the dreamer's past (from more distant to recent ones)

Context of sleep

The cerebral-psychological-semiotic-social conditions of the dream

– Removal of interactions (relative silence and immobility) and absence of external distractions or constraints
– Nocturnal perceptions integrated/retranscribed into the logic of the dream
– Loss of reflexive control and a reduced attention to the organisation of narrative
– Self-to-self communication (implicit internal language)
– Weakening of formal and moral censorship

Analogical mechanism transforming schemas of experience into oneiric schemas

Visualisation, exaggeration/dramatisation, symbolisation, metaphorisation, condensation

Waking post-dream situation

Recollection of the dream

Oral account to someone else or written account of the dream

Secondary elaboration: reactivation of constraints of communication from self to others

Incorporated past, unconscious without being the result of repression

Childhood past

First incorporated schemas/dispositions and associated images/memories

↓

Adolescent past

First incorporated schemas/dispositions confirmed or modified and new associated images/memories
+
potential new incorporated schemas/dispositions and associated images/memories

↓

More recent adult past

Older schemas/dispositions confirmed or modified and new associated images/memories
+
Potential new incorporated schemas/dispositions and associated images-memories

Figure 2 Incorporated past and contexts relevant to the study of dreams

dispositions or schemas). All of this contributed to the development of internal stimuli (associated with particular elements of the existential situation)[141] which, in the context of sleep, in turn trigger the dream. It will be observed that these stimuli become active only in periods of relaxation, of inactivity or of routine activity of a kind propitious to dreaming or daydreaming. They act therefore in *deferred time*, as stimulations which will in a sense be held in reserve and reactivated in periods of thought unconstrained by the immediate environment.[142] Finally, on waking up, the dreamer recalls the dream and can, in certain cases, describe it in a new context (for example, by confiding in a family member or a friend, a process which, consciously or not, may modify what he or she remembers and is able to say) and with predetermined (in this case specifically linguistic) dispositions (remembering that all dreamers do not have the same lexical, syntactical or narrative skills) (see figure 2).

The formula for interpreting dreams is closely related to the one which can be applied to certain examples of short literary creations. Some of Kafka's short stories which were written very quickly (in the space of a few hours) can thus be linked to *circumstantial elements* (an event which had taken place the day before or a few days previously), to *current circumstances* (the type of situation in which he had found himself over a period of several weeks, months or years) and to the *structural elements of his own inherited stock of dispositions and of his existential situation*. Their creation can be understood only by identifying the various threads attaching them to all these elements (circumstantial, current and structural). A balanced interpretation always implies clearly identifying and linking the incorporated past (dispositions and the nature of the existential situation) and the *triggers* or *activators* of elements of this incorporated past which provoke the dreamer to deal with particular 'problems' or 'preoccupations' during sleep.

The dream can be studied from the perspective of different disciplines or from different angles within the same discipline, though unfortunately this can somewhat disrupt the components of this formula. These might include a strictly *neuroscientific* perspective on the functioning conditions of cerebral activity during the different phases of sleep, a *linguistic* one focusing on the role of metaphor and word play in dreams, the absence of narrative coherence or the recurrences of subject categories in dream accounts, a *sociolinguistic* or *psycholinguistic* focus on the implicit nature and the presuppositions of an internal language, or a *psychological* exploration of diurnal residues, of the weakening of control, of reflexivity and of planning in dreams or of the loss of a sense of what is and is not real, etc.

Each of these perspectives implies setting aside or ignoring a certain number of precisely those elements the formula sets out to bring together. Yet, since each of the points studied has its own characteristics, its own structure, its own logic, etc., disciplinary and specialised study appears to be perfectly satisfactory from a scientific point of view. However, it is by refusing to split the problem into its different components, by showing the deep and systemic links between the different constituent parts of the problem, that progress can be made towards a science of dreams and, more broadly, of forms of human expression.[143]

The difficulty in bringing about an understanding of the process of dream production lies in the fact that this requires an overarching view that analyses of dreams rarely fully achieve, either because of a lack of information on a particular aspect of this process or simply as a result of reducing the object under scrutiny to a series of micro-processes resulting from the specialisation and social division of scientific study. For example, in a work which is remarkable from more than one point of view

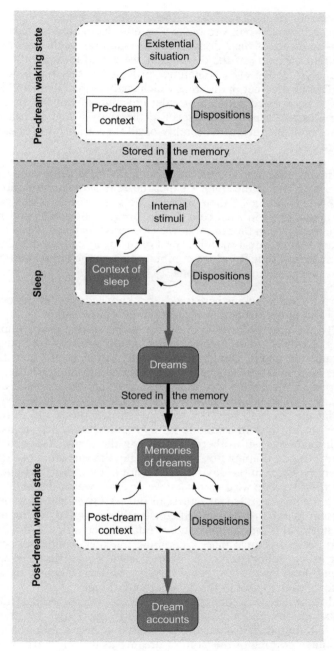

Figure 3 The process of dream production

and yet rarely cited in studies on the dream, the French psychoanalyst René Allendy was at pains to make a careful distinction between dreamers' own accounts of their dreams, the associations made with regard to the different elements of the dream and the actual interpretation by the psychoanalyst.[144] He even sometimes provided a succinct biographical context for the dreamer in question which enabled the dream and its associations to be situated within a broader life context. But the dreams only serve to illustrate a particular aspect of the analysis and do not provide the meaning of the integrated totality of all the various processes at play in the dream:

> the dreams cited are, for the most part, far from being analysed in depth, with the whole range of their current overdeterminations or in the intertwining of their ancient roots, a process which would have necessitated in each case dozens of pages of details and many considerations. On the contrary, they are presented summarily purely in order to illustrate a specific aspect of the oneiric phenomenon. It is their sheer multiplicity which combines to give the impression of the wide-ranging potential of dreams.[145]

What is most sadly lacking here is a deeper knowledge of the history of the dreamer and of the structures of the dreamer's personality.

Finally, the general formula of dream interpretation enables an understanding of why it is that, on awakening, the dreamer cannot immediately understand the oneiric images that were nevertheless of his or her own making. This situation can be largely explained by the fact that human beings come with a history of their own, and that this past life does not disappear but, instead, continues to exist in the form of embedded experiences that are ready to resonate with present situations and to resurface at any moment, both in a waking state (in our solitary actions as well as in our interactions with others) and during the night. As Erich Fromm observed: 'In our sleeping life, we seem to tap the vast store of experience and memory which in the daytime we do not know exists.'[146] In answer to the question 'Why do we dream what we dream?', we must therefore reply: 'Because the incorporated structures of our past lives and the contexts of our present lives constrain us and constantly determine the limits of our mental horizon, of our actions and of our preoccupations.' But this past and this present change places, combine together, condense, symbolise and act as metaphors for each other in such a way that the processes governing these operations, based largely on the mechanism of analogy, are no longer intelligible to the dreamer on waking.

We do not all have the same past, we do not experience the same present situations, and it is therefore entirely logical that our dreams are socially differentiated, just like our gestures, our speech or our behaviours. Dreams have nothing of the 'stuff of dreams' as it is ordinarily conceived when we refer in such terms to our wildest desires ('I dream of becoming rich and famous'). They are existentially and socially anchored; they are profoundly realistic and only appear crazy, absurd or strange because the conditions and the means used to present experience in a symbolic way confuse matters.[147]

Dreams contain no 'unfathomable mystery' to be unveiled, no 'secret' to be uncovered, or any 'mysterious code' that could potentially be cracked. Instead they contain existential preoccupations which express themselves in a form unlike any they might take in the socially varied moments of waking life. We are, however, dealing with one of the forms of expression of experience which is the least marred by structural, moral, religious, political or cultural censorship, one of the purest ways of expressing our experience *for ourselves, from self-to-self*. Unravelling the threads of oneiric representations is thus a way of learning to understand better our socially confined mental processes and of offering each of us the possibility of gaining a little more control of what is constantly and secretly at work within us.

3

Psychoanalysis and the
Social Sciences

No book on the sociological interpretation of dreams can avoid a confrontation with psychoanalysis, the scientific image of which has never been as tarnished. Is it a pseudo-science, a non-science or a scientific revolution now overtaken by scientific progress in experimental psychology and neuroscience? Negative opinions on the Freudian oeuvre and the various extensions of it abounded in Freud's day and continue to be voiced more than a century after the founding work of psychoanalysis.

At the same time, through a process of indirect homage which is not always intended, all those who work on dreams continue to refer, whether negatively or positively, to *The Interpretation of Dreams*. These include neuroscientists such as John Allan Hobson and Michel Jouvet and psychologists specializing in the analysis of dream content (Calvin S. Hall, Robert L. Van de Castle or G. William Domhoff), who are sometimes fiercely critical of psychoanalysis, along with those who, as neuroscientists (Mark Solms), cognitive psychologists (Jacques Montangero), historians (Jacques Le Goff, Peter Burke), anthropologists (Abram Kardiner, Cora Alice Du Bois) or sociologists (Roger Bastide, Norbert Elias), refer implicitly or explicitly to psychoanalysis in conjunction with other disciplines.

Over the course of time, in the human and social sciences in particular, many attempts at reconciliation between the various factions have been made by researchers belonging almost exclusively to the same generation: the anthropological movement referred to as 'Culture and Personality', with Abram Kardiner (1891–1981) and Cora Alice Du Bois (1903–1991), has inspired sociologists and anthropologists such as Roger Bastide (1898–1974) or Georges Devereux (1908–1985), and authors as different as the sociologist Norbert Elias (1897–1990) or the psychoanalyst Erich Fromm (1900–1980) have managed to bring together sociology or Marxism and psychoanalysis.[1]

Ever present throughout this book, Freudian thinking and the criticism that can be directed at it cannot be confined to a single chapter which would deal exhaustively with the matter and then close the file. For rather than closing psychoanalysis in upon itself, and with these many arguments or internal fracture lines, it should, on the contrary, be permanently reinserted into the culture of human and social sciences by demonstrating that the questions it asks, as well as the answers it brings, are general questions which are of just as much interest to the sociologist, the anthropologist, the linguist or the historian as they are to the psychoanalyst.

In the course of this chapter therefore we will focus simply on a few points of contention (the relationships between the biological and the social, the strong tendency of psychoanalysis to centre explanations on childhood and sexuality) and of agreement (on the formula for interpreting human behaviours) between psychoanalysis and the social sciences. Other aspects (the theory of the unconscious, the theory of censorship, the dream-work, the event-focused approach, the function of dreams, etc.) will then be examined in subsequent chapters, when the logical sequence of the argument demands it.

Between biological and social

One of Freud's major ambiguities concerning the question of the individual lies in the fact that he never succeeded in making a clear choice between two conceptions of the individual: that of a socialised individual whose psychological activity (unconscious, ego and superego) is socially determined entirely by early intra-familial relationships and that of a biological individual very largely dominated by a libido and natural instincts, sometimes even by the heritage of a far distant past. This ambivalence explains the fact that writers can either view Freud as the founder of a discipline which places social relationships at the heart of the formation of personality or, alternatively, take issue with his biologism.

Freud himself observed that, all too often, 'individual psychology' and 'social . . . psychology' are seen in opposition to each other, whereas in reality 'only rarely and in exceptional cases is individual psychology in a position to disregard the relations of this individual to others', for

> someone else is invariably involved, as a model, as an object, as a helper, as an opponent, and so from the very first Individual Psychology is at the same time Social Psychology as well – in this extended but entirely justified use of the words.
>
> The relations of an individual to his parents and to his brothers and sisters, to the object of his love, and to his physician – in fact all the relations which have hitherto been the chief subject of psychoanalytic research – may claim to be considered as social phenomena.[2]

Successors to Freud, Marie Bonaparte, Anna Freud and Ernst Kris could therefore emphasise the clearly social point of view of psychoanalysis which differentiates itself from the biology, medicine, physiology and neurology of its time:

> Freud's self-analysis, which opened the way to an understanding of the conflicts of early childhood, brought about a shift in his interests. Insight into the conditions in which individual conflict arose in the course of the interaction between the child and its environment – in other words the intervention of the social aspect – meant that the need to explain psychological process by immediate physiological factors had lost its urgency.[3]

Nevertheless, if he accords more importance to intra-familial social relationships, Freud accompanies this sociological gesture with a universalisation of the forms of social relationships he analyses. The little boy's love for his mother and the jealousy or rivalry vis-à-vis his father are immediately transposed into a universal fact of early childhood; the Oedipus complex becomes one of the great universal organising forces of the male human psyche.[4] And the same applies in the case of Jung's Electra complex. However, as Bronisław Malinowski and Margaret Mead so clearly demonstrated, such complexes are based on a certain type of family structure, which is that of a powerful, respected father who has occupations outside the home and makes little contribution to daily domestic life, a mother dominated by the father but who nevertheless occupies a central role at the heart of the family structure, and a child who, depending on his or her gender, learns to love and be attracted by members of the opposite sex, and who therefore sees someone of the same sex as a potential rival or competitor. In addition, moreover, the same child, witnessing the arrival of a little brother or a little sister and the transference of his parents' attention elsewhere, experiences frustrations and jealousies towards his or her siblings: 'Freud's great mistake', writes Roger Bastide, 'was his biologism, which led him to believe that what he had discovered in analysing nineteenth-century Westerners could be universally applied. The complex is a social matter and as a result occurs in any number of civilisations and any number of social backgrounds even within a particular civilisation. It is not a phenomenon of nature but the result of "culture".'[5]

Moreover, if he does indeed place the child in the context of his or her family, and more precisely in the very fabric of familial relationships, Freud hardly ever classes members of the family according to the social properties which every sociologist considers to be fundamental, particularly for an understanding of the nature of intergenerational social transmission. Fathers, mothers, brothers, sisters do not have qualifications or professions, no age or national loyalties are mentioned, no religious affiliation or cultural or political activities . . . Freud essentially sees them only on the basis of the different types of psychological difficulties they may have and on their place in the original or current family universe. Not only does Freud forget that Oedipus was a king, as Carl Schorske points out, but he also ignores anything else pertaining to him except his familial status as a son (to Laius and Jocasta). No association with a particular social class and no objective relationships of inheritance between parents and children: 'The father is not the entrepreneur, and the son is not his heir – the father is only the mother's lover and the son is his rival!'[6]

Relations with the father and the mother, with brothers and sisters, never, however, exist in isolation from their social roots. They have social origins, professions, educational backgrounds, denominational characteristics, cultural tastes, moral attitudes, etc., and intergenerational relationships are as much about the 'transmission' of material and immaterial resources as they are relationships marked by sexual desire (*libido sexualis*). Inversely, social actors are clearly born not into social classes or into commercial organisations but into families; they learn about their class through close, emotional relationships of identification and counter-identification which they maintain with members of their family rather than in an abstract way. Sociologists and psychoanalysts should never lose sight of the fact that actors are fundamentally individuals capable of forming relationships and with their own inherent social properties.

The neglect of many extra-familial social structures by Freud and his followers is essentially because, on the one hand, they focused their attention on specific psychological problems (hysteria, paranoia, persecution mania, obsessional neurosis, phobias, anxiety, depression) rather than on ordinary and non-pathological social practices and, on the other hand, their patients all belonged to the same social class and to the same type of society:

> The objects of their investigations were, first and foremost, sick and healthy members of modern society and largely of the middle classes; in short, they were members of the bourgeois class, with the same social background. What determined and differentiated their individual lives, then, were the individual, personal and, from a social standpoint, accidental experiences above this generally shared foundation. All the persons studied shared the same psychic traits, insofar as these traits were the product of an authoritarian society organized around the facts of class structures and the methodical pursuit of maximal profit. They differed psychologically only insofar as one had an overly strict father who terrified him in childhood, another had an older sister who was the focus of all his love, and still another had such an overly possessive mother that he was never able to break his libidinal ties with her.[7]

Finally, in certain texts, Freud can provide fresh ammunition for an evolutionist psychology, albeit one with an extremely fragile empirical basis. The dream reveals 'impressions from the dreamer's early childhood' which have become unconscious 'owing to repression', but also 'material which cannot have originated either from the dreamer's adult life or from his forgotten childhood' and which forms 'part of the *archaic heritage* which a child brings with him into the world, before any experience of his own.' These elements are close to 'the earliest human legends and . . . surviving customs', and dreams could provide 'a source of human prehistory which is not to be despised'.[8] Freud's work is therefore typically a compromise formation and sometimes oscillates 'between classical psychology, which considers every person's spirit as though they were isolated islands, completely inaccessible to each other, and the sociology of collective representations, of fixed institutions.'[9]

Psychoanalysis and the general formula for interpreting practices

Looked at with a certain amount of hindsight, psychoanalysis turns out to be using a schema of intelligibility of behaviours which is not very far removed from the dispositionalist-contextualist schema I have formulated. Both refer to triggering elements and to contexts which trigger deep-rooted tendencies going back to early childhood. This similarity in theoretical models cannot be attributed simply to the effect of 'culture' or to the popularity of a certain mode of reasoning. It is an indication that the structures of the real world are revealed step by step and that the various elements which allow an understanding of the actions, the representations and the sensations of individuals within society are elements which have an empirical foundation. The fact that the dispositionalist-contextualist sociologist and the Freudian psychoanalyst should both have closely related schemas of intelligibility can be explained by the fact that both of them come up against the same realties, the same lines of force of the real. Through the (relative) similarity of these two different approaches the structure of reality can therefore be glimpsed.

It was as a result of studying cases of hysteria with Joseph Breuer that Freud gradually began to establish a link between *recent triggering events*, which he referred to by the term 'day residue' (or 'diurnal residue'), and an incorporated past, which he calls 'the unconscious' and which is, according to him, the product of repression. Henri F. Ellenberger, the psychiatrist and historian of psychoanalysis, made a clear link between the early work on hysteria and the study of dreams:

> In the latent content, Freud finds as one constant element the *day residue*, that is, some more or less insignificant event of the day preceding the dream. And just as he connected a pubertal trauma with an early forgotten sexual experience, Freud also found a connection between the day residue and childhood memories. Among the many trivial events of the day, the dream chooses the one that shows some relationship to a childhood memory, and as Freud puts it, the dream stands with one foot in the present and one foot in childhood.[10]

The symptoms of the patient suffering from hysteria correspond to the manifest content of the dream, and, in both cases, an unconscious intervenes to structure the behaviour or representations involved.

The attraction of psychoanalysis for a dispositionalist-contextualist sociology which focuses on individual dispositional singularities is its *field of study* – that is to say, the individual psyche in all its complexity – and its *scale of observation* – in other words, the individual scale which enables a detailed study of interpersonal social relationships and, in particular, of early intra-familial relationships. Psychoanalysis turns its attention predominantly to the psyche and its pathologies, using a semi-methodological semi-therapeutic approach which consists in a particular type of verbal exchange (psychoanalytic therapy). It focuses its attention on the familial experiences of the individuals studied, independent from any questions about the economic and cultural conditions of their lives, and awards a prime place within any explanation of behaviours to early familial experiences and particularly to the 'sexual' dimension of experiences. The behaviour patterns of a given individual are therefore, for both psychoanalysis and dispositionalist-contextualist sociology, the product of an encounter between an internalised past in the form of 'mnesic traces' and the new contexts in which the individual is operating. *Homo psychanalyticus* is a creature of relationships with a history of incorporated familial relationships, but whose economic, cultural, educational, professional, religious, etc., properties are left unexamined. The Freudian interpretation of behaviours is based therefore on the following formula, which represents a particular variation of the generic formula previously set out:

Incorporated familial past <—> Contexts of existing interpersonal relationships => Behaviours

or:

Internalised childhood familial experiences, with emphasis on the libidinous aspect of intra-familial relationships <—> Contexts of existing interpersonal relationships => Neuroses, psychoses, lapses or slips, parapraxes, dreams, etc.

From a sociological point of view, the psychoanalytical model of interpretation of behaviours involves even more limits than those already mentioned. First of all, Freud tends to reduce past experience to key events rather than seeking to reconstruct sequences of relatively similar events capable of giving rise to schemas of experience or to dispositions. Psychoanalysis also tends to drift towards a certain mechanistic dispositionalism by ignoring the context of current relationships and the active role this can play, and by prioritizing explanations essentially rooted in the incorporated familial past. It is a case of 'a linear determinism envisaging nothing but the action of the past upon the present',[11] with the patient's behaviours being linked only to their 'childhood past', which, without therapeutic intervention, would determine his or her entire future.[12] Finally, Freudian psychoanalysis managed to take account in explaining human behaviour of the important role of family structures, given their key importance in the lives of individuals, and the fact that, in Freud's time, there was little competition from other types of socialisation. It is through this configuration of relationships of interdependence that children discover social reality through the mental and behavioural schemas of members of their family. But this almost exclusive focus on familial experience in its purely interpersonal aspects, even if it is seen as fundamentally social,[13] results in a blind eye being turned to other contexts of socialisation. So much for school, the peer group, religious, political, cultural or sports institutions or those associated with the professional milieu, within which individuals continue the process of psychological and behavioral modelling!

In spite of such limitations, Freud tried to make sense of dreams by linking the question of the elements triggering the dream with that of the significant and driving forces that give dreams their meaning and their coherence. It is undoubtedly in his study of the patient Dora that he is most lucid about his system of analysis and comes closest to a balanced general formula for interpreting dreams. 'A regularly formed dream', wrote Freud,

> stands, as it were, upon two legs, one of which is in contact with the main and current exciting cause, and the other with some momentous occurrence in the years of childhood. The dream sets up a connection between those two factors – the event during childhood and the event of the present day – and it endeavours to re-shape the present upon the model of the remote past. For the wish which creates the dream always springs from the period of childhood; and it is continually trying to summon childhood back into reality and to correct the present day by the measure of childhood.[14]

The way in which the problem is presented always suffers from a certain event-focused vision and from an overemphasis on childhood and the family experience, but the balance sought for here is highly relevant.

Determining event from childhood <—> Current cause of the dream => Dream.

And a little further on in the same study, Freud is even more pertinent when he makes a distinction between what is merely the *trigger for the dream* (the 'waking thoughts ... which are continued into sleep') and what constitutes the real 'motive power' (the unconscious wish), a sort of virtual power waiting to be triggered. He returns to the metaphor of the entrepreneur and of capital, which he also includes in *The Interpretation of*

Dreams, to explain the respective roles of recent events experienced by the dreamer and unconscious desire:

> The position may be explained by an analogy. A daytime thought may well play the part of an *entrepreneur* for a dream; but the *entrepreneur*, who, as people say, has the idea and the initiative to carry it out, can do nothing without capital; he needs a *capitalist* who can afford the outlay, and the capitalist who provides the psychical outlay for the dream is invariably and indisputably, whatever may be the thoughts of the previous day, *a wish from the unconscious.*[15]

Unconscious wish (motive power) <—> Waking thoughts => Dream
Capital <—> Entrepreneur => Dream.

Freud is tentatively trying to establish what should be linked and how it should be linked in order to explain the oneiric process. He tries nevertheless to retain a link between the incorporated past (which he reduces, wrongly, to 'childhood experiences' alone, and sometimes even to *events* from infancy) and the recent elements triggering the dream ('recent experiences').[16]

Infantile hypothesis

> First of all I have accomplished a piece of self-analysis which has confirmed that fantasies are products of later periods which project themselves back from the present into earliest childhood.
> (Sigmund Freud, *The Origins of Psychoanalysis*, pp. 270–1)

It is to his credit that Freud understood the importance of family in the social make-up of individuals. The earliest experiences of socialisation, the types of experience and relationships associated with early infancy, have a powerful influence on the personality and later tendencies of the child who will, for the rest of his or her life, continue to be marked by these experiences of affection or lack of affection, of unconditional, conditional, or complete absence of love, of attachment or detachment, of relations towards the parental authority, of relations of competition or rivalry with brothers and sisters, etc. Utterly dependent on the adults surrounding him or her, the child learns ways of seeing, feeling and acting in the world, and these then form the dispositional foundations for his or her future actions and reactions.

From the standpoint of a very different kind of psychology, Jean Piaget nevertheless acknowledged the role of psychoanalysis in the discovery of the earliest relationships repeated and internalised in the form of schemas:

Day to day observation and psycho-analytic experience show that the
first personal schemas are afterwards generalised and applied to many
other people. According to whether the first inter-individual experiences of the child who is just learning to speak are connected with a
father who is understanding or dominating, loving or cruel, etc., the
child will tend (even throughout life if these relationships have influenced his whole youth) to assimilate all other individuals to this father
schema. On the other hand, the type of feelings he has for his mother
will tend to make him love in a certain way, sometimes all through his
life, because here again he partially assimilates his successive loves to
this first love which shapes his innermost feelings and behaviours.[17]

Freud recalls his discovery of the importance of very early experiences
in the course of his research on the origins of neurotic symptoms:

> I was carried further and further back into the patient's life and
> ended by reaching the first years of his childhood. What poets and
> students of human nature had always asserted turned out to be true:
> the impressions of that remote period of life, though they were for
> the most part buried in amnesia, left ineradicable traces upon the
> individual's growth and in particular laid the foundations of any
> nervous disorder that was to follow.[18]

During psychoanalytic therapy, 'in his transference-attitude he [the
patient] is re-experiencing emotional relations which had their origin in
his earliest object-relationships during the repressed period of his childhood.'[19] And, in dreams, Freud believed he could detect that what had
'instigated the dream' in fact 'derived from childhood'.[20]

If Freud was right to emphasise this period so rich in experience, he was
nevertheless wrong to confine socialising influences solely to this stage of
life, as though, in between the adult coming to consult the psychoanalyst
and the events of early infancy, nothing else had really happened, except
for the repetition of the same schemas of experience, of the same types
of relationships, of the same kinds of reaction. Yet, throughout their
lives, individuals are developing and transforming themselves in the
course of multiple experiences and multiple relationships which are by no
means restricted to those of a family nature; they include socialising with
friends, educational, professional, religious, political, cultural, sporting
experiences, etc., all of which have contributed to reproducing, repeating
or modifying those early dispositions. And the problems to be faced, the
preoccupations and centres of interest, change throughout the course of
our lives, depending on new circumstances, new configurations, specific
moments in the life cycle, etc.

Freud can therefore be reproached for a certain *infantile determinism*
which ignores the fact that, if the experiences of early childhood are key
to the way subsequent experiences are dealt with, they are nevertheless

continuously reshaped as new experiences come along. It is never the 'first' experiences that are exclusively determinant, still less a handful of events or a few key scenes from early childhood,[21] but rather the relatively coherent corpus of a series of relatively analogous experiences. 'The Oedipus complex' cannot possibly be made 'the key to the human condition',[22] nor can isolated childhood experiences be made into determinants which would act directly on the present, without looking at the sequence of similar experiences which succeeded them.

Criticism of the approach that seeks to explain everything solely in terms of childhood experiences came eloquently from Erich Fromm. Before Freud, nobody was aware of 'what importance the experiences of the child and particularly the very young child had for the development of his character and thereby of his whole fate. . . . For the first time one began to take the child and what happened to him seriously, so seriously indeed that one believed one had found the key to all further development in the events of early childhood.'[23] This insistence on the role of early childhood had the consequence of 'an underestimation of the importance of later events'[24] in the interpretation of behaviour.

Fromm distinguishes himself from Freud by stating, for example, that 'the contents of a dream are not necessarily of an infantile nature.'[25] In the case of dreams, as for any other symptom or compromise formation, Freud indeed rapidly came to the conclusion that everything was deeply rooted in the period of infancy. If in *The Interpretation of Dreams* (1900) he remained prudent when saying that the childhood experience is 'one of the sources from which dreams derive material for reproduction',[26] his theory loses any such nuance when, in lectures given in 1916–17, he declared:

> We have not only found that the material of the forgotten experiences of childhood is accessible to dreams, but we have also seen that the mental life of children, with all its characteristics, its egoism, its incestuous choice of love objects, and so on, still persists in dreams – that is, in the unconscious, and dreams carry us back every night to this infantile level. The fact is thus confirmed that *what is unconscious in mental life is also what is infantile.*[27]

As is so often the case, Freud was generalising excessively in claiming that 'the evil impulses of the dream are merely infantilism, a return to the beginnings of our ethical development, since the dream simply makes children of us again in thinking and in feeling.'[28] In those moments where generalisation was at its peak, Freud went as far as to claim that 'all dreams are the dreams of children and they all work with infantile materials, through childish psychic stimuli and mechanisms',[29] and that 'a wish which is represented in a dream must be an infantile one.'[30]

Rather than correcting this infantilist interpretation, the psychoanalysts who came after Freud sometimes accentuated this tendency. For example,

René Allendy, the co-founder of the French Society of Psychoanalysis, referring both to Freud and to Otto Rank's *The Trauma of Birth* (1924), urged practitioners to carry out research on the 'infantile roots' of the dream, which, according to him, 'go even further back than the experience of weaning'.[31] He then provides examples, which are completely unprovable, of 'inter-uterine dreams' which 'may or may not entail the representation of the difficult and anxious journey of birth.'[32]

Sexual hypothesis

It is a well-known and sometimes caricatured fact that Freudian anthropology makes sexual desire (*libido sexualis*) the driving force of human action. Like the univocal theory of the *homo œconomicus*, who sees only the economic interest in all forms of human behaviour, the *homo psychanalyticus* is centred on his *libido sexualis*. For Freud, the other forms of libido are, ultimately, merely sublimated ways of assuaging impulses of a sexual nature. For example, 'the impulse which drives us to acquire knowledge has its source in infantile sexual researches, i.e. in the wish shared by all of us to know where babies come from and what part in that is played by father and mother.'[33] But if Freud makes it an underlying biological principle (all dreams are to a greater or lesser extent attributable, according to him, to unsatisfied sexual desires), paradoxically he appears to be extremely embarrassed about dealing directly with the question of sexuality when it appears in dreams. It is rather as though Freud dismisses any dreams with an obvious sexual content in order to preserve the purity or the strength of his interpretive model which is based on repressed sexuality. Sexuality is a central explanatory principle, but it is not strictly speaking an object to be explored by the psychoanalyst.

Before he turned his attention to dreams, Freud drew attention to the sexual origins of hysteria among young women. Initially this was in conjunction with Joseph Breuer: 'sexuality seems to play a principal part in the pathogenesis of hysteria as a source of psychical traumas, and as a motive of "defence" – that is, for repressing ideas from consciousness.'[34] Cases of hysteria, like that of Dora, are evidence of the relations of domination which make young girls become the object of male seductions, of the lead weight cast by society over sexual matters, and also of the omnipresence of sexual issues in the lives of bourgeois young women (in Dora's case, she was made aware of sexual matters at a very young age through a governess who was well read on the subject).

Whether desired, imposed or refused, sexuality saturates Dora's universe. She was eighteen years old when her father, an important industrialist, persuaded her in 1889 to consult Freud. She had told her parents about an attempted 'seduction' (which today would be described as 'sexual harassment') on the part of Mr K. The latter first tried to kiss her in his shop when she was only fourteen years old, whereupon she ran away. He then made advances to her during a walk near a lake, and she slapped him and again ran away. Subsequently, during a family visit to the Ks, Dora woke up to find him standing in front of her in her bedroom and was unable to preserve her privacy since the key to the bedroom had mysteriously disappeared. But Dora's father thought all this was simply a sexual fantasy. Mr K denied having attempted to seduce Dora and, in the end, nobody believed her account, and this led to her developing symptoms of hysteria (breathlessness, nervous cough, aphonia, depression, etc.). Symbolically reinforcing male domination, in his interpretation, Freud attributed to his young patient feelings of desire for Mr K, even though she constantly condemns the assaults of which she had been the victim. He makes comparisons with the situation of her father standing in front of her bed when she suffered from enuresis – around the age of seven or eight – and that of Mr K appearing beside her bed: soaked by urine in one case and by desire in the other. The mother, for her part, poorly educated and withdrawn, was sexually abandoned by her husband and channelled all her energy into obsessional housework. She withdrew emotionally from her children and made family life difficult to endure. The Ks were friends of Dora's family. Dora's father, suffering from tuberculosis, had met the K family in Merano and since that time had been in an adulterous relationship with Mrs K, a handsome woman of Italian origin.

'If it is true that the causes of hysterical disorders are to be found in the intimacies of the patients' psycho-sexual life, and that hysterical symptoms are the expression of their most secret and repressed wishes, then the complete elucidation of a case of hysteria is bound to involve the revelation of those intimacies and the betrayal of those secrets.'[35] Freud is convinced that not only hysteria but, more broadly, all neuroses have sexual causes. For him, the 'emotional excitation' at work behind the phenomena of the neurosis is 'habitually one of a sexual nature' arising as the result of a 'current sexual conflict' or 'the effect of earlier sexual experiences'.[36] He wrote to Bleuler on 22 February 1925: 'I am firmly convinced that sexuality is the *specific* etiology of neuroses and, in this sense, I am totally convinced of the exclusive character of the sexual etiology.'[37] Freud would therefore generalise his initial results – not abruptly, but little by little, sometimes even denying his focus on the sexual when he was reproached on that score.[38]

The historians Lydia Marinelli and Andreas Mayer point out that, in the first version of *The Interpretation of Dreams*, 'neither was the Oedipus dream the typical dream prototype, nor did Freud describe the dream wish as exclusively sexual.'[39] His famous phrase – 'A dream is a (disguised) fulfillment of a (suppressed or repressed) wish' – 'deliberately left the basic formula of the dream open.'[40] In the very first edition of his book, 'the underlying wish could have a variety of purposes',[41] and it was only in the third edition that Freud added a note on the importance of 'infantile sexuality'. But Freud's sexualisation would continue to grow, and it was only twenty years later that the study of dreams about accidents in traumatic neurosis would lead him to restrict the purpose of dreams as the fulfilment of desire in his famous *Beyond the Pleasure Principle*.[42]

However much he denied it, it was Freud himself, along with some of his close colleagues (notably Otto Rank), who contributed to confining his interpretation to 'the sexual factor'. In his *The Interpretation of Dreams*, it is he who, on the subject of 'innocent' dreams, declares that 'the motive for the censorship is obviously the sexual factor.'[43] And it is he again who, without proof, links his dreams to 'reprehensible sexual acts'[44] during childhood, who confirms that 'all complicated machinery and apparatus occurring in dreams' represent 'the genitals',[45] he again who transforms long and firm objects such as umbrellas, tree trunks, rods, walking sticks, weapons such as daggers, knives or pikes into symbols of the penis, and objects such as trunks, boxes, caves, chapels and wardrobes into vagina substitutes,[46] or who associates the impression of déjà-vu in dreams with the mother's genital organs (even writing that this 'invariably' refers to the organ in question).[47] Finally, it is he who interprets in dreams the 'up above' and the 'down below' by rejecting any social (hierarchical) dimension, associating 'down below' with the genital organs and 'up above' with the mouth, the face or the breasts.[48]

And in *On Dreams*, which is in some way a summary of the arguments in *The Interpretation of Dreams* and was published one year later, in 1901, Freud pursues this same reduction:

> No one who accepts the view that the censorship is the chief reason for dream distortion will be surprised to learn from the results of dream interpretation that most of the dreams of adults are traced back by analysis to *erotic wishes*. . . . A great many other dreams, however, which show no sign of being erotic in their manifest content, are revealed by the work of interpretation in analysis as sexual wish fulfilments, and, on the other hand, analysis proves that a great many of the thoughts left over from the activity of waking life as 'residues of the previous day' only find their way to representation in dreams through the assistance of repressed erotic wishes. There is no theoretical necessity why this should be so; but to explain the fact it may be pointed out that no other group of instincts has been submitted to such far-reaching suppression by the demand of cultural education, while at the same time the sexual instincts are also the ones which, in most people, find it easiest to escape from the control of the highest mental agencies.[49]

In this way, everything in dreams, even the most anodyne, can be the symbol of 'parts of the body and activities invested with erotic interest'.[50]

Before the social sciences, psychologists and even psychoanalysts had already distanced themselves with regard to the sexual aspects of the Freudian hypothesis. Théodore Flournoy, a Swiss psychologist, criticised Freud in 1907 on this issue.[51] For him, dreams expressed not only 'wishes', as Freud claimed, but 'all our tendencies'. He was critical of the fact that Freud was only interested in dreams linked to the repression of inexpressible or unpleasant matters, particularly those of a sexual nature, and considered that the foundations for interpretation as proposed by Freud were too narrow. Whatever is emotionally on our minds can become the subject of a dream, but sex is not the only source of emotion: anything which frightens, distresses, worries, moves, saddens or inspires passion can therefore give rise to dreams.[52] Similarly, the Swiss psychiatrist Eugen Bleuler, who took a very active interest in psychoanalysis and for a long time corresponded with Freud, announced in a conference given in Zurich in 1912 'that the "essentially sexual significance" of the unconscious as the place of repressed childhood desires was a theory which was "too narrow and, moreover, unnecessary".'[53]

Again, in 1920, Yves Delage criticised Freud's apriorism and his tendency to generalisation:

> Freud and those who have followed in his footsteps seem to me to be victims of a sort of psychosis which makes them constantly look for a sexual influence behind all our thoughts and actions, even in the most unlikely conditions. The importance of this factor may indeed be significant, but it is wrong to systematically trace everything back to this *a priori*. . . . In spite of his depth of knowledge, his hard work, his detailed research and his insight, Freud will continue to represent a misguided approach, someone who, in thrall to systematic conceptions, allowed himself to end up attributing a universal character to a factor which applies only to certain particular cases, and this then led him to distort the facts and explanations in order to make them fit his preconceived idea: he attributed to the human mind a teratological deformity of which he was the principal victim.[54]

Alfred Adler too, breaking with Freud from 1911 onwards, criticised his sexualist tendency. For 'to explain anything that is not understood as a sexual symbol, and then to discover that everything springs from the sexual libido, does not stand up to intelligent criticism': 'when he forced himself to group all psychical phenomena round the single ruling principle that he recognizes – sexual libido', it was inevitable that Freud 'should go wrong'.[55]

Finally, it is worth citing the criticism made by Erich Fromm, who also believed that Freud too often reduced all desires and wishes to their sexual dimension, whether incestuous desires, fear of castration, etc.[56] Fromm acknowledged the fact that Freud had understood the powerful attachment of the child to the mother (or to a mother substitute). This relationship of total dependency for both physical and emotional nourishment means that 'Without her help he would die, without her tenderness he would become mentally sick': 'She is the one who gives life and on whom his life depends. She can also take life away by refusing to fulfil her motherly functions.'[57] But what Fromm criticises in Freud is that he attributed 'the attachment to mother as essentially one of a sexual nature',[58] whereas in fact it stems from maternal protection and the child's sense of security.

Fromm also disputes Freud's interpretation of the Oedipus myth, pointing out that 'not sexual desires but one of the fundamental aspects of interpersonal relationships, the attitude toward authority – is held to be the central theme of the myth.'[59] Freud projects onto this myth, as onto the dreams he interprets, a sexual perspective. Yet, for Fromm, 'the myth can be understood as a symbol not of the incestuous love between mother and son but of the rebellion of the son against the authority of the father in the patriarchal family.' And, as a result, 'the marriage of Oedipus and Jocasta is only a secondary element, only one of the symbols of the victory of the son, who takes his father's place and with it all his privileges.'[60] The father–son conflict has its own logic, and if the son seeks to kill the father, or hates him, it is because this father dominates, oppresses, crushes or controls him. Whether mother–son relationships or father–son relationships, these are relationships of dependence and of power, of love-dependence with the mother and of authority-dependence with the father.

And if, on several occasions and against all the evidence, Freud denied reducing the explanation he proposed for both neurotic symptoms and dreams to a sexual one, the psychoanalysts who came after him would sometimes have less hesitation in sexualising everything. 'In the development of orthodox Freudian psychoanalysis, infantile sexuality still remains the cornerstone of the system',[61] writes Erich Fromm. The same goes for the Hungarian psychoanalyst and ethnologist Géza Róheim (1891–1953), who, in a book devoted to dreams, sets out his sexualised vision of oneiric phenomena. For him it all comes down to symbols of genital organs, pubic hair, breasts, the act of masturbation or the orgasm. On the subject of a dream such as 'I jump from a rock to rescue a child in the ocean. By the time I get there it is only a doll. Then I see it on the beach, safe and alive', he offers the following interpretation: 'The ocean he jumps into is his wife's vagina. The jumping figure is the phallic body . . . The dream means coitus, uterine regression and birth on the beach.'[62]

Similarly, in 1926, René Allendy, the co-founder of the Societé Psychanalytique de Paris, resorted to many examples of unequivocally sexual interpretations of dreams in what is an extremely detailed study (each dream is written down, contextualised, accompanied by any associations made by the dreamer and interpreted). An 'elongated barrel' symbolises 'the paternal phallus and the virility which must be assimilated',[63] 'going up in a plane signifies sexual fulfilment', the figure 6 has 'a phallic meaning' (when it is six o'clock 'the clock hands are positioned vertically on the dial (also a phallic image)' and 'the word six has associations, via assonance, to sex'), 'the tree thrusting its roots into the earth is a sexual image', 'dreams of flying, of levitation, have an erotic meaning', 'doors, thresholds to be crossed, openings, generally suggest penetration in the sexual act', 'elevation and ascension generally indicate sexual desire, and staircases the sexual act', *and so on and so forth*.

Rather than aiming for a monocausal explanation, we should instead today be aiming for a plural model of socially constituted desires. There are essentially as many kinds of possible desires (or interests) as there are social dimensions explored by human beings: sexual, emotional, physical, technical, cognitive, moral, aesthetic, political, warlike, religious, economic, etc. For example, there are as many manifestations, both in social reality and in dreams, of the desire to dominate (*libido dominandi*) as there are of sexual desire (*libido sexualis*), and, if there is indeed an element of domination within the sexual, it cannot be simply reduced to that. In a dream introduced and interpreted by René Allendy, we see how what is at stake are the struggles and rivalry for professional recognition, even if, as the analyst himself does here, the virility of the dreamer is also referred to:

A young lawyer dreams that a new war has broken out. He finds himself in the recruitment office with a colleague of his own age and notices to his satisfaction that he is a sub-lieutenant while the colleague is just an ordinary private soldier. When it becomes clear that the dreamer has been jealous of his colleague because of his success at a legal conference, the dream takes on a very clear meaning, which is that of re-establishing superiority for himself by using a military advantage. The war implies the idea of professional rivalry, the need to be active and virile. . . . In the previous example, in particular, the dreamer did not wish for war at all: he did not see it as a symbol of rivalry and a pretext for superiority.[64]

As the expression of dreamers' preoccupations, dreams reveal the diversity of human preoccupations and consequently cannot be simply reduced to the sexual dimension of experience. Norbert Elias pointed out 'the possibility of there being very strong emotional bonds of many kinds without any sexual overtones.'[65] This 'elementary and biologically based dependence on others' is not confined 'to the satisfaction of *sexual* needs', since 'people look to others for the fulfilment of a whole gamut of emotional needs',[66] not all of which can be reduced to the *libido sexualis*. For Elias, the psyche of each human being represents a configuration of 'valencies' of very different natures, which can come together or establish themselves, durably or more fleetingly, within interpersonal relationships or very varied types of activity. This 'personal configuration of valencies', closely related to what I term an individual heritage of dispositions and skills, starts to take shape during infancy, within the familial structure. It is therefore initially highly dependent on the types of relationships and activities – historically and socially very varied – which develop within the family and then continue to take shape and to change shape according to relationships of interdependence and situations experienced.[67] Such a concept takes us from an omnipresent *libido sexualis* or an omnipresent *sexual valency* to a multiplicity of *libidines* or of *valencies*.

The highs and lows of the dream: sexuality and domination

> If a man dreams that he is flying not very far above the earth and in an upright position, it means good luck for the dreamer. The greater the distance above the earth, the higher his position will be in regard to those who walk beneath him. For we always call those who are more prosperous the 'higher ones' . . . Flying with wings is auspicious for all men alike. The dream signifies freedom for slaves, since all birds that fly are without a master and no one above them. It means that the poor will acquire a great deal of money. For just as money raises men up, wings raise birds up. It signifies offices for the rich and the very influential. For just as the creatures of the air are above those that crawl upon the earth, rulers are above private citizens.
>
> (Artemidorus, *The Interpretation of Dreams: Oneirocritica*, p. 132)

Having taken a close look at structural domination,[68] it seems to me logical, and even essential, to turn my attention to internalised domination, which structures our representations even in our dreams. Domination observed in its unfolded, overt state, in institutions, interactions, inegalitarian structures, etc., does not come without domination in a folded, more hidden form, in the schemas of perception internalised by individuals. If our mental representations, whether conscious or unconscious, are structured by power relations, the dream must be able to demonstrate the existence of such relations. The social world, with its interwoven threads of relations of domination and struggles for power of various types, inevitably penetrates the oneiric world. This is in any case the hypothesis I intend to demonstrate by embarking on this area of study.

Subjects dream of power and about power, of the power they wield over others or that which is wielded over them; their dreams feature figures of power and relations of power, people who dominate and others who are dominated. And as the dream proceeds semiotically according to its own possibilities, which are essentially visual, dreams can depict domination through spatial dispositions and movements of the body: being high up or being low down, looking up or looking down from above, climbing, ascending, rising or slipping down, falling down, having ascendency over, being above or below someone, getting the upper hand or losing out, being under the responsibility or the control of. . . . There are also summits, high places and deep holes, cellars and underworlds.[69]

Yet, out of all of that, Freud wished only to see the sexual dimension. And reducing relations of domination to the sexual was all the easier given that sexual relationships also involve relations of domination. But projecting a sexual dimension onto all relations of domination seems to be taking advantage of the homology of the situation by using the language of a specific domain of behaviour (sexual) to refer to the whole range of existing practices, all of which moreover have their own ways of operating.

We shall thus see, by looking at many examples of dreams, how the issues of power, hierarchy and domination which structure social experience in the waking state within the family, in the professional field or in the broader social domain manage to find metaphorical expression in dreams through spatial oppositions or more directly through the use of social markers of distinction, hierarchy or power. The many examples looked at will show that the 'political' dimension of oppositions between above and below, superior and inferior, high and low, etc., cannot be reduced simply to the sexual dimension of opposition between male and female, and that the desire to dominate, to have or to take the upper hand or, conversely, the fear of being humiliated, dominated, looked down on, or falling, continues to haunt dreamers.

Family, power and sex

If power appears just as important a structuring force as sexuality, given that the two are not entirely separable, it is because the earliest relationships between parents and children are relationships of power and that, however gentle or affectionate they may be, from the outset they contribute to making human subjects into beings who are enduringly dependent on adults and on their authority.[70] After the father and the mother, along comes the teacher, the lecturer, the coach, the doctor, the policeman, the office or team manager, the director of this or of that, the emperor or the empress, the king or the queen, the president, etc.

Freud clearly interpreted dreams about kings and queens as dreams depicting fathers and mothers,[71] but the fact that these are figures of authority and power was not sufficiently emphasised. For him, this was no more than a mask of social appearance which hides the familial truth interwoven into the backdrop of the social comedy enacted in the world of the dream. The prosaically social interested him only as a symbol of intra-familial relationships. It was as though he refused to consider the manifest social content of the dream because he was convinced that, behind this puppet theatre, the real actors are the mother, the father, the children and their relationships controlled by an unconscious libidinous regime. But instead of choosing sides (that of the psychoanalytical family-based interpretation versus that of a more political and institutional interpretation) we should strive to keep together all the experiences which resonate in the mind of a subject who has experienced them all, and in the order in which (except for the children of kings and queens who, from the start, experience the identification of the father and the king, the mother and the queen) institutional figures of power are generally presented in the history of subjects as *analogons* of primordial figures of power. As Pierre Bourdieu writes: 'individual history, in its most individual aspects, and even in its sexual dimension, is socially determined. Carl Schorske put it very well when he said: "Freud forgets that Oedipus was a king."'[72]

Freud knew very well that dependence in relation to parents or the power they exert over their children are not the only kinds of relationships which involve forms of domination. Rivalries, competition, oppression, jealousy, abuse, also structure relationships between brothers and sister and, further afield, with playmates or schoolfriends, etc. Fathers very often dominate mothers, parents dominate children, sons become rivals of their fathers, daughters of their mothers, children view the arrival of their little brothers or sisters and fear they will steal their parents' attention, love or support, and so on.[73]

And Freud is sometimes also able to identify hierarchical social structures in dreams of the high/low type, but he then interprets these in terms of 'phantasies of a sexual nature'. The case entitled 'A lovely dream'[74] is a case in point. The dream is structured on the basis of oppositions: those up above/those down below, first floor/ground floor, rich/poor (modest), going up/coming down, superimposed onto the opposition of brother/dreamer. With the help of associations made by the dreamer, Freud concludes that part of the dream draws its scenario from a play he had seen at the theatre the previous evening which told the story of a girl who had affairs with 'members of high society', who 'went up in the world' but then went 'down in the world'. The X Street of the dream, in which there was an 'unpretentious inn', turns out to have been the address of an actress with whom the dreamer had been involved in a relationship. When he had gone to visit her one summer, he had found himself obliged to stay in a shabby hotel in the area where he was relieved not to 'have picked up any vermin', his coachman having told him it was not a hotel but only 'an inn'. Moreover, Freud notes the reversal of the relationship between high and low in the context of the dreamer and his brother: whereas in the dream the brother is upstairs, in real life he occupied a lower status, having lost his position in society. The dream is therefore full of references to matters of hierarchy, even including the reference to the king of Italy, to whom insults are directed at the end of the dream. For the contemporary reader, the absence of any further information than that provided by Freud makes it difficult to understand all the aspects of the dream. It would be helpful, for example, to know more about the dreamer's relationship with his brother and why he placed him in the dominant position in the dream. But the sexual interpretation by Freud leaves little room for consideration of the many indications referring to a social structure of domination. For Freud, in this dream as in many others, the high and the low, the action of going up and that of going down, refer in a clear and unequivocal way to sexual matters: 'Steps, ladders or staircases, or as the case may be, walking up or down them are representations of the sexual act.'[75] Similarly 'down below' refers to the genital organs and 'up above' to the mouth, face or breasts.[76] Yet how is it possible to ignore that above and below are indicators of power and importance? Going up and down can, of course, refer to the sexual act, but also to social elevation (climbing, rising) and decline (falling, coming down).[77]

Dominating or being dominated

As early as 1851, however, the French philosopher and archaeologist Antoine Charma had observed the existence of dreams of power which could, for example, in oneiric terms, take the form of differences in position between a dreamer who glides or flies and other people who are crawling – a vivid way of saying, essentially, that vanity, high self-esteem or pride 'gives us wings', as the expression says. 'Do you allow yourself to be carried away in a surge of pride which raises you in your own esteem above those around you? The sheaves of your brothers will bow down before your own, or you will soar in the skies, while the crowd, which you have left behind, will crawl humbly on the ground.'[78] Or,

As for this power which sleep sometimes accords us where we are lifted up and moved through the air, many experiments, carried out first of all on myself and then on a few people whose confidences I trust all the more in that they can have no suspicion of the uses to which I may put them, have proved to me that it is indeed vanity satisfied during the day which in the night gives us wings and raises us physically above our fellow creatures.[79]

After his split from Freud, Alfred Adler, the Austrian doctor and psychotherapist, developed an individual psychology which proved to be much more sensitive to the social and political dimension of dreams. In 1933, for example, he wrote:

Dreams of falling (surely the commonest of all) indicate that the dreamer is anxious about losing her sense of worth; but at the same time they show by spatial representation that the dreamer is under the illusion that she is 'above'. *Flying dreams* occur in ambitious people as the precipitate of their struggle for superiority – the struggle to perform something that will exalt the dreamer over everyone else. This dream is frequently accompanied by a *falling dream* as a warning against an ambitiously risky struggle.[80]

Yet another social dimension of the flying dream which Freud failed to notice. For him, flying refers to the family practice involving games where little children are made to fly: 'There cannot be a single uncle who has not shown a child how to fly by rushing across the room with him in his outstretched arms or who has not played at letting him fall by riding him on his knee.'[81] It is indeed possible that dreaming of flying or falling comes from exactly that, but these dreams have associated meanings which in certain cases are difficult to clarify: dreams of omnipotence, of domination, of flying high, of self-confidence, of a sense of ease and of joyful lightness.

Adler makes the connection between the ontogenetic, individual dimension and the collective and structural dimension. Each individual experiences the sense of gaining in recognition and in dignity by moving from the state of the crawling child to that of the child walking on two feet and who is no longer 'down' and 'clinging to the floor'. On the basis of this first experience, already structured by social relations of domination – it is socialised adults who teach the child the sense of good and bad, worthy and unworthy, right and wrong, etc. – other social meanings are gradually superimposed or added:

> The abstraction of the concept, above-beneath, obviously plays an extremely important role in the civilization of mankind . . . ; a certain proof is to be found in the conduct of small children who throw themselves on the floor angrily and thus try to make themselves dirty in order to attract the attention of their parents but betray thereby that the idea of 'being down' as a fiction of what is forbidden, dirty, sinful is developing in them. . . . In this category of 'down-up,' one of which cannot be thought of without the other, is further found intermingled trains of thought (in both neurotics and normal persons), which express the antithesis of conquest and defeat, of triumph and inferiority.[82]

Adler emphasises the analogy between 'moral superiority' and spatial superiority and makes the point that many religious visions were based on an opposition between the 'high' and the 'low'.[83]

Given that dreams favour the visual aspect of the narrative, all actions and all meanings must be presented in spatial terms: 'Frequently this "will to be up" is expressed in a strongly figurative manner, in both dreams and in symptoms, and takes the symbolic form of a race, of soaring, of climbing mountains, of emerging from water, etc., while the "down" is represented by falling, in short by a motion downwards.'[84] Adler listens to what his patients tell him, with particular attention to these oppositions between high and low, and without relating them exclusively to any sexual signification they might suggest.

On the subject of a female patient who tried to explain her dream to him, Adler notes that 'a series of ambitious thoughts emerged which takes the form among others of a sexual picture of domination over her future husband' and that 'She remembered dreams of earlier times which represented her as riding on a man, on a horse.' He then continues his analysis by observing that 'the dream of flying, of climbing stairs, etc.', can be seen 'as a dynamic expression of the "will to be up" in the sense of the manly aggression'.[85] Or, similarly, when the patient says that, in her dream, she 'climbed onto the heads of everybody', Adler sees this as 'a form of speech to express that she is superior to all others.'

> The sequence of ideas which make up this dream reveal the neurotic predispositions of the patient. In reality, her masculine protest, her inclination to belittle others, her ambition, her sensitiveness, defiance, unyieldingness, obstinacy, are all evident and the psychic significance of her headaches is also revealed in this dream. Analysis had shown in particular that the symptom always made its appearance when the patient experienced a feeling of defeat, of belittlement, of emasculation, when – in the words of the dream – anyone 'mounted her head'.[86]

If the opposition high/low also characterises relations between the masculine and the feminine, the relation of domination is not therefore exclusively sexual.

The social (economic or cultural) hierarchy sometimes structures dreams in an even more direct way. One of Adler's patients had the following dream: 'I was with my old friend and was speaking with him about a mutual friend. He said, "Of what use is his money to him, he has learned nothing?"' As a result of a sound knowledge of the patient and of his relationship with this 'old friend', Adler understood that the patient was dreaming of winning in social terms in order to be victorious in a romantic rivalry:

> The old friend, who had cut our patient out in the courtship of a girl, had failed in the technical school and had given up study. The patient was superior to him for he had finished the course. He embraced the sublime principle 'Knowledge is more than money,' especially as this profession served his fiction to be 'above' and comforted him. The mutual acquaintance is placed here instead of the rich girl who was courted by both. The contest begins anew. Our patient is declared victor by his rival.[87]

This desire for domination manifests itself also in the way the patient declares that, in fact, 'an uneducated girl from the country serves his purpose, as he can always remain her master.'[88] And another of his patients, whose 'dislike for those above him is boundless and deep-seated', dreams that the choir to which he belongs was due to give a concert and that the director was not there. Adler knows that this situation has already arisen in the life of this patient and, having learned how to understand his deepest dispositions, makes the following observation: 'This situation appeared to him better than any other. "We need no director," he thought. This is his usual attitude in all situations in which he himself is not the director.'[89]

In 1914, even though he emphasised the rarity of dreams of greatness among the dreams of ninety fifteen-year-old schoolchildren (in comparison with their daydreams),[90] Paul Borel mentions two cases from among the dreams in his survey: one person dreams they are in charge of torpedoing the German fleet in order to protect a food convoy coming from the USA, and another says: 'I dream of vast and wealthy kingdoms of which I am the master.' Similarly, in their disjointed sociological survey of the dreams of French people carried out during the late 1970s, Jean Duvignaud, Françoise Duvignaud and Jean-Pierre Corbeau mention cases of dreamers who are confident of their success and of their dominant position and whose dreams are clearly visual transpositions of expressions such as 'looking down on people', 'feelings of superiority', 'having the upper hand over' or 'being highly placed'. One person dreams he is in a plane 'very high in the sky' and that the island on which he needs to land is 'too small for the plane'; another sees himself 'on a sort of watchtower', sees 'people around him' but finds that he feels 'too good to want to go down'; and another says that he sometimes finds himself 'flying over a beach and knowing that people are watching him and calling out to him.'[91]

The main tendencies and attitudes in relation to class or to career paths are reflected in the dreams recorded by sociologists, in particular 'the euphoria of domination and intense pleasure' (dreams of swimming pools, beautiful women, magnificent castles, the latest ski equipment, etc.), the certainty about one's social importance ('I know people have expectations of me'; 'a feeling of extraordinary completeness') or, among male executives, the 'fear of falling'.[92] For example, a high-ranking executive who is afraid of being downgraded dreams that he falls into a hole (as in the expression 'to be at rock bottom') and that his colleagues are watching him but cannot get him out.[93] Or another executive, who dreams of professional success (along with sexual power), seeing himself 'dancing superbly and with all the girls' or in the role of 'the conductor of an orchestra' who gets everyone dancing and is 'congratulated' by everyone.[94] Similarly, another young executive who dreams he is the factory owner and can exert his power over the pretty female employees: 'I'm dancing with our female employees and they are all really pretty, I promise to make them secretaries so they don't have to dirty their hands; everyone is happy and I myself have become rich.'[95]

Sometimes, hierarchies are implicit or very discreet, even though they structure the overall meaning of the dream. For example, a man dreams that an individual wearing a big cloak is running, bent forwards, and that he falls and hurts his head. When the dreamer goes back over the details of his dream, he says that his brother used to run in a bent-forward position and that the cloak is like one belonging to his brother-in-law. The individual who is running is therefore a composite of his brother and his brother-in-law. But what do the two have in common? The dreamer says that 'the first was older, stronger and dominated him' through his childhood and that his 'brother-in-law is richer'. As a result, 'the dreamer wishes to witness the fall of all those who are in any way superior to him or who, in general terms, incite his jealousy.[96] Or, again, another man dreams that he is in officer's uniform and that he meets his colleague X, a private soldier. In discussions with the analyst, the dreamer explains that the colleague in question obtained significant professional success and that another colleague who aroused his jealousy had told him about his antimilitaristic opinions, which displeased him. The effect of this double professional revelation on an existing tendency for rivalry in the dreamer triggered the dream. The colleague X in his military uniform thus combines the two colleagues who are *analogons* in waking life. The rank of the private soldier is a way of allowing the dreamer to express a desire for superiority over a colleague (he sees himself as an officer in the dream), a disposition which is already solidly anchored in him: 'It is obviously about a desire for superiority over a colleague, but this spirit of rivalry is a constant in the dreamer, compensating for a neurotic fear of inferiority by which he is affected.'[97]

The fear of not being equal to the task is similarly significant in a personal dream reported and discussed by Maurice Halbwachs, who was slightly 'mortified' one day by not knowing the chemical substances indicated on a medical prescription. That evening, he dreamt that he was with his friends from the École normale supérieure, that they were talking about chemistry and that he was unable to answer some questions about lime. He notices, moreover, that in his dream some of his friends were sporting medals. The uncomfortable sense of ignorance from the previous day had revived his fear of not being up to the level of his distinguished (medal-wearing) university friends. He therefore felt humiliated by not knowing things that they knew.[98]

This dream is an echo of the famous dream of 'the injection given to Irma' interpreted by Freud.[99] In this personal dream, Freud is particularly worried about his reputation among his colleagues. Irma had been his patient, and Otto Rank had said of her the previous day: 'She is better, but not quite well.' Freud felt that Otto was taking advantage of the situation to criticise his treatment. The tone he had used and the way he mentioned that she was better, 'but not quite well', led Freud to think that Otto was essentially delighted with this opportunity to denigrate his action. Yet in the dream he sees Otto and makes him responsible for the effects of an injection, making the point that 'the syringe had not been clean' – a way of alluding to the fact that Otto's attitude to him was not as it should be. Freud wrote thus: 'the dream gave me my revenge by throwing the reproach back onto him.'[100]

In his study conducted among 266 students from Volda in Norway, Jan Frederik Hovden also shows the influence of domination on dreams.[101] Looking at memories of recurrent dreams, he manages to establish that dreams about situations of extreme distress and weakness (being tied up and incapable of moving, being buried, being pushed down, smothered, being dead, seeing dead bodies, etc.) are more often experienced by female students and by people from less cultivated backgrounds, and that dreams of power and superiority (being able to fly, becoming suddenly rich, finding money, having superior artistic or mental abilities) are more often associated with male students and people from more cultivated backgrounds.[102] Even though the study unfortunately focuses not on accounts of precise dreams but on the responses to pre-coded questions about memories of recurring dreams (which contributes a little further to distancing the dream object itself), the feelings of domination or of being dominated can be seen, here too, to structure the oneiric experience.

The dream under a totalitarian regime

It is, however, in a study by Charlotte Beradt on dreams under the Third Reich that we find the strongest and most impressive proof of the way in which the political sphere invades the subjectivity of citizens and intrudes on their privacy, even in moments when the human being seems to have withdrawn from society and its constraints. Beradt does not concern herself with the dreamers' personal histories. She links the dreams not to a series of individual experiences but, rather, to the general characteristics of a period in which Nazism was on the rise. The dreams, which she meticulously collected from German people from 1933 onwards, show how the oneiric stage becomes the theatre of all the feelings of dispossession, depersonalization, humiliation, acceptance, submission or guilt, but also of the fascination or attraction exerted by torturers, associated with the gradual establishment of a totalitarian regime.

The dreamers imagine they are being listened to at the very heart of their private space by authorities who have placed microphones everywhere; they even feel their most intimate thoughts are under scrutiny and dream that the walls of their apartments, like those of neighbouring buildings, have completely disappeared. Constantly watched, they feel threatened by booming loudspeakers, political images and slogans or military uniforms; they dream of behaving in a docile manner, of bowing down before authority and taking comfort in conformist attitudes. They are paralysed by fear or anxiety. Beradt sees these as attempts to 'toe the line' and as 'initiation rites into the totalitarian scheme',[103] but they could just as easily be seen as opportunities to play out whatever is feared in order to be able to face up to it. The dream sounds the alarm and acts as a warning of danger, just as much as it internalises and accepts the reality imposed on it. In the dream, the dreamer describes 'more precisely and with greater subtlety than he could ever have while awake' the mechanism of 'totalitarian rule'.[104] And what the dream is doing here cannot be unequivocally situated either as a form of resistance or as one of utter submission to the order being established.

Unlike the approach favoured in psychoanalysis, the author does not want to separate manifest content from latent content.[105] Because she fears the denial of the obviously political content of the dream, she rejects the idea of an interpretation which would be completely at odds with what the images seem to suggest literally, by focusing on family relationships in early childhood, for example. Nevertheless, the two points of view are compatible. The sense of a dispossession of the self, created by the political situation experienced by the dreamers, cannot fail to reflect, to resonate or to suggest through analogy situations from childhood (vis-à-vis their parents) or from later in their lives (in relation to different types of authority encountered) that dreamers have experienced. Without being able to question the dreamers directly, there is nothing to suggest whether behind the oneiric images which refer to the present time there is not also a whole series of wounds, humiliations or needs of a completely different nature.[106]

And, moreover, the dreams themselves sometimes set the scene for a mixture of registers by condensing an educational setting with more obviously political elements.

> A schoolgirl whose father had once been a communist had the following typical dream: 'I receive the same comment on all my report cards and on all the class work I do: Very good, but unsatisfactory because subversive.' This old nightmare about schools and examinations (in the case of the schoolgirl, it was a direct reflection of her own situation) appears to have occurred in many variations among adults. I received a number of such reports, such as: 'I am not promoting you because you belong to the Church,' or '... because you are ideologically intolerable.' Or, posted on a university notice board – and this, again, is almost parody: 'So-and-so has failed because he is an enemy of the people.'[107]

It is not difficult to see, in such a scenario, how the relationship of authority between citizen and state echoes the relationship of authority between pupil and teacher. The dreamer confuses the two registers, aware of the analogy between the two situations. If, in chronological order, family or school experiences precede professional, political or religious experiences, this in no way undermines the specific nature of the different registers of experience which each individual links psychologically and between which he or she sometimes creates equivalences.

Politics always contains more than exclusively political experiences. Yet does that imply that the political can be reduced to issues of family and structures of domination or struggles for power to the sexual dimension of human relationships? The psychoanalyst is certainly right to say that the manifest content of a political type 'prevents access to a completely different regime of thinking, which is hidden behind that one, uses it for its own ends and finds in it a secret satisfaction.'[108] Yet it can just as surely be said that political experience, or, more widely, the experience of domination, is based on, and uses to its own ends, dispositions constituted in very different social contexts. For it would be inappropriate to say – and this is precisely what Charlotte Beradt seeks to avoid – that the weight of political oppression felt by the dreamers is merely a façade behind which childhood sexuality could hide.[109] The important lesson to take away from Charlotte Beradt's work is that the interpreter should not neglect the explicit, manifest content of the dream, since this could hinder understanding of very real current experiences and structures – which are sometimes political – through which more distant sufferings of all sorts can sometimes be expressed.[110]

Hobson's dream of greatness

For a number of decades, the American neuropsychiatrist John Allan Hobson has been developing an approach which goes in the opposite direction to research acknowledging the interest of interpreting dreams. In spite of this, he has embarked on the study of one of his own dreams. As is often the case with self-analysis, the interpreter turns out not to be in the best position to understand the dream and to provide an interpretation which brings out the dispositional properties indicated in it. In this particular case, the dream, along with the commentaries accompanying it and other personal dreams also mentioned, could reasonably be seen to suggest a tendency to dominate and longings for greatness which the researcher seems inclined to underestimate or ignore altogether.

Hobson, whose wife is programme director at the Museum of Fine Arts in Boston, has the following dream, accompanied by comments in square brackets:

My wife, Joan, and I are at the Museum of Fine Arts in Boston to attend a concert in the larger Remus auditorium. It is someone (perhaps John Gibbons) playing a Mozart piano (concerto?) on a large Steinway (no orchestra, but image vague anyway). [The piano is reminiscent of the large Steinway grand in the great hall of the Phillips Collection in Washington, which I visited the previous Saturday.] As is usual on such 'museum' occasions, I am restive, feeling like the third wheel on Joan's business bicycle, and hence inattentive. I decide to explore and go down to the smaller, older theater (near the Egyptian sarcophagi). This theater is now limited to small lectures but was, twenty years ago, the place where, as young members, Joan and I attended museum programs of the type that are now in Remus, and now under Joan's direction. I hear music and the faint bustle of excitement. Opening the door a crack, I am amazed to realize that Mozart himself is on stage, playing the same concerto (again without an orchestra) on an antique harpsichord from the museum collection (not the Mozart Pianoforte). Although the door is open only for an instant, I notice Mozart's rich red brocaded frock coat (the curlicues are gold-embossed) and his white powdered wig. He has a beatific smile, and the arpeggios stream through the door into my ear. I also notice that Mozart has gotten a bit overweight, and wonder why. I close the door with a shhh! and try to figure out how to tell Joan of my discovery. Then I wake up.[111]

The analysis begins quite well, with Hobson acknowledging: 'I am prepared to admit that this dream might have a psychoanalytical "meaning": I *am* ambitious. I *do* admire Mozart. I *would*, consciously, like to be as brilliant as Mozart. Some of my most devoted friends have even called me "Mozart."' Yet in spite of that, he suggests 'under the suspended cognitive rules of REM sleep, Mozart is Mozart' and not, he insists, a 'stand-in for my father'. But it is hard to see why a psychoanalyst could suggest seeing Mozart as a paternal figure. Friends nicknamed him Mozart and he himself would love to be the Mozart of neuropsychiatry. Moreover, he sees in his dream a Mozart who has put on weight and himself indicates in his commentary that this is not entirely without connection to his own case: 'The body-type file has been opened and incongruous plot features are the result: *my* belly has begun to bulge!' Yet there is in fact no incongruity or coincidence in this historical detail, since it is indeed himself that the dreamer sees on the stage. And moreover this stage is now a lecture theatre, which once again refers back to an important aspect of his professional activity. In another personal dream which he describes, Hobson describes a situation where his application for a series of lectures is rejected by the members of a committee who instead opt for a lecturer who will help them with fundraising, thus demonstrating that giving lectures is an important means of recognition in his professional universe.[112]

What Hobson fails to see is that everything in his dream, and in the comments he makes on it, suggests that the dream is enacting the process of his taking power back from his wife. The latter drags him along with her to the museum (her workplace) and he is bored. He therefore goes to a part of the museum which is now used for lectures (which represent an important part of his career) and sees himself on the stage in the person of Mozart, complete with paunch just like him, alone and without an orchestra, like a lecturer. These elements contribute in this way to turn the dream into the stage for a power struggle with his wife. He would like to be Mozart, alone on the stage, famous and dressed in gold, admired by his wife, instead of someone who gets dragged along to watch another person shine. And even the remarks he makes on the interpretation of this dream indicate the fact that the Mozart of the dream is indeed himself and that he would like his wife to feel proud at seeing him on the stage: 'I would love to see Mozart, to have my wife "score" by attracting him to the museum and to discover him there so that I could report her coup to others.' He then adds this magnificent commentary, which becomes almost ironic if you bear in mind that the dream is a way of saying that he is not in the least bit interested in what his wife does and would prefer instead for her to admire him on stage during one of his lectures: 'I found the dream pleasant, surprising and gratifying. I also enjoyed telling my wife this story. From a social point of view, my dream was a belated wedding present!' If his dream is a wedding present, it looks more of a poisoned chalice than anything he might consciously envisage.

If psychoanalysis had very sound reasons for highlighting the largely neglected importance of family, early childhood experience and the sexual dimension of human desires and behaviours, if it also sought to find an interpretative equilibrium between the triggering elements from the present and the past experiences of the individuals in question, it undeniably succumbed to the temptation of the naturalisation of wishes, overestimated the autonomy of the family structure, put too much value also on the impact of certain events of early childhood, and over-interpreted the sexual nature of human motivation.

Psychoanalysis allowed itself in this way to forget that a social world encompasses the family universe, that individuals cannot be reduced to their status as father, mother, son or daughter, brother or sister, husband or wife, but throughout their lives are part of a sequence of other hierarchised social universes (social, professional, religious, political, sporting, military, etc.) where other power games are played out, and that they are driven by a whole host of socially constituted wishes rather than simply by sexual and natural ones. As the most intimate and personal form of human expression, the dream is nonetheless a space in which the social structures of domination and the multitude of *libidines* placed at the disposal of dreamers by the social world, depending on the state of its development, may still be observed.

4

The Incorporated Past and the Unconscious

Days when a flash of lightning brings coherence into the picture, and what has gone before is revealed as preparation for the present.
(Sigmund Freud, letter to Wilhelm Fliess, 27 October 1897, in *The Origins of Psychoanalysis*, p. 226)

One of the important components of the general formula for the interpretation of dreams[1] is what is referred to in sociology as the incorporated past. The exact nature of this embodied past is made up of a number of different elements. These include the question of the formation, reinforcement or adjustment of schemas or dispositions over the course of a series of socialising experiences of varying degrees of coherence, the way in which these schemas or these dispositions are transposed onto dreams in the form of oneiric schemas, and the unconscious – though not repressed – nature of this incorporated past, all of which will be our focus here.

Dreams, like any other form of expression, and forms of expression like any other practice, are marked by the presence of schemas or dispositions which bear witness to a multi-layered past, sedimented within the socialised body of the dreamer. In order to genuinely understand dreams, therefore, we need to identify the historically and biographically constituted structures which lie hidden behind an apparently incoherent dream account.

To do so, we can only adhere to the realism of the structure which led Thomas M. French and Erika Fromm to say that 'the logically articulated system that we seek is already implicit in an unverbalized cognitive structure that underlies all that the patient says and does' and that 'Our basic task is to expose this cognitive structure to plain view without destroying it.'[2] The structure in question, or, more precisely, the structures governing the production of dreams and of all other acts or forms of expression, pre-date analysis and are the products of an incorporated history made up of schemas or dispositions which are internalised by individuals.

The concept of 'schemas' or 'dispositions' – but the same applies equally to a whole range of other concepts, like that of 'structure' – represents a genuine challenge to positivism, which insists on *seeing* things in order to accept their existence. Both a schema and a disposition are realities which cannot be directly observed but which we have to assume are active in order to explain the coherence of what we observe. For example, an ascetic tendency can reveal itself just as clearly in a past attitude to schoolwork, in a present-day attitude to work, in the way the family budget is managed, in choices relating to sports and ways of practising sports, etc. To claim that no one had ever seen a disposition or a schema in order to refute a dispositional approach would be a grossly positivist error. No dispositionalist has ever claimed that a disposition is observable in itself. What is observable are the effects it produces in practices and in representations.

This was the argument used by the American anthropologist Ralph Linton regarding the importance of the concept of 'personality' (or of 'personality structure'):

> Moreover, they are not susceptible to direct observation. We can only deduce their qualities from the overt behavior in which these qualities find expression. Going a step farther, the only grounds for assuming the existence of personalities as operative entities persisting through time is the consistency in the overt behavior of individuals. The individual's repetition of similar responses to similar stimuli, in those cases where such responses are complex and obviously not instinctual, can only be accounted for on the assumption that experience is, in some way, organized and perpetuated.[3]

Sigmund Freud also set out an implicit dispositionalist argument when he distinguished the 'latent thoughts' or the 'latent content' of the dream from the 'manifest thoughts' or 'manifest content'. The notion of 'latency' refers to a virtual existence, to a potential, to something not demonstrated but which could potentially be demonstrable. The status of the unconscious is therefore close to that of a disposition: it is an incorporated or embodied past which has a structuring effect but which manifests itself only in given situations or circumstances. But 'latent' can also sometimes mean 'hidden' or 'disguised', and this allowed Freud to develop his questionable vision of what is censored/disguised/hidden.[4] However, the invisible but nevertheless structuring nature of the background comes from the schema or the disposition and is not the effect of a censorship.

This chapter will focus on some different modes in which the incorporated past resurfaces in the present (in the form of memories, symbolic expressions such as games or dreams, or actions), on the contribution made by neuroscience, psychology and sociological dispositionalism to the study of the phenomena of the internalisation of objective regularities and of practical anticipation, on oneiric schemas which are linked to socially constituted schemas and dispositions, and on the criticism of Freud's event-focused vision, which too often seeks to uncover the significant events of early childhood rather than to piece together sequences of recurring and relatively similar events which have the most enduring impact on the incorporated past of each individual.

Ways in which the incorporated past is actualised

Freud identified two ways in which the incorporated past manifested itself in the present. The first is the conscious process of remembering (memory), and the second consists in experiencing a repetition of a schema (whether relational or emotional) that is part of the unconscious actualisation of incorporated dispositions, whether in the context of psychoanalytic therapy (through the phenomenon of 'transference' onto the person of the analyst)[5] or in ordinary life. This distinction is fundamental and should be kept in mind so as to avoid reducing the return of the past into the present purely to the exercise of memory or referring to the effects of habit in the language of memory, as Piaget did when he wrote: 'The child will try . . . to make the new object enter into each of his habitual schemata, one by one. In other words, the child will try to "understand" the nature of the new object.'[6] For we do not 'remember' a cognitive or sensorimotor schema in the way we do a past event. Habit-memory, as Bergson said, has nothing to do with recollection-memory: 'Habit rather than memory, it acts our past experience but does not call up its image.'[7] It is a 'bodily memory' which makes itself visible in ways of being and of doing and not in 'memory-images'.

The second mode is the most crucial in understanding that individuals constantly play out scenes they have lived through in the past without knowing that they are doing so. They adopt the same attitudes, place themselves in the same positions or situations, act or react in the same way, and sometimes produce the same effects. Involuntary memory, 'an urge to action', the past takes the form of dispositions and therefore does not resurface only in the guise of detailed memories of actions, words, feelings or thoughts. The incorporated past acts on our perceptions, our representations, our emotions or our actions without our even being aware of it. Hume was already emphasising that our 'past experience' acts on the mind in a way so 'insensible' that it can escape our consciousness altogether. And it is precisely remembering without memory which is at work when a man 'stops short in his journey when meeting a river in his way' and 'foresees the consequences of his proceeding forward' thanks to practical knowledge provided by his past experience:

> But can we think, that on this occasion he reflects on any past experience, and calls to remembrance instances, that he has seen or heard of, in order to discover the effects of water on animal bodies? No surely; this is not the method, in which he proceeds in his reasoning. The idea of sinking is so closely connected with that of water, and

the idea of suffocating with that of sinking, that *the mind makes the transition without the assistance of the memory*. The custom operates before we have time for reflection.[8]

It seems to me, however, that this second category would benefit by being extended to include all kinds of schemas and dispositions and by taking into account the difference between the practical scenes of waking life and all the scenes of waking life which are moments of symbolic expression, outside of any practical urgency and without any immediate considerations and direct consequences. There would then be three main ways in which the incorporated past would act on the present: 1) the practical activation in the actions and interactions of everyday life; 2) the implicit staging in the form of symbolic expressions (e.g. a child's game with characters or objects, a spoken or written story, a drawing, a painting, a dream, a daydream, etc.) which are structured by the disposition or schema in question; and 3) the mental or verbally retrieved memory of scenes in which these schemas of experience are revealed (memories which can resurface in the ordinary situations of life or as a result of sociological interviews, analysis, psychotherapy, etc.).[9]

In all cases, whether the past returns in the form of a 'that reminds me' or of a 'that makes me act, think, or feel like this or like that', it is present situations which open or close the possibilities of a reactivation of our incorporated past. Incorporated past and present context are inseparable elements. At any given moment, we perceive the situations in which we find ourselves on the basis of what our incorporated past has taught us to perceive; at each moment, the situations with which we are faced, not all of which we can control, reactivate our embodied past without any conscious decision needing to be taken.

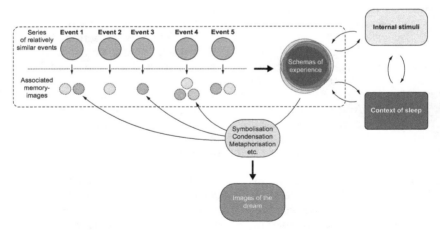

Figure 4a The comparative processes involved in the production of dreams

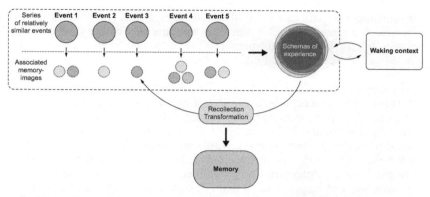

Figure 4b The comparative processes involved in the production of memories

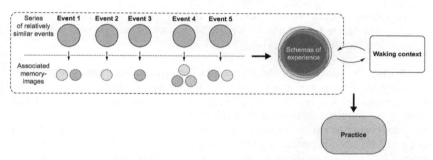

Figure 4c The comparative processes involved in the fabrication of practice

An awareness of these different modalities of the actualisation of the incorporated past is a way of highlighting the risk of overestimating the effects of verbalisation during psychoanalytic therapy and many forms of psychotherapy.[10] Getting patients with psychological disorders to talk undoubtedly helps them on the road to recovery, but not everything can be brought down simply to a question of increased awareness, to the liberating expression of repressed, hidden or buried experiences, or to the liberating effect of speech. There are also dispositions which make us act in a certain way, dispositions which affect how we believe, think, feel, etc., all of them firmly anchored, with the result that the same problems are constantly repeated. Disorders are compulsive[11] only because they are associated with socialised individuals, with their customs and habits, whose dispositional forces lead them to reproduce the same problems, repeat the same sequences of action or interaction, or put themselves constantly into the same problematic situations.

Freud sometimes saw the role of psychoanalytic therapy as a technique for 'curbing the patient's compulsion to repeat and for turning it into a motive for remembering'.[12] Yet he was conscious of the discontinuity between what is a matter of 'memories' or of 'remembering' and what he himself called 'repetitive actions':

> We may say that the patient does not *remember* anything of what he has forgotten and repressed, but *acts* it out. He reproduces it not as a memory but as an action; he r*epeats* it, without, of course, knowing that he is repeating it. For instance, the patient does not say that he used to be defiant and critical towards his parents' authority; instead, he behaves in that way to the doctor. He does not remember how he came to a helpless and hopeless deadlock in his infantile sexual researches; but he produces a mass of confused dreams and associations, complains that he cannot succeed in anything and asserts that he is fated never to carry through what he undertakes. He does not remember having been intensely ashamed of certain sexual activities and afraid of their being found out; but he makes it clear that he is ashamed of the treatment on which he is now embarked and tries to keep it a secret from everybody. And so on.[13]

Making the schemas or dispositions which individuals carry with them verbally explicit is not enough to miraculously change their state. For the non-verbalised structures of behaviour are not themselves modified simply by a heightened awareness of them. In this sense, the sometimes very extended duration of psychoanalytic therapy can be justified by its capacity to act in a procedural way rather than simply through verbalisation. The psychoanalyst presents his or her patient with a new model of relationships and feelings. The analyst does not seduce or punish but instead listens, is patient, etc., and, over a long period, such relationships can contribute to modifying both the patient's 'emotional heuristics' (or 'habits of feeling') and their relational ones: 'It seems likely that, if a psychoanalytic therapy (and any other therapy) which aims to bring about any kind of lasting restoration of new emotional heuristics lasts such a long time, it is also because, in order to modify past procedures, the constant repetition of experiences is necessary.'[14]

In a text written in 1885, the Belgian psychologist and philosopher Joseph Delbœuf highlighted the importance of the habits which constantly shape our actions and our thoughts, whether waking or sleeping:

> If we group together under the generic term of habits all the acquired dispositions which have the effect of reducing effort and, consequently, attention, we can say that habits, as habits, are always part of our current knowledge; whether at rest or active, they are always at our service; in short, they do not sleep. Our habits therefore, both the most recent and the oldest, are part of ourselves. They are with us in all our normal states. Whether we are awake or lost in reverie or

deep in the realm of sleep, they are interwoven into all our thoughts and all our gestures.[15]

Given that socialisation is a permanent and ongoing process extending from the birth of an individual to his or her death, these habits may have been formed long ago or acquired more recently.

But the fact that the past is condensed in the form of habits (schemas, dispositions, abilities, etc.) means that there is no such thing as an out-of-date past. There is nothing more present than these condensed past experiences (Piaget used the expression 'summaries of experience' to refer to emotional, perceptive or sensorimotor schemas): 'For the common man', wrote Delbœuf,

> the past is what has gone by. Error! It is, on the contrary, reality in its most concrete form, that which cannot be undone. . . . The present is not pregnant with the future: *it is impregnated with the past*; it is the sum of and, in a manner of speaking, the fossilisation of all the past. In this way, nothing in nature is lost. The present has absorbed everything. This is, under its physical aspect, the significance of the complex and famous axiom. Beneath the psychic aspect, it expresses the great law governing the evolution of all beings. Their present faculties are the result of the accumulation of all the experience of the past.[16]

And, in this astonishingly apt observation, Delbœuf was already setting in place an approach to the interpretation of dreams which took into account habits and the circumstances that triggered them:

> In all our feelings, as in all our actions, there is always an element of chance and an element of necessity. The element of chance might be some impression or other, coming from outside, which triggers our sensibility and our activity; the element of necessity is what follows on from this impression in the organism and the activation of habits it encounters in its path. In musical boxes, the engineer has positioned raised points in a specific order on a cylinder. When a button is pressed, the box plays a tune and when a different button is pressed, it plays another tune. The mind is just such a musical box; . . . it is like a book of phonographic sheets. External agents constantly coax music out of it, sometimes complete tunes, sometimes fragments of tunes. The tunes that it plays are the habits it has acquired. The principles which we have set out here will serve to classify and to explain dreams.[17]

When Freud was forced to revise his general theory of dreams as the disguised fulfilment of unconscious repressed wishes in order to take into consideration the post-traumatic dreams of soldiers from the First World

War, he became aware of the fundamental importance of repetition in the process of human psychology.

> Thus we have come across people all of whose human relationships have the same outcome: such as the benefactor who is abandoned in anger after a time by each of his protégés, however much they may otherwise differ from one another, and who thus seems doomed to taste all the bitterness of ingratitude; or the man whose friendships all end in betrayal by his friend; or the man who time after time in the course of his life raises someone else into a position of great private or public authority and then, after a certain interval, himself upsets that authority and replaces him by a new one; or, again, the lover each of whose love affairs with a woman passes through the same phases and reaches the same conclusion. This 'perpetual recurrence of the same thing' causes us no astonishment when it relates to *active* behaviour on the part of the person concerned and when we can discern in him an essential character-trait which always remains the same and which is compelled to find expression in a repetition of the same experiences.[18]

But Freud firmly fixes the return of these same sequences of actions, attitudes and reactions in the biological workings of instincts or drives. For him, the instinct is 'an urge inherent in organic life to restore an earlier state of things which the living entity has been obliged to abandon under the pressure of external disturbing forces'; it is an 'expression of the inertia inherent in organic life'.[19] Had he used Spinoza's vocabulary, Freud would have said that everything strives to persevere in its being: 'all instincts tend towards the restoration of an earlier state of things.'[20] And the instinct, or drive, like a disposition, can be modified only as a result of 'external disturbing and diverting influences'.[21] If Freud had not made the pleasure principle, which fitted with his theory of repressed unconscious, the explanatory principle of all dreams, things might have been much more straightforward for him, and he would no doubt have been able to place at the heart of psychic processes this repetition which lies at the very core of the dispositionalist approach: 'If it is really the case that seeking to restore an earlier state of things is such a universal characteristic of instincts, we need not be surprised that so many processes take place in mental life independently of the pleasure principle.'[22]

The statistician brain or practical anticipation

Through the various channels and means at their disposal, the neurosciences deal with the same kinds of problems as those upon which Humean philosophy or dispositionalist sociology, among others, have always worked. Human beings are creatures of experience who, without realising it, constantly rely on their past experiences in order to be able to act in the present. They make sense of what they see, hear, etc., according to what they have experienced in the past, and they unconsciously anticipate, on the basis of their incorporated past, things yet to come: the things yet to be said, the gestures to be made, the events which will occur, etc.

The Bayesian brain[23] or the statistician brain is the theoretical framework which guides much of the work carried out in cognitive neuroscience on perception, language and action. According to this model, the brain is a complex system of unconscious probabilistic calculations. It is as though the brain is constantly gambling on the fact that everything that happens or will happen is no more than the extension of internalised past experiences; it 'uses the past to predict the present.'[24] Essentially, we could say that this represents all the non-conscious probabilistic calculations carried out by the brain, which are collectively referred to as intuition or the sense of what might lie ahead. 'The hypothesis of the "Bayesian brain"', writes the cognitive psychologist Stanislas Dehaene, 'postulates that our brain infers, from sensory input, an internal model of the external world. In turn, this internal model can be used to anticipate sensory data. The hypothesis of predictive coding assumes that the brain constantly generates this type of anticipation, and generates a signal of surprise or of error when such predictions are violated by unexpected sensory data.'[25]

These advances in neuroscience show that at each moment the fine flux of conscious operations hides a multiplicity of unconscious operations or calculations whose task is to interpret the sensory information and to ascertain which elements of this should be transferred to the conscious space. 'Clearly', wrote Dehaene, 'many complex sensory operations unfold sub rosa to assemble the scene that eventually plays out seamlessly in our mind's eye, as if coming straight from our sensory organs.'[26] But, as all of these operations which are taking place within us are inaccessible to our consciousness, we think subjectively that the only intellectual effort our brain is making is focused on the moments where we are involved in a challenging intellectual task. And even in such moments of intense intellectual effort, such as in the case of solving a mathematical problem, non-conscious processes are still at work: 'our mind's subliminal operations exceed its conscious achievements. Our visual system routinely solves problems of shape perception and invariant recognition that boggle the best computer software And we tap into this amazing computational power of the unconscious mind whenever we ponder mathematical problems.'[27]

Dehaene adopts the socio-political metaphor to portray this imbalance between the conscious tip of the iceberg and the enormous submerged unconscious mass:

> Modern cognitive psychologists have developed a variety of essentially equivalent metaphors, picturing conscious access as a 'central

bottleneck' or a 'second processing stage', a VIP lounge to which only the happy few are admitted. A third metaphor emerged in the 1960s and 1970s: it depicted consciousness as a high-level 'supervision system', a high-powered central executive that controls the flow of information in the rest of the nervous system.[28]

But how, we might well ask, can all these calculations result in a relatively coherent and stable structure of the world? In my view, the response lies in the structure of the world itself (both physical and social). These calculations are practical anticipations, pre-reflexive and non-conscious predictions, based on sequences of relatively coherent past experiences internalised by individuals and referred to by dispositionalist sociology as dispositions. In philosophical debates between the most radical empiricists (Berkeley) and the apriorists (Kant), the apriorists confront their adversaries with the argument that the multitude of experiences in which we are involved would make perception and structured representations of the world impossible if we did not already possess a previously structured mind. The solution to the problem raised by these debates will therefore lie in the existence of innate structures of perception and representation which would pre-date all experience.

What both apriorists and empiricists forget is that the world is always already structured and that the brain is capable of detecting the regularities or recurrences which it encounters, whether these are social (the way in which others interact with that individual) or physical (the natural phenomena which he or she encounters). Thanks to the capacities of their brains, human beings therefore manage to deduce mental and behavioural regularities from the regularity of the world:

> From birth on, the brain receives intensive training in what the world looks like. Years of interaction with the environment allow it to compile detailed statistics of which parts of objects tend to frequently co-occur. With intensive experience, visual neurons become dedicated to the specific combination of parts that characterizes a familiar object. After learning, they continue to respond to the appropriate combination even during anesthesia – a clear proof that this form of binding does not require consciousness.[29]

Rather than a mind pre-structured before any experience, we have a brain which is waiting to be structured by its experiences of the world. This means that a human brain is made to seek out structures, forms, relatively unvarying realities in the world, but that it is ready to assimilate any possible form imaginable, from the moment any such forms become discernible. 'Our brain acts as a sophisticated statistician that detects meaningful regularities hidden in seemingly random sequences. Such statistical learning is constantly running in the background, even as we sleep.'[30] The dispositions or schemas sociologists are able to identify therefore have a neuronal foundation on which the neurosciences are currently focusing:

> Even prior to birth, our neurons sample the statistics of the world and adapt their connections accordingly. Cortical synapses, number-ing in the hundred thousand billions in the human brain, contain dormant memories of our entire life. Millions of synapses are formed or destroyed every day, particularly during the first few years of our lives, when our brain adapts the most to its environment. . . . Everywhere in the brain, such connection strengths lie at the founda-tion of our learned unconscious intuitions. In early vision cortical connections compile statistics of how adjacent lines connect to form the contours of objects. In auditory and motor areas, they store our covert knowledge of sound patterns. There, years of piano practice induce a detectable change in grey matter density.[31]

These contributions from neuroscience reinforce sociological disposi-tionalism based on very different methods (long interviews and observa-tions); the brain detects regularities in a structured environment (by forms of social life, the laws of physics, of biology, etc.) and internalises them in the form of schemas and dispositions which function in the same way as practical anticipations. This is what we shall now examine.

The internalisation of the regularities of experience

In his *A Treatise on Human Nature*,[32] David Hume stresses the importance of our experiences, which, when repeated, create mental habits and func-tion, in practice, like pre-reflexive anticipations of phenomena to come. Fire is *associated*, in the mind of someone who has already experienced it, with heat, and even with the possibility of getting burnt, just as water is *associated* with the impossibility of breathing under water, and these associations, whenever there is contact with these elements, immediately lead to attitudes of prudence or fear. Someone who has had experience of fire or of water has been able to observe the same phenomena on each occasion and ends up anticipating, without the need for any calculation or thought, the effects of contact with these elements.

It is therefore on the basis of a repeated experience that a disposition or schema is, through *habituation*, gradually formed. And it is this disposi-tion or this schema which allows the perceiving and acting individual unconsciously to project into the future the internalised product of his or her past experiences by supposing that the future will be 'conformable to the past': 'We may observe, that the supposition, *that the future resembles the past*, is not founded on arguments of any kind, but is deriv'd entirely from habit, by which we are determined to expect for the future the same train of objects to which we have been accustom'd.'[33] Whether it is types of interaction with people, objects, or animals,[34] or moral, cultural, aesthetic or political types of behaviour or attitudes, or ways of exercising authority or modes of reasoning, the individual incorporates a whole host of habits which in practice are constantly in the process of being modified and combined. Faced with any given situation, the individual acts or reacts according to what they immediately believe they recognise among the imperatives associated with this situation in accordance with their past experience. Present action is pregnant with an entire incorporated past.

Hume even reveals himself to be a very shrewd analyst of the processes of analogical connections by linking custom, habit and analogical transfers, and by making a distinction between identical cases that allow habit to be used without any difficulty and cases that are only similar and require more significant adjustments:

> Our judgments concerning cause and effect are deriv'd from habit and experience; and when we have been accustomed to see one object united to another, our imagination passes from the first to the second, by a natural transition, which precedes reflection, and which cannot be prevented by it. Now 'tis the nature of custom not only to operate with its full force when objects are presented, that are exactly the same with those to which we have been accustom'd; but also to operate in an inferior degree, when we discover such as are similar; and tho' the habit loses somewhat of its force by every difference, yet 'tis seldom entirely destroy'd, when any considerable circumstances remain the same. A man, who has contracted a custom of eating fruit by the use of pears or peaches, will satisfy himself with melons where he cannot find his favorite fruit; as one, who has become a drunkard by the use of red wines, will be carry'd almost with the same violence, to white if presented to him. From this principle I have accounted for that species of probability, deriv'd from analogy, where we transfer our experience in past instances to objects which are resembling, but are not exactly the same with those concerning which we have had experience. In proportion as the resemblance decays, the probability diminishes; but still has some force as long as there remain any traces of the resemblance.[35]

The sociologist's dispositionalist vocabulary, like the Humean philosophy of experience, carries within it the idea of recurrence, of some form of repetition, of series or of classes of events. An individual's brain detects regularities because there are objective regularities in the world (both the physical and the social world) to detect. It is because parents have a *style* of behaviour and of *habits* that children can internalise shortened or condensed forms of experience in the form of incorporated *schemas* or *dispositions*, which as a result function on the basis of practical anticipation and of the projection onto the present situation of the product of past experience. Regularity is as much in the world outside each individual as it is inside each of them.[36]

When it turns its attention to the internalisation of conflicts or to parent–child relationships, psychology is, from my own point of view, a refined sociology of processes of incorporation or of internalisation. Jean Laplanche and Jean-Baptiste Pontalis thus wrote that the concept of internalisation in psychoanalysis refers to the 'process whereby intersubjective relations are transformed into intrasubjective ones (internalization of a conflict, of a prohibition, etc.)': 'We only speak of internalization when it is a *relationship* that is transposed in this way – for example, the relation of authority between father and child is said to be internalized in the relation between super-ego and ego. This process presupposes a structural differentiation within the psyche such that relations and conflicts may be lived out on the intrapsychic level.'[37] But the processes of internalisation apply both to affective schemas of perception, representation or action and to relational schemas.[38]

The example of relationships between anxious or depressive mothers and their babies used by Martin Dornes, the German psychoanalyst and psychologist turned developmentalist, demonstrates the development in the very young baby of schemas of action and reaction through repeated interaction with their mothers. If there is ever a single actor who is particularly dependent on the present situation and without any (significant) past, it is unquestionably the newborn. For pragmatists, this actor par excellence is infinitely more sensitive to contextual, and in this instance interactional, determinations given that its dispositional foundations are negligible: 'The newborn does not bear grudges', explains Dornes, 'and he cannot do so because his emotional state depends on the current interactional reality, and any change to this also changes his emotional state. An offended adult, because he can fantasise constantly about the offending situation, can maintain a feeling of offence or of vengeance independently of, and beyond, such situations.'[39] The newborn does not speak and does not have an adult's capacities for observation and analysis, but he internalises the anxieties of the mother by responding to her behaviour in the course of their interactions:

A mother can, for example, have the conscious or unconscious fantasy that her newborn could die of hunger. The newborn cannot understand this fantasy even if it is communicated to him or her. What he or she does understand, however, is the following: in order to control her anxiety about the failure adequately to nourish her child, the mother will feed the newborn on every possible occasion, whether appropriate of not. . . . This compulsion to feed permeates the interaction to which the newborn reacts with aversion. The baby chokes, vomits, refuses to feed, therefore taking the first steps towards starvation and carrying out or 'introjecting' the maternal fantasy. Introjection at this very early stage therefore means that the fantasies and emotions of the parents are communicated by interactional correlates and that, in this way, they are understood by the newborn. *Introjection in the newborn is not an intentional psychological process activated where an alien psychological content is introduced; it is the taking up, the assimilation of the correlates which are an expression of parental fantasies, or a reaction to these.*[40]

As a result, the newborn ends up refusing to feed in order to resist the mother's overfeeding, confirming the latter in her fears.

In the same way, in cases of depressive mothers with reduced motor function, a sad expression, sluggish body and listless voice, newborns model their interactions on their mother's behaviour and end up in this way internalising the signs of a depressive state:

> After initial and tenacious efforts to renormalise the mother's behaviour – the newborn smiles at her even more, makes more attempts to communicate vocally and generally intensifies attempts to interact – the baby withdraws from interaction. His eyes lose their sparkle, his breathing becomes shallow; while some newborns simply remain in this state, others start crying and still others refuse any visual contact. In the majority of cases, a state of withdrawal on the part of the newborn inevitably follows on from the apparent depression of the mother.[41]

In certain cases, too, when attempts by the newborn to 'reanimate' his mother are crowned with success, he may deduce that he needs to remain active and to do all he can to seduce and charm in order to avoid a return of lethargy in the mother and to get her attention and feel loved.[42] Dispositions and schemas of behaviour are thus transmitted by the adoption of a 'slowed down interactional affectivomotor style' from the parents 'if it becomes chronic': 'An "introjection" of depression on the behavioural and physical level takes place.'[43] And, towards the ninth month, the baby is able to calibrate his reactions with others on the basis of interactional habits developed with his parents.

The work of a researcher such as Daniel Stern, who also combines being a psychoanalyst and a developmental psychologist, indirectly confirms the hypothesis of a Bayesian brain detecting regularities and invariants: 'One of the central tendencies of mind that infants readily display is the tendency to order the world by seeking invariants. A format in which each successive variation is both familiar (the part that is repeated) and new (the part that is new) is ideally suited to teach infants to identify interpersonal variants.'[44] Stern also demonstrated that the repeated interactions between mother and child allow the latter correctly to anticipate both the mother's gestures and the behaviour to adopt: 'This generalized memory is an individual, personal expectation of how things are likely to proceed on a moment-to-moment basis.'[45]

For example, mealtimes represent rituals which can have minor variations, thereby allowing the baby to store in memory not every single
episode of mealtimes but the prototype 'of a "breast-milk" episode',
which is like the 'average experience' or the invariant structure gradually
constructed from the relatively coherent series of breast-milk episodes.
What the newborn internalises therefore is the schemes or schemas of
interaction and not the large number of interactions which have actually
taken place. Each '*schema-of-being-with*' is made up of actions, sensations,
visual perceptions and affects and forms a whole that the baby masters in
a practical, physical way. Babies do not remember previously experienced
situations but 'instead indicate *by their behaviour alone* that something has
been stored in the past that is capable of influencing current behaviour.'[46]
And what Stern also showed was the fact that, the more a type of interaction or situation is repeated, the more a prototype is strengthened, and
the more difficult it is for the child to incorporate changes in his own
behaviour: 'the more past experience there is, the less relative impact for
change any single specific episode will have. History builds up inertia.'[47]

These schemas (relational, emotional, sensorimotor, cognitive, evaluative, etc.) are ones we construct through regularities of behaviour which
arise from the relationships we have with other people and with the objects
around us. Jean Piaget, a major theoretician of schemas, disagreed on this
point with Freud, who reduced behaviour too much to concrete relationships between people and particular scenes between these people:

> When an individual has rebelled inwardly against excessive paternal
> authority, and subsequently adopts the same attitude to his teachers
> or to any constraint, it does not follow that he is unconsciously
> identifying each of these persons with the image of his father. What
> has happened is merely that in his relations with his father he has
> acquired a mode of feeling and reacting (an affective schema) which
> he generalizes in situations that are subjectively analogous. Similarly,
> though he may have acquired the schema of free fall by dropping a
> ball from his cot, it does not follow that he subsequently identifies all
> falling bodies with that ball.[48]

On the subject of interfamily relationships and of ludic-symbolic
transpositions of such relationships, Piaget has this to say: 'All those with
whom the child lives give rise to a kind of "affective schema", a summary
or blending of the various feelings aroused by them, and it is these schemas
which determine the main secondary symbols, as they often determine
later on certain attractions or antipathies for which it is difficult to find
an explanation except in unconscious assimilation with earlier models
of behaviour.'[49] Taken together, all the schemas (or dispositions) which
individuals, as the result of their experience, carry within them form what
is commonly referred to as their 'personality' or their 'character': 'Just as
there are motor schemas and intellectual schemas, so there are affective

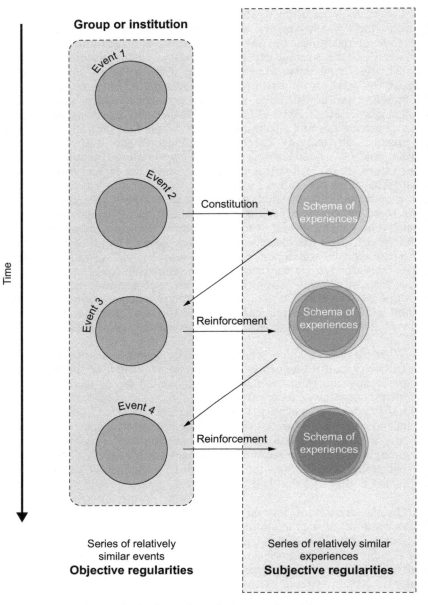

Figure 5 The formation of schemas of experience

schemas ... and it is the organized ensemble of these schemas which constitutes the "character" of each individual, i.e., his permanent modes of behaviour.'[50] These schemas, which shape interpersonal relationships as well as the practice of play, are also interwoven into the fabric of our dreams.

Oneiric schemas and the incorporated past

In order to be able to comprehend dream accounts, we need to be in a position to identify the underlying structures behind the images and emotions which can sometimes take on the appearance of a completely random sequence. Only discussions with the dreamer about his or her dream will enable these structures to emerge, but, once these have been identified in one dream, they are more easily recognisable in other dreams from the same night or the same period of time. The difficulty lies in the fact that what we see in dreams are not of course 'schemas' but images, which may be borrowed from different periods in the dreamer's life: 'It is true that sometimes in his dreams, some person with whom he has quarrelled will appear in situations taken from his childhood, and will be symbolized by characteristics belonging to his father. Moreover, if his dream were to be analyzed he would easily see the close inter-relation of past and present situations.'[51] But these images are not the only, or even the most important, part of what there is to see in the dream. Variable and interchangeable, they are the unique and visual actualisations of schemas.

In an article dated 1904, the philosopher and psychologist Henri Delacroix put forward the hypothesis that themes or ideas unconsciously structure our dreams, that they keep coming back like some kind of obsession which haunts and gives shape to oneiric images:

It would seem to us that underlying most dreams is an idea, a given, which is essentially modifiable and fluid and which is part of the group of images that first appears and which this group of images represents. This idea may lie deeper than the group of images; it may be underlying – that is to say, that it can control the movement of images without actually being present, without expressing itself in explicit terms, as when a secret desire or a subconscious preoccupation appears in our consciousness in the form of representations whose true significance and sequence we cannot immediately understand. Pathology show us how this normal phenomenon can be exaggerated by subconscious obsessions that, unknown to the patient, nevertheless partly control the flow of their images.[52]

These same themes, charged with emotions, are, according to Delacroix, present both in our dreams and in our daydreams, or in our artistic creations where these exist:

In our thoughts there are groups, systems of images orientated around one or a number of main images, clear themes which take shape, are maintained, become richer and fade away in the course of our experience. These themes contain a whole variety of tendencies, emotions, representations. . . . the study of ordinary daydreams and of artistic creation is particularly apt at showing, by accentuating it, the role that these themes play in all thought. It has been established, with much wisdom, that we all have certain preferred themes in our daydreams which, when the time is right, unleash the images they contain in either an active or a latent form. . . . Now many dreams are similar to these daydreams of waking life; either they originate from a new theme, not present in the waking state or else they build on a theme from the previous day which had remained in a latent state; and, for these, we are forced to admit that the sleeping dreamer, like the daydreamer, does not confine his thoughts merely to a sequence of images without any internal liaison.[53]

Whether the structuring principle of a dream is called an 'idea', a 'theme', a 'structure' or a 'schema' is, in the end, of little importance. What matters is the recognition that even in the most apparently incoherent dream there is in fact coherence and that consciousness 'does not immediately become lifeless' as we fall asleep but only loses its 'central element', which, in the waking state, usually coordinates images. Both coherent and extremely incoherent dreams

are the largely continuous developments of a mental theme, a more or less harmonious combination of several themes. One main theme can reappear after varying intervals of time, as familiar dreams demonstrate. In sleep as in waking, the theme, constantly threatened by the surge of new sensations and by the play of secondary images, survives or fades away depending on its importance and on the current state of mind: dreams or daydreams come to nothing for the same reason or survive in the same manner. If in the waking state thoughtful concentration sometimes contributes to the evolution of the image, in sleep the lowering of consciousness and the raising of the threshold of stimulation strengthen the monoideic nature of the theme which is taking shape; the result is a generalised distraction, a systematic anaesthesia in relation to any sensation which is unable to penetrate the current system, and a remarkable aptitude, provided they are not resistant to it, to incorporate inopportune sensations (which is demonstrated by those dreams in which we interpret a sensation in relation to what we are dreaming).[54]

When examining a series of dreams from a single dreamer (or from a group of similar dreamers), we can try, by looking at a great many dreamt scenes, to identify common structures or *immanent schemas*. Immanent, because dreams cannot be interpreted by using an external framework of reference, such as could for example be provided by a dream book or by certain stabilised schemas from Freudian theory. Instead, for each dream, it is a matter of showing what it has in common with other dreams belonging to the same series. The existence of these oneiric schemas is inferred not from pre-established interpretive grids but from structured comparisons of collected dreams.

In order to give some idea of the work of an interpreter, we could start with the example taken by Douglas Hofstadter (a researcher in cognitive sciences) and Emmanuel Sander (a developmental psychologist) looking at Aesop's fable 'The fox and the grapes', which has subsequently been reworked by numerous writers, including La Fontaine. The schema which emerges from the fable can be expressed in the following manner: it is about 'things that one once craved deeply but that one failed to obtain, and that one therefore disparages',[55] or, put even more briefly, 'disparagement of an unrealized yearning'.[56] Hofstadter and Sander come up with numerous situations which all share the same structure. For example, a man who did not succeed in buying his plane tickets on the internet decided to abandon the idea of going on holiday, but said he was in fact relieved because his chosen destination was too crowded and that would have spoilt his enjoyment. Similarly, another man dreamt of becoming an actor, but when he did not succeed in doing so declared he was glad it had not worked out, since theatre is an unhealthy milieu which would not have suited him, and he said he was happy to be leading a more balanced life away from the footlights. And so on and so forth. The many individual situations put forward by the authors 'belong to a single category whose members, though very different, all share the same core – namely, the moral of the fable of the fox and the grapes. Each of these scenarios exemplifies, in its own way, the notion of failure followed by belittling of the original goal.'[57] In the same way, the different dreams which make up an individual series feature similar structures in situations which are often very different. The apparent diversity of oneiric scenes sometimes makes it difficult to see the coherence of oneiric schemas.

It is as though 'an individual stripped of his soft parts, the skeleton plunged in an appropriate milieu, put on another flesh', or as though 'a theme [was] played in another tone and timbre.'[58] The same general formula can be exemplified by a great many relatively equivalent elements, and it is the variety of situations which makes it difficult to see the unity of the underlying structure: 'Just as a play is set in a sitting room – but an infinite number of sitting rooms can be painted: by such and such an actor, but there are a hundred species – tall ones, small ones. It is *the play itself which matters*.'[59]

The process whereby schemas are reconstructed finds some of its origins in the surrealist tradition. It can be seen in action in the work of the linguist and religious historian Georges Dumézil who, during the 1930s, discovered the schema of trifunctionality.[60] On the basis of a compared

Indo-European mythology, he effectively identified similar narrative structures which he linked to the three fundamental functions of priests, warriors and 'producers' (farmers and labourers). Claude Lévi-Strauss also used this same method to analyse myths,[61] and the art historian Erwin Panofsky turned to it to explain the formal links between Gothic architecture and scholastic thought.[62] But, unlike the structuralist, the dispositionalist researcher tries to reconstruct the socio-genesis of schemas by making links between oneiric schema and the types of social experience repeatedly experienced by the dreamers. For the existing structure that can be sensed at any moment in time is simply the crystallisation or sedimentation of a series, either long or short, of relatively similar past experiences. *Morphology of necessity requires an archaeology.* If it is impossible to associate types of dreams directly with categories of socially homogeneous dreamers, the objectivisation of oneiric schemas nevertheless assumes its sociological dimension only once these schemas are linked to schemas of experience.

These oneiric schemas are therefore indissociable from the incorporated schemas and dispositions internalised by the dreamer throughout the course of his or her life. At any specific point in the dreamer's existential situation, it is these schemas which push the dreamer to dream in one way rather than another. For example, a relationship of conflict towards figures of authority, an emotional schema of anxiety which manifests itself whenever any conflict situation arises, a tendency to dependency or to self-doubt, a recurring feeling of guilt or of inferiority, of superiority or of social envy, and sometimes a combination of these, can dictate the structure of dreams.

It is for that reason that the relationship of the incorporated past to the present of the dream is an active rather than a passive one. The past cannot be reduced to an amorphous stock of image-memories upon which the dreamer can draw as his fantasy takes him. It *informs* the dreamer's consciousness, nudges him in a given direction and *arranges* the images in a particular way. For this reason, any overly static formulations which see the past merely as a supply of potential schemas or themes should be avoided. Thus, when Jacques Montangero writes that 'memory and general knowledge provide the elements of dream content',[63] or when he refers to the memory as a 'reservoir' 'from whence the elements of autobiographical reminiscences can be drawn',[64] he is giving the impression that the incorporated past is a passive supply, whereas, quite the contrary, it is an active structure, a principle for action, a powerful motor which contributes to defining what is significant and important and what is not.

Researchers who have been able to analyse a long series of dreams experienced by a single person observe, regardless of changes in the dreamer's life, relative recurrences and constants which can be explained by the role of incorporated schemas and dispositions: 'When one analyzes a dream diary that has been kept over a number of years, a large amount of consistency in what the person dreams about is found from year to year. He is dreaming about many of the same themes at the age of fifty as he was at the age of twenty-five. This consistency occurs in spite of fairly drastic changes in the conditions of his waking life.'[65] The coherence of a dream can be grasped through discussions with the dreamer, who, describing the different elements that made up the dream, reveals elements of coherence, sometimes hidden, between images and scenes that at first sight seemed to be unconnected. But the series of dreams is even more useful in terms of revealing such coherences:

> When a person begins to keep a record of his dreams, he will not, at first, recognize any connection of subject matter from one night to the next. The dreams will appear completely dissociated from each other, occurring in random fashion. As the number of dreams in the record increases, then the dreamer will begin to recognize repetitions, regularities, and consistencies. The same characters, situations, activities, and objects, the same themes repeat themselves.[66]

Calvin S. Hall and Vernon J. Nordby consequently put forward the hypothesis that the coherence of dreams is a reflection of constants in the personality of the dreamer: 'We believe the person is a fairly stabilized organization of personality traits, attitudes and behavioral patterns. He is, as the saying goes, a creature of habit. No matter where he goes, these habits of thinking, feeling, and acting go with him. They even follow him into the world of sleep, so that he is the same person awake or asleep.'[67]

A critique of the event-focused approach

Psychoanalysis rightly, albeit somewhat too exclusively, attributes a crucial importance to early social experiences. But it combines this approach with a sort of *cult of the determining event*. Right from the time of his study on hysteria with Joseph Breuer, the search for the event, and even for the precise *incident*, is a major element of Freud's thinking. While they admit that, in 'common hysteria', 'instead of a single, major trauma, [they] find a number of partial traumas forming a *group* of provoking causes. These have only been able to exercise a traumatic effect by summation and they belong together in so far as they are in part components of a single story of suffering',[68] the two scholars say they are nevertheless investigating 'a great variety of different forms and symptoms of hysteria, with a view to discovering their precipitating cause'.[69] The one-off, detailed event would therefore be the cause of the symptoms of hysteria. Freud and Breuer themselves emphasised the 'disproportion between the many years' duration of the hysterical symptom and the single occurrence which provoked it',[70] but were not surprised by this.

And if Freud could refer clearly to the idea of a series of relatively similar events in the context of a patient's case ('the symptom was not the precipitate of a single such "traumatic" scene, but the result of a summation of a number of similar situations'),[71] he nevertheless continued to emphasise the significance of the event: 'Analytic experience has convinced us of the complete truth of the assertion so often to be heard that the child is psychologically father of the adult', wrote Freud, 'and that the events of his first years are of paramount importance for his whole later life. It will thus be of special interest to us if there is something that may be described as the central experience of this period of childhood.'[72]

Psychoanalysis tends to look for key events or key people in the patient's past, whereas, as we have seen, it is the relatively coherent series of events, or sequences of events, or the relatively similar types of people, that are significant in terms of the dreamer's personality. Prototypes of interaction (Daniel Stern) or emotional heuristics (Martin Dornes) are effectively 'averages' or 'generalisations' which wipe out variations and preserve only the invariant part. Considered from the point of view of schemas, the specific incident, or the particular person, appears only as an element among others taken from series of relatively similar events or people. We need therefore to get away from an event-focused vision and from the personification of problems.

Freud was always looking for detailed interpersonal events. He helped patients to remember a *specific* traumatic scene or a *specific* act from their early childhood which was supposed to provide the key to their current sufferings, and so leant towards a sort of event-focused explanation which ultimately precluded any understanding of mental and behavioural processes that had developed over time, as opposed to isolated shocks produced as a result of specific events, no matter how important. Condensed forms of more or less analogous experiences which may encompass very different people, places and situations are incorporated and resurface in the present. Just as 'Rome was not built in a day', mental and behavioural dispositions require time and repetition in order to become established.

It was moreover Freud himself who, referring to the relationship between collective and individual psychology, commented on the difference between the clearly differentiated people from the family circle and the multiplicity of people who have contributed to making an individual into the person he or she is:

> the individual in the relations which have already been mentioned – to his parents and to his brothers and sisters, to the person he is in love with, to his friend, and to his physician – comes under the influence of only a single person, or of a very small number of persons, each of whom has become enormously important to him. Now in speaking of social or group psychology it has become usual to leave these relations on one side and to isolate as the subject of inquiry the influencing

of an individual by a large number of people simultaneously, people with whom he is connected by something, though otherwise they may in many respects be strangers to him. Group psychology is therefore concerned with the individual man as a member of a race, of a nation, of a caste, of a profession, of an institution, or as a component part of a crowd of people who have been organized into a group at some particular time for some definite purpose.[73]

But how could Freud's patients fail to recall specific events they had experienced or, at least, specific events which had been told to them in the family context? How could they speak the language of repetition, of series, of the coherent sequence of similar experiences? Freud simply took his patients too literally and failed to see how the account of a particular event could conceal an entire forest of similar events. Psychoanalysts such as Stern or Dornes, who managed to combine the psychoanalytical approach with adults and the direct study of early childhood (interactions between parents and children), clearly understood the limitations of the explanation based on the single event:

It is becoming clear that it is not in a single moment that the mother withdraws her investment in the child and that the newborn introjects the image of the depressive mother, but that it is in the interactions and fragments of interactions repeated on a daily basis that this withdrawal takes place. The accumulation of these contributes to the effect which, in the context of analysis, appears to be the result of a single event. . . . That which, in the process of reconstruction and in memory seems like a single moment is in actual fact a constantly repeated sequence. However, the 'false' reconstruction and memory of the abrupt withdrawal contains the essence of the atmosphere and the emotional flavour of the early interaction, and, in this respect, they are absolutely 'true'. The fantasy of the sudden withdrawal condenses a large number of micro-episodes into one single moment, and this moment encompasses the truth of feelings about a former or ongoing interaction, even though, as a *moment*, it had never actually existed in childhood.[74]

Even the trauma of rape or sexual interference during childhood is rarely a single incident which single-handedly turns the victim's life upside down; rather, it is more often the repetition of these acts over a significant period of time. This is highlighted by Juan-David Nasio with reference to the case of Isabelle, who had an incestuous relationship with her older brother between the ages of ten and fourteen: 'We might think that, during the four years of the incestuous relationship with her older brother, she was the victim not of a violent single incident but of a series of regular micro-traumas. In reality, the psycho-trauma does not necessarily appear as a sudden and violent intrusion; it can happen gradually and subtly over quite a long period of time.'[75]

The case of Freud himself can be cited on the basis of what he reveals of his own history in *The Interpretation of Dreams* and in Peter Gay's biography. 'So far as I knew, I was not an ambitious man',[76] declared Freud in interpreting one of his dreams. Yet it was the same man who, at the same period but in a private context, refers to himself as some sort of conqueror: 'Writing to his friend Wilhelm Fliess in 1900, he said of himself, "I am not a man of science at all, not an observer, not an experimenter, not a thinker. I am nothing but a *conquistador* by temperament, an adventurer if you want to translate this term, with all the inquisitiveness, daring, and tenacity of such a man."'[77] Biographically, everything points to the fact that Freud was an ambitious child, adolescent and then adult. Initially this was because his family was very ambitious for him. The son of a wool merchant, he had always benefited from a good education and from the attention and particular care of his parents, Jakob and Amalia. This attention was somewhat selective, and his brothers and sisters did not have the same privileges as he did. Peter Gay said he was 'the declared family favorite' and recalls that 'His sister Anna testifies that he always had a room of his own, no matter how straitened his parents' circumstances.'[78] The whole family was anxious to preserve the tranquillity of the young man who was doing so brilliantly in his studies:

The family accepted Freud's boyish imperiousness with equanimity and fostered his sense of being exceptional. If Freud's needs clashed with those of Anna or the others, his prevailed without question. When, intent on his school books, he complained about the noise that Anna's piano lessons were making, the piano vanished never to return. It was much regretted by his sister and mother alike, but without apparent rancor. The Freuds must have been among the very few middle-class Central European families without a piano, but that sacrifice faded in the face of the glorious career they imagined for the studious, lively schoolboy in his cabinet.[79]

Encouraged, protected, supported and rewarded by his family, Freud also achieved educational recognition and saw his ambitious tendencies legitimised by the educational institution:

Ambitious, outwardly self-assured, brilliant in school and voracious in his reading, the adolescent Freud had every reason to believe that he had a distinguished career before him, one as distinguished as sober reality would allow him to pursue. 'At the Gymnasium,' he tersely summed up his record, 'I was first in my class for seven years, held a privileged position, was scarcely ever examined.' The report cards he preserved repeatedly pay tribute to his exemplary conduct and his outstanding work in class. His parents naturally predicted great things for him, and others, like his religion teacher and paternal friend Samuel Hammerschlag, gladly substantiated their fond and extravagant expectations.[80]

Three anecdotes from his childhood sum up this potential for success. First of all, from his earliest childhood, Freud had been told the story of how 'an old peasant woman had prophesied to my proud mother that with her first-born child she had brought a great man into the world.'[81] Freud tells this story but does not seem to realise that this myth of the 'great man' has been exaggerated within the family and is merely the indication of a family desire to make the child succeed. A great number of 'old peasant women' have certainly said exactly the same thing to a great number of other mothers. But the question remains nevertheless as to why his parents told this story on numerous occasions ('an anecdote I had often heard repeated in my childhood').

Another episode which Freud recalls is one where, aged eleven or twelve, he was with his parents in a restaurant.[82] A man was going from table to table and improvising verses by invitation in exchange for a small sum. The young Freud was sent to invite the man to their table, and before any request had been made he had recited a few verses to the child which said he would probably one day become a 'cabinet minister'. It was that very liberal time when a 'Bourgeois Ministry' had been established between Austria and Hungary. And among the ministers there were even several Jews, which gave hope and ambition to young Jewish schoolboys. The two events were visibly linked in Freud's head. But, once again, recalling the event in such detail simply indicates the dispositional ground on which this would take on its fullest meaning.

Finally, when we see the way Freud recounts his reaction to the story of a humiliating experience to which his father was subjected, the ambitious tendencies which were firmly anchored in him become even more apparent. He tells how, around the age of ten or twelve, his father would take him on his walks and would recount to him the events of his own childhood.[83] He told him that one day he had gone for a walk wearing a new fur cap and that a Christian had come up to him, knocked the cap onto the ground in the mud, shouting 'Jew! Get off the pavement!" His son asked what he had done, and his father replied that he had simply stepped into the road and picked up his cap. Freud was somewhat disappointed by this reaction, which 'struck me as unheroic conduct on the part of the big, strong man who was holding the little boy by the hand.' He mentally compared this scene to one he had learned about at school, where Hannibal's father, with whom he identified (he refers to his 'enthusiasm for the Carthaginian general'), makes his son swear to take revenge on the Romans. Freud aspired to be this Hannibal who takes power and attempts to conquer Rome. He is a Jew who wants to be a great man and a conqueror in a world which is not on his side. Ambitions and dreams of grandeur, desires to avenge his both his family and the Jews, begin to take root at a very early stage. And these are feelings which grow stronger, year after year, in the course of a thousand experiences which nobody is ever able to remember in their entirety. In the course of these isolated scenes selected by Freud's memory, what emerges are the ambitious tendencies that took shape very early on and which were subsequently constantly confirmed, strengthened or thwarted by many series of experiences from which only a few moments are seized.

5

Unconscious and Involuntary Consciousness

The study of dreams provides an opportunity for the thorny question of consciousness to be revisited. What does it mean to be conscious? Do different forms of consciousness exist? What role do the conscious and the non-conscious play in human action and thought? Is the dreamer conscious of his or her dream and, if so, what kind of consciousness are we dealing with when the conscious subject does not have control over his or her own mental representations? What does the fact that dreamers themselves do not understand their own dreams tell us about the way the psyche functions? And, if that functioning process involves the unconscious, what form does it take?

We have seen that the unconscious *is* the incorporated past within each individual and that, rather than deriving its properties from mechanisms of repression linked to forms of censorship, these stem from an amnesia of its origins, from the conditions governing the embedding of dispositions (or schemas), and from the limits of voluntary or reflexive consciousness in carrying out actions.

The involuntary consciousness of the dreamer

The study of dreams makes us aware of the often involuntary, uncontrolled and opaque nature of human psychic life. Before broaching the question of the Freudian unconscious, inextricably linked to the notions of repression and censorship, we should turn our attention to the fact that human beings can at the same time be conscious and apparently aware of what they are doing, that they can also be conscious and have no control over the nature of their flow of consciousness, and that they are very often conscious without knowing what determines the products of their consciousness and in ignorance of almost all the cognitive processes they are deploying.

On the basis of what psychological study, and particularly the study of dreams, reveals about the facts of consciousness and non-consciousness, the classic sociological question of 'the meaning actors give to their actions' appears particularly naive. Believing that individuals are best placed to know what they are doing when they act, think or feel is tantamount to believing that human beings are transparent to themselves. However, the meaning that actors – sometimes – give to what they do is no more than the tiniest exposed part of the submerged continent of their psychological and physical lives. When sociologists conduct rapid interviews in which they ask interviewees questions about what they think, enjoy or do, they succeed only in obtaining what those questioned are able to perceive, recollect and put into words.[1] When they conduct longer interviews and ask questions designed to elicit more detailed accounts of practices or particular experiences, they obtain more information about what, in part non-consciously, structures the lives of the interviewees. When they are in a position directly to observe individuals acting and speaking, they are able to gain access to the practices and realities that individuals experience or of which they are part, but which they do not necessarily see or talk about themselves, or which they talk about but end up describing things differently to the way in which they actually happened. Finally, the study of dreams gives us access to narratives created involuntarily by dreamers which unfold outside their control, and which, for the duration of the dream, they take for reality itself but rarely understand at the moment of waking.

Belief in the reality of the dream

Absorbed in their dream, the dreamer is convinced that they are experiencing a real situation rather than something they are imagining – that is to say, mentally inventing. The individual experiences emotions just as in waking life and feels as though subjectively immersed in the very heart of the action, absorbed by the unfolding events even when these appear strange and fantastical when judged by the criteria applied in waking life.[2] This sense of reality rapidly fades on waking, and what seemed real during the dream is restored to the 'imaginary' or 'symbolic' realm to which waking consciousness assigns it. If this is so, it is precisely because the waking consciousness has the means to *compare* the state of the real world and the state in which the dreamer was plunged just a few minutes earlier. The perception of the real-life situation permits a redefinition of the symbolic activity which, *without comparison*, appeared to the dreamer like a real experience. The dream wipes out any differences between the real and the symbolic; waking consciousness re-establishes it.

With the absence of 'critical perspective', the lack of 'the reflective self-awareness that helps us test reality during the waking state',[3] the 'loss of "the reality test"',[4] it is indeed the absence of means or of points of comparison that makes the dreamer so credulous. Freud summed up the thinking of Joseph Delbœuf (1831–1896) in the following manner: 'We believe in the reality of dream-images', he says, 'because in our sleep we have no other impressions with which to compare them, because we are detached from the external world.'[5] And Yves Delage reiterated this same point of view: 'The dominant fact is that, except with some rare exceptions, the dreamer believes in the objectivity of his dreams, and he does so on account of the simple fact that there is no reason not to believe in them in the absence of any possibility of comparing them with waking life, the existence of which he is ignorant during his dream.'[6]

It thinks in me: another image of the human being

'Social subjects' would be much more of a subject if they knew
that they are very rarely subjects and that in fact 'it speaks'
through them.
(Pierre Bourdieu, *Habitus and Field*, p. 69)

This credulity on the part of the dreamer who believes in the reality of what he or she is dreaming seems almost trite. It is, however, yet another proof of the relatively feeble control human beings exert over their own forms of expression. They are indeed the ones producing these dreams and yet, for the duration of the dream, they take them for realities. And when they wake up and realise that 'it wasn't real' and that 'it was only a dream', they themselves often do not understand what they alone have invented. 'Dreams', wrote Freud, 'make an unrestricted use of linguistic symbols, the meaning of which is for the most part unknown to the dreamer.'[7]

It is easy to understand why the strange quality of part of our dreams could at other periods have been considered, and still is today by other societies, as a sign of messages sent by ancestors, spirits or gods. For how is it possible to have no understanding whatsoever of something we have ourselves created? It would seem almost more natural to attribute these narratives to others rather than to oneself.

To accept the fact that these accounts make sense, even if they generally fail to do so in the eyes of those who have constructed them and who sometimes put them into words, requires a profound rethink of the image of the human being, of what he or she is capable of and conscious of. It means, for example, acknowledging that human beings are subject to processes and mechanisms, of a psychic as well as a physiological nature, over which they do not have complete control – and acknowledging, too, that human beings generally lack the capacity spontaneously to understand the end products of these processes and mechanisms.

In spite of all the scientific research which, from Freud's theory of the unconscious to the most recent theories in neuroscience of the cognitive unconscious, and including Bourdieu's theory of the logic of practice, has demonstrated that the human being cannot in any sense be considered entirely as a sovereign individual who is conscious, intentional, in complete control of all decisions, thoughts and acts, transparent to him- or herself, etc., many researchers remain resistant to the idea that *it* could think, or that *it* could imagine outside of a reflexive consciousness or of a self capable of the perfect mastery of his or her thoughts: 'Sigmund Exner, who was Freud's colleague in Vienna, had stated in 1899: "We shouldn't say 'I think', 'I feel', but rather 'it thinks in me' [*es denkt in mir*], 'it feels in me' [*es fühlt in mir*]" – a full twenty years prior to Freud's reflections in *The Ego and the Id* (*Das Ich und das Es*), published in 1923.'[8] In this way, it could be said that certain processes are 'at work' while we sleep, and that the dream is this thought or this symbolic expression during sleep which is inaccessible to the immediate understanding of the waking subject.

The dream is there to remind us that, although it is the dreamer who is dreaming, the dream is not the product of any voluntary desire to dream. 'The psychic relaxation of sleep seems to involve a resting of the will',[9] claimed Durkheim in 1884. In that case we need to accustom ourselves to saying that 'something is dreaming within him' rather than 'he is dreaming'. For, as Alfred Maury so clearly put it, 'in thought there operates a process exactly like the one for which our purely organic functions form the theatre. We digest, we breathe, without realising it; we even carry out certain external movements in a purely instinctive manner . . . I witness acts in which I intervene, without knowing either why or how.'[10] Not only is the dream not dependent on a decision on the part of the dreamer, but the dreamer discovers and sometimes attempts to understand the dream as though it were a text written in an unknown language or a product of someone else's (rather feverish) imagination. *Something* dreams, s*omething* is at work in the dream, and detailed analyses of dreams provide every reason to think that the result of this work is anything but incoherent, that it is not the completely chaotic product of images randomly produced by a brain in a sleeping state.

Our uncontrolled psychic and symbolic functioning is present not only during time spent dreaming but also in the daydream and, indeed, in all those times when, in spite of the conscious control of part of our acts and of our utterances, unconscious psychic mechanisms continue to function and to underpin our behaviour. We can only agree with Joseph Breuer when he declares that 'the whole conduct of our life is constantly influenced by subconscious ideas.'[11] But Breuer had only an intuition of phenomena that we now know to exist: 'Oblivious to this boiling hodge-podge of unconscious processes', wrote Stanislas Dehaene, 'we constantly overestimate the power of our consciousness in making decisions – but in truth, our capacity for conscious control is limited.'[12] In order to progress scientifically, scholars should have left behind ancient spiritualist conceptions like those held by Maine de Biran, who contrasted the notion of a situation without 'self', into which sleep would plunge us, to waking situations in which an intentional 'self' would steer all our behaviour and our thoughts.[13]

What Alfred Adler suggested in 1933 was that individuals understand scarcely any more what they do in many situations of waking life than when they are dreaming. They act in a perfectly coherent way, but this

coherence is guided by a knowledge which we could describe as practical
– in other words, by their dispositions – without being immediately
accessible to that individual's understanding:

> how are we to explain that no one understands their dreams or pays
> any attention to them, and that in most cases they are forgotten? . . .
> People know more than they understand. Is their power of knowing
> alert in dreams while their understanding is asleep? If this be so,
> then we must also find evidence of something like this in waking
> life. And in fact, people understand nothing about their goal, but
> they pursue it none the less. They understand nothing about their
> life-style, yet they are permanently shackled to it. And if, when
> confronted by a problem, the life-style indicates a certain path, like
> going to a drinking party or undertaking something that promises to
> be successful, then thoughts and images always arrive on the scene
> . . . for the purpose of making this path attractive, although they are
> not necessarily obviously connected with the goal. If a woman is very
> dissatisfied with her husband another man often seems more desirable
> to her, without her making the connection between the two clear to
> herself, to say nothing of understanding her implied accusation and
> revenge. Her knowledge of the things that are nearest to her will not
> become understanding until she has seen them in connection with her
> life-style and her immediate problems.[14]

If the dreamer does not know on waking exactly what he or she has
dreamt about and waking thought takes over again, if these flashes of
nocturnal brilliance are not accessible to the dreamer's immediate understanding, in the end none of that is any more surprising than for a child
to set out in the form of games the problematic situations of their life,
without knowing exactly what it is they are in the process of 'recounting'
in their play. Once awake, the dreamer often feels estranged from their
own dream; they regard it with astonishment as though they were not
themselves responsible for it. As Wittgenstein wrote, 'man possesses the
capacity of constructing languages, in which every sense can be expressed,
without having an idea how each word has meaning or what its meaning
is and what each word means – just as people speak without knowing how
the individual sounds are produced.'[15]

These initial reflections on the often involuntary nature of our psychic
activity and on the limits of reflexive consciousness impel us to take the
question even further.

Unconsciousness or involuntary consciousness

Freud claimed that psychoanalysis was 'energetically denying the equation between the mental and the conscious': 'No; being conscious cannot

be the essence of what is psychical. It is only a quality of what is psychical, and an inconstant quality at that – one that is far oftener absent than present.'[16] Freud's way of expressing himself here might suggest that the dream is not a conscious activity. The different uses of the term in daily life contribute to making it difficult to define. After all, don't we say of a person who has passed out that they are not conscious and even that they have 'lost consciousness'? Is the moment of falling asleep one of loss of consciousness and that of waking a regaining of consciousness?[17] Yet memories of a dream on waking prove that the dreamer was indeed conscious of what he or she dreamt. If he or she was really dreaming without knowing it, unconsciously, there would be no possible access to the dream, and we would not even be able to put a name to something of which we would be utterly ignorant. Certain researchers in neuroscience (such as Lionel Naccache and Stanislas Dehaene)[18] are correct in citing the criteria of 'reportability' in order to define the conscious, or unconscious, nature of a psychic activity: what I do not perceive and what I can therefore not speak about is unconscious, but what I perceive and can speak about is necessarily conscious.[19]

'When we dream', says Donald J. de Gracia, 'we are consciously aware of visual, auditory, tactile, kinesthetic and emotional content, as well as thought (both cognitive and metacognitive) and to lesser extents smells, taste and pain. With respect to sensory perceptions during dreams, these are presumably hallucinations, but they are conscious experiences nonetheless.'[20] The dreamer is indeed conscious and can, therefore, remember the dream, but he or she is conscious *in a particular way*. The fact that the dreamer is conscious does not mean that they know they are in the process of dreaming, or that the dream is intentionally produced, that it is in some way voluntary, that the motivations or determinants behind it are known to the dreamer, that its scenarios are controlled, that the processes which govern its production are conscious ones, and that on waking the dreamer knows exactly what their dream means. The dreamer is by no means conscious of the whole process and of the various mechanisms which lead him or her to dream a particular dream, but he or she is nevertheless totally conscious of the dream and even experiences it as though in a waking state.

We need therefore to establish the difference between four main situations relating to consciousness:

1. It is possible to be conscious without being intentionally in control of the flow of consciousness or of the sequence of our acts. This applies to dreams, to daydreams and to any kind of hallucination or delirium but also to all the routine acts of ordinary waking life which we often carry out 'on auto-pilot'.[21] Our dreams are forms of expression of which we are indeed conscious, that we can remember and recount on waking, but whose production lies outside the control of our will. We dream, the dream happens in us and we are aware of it, just as certain things touch us and our tears are the sign of that. But we do not control all these

processes which are present within us depending on what we have experienced and on the present circumstances in which we find ourselves. According to whether we are playing, engaging in a practical task, writing, dreaming, raving in delirium, etc., our forms of expression and the modalities of our consciousness constantly vary without us organising or regulating them in a conscious way. Dreaming is therefore the form our consciousness (and our expression) takes when we are asleep and, consequently, are cut off from interactions with the world and with others. If we consider, like Maine de Biran, that the 'self' is inevitably an 'intentional self', then we might be led into thinking that the 'self' is completely cancelled out during sleep. But this dichotomous thinking (self vs. non-self), based on a limited conception of 'self', brings our understanding to a dead end.[22]

2. It is possible to be conscious of something without being conscious of what determines us to do or to think this thing. For example, a person can be perfectly conscious that they like things to be tidy without being conscious of what it is that drives them to be tidy; someone can enjoy reading detective novels without knowing what it is that gives them a taste for this particular literary genre. This non-consciousness of cause is the most frequent situation in both waking life and sleep. As Spinoza said:

> Men are deceived because they think themselves free, and the sole reason for thinking so is that they are conscious of their own actions, and ignorant of the causes by which those actions are determined. Their idea of liberty therefore is this – that they know no cause for their own actions; for as to saying that their actions depend upon their will, these are words to which no idea is attached.[23]

Our actions can at the same time be conscious at a certain level and supported and guided by non-conscious forces, just as they can be carried out according to non-conscious modalities. Every single action and every single thought draws on the experiences of the embodied past in the form of schemas which remain outside our consciousness.

3. It is possible also to perceive things without being conscious that we have perceived them but still benefit from the practical consequences of what we have perceived, as in the case of subliminal perception of images used by researchers in certain tests. Neuroscientific proofs of the existence of unconscious perceptions come as a result of being able to measure the effect of these perceptions on the behaviour of the subject who has subjectively no sense of having perceived anything whatsoever. For example, people with a cortical scotoma cannot consciously see a point of light, but when they are asked to look in the direction of the light, even if they have the impression they are 'responding' in a completely random way, they turn their gaze in the right direction.[24]

On a more ordinary level, we can observe what researchers call the 'cocktail party effect'.[25] We have all had the experience of finding that in a noisy, crowded room, outside our own immediate linguistic exchanges, other conversations appear as just a general hubbub or a hum of background noise. And yet, if the first name of one person is suddenly uttered by somebody in the room, that person's attention is captured and they are able to hear it. That means that the person in question was perceiving without being aware that they were perceiving and that their selective perceptive system enabled them to switch off from surrounding conversations in order to be able to concentrate on what was being said in their immediate vicinity, but that the same perceptive system is capable of bringing a single word to the foreground of their attention, causing them to switch off from the immediate conversation and instead focus their attention on other conversations. In a similar way, in the case of new parents, even a faint nocturnal cry will wake them up, whereas sounds which have no particular significance or no suggestion of danger will not disturb their sleep. These kinds of perceptions can be compared to the 'small perceptions' identified by Leibniz, considered by Ellenberger, in his book *The Discovery of the Unconscious*, to be the first theoretician of the unconscious. Such perceptions are those which lie below the threshold of consciousness or attention 'even though they play a great part in our mental life.'[26] Without paying attention, we perceive things which can nevertheless influence our actions or thoughts – for example, when we speak more loudly because of a noise to which we have become accustomed and to which we no longer pay attention. All these cases constitute proofs of 'unconscious cognitive processes'.

The results of neuroscientific work on the ongoing 'probability calculations' carried out by the brain in order to perceive and interpret the surrounding world should logically – if scientific results travelled between different disciplines – have major consequences in the study of the processes of socialisation. This means that a large part of what informs the brain depends on the whole on a seen–perceived–interpreted environment and not just on deliberate educative actions or on interactions intentionally tailored to an educative end. The reconstitution of the objective circumstances of life is, therefore, fundamental. It allows an understanding of the objective background which is gradually internalised in a non-conscious way by the child. Conscious acts of education, deliberate actions of socialisation, are only the *minuscule visible part of the iceberg*. The example of the word suddenly heard during a cocktail party when all the surrounding conversations seemed to be just a vague and imperceptible hubbub shows that, even if we are not always conscious of what is happening around us, our brain nevertheless continues its ceaseless task of capturing and sifting through acoustic, visual, olfactory information, etc., all of which remains at a non-conscious level until the brain identifies some relevant information. And it is only at that point that consciousness processes the information in question.

The child is just as much influenced, shaped, transformed, constituted by the non-spoken and the non-conscious as by what is said to him or her explicitly. Parents may tell the child one thing and do another, or they can tell the child certain things which are then contradicted or contravened by the physical environment (such as the mother who tells her children not to drop litter on the ground, whereas the local area, the block of flats or the lift used each day clearly demonstrate that everybody drops litter; or the parents who urge their children to read when the books on the family bookshelves are very rarely opened). The idea that children are like 'sponges' capable of feeling things that adults are persuaded to sweep under the carpet has a certain pertinence. For adults give themselves away (give away their problems or the situation in which they find themselves) in a thousand different ways (in their expressions, their intonation, their silences, their gestures, their behaviour or their absence of reaction); and their physical environment also speaks for them, even when they say nothing.

4. Finally, there are all those psychic operations which occur without the dreamer's knowledge, and which the dream analyst gradually manages to deduce from the oneiric material in combination with the free associations obtained during analysis. These include, among others, processes of symbolisation, metaphorisation, condensation, displacement or substitution, all of which are based on practical analogies. In this we come close to the 'imperceptible thoughts' referred to by Pierre Nicole in 1715 in his *Traité de la grace générale*.[27] Such a phrase represents a veritable heresy from a Cartesian point of view. For Descartes, a thought cannot, by definition, fail to be perceived. A thought is indissociable from the act of thinking it. But Nicole argued, quite rightly, that the imperceptibility of certain thoughts is linked to a lack of attention. And, all things considered, it is the Cartesian argument which appears to be on dangerous ground, for thinking is an action like any other and can never be permanently accompanied by a reflexive consciousness of itself. We are immersed in our thought and not in the thinking of that thought, in the same way as we are usually immersed in walking and not in thinking about walking.

These four scenarios represent a genuine challenge to Cartesian thought on the subject. They show that we cannot be conscious of everything, that we can be conscious without its being deliberate or considered, and that we can perceive realities by taking objective account of them in our actions, but without paying attention to them. The 'subject' is the seat of psychic processes and unconscious perceptions, or perceptions which are conscious but not intentional – a far cry from the reflective, all-powerful consciousness of a supreme subject conscious of themselves and of the world. Freud was right to point out the antagonism of philosophers to the idea of a thought which could be unconscious: 'This, of course, provoked a denial from the philosophers, for whom "conscious" and "mental" were identical, and who protested that they could not perceive of such a monstrosity as the "unconscious mental".'[28] In the view of many philosophers, not only could the psychic ('mental') only be conscious, but consciousness could only be reflexive. And when, in the nineteenth century, the idea of an unconscious began to take hold in the West, the unconscious part of our thoughts would be seen as the 'primitive', stupid, inferior part.[29]

Dreaming is a mode of consciousness, but it is neither the consciousness of the dreamer (the dreamer generally tends to believe he or she is really experiencing the things they dream about), nor the consciousness of the past and present determinants of the dream, nor the conscious control of the flow of oneiric consciousness, nor the consciousness of the (analogical) thought processes involved in the act of dreaming. The dreamer, like the daydreamer, is totally immersed in what he is dreaming and therefore highly conscious of the images which appear in the dream or the daydream. He is not, however, conscious of what is happening around him while he is sleeping and believes he is somewhere other than where he actually is.[30] Nor is he conscious of what he is doing in the moment of the dream (convinced that this is a real experience), or even of what it is that makes him dream that particular dream. Consciousness is always a *consciousness of something* and not of everything; it is never a constant property but always *temporary*, and it rests also on *motivations or causes of which the main protagonist is most often not conscious.*

For all these reasons, rather than overloading the term 'consciousness' by assigning to it properties it does not always have, we need to make a distinction between consciousness, wakefulness, attention or vigilance, intentionality-will, control-mastery and reflexivity. For example, solving a complex mathematical problem means being awake, having the intention and the will to do so (a complex problem cannot be solved inadvertently), concentrating on the task in hand and controlling what we are doing, even if the problem can continue to preoccupy us in moments when we are not supposed to be working on it (during sleep, leisure time, practical activities, etc.). It is nevertheless impossible to solve a mathematical problem thoroughly while asleep. Daydreaming can be more or less voluntarily controlled and, by its very nature, involves being awake but switching off temporarily from the immediate environment and from potential demands. Finally, the dream only takes place during sleep, is only very exceptionally directed,[31] and cannot be controlled and mastered while still holding the full attention of the dreamer who experiences the dream as though it were real, which implies a relative loss of consciousness of the immediate surroundings and of the true status of the images observed.

The unconscious without repression

> There is an underlying, hidden level of culture that is highly
> patterned – a set of unspoken, implicit rules of behaviour and
> thought that controls everything we do. This hidden cultural
> grammar defines the way in which people view the world, determines
> their values, and establishes the basic tempo and rhythms of life.
> Most of us are either totally unaware or else only peripherally aware
> of this.
>
> (Edward T. Hall, *The Dance of Life*, p. 6)

All the preceding arguments allow us to approach the important question
of the Freudian unconscious. For Freud, the unconscious is essentially
made up of experiences which cannot be expressed or admitted; it is the
product of repression (of 'infantile sexuality'). Freud even claimed that
'The theory of repression is the corner-stone on which the whole structure
of psychoanalysis rests. It is the most essential part of it.'[32] Had the theory
of repression indeed been such a corner-stone, then psychoanalysis would
have collapsed long ago. Fortunately, however, psychoanalysis is far more
than just simply a theory of repression.

A theory of *repressed* unconscious is problematic not only from the
point of view of the neurosciences and of cognitive psychology but also
from that of dispositionalist sociology which shows that the realm of
the non-conscious is made up of all the previous constituent experiences
of an individual, even though the conscious memory of these cannot be
permanently stored. Not because these experiences would necessarily be
painful, inexpressible and therefore to 'be repressed', but because the child
and then later the adolescent and the adult cannot 'learn' to act, see, feel,
etc., in a certain way while at the same time knowing precisely and clearly
what it is they are in the process of learning. It is a case, as Bourdieu put it,
of 'genesis amnesia'. Our successive past experiences, from birth up until
the present moment, are what constitute our personality, our perceptions,
judgements, representations and actions, without our being necessarily
conscious of it. The individual does not hold his past experiences in
front of him or her like something he or she 'possesses' or as something
'acquired'. They are a component part of each individual which partly
determines, without he or she being conscious of it, their representations
or their actions. In all relationships, the individual draws on unconscious
elements (we should, in a less reified manner, refer to non-conscious
elements)[33] from their past which have sedimented in the form of ways of
seeing, of feeling and of acting – or, in short, of general or specific dispositions (or schemas) and abilities. 'The "unconscious"', wrote Bourdieu, 'is
never anything other than the forgetting of history which history itself
produces by incorporating the objective structures it produces in the
second natures of *habitus*.'[34]

Not only is the unconscious nature of the incorporated past the result of genesis amnesia – or, in other words, our incapacity to remember what it is that has made us what we are; it is also linked to the fact that a large part of what we incorporate is neither explicit nor conscious. Cognitive psychology 'shows, for example, that, in the area of sensory perception and the use of language, unconscious rules are often used which can in part never be conscious, without, however, being repressed.'[35] Moreover, children usually deduce the rules of behaviour in a practical way rather than needing to having them specifically inculcated:

Firstly, parental reactions are communicated at an early age, and, secondly, this happens implicitly. The mother who reacts with depression or asthma when the child starts to distance itself or the father who becomes angry when his son outdoes him are 'implicitly' communicating a 'rule': 'Do not leave me or I will suffer.' 'Do not outdo me or I will get angry' ... This is why the association of the child's tendencies to distance itself with a threat to the mother or that of the need for rivalry with a threat to the father is, from the beginning, unconscious. It does not *become* so through repression, but it *is* because of implicit communication, and it *remains* so because it is not explicitly – in other words, linguistically – encoded and communicated.[36]

And if the child 'wanted to or could put it explicitly, he or she would probably be verbally contradicted by the parents.'[37] For not only do children learn, from the situations they experience with their parents, types of behaviour that nobody ever explicitly explains to them, but 'they often learn the opposite of the rules communicated to them verbally, since the parents' actions speak a clear "language" (for instance, when an example of aggressive behaviour by the child is indeed verbally condemned but at the same time is greeted in a non-verbal way by visible signs of joy).'[38]

Children therefore carry within them schemas of experience – interactional, affective, perceptive, evaluative, etc., schemas of whose existence they are unaware and have not consciously sought. There is no need to presuppose a mechanism of repression for a reality which would be taboo, embarrassing, disturbing or traumatic in order to make sense of the unconscious nature of these schemas. But when realities which are taboo, troublesome, disturbing or traumatic are buried, *like any others* – that is to say, *no more or less than any others* – in the unconscious of individuals, they can trigger disorders which they can subsequently find it difficult to cast off. The most anodyne experience is no more accessible to consciousness than is the most traumatic experience. The fact that it is unconscious is simply less problematic for the person involved.

As a psychoanalyst, Martin Dornes nevertheless challenges the notion of an unconsciousness exclusively made up of repressed experiences. For example, if a baby sees that each sign of autonomy on his or her part – for example, moving away from the parents on all fours – provokes 'subtle or clear signs of parental suffering', he or she will conclude in a practical way (without expressing it) that it would be better to impose a brake on any desires for autonomy that they might feel: 'He will sense anxiety or anger when he moves away and, in the long term, will avoid expressing such tendencies without knowing why he is doing so.'[39] There is no repression in this particular dispositional unconscious which is formed from the internalisation of *practical deductions*.[40] This is instead what Dornes refers to as 'a procedural unconscious ':

> The main point that concerns me in these developments is the establishment of the idea of a procedural unconscious; there is an unconscious knowledge which determines behaviour and feelings in emotionally heightened situations, without this knowledge being repressed or being prevented from becoming conscious by some kind of resistance. I consider this procedural knowledge (or perhaps these emotional heuristics) as the 'prime cause' of what, subsequently, can be formed or reconstructed as unconscious fantasy.[41]

Children learn 'at a procedural level' – in other words, unconsciously – over the course of numerous repeated episodes a certain amount of interactional knowledge, but they are unaware that they know it. They do not know that they have learned these things, and, when they acquire the ability to speak, they are quite incapable, except with external help, of verbalising this knowledge:

> If a child of eight months repeatedly experiences the fact that moving away on all fours results in panic on his mother's part, he then develops uncomfortable feelings about this situation; he restricts his movements and that restriction becomes automatic. But, at this age, he does not yet make any *symbolic* association between his 'moving away' and 'a threat to his mother', even if his mother's reactions when he crawls away from her suggest the conclusion that she feels threatened. The eight-month-old child does not 'think': 'If I move away, I am threatening my mother/my mother feels threatened', since he has not yet developed concepts such as 'distance' or 'threat', or, consequently, the 'thoughts' where such concepts might be found. Instead he perceives an affect in his mother and he adjusts his behaviour accordingly. He will seek a compromise between proximity and distance which will be tolerable to them both. The emotional heuristic thus developed from the autonomy/limitation of the distancing process *can subsequently be reconstructed* as a rule which can be formulated linguistically or as an unconscious conviction/fantasy – 'If I go too far away, I am threatening my mother' – but which does not yet exist as such in the mind of the infant. It exists initially only in the

form of interactional knowledge without any linguistic expression and without any kind of fantasy.[42]

These schemas of interaction and affective schemas are the product of practical deductions rather than explicit, verbalisable knowledge:

> The effective cause lies in experiences which are repeated often throughout the life history and which happen in an automatic way. . . . the patient behaves as though he believed/thought/imagined that 'moving away' and 'threatening the other person' are one and the same thing. But it is likely that he believes this to be the case only at a procedural level. He *acts and feels* according to this belief without its actually existing in the form of a linguistically formulated notion. But it *can* indeed be formulated linguistically, and this is precisely what the analyst is attempting to do.[43]

The very fact that Freud refers to a 'forgetting' of the past, which would be explained by a process of repression, indicates, moreover, that his focus is more on memories than on an incorporated past which comes back by reactivation, updating, triggering schemas or dispositions in current situations. Giving the impression that, were it not for repression, patients would be capable of remembering absolutely all their experiences, he neglects the existence of other ways in which the past can be reactivated other than simply through memory:

> Everything that had been forgotten had in some way or other been distressing; it had been either alarming or painful or shameful, by the standards of the subject's personality. It was impossible not to conclude that that was precisely why it been forgotten – that is, why it had not remained conscious. In order to make it conscious again in spite of this, it was necessary to overcome something that fought against one in the patient; it was necessary to make efforts on one's own part so as to urge and compel him to remember. The amount of effort required of the physician varied in different cases; it increased in direct proportion to the difficulty of what had to be remembered. The expenditure of force on the part of the physician was evidently the measure of a *resistance* on the part of the patient. It was only necessary to translate into words what I myself had observed, and I was in possession of the theory of *repression*.[44]

Freud had been aware of the difference between the unconscious, as he defined it, and other forms of unconscious notably made up of latent representations, which are not conscious yet which have not been repressed, and which it is not the purpose of psychoanalysis to bring to light.[45] But by more often than not reducing the unconscious to what is repressed, psychoanalysis develops a moral or political vision of the psyche as one where certain things are hidden, unsayable, secret, kept in the shadows by the existence of a sort of police force or moral censorship. It is undoubtedly this vision of things which gives psychoanalysis some of its seductive power, since it is a vision which claims to reveal to the subject the most secret, taboo, unspoken and even horrific things that are playing out within them but without their knowledge. Declaring, for example, that the hidden or the repressed is essentially of a *sexual* nature could well have had a seductive appeal because of the provocative nature such a hypothesis represented at the time.

This insistence on repression (in the strict Freudian sense of the word, there is no unconscious except a *repressed* one) comes certainly from the fact that, in spite of his laudable attempts to extend his study from the pathological to the normal, Freud worked first and foremost on cases of patients suffering from very significant psychological disorders such as hysteria or paranoia. The traumatic experiences, whether sexual or otherwise, experienced in childhood by his patients, and very difficult to bring back to memory, marked him to such an extent that, for him, the concept of the unconscious was inextricably tied in with that of repression. But, as we have seen, it is not only the traumatic experiences of this period of life which are forgotten but indeed all experiences, including the most banal and anodyne ones.

The unconscious nature of what preoccupies human beings, in their waking life as well as during sleep, does not therefore need the mechanism of repression in order for it to be explained. All those scholars who formulated a hypothesis of the unconscious, both before and after Freud,[46] emphasised a reality completely central to the psychic and behavioural lives of human beings, and the hypothesis of repression can be dismissed without in any way calling into question the existence of unconscious psychic processes. But the discussion needs to be taken a little further still, for repression makes sense for Freud only in relation to a censorship which is itself supposed to explain the particular structural qualities of the dream (products of the circumvention of the censorship).

6

Formal Censorship, Moral Censorship: The Double Relaxation

> I drew the curtains in the bedroom and got into bed. It was one of the few moments of profound relief in the day. No stranger, no stranger's gaze, perhaps not even a stranger's ear followed me into this room. I tasted that inexpressible pleasure of being alone, of not being observed or having any demands made on me. Of not thinking, not working. Not trying to find anything or to know anything. Of lying down peacefully on my back, my eyes closed, breathing. Breathing. I breathe. I do not think. I am calm.
>
> (Christa Wolf, *Ce qui reste*, p. 64)

For Freud, the unconscious, which is composed of all the past experiences repressed beyond the realm of the conscious, tries to find a means of expressing itself but comes up against the forces of the censorship, which force it to dissimulate, disguise, distort, conceal, mask, or transform – these are all terms used by Freud – this expression in order to render it acceptable. This censorship is linked to the superego, which is at one and the same time a sort of internal (moral) court and a (political) office of censorship, a judge coupled with a censor in the form of an internalised product of interdictions and limits, set in place by the parents but more broadly linked to the norms and forms of censorship characteristic of a given era and milieu.[1] The power struggle between the forces of unconscious desires and the forces of the censorship results in a form of an expression (e.g. oneiric) or a symptom (e.g. neurotic) which is what Freud calls a 'compromise formation'.

Suppression, repression, censorship, struggle, power struggle, circumvention of the censorship, compromise, etc. – all expressions to emerge from Freud's writing – the Freudian psychic system resembles a political zone at the heart of which battles between opposing forces are constantly played out. The political or polemological model for the function of the psychic apparatus gives the impression of a world of high surveillance where every message must be coded and where an extremely sophisticated and almost Machiavellian encrypting machine transforms everything, so that the initially unacceptable message, that of the unconscious, can no longer be recognised by the supervising powers. Not convinced by this model, the Russian philosopher Mikhail Bakhtin wrote (under the name of a close friend, V. N. Volosinov): 'how delicately this "unconscious mechanism" detects all the logical subtleties of thoughts and all the moral nuances of feelings! The censorship exhibits enormous ideological erudition and refinement; it makes purely logical, ethical, and aesthetic selections among experiences.'[2]

For Freud, this central idea of bypassing censorship was the key to explaining the often incoherent or strange character of the dream: 'Dream distortion is what makes a dream seem strange and unintelligible to us.'[3] And forgotten elements, gaps, incoherence or strangeness were simply indications of the impressively efficient action of the censorship process: 'Wherever there are gaps in the manifest dream, the dream censorship is responsible for them. We should go further, and regard it as a manifestation of the censorship, wherever a dream-element is remembered especially faintly, indefinitely and doubtfully among other elements that are more clearly constructed.'[4]

It could be said that a false hypothesis nevertheless enabled Freud to make a highly significant breakthrough in understanding dreams, given that it encouraged him to begin to explore what was being constructed in the oneiric process and what exactly was involved. The dream is supposed to disguise the (concealed) fulfilment of an unconscious (repressed) wish in order to allow it to slip through the net of the censorship. Instead of regarding these incomprehensible narratives as the products of a somewhat deranged brain, Freud transforms the very incomprehensibility of the dream into a successful and perfectly coherent masking operation: 'the dream had to be obscure so as not to betray the proscribed dream thoughts.'[5] And if the incoherence of the dream has a meaning, then it is important to try to unlock that meaning and to describe all the processes involved in the encoding (symbolisation, condensation, displacement, substitution, etc.) which deliberately masked the message.

'It is, indeed, not easy to form any conception of the abundance of the unconscious trains of thought, all striving to find expression, which are active in our minds',[6] said Freud, describing the colossal task of decoding that he has put in place. He sees his work as that of a codebreaker, given that 'interpretation means finding a hidden sense.'[7] And such meaning is not hidden by chance, but deliberately, because it has to be concealed in order to escape detection by the censorship. Freud admits himself that his way of presenting things belongs to a sort of 'demonology', for it is as if a cunning little genie had evoked the forces of censorship: 'The impression left is that the formation of obscure dreams proceeds as if a person had something to say which must be agreeable for another person upon whom he is dependent to hear.'[8]

With the exception of childhood dreams which are 'short, clear,

coherent, easy to understand and unambiguous',[9] the *manifest content* of
the dream is, like a coded political or military message which hides its true
meaning, a false message which hides a true message, one which Freud
calls the *latent content* of the dream. 'Les carottes sont cuites', announced
on the radio from London during the Second World War, did not refer to
a culinary activity but was the signal to begin operations in the territories
occupied by the Germans. And, in the same way, what the dream seems to
say cannot be taken literally, since it conceals deeper thoughts.

Freud formulated the hypothesis of a force of censorship and that of
the repression of desire at a time and in a society where the taboo of sex
was particularly strong and where ideological censorship was not a matter
to be questioned. The tendencies 'invariably of a reprehensible nature,
repulsive from the ethical, aesthetic and social point of view' that he saw
at work were for him essentially sexual: 'first and foremost manifestations
of an unbridled and ruthless egoism'.[10] The political model of psychic
activity is in Freud's eyes extremely relevant. In a letter to Wilhelm Fliess
of 22 December 1897 he wrote: 'Have you ever seen a foreign newspaper
after it has passed the censorship at the Russian frontier? Words, sentences
and whole paragraphs are blacked out, with the result that the remainder
is unintelligible. A "Russian censorship" occurs in the psychoses and
results in the apparently meaningless deliria.'[11] Freud was already using
this political situation to help him to reflect on psychoses, just as, a few
years later, he would use it in order to understand the dream.[12] And
the moral straightjacket which he detects in his own society is first and
foremost associated with sex, the effects of which he saw for himself
when, for example, before a lecture he was due to give, he was asked to
announce that he was 'coming to risqué matters' and so would 'call for an
intermission so that the ladies could leave the hall'.[13]

A young friend and contemporary of Freud, the writer Stefan Zweig,
conjures up the moral climate of the period before 1914 with great clarity
in *The World of Yesterday*, in which he describes his discovery of a general
hypocrisy regarding sexuality: 'School and church, salon and courts,
newspapers and books, modes and manners . . . and even science', 'all
authorities were united in a boycott of hermetic silence.' They demanded,
he said, 'secrecy and reserve'. A 'middle-class morality of the nineteenth
century, which was essentially a Victorian morality', 'anxiously evaded the
sexual problem'. This era 'limited its morality, not by forbidding a young
man to carry on his *vita sexualis* but by demanding of him that this painful
matter be attended to in as inconspicuous a manner as possible.' The
need to conceal also imposed a second need, one which meant 'constantly
tracking down' sexuality with the result that society 'was actually forced
to think constantly of the indecent'.[14] There is nothing more obsessed with
sexual matters than a society which is constantly determined to conceal
anything relating to them: 'As a matter of fact, nothing increased and
troubled our curiosity as much as this clumsy business of concealment;
and since all that was natural was not permitted to run its course freely and

openly, in a big city curiosity created its own not very clean underground outlets.'[15] In his political metaphors and in his sexual obsession, Freud was very much a man of his time.

And as in the case of the unconscious, which he at times accepted was not necessarily the product of repression, Freud can sometimes open the door to other explanations concerning the characteristics of oneiric images: 'We have not, of course, maintained that the censorship is the sole factor responsible for the distortion in dreams, and in fact when we study them we can discover that other factors play a part in producing this result.'[16] He mentions in particular the constraint of visualisation imposed by the dream: 'The dream content consists chiefly of visual scenes: hence the dream ideas must, in the first place, be prepared to make use of these forms of presentation . . . it will be easy to understand the transformations to which the dream work is constrained by regard for this dramatization of the dream content.'[17] Yet it is indeed the censorship and nothing but the censorship to which Freud refers constantly in order to make sense of the symbolisations, condensations, displacements, substitutions, forgetting and lacunae which he observes in accounts of dreams: 'The distortion in the dream is thus shown in fact to be an act of the censorship.'[18] And, in a note added in 1919 to *The Interpretation of Dreams*, Freud wrote, again without ambiguity: 'the kernel of my theory of dreams lies in my derivation of dream-distortion from the censorship.'[19]

The most private of the private: on stage and behind the scenes

There is something paradoxical in Freud's reasoning. While he tends to explain all the structural and moral properties of the dream on the grounds of the need to outwit and therefore come to a compromise with the censorship, he also puts forward the idea that the censorship will be at its weakest during sleep and will re-establish itself at the moment of waking. 'Under certain conditions, of which the state of sleep is one, the relation between the strength of the two agencies [the unconscious and censorship] is modified in such a way that what is repressed can no longer be held back.'[20] Or again: 'it appears to be compelled by the psycho-physiological conditions of sleep to relax the energy with which it is accustomed to hold down the repressed material during the day.'[21]

Freud clearly takes this notion of the relaxing of the moral censorship in the dream from authors such as Antoine Charma (1851), Karl Albert Scherner (1861) or Alfred Maury (1861). Charma wrote that 'enslaved nature, humiliated during waking hours, liberates itself and takes its revenge during the hours of sleep!'[22] Scherner, for his part, claimed: 'The body's instincts turn on themselves; it is they who are the masters now. What do they care for the standards of the moral law? They are free! Without constraint, as their physical nature created them, they throw themselves into action in order to set themselves free. They exhort the imagination to provide them with troops of images in order to express despair or ardent pleasure.'[23] And Maury refers to the intelligence of the dreamer as 'intelligence undressed', which begins to act 'when it shakes off this ceremonial costume which we call reason and this somewhat tiring bearing which we name consciousness.'[24] Maury even described in detail the absence of repression of intense desires in the dream. The dream is liberated from censorship to such an extent that 'we commit, in our imagination, reprehensible acts, even crimes of which we would never be guilty in real life.' If in a waking state we can 'fight' against our bad instincts to avoid giving into them, the dream is the space where they express themselves unrestrainedly:

> In my dreams I always give way to them, or, to put it better, I act on their impulse, without fear or remorse. I abandon myself to the most violent outbreaks of anger, to the most reckless desires, and when I awake I am almost ashamed of these imaginary crimes. Clearly the visions which run through my thoughts and which appear in the dream are suggested to me by the provocations I feel and that my absent will does not seek to suppress. The nervous excitement which sometimes accompanies sleep and which provokes dreams where our passions, such as licentiousness, anger or fear, flow freely can impart to our actions and our feelings an element of violence which they do not have in the waking state. . . . In dreaming, man therefore reveals himself totally as he is in his native nudity and misery. As soon as he ceases to exercise his will, he becomes the plaything of all those passions from which, in the waking state, conscience, the sense of honour and fear protect us.[25]

Freud thus partially borrowed from these writers the concept of the relaxation and the absence of control or will, at the same time introducing the idea that there would be disguises or misrepresentations because of the censorship, in order to explain the formal properties of the dream which are in fact due to very different reasons.[26]

After Freud, other writers would continue to support the idea that the desires 'we repel when awake reappear during sleep.' This is, for example, the position of Marcel Foucault, who, in 1906, claimed that, during sleep, 'moral and higher faculties are suspended' and that 'all the mental and moral forces that reason controls during wakefulness are unleashed':[27] 'The main reason for the predominant place occupied in the dream by repressed desires and unreasonable fears seems to me to lie in the suspension or weakening of the power to control and supervise during sleep: all the forces that the waking man's reason pushes back into unconsciousness resurface when the activity of the critical faculties is withdrawn.'[28] The same is true of Yves Delage, who, in 1920, associated repression with waking life:

As a result of all that has been demonstrated in the course of this book, we conclude that dreams for the most part reproduce ideas which, in real life, have been held in check, repressed, either by intercurrent circumstances or by an act of our own will. Those ideas repressed by intercurrent circumstances are unimportant and need not be systematised, since they are simply those which, by chance, happened to occupy the thoughts at the moment when the circumstance which drove them out intervened. The same is not true for the ones we have repressed advisedly. If we have acted thus in their case, it is because they were of a particular nature, intrusive or shocking, because they somehow offended our feelings. Now the things which hurt or shock us are often those which we do not like to admit to ourselves, those to which we unconsciously or deliberately turn a blind eye, in order to delude ourselves. However, these things, these feelings, these tendencies, these impulses which we keep hidden from ourselves are brought brutally into our view by the dream, and, in doing so, the dream renders us a service provided we know how to make good use of it.[29]

It is difficult therefore to see whether it is the censorship or the relaxation of the censorship which explains the dream images: a matter of balance, it might be said, since it is a matter of a compromise formation. The censorship would be diminished, weakened, but not removed entirely:

Under certain conditions, one of which is the sleeping state, the balance of power between the two procedures is so changed that what is repressed can no longer be kept back. In the sleeping state this may possibly occur through the negligence of the censor, what has been hitherto repressed will now succeed in finding its way to consciousness. But as the censorship is never absent, but merely off guard, certain alterations must be conceded so as to placate it. It is a compromise which becomes conscious in this case – a compromise between what one procedure has in view and the demands of the other.[30]

There is, however, a tension between the idea of a maximum easing of the censorship and that, more often cited, of a permanent concealment, of a disguising or a coding which implies the oppressive omnipresence of this same censorship: 'Whosoever has firmly accepted this censorship as the chief motive for the distortion of dreams will not be surprised to learn as the result of dream interpretation that most of the dreams of adults are traced by analysis to erotic desires.'[31] Either the censorship is absent from the dream or extremely feeble, or it structures it to such an extent that all its latent thoughts are transformed into morally correct manifest thoughts. Wanting to hold both these views at once calls for argumentative gymnastics. The techniques of camouflage are so sophisticated that we might wonder to what extent the censorship is indeed relaxed, if at all. This ruthless censorship seems to be even more devious in the dream than in waking life. But why then does Freud accept the possibility of a weakening of the censorship which 'resumes complete sway'[32] on awakening? It is in answering this question that we can understand the extent of the error which has been made.

The social conditions of the elimination of the moral and structural censorship

> A young man wished his parents to separate, because his somewhat tyrannical mother was spoiling his father's life. She was a Parisian and he had a southern French name. In his dream the son was leaving the station at Avignon and was struck by the unusually tidy and clean appearance of the streets. He was then told: 'Everything is better than it used to be, now that the south of France has become an independent republic.' Here there is clearly symbolism, almost comparable to that of an imaginative game, but it is difficult to see where censorship comes in, since the meaning is obvious.
>
> (Jean Piaget, *Play, Dreams and Imitation in Childhood*, p. 192)

It is difficult not to revise the Freudian theory of repression and censorship in the light of what researchers in the social sciences have contributed in terms of the study of censorships imposed by relations of domination on discursive or non-discursive behaviours. Writers such as James Scott (who has pointed out the variations in the behaviour and speech of those dominated, depending on whether they were actively engaged in interaction with the dominators or not)[33] or Pierre Bourdieu (who in his 'The Economy of Linguistic Exchanges' discusses the results of the sociologist William Labov)[34] are central figures in this debate. Their work makes it possible to put into perspective the Freudian theory of censorship and of the 'dream work', which essentially consists in a coding (disguising, masking, etc.) of the latent thoughts of the dream in order to get around the censorship.

The central idea of James Scott is contained in just a few phrases. There are two types of 'transcript' (speech, gestures, attitudes) for those who are dominated: a 'public transcript', which those who are dominated adopt in the presence of the dominators to avoid the risk of sanctions, and a 'hidden transcript', which is manifest only when the dominated are in locations that are not under the immediate control of the dominators ('outside the intimidating gaze of power'),[35] either 'offstage' or in the wings,[36] or in the intimacy of their peers – in other words, in relatively autonomous locations (family milieu or friendship circle) – or in their 'heart of hearts' when they find themselves reflecting on what they have experienced. In his attempts to make sense of class relations in a Malay village, Scott observed that 'the poor sang one tune when they were in the presence of the rich and another tune when they were among the poor. The rich too spoke one way to the poor and another among themselves.'[37] Or again: 'Who among us has not had a similar experience? Who, having been insulted or suffered an indignity – especially in public – at the hand of someone in power or authority over us, has not *rehearsed an imaginary speech* he wishes he had given or intends to give at the next opportunity?'[38] The 'public transcript' is therefore always the product of a *repression of expression* (dissimulation, repression, masking, disguise) and the 'hidden transcript' the product of an 'unrestrained expression' with regard to the dominators.

We could even say that the immediate absence of a judge, or of a censor, and the presence of peers *pushes* and *constrains* expression towards subversive bravado or criticism in the interests of honour and of the re-establishment of dignity. For it would be a mistake to make the 'hidden transcript' an 'authentic', 'true' and 'free' transcript and the 'public transcript a constrained, forced, inauthentic or hypocritical transcript. In reality, the truth of social behaviours lies in the variety of 'transcripts' produced according to the different situations, and the constraints which weigh down the hidden transcripts are no less powerful than those which structure the public transcripts. The sociologist's task is simply to link each particular transcript to the specific conditions of its enunciation or of its production. Scott says that we should not take the public declarations made by those over whom some kind of power is exercised 'at face value'.[39] But he should say the same thing about private declarations made 'in confidence'. Part of the truth of social relationships lies in the fact that the dominated are forced in many situations to put on a 'brave face' in public. That truth does not therefore lie only in critical discourse or in the mockery or anger that goes on behind the scenes or in locations outside the immediate control of the dominant. Constraints of another nature weigh on these contexts of expression which might be esteemed to be more 'free': expression is 'free' in so far as it is freed from the direct link with the dominator, but this liberation results in that individual being constrained by other social contexts such as that of the family or of friendships, the mental contexts of daydreams or of dreams during sleep.

The situations which give rise to 'public transcripts' correspond to what Bourdieu calls the 'formal' or 'official' markets, or, in other words, to markets 'dominated by the dominators'. The dominant markets impose specific forms of censorship (ways of behaving, of speaking, dressing, etc.), and this legitimate censorship is all the more powerful because the situation is official and tightly controlled. Situations where 'hidden transcripts' can be seen are, on the other hand, 'free markets', in which censorship imposed by the dominators is suspended. When Pierre Bourdieu speaks of those who 'let themselves be carried away by their own words', and who surrender 'without restraint or censorship to their expressive impulse',[40] he is implying, like Scott, that the free markets and free speech are subject to no rules or constraints and come closer to an incontrollable or unrestrained 'nature', an impression reinforced by the impulsive nature of the vocabulary involved.

Bourdieu owes this analysis largely to the American socio-linguist William Labov, who established that the variation in linguistic behaviours depending on the degree of 'formality' or 'tension' of the situation in which the speaker is placed does not apply only to the utterances as signifying productions but also to the most formal aspects of speech (pronunciation, lexical or syntactical register, style of utterance) which are rarely consciously controlled. In doing so, he proved that the effects of the formal, structural censorship exercised by certain situations, provided those involved are sufficiently aware of them, result in unconscious adjustments being made which have to do more with a practical linguistic sense than with any intentional control of linguistic 'choices'. Pierre Encrevé summed up the results of Labov's work as follows: 'The more the context is a "formal" one, the more, in all speakers, variants appear related to "prestige" (those used most by the upper classes).'[41]

Bourdieu introduces a whole range of utterances which go from speaking in public on the official markets to speaking in private (with friends or family) on the 'free' markets:

> the unification of the market is never so complete as to prevent dominated individuals from finding, in the space provided by private life, among friends, markets where the laws of price formation which apply to more formal markets are suspended. In these private exchanges between homogeneous partners, the 'illegitimate' linguistic products are judged according to criteria which, since they are adjusted to their principles of production, free them from the necessarily comparative logic of distinction and of value. Despite this, the formal law which is thus provisionally suspended rather than truly transgressed, remains valid, and it reimposes itself on dominated individuals once they leave the unregulated areas where they can be outspoken (and where they can spend all their lives).[42]

Like Bourdieu, Scott never specifically turned his attention to dreams. In his discussions on the 'transcripts' (hidden or public), he comes up with a whole range of situations which go from the 'inner depths' of daydreaming right to the concentration camps, taking in on the way 'dialogue among friends of equal status and power'.[43]

According to Scott, those who are dominated 'conceal', 'mask', 'disguise' their intentions, their feelings, their spontaneous ways of feeling and of acting in order to avoid being sanctioned by those who hold power. There is therefore work to be done in order to 'shape', and even to 'repress' or 'suppress', these expressive 'impulses', which Bourdieu analyses very clearly using a Freudian vocabulary:

every expression is an accommodation between an *expressive interest* and a *censorship* constituted by the field in which that expression is offered; and this accommodation is the product of a process of euphemization which may even result in silence, the extreme case of censored discourse. This euphemization leads the potential 'author' to produce something which is a compromise formation, a combination of what there was to be said, which 'needed' to be said, and what *could* be said, given the structure of a particular field. In other words, what is sayable in a given field is the result of what might be called a form-giving process [*une mise en forme*]: speaking means observing the forms.[44]

Even if they are not referring specifically to the question of dreams, the analyses made by Scott and Bourdieu nevertheless draw attention to the fact that the dream is situated at the extreme limit of the private domain. In the terminology used by Scott, we could say that the dream is the *most hidden of hidden transcripts*. And in that of Bourdieu, we could say that it is a symbolic production which emerges from the *most open of open* markets: that of the dialogue with the self, of self-to-self communication.[45] The dreamer's interlocutor, who is none other than himself, combines two fundamental properties that *permeate* the dream: he or she is of *perfectly equal social value* (the social homogeneity is pure and perfect) and shares exactly the *same existential and dispositional background* (which is only ever partially shared between the closest social partners: spouse, brothers or sisters, father or mother, longstanding friends or colleagues, etc.). As the product of the most open of open markets, the *dream* is radically different from the *silence* of someone who, in the presence of the dominator or of all the potential bearers of legitimate norms, sees their speech prevented from finding expression. The dream is therefore, among all the existing forms of expression, the one which, by virtue of the exceptionally protected nature of its conditions of production, is the least susceptible to the powers of censorship, whether formal or moral. By drawing attention to the censorship which would give rise to the dream-work, Freud paradoxically put his finger on the distinctive property of the dream – that is, the weakening of the censorship in relation to all the social situations where the legitimate norms and powers permanently make their presence felt.

Pierre Bourdieu writes in a very interesting manner, one to my knowledge almost never discussed in the sociological field, that 'the Freudian model' should be perceived 'as a particular example of a more general mode, which makes any expression the product of a transaction between the expressive interest and the structural necessity of a field acting as a form of censorship.'[46] In saying this, he is opening up the possibility that the dream can be seen as a particular case of the possible, a case of a form of expression which can be understood only at the intersection of an expressive interest (i.e. what I would call the existential situation of the dreamer – the most frequently occurring and structuring preoccupations of his or her existence – and what this reveals about his or her mostly deeply rooted dispositions) and the conditions in which it is expressed.

But Bourdieu does not take his intuition far enough and circumvents the problem. Firstly, instead of sociologising it, he allows for the possibility that this expressive interest might be just as much a 'biological drive' as a social one. Furthermore, he does not challenge the general relevance of his concept of field and instead subjects it to a problematic extension, for example by making the family a field. He writes: 'The social repression that occurs in the domestic context, as the field for a particular type of relation of power (whose structure varies according to the social conditions), is very specific in its form (one of tacit injunction and suggestion) and applies to a very specific class of interests: sexual drives.'[47] It will be observed, moreover, that in this citation the domestic space is supposed to be characterised by the repression of sexual drives, a notion indicating that Bourdieu is turning back to Freudian arguments on repression and its sexual explanation but without questioning them.

But, above all, in integrating the Freudian model in his argument, Bourdieu does not challenge the power of the censorship which, according to Freud, is exercised on dreams and, instead, behaves as though dreams, like philosophical productions (those of Martin Heidegger which he studied), are subjected to this censorship with the same degree of intensity. He writes therefore: 'the Freudian analysis of the syntax of dreams and of all "private" ideologies provides the instruments which are necessary for an understanding of the labour of euphemization and imposition of form which occurs each time a biological or social drive must come to terms with a social censorship.'[48] With his attention firmly focused on public symbolic productions, produced in a state of waking consciousness, he finds nothing more to add to the model of the censorship of impulses applied to the dream. However, the very fact that the Freudian model, as he emphasises, functions particularly well in the context of the analysis of literary, political or philosophical symbolic productions which are nevertheless a million miles away from oneiric productions should have alerted his critical attention. Bourdieu overlooks the Freudian error, failing even to see it. This error consists in making censorship a powerful principle for the explanation of the dream (of the form it assumes) as the disguising of a latent thought which must escape the control of the censorship, even though the forces of censorship are noticeably absent in these times of private, self-to-self communication.[49]

For his part, Freud does not distinguish situations according to whether they are private or public, unofficial or official, intimate or impersonal, mental or verbal, asleep or awake. The closer the focus on the private, the intimate, the mental state, the less powerful both moral and linguistic control becomes. On the other hand, public situations imply a much higher level of tension, a higher degree of self-control and a very active moral and linguistic hypercorrection. From this point of view, dreams can be differentiated from daydreams, which in turn differ from the informal face-to-face interaction with a close acquaintance, which differs again from the more formal interaction with a colleague, which in its turn differs from the official discourse in public or the school exam, etc. Freud's theoretical model of the psychic system takes almost no account of variation in contexts, and this also prevents him from identifying the specific nature of the dream in comparison with other forms of expression.

In this way, Freud regards the intra-psychic situation of the dreamer as analogous with that of communication between two people, one of whom occupies a superior position:

> where the wish-fulfilment is unrecognizable, where it has been disguised, there must have existed some inclination to put up a defence against the wish; and owing to this defence the wish was unable to express itself except in a distorted shape. I will try to seek a social parallel to this internal event in the mind. Where can we find a similar distortion of a psychical act in social life? Only where two persons are concerned, one of whom possesses a certain degree of power which the second is obliged to take into account. In such a case the second person will distort his psychical acts or, as we might put it, will dissimulate. The politeness which I practice everyday is to a large extent dissimulation of this kind.[50]

A genuine comparison would lead him to realise that the two situations have little in common in terms of the effect of the censorship. The interest of the work carried out by researchers in the social sciences lies precisely in its ability to demonstrate that the censorship is not the same everywhere, whatever the context of the expression. The same person, speaking with their close friends about a particular individual who has power, will already not say the same things. But we may well wonder why, whereas in the dream everything takes place self-to-self, without an external interlocutor or an audience, the dreamer should feel the desire to disguise his or her feelings in the manner of a subaltern confronted by someone who holds power.

Similarly, Freud draws an analogy between the situation of the dreamer and that of a writer who is seeking to publish a text which is critical of the power currently in place:

> A similar difficulty confronts the political writer who has disagreeable truths to tell to those in authority. If he presents them undisguised, the authorities will suppress his words – after they have been spoken, if his pronouncement was an oral one, but beforehand, if he had intended to make it in print. A writer must be aware of the censorship, and on its account he must soften and distort the expression of his opinion. According to the strength and sensitiveness of the censorship he finds himself compelled either merely to refrain from certain forms of attack, or to speak in allusions in place of direct references, or he must conceal his objectionable pronouncement beneath some

apparently innocent disguise: for instance, he may describe a dispute between two Mandarins in the Middle Kingdom, when the people he really has in mind are officials in his own country. The stricter the censorship, the more far-reaching will be the disguise and the more ingenious too may be the means employed for putting the reader on the scent of the true meaning.[51]

Would the censorship be as powerful when it is internalised as it is when it is being exercised by a powerful institution of power such as the state? Freud does not ask himself this question and fails to see the problem that would have permitted him to abandon the hypothesis of the censorship and to turn instead to the study of the properties of the context of sleep.[52] A neuropsychologist such as Mark Solms, who is far from hostile to Freudian theory (he is the founder of neuropsychoanlysis), nevertheless thinks that today there is undoubtedly 'no need to introduce the additional function of censorship'[53] in order to make sense of the dream-work.

Because he turned his attention towards the social contexts of memory and was very familiar with the psychological literature of his time, Maurice Halbwachs understood why the censorship, both formal and moral, is absent from the dream. First of all, nothing in the dreamer's situation obliges him or her to be explicit and coherent. He, or she, simply has to conjure up scenes which echo the dreamer's own experience, since they are not addressing anyone other than themselves: 'The sleeping man escapes from the control of society. Nothing obliges him to express himself correctly, since he is not seeking to be understood by others.'[54] But we can also see behind this absence of narrative or structural discipline the absence of moral control over what is permitted to be said:

> We observe that man is trained to understand what he sees and what he feels by social discipline and that his intelligence is made up of ideas (almost all of them partly verbal) which come to him from his immediate or more distant human entourage. Certainly, ... during sleep, this discipline slackens considerably; the individual escapes from the pressure of these groups. He is no longer under their control. But, at the same time, he is deprived of some of the support he received from them. That is why he is unable to recall, in the form of coherent sequences of clearly situated events, certain periods or scenes from his past life.[55]

But it is to a philosopher, linguist and theoretician of Russian literature, Mikhail Bakhtin, that we owe the most pertinent formulation of the problem of the censorship. The proximity between speaker and person addressed – and in the dream the proximity is transformed into identity – explains the weakening of the censorship. Both family genres and intimate genres share the fact that they perceive the person addressed 'outside the frameworks of hierarchy and social conventions, "without rank" as it were':

> This gives rise to a certain *candor* of speech (which in familiar styles sometimes approaches cynicism). In intimate styles this is expressed in an apparent desire for the speaker and addressee to merge completely. In familiar speech, since constraints and conventions have fallen away, one can take a special unofficial, volitional attitude to reality. (The loud candor of the streets, calling things by their real names, is typical of this style.) ... Intimate genres and styles are based on a maximum internal proximity of the speaker and addressee (in extreme instances, as if they had merged). Intimate speech is imbued with a deep confidence in the addressee, in his sympathy, in the sensitivity and goodwill of his responsive understanding. In this atmosphere of profound trust, the speaker reveals his internal depths. ... Familiar and intimate genres and styles (as yet very little studied) reveal extremely clearly the dependence of style on a certain sense and understanding of the addressee ... and on the addressee's actively responsive understanding that is anticipated by the speaker. ... Unless one accounts for the speaker's attitude towards the *other* and his utterances (existing or anticipated), one can understand neither the genre nor the style of speech.[56]

The last sentence in this illuminating extract acts as a fairly radical criticism directed at Freud, who failed to take into account the nature of the *context of expression* in order to understand the particular form of expression with which he was dealing. We can only regret that Bakhtin did not include the dream account in his discussion, since he would have found in it further confirmation of the pertinence of his analyses. This fusion of speaker and person addressed serves to explain the moral relaxation as well as the elliptical and apparently illogical nature of the dream.

What does the censorship do?

Instead of attempting to describe the properties of the context in which an expression like the dream takes place, Freud tries to save his theory of the censorship by embarking on argumentative acrobatics or by keeping a discreet silence on certain facts.

With regard to argumentative acrobatics, Freud firmly maintains the idea that the manifest content of the dream is a distorted version, under the influence of the censorship, of the latent content of the dream, but he is nevertheless obliged to provide some explanation for certain dreams where dreamers do or witness terrible things. At that point, he finds himself obliged to advance the hypothesis that the latent content is 'entirely eluding censorship and passing into the dream without modification.'[57] But this kind of explanation is not very satisfactory. Why should the censorship suddenly vary in its effects? Rather than coming up with a censorship which could sometimes fail, Freud should have accepted the fact that the censorship is scarcely present in dreams, and that this is precisely what constitutes the fundamental interest of studying dreams. If Scott was right to see some 'hidden transcripts' of resistance behind the scenes of relations of domination, then the dream represents the 'hidden transcript' which is most thoroughly liberated from censorship.

In one of the dreams analysed by Freud in *The Interpretation of Dreams*, a woman is in love with a man whom she last saw standing beside the coffin of her dead nephew (her sister's son Otto). She wants to see this man again and therefore dreams that her sister's other son (Karl), of whom she is much less fond than she was of Otto, is dead.[58] Freud says that this is a dream of impatience and that the woman in question was associating the man with the terrible circumstances in which she had last seen him. But what is most extraordinary about this dream is that, although dreaming about the death of another child is hardly acceptable from a moral point of view, this is nevertheless the way in which the dreamer chooses to express her wish to see this man again. The very fact that she is less fond of Karl than she was of Otto means that she is not troubled by any censorship and can therefore make him die in the dream, for only the expected effect of his death, that of seeing this man at his funeral, matters in her eyes. The dream therefore condenses both her relationship with Karl and her desire for a man, which are linked together in her mind.

In another case, a jurist dreamt that he was arriving at his house with a lady on his arm but found the police waiting for him, ready to arrest him on a charge of infanticide.[59] It turns out that, the previous evening, he was with his mistress, with whom he had spent the night. She was a married woman, and as he did not want her to become pregnant he practised coitus interruptus, which is a way of not having a child and, in a sense, of killing the child he could potentially have with her. His wish, and Freud was probably correct on this point, was to avoid having a child with this woman. But, once again, Freud does not realise that the atrocity is more in the manifest content of the dream than it is in its latent content (not wanting to have a child is not the same as dreaming that you have killed one!). What such a dream proves is, rather, that the dreamer let go of the reins of social control and of censorship. He imagined something far worse than what he actually wished for, and it is hard to see what he is hiding (from himself) in this dream.

On the subject of silences, Freud does not dwell on erotic or more directly pornographic dreams even though these certainly exist; they feature only very marginally in his own corpus of dreams. In *The Interpretation of Dreams*, he even admits in a simple footnote to having 'avoided analysing dreams of obviously sexual content'.[60] Upholding the idea that what cannot be discussed is most often sexual desire, or that sexual desire cannot be talked about except in a disguised form, he could be embarrassed only by overtly and even crudely sexual dreams. How can what we are supposed to hunt down and flush out from behind very banal, anodyne or strange reality burst onto the oneiric stage, in full daylight?

For example, in *The Interpretation of Dreams* Freud mentions a dream experienced by a colleague of Otto Rank. This man dreams that he is running down a staircase, chasing a little girl. He catches her and, right in the middle of the staircase, rubs his genitals against hers: 'I suddenly found myself . . . copulating with the child (as it were in the air). It was not a real copulation; I was only rubbing my genitals against her external genitals, and while I did so I saw them extremely distinctly, as well as her head, which was turned upwards and sideways.'[61] The distortion and even omission of the sexual element essentially applies to the title Freud gave to the dream, in that he modestly entitles it 'A staircase dream'. The dreamer, for his part, describes the scene explicitly and describes to the analyst a sexual activity without penetration involving a young girl. We may wonder, in this case too, what had happened to the forces of moral censorship!

As early as 1861, Scherner was observing that 'oneiric manifestations of nudity and of sensuality are frequently to be found . . . even where the individual is highly moral in waking life': 'We see ourselves and we see others openly satisfying natural bodily needs, which the waking man zealously conceals: very often, the dreamer sees himself in the company of tender young women in places that all the inhabitants of the house must pass through in order to relieve a pressing need.'[62] Similarly, Calvin S. Hall and Vernon J. Nordby, who worked on thousands of dreams, observed that certain dreams were not described because the dreamers were ashamed of them. These dreams involved people close to them and were sometimes extremely improper.[63] The censorship thus reappears on waking, but is conspicuous by its absence during the dream. The effects of the censorship can even be set aside on wakening, since many dreamers shared their dreams without hesitation even when they included material which was taboo, shameful or unpleasant, because they had been promised anonymity and because they had no particular connection with the researcher. Certain dreamers also recounted dreams which were undoubtedly awkward on the grounds that they did not feel responsible for their thoughts during sleep.[64] Violent dreams (a dreamer who killed her father with a friend, or another dreamer who killed his close relations one by one)[65] or sexual dreams (featuring dreamers having sexual relations with people of the same sex or with the opposite sex, with animals, and a whole range of sexual practices including masturbation, sodomy, fellatio, etc.)[66] are frequent. And Hall and Nordby say that dreams allow people to express their motives often in a 'more thinly disguised form' than in waking life.[67]

There is no end to the supply of citations from scientific literature on dreams which could be used as examples of situations which are overtly sexual or explicitly aggressive.[68] For example, René Allendy reports the following dream from a young girl: 'I was up on the roof with a young woman and I had to get down with her, without falling. Her lover was waiting for her down below. I reached the ground. The man indicated that he desired me and I gave myself to him on the pavement.'[69] To discover the meaning of this scene clearly involves going beyond its manifest content, for example, by questioning the dreamer about whether she has ever found herself on a roof, or if this scene reminds her of a scene from a film or a novel, asking her if she recognises the young woman or the lover or if these two characters remind her of people she knows, and whether she has ever had a sexual relationship with someone who is already in a relationship. But any meaning that can be uncovered will have little to do with any attempt to circumvent some very distant censorship. It will instead be linked to the dreamer's past experience and existential background, and it is these which the interpreter must learn to uncover.

The same writer, who has carefully noted a large body of dreams along with their contexts and any associations made by the dreamers, expresses his astonishment at certain dreams which, quite clearly, cannot be explained as the result of a censorship:

> Now the distorting effect of the censorship is exerted more or less according to the dreams and to the individuals concerned, perhaps also according to whether the subject is sleeping deeply enough to be capable to some extent of losing sight of the mostly recently acquired elements of the censorship. The fact remains that in our dreams we cold-bloodedly carry out atrocious acts or monstrous desires, at least when judged from the point of view of our conscious ethics. So, for example, dreams often show the death of people who have, in however slight a way, offended our instincts, even though these may be people we nevertheless think we love. . . . It seems to us difficult to explain such irregularities in the mechanism of the censorship.[70]

Finally, we will look at a dream studied by Jacques Montangero, which shows not only that the censorship is almost non-existent but that the dream is much more candid and direct than the real situation from which it arose. The dreamer is a married man of about fifty, who has written a letter to a young woman who had made her details known with the suggestion that she was interested in meeting sexual partners. The letter remained without reply, but three months later the man encountered one of his nieces who resembled the description of the young woman, and he felt deeply ashamed at the idea that it might indeed have been her. Sometime later, he dreamt that he was with the daughter of his cousin and was wondering, awkwardly, how to tell her that she would receive a letter at her home containing a used condom. 'With this dreamlike sense of exaggeration', Montangero observes, 'the staging of the dream is very crude, indicating that the letter had been sent to a family member of the next generation, that it was associated with sexual activity and that it was very shocking to have sent it.'[71] Not only is the dream clearly not seeking to get around any form of censorship, but it is exaggerating the feeling of shame experienced in the waking state.

A dreamlike lucidity?

The dream is not distorted in order to escape from an almost non-existent censorship. Rather, it is the most 'pure' element of self-expression (or expression of individuality, as Bakhtin put it), the one which is most unfettered by any need for compromise. It is not therefore the 'compromise-formation' Freud wanted to see in it, but a self-to-self form of expression which is capable of freeing itself at the same time both from the linguistic or formal obligations of communication (both oral and written) with others and from the moral obligations of expression normally censored so as to avoid shocking or provoking disapproval. The absence of formal, structural censorship is what gives the dream its sometimes disjointed, illogical, non-chronological, incoherent nature (at the moment of waking, the dreamer must nevertheless try to recount the dream in an acceptable form).[72] The absence of political or moral censorship is what enables the dream to be more directly anchored in the dreamer's own problems. The dream goes to the very heart of whatever the dreamer's preoccupations are, but in forms which perplex the dreamer in his or her waking state. And it is for this reason that attention has sometimes been drawn to the lucidity of dreams or their capacity to identify problems without putting on kid gloves or beating about the bush, and even sometimes by dramatising them, and thus making them appear clearer and more imposing than they seemed to the waking consciousness.

It was Léon d'Hervey de Saint-Denys who, in 1867, pointed out the perspicacity of the mind in the dream, precisely on account of the total disconnection of the dreamer from any elements which could provide any distraction from his or her thinking: 'It is surely one of the most interesting aspects of the subject which we are examining; this powerful perspicacity, this sort of intuitive divination to which the mind can sometimes raise itself, in the dreaming state, thanks to the absolute concentration of all the dreamer's powers of attention.'[73] He cites the doctor and philosopher Pierre Jean Georges Cabanis, who explains that sometimes we dream that someone is not altogether straightforward and honest, even though they may be someone we like in waking life, and that the facts end up proving that the dream was indeed right.[74] Fleeting feelings, semi-conscious in waking life, and which end up going unnoticed, can give rise to much sharper images in the dream.

Again, in 1920, Yves Delage claimed that the dream was the area likely to cast most light on the dreamer's personality:

The dream renders the invaluable service of brutally pulling off all the veils and revealing us to ourselves exactly as we really are: it is up to us not to spurn these revelations. . . . The dream is a flaming torch which lights up the lowest depths of our intimate nature. Is it wise to close our eyes to its light under the pretext that it is the imagination and not reason which clasps it in its hand? *In vino veritas*, as the Ancients used to say. We propose adding another saying to this one: *In somnio veritas.*[75]

Delage recounts a personal dream which he had on the night of 11–12 April 1914 ('Dream of the inopportune visitor')[76] which proves the lucidity of the dreamer, or at least the capacity of the dream to reveal the truth of a situation which cannot be seen clearly in waking life. The writer dreamt that he made a surprise visit to a couple of very close friends, M and Mme X, and that these, and in particular Mme X, received him with extreme coldness (first ignoring him and then being excessively distant towards him). In his waking life, nothing would lead him to imagine such a reaction on the part of his friends, but Delage notes: 'A certain rigidity concerning the consideration that she [Mme X] believed to be her due is not altogether alien to her character, with the result that fleeting images instantly suppressed in the waking state could well have crossed my mind, depicting her in the light in which my dream had shown her.' In the intimacy of the dream, what is only a half-conscious thought in the waking state manifests itself without any nuances: 'The dream shows us, without any veil, I would say without modesty, the judgements, the opinions, resulting from the unconscious cerebration. Viewed from this perspective, many things become clear which would not otherwise be so. And this is how the dream renders us the service of setting before our eyes those of our own thoughts that we would not admit to ourselves.'

Similarly, in the work of Erich Fromm, we find the most detailed idea of the lucidity, the perspicacity or the 'truth' of the dream. Fromm explains this increased lucidity by the fact that, during sleep, dreamers are 'free from the burden of work, from the task of attack or defense' and therefore 'from watching and mastering reality'.[77] No longer subject to the distractions of the environment, the dreamer can devote wholehearted attention to his or her thoughts with an intensity that would be impossible in waking life: 'penetrating thinking requires an amount of concentration which we are often deprived of in the waking state.'[78] Fleeting sentiments or passing intuitions from waking life can be expanded on. In this way, Fromm recounts a dream where the dreamer demonstrates more 'insight' vis-à-vis a certain person than in diurnal life. In waking life, this person is regarded with admiration and is idealised, whereas during the dream a certain cruelty appears (which will be confirmed by the facts). He describes 'a more penetrating and truer judgement than that of the waking state'.[79] This does not imply a return to the pre-scientific notion of the premonitory nature of the dream. The conditions of expression within the dream simply allow the unconscious perceptions of wakefulness, or those which are conscious but fleeting, to express themselves more clearly.

Finally, the more recent work carried out by Ernest Hartmann also highlights the same phenomena of 'perspicacity' or 'lucidity' within the dream.[80] For example, Hartmann claims to have heard more or less the same type of dream recounted by six women in the course of his studies on dreams. This dream went something like this: 'I was dreaming about my boyfriend "Jim", and then he turned into my father.' In their daily lives, these people were no doubt guided in their behaviour towards their father and their boyfriends by the unconscious perception of analogies. But consciously, in the waking state, they were completely unaware of this. The dream expresses symbolically what is 'acted out' in waking life. On waking in the morning, certain women said they had not noticed the similarity between boyfriend and father before their dream. There is therefore a certain lucidity in the dream. Dreamers see what is unconsciously perceived in waking life.

Yet this lucidity nevertheless has obvious limits. The dream brings lucidity only to those who not only remember their dream but are able to focus on it long enough for them to extract from it some elements of self-knowledge and knowledge of others. For, if the dream reveals a lucidity that seemed unexpected on the part of a sleeping person, it nevertheless presents itself in a somewhat encrypted form to the person who remembers it on waking. We should therefore refer instead to a potential access to a certain form of lucidity which emerges through the task of interpreting the dream.

All dreams are not the fulfilment of an unsatisfied wish

Freud's theory of the unconscious, indissociable from repression, from the resurfacing of repressed wishes and from the notion of a censorship, led the father of psychoanalysis to see the dream as the (disguised) fulfilment of a (repressed) wish left unsatisfied in waking life. This generalisation, seen as ill-founded both by his contemporaries and by many researchers who have come after him, prevented him from realising that the dream can be as much an opportunity to express a current or anticipatory fear, to relive a past traumatic situation, or simply to set out a problem as it can be the chance to fulfil in the imagination a wish that has not been satisfied in waking life.

Freud deliberately simplifies and generalises his central argument of the veiled fulfilment of an unconscious wish. This is a necessary element in his theory:

> I might then have gone on to say that the meaning of a dream turned out to be of as many different sorts as the processes of waking thought; that in one case it would be a fulfilled wish, in another a realized fear, or again a reflection persisting on into sleep, or a resolution (as in the instance of Dora's dream), or a piece of creative thought during sleep, and so on. Such a theory would no doubt have proved attractive from

its very simplicity, and it might have been supported by a great many examples of dreams that had been satisfactorily interpreted, as for instance by the one which has been analysed in these pages.[81]

On a variety of different pretexts, he would thus continue his search to seek out the hidden unfulfilled wish, even at times resorting to some interpretive acrobatics.

But the exercise has its limits. If dreams do not appear explicitly as the fulfilments of wishes, it is because the wish is so well hidden, and Freud recognised the 'influence of the censorship'[82] at work in dreams. When the dream is clearly too painful to be considered as the fulfilment of a wish, Freud changed his tune only to carry on singing the same tune! The painful dream would still fit the description of the dream-wish, except that the wish is no longer that of the unconscious but that of the ego or of the censoring agency.[83] In this way, 'punishment dreams' would still be wish-fulfilments, but coming from the ego, who would react to the suppressed unconscious wish by wishing to be punished.[84] And when a patient, doubting the pertinence of the argument of the fulfilment of a wish in the dream, presents him with a dream that appears not to be the fulfilment of a wish, Freud claims that she has indeed fulfilled an unconscious wish, notably that of contradicting him, of proving him wrong by having such a dream[85] – a fine example of how to act as though everything confirmed his argument, even when everything appeared to prove him wrong!

Freud himself came late to an awareness of the importance of dreams provoked by the 'repetition compulsion'. In *Beyond the Pleasure Principle* (1920),[86] he acknowledges the existence of a principle which is not that of pleasure but that of the compulsive repetition of the same disturbing or even totally traumatic situations (train crashes, accidents, wars, etc.). Dreams, but also children's games or the interactional framework of psychoanalytic therapy, are moments among others where the reactivation of situations that are not always desirable or associated with pleasure can be observed. The war of 1914–18 would cause Freud to change his stance by making it possible for him to envisage other grounds for oneiric expression. The dreams of soldiers (as of those afflicted with traumatic neuroses), which repeat the unbearable shocks of the war, led Freud to modify his interpretation. Traumatised individuals who had not been able to control an event that had happened out of the blue, they repeated the distressing event in their dreams in order to control symbolically what they had experienced 'passively'. Yet, for all that, Freud did not modify subsequent editions of *The Interpretation of Dreams*.

Like ordinary language, the language of dreams does not have only one orientation. To say that the dream is restricted to the expression of unconscious wishes amounts to saying that verbal language allows us to express only the wishes of subjects or speakers. Yet language, whether it is visual and oneiric or verbal and used during waking life, performs a whole range of functions, expressing wishes, anger, anxiety, fear, doubt, ambivalence, commands, etc. It is as though Freud wanted to reduce all the operations of oneiric language to one single linguistic operation, notably one in which the dreamer expresses a wish that their waking life has not allowed them to fulfil:

> It is probable that there are many different sources of dreams, and that there is no single line of explanation for all of them. Just as there are many different sorts of jokes. Or just as there are many different sorts of languages. . . . [Freud] wanted to find one explanation which would show what dreaming is. He wanted to find the *essence* of dreaming. And he would have rejected any suggestion that he might be partly right but not altogether so. If he was partly wrong, that would have meant for him that he was wrong altogether – that he had not really found the essence of dreaming.[87]

The dream too, can have a great many uses.

In 1903, Théodore Flournoy (1854–1920), a Genevan doctor and psychologist, published in the Geneva *Archives de psychologie* the first commentary in French of the *Traumdeutung*. He commented positively on the fact that Freud attributed a significance to the dream instead of considering it as 'simply an incoherent and haphazard jumble of mnesic debris'. But he identified some limits or defects, including that of the misuse of generalisations:

> Some will even find that he is sometimes too ingenious, and that his interpretation of some of the dreams is extremely far-fetched. And we must admit that the universality he gives to his argument leaves us perplexed. No doubt, a great many of our dreams, when closely examined, are indeed no more than 'the disguised fulfilment of a repressed wish'; but to say that this applies to all dreams seems to us more difficult to accept.

Flournoy observed that in certain cases the dreams are based on a fear rather than on a wish or a desire, and he attributes the dream with a preparatory function rather than just that of remembering the past.[88] In short, Freudian theory seemed to him much too narrow, and he summed up these points of disagreement by stating that dreams 'express all our tendencies – not only wishes, but fears', that 'these are not only repressed tendencies but also tendencies that the self perfectly admits' and that 'not everything is disguised'.[89]

Sometime later, Marcel Foucault expressed the same reservations about Freudian theory. He acknowledges the existence of dreams that correspond to the model of the fulfilment of an unfulfilled wish. For example, a pupil forbidden from leaving the premises by his school dreams that, by subterfuge, he succeeds in joining his classmates. Another pupil dreams that he misses the train which would have taken him to school for the beginning of term, thus expressing a wish to prolong the pleasure of the holidays.[90] But, for Foucault, both fear and desire contribute to generating dreams that are 'a mental rumination', a means of preparing for action to come and of facing the difficulties which arise, and not just a compensation. For example, when a very gifted pupil dreams that his name is not inscribed on the roll of honour,[91] he is revealing the fears of someone who seeks to maintain his educational status:

> I do not believe that Freud's theory, according to which every dream is the fulfilment of a wish, can explain the facts I have just cited; but I think rather that fear acts as an organising force in the dream in the same way as positive desire. . . . positive desire is inventive; it suggests the means through which it can be immediately satisfied or else those which will mean its future satisfaction is at least prepared for. In this way this mental rumination which forms the dream is useful: it provides the mind with the means, of an extremely variable value moreover, to achieve the ends to which it aspires . . . fear acts in the same way; it also suggests means of action, namely, the means through which the threatened danger can be avoided.[92]

But, in all fairness, we can understand why Freud, against all factual evidence, chose to uphold his argument about the fulfilment of a wish in the dream. Like the hypothesis of a censorship which made possible and even necessary the search for all the ways in which the dream is supposed to elude the surveillance of the censorship, the argument of the fulfilment of a wish supports the idea that dreams do indeed have meanings which can be sought and that they are not simply an incoherent and meaningless series of images. In an enthusiastic letter to Fliess on 16 May 1897, Freud makes this significant comment: 'I have been looking into the literature on the subject and feel like the Celtic imp: "How glad I am that no man's eyes have pierced the veil of Puck's disguise." No one has the slightest suspicion that dreams are not nonsense but wish fulfilment.'[93]

The undeniable achievement of Freud's work, consisting as it does in a refusal to reduce the dream to biological or neurological elements, in contradicting all those who saw in dreams only something shapeless, incoherent and unintelligible and in endeavouring to describe all the cognitive processes at work in dreams (visualisation, dramatisation, symbolisation, condensation, displacement, etc.), blinded him to the reduction he was enforcing by reducing all dreams to the disguised fulfilment of a repressed unconscious wish. It is as though Freud were using a key which allowed him to leave firmly closed those wrong doors labelled 'organic-biological reductionism' and 'unintelligibility of the dream', all of which lead to dead-ends, but that the key opened only a small door in a huge edifice which cannot be completely accessed in that way. It should be added that this key also enabled him to bring together a series of problems and, as a result, to unlock solutions to a whole range of neurotic symptoms, including those associated with hysteria, as well as dreams.[94]

But we can put aside the idea of the fulfilment of an unconscious wish, and of the disguising of this wish because of the censorship, without abandoning the idea that the dream makes sense and that the modalities through which it is expressed, which are linked to the specific constraints imposed on it, merit description. Freud's error is also an error about what a theory can or should be. He feels the need to find the *key* which will open all dreams, whereas any such attempt is by nature doomed to failure.

A general theory is entirely possible and even desirable, but it cannot amount to one single principle that enables all dreams to be explained. The sole purpose of such a theory must be to uncover the processes or mechanisms at work in the dream, to show us what the images of dreams are made of, and what is needed – what kind of information on dreamers' lives – in order to link these images in such a way as to enable them to be interpreted. Such a theory does not provide an interpretation grid or a general principle to explain where all dreams come from; rather, it simply offers a way of proceeding so that, with each new dream, the task of questioning the dreamer, of clarification, of bringing together relevant elements and of interpreting all of that can be repeated.

7

The Existential Situation and Dreams

> All our feelings betray themselves in dreams: all our life repeats
> itself in them, our heart is laid bare; we dream of our loves, of our
> anxieties, of our hopes, of our past, more often than we think.
> (Gabriel Tarde, *Sur le sommeil*, p. 73)

The expression 'existential situation', which is used in the general formula for the interpretation of dreams,[1] refers to the whole range of problems, cares and preoccupations, at varying levels of consciousness, which each individual must face within the context of their own personal history – a history which itself depends on that of the groups and institutions frequented by that individual either now or in a near or more distant past (family, friends, school, church, work, political party, union, clubs or associations, etc.). In order to understand the particular existential situation an individual might be facing, we need therefore to put in place sociological methods which objectify biographical paths rather than relying on philosophies of existence.[2]

If researchers in human sciences have succeeded in sociologising a notion such as that of 'suffering',[3] they have more or less totally abandoned the question of 'care' (*Sorge*) or 'concern' (*Besorgen*) to the derealising philosophy of someone like Martin Heidegger,[4] just when the German philosopher was trying to draw a clear distinction between his conception of 'care' and the 'cares of life' experienced by individuals living in society, on which the social sciences should be primarily focusing. In spite of its philosophical connotations, the term 'existential' in the notion of 'existential situation' does not therefore refer to anything other than the ordinary, prosaic problems of the real existence or co-existence of individuals.[5]

The existential issues of any one individual consist of the galaxy of more or less interconnected problems which they come up against and which evolve throughout their lives. These problems, initially rooted in the family unit, and which tend to appear or to alter at each stage in the life cycle and whenever there are changes of direction or other biographical changes of varying degrees of importance, can sometimes be linked to troubling or problematic dispositions (anxious, fearful, depressive dispositions, tendencies to self-blame, to a lack of self-esteem, etc.), sometimes to a clash between opposing dispositions (which lead to tensions or to permanent doubts), or sometimes to crises triggered by an imbalance between an individual's dispositions and their life context (frustrated, thwarted or inappropriate dispositions with feelings of failure, shame or malaise). But often these are issues linked to particular spheres of activity, to levels of social engagement, to specific relationships or situations such as relationships with men or women, with authority, an inferiority or superiority complex in one area or another, issues associated with sexuality, with illness, with the body, etc.

I initially came up with the expression[6] 'existential situation' in order to explain the processes of literary creation in the work of Franz Kafka.[7] The writer is tormented by a series of problems linked to his father, to his creative output, to his relationships with women and with marriage, to the tensions he experiences between professional demands and creative work, etc. In his writing Kafka explores his pressing existential questions, his internal tensions, his feelings of guilt and of oppression, turning to literature as a means of liberation in an attempt to untangle his *existential knots*.[8] The different elements of the existential situation find expression equally well, moreover, in oneiric productions[9] as they do in literary productions, and, as is the case with the creative text, dealing only with the verbal surface of the dream account without linking the account or the text to the underlying elements of the dreamer's existential situation would, to my mind, make no sense whatsoever.

As Thomas Morton French demonstrated so perfectly, if the dream does not at first sight seem to make sense, it is because we still do not know how it fits in relation to the context of the dreamer's life and in particular because we are unaware of the problems with which he or she is wrestling at the time of the dream.[10] French uses the expression 'cognitive structure' – a somewhat unfortunate one given the centrality of the emotional dimension in the dream – to refer to the way in which the meanings of the dream fit together like the pieces of a jigsaw puzzle, and how this puzzle fits in with the reality of the dreamer's life. The cognitive structure of the dream is a galaxy of related problems, among which is to be found the 'focal problem[11] of the dreamer at the time of the dream. In order to interpret the dream correctly, we must then, according to French, learn to identify both the focal problem, which has its own history and more often than not focuses on questions of interpersonal adaptation, and the triggering stimulus which actively provoked it.

The concept of the existential situation seems to me to be particularly suited to the study of dreams, given that no dream is ever totally without significance, nor does it ever deal only with perfectly anodyne situations. On the evidence of the current state of knowledge relating to oneiric productions, we can reasonably put forward the hypothesis according to which *the dream space is the treatment centre for problems currently unresolved but which echo problematic situations from the past*: preoccupations, intra-psychic or interpersonal conflicts or tensions, frightening, awkward, troublesome or distressing situations, etc. We can therefore say, in the words of Roger Bastide, that 'personal dreams evoke the dreamer's struggles with existence.'[12]

The dreamer is always at the heart of the dream,[13] even if they do not necessarily appear in all the dreams or if their place is not always very clear (they can experience the scene and see people as though through the lens of a subjective camera without seeing themselves; they can also see themselves in first one character and then another, or in several characters at a time). But, in all cases, unsolicited and unintentionally produced by the dreamer, the dream is necessarily a projection of their thoughts or preoccupations: 'Dreams are completely egotistical',[14] as Freud so rightly said. The study of dreams means going to the very heart of the problems facing the dreamer in waking life and understanding how he or she deals with them: 'Oneiric dreams do not limit themselves to representing the preoccupations and aspirations of the individual; they are often indicative of the way he thinks about the world and reacts to other people.'[15]

Even if their approach is, as we have seen, somewhat superficial, quantitative and qualitative content analyses of dream accounts succeed in highlighting these links between the problems of waking life, which vary according to the situation in which dreamers find themselves, and oneiric themes. So, for example, brothers and sisters with a disabled sibling dream of the problems associated with being disabled, children living in conflict zones dream of scenes of war, trauma victims dream or have nightmares about the traumatic event, incarcerated former members of the Red Brigade dream of the same situations, sports or music students respectively dream more often about sports or music than others, etc.[16]

A study on pregnant women found, for example, that their dreams reflected their preoccupations concerning fertility, pregnancy and birth as well as those about the sex and the health of their children to be. The same study found that women who had good reason to be more anxious were more likely to express or to resolve these feelings through dreams.[17] Summing up her extended research on dreams, Isabelle Arnulf writes, 'The vast majority of dreams deal with the ordinary preoccupations which relate to the family, to loved ones, to leisure activities, and to interactions with people with whom the sleeper studies or works.'[18] And if we dream about people close to us (family, friends, colleagues), it is because, for better or worse, these are the people with whom we are emotionally involved.

In 1972, Calvin S. Hall and Vernon J. Nordby reported a very significant result from quantitative studies, namely that sad dreams or dreams about misfortune are always more frequent than happy dreams, in all the series of dreams experienced by the same individual or by groups of individuals.

For the seven individuals, who reported a total of 709 dreams, 582 contained an aggression, misfortune, or failure, and 313 contained a friendly act, good fortune, or success. . . . These findings for seven dreamers compare favourably with an analysis of 1000 dreams obtained from 200 young adult males and females. There was an aggression, misfortune, or failure in 931 dreams, and a friendly act, good fortune, or success in 573 dreams. The conclusion is obvious. Many more bad things than good things happen in dreams. This conclusion is highlighted by the results obtained from an analysis of emotions experienced in dreams. The emotions of sadness, anger, apprehension, and confusion are mentioned 565 times in the 1000 dream reports of young adults. Happy emotions are mentioned only 137 times.[19]

The study carried out by Hall and Van de Castle mentioned in the second example[20] established that, out of more than 700 emotions expressed in the 1,000 dream accounts, around 80 per cent were negative and only 20 per cent were positive, and that there were 411 cases of 'misfortune' (accidents, injuries, illnesses, losses, obstacles, etc.) and only fifty-eight cases of 'good fortune' (the situations of misfortune are thus seven times more frequent than those of good fortune). Another more recent study confirms these facts.[21] The authors collected 419 dreams and 490 events of waking life from thirty-nine university students (sixteen men and twenty-three women, aged between nineteen and thirty-six) over a period of two weeks and interviewed them about frightening experiences in their lives (n = 714). The results of the study show that three-quarters of the dreams collected featured frightening events compared to only 15 per cent of the events of ordinary life recorded. All this would suggest that dreams are much more about preoccupations than about things which do not pose any particular problem.[22]

To paraphrase Aragon, we could say that 'there is no such thing as a happy dream'. That does not imply that dreams are the overflow channel for all misfortunes, but psychic activity is involved more in unresolved problems (even in the case of happy situations), frustrated desires, the tensions and contradictions of daily life, small and major traumas, and the anticipation of stressful or exciting events scheduled to take place in the near future (exams, job interviews, trips, etc.) than with everyday situations which do not particularly detain the dreamer's attention. If this is the case, then dreams certainly do not allow us to determine the entire heritage of dispositions at the dreamer's disposal or to grasp his or her personality in full, but simply to ascertain the most striking and problematic issues *at work* within him or her. A platform for all worries, all preoccupations, all problems, all conflicts, all tensions, the dream is not the place for the expression of 'the obvious'. The dreamer's problems are like magnetic fields which draw everything towards them, the fixation points towards which images and emotions gravitate: 'The fact is that whenever you are preoccupied with something, with some trouble or with some problem which is a big thing in your life – as sex is, for instance – then no matter what you start from, the association will lead finally and inevitably back to that same theme.'[23]

And it is because the problems which make up the existential situation are relatively stable that there is recurrence in dreams in spite of the apparent diversity of oneiric situations or scenarios. So-called recurrent dreams are therefore only the visible part of a less visible or more discreet coherence rendered possible by the slowly changing structure of the existential situation. Erich Fromm wrote that recurrent dreams 'are expressive of the main theme, of the *leitmotif*, in a person's life, often the key to the understanding of his neurosis or of the most important aspect of his personality.'[24] But we need to know how to search beneath the teeming surface of dreams for the most stable of those slowly moving plates which silently structure the whole.

The dream therefore has nothing to do with the acting out of situations which are 'dreamt of' (wished for, desired, etc.). It is even somewhat paradoxical that, in its commonly understood meaning, the word 'dream' should be used to refer to situations that are very enviable or desirable but which represent ideals, unhoped for, illusory and far removed from reality ('I dream of going round the world', 'I dream of getting rich', 'It's a childhood dream', the 'American dream', 'It's just a dream', 'There's a gap between dream and reality', 'mistaking dreams for reality', etc.). The dream is the exact opposite of such idealised productions. If it takes fantastical and incoherent forms, it is nevertheless extraordinarily realistic, in that it 'works on' elements drawn from the dreamer's real experience both past and present, sometimes dating from the very distant past or, on the contrary, sometimes from much more recent experiences. No doubt the double significance of the word 'dream' has been a factor in impeding the understanding of the dream as a form of expression which takes place during sleep. And we might well wonder if Freud's definition of the dream as 'the fulfilment of an unrealized wish' has not also been contaminated by this rather confused semantic situation.

Dream and outside the dream

In order to interpret dreams correctly, should they be linked to the external circumstances at the time of the dream, to the physical sensations of the dreamer during sleep, to the context of his or her immediate life or indeed past life, and, in particular, to his or her childhood? Scholars who have studied the dream have all responded, in one way or another, to the question of the relevance of what happens outside the dream. And even the choice made by certain content analysts, acting as good formalists, to focus only on dream accounts is a radical way of responding to this question.

The idea that dreams deal with the preoccupations of the dreamer is not a recent one. In his famous *De rerum natura*, Lucretius (first century BC) was already observing how the preoccupations of daily life made their way into our dreams, so that the lawyer sees himself pleading, the general sees himself in the battle, the sailor finds himself facing a storm at sea, etc. And the same idea recurs in *The Interpretation of Dreams* by Artemidorus of Daldis:

> It is the nature of certain experiences to run their course in proximity to the mind and to subordinate themselves to its dictates, and so to cause manifestations that occur in sleep. .... For example, it is natural for a lover to seem to be with his beloved in a dream and for a frightened man to see what he fears, or for a hungry man to eat and a thirsty man to drink and, again, for a man who has stuffed himself with food to vomit or to choke. .... It is possible, therefore, to view these cases in which those types of experiences occur as containing not a prediction of a future state but rather a reminder of a present state.[25]

Artemidorus emphasises the dreamer's emotions, and it could be said that, if the lawyer sees himself pleading and the sailor imagines he is caught up in a storm, it is because these situations are important to them and are at the emotional heart of their ordinary life: 'A man will not dream about things to which he has never given a thought', writes Artemidorus. 'For what men dream even about private things if they have not previously reflected upon them?'[26]

Artemidorus was already advocating a close scrutiny of dreams, particularly with a view to seeing if the dream had any bearing on 'whether he felt happy or unhappy',[27] and attempting as far as possible to find out as much as possible about the dreamer, his age, his sex, his profession, his financial situation, his social status (e.g. whether slave or master), his customs and habits, his physical and psychological state, etc. Handing down his advice to future oneirocritics, he wrote:

> It is profitable – indeed, not only profitable but necessary – for the dreamer as well as for the person who is interpreting that the dream interpreter know the dreamer's identity, occupation, birth, financial status, state of health, and age. Also, the nature of the dream itself must be examined accurately, for the following section will make clear that the outcome is altered by the least addition or omission, so that if anyone fails to abide by this, he must blame himself rather than us if he goes wrong.[28]

The oneirocritic is even particularly vigilant with regard to the quality of information gathered: 'You must examine closely, moreover, the habits of men before the dream, that is, you must carefully inquire into them. And if you are unable to find out anything definite from their own mouths, you should put them aside for the present and find out about them from other people, so that you will not make a mistake.'[29] Artemidorus goes on to point out that, by knowing these habits, it is possible to ascertain whether what was seen in the dream was a habit from daily life or a way of referring to something else – in other words, the use of symbolisation.

Artemidorus is therefore a long way removed from the dream books which, from the Middle Ages right up to today, offer all-purpose dictionaries of symbols by matching univocal meanings to signs. Not only are elements of dreams (places, objects, animals, people sometimes only fleetingly captured) decontextualized (very few long accounts of dreams are included), but such guides assume a universality of meanings and pay no attention to the existential backgrounds of the dreamers. In the Middle Ages, for example, dream books linked 'this reduced content of few words and a univocal meaning also presented in a condensed form'.[30] For example, 'the dreamer saw a cithara, but nothing is said about his relationship with this object.'[31] The object is supposed to mean something in its own right, independently of the dreamer's relationship to it.

But certain practices free themselves from dream books in order to put into practice this connection between the dream itself and information about the state of the dreamer as suggested by Artemidorus. Jean-Claude Schmitt pointed to the existence of this move to focus more attentively on the situation of the dreamers: 'The mother of Guibert [de Nogent] did not rely on any kind of dream book. She discussed the content of the dreams at length with the person concerned and suggested an overall interpretation taking into account the dreamer's spiritual and moral state. Thus, according to her son, "she reviewed with me my devotion to study, my actions and my occupations."'[32]

Eighteenth- and nineteenth-century scholars regularly cited writers such as Lucretius or Artemidorus, either to support the superstitions they themselves believed in or else to note relevant elements from a perspective of a science of dreams. Thus Abbot Jérôme Richard cites Lucius Accius (170–86 BC), who emphasises the links between diurnal preoccupations and nocturnal imagination: 'A very ancient poet said, with as much verity as elegance, that one should not be surprised if men are struck in dreams by the same objects they see and are preoccupied by in the ordinary course of their lives.'[33] Richard is of the opinion that oneirocritics are hardly ever wrong in their interpretation of dreams, because the dreamer provides them with information about his situation: 'Whosoever wishes to become involved with explaining a dream must know who the person who has dreamt it is, what he does, the circumstances of his birth, the state of his health, his age. It was Artemidorus himself who spoke of all these precautions.'[34] For him, it is clear that the dream images are linked 'to what has most strongly affected the mind during waking hours, and to the objects which are most often its concern'.[35] But he emphasises too that the very form of the dream can result in such links going unnoticed. Involuntary and often strange, this form of human expression is nevertheless linked to our thoughts, our feelings and our actions in the waking world:

> Our attention is so absorbed by what the dream presents to us as extraordinary and new that it seems that we dare not go back and remember that we existed, that we had ideas, listened to speeches, made plans, carried out actions, all of which caused it to exist. The disorder in which, during sleep, the imagination presented these different images, and which had a powerful effect on the mind, is all that is noticed on waking; we are filled with amazement and surprise; whereas the habit of reflecting on what has happened would persuade us that we had indeed formed these dreams ourselves without being aware of it, like the thousand other natural and necessary actions which do not require attention even though they are no less perceptible, but which we see as purely natural, and do not try to seek anything marvelous or divine in them.[36]

Almost a century later, Karl Albert Scherner called for a deeper knowledge of the dreamer, essentially from the perspective of the recent circumstances that had provoked the dream:

> With close attention, [the researcher] determines at the same time the circumstances in the dreamer's life before the dream; he reads, in the attitudes and moods of the mind still present in the morning, the kinds of motives which have given rise to the dream, then compares them with what has been said and done; often he reads deep within the mind of the dreamer, far beyond what the dream seems to mean to the person who recounts it, and all his intimate secrets are revealed through the images of dreams produced involuntarily during the night. Nevertheless, a very precise knowledge of the individual situation of the dreamer is necessary in order to follow the trail leading to the true situation and the truth behind the most striking oneiric images, which most often serve as the keystone for the other images in the dream; for the main images of the dream are determined most often by the interests of the dreamer experienced in the preceding day and by their real incarnations.[37]

For Scherner, it was impossible to shed light onto 'the shadowy life of the dream' unless a comparison was made between the dream and the 'real circumstances' of the dreamer. The latter 'can be glimpsed' or 'seek to reveal themselves' in the dream. Even if Scherner did not take into account the fact that any current preoccupations form part of a history and cannot be separated from the dispositions and schemas incorporated by the dreamers, and even if he did not have access to Freud's technique of free association or the methodological tools represented by sociological interviews of a biographical type, he nevertheless understood that oneiric language cannot be deciphered without detailed knowledge of the dreamer.

Armed with this conviction, Scherner set about the task of analysis and embarked on the quest to find the origins of the different images which make up the dream. He succeeded in showing that the elements of the dream were drawn from the dreamer's life, but, unlike Freud, he did not seek to establish what these different images referred to and what they had to say about the existential situation of the dreamer:

> A young man dreams that his aunt surprises him by giving him a present, and that, when he opens it, he discovers to his astonishment that it contains four pairs of short swimming trunks, each one a different colour: white, red, yellow, blue. Who could make sense of this dream without knowing the true origins of the powerful impressions underlying it? And yet it is just a very simple dream. In fact, the dreamer genuinely expected a present from his aunt, having heard about it from a third party; the day before the dream, he had been in the town hall, which had been decorated with lots of multicoloured flags in honour of some important people; furthermore, the dreamer was an outstanding swimmer and practised his art on a daily basis with great pleasure. It was therefore these three significant moments that constituted the dream: the anticipated present from the aunt, the flags at the town hall, and the swimming trunks. From these the significant elements of the dream are skilfully woven, the dream taking as its starting point the most intense element, the expectation of the present, continuing it in the multicoloured flags, and transforming in their turn the latter into swimming trunks of identical colours.[38]

If we link the three elements cited, the dreamer seems to be waiting for some kind of recognition. The present refers to the idea of gratification and of a pleasant surprise. The colour of the flags, with their association with important figures, could mean that he himself was expecting to become an important figure (gratified). And the fact that swimming trunks feature is undoubtedly linked to the fact that the dreamer is an outstanding swimmer and that his skill is acknowledged. Awaiting acknowledgement for what one does and becoming a distinguished figure are, in all likelihood, what the dream in question is about. But, to be totally sure of that, we need to know the dreamer's dispositions (ambitious or timid) and the broader context of his existence (Is he satisfied with his situation or not? Does he hope for changes?).

Freud drew inspiration from this long tradition of studying the links between waking life and dream life: 'dreams are never concerned with things which we should not think it worthwhile to be concerned with during the day, and trivialities which do not affect us during the day are unable to pursue us in our sleep.'[39] He restored to the secondary place the deserved arguments on the role of external circumstances or physical sensations during sleep[40] and described diurnal residues as stimulators (but not the driving force) of the dream. Freud's strength was therefore in seeing that there was a driving force which carried the dream along, and that the 'material' of the dream drawn from the experiences of the previous day was simply what the dreamer was using to express this expressive impulse, the state of sleep favouring such an expression given the accompanying detachment from all the interests of life. But, unfortunately, he placed at the very heart of interpretation an unconscious made up, according to him, of all the repressed events originating for the most part in early childhood, came up with a mechanism of repression linked to the notion of censorship which was to prove problematic, and made the central driving force of the dream correspond to an essentially sexual motive ('a wishful impulse, often of a very repellent kind').[41]

Alfred Adler, for his part, rejected any hypothesis based purely on sexual experience from childhood and linked the dream essentially to the current preoccupations of the dreamer. The dream '"puts an edge" on the dreamer for the solution of a problem in his own particular way':[42]

> The dream is a sketch-like reflection of psychic attitudes and indicates for the investigator the characteristic manner in which the dreamer takes his attitude in regard to a certain problem. It coincides therefore, with the form of the fictitious guiding line, yields only efforts of premeditation, tentative preparations of an aggressive attitude and therefore can be utilized to great advantage for the purpose of understanding these individual preparations, predispositions, and the guiding fiction itself.[43]

Likewise, the psychiatrist and psychotherapist Alphonse Maeder, who was initially close to Freudian psychoanalysis before turning instead to the individual psychology proposed by Adler, sees the dream as 'a "preliminary exercise" for the problems that presented themselves in waking life'.[44] In a letter to Freud on 24 October 1912, Maeder refers to two sides represented in the dream: 'the compensatory meaning' in relation to something lacking in waking life and the 'preparatory exercise to the attainable resolution of conflicts'.[45]

A great many researchers have noticed the reductionism employed by Freud in reducing all dreams to the fulfilment of a wish and all wishes and desires to a sexual dimension. The problems that are worked on in dreams are varied in nature, and their relationship with the real situation of dreamers is equally varied. But challenging Freud, with good reason, on certain specific points, however central, will not be enough to rock the foundations of his general model of interpretation. Instead, what is now needed is the framing of more pertinent proposals on the question of what is expressed in the dream and the linking of these to the more general issue of the processes behind the creation of dreams. Yet both Adler and Maeder were very far from achieving this.

The driving force of emotions

When Maurice Halbwachs turned his attention to dreams, he stressed the importance of 'largely hidden tendencies of our sensibility'[46] and of the 'quite marked emotional tonality [of our dreams]: oppression, preoccupation, painful sensation of not doing what we should be doing, micromania, etc.'[47] The feelings which emerge in our waking lives reappear in dreams: feelings 'of anxiety, of fear and sometimes even of terror, of shame, of embarrassment and also of dissatisfaction caused by powerlessness and failure.'[48]

The importance of emotions has been emphasised repeatedly in studies on dreams: we dream of people, objects, places or situations with which we have emotional involvement. Among the theorists of the dream, Ernest Hartmann in particular succeeded in grasping the full significance of emotions in the oneiric process. Hartmann analysed the dream as a time of connection between recent events and events which resonate with them from a more or less distant past. And, for him, 'emotion . . . is the force which drives or guides the connecting process and determines which of the countless possible connections are actualized at a particular time and thus which images appear in the dream. Dreams "contextualize" the dominant emotion.'[49] But the emotions to which Hartmann is referring are not floating in a vacuum: they are attached to preoccupations, concerns or questions left in suspense. For example, rather than fear in general being played out in the dream, it is the fear of doing wrong, of dying, the fear of failure or of harming others, etc. These are emotionally problematic situations.

If we take the particularly striking case of someone who has recently been involved in a major traumatic event (for example, someone who has escaped from a fire, a rape victim or a survivor of a serious rail crash), there can be no doubt about the problem which preoccupies that individual, invading their thoughts and resurfacing even in their dreams. The connections between the traumatic event experienced and relatively similar events from the past or images seen on television, in the cinema or theatre, or in books, etc., are guided by the emotional preoccupations of the dreamer:

> First the trauma is replayed vividly and dramatically but not necessarily in precisely the way it occurred: there is often at least one major change in the dream, something that did not actually occur. Very rapidly the dreams begin to combine and connect this traumatic material with other material that appears emotionally similar or related. Often, . . . a person who has been through one kind of trauma dreams of all kinds of other traumas that may be related to this same feeling of helplessness, terror or guilt. In some cases this connecting involves reactivating previous trauma and other emotionally important personal themes evoked by the trauma ('rekindling').[50]

Hartmann judiciously uses the case of post-traumatic dreams to reflect on more ordinary dreams, since the post-traumatic dreams tend to magnify the processes at work in the dream:

> But however common or uncommon it may be in our lives, I suggest that trauma can be seen as a paradigm or a simplest case in which we can see most clearly what happens in dreams, and that probably other dreams follow the same pattern though it may be more difficult to discern. In someone who has just experienced a severe traumatic event, we can be quite certain of the dominant emotions even without knowing the person's life in great detail. Of course, past experiences, day residues, etc. are not irrelevant; they are, in fact, what is swept up by the emotion to form the pictures of the dream. I believe, if we move on from trauma to somewhat less dramatic situations, we can still see the same patterns though not always as clearly.[51]

The emotional preoccupations of the dreamer are rarely as powerful as those associated with serious trauma. The emotional force of trauma means that a central, inescapable problem imposes its presence in the dreamer's mental space. But when dreamers have less intense preoccupations, and when several of these combine in dreams, they are much more difficult to recognise and so render the analyst's task infinitely more complex. Only a detailed knowledge of the dreamer, through relatively long-term therapy,[52] psychoanalytic therapy[53] or a series of sociological interviews on dreams and dreamers' lives,[54] will enable the missing elements of the problem or the missing pieces of the puzzle to be retrieved.

The therapeutic and political effects of making problems explicit

If dreams deal with problems of many different sorts, highlighting these problems in the course of interviews, and then through the interpretation of any oneiric and biographical material which has been obtained, will inevitably produce effects which could be called therapeutic, even if these were not deliberately sought by the researcher. In the course of such interviews, dreamers are persuaded to give explicit voice to areas of their experience which they rarely have the time or the opportunity to recount or discuss in the course of ordinary life. By clarifying certain aspects of their preoccupations and establishing links between experiences they would not necessarily have associated without the support of the interview, dreamers become aware of what is on their minds and what it is that is driving them to act, feel or think in a certain way. Because it encourages the verbal expression of experiences, the sociological interview provokes a heightened consciousness which forms the basis of many kinds of therapy.

But the therapeutic effects produced can go hand in hand with political effects, in the broad sense of the term, when, as in the case of sociological interpretation, the interpretation ends up revealing what is collective within the individual and what is impersonal within the most personal experience. Through his tendency to reduce all problems to sexuality, Freud contributed either to 'personalising' his patients' problems or to confining them within the restricted limits of the family sphere. If the problems are of a purely personal nature, the patient must essentially rely on self-analysis in order to resolve them. If the 'personal' problems are of a family nature, the question can then be asked as to how the nature of family relationships can be changed so that such problems become less marked or disappear.[55] And if it turns out that the 'personal' problems are related to structural questions of various sorts (familial, educational, professional, sexual, religious, political, etc.), then their resolution will be largely through a *political process* designed to modify social structures.

This is what Frantz Fanon was suggesting when he discussed the dream of a black friend and patient who was finding it difficult to 'progress' in his professional career.

> I had been walking for a long time, I was extremely exhausted, I had the impression that something was waiting for me, I climbed bar-ricades and walls, I came into an empty hall, and from behind a door I heard noise. I hesitated before I went in, but finally I made up my mind and opened the door. In this second room there were white men, and I found that I too was white.[56]

If the psychoanalyst sees in this the fulfilment of an unconscious wish, Fanon for his part emphasises the profoundly social (and, in this instance, racial) dimension of this wish. The dream reveals 'an inferiority complex' from which he must try to free his patient, but,

> if he is overwhelmed to such a degree by the wish to be white, it is because he lives in a society that makes his inferiority complex possi-ble, in a society that derives its stability from the perpetuation of this complex, in a society that proclaims the superiority of one race; to the identical degree to which that society creates difficulties for him, he will find himself thrust into a neurotic situation.[57]

The consequence of such an interpretation which links the dream to 'the context of the world' is clearly eminently political:

> the black man should no longer be confronted by the dilemma, turn white or disappear: but he should be able to take cognizance of a pos-sibility of existence. In still other words, if society makes difficulties for him because of his color, if in his dreams I establish the expression of an unconscious desire to change color, my objective will not be that of dissuading him from it by advising him to 'keep his place'; on the contrary, my objective, once his motivations have been brought

into consciousness, will be to put him in a position to choose action (or passivity) with respect to the real source of the conflict – that is, towards the social structures.[58]

As soon as the problem at the heart of the dream (the alienation of someone for whom success means becoming white) is recognised as a problem which is rooted in social structures, and therefore external to the patient, treating the patient's neurosis will ultimately mean seeking a way to transform those social structures.

Fanon's comments essentially raise the question of the therapeutic-political function of a sociology of dreams. The use of repeated interviews about dreams and the biography of dreamers inevitably produces therapeutic effects of increased consciousness in dreamers. But, unlike psychoanalysis, sociology forces dreamers to realise that the problems they are working on in their dreams, the concerns or the preoccupations which torment them even when they are asleep, are not unconnected to the structures of the social world and, in particular, to the groups they belong to or have frequented in the past.

8

Triggering Events

> We often have the impression that the dream has seized one or
> more mental issues put aside the day before or in the preceding
> days. These have been abandoned, and tonight's dream picks out
> remnants which had completely disappeared and makes them into
> something scarcely recognisable.
> (Paul Valéry, *Questions du rêve*, p. 105)

The general formula for interpreting practices, like the general formula
for interpreting dreams,[1] which we continue to unfold, chapter by chapter,
reveals the role of triggering elements in the production of practices such
as dreams. The incorporated past (schemas or dispositions), along with
elements of the existential situation, are activated by events (words, specific gestures, or more general situations) which transform the virtual into
the real, potential into action.

The affective schemas, schemas of experience or dispositions which
dreamers carry within them, make their presence felt in the dream only
because they have been *triggered* by the events or circumstances of waking
life, either on the day of the dream itself or in the preceding days. 'I must
begin with an assertion that in every dream it is possible to find a point of
contact with the experiences of the previous day',[2] wrote Freud. Before
him, in 1861, Scherner spoke of the 'sensory impressions of the day, very
vivid and recently felt, the echoes of which reverberate in the dream life,
or as a following on from real objects which have particularly aroused our
inner interest on the previous day.'[3] In the same year, at a time when he
was keeping a dream notebook and noting down each time his 'frame of
mind' before falling asleep, Alfred Maury also emphasised the role of 'circumstances' in the construction of the dream: 'The recollection of images
and sensations lost during the waking state usually provides the dream
with its elements. We dream of what we have seen, said, desired or done.'[4]

The experiences which have occurred during the day (or in the preceding
days) 'provoke' the dream even if they are not strictly speaking the driving

force. This is what Freud called the 'day residue', and the phenomenon has continued to be confirmed, verified and clarified ever since by researchers from all disciplinary horizons. For example, between December 1970 and August 1978, the neurobiologist Michel Jouvet worked on 2,525 personal memories of dreams recorded either during the night or immediately on waking in the morning. From this corpus, he took 400 memories of dreams (130 in the context of ordinary life and 270 during or after trips abroad) for which it was possible to date with precision (between zero and fourteen days) the event which constituted the manifest content of the dream. Out of the 130 ordinary dreams, forty-five incorporate elements from the day itself (34.6 per cent), after which the figure declines rapidly until the sixth day before the dream, but with a significant peak (i.e. 10 per cent) after one week.[5] Ernest Hartmann's study, also based on personal oneiric experiences, indicates the presence of day residues from the day of the dream in 94 per cent out of 800 cases.[6] Another study led by Ari W. Epstein[7] shows that, out of fifty dreams for which a link with a day event could be clearly established, in a little more than half of these the time between the event and the dream was between zero and twenty-four hours, in a little more than a quarter of cases it was between twenty-four and forty-eight hours, in a little less than a fifth of cases it amounted to between forty-eight and seventy-two hours, and in only one case was it even longer. And, summarising research on day residues, Tore A. Nielsen and Russell A. Powell[8] concluded that dreams are about twice as likely to incorporate events which have taken place in the day before the dream (65 to 70 per cent), than they are to include events which took place two days before the dream (30 to 35 per cent).

But, in order to understand the precise nature of this day residue, we need to resituate it in the context of the overall dynamics governing the production of the dream. The recent events from the dreamer's life which can feature in the dream are by no means randomly selected. Such events serve to reawaken episodes from the dreamer's incorporated past and are linked to elements of his or her existential situation that lie at the heart of the dream. In order to understand why these recent events, along with the elements from the past which can find an echo in them, resurface in dreams, we must assume that these recent actualisations have a deferred action during sleep.

Freud grasped the essence of the matter by linking recent events and tendencies hidden deep with the unconscious, even if, in my view, the exact nature of that link was not always correctly formulated. He wrote, for example, that 'Something which is derived from our conscious life and shares its characteristics – we call it "the day's residues" – combines with something else coming from the realm of the unconscious in order to construct a dream.'[9] This concept of combination suggests some kind of harmony between the two elements, whereas in fact it is more the case that the recent events, which the dreamer is sometimes capable of remembering, have reawakened incorporated schemas or dispositions constituted over the course of past experiences and of which the dreamer is no longer conscious.

Freud is on firmer ground when he refers sometimes to 'the source of the dream'[10] or to 'the experience of the previous day which provoked it'[11] in order to describe the role of these recent events. Present events permanently reopen segments of our past which the demands and imperatives of the day prevent us from dwelling on. Conversely, it could also be said that these events attract the dreamer's attention only because they echo sequences of past experiences and the problems associated with them. Recent triggers (those of the previous day) are effective only because the schemas of experience are present in an incorporated form and because the dreamer is ready or willing to perceive and respond to these events. The triggering event can play this role successfully only because the dreamer is susceptible to it. Without a particular framework of sensitivity, the dreamer would not therefore be affected by the event or situation in question and would not dream the dream that he or she does.

Freud talks about the 'unimportant details'[12] of the day which the dreamer brings into his dream. But this apparently unimportant, insignificant or trivial characteristic of the life circumstances of the dreamer is in no sense a way of eluding the censorship by distracting attention from the important to the secondary. These 'details' only appear unimportant to the outside gaze of the analyst who fails to see how the most insignificant present is infused with the dreamer's own incorporated past. The most trivial recent impression can reactivate far more traumatic past experiences: 'I knew a university lecturer', wrote René Allendy,

> who, each time he found himself in an unpleasant situation (illness, worries), would dream he was sitting the final exams of his teaching course, which, in his case, had taken place in a state of great anxiety and poor health. . . . The most trivial emotions of the day can bring back very intense memories of the past (a minor dispute with a colleague can reignite stories from the war and bayonet attacks).[13]

Yet these 'unimportant details' are simply one of the two elements which make up the ensemble formed by the incorporated past (dispositions or schemes and the nature of the dreamer's existential situation) and the context of recent life.

The internal stimuli which trigger the dream only have meaning therefore at the intersection between the incorporated past and these recent situations. The dream creates a story which is a blend of past situations and experiences and present situations and experiences. And this blend is capable of taking the form of condensed hybrid images or of bringing together people, places or objects which would never come into contact in real life, thus giving the dream an incoherent or incongruous appearance.

Two opposing errors should thus be avoided when interpreting dreams: 1) that which consists in seeing in the dream only the (disguised) expression of a childhood past and 2) that which consists in seeing in the dream only the manifest (totally transparent) expression of current preoccupations. The former is the one most often made by psychoanalysis and the latter by content analysts, who focus exclusively on the manifest content of dream accounts. In order to take both of these into account simultaneously, and to know what provokes the presence in the dream of specific people, objects, places, etc., it is imperative to be familiar both with the context of the dreamer's recent life (and in particular that of the day(s) preceding the dream) and with the links that this recent situation shares with a series of relatively similar past situations.[14]

The day residue: theoretical and methodological inaccuracies

But let us return to the question of the triggering event. A great many studies focusing on 'day remains' or 'day residues' – in other words, on the elements of the day preceding the dream and which feature in it – often suffer from a certain degree of imprecision concerning their nature.[15] The question needs to be asked, for example, before embarking on any kind of calculation, as to whether estimating the time involved for the day residue to be incorporated in the dream makes any sense at all, something these researchers have failed to do. Some research goes to great lengths to date day residues precisely and attempts to identify consistencies and even rules, centred notably on the peak of memories dated around seven days before the dream, even though there is no sense of clarity about the precise nature of what is actually being 'measured' and on the method applied in order to do this 'measuring'.

First of all, the term 'remains' or 'residue' tends to make these elements into a *passive* component which, detached from the course of waking life, finds itself incorporated into the oneiric structure. Yet these elements are, in the chronological order of experiences, *triggers* of associations, *stimuli* which activate the processes of analogy.[16] They therefore play a fully *active* role in the process. They become passive material only if we neglect to think of things in the context of their dynamic process. This is what occurs when we adopt the point of view of the learned *lector* who has the dream account in front of his eyes and who speculates about the origin of the elements which make up the dream.

Next, we should examine the methods used by researchers to collect these elements of diurnal life, for example by 'objectively' comparing the waking life diary kept by the dreamer – but with what guidance about how to keep such a diary? – and dream accounts? – or by asking the dreamer to identify which elements of the dream remind him or her of aspects of waking life on the preceding day. Or else by questioning dreamers about each element of the dream in order to find out what it makes them think of, a technique which comes close to the practice of free association advocated by Freud.

Asking dreamers to keep a diary of the events of their waking life in order to be able to compare it to their dream accounts can present considerable problems of which many scholarly researchers seem to be unaware. In reality, a potentially infinite number of facts, events, objects, people, places, animals, etc., could occur in the days preceding the dream (and one can only imagine the complexity of the situation the further back in time one goes), and it is clearly not possible for the dreamer to note them all. If no advice is given as to the nature of what is being sought, the dreamer may perhaps make a selection depending on what he or she considers to be important or in relation to the amount of time spent in doing certain things. And if the dreamer is explicitly asked to note down events with significant emotional impact, then only a tiny part of the elements of waking life will be selected, and, without putting it into so many words, we are clearly running counter to the Freudian hypothesis on the sometimes apparently insignificant or banal nature of the daily residue. Without acknowledging it theoretically, the researcher often considers that only those elements which qualify as 'striking', 'powerful', 'emotionally charged', can constitute day residue, whereas the memory of the micro-events of waking life can be unreliable precisely because they are too 'small' or too 'trivial' to be systematically memorised.

But the blindness is at its most evident when researchers decide to ask people external to the research (referred to not without significance as 'judges', these do not in principle have any interest in underestimating or overestimating the presence of day residues) to compare the diaries of waking life and the dream notebooks in order to establish what is day residue and what is not.[17] The falsely scientific objectivity which is aimed for is supposed to be obtained thanks to the impartiality of the judges without fundamentally questioning either the materials they are asked to compare or the cognitive operations they need to apply in doing so. How can such impartial 'judges' see the connections between situations about which they know very little? For example, if the dreamer dreams about a hat, and one of the striking things he had experienced in the days before the dream involved a person who was wearing this kind of hat, nobody except him is in a position to detect this connection if he had omitted to mention the hat in his diary.

Starting out from the finished dream in order to ask the dreamer what, retrospectively, reminds them of things they have experienced in waking life is already a lot less artificial. The dreamer is indeed best placed to say what, in the dream, reflects their diurnal experiences. But the situation is nevertheless not without its difficulties, for asking a dreamer to carry out this task of making connections (between diurnal life and dreams) unaided presupposes they have a spontaneous capacity to recollect scenes, objects, people, places, etc., encountered during the days preceding the dream. In reality, nothing could be more difficult. And that is why Freud's practice of free association or the sociological interview about the dream represent the most pertinent solutions, in so far as they offer the dreamer some support in the somewhat systematic search for relationships or links. On this point, Freud shows himself to be infinitely more subtle and relevant than those who often reproach him for not having adopted a genuinely scientific approach (by which they mean an experimental rather than a clinical approach).

We may wonder too what leads researchers to consider that two elements – one taken from waking life, the other taken from dream accounts – are sufficiently similar to enable them to decide whether the element from waking life is a diurnal residue or not. Is a sometimes rather hazy analogy in terms of situation ('travelling', 'going somewhere with a feeling of anxiety', 'crossing a road', 'buying something', etc.) enough to qualify the element in question as a day residue? Should we, for that matter, identify the day residue on the basis of isolated elements (dreaming about a cat, a knife, a hat, a town or a building, a particular person), an approach which might lead to doubts about whether this is indeed a day residue in the sense Freud intended (if I dream about a cat – and not about a cat which does something specific in a specific situation – how can I know if this relates to a cat I encountered yesterday or to one I saw a fortnight ago, or to all the cats I have encountered in the course of my existence?), or on the basis of situations (e.g.: a cat playing with a ball, a cat which scratches, etc.)? And if only the broader situation seems to correspond (e.g. 'going somewhere but feeling scared of missing something'), but without any specific element corresponding (going to an airport but a completely different airport than one actually visited, going to the station rather than to the airport, going to the bank but being worried it might be closed, etc.), can it nevertheless be considered a day residue? So many questions which are never raised by those preoccupied with measurement.

Finally, we may wonder how it is possible to determine the exact moment in time of the 'day residue'. When the elements concerned are very specific and unique (e.g. seeing a woman with a very particular hat the day before the dream; knocking over a pan of boiling milk, etc.), they can be easily situated. But when they are the ordinary and frequently occurring elements of everyday life, it makes little sense to situate them precisely in time (e.g. the dreamer saw his mother in a dream, but he sees her every day; the scene takes place in the kitchen, but that is where they eat every day, etc.). Michel Jouvet himself highlights this 'difficult issue of the *precise* dating of an event when the dreamer's experience remains unchanging': 'How can we date a banal event with any precision if it is something which happens on a regular basis in the same house, the same workplace, the same street, the same town, even the same country?'[18]

Rather than making so much effort to collect data which are inexact in terms of their validity and acquired in conditions potentially subject to doubt, a far more urgent task would be to explore how the elements of waking life, from the most recent to the most distant, link together, and how these combine with the incorporated past of dreamers to produce, in the specific context represented by sleep, dreams which can only be accessed thanks to the accounts of them provided by dreamers.

The day residue: the inertia of habit

Various different studies appear to show that there is a force of inertia exerted on dreams by the past. The case of dreams experienced by people while travelling effectively proves that a change of environment does not immediately result in the new environment featuring in dreams. The brain needs to have begun to assimilate new habits in order to integrate elements of the current life into dreams. 'In the case of my own dream bank', writes Michel Jouvet, 'I listed 306 dream memories, collected over ten to twelve days after twenty trips abroad (either for a period of five days or for periods of ten, fifteen or twenty days). ... The results demonstrate that, the longer the trip, the greater the percentage of memories of dreams related to the new environment (from 7 per cent for the first week to 42 per cent for the third week).'[19] Similarly, the case of Tama, a Bassari from south-east Senegal, has been closely studied by ethnologists. Born in 1939 or 1940, he came to France in 1964, following an invitation by anthropologists, for a period of 148 days (221 dreams), and again in 1967 for 134 days (278 dreams). In Tama's case, only 15 per cent of day residues were found in the dreams he had while he was living in France, whereas when he was at home in Senegal the figure rose to 85 per cent; and the situation was the same on his return to Senegal. Michel Jouvet concludes from this that his unconscious 'has not assimilated life in France':[20] 'Tama dreams only of his native village, of his friends, and of his activity as a stockbreeder and farmer, even though he is wandering through the streets of Paris every day. Each night, his unconscious unlocks a suitcase in which he finds his father, his mother, his wives and his brothers.'[21] These results are consistent with those of researchers who have worked on the dreams of cosmonauts. 'They collected many dreams experienced by cosmonauts during their space missions, in a state of weightlessness, and noticed that these cosmonauts dreamt that they were at home, with their families or in a terrestrial environment, whereas they had only 3 per cent of *Traumtag* relating to their weightless condition.'[22]

There may seem to be incompatibility between the facts presented by Michel Jouvet (you need to be in an environment for a long time before it really starts to feature in dreams) and those put forward by Freud on the subject of the day residue (which suggest that events from the day preceding the dream can feature in it). But this is by no means the case. Elements of the immediate present (people, places, objects, etc.) enter explicitly into the dream when this has already acquired a certain historic weight for the dreamer; it is therefore only a false present. It is not only the immediate present that finds its way into the dream but anything to which the dreamer is accustomed. This fact becomes evident whenever there are abrupt changes in a dreamer's life circumstances, as is the case for travellers or migrants, where it is often several weeks before new habits are established and the new circumstances begin to feature in dreams. However, it is the events, interactions and problems that feature in this new context which activate elements of the incorporated past. The present always activates the past, but it enters the fabric of the dream only in an explicit, manifest way when it has attained a certain weight or the necessary existential significance for the dreamer.

The deferred effects of triggering events

One of the particularities of the dream lies in the fact that the present triggering context – the day remains or residues – is not the immediate context of the dream production. The context of sleep provides a stage where all the associations provoked or triggered by events, of varying degrees of significance in the eyes of the dreamer, which took place on the day of the dream or in the preceding days can be played out. It is as though the context of sleep leaves the way clear for the action of internal stimuli which are 'kept in reserve' and linked to recent triggering events, providing an opportunity for the embodied past to find expression through a series of connections between analogous situations.

Unlike the external stimuli of waking life, the stimuli which trigger dreams are produced internally. Many of the demands – both formal and moral – associated with waking life are absent during sleep, and 'reactions' to internal stimuli can only be mental rather than physical ones. 'When we sleep', write Katherine Macduffie and George A. Mashour, 'our primary sensory zones are deactivated. Therefore, all the information supplied to the dreaming brain is endogenously generated. Motor output is also blocked, and thus all responses are similarly internally restricted.'[23] The dreamer's reduced awareness of the external sensory stimuli combined with the weak activation of the prefrontal cortex responsible for all the reflexive operations of control and planning facilitate the formation of connections between past and present experiences of a recent or more distant nature: 'In the absence of external stimulation, and with a hypoactive PFC [prefrontal cortex], the dreamer is both "off-line" and "off the clock". Rather than restricting the brain to silence, the inhibition of these two elements of waking consciousness can free the brain for hyperassociation.'[24]

As in children's games or in daydreams, the absence of *immediate* external stimulations provides the individual with an opportunity to 'replay' the unlocking of an entire incorporated past through a context which is recent but not present at the moment of the dream. For this reason, the dream can be described as one of the main access routes to elements of the existential situation and to the incorporated past of the subject (even if access to this pathway is often impeded on account of the specific properties of oneiric images).

The dream is therefore the *deferred* expression of an elaboration which began to germinate in the waking state and which was halted, inhibited, by the multiple ordinary demands of waking life (all the things an individual feels they need to do or say). It is in this respect that dreams closely resemble artistic creations and represent a space set aside from the flow of practical activities for the expression of a certain number of problems that are preoccupying the creator. Even those individuals with little cultural connection and those most caught up in practicalities and action are, for the duration of the dream, plunged into a *creative form of expression beyond the reach of any practical injunction*. At work within them, and beyond their volition, are all those things, both positive and negative, that concern and preoccupy them.

Nocturnal perceptions and sensations

One final point relating to the question of triggering events needs to be addressed. Some of those who have seized upon dreams in a resolutely scientific perspective have attempted to see oneiric language as the effect of internal physical sensations (notably pain of various kinds: stomach pains, muscular cramps, high temperatures, etc.) and external sensory stimulations (essentially auditory, visual, olfactory and tactile) on sleeping thought. For example, Abbot Jérôme Richard (1766) was convinced that dream images were linked to 'the state of the organs' of the dreamer.[25] And, according to Moreau de la Sarthe (1820), 'to dream of an open window, you must feel cold in bed and transform this sensation into a nocturnal vision.'[26] In this way Moreau links the account of the dream to the description of nocturnal physical sensations. In the same way, Alfred Maury (1861) dreamt as a child that his head was resting on an anvil, that someone was hitting him with a hammer and that his head melted like ice. When he awoke his head was bathed in sweat because of the heat and he could hear hammer blows. He concluded that the effects of the heat and the sound of the hammer blows had brought about the images of his dream.[27] Maury even carried out further experiments which proved that the sounds, smells, physical contacts, etc., perceived during sleep find their way into dreams. For him, 'external sensations are very much present in dreams ..., they are often the starting point.'[28] Yet, all the examples he gives show that it is interpretations or transpositions of these sensations which find their way into dreams.

The idea of linking dreams with elements of the dreamer's life (and, specifically, with events taking place during sleep) implies already having a materialist conception of man, like that made possible by Descartes two centuries previously. From this point of view, Freud could be said to be just as much a materialist as some of his predecessors, but his materialism is neither organicist nor perceptionist. If dreams are indeed associated to the experiences of dreamers, the link is generally not to nocturnal sensory experiences, whether internal or external, but to the experiences from both the past (dating back to early childhood) and the present (the day or the hours preceding the dream), acquired as a social being. But that kind of materialism, which we could call 'socio-psychic' since it situates the origin of dreams in human relationships and focuses only on the psychic or mental traces that these relationships have left in the socialised body of the dreamer, and which can be partially accessed only through conversations with the patient or in psychoanalysis, implies an antipositivist scientific approach. Freud commented that he was not surprised to observe the overestimation of non-psychic stimuli, since these were after all the easiest to detect and to confirm through experiments, and the psychiatric thinking of his time is very marked by this 'somatic view of the origin of dreams'.[29] In order to make the question of dreams progress scientifically, Freud had to take up a position somewhere between a physiological materialism and an unfounded spiritualism.

Freud did not deny that certain physical perceptions or sensations could occur in dreams: 'It is generally recognized that sensory stimuli arising during sleep influence the content of dreams: this can be proved experimentally and is among the few certain (but incidentally, greatly overvalued) findings of medical investigation into dreams.'[30] But when this is the case, such perceptions or sensations are neither the core nor the driving force of the dream and appear only in a *transposed* form in the highly visual account which has its own logic and which sometimes absorbs elements as they occur.[31] Dreams can therefore make use of the dreamer's physical sensations or of external events, perceived by the dreamer while sleeping, in order to pursue their narrative. In doing so, they 'do not simply reproduce the stimulus; they work it over, they make allusions to it, they include it in some context, they replace it by something else.'[32] During the night, there might be a bright light, the sound of a bell or an alarm, a smell, a sensation of feeling cold, an insect bite, etc. But these sensations or these perceptions, when they are not quite simply ignored altogether,[33] do not form the whole of the dream and are transposed into it so that a thunder clap can be integrated in the form of a gunshot and the creaking of a door as robbers breaking in, a foot poking out of the bed turns into a dream about a collapsing floor, etc. Proof that the logic of the oneiric narrative is more important than the particular elements integrated into it, and that these do not constitute the central explanation of the narrative, lies in the fact that the same stimuli appear in very different forms in different dreams; the ringing of an alarm can become the sound of a church bell, a bell round an animal's neck, the sound of breaking crockery, etc.[34]

Freud was not the first person to think along these lines. For example, in 1861, Karl Albert Scherner described the dream material as originating from 'organic somatic stimuli' but pointed out that these 'only furnish the mind with elements which it then uses according to the projects of its imagination.'[35] Léon d'Hervey de Saint-Denys also expressed doubts in 1867 about the significance of organic causes:

For my own part, having drawn on a long observation of more accurate, and particularly more positive, evidence, I am a long way from attributing to organic causes such an important influence on the origins and the workings of all our dreams. . . . Using my analysis of several dreams, I shall attempt to demonstrate that it is the association of ideas alone, in general, which governs the course of the dream.[36]

For these writers, as for Freud, the logic of the dream comes first, and the effects of both internal and external stimuli are secondary and form part of this logic. Although critical of numerous aspects of psychoanalysis, research in neuroscience and cognitive psychology does not contradict it on this point.[37]

9

The Context of Sleep

Defining dreams through sleep
(Gabriel Tarde, *Sur le sommeil*, p. 50)

In the course of the preceding chapters, we have seen how the incorporated past, the existential situation and triggering elements interlink in the process of oneiric production. The final key element of the general formula for the interpretation of dreams[1] is the *context of sleep* – that is to say, the context within which the dream images unfold.

The dream is a form of expression with structural properties that are linked to the particular conditions of its enunciation. In spite of his hesitations about turning it into an object of sociological study, Maurice Halbwachs correctly identified the problem of the dream by observing that the difference 'between dream thoughts and waking thoughts' lies in the fact that 'they do not both develop in the same context.' In spite of their differences in approach, Maury and Freud nevertheless were in agreement on this question:

> When Maury compares dreams to certain forms of insanity, he senses that, in both cases, the subject is living in his own world, where relationships are established between people, objects, words, which make sense only to him. Outside the real world, forgetting both the physical laws and the social conventions, the dreamer, like the lunatic, undoubtedly engages in an internal monologue. . . . But when Freud attaches to the dream visions the value of signs whose meaning he looks for in the hidden preoccupations of his subject, he is essentially saying the same thing.[2]

In order to be properly understood, the context of sleep should be described as a context marked at the same time by social, semiotic, psychic and cerebral properties.

Cerebral and psychic constraints

Contrary to the image we may have of him today from a neuroscientific point of view, Freud was already writing in his *Interpretation of Dreams* that, in order to understand dreams, it was vital to acknowledge that the 'the state of sleep' entailed 'modifications in the conditions of functioning of the mental organizations'.[3] As we have already seen,[4] in a sleeping state, the brain and the rest of the body are not in exactly the same state as in waking life. The body experiences phases of muscular atony (in paradoxical sleep) or of muscular relaxation (in deep sleep), the sensory system sifts external information in order to protect the sleeper's sleep,[5] the brain demonstrates activity of varying levels of intensity (particularly intense during periods of paradoxical sleep), with, however, a decrease in the activity of the prefrontal cortex, which is the seat of reflexive consciousness (planning, reflexive or executive control, reorganisation of information, maintaining attention/concentration, controlling actions, etc.).[6]

The neurobiological conditions for the production of forms of expression are just as important in waking life as they are during sleep. But since sociologists generally work on waking individuals, these universal neurobiological conditions end up being neutralised and forgotten. It is only in trying to find links between life during sleep and waking life that the differences in neurobiological functions become apparent. But, contrary to what the American neuropsychiatrist John Allan Hobson thought, it makes no sense to separate the *form* of the dream ('detailed sensory imagery, the illusion of reality, illogical thinking, intensification of emotion, and unreliable memory'),[7] which would be universal and would be a matter for physiology, and the *content* of the dream, 'attributable to specific individual experiences'.[8] Both form and content can be explained by sociological, linguistic and psychological reasons as much as by the neurobiology or the neurophysiology of the brain. Each type of determination is, in the end, simply a version within its own specific context of what is also being enacted within each of the other contexts. For example, the 'strangeness of dreams' comes not just from 'distinctive physiological features of REM-sleep generation' or from a 'change in brain-mind mode',[9] but equally from the conditions of self-to-self communication.

Théodore Jouffroy said that what disappeared during sleep was 'the effort demanded to manage our capacities'.[10] The images which we see are no longer 'regulated by the will'.[11] Karl Albert Scherner, for his part, emphasised the loss of the 'centralising power' which manifests itself during sleep. The 'central force of the Self', which, during waking life, can 'master' or 'tame the elements of the life of the mind', disappears, leaving the way open for the 'life of oneiric images totally liberated from its central power'.[12] And Freud defined sleep as 'motor paralysis' and 'a paralysis of the will'.[13]

Ignace Meyerson saw in the dream 'a certain relaxation, a certain weakening of precise attention to the external world',[14] and noted the absence of voluntary control and of the possibility of retrospective correction of the images produced. The 'symbols (images or words) . . . will no longer be corrected, as in a waking state.'[15] This lack of reflective control partly explains the sense of incoherence often provoked by the memory of the dream on waking. The dreamer does not have the cognitive means of constructing a coherent visual account, an integral narrative whole with a beginning, a middle and an end. 'Dreams lack the principle of synthesis which reigns over our ordinary memories in order to maintain the association of the various constituent elements in line with reality.'[16] But the dream narrative, though disjointed in a structural sense, is nevertheless coherent in terms of the problems it addresses and the analogies on which it draws in the images involuntarily selected.

Withdrawing from the flow of interactions

Sleep implies a withdrawal from ordinary social interactions. The dreamer is relatively isolated, solicited by the surrounding environment far less than during waking life (the brain can nevertheless detect worrying or unusual sounds which cause the dreamer to wake up: a child's cries, an unusual sound, an alarm going off, etc.), he or she is silent, usually in darkness or half-light and either lying down or sitting. And since there is no need to respond to external demands, to say or do anything with any degree of urgency, to manage any kind of practical tasks, or to resolve a specific problem which requires full concentration, the dreamer can concentrate on the images from the dream and experience them as though they were real.

In the waking state, psychic activity is usually under siege from demands coming from outside (things that have to be done or words, sounds, events or people that we encounter and which are of direct or indirect concern to us and require our attention). During moments of pause in waking life (daydreams) and especially during the night (dreams), this endless flow of 'distractions' ceases, and psychic activity can turn its attention to the questions preoccupying the dreamer. Antoine Charma compared the 'bed in which we bury ourselves' to a 'tomb which cuts us off from everything that could allow life in': 'We remove light from our sight, sound from our hearing, perfumes from our sense of smell, flavours from our taste, the contrasts of cold and of heat from our touch, the movement of the air, disturbances and annoyances of all kinds.'[17] For sleeping means 'severing any dealings with the milieu in which we are steeped; it is in a sense like being dead to the external world.'[18]

This maximum withdrawal from the course of ordinary life which enables sleep, this isolation of the dreamer, means that psychic activity no longer has to turn to the outside but can reverse that movement by focusing on the inner depths. The 'centripetal activity comes to a stop'[19] and a centrifugal force comes into action.[20] But these inner depths to which the dreamer now turns are made up of everything which has been provoked within him or her by interactions with the external world. It is therefore still the social world that the dreamer finds within themselves, but one they have made their own, which demands their attention and continues to work within them in connection with their own history.

As Antoine Charma observes, the absence of immediate external demands means the focus can turn purely to internalised demands (stimuli):

> Sleep suppresses all five senses at once. When, in your waking state, you ponder questions of psychology or geometry, I imagine that, as far as possible, you put aside poetic or other faculties the influence of which, far from helping, would damage the action of the intellectual power that, for the moment, you wish to bring exclusively to the fore. You do your utmost, but the state of abstraction you seek to establish will not, cannot, entirely stifle everything that lives and moves around the centre where you shut yourself away. As soon as you sleep, on the contrary, the sympathetic link, which brings together your various faculties, relaxes to the point where it sometimes appears to be completely severed, and the spirit allows itself to be entirely enclosed within a circle of ideas, where outside emotions will not disturb it, and where consequently it will perform wonders.[21]

Charma remarks, moreover, that the intense concentration of the dreamer is also that sought, and partially obtained, by someone striving to create a work of art or resolve a problem.

By stepping back temporarily from 'daily matters', by switching off from the constant flow of actions and interactions, the dreamer can create a world of images so compelling that he or she believes they are seeing reality itself: 'We may call what we wish the illusions of sleep, ecstasy, delirium, and even madness; but we must recognise that this is a phenomenon unique in its essence, the isolation from the surrounding world, the withdrawal of the mind into itself, and as a result belief in existence and in the real succession of facts which exist only in our minds.'[22] Without any point of comparison, the internal world has become the only world there is, and the dreamer reacts within that world as though they were genuinely experiencing what they are in fact in the process of creating.

Self-to-self communication: internal language, formal and implicit relaxation

In this very particular context of sleep, the dreamer's expression is fundamentally one of *self-to-self communication*. It is an internalised or private language, without any audience, and consequently without the need to be understood by others (formal censorship) or the fear of not being morally correct (moral censorship). As self-to-self communication, the dream is characterised by contiguous analogies or associations which are unique to the dreamer, by the absence of continuity or by abrupt changes of subjects, by all sorts of implied or unsaid things, by shortcuts and, more generally, by an elliptic mode of expression.

One of the major gaps in Freudian thinking on the dream and beyond lies in the linguistic, psycholinguistic or sociolinguistic question of the context of expression of the dream as one of self-to-self communication. An awareness of this central aspect of oneiric expression enables us to make sense of much of the dream-work and of the structural properties of the 'dream narrative' without the need to formulate a notion of disguise or misrepresentation of thoughts in order to thwart the censorship. What Freud introduced as 'distortion'[23] is in fact no more than the properties inherent in a form of expression which, like any other, is adapted to the particular conditions of expression. The 'dream-distortion' is a consequence not of 'the censorship' but of self-to-self communication.

'In the dream', Maurice Halbwachs said, 'we are not concerned with anyone but ourselves: at that moment all language expresses and all structure represents everything we have at that moment in our mind, since there is nobody and no physical force to prevent it.'[24] The dreamer is not addressing anyone other than him- or herself and, unlike the egocentric language of children talking to themselves (asking themselves questions, answering, commenting on their actions, etc.), oneiric language is visual, sometimes auditory, tactile and kinaesthetic (and very rarely gustatory or olfactory).

The dream and codes of intimacy

We know that private exchanges between people close to each other are infinitely more informal and implicit than public exchanges in official and less relaxed circumstances. Making ourselves understood by being careful to make what we have to say explicit and not assuming that other people know what we are talking about, because in fact they have no experience or knowledge of it, are factors which ordinarily weigh heavily on oral or written public speeches. 'When speaking', wrote Mikhail Bakhtin,

> I always take into account the apperceptive background of the addressee's perception of my speech: the extent to which he is familiar with the situation, whether he has specialised knowledge of the given cultural area of communication, his views and convictions, his prejudices (from my viewpoint), his sympathies and antipathies – because all this will determine his responsive understanding of my utterance. These considerations also determine my choice of a genre for my utterance, my choice of compositional devices.[25]

When we talk about self-to-self communication, we are therefore referring to maximum 'shared knowledge' or 'shared experience'.

Long-term friends and couples who talk to each other and understand each other without having to spell things out need to make far fewer formal efforts than strangers or people who are socially a long way apart from each other. Sometimes they need do no more than simply exchange a glance or a smile, a laugh or a look of complicity, without uttering a single word, because they are taking part in the same event, reacting to the same suggestion or the same situation, and thinking exactly the same thing thanks to their shared past experience. 'Listen to conversations between close friends in cafés or bars or at home in the evening: they are punctuated with allusions instead of precise descriptions and are marked by sudden changes of subject rather than by continuity.'[26]

According to the English sociologist Basil Bernstein, this kind of conversation typically consists of a restricted sociolinguistic code. The speech pattern is 'fast and fluent, articulatory clues are reduced; some meanings are likely to be dislocated, condensed and local; there will be a low level of vocabulary and syntactic selection; *the unique meaning of the individual is likely to be implicit*.'[27] A restricted code occurs 'where the form of the social relation is based upon closely shared identifications, upon an extensive range of shared expectations, upon a range of common assumptions.'[28] It is the 'code of intimacy',[29] the code of exchanges between close friends or partners sharing the same values or the same experiences, the code of those who do not need to explain everything or to use formal structures:

> If we think of the communication pattern between married couples of long standing, then we see that meaning does not have to be fully explicit, a slight shift of pitch or stress, a small gesture, can carry a complex meaning. Communication takes shape against a backcloth of closely shared identifications and affective empathy which removes the need to elaborate verbal meanings and logical continuity in the organization of the speech.[30]

But when speaker and person spoken to are one and the same, as is the case in the dream, and existential complicity is therefore total, the mind can draw on a huge stock of experiences in order to work on its preoccupations. The dreamer has access to a full apperceptive background which enables him or her to understand what it is he or she 'says' *to him- or herself*. As a result, the oneiric genre is marked by this context of the perfect concurrence of a sleeping speaker addressing a sleeping interlocutor. Without specifically focusing on the case of dreams, Bernstein nevertheless emphasises the use of 'condensed symbols' in the restricted code ('intensifications and the condensations of such communication') and of metaphors[31] which reflect analyses on the structural properties of dream.[32]

This largely explains, as we shall see, both the moral relaxation (the absence of external moral judgement) and the more structural relaxation.

Things left unsaid, ellipses, actions interrupted without reason and abrupt changes of subject, people who suddenly appear, disappear or are transformed without explanation, similarly untimely changes in terms of places, objects, decors, feelings, the absence of integrated totality replaced by a not very explicit series of micro-episodes, narratives, etc.,[33] all make sense if the dream is seen inside its context of expression. But the situation becomes much less clear between a sleeping speaker and an interlocutor in a waking state. What made perfect sense to the dreamer appears strange or incoherent to the awakened individual.

In 1964, French and Fromm had pointed out the fact that, 'while he was sleeping, the dreamer had no need to put his thoughts in a form that could be communicated.' He was simply 'struggling, often unsuccessfully, for a solution to a practical emotional problem of his own'. And when he describes his dream to his analyst, he 'is not trying to explain . . . what he was thinking about', for he is rarely conscious of the problem referred to in his dream.[34] Self-to-self communication is the reason why the dreamer has absolutely no need to provide any clarification or any logical or simply syntactical guidelines for the account he produces: 'The logic that we miss in the dream work is the syntactical logic of speech. . . . Speech was designed primarily for communication. When we dream, we are not particularly interested in communicating our thoughts to others or in reasoning from propositions. Therefore we can dispense with syntactical logic.'[35] Freud could observe, on the subject of one dream, that 'a great part of the impression of absurdity in this dream was brought about by running together sentences from different parts of the dream-thoughts without any transition',[36] but he failed to see that the absence of transition in question, far from being a way of scrambling the message, is linked to the fact that the dreamer regards it as pointless to explain the links that, in the moment of the dream, he is able to grasp immediately.

The dream as reality

We have already pointed out that the dream account was an account of lived experience, even if this experience is purely imaginary. The dreamer is a participant in the dream; he or she actively lives the dream rather than simply being a spectator to it. The use of the expression 'internal cinema' to refer to the visual constraint imposed on the dreamer's thoughts is, however, not entirely satisfactory, since it gives the impression that the dreamer is somehow external to the oneiric scene. Yet dreamers *see themselves and believe themselves to be actually there*. They are fully fledged actors in the events and can, as a result, sometimes experience very powerful emotions.

Since the dreamer thinks they are experiencing whatever it is they are dreaming about, everything in the dream is experienced in the present rather than as the memory of past events or in anticipation of events to come. The ability to remember or anticipate means having reference points outside the present action which are not accessible to the sleeper's consciousness. What in daydreaming can be experienced in the form of recollection or of the mental preparation for future scenes (exams, appointments, etc.) 'becomes a present-day reality for the sleeping dreamer'.[37]

And because the dreamer actively experiences the dream rather than simply seeing it, the description or account they give of it will never be as coherent as it would be if they were more distanced from the events and were constructing a narrative whole. Mikhail Bakhtin thus distinguished between the 'ethico-practical' viewpoint of someone who navigates the social world by steering a course through 'ethical and practical cognitive categories (those relating to what is good, true and those with practical purposes)',[38] and for whom any event is always 'open and risky',[39] and the 'aesthetic' point of view which places the narrator in an 'exotopic position' and allows them to construct a structurally explicit account which is both logical and coherent. For example, the child who plays with his friends at being the

> leader of a band of robbers, experiences his life as a robber from the inside. It is through the eyes of a robber that he sees a second child run out in front of a third child, who is the traveller. . . . The relationship each of them has with the life event they have decided to play out – an attack on the stagecoach – is none other than the desire to take part in the event, the desire to live that life as a participant. . . . This relationship with life which manifests itself in the desire to experience it for yourself, in person, is not an aesthetic relationship to life; in this sense, the game is the same as a daydream or a somewhat simplistic reading of a novel which means identifying with the main character in order to experience, in the category of the first person, their reality and their interesting life. Put another way, when we dream, we are quite simply under the direction of an author, but this does not in any way resemble an artistic event.[40]

The 'exotopic' position – in other words, one which remains outside the situation, the actions, the characters – is the only position which allows the dreamer to avoid the implicit, to situate the characters, places, moments, actions in relation to each other, to respect a chronological order[41] and to provide coherent meaning by organising the facts into a system, according to Aristotle's concept. Yet the dreamer is in no sense a *deus ex machina* and has neither the cognitive-cerebral means (planning, metalinguistic control, etc.) to be one nor the communicational need (he or she is only addressing themselves) to achieve such a goal.

Dream accounts and poor school compositions

The dream account or narrative in fact closely resembles informal oral exchanges between people who know each other well or the oral or written narratives produced by schoolchildren with significant learning difficulties.[42] Such accounts, full of implicit elements, not necessarily in chronologic order and made up of incomplete phrases and of disjointed fragments of narrative, naturally appear to teachers as 'incoherent', 'confused' or 'incomprehensible'.[43] The children tend to relive, replay and mime stories rather than narrate them properly. It is less a matter of words to listen to or of written accounts to read than of stories to live out (with the use of intonation that re-creates the emotions of people, of gestures, of mimes or physical movements to show the actions that took place, of onomatopoeia which reproduces the sounds described). As in these heavily criticised examples of schoolwork, the dream is made up of elements which only make sense if they are regarded as *extracts* from more complex situations and from a presupposed overall experience on the part of the dreamer rather than as elements capable of fitting together to create a coherent world. Scholars working on dreams have often reserved for them exactly the same kinds of comments as those pronounced by schools on 'poor quality essays', accusing them of being confused, implicit, illogical, fragmented, incomprehensible, jumping from one subject to another, etc.[44] It is because it refers to a whole implicit incorporated past that the dream can function as a series of small narrative sequences apparently unrelated to each other and which merely suggest or evoke using the pared-down means at the disposal of the dreamer (visual symbolisation, metaphor, condensation, etc.).

Just as spoken language 'contents itself with emphasizing the main lines of thought', as Vendryes says, and as 'the logical relations of words, and component parts of a sentence, are either imperfectly indicated, with the help, if necessary, of intonation and gesture, or are not indicated at all and have to be supplied by intuition',[45] the different elements which make up a dream are like the visible part of an iceberg, where the much larger submerged part (dispositions, existential situation, recent life circumstances) remains invisible, and do not need to be made clear by the person dreaming.

As long as no account is taken of the submerged parts of the iceberg and the meaning of the dream is sought purely in the words of the dream account, as is the case with those rigorous analysts of dream content, without heed for any theoretical considerations, it is impossible to understand exactly what is going on behind the narrative in question. Freud therefore justified the need for associations established in connection with the dream by the fact that the elements of the dream, if we are to understand them adequately, cannot be detached from all the dreamer's presuppositions: 'By following the associations which arose from the separate elements of the dream divorced from their context, I arrived at a number of thoughts and recollections, which I could not fail to recognize as important products of my mental life.'[46] Their role is to *contextualise* the elements of the dream which are like incomplete notes (symbolic shorthand). All the associations 'throw a surprising light on all the different parts of the dream, fill in the gaps between them, and make their strange juxtapositions intelligible', and if we want to explain the 'relation between them and the dream's content', 'The dream is seen to be an abbreviated selection from the associations, a selection made, it is true, according to rules that we have not yet understood: the elements of the dream are like representatives chosen by election from a mass of people.'[47] All the work of association and of clarification makes it possible to grasp the incoherencies, the implied content, the hidden meanings, etc., that the dreamer does not need to present in the dream.

The dream is a form of shorthand and retains salient points only in the form of condensed symbolic images which acquire meaning only when linked to the circumstances and the series of experiences underpinning them. As Abbot Richard wrote in 1766, it is very difficult to grasp the coherence of thought from the outside 'when the rapidity of the imagination causes a quick succession of ideas to follow one after the other, seemingly haphazardly but in fact not so, since they are part of this sequence of perceptions that others do not know, and which are a reminder of facts which can only be connected by the spirit which experiences them.'[48] Only a scientific reconstruction of the missing pieces can compensate for the problem posed by this exteriority.

Yet, paradoxically, the dream which 'aims for the essence (to conjure up some meaning) without being burdened by all those things habit or convention would forcibly bring up',[49] like the 'poor school compositions' which tend to be more like narratives to experience directly than accounts to listen to or to read, forcibly expose the arbitrary and artificial nature of ordinary narrative structures, notably based on a scholarly type of discourse, which relies on the *construction of a plot* and the *use of a linguistic framework to render the experience coherent*. This permanent linguistic straightjacketing (usually narrative) through which we are accustomed to seeing the world, and which we generally consider as 'obvious' and 'natural', nevertheless prevents us from understanding the real processes (analogical, intermittent and unconscious) of psychic activity and the logic of forms of expression which vary depending on the context in which they are generated.

As soon as they wake up, the dreamer tends to become caught up in the ordinary contexts of the narrative formulation of their experience and thus loses contact with the analogical activity unique to the sleeping state, which is perfectly coherent. Not that they are de-socialised at the time of the dream, since in fact they are just as much socialised there as in their public interactions, but because the context of sleep renders possible, and even necessary, a self-to-self communication which is more condensed, less integrated into a whole, and more implicit, which is no longer directly accessible to them once they have returned to the waking state. The same person dreams of things that are perfectly coherent and then is incapable of understanding them on waking. For, even in the dream, the 'I' is another.

Inner language, solitude and the dream

A considerable number of the formal and structural properties of the dream can be easily understood once we take into account the fact that we are dealing with an inner language without any external audience. This 'inner language' ('inner speech', 'endophasia') has been studied by psychologists. But the problem with this concept is that this language has often been thought of as essentially a verbal one, in the manner of a monologue or of an inner *verbal* dialogue, whereas what we are gradually realising on the subject of the dream or the daydream is that inner thought or psychic activity are not made up essentially of words but rather of images, and even of relatively intermittent series of visual narrative sequences. The expression 'internal cinema' is the most accurate from this point of view, as long as it is clear that the dreamer is the principal actor and not merely a spectator. We need therefore to adapt the verbally centred notion of 'inner language' to this key fact.

A large part of our mental life, which we call 'thought', occurs in the form of mental images and not only words.[50] When someone thinks about which clothes to wear, when an architect draws up plans for a house, when an individual is playing chess, when they picture the route to get to a friend's house, etc., it is images and scenes that come into their heads just as much as words or utterances, even if monologues or inner dialogues may also feature. Similarly, memories of the past often come in the form of visual scenes. But sleep enables a form of expression, that of the dream, imposing on it a powerful need for visualisation[51] which means that the dreamer cannot speak, write, read, draw, etc., but imagines he or she is living the various scenes. The dreamer can also hear words or sounds, have physical sensations or feel the imagined movements of his or her body (the feeling of falling, of flying, or of being incapable of advancing, etc.) and can experience powerful emotions (sadness, joy, fear, oppression, etc.).

Inner language is defined very aptly by the Russian psychologist Lev S. Vygotsky as 'speech for oneself' as opposed to 'external speech', which is speech 'for others' (written language being one which 'must explain the situation fully in order to be intelligible').[52] This absence or presence of addressees is what determines any structural differences: 'It would be surprising indeed if such a basic difference in function did not affect the structure of the two kinds of speech.'[53] If the inner language can be very elliptical and implicit, it is because for the speaker 'the subject of our inner dialogue is already known.'[54] And, for Vygotsky, 'to understand another's speech, it is not sufficient to understand his words – we must understand his thought.'[55] The comparison between an inner language developed in the waking state and an inner oneiric language probably stops there. For, unlike the awakened individual, the dreamer does not understand what he or she has very subtly (analogically) expressed during sleep.

In spite of his doubts about the sociological status of an object such as the dream, Maurice Halbwachs was one of the first scholars to turn his attention to the specificity of the 'inner language' which constitutes oneiric language. For him, this inner language is the 'intermediary between the events of waking life and the scenes from the dream'.[56] It is an 'incoherent language which is automatic, often rushed, voluble, sometimes inter-rupted, interspersed with gaps',[57] a language which 'is characterised by lots of repetitions, contradictions, absurdities, one which would not be tolerated in an exchange between waking individuals, that we would not accept ourselves if, in our waking state, we were talking in a monologue, speaking to ourselves.'[58] Halbwachs imputes to it all the characteristics of implicit language which does not set out to be understood by anyone else and which reveals the omnipresence and the omniscience of the dreamer: 'In the descriptions of the dream, we make the characters talk, as in a puppet theatre where the puppeteer gives to first one, then to the other, words which he himself pronounces. But, if there were no spectators, he could dispense with saying the words aloud and simply think what each should say. It seems that this is often the case in the majority of dreams.'[59]

Avant-garde literature (authors such as James Joyce, Virginia Woolf, William Faulkner, etc.) explored the characteristics of inner language in considerable depth. For example, Bloom's inner monologues in *Ulysses* are rarely made up of whole phrases. More often they are incomplete, interrupted, with the use of ellipses, separated from their articles, from their subject pronouns, their prepositions and their copulative verbs, and it is 'likely that Joyce . . . aimed at an accurate representation rather than an artful stylization of mental language.'[60] Dorrit Cohn even observes that the phrases of Bloom's monologues correspond to Vygotsky's definition of inner language: 'Vygotsky defines this syntactical peculiarity as "a tendency toward an altogether specific form of abbreviation: namely, omitting the subject of a sentence and all words connected with it, while preserving the predicate." This radical ellipsis has the simplest reason: it is because we can already know what subject we are thinking about that we can condense verbal thought to pure predication.'[61]

The social situation that most closely resembles the one in which the daydreamer or the dreamer finds themselves is that of Robinson Crusoe before meeting Friday. For Crusoe, verbal expression, which is now entirely soliloquy, can no longer be clearly distinguished from inner monologue or from a stream of consciousness made up of images more than of words. Deprived of any interlocutor, he has no external injunction to put into words what he is thinking or doing, is about to do, or has done. He feels no compulsion to be explicit (for someone else's benefit) about what he is saying and can regress to a highly implicit self-to-self language. This regime of permanent daydream, coupled with dreams during sleep, leads to a loss of coherency in terms of images, and of the world. For what structures our perception of the world, without our being aware of it most of the time, are interactions with others and the necessity of stepping out of ourselves in order to communicate in an acceptable and comprehensible manner (clearly, more or less explicitly, coherently) with someone else.

Without this repeated external demand, incoherence, illogicality, images which make sense only to the self or idiosyncratic symbolisms would dominate:

> I know now that every man carries within himself – and as it were above himself – a fragile and complex framework of habits, responses, reflexes, preoccupations, dreams, and associations, formed and constantly transformed by perpetual contact with his fellows. Deprived of its sap, this delicate growth withers and dissolves. My fellow-men were the mainstay of my world . . . Each day I measure my debt to them by observing the fresh cracks in my personal structure. I know what I would suffer should I lose the use of words and with all the power of my anguish I seek to combat that final surrender. But my relationship to material things is also undermined by solitude. When a painter or engraver introduces human figures into a landscape or alongside a monument they are not there merely as an accessory. Human figures convey the scale, and what is still more important, they represent attitudes, possible points of view, which enrich the picture for the outside observer by providing him with other, indispensable points of reference.[62]

If, as we shall see,[63] there can be no general dictionary of symbols or a universal key to dreams, it is precisely because the dreamer does not speculate as to whether he or she can be understood by anyone else. The dream is distinguished by the absence of an immediate interlocutor and of an external social context of interaction. Without any external presence, the dreamer has only the ghosts of past interlocutors (recent or more distant), who made it possible in particular for him or her to develop a language and even the possibility of a stream of consciousness, however loosely structured.

10

The Fundamental Forms of Psychic Life

In order to advance our understanding of the general formula for interpreting dreams,[1] it is important to specify the fundamental properties of the processes underpinning the production of dream images. Analogy is a central element in both dream and waking thought, bringing together things that share some resemblance. But, in addition to association through analogy, there is also association through contiguity, which means that two things are mentally indissociable, the image of one immediately conjuring up the image of the other, because they are often linked in the dreamer's actual experience.

Practical analogy

What lies behind this universality of analogy-making? In order to survive, humans rely upon comparing what's happening to them *now* with what happened to them in the past. They exploit the similarity of past experiences to new situations, letting it guide them at all times in this world.
(Douglas Hofstadter and Emmanuel Sander, *Surfaces and Essences*, p. 28)

By referring to transference and counter-transference in the context of psychoanalytic therapy, by developing the technique of free association of ideas, and by highlighting the central processes at work in the 'dream-work' (symbolisation, metaphor, condensation, displacement or substitution), Freud inadvertently put his finger on a fundamental aspect of relational and psychic life. For, as he himself observed on certain occasions, associations and transference are by no means confined to the relationship between the analyst and the analysand, and these processes or mechanisms, like oneiric operations, are underpinned by practical analogy.

Practical analogy, involuntary and unconscious, lies at the heart of human psychic activity, *in both dreams and waking life*. The use of different terms to indicate a whole range of mental operations underpinned by analogical processes can sometimes tend to cloud the view of this key aspect of psychic activity, fundamentally linked to the *historic nature of human beings*. What is perceived, felt, represented or interpreted in the present moment is necessarily based on a somewhat approximate unconscious analogical connection between the new situation which presents itself and past situations already experienced, the traces of which are stored in the brain in the form of schemes or dispositions (prototypes, models, schemas, patterns, cognitive structures, etc.). It is therefore because human beings are capable of internalising their past experiences in the form of schemas or dispositions, and because moreover they are constantly subjected to new situations, because they are the products of history and have an ongoing history of their own, that analogy is a central phenomenon in their psychic functioning. Hofstadter and Sander sum up this point perfectly: 'No thought can be formed that isn't informed by the past; or, more precisely, we think only thanks to analogies that link our present to our past.'[2] *We could say that analogy is unique to mankind and that it is the sign that the human being is a historic being.*

With their distinctive brains and nervous systems, human beings are therefore naturally compelled to make analogical connections between past experiences and the new situations with which they are confronted. Such connections are almost like a form of jurisprudence with the present 'case' and 'cases' already experienced in the past ('precedents'), which means that the present is always perceived and even anticipated on the basis of the past. As these creatures of history, caught up in an *ineluctable chronological succession of experiences*, human beings cannot escape the processes of practical analogy, which generally take the form of pre-reflective anticipation. Such anticipation can be confirmed or invalidated, but on each occasion it perceives the present only from the perspective of structures of perception and of representation which have been established in the course of previous experiences.

The 'human ability to make analogies' is the 'fuel and fire of thinking'.[3] Practical analogy is present in the very earliest non-verbal acquisition of schemas of interaction internalised by infants, who base their actions and reactions on the basis of anticipations that past rituals of interaction have enabled them to acquire. Recognising past schemas of interaction in the present contexts of interaction with their parents, they are constantly making non-conscious associations, and where necessary adjustments, between the past and the present and between the habits formed from past exchanges and the beginnings of present exchanges.[4]

This kind of internalisation of relational and affective schemas, which begins even before the acquisition of speech, will continue throughout the individual's life. In each 'new' situation, the socialised individual acts by unconsciously mobilising the incorporated schemas or dispositions triggered by the situation. And *practical analogy* plays a central role in the opening up of the incorporated past by the present. It is in their capacity to find – in a practical and all-encompassing way rather than analytically – resemblances between the present situation and coherent sequences of past experiences incorporated in the form of summaries of experiences (schemas) that the individual can activate the dispositions or the skills which allow him or her to act in the most appropriate manner.

The process of analogy continues throughout the acquisition of language and of perception, as the child gradually learns to name the beings and objects around them. The action of naming is based on the capacity to identify analogies between new objects and objects already recorded. For example, the child learns to use the word 'dog' for a large variety of animals which have, in spite of their difference, a 'family resemblance' (Wittgenstein). Their size, their fur, their colour, their build, the shape of the head or the body can vary without necessarily threatening their shared association to the category of dogs.

Children's capacities of discrimination or recognition become refined and sharper in the course of the process of linguistic socialisation, which is intrinsically linked to the child coming into real or figurative contact with different cases belonging to the same category. In the early stages of learning, a child can refer to almost all the four-legged animals he or she encounters with the word 'dog'. By using the word for a specific category of animals to designate those belonging to other categories, but which nevertheless possess shared features (just as dogs, cats, sheep, goats or ponies have four legs and usually have fur), the child reveals the involuntary work of analogy which establishes connections, in a relevant manner, between objects that are in fact different. In the same way, the small child who is beginning to talk may try to communicate with the family dog because, in some aspects of its behaviour, it displays some similarities with human playfellows.

Words therefore function as schemas, in the sense that they represent the accumulation of a multiplicity of more or less analogous real situations experienced by the speaking subject. In order to move from the specific use of 'mummy' (which links a word to a single reality) to a more abstract, generalised or less specific use (which means that there is not just one single mummy), the child embarks on a process of semantically integrating into the word 'mummy' a whole series of similar cases (there is 'my mummy', but 'my mummy' also has a mummy, my friends also have a 'mummy', etc.):

> At the outset, there is a concrete situation with concrete components, and thus it is perceived as something unique and cleanly separable from the rest of the world. After a while, though – perhaps a day later, perhaps a year – one runs into another situation that one finds to be similar and a link is made. From that moment onward, the mental representations of the two situations begin to be connected

up, to be blurred together, thus giving rise to a new mental structure that, although it is less specific than either of its two sources (i.e., less detailed), is not fundamentally different from them.[5]

Subsequently, and particularly thanks to the pedagogical activity associated with school, the child will learn to distinguish between objects in a more analytical, deliberate and thoughtful way, but this new way of discriminating between realities on a more rigorous basis will always be less obvious than the practical analogical skill which is the foundation of the child's perceptions and reasoning. The ordinary recourse to a practical sense of overall resemblance is always less precise than a systematic analysis based on the criteria of the object, but it is also incomparably more economical, faster and more efficient, as René Allendy observes:

> Initially, visual representation is infinitely faster than the analytical description of a situation; it is a synthesis. For example, it is a long and complicated process to express the state of mind of someone in a state of indecision, racked with worries, dogged with problems, held back by his physical or moral shortcomings. On the other hand, instantly conjuring up in a picture, this same man mired in a bog, describing him as *bogged down*, is by means of symbolism a way of instantly conveying an impression of the situation.[6]

Analogy in dreams

The dream establishes analogical links between the dreamer's present situation and various crucial elements from the past, whether recent or more distant. *Practical analogy*, which also guides our behaviour in waking life by enabling us to understand, interpret, act, react and even anticipate the course of things by linking the past and the present, does not, however, with some exceptions (e.g. parapraxis or delirium), lead to *fusion* or *conflation* in waking life: the past and the present are usually *clearly distinguished* from each other, and only the elements belonging to the present penetrate the conscious, except in cases where a memory is explicitly recollected in the form of a daydream or by a word which evokes a particular memory.

The dream, on the other hand, can indiscriminately *fuse* scenes, places, people and objects from our present with analogous scenes, places, people and objects from our past. The *analogons* of the past are set free during sleep and make their way to the surface of the dreamer's involuntary consciousness. At that point, the elements of the past which are at play in analogical links cease to be implicit (as they are in ordinary waking life) and mingle with elements of the present in the confines of the oneiric space taking the form of symbolisations, condensations, metaphors or substitutions. They erupt into the zone of the sleeping consciousness, whereas in *waking consciousness they remain in the background*. In a sense they *determine* us while remaining in the *wings* during waking life, without us being aware of them and without appearing directly, whereas in dreams they *take centre stage*.

As Ernest Hartmann said, the dream *reveals* the hyper-connectivity of our mental functioning, linking different moments from the past with the dreamer's present.[7] But this hyper-connectivity is the ordinary functioning of our brain which, constantly, both in waking life and during sleep, connects the new with the already known or makes sense of the new from the perspective of the already known. *The specificity of the dream lies therefore in fusing what was previously kept separate by the waking consciousness, in order to focus attention on a particular problem.* The blend or mix of past–present operates without providing any manual for these processes. If different elements, taken from different moments in the past, can come together in the same *oneiric space*, the reason for their presence nevertheless remains completely *implicit*, since *the dreamer addresses only him- or herself.*

And it is for this reason that, once the dreamer has woken up, the significance of the dream images evades his or her watchful consciousness, which does not function in the same way as it does during sleep. The interpretation of the dream is therefore the surest route to an *awareness of the processes of analogical connections* unconsciously set in place by the dreamer. It is also the most direct *means of access to the problems of the dreamer's life*. Yet we should not imagine that studying dreams allows us to grasp realities that would be completely inaccessible by any other means, since the dispositions and elements of the existential situation which are expressed in dreams constantly express themselves, though in very different ways, in the waking life of the dreamer. Taking the dream as the object of study is simply a way of focusing attention on the way in which these elements function and find expression in the specific context represented by sleep, rather than a way of accessing the secrets of the mind or of the psyche.

It is as though, for the brain, past and present elements were interchangeable or equivalent and could be substituted or combined once the schema of incorporated experience had established an analogical relationship between them – that is to say, a relationship between the different elements of the present, between the different elements of the past, or between the elements of the past and those of the present. If the father and the boyfriend of a female dreamer are clearly distinguishable in waking life, in the dream they can be considered as equivalent and be treated as such, because the dreamer's brain has established links between the two by identifying similarities or shared characteristics. All those things which resemble each other can potentially be condensed into one or can be substituted for each other within the dream.

The mechanisms of analogy are permanently active in the dream. Their activity explains why there are no boundaries of fields or of worlds between situations, people, places, objects, etc. Experiences from within the social world that take place in different times and spaces are experienced by the individual as experiences which communicate with each other, are linked, reflect or contradict each other. Nor is there any separation between the past and the present, since experiences (situations, people, places, objects, etc.) from the most distant past and those of the most immediate present live, mix together and communicate in the same symbolic space.

Finally, the dream makes no distinction between what is essential and what may seem purely incidental. With his concept of displacement, Freud was referring to the process whereby the most important elements and those of secondary importance were inverted, a somewhat sly way of diverting the attention of the censorship. Yet the displacement in question amounts only to the simple substitution of one thing (person, place, object, situation, etc.) for another (person, place, object, situation, etc.), generally based on an analogy subjectively perceived by the dreamer. We may therefore wonder who is in a position to decide what is essential and what is secondary in the dream. Diurnal events which trigger the stimuli responsible for dreams can sometimes appear from outside to be mere details or anodyne events, with no particular significance. But the dreamer, on the other hand, with the schemas and dispositions at his or her disposal, has, consciously or not, perceived the analogy between the objects or the situations in question.

If the terms of the specific problem which are addressed in the dream are not always very clear to the waking individual, it is not because censorship imposes concealment, diversion or disguise. Nor is it because the dream sets out to violate the 'natural laws' by allowing people, places and time zones to change without warning, or that there are impossible fusions or combinations of people, places, times, situations, etc.[8] It is simply that the *analogons* are mobilised in the dream in so far as they are considered by the brain as being equivalent to elements of the problems addressed in the dream. It is as though we are dealing with an equation in which each term can be replaced by an equivalent term (or series of terms). In order to locate the underlying problem of the dream, each element of the dream needs to be decoded with a view to identifying the unspoken element for which it is the *analogon*. Sometimes a dream can say several things at once, and its heterogeneous and vivid character is the result of the combination of all the analogies or the problems involved.[9]

One of the personal dreams of the philosopher and psychologist Marcel Foucault demonstrates an oneiric substitution based on a situational analogy. When he was a high school [*lycée*] teacher, he was particularly afraid of the principal of the establishment. One night, he dreamt that he was a pupil and that he was struggling to remember the lines of a poem he was supposed to have learned and was about to recite. This filled him with anxiety, 'because of the reputation for strictness of the teacher, Mr X', who was none other than his principal in real life: 'Thus the vague anxiety I felt towards my principal in waking life increased in my sleep, and the fear of being found out became a reality in the dream because I did not know the poem and was incapable of learning it.'[10] The analogy between the hierarchical relationship between teacher and principal and the hierarchical relationship between pupil and teacher explains the substitution of one for the other.

In a case studied by George Lakoff,[11] a woman dreams that she is in the class of her favourite professor in the university. He came up to her and told her that she was not working hard enough and would fail her exams. In real life, the dreamer is married to a professor who is a colleague of the one in the dream. When she got married, she had given up a job she hated and was no longer involved in any kind of professional activity. She was therefore afraid that not working might put her into a financial situation which would lead to a breakdown in the marriage. In fact, in her dream she had replaced her husband with his colleague and transposed into an educational context (working to ensure educational success) her fears relating to her marital situation (working in order to ensure the success of her marriage). In her dream, she was essentially imagining that her husband was reproaching her because the fact that she was not working was the reason for their marital difficulties (educational failure reflecting conjugal failure).

Calvin S. Hall and Vernon J. Nordby also come up with a case where analogies between people and situations integrally structure the dream of a young single woman suffering from anxiety. She describes the following dream to her therapist: 'An elephant was chasing me. I ran home but the door was locked and I couldn't get in.'[12] The associations made by the dreamer reveal that she has been deeply afraid of elephants ever since her father took her to a circus when she was a child. On that occasion she was terrified by the elephants performing their act and cuddled close to her father. She recalled that his breath smelled strong and his eyes were half-closed and bloodshot. Later, when she became an adult, she realised he must have been drunk that day. In the description she gives of her father, he is a big man, with a large red nose, and as a child she was afraid of him. She started to cry and wanted to go home. She remembered that she wanted to go back to her mother, who would protect her from her father when he became violent. But, as time went on, her mother cut herself off from the family and no longer seemed to care about her. The dream therefore, with the help of a number of analogies, staged the situation of a threatening father chasing after her and her mother's failure to protect her. The terrifying elephant is an *analogon* of the father (big, with a large nose, and terrifying); the chase scene is analogous to situations from her childhood with her father; the closed door is the visual *analogon* of her mother's withdrawal of help or protection; and the house is the *analogon* of a safe place.

The analogy of situations (present and past) and people which leads to a process of condensation can be observed in the following example given by Erich Fromm:

A man who works under an authoritarian boss may be unduly afraid of this man because of the fear he had of his father as a child. The night after the day on which his boss criticized him for one reason or another, he has a nightmare in which he sees a figure, which is a mixed compositum of his father and his boss, trying to kill him. Had he not been afraid of his father as a child, his boss's annoyance would not have frightened him. But if his boss had not been annoyed that day, this deep-seated fear would not have been mobilized and the dream would not have occurred.[13]

And a similar analogy between past and present situations provides the key to understanding dreams cited by René Allendy:

> For example, a man falls asleep thinking about the thanklessness of his daily routine and the monotonous nature of his job. In his dream he revisits memories of his secondary school days. Assuredly there seems no logical link, in terms of any rational concepts, to link a school classroom with its dismal lighting with the job of sup- plying commercial products to retailers, but when we understand what feelings of tedium, of constraint, of monotony the subject has experienced during his studies, we realise that, in order to characterise his disgust of a profession in which he now feels trapped, no other memory could hold a more appropriate emotional note. Another person, a university professor, frequently sees himself in his dreams at a particular stage in his training, taking his teacher training exams and confronted with a whole range of difficulties. When we find out that he was in poor health at the time of the exam and that he is now once again facing anxieties about a health issue, the dream takes on an obvious significance. The exam in question has become an allegory, the concrete image of poor health, and appears in direct relationship to the feeling of being physically unwell.[14]

Maurice Halbwachs regarded Freud's interpretations as 'both very complicated and very uncertain',[15] notably because of the multiplicity of associations which could reflect elements of the dream. The fact that, 'behind the same name, there might be several different characters, which are moreover all ready to change into each other', and that the same 'is true for most of the events and objects of our dreams',[16] left the sociologist feeling puzzled. But if oneiric schemas are linked to schemas of experience, which are summaries of experience, then the list of possible substitutions is a very long one and can of course keep growing indefinitely. The fact that associations can be endless nevertheless confirms that in a sense all relatively analogous past experiences are in action in the oneiric scheme in question. By asking the dreamer to associate the different elements of the dream to other elements, the analyst is simply bringing together a few cases belonging to the same series of experiences but can by no means reconstitute the totality of cases. It is not even certain that the cases on which he or she ends up focusing were the ones most significant in the elaboration of the dream. Yet that in no way diminishes the relevance of any attempt to uncover the coherence of the series schemas underpinning the dream.

Transference in analysis as analogical transference

The famous transference associated with analysis when the analysand projects or transposes onto the analyst relationships (types of relationship, feelings, desires, fantasies, etc.) he or she has had with other significant people in his or her entourage (generally reduced to significant people from childhood) certainly exists, but it is by no means confined to psychoanalytic therapy. The sociological interview is not dissimilar, in that it provokes certain questions on the subject of the status conferred on the interviewer by the interviewee and what role he or she has adopted in the exchange (quasi-father, quasi-mother, quasi-son, quasi-brother, quasi-colleague, etc.). But, more generally, any new interpersonal relationship that is established enables each of the participants to transfer (transference or counter-transference by the two people involved in the relationship), without being conscious of it, certain ways of acting which have already been tried out in the past with other people. And this transference of past relationships onto present relationships is underpinned by practical analogies. It is precisely because an individual sees the other person as an *analogon* of other people that he or she projects certain representations onto them and behaves with them in a way analogous to that deployed in the past.

Freud undoubtedly placed too much emphasis on the personal nature of the social relationships with which he was dealing. After all, the older the person analysed, the more likely it is that the type of relationship involved will have been established and formed through the course of a very long series of empirical experiences involving people rather than being simply a relationship with one specific person. Referring to the transference between Dora, being treated for hysteria, and Freud, Jean-Michel Quinodoz points out the multiplicity of relationships implicitly involved:

> Transference could be described as a drama which, in the course of an analysis, is enacted with respect to a significant person in the patient's past who is projected into the present and on to the psychoanalyst. In Dora's case, it was not just one important person from her past who was transferred on to Freud, but two: Freud represented not only Herr K but also an earlier seducer, Dora's father, who in turn had been relayed by Herr K. Thus, in the course of the analysis, a real event which had recently taken place in Dora's life echoed something

from her childhood: the fantasy of being seduced by her father when she was a little girl.[17]

We see therefore that relational schemas are in action in therapy or in the sociological interview, just as they are in any other kind of interpersonal relationship. The only difference lies in the fact that both the analyst and the sociologist strive to be aware of these transferences and to put them to good use in order to gain a better understanding of the analysand or of the interviewee.

If 'an analysis without transference is impossible', it is because *all interpersonal relationships* involve transferences. As Freud himself said, 'It must not be supposed, however, that transference is created by analysis and does not occur apart from it. Transference is merely uncovered and isolated by analysis. It is a universal phenomenon of the human mind, it decides the success of all medical influence, and in fact dominates the whole of each person's relations to his human environment.'[18] In Dora's case, the social structure of the relationship combined with the age and the gender of those involved, the nature of the relationship of dependence between the patient and her analyst,[19] and no doubt too the authority of the specialist pave the way to a father–daughter type relationship. 'At the beginning it was clear that I was replacing her father in her imagination, which was not unlikely, in view of the difference between our ages. She was even comparing me with him consciously.'[20]

Depending on the case, transference is generally an identical repetition or an adaptation, an adjustment, an accommodation (in Piaget's sense of the word):

Some of these transferences have a content which differs from that of their model in no respect except for the substitution. These, then – to keep to the same metaphor – are merely new impressions or reprints. Others are more ingeniously constructed: their content has been subjected to a moderating influence – to *sublimation*, as I call it – and they may even become conscious, by cleverly taking advantage of some real peculiarity in the physician's person or circumstances and attaching themselves to that. These, then, will no longer be new impressions, but revised editions.[21]

But identical transference or the pure and simple repetition of a past relational schema is certainly not the situation most frequently experienced by socialised individuals. The dynamics of relationships mean that the modes of behaviour adopted begin by referring to similar experiences from the past before adjusting and modifying in the course of getting to know the person in question.

In *all human interactions*, transferences and counter-transferences of relationships and behaviours are constantly played out between interactants. A female writer might see in her editor a sort of protective mother

figure whom she loves, fears and respects all at once; an apprentice might
see his boss as an intimidating paternal figure and act like a son in the face
of an authoritarian father; an employee might project onto a somewhat
older colleague the image of an older brother of whom he was once jealous
and interact with him accordingly; a woman might behave towards her
new partner as though he were her ex-husband, etc.

Association: analogy and contiguity

> And even in our wildest and most wandering reveries, nay in our
> very dreams, we shall find, if we reflect, that the imagination ran not
> altogether at adventures, but that there was still a connexion upheld
> among the different ideas, which succeeded each other.
> (David Hume, *An Enquiry concerning Human Understanding*,
> p. 16)

'Association' is sometimes referred to in a manner which confuses two
different types of link: the *analogy* between two realities (people, places,
objects, situations, etc.) and the link of spatial, temporal or logical *contiguity* (the two realities are contextually linked in the dreamer's experience,
the two realities follow on from each other, one is the consequence of the
other). In the first scenario, the subject associates things because he or she
perceives them as analogous, and therefore equivalent and substitutable.
In the second scenario, smoked salmon, for example, features in a dream
because it is a friend's favourite food and dreaming of smoked salmon
amounts to dreaming of that friend,[22] the scent of orange blossom plunges
the subject back into his or her native Morocco, the sight of a yellow
oilskin spontaneously calls to mind the family boat, and the evocation of a
pine forest is mentally associated with the fire witnessed one summer: the
realities in question are not analogous but they nevertheless go together. In
his *Philosophy Lectures: Notes from the Lycée de Sens Course, 1883–1884*,
Durkheim was already pointing out the existence of these two types of association: 'This means we should recognize at least two types of associations
of ideas – association by contiguity and that by resemblance.'[23]

Karl Albert Scherner refers to the 'law of associations' and to 'associative dreams' in which 'associations of ideas' can be observed. He mentions
first of all dreams which link together analogous situations. For example,
a boy dreams that he is climbing a tree in order to reach a magpie's nest
and that the parent magpies are flying around above his head in a menac-
ing manner, then that he is in his classroom at school and his teacher is
threatening to hit him on the head with his cane because he has learned
his lesson badly. In both these cases, the dreamer has done something
wrong and is threatened with punishment or sanction.[24] But Scherner also
refers to 'associative dreams in the form of contiguity and simultaneity':
'Their law is as follows: things one has seen or experienced in reality in the

same place (contiguity) or at the same moment (temporal circumstances, conjunctures, etc.) each evoke the other, as objects representing the dream, in order to set up connections.'[25]

In his research, Jacques Montangero clearly demonstrated that what appears in the dream could be linked to the phenomena of analogy or contiguity. So, for example, if Uncle John is dead, the thought of the uncle can trigger elements analogous to the category of 'uncle' or to categories to which he belonged.[26] For example, anyone who looked like or could remind you of the uncle in question (adults, uncles, quick-tempered individuals, authoritarian types, alcoholics, etc.) could be substituted for him. Moreover, elements 'contiguous' to the uncle could feature in the dream: 'The place where he lived, the particular cap he would wear in the winter, the old furniture he collected.'[27] Similarly, the old friend of a female dreamer appeared in her dream with her brother's face because 'both of them provoke the same sense of helpless rage in her.'[28] Or, in another example, when he is about to submit a thesis in front of five members of a jury, a student dreams he is trying to convince five stars in the sky that his ideas are good ones – a vivid way of saying that the members of the jury are, for him, like brilliant and inaccessible stars.[29]

The method of 'free association' practised by Freud is a 'method according to which voice must be given to all thoughts without exception which enter the mind, whether such thoughts are based upon a specific element (word, number, dream-image or any kind of idea at all) or produced spontaneously.'[30] The patient is encouraged to let go of his or her thoughts so that the analyst can access the entire universe of associations particular to that individual, whether these are analogies or contiguities. Freud asks the dreamer to 'divert his attention from the dream as a whole on to the separate portions of its content and to report to us in succession everything that occurs to him in relation to each of these portions – what associations present themselves to him if he focuses on each of them separately.'[31] These associations provide a variety of materials, from memories of the day before the dream to memories of more distant periods, without which the dream would be incomprehensible. Freud's theory is that during the dream these same associations – or associations of the same type – are at work and render the dream possible. For at the heart of the dream-work are practical analogy (resemblance) and association through contiguity (indissociation) that were not always clearly distinguished by Freud. 'One and one only of these logical relations is very highly favoured by the mechanism of the dream-formation; namely, the relation of similarity, consonance or approximation – the relation of "just as". This relation, unlike any other, is capable of being represented in dreams in a variety of ways.'[32]

In the dream of one of his patients, Freud identifies, for example – thanks to information and associations provided by the dreamer – an association by contiguity, an almost homonymic literalisation, and an implicit analogy: 'As part of a longish dream a patient dreamt that *several*

members of his family were sitting round a table of peculiar shape, etc.' The
table in the dream reminds the dreamer of one he once saw when visiting
a family where relations between the father and the son were strained,
and the dreamer spontaneously explains 'the same thing was true of the
relationship between himself and his own father.' The table is therefore
associated with a particular family, and the fact that he sees his own family
grouped around it is an effective visual way of saying that the two families
are analogous. It amounts to saying: '*We are in exactly the same position
as they are*.' But the choice of the table to associate the two families and
to suggest this analogy is motivated by what is almost a homonymy, since
the family who own the table were called *Tischler* [literally, 'carpenter']:
'By making his relations sit at this *Tisch*, he was saying that they too were
Tischlers.'[33]

A dream published by René Allendy clearly demonstrates associations
through contiguity and analogy of situations.[34] A young man dreams he
is in Arcachon and that he is sledging over pine needles. In discussions
with the dreamer, the analyst discovers that, for him, Arcachon is the
town where he was treated for tuberculosis. At that time, he was both
attracted to women and afraid of them, a situation which caused him to
miss out on many romantic opportunities. Arcachon is therefore associated with a negative experience of illness during which things did not go
well for him on a sentimental level. The sledge ride over pine needles,
on the other hand, refers back to his very positive experience of sledging
down the slopes at La Bourboule when he was a child (aged eight). He
was at the time very proud of being the only one to do so, a fact which
provoked envy among other children. His treatment was moreover very
positive. Consequently, associations-contiguities allowed him to convey
his wish to find himself in a situation likely to provide sentimental opportunities (such as that in Arcachon) but with the success and the pride
which he felt when he was sledging down the slopes (at La Bourboule).
Like his friend who had just got engaged, he hoped for success on a
sentimental level.

René Allendy provides another dream which is clearly based both on an
association through analogy and on association through contiguity:

A young man had been much affected by the loss of his sister, who
had died at the age of twenty. So great was his grief that he forced
himself never to think about her and never to speak about his loss.
He dreams: *Dream* – I saw a little dog we used to have at my parents'
house (and which is, in fact, dead). I was amazed to see it was still
alive, I admired its longevity and I felt an overwhelming love for it.
Interpretation – When we know that the dog in question belonged
particularly to the dreamer's sister, and that it died not long before
she did, it is clear that the desire for resurrection and the deep feelings
of tenderness go back in reality to the dead sister. The displacement
enables the overwhelming emotions to be somewhat filtered and

justifies an overflowing of love which would have been incongruous considering the actual object.[35]

There is therefore an analogy of situation (dead sister/dead dog) and an association through contiguity (the dog belonged to his sister). As in post-traumatic dreams which express the trauma by transforming the initial traumatic situation so as to render it less painful or terrifying and to reduce the emotional involvement,[36] the substitution is brought about not by censorship but by a *process of connecting* the present with the past. What Allendy does not specify is whether the dreamer had seen a dog during the day or if he had simply heard some mention of this dog or seen a photograph of it. But the dreamer does not need to circumvent a non-existent censorship since, in his heart, he knows that his sister's dog is the *analogon* of his sister.

11

The Oneiric Processes

> The description of the oneiric structure (impossibility of
> expressing, dictatorship of figuration, condensation as sole means
> of expression) would attribute the disguise of latent thoughts as
> much to the condition of the dream as to [the] censor-repressed
> struggle. . . . The unconscious is the abandonment of the norms of
> wakeful expression.
> (Maurice Merleau-Ponty, *Institution and Passivity*, p. 158)

Armed with these two key notions of psychic functioning in the form of association through analogy and association through contiguity, we can now look more closely at the oneiric processes involved in the course of the production of dreams.

Freud often thought of the dream-work in terms of a translation from one language (latent) into another (manifest). Except in the case of the dreams of young children, which are, according to him, the 'open fulfilment of a permitted wish', the ordinary 'distorted dream' is the 'disguised fulfilment of a repressed wish'.[1] Given the central place of the dream censorship in his conception of the psychic mechanism, this translation is in fact a kind of 'coding', of 'ciphering' or 'encrypting'. For Freud, therefore, the dream-work is made up of all the processes through which latent thoughts allow themselves to be glimpsed in manifest thoughts. Freud talks about 'the transformation of the latent dream thoughts into the manifest dream content' and even about 'psychical material being changed over from one mode of expression to another, from a mode of expression which is immediately intelligible to us to another which we can only come to understand with the help of guidance and effort.'[2]

The problem with such a vision is that it implies the existence of a 'latent dream' waiting to be translated into a 'manifest dream', whereas in fact no previously formed message lurks in the depths of the unconscious waiting to be transformed and encrypted by the dream-work into a manifest message acceptable to the censorship. The 'latent dream' is more like a hypothesis which the interpreter feels obliged to formulate in order to understand the 'manifest dream'. Making this into a means of expression, a language or an existing content would, as Bourdieu said, mean shifting from the model of reality to the reality of the model.[3] Believing that the manifest content of the dream is simply the translation of a latent content, imagining that a message which starts out as perfectly clear would be transformed into a 'remarkable and puzzling form',[4] is akin to suggesting that linguistic productions are merely the transposition of a thought already formulated deep within the mind.[5]

It would in fact be preferable to say that the manifest content of the dream, that which can be accessed through the dream account, cannot be understood, and therefore interpreted, without some reconstruction of elements of the dreamer's life, of a 'non-dream state' (the circumstances which preceded the dream, his or her past experiences, and the current and past nature of his or her preoccupations), and without taking into account all the psychic operations that contribute to the creation of the dream in the particular circumstances of expression that correspond to the context of sleep.

Ordinary objects, people or actions in inappropriate contexts; unusual objects, places or people in ordinary contexts; objects, places or people who metamorphose into other objects, places or people; people who are physically recognisable but who, in the mind of the dreamer, take on the identity of other people; objects, places or people who are blends of a number of objects, places or people; people who behave in a very unusual manner in comparison with their usual behaviour in real life; sudden disappearances of objects, places or people; unexpected temporal or spatial jumps, etc.[6] – all these elements contribute to making the dream narrative seem absurd, strange or incongruous. But this strangeness disappears when we understand the nature of the oneiric processes at work and their relevance from the perspective of the dreamer's experience.

Verbal language, symbolic capacity and dream images

We dream first and foremost with visual images, and our memories are therefore more often visual than linguistic. Characters in dreams do not always speak, but the dreamer is an omniscient narrator who knows what they are thinking or feeling. Nevertheless, our symbolic capacity to visualize mentally scenes which are imagined rather than seen, our capacity also to construct images which are not lacking in coherence from a narrative perspective and which are organised into plots ranging from the very simple (a single action) to the highly complex (a sequence made of up of many actions), is linked to our lexical, syntactic and narrative linguistic skills. When we know, moreover, that a great many dreams are based on literalisations of culturally diverse metaphors ('to have the upper hand', 'to be above all that', 'to get it in the neck', 'to have it up to here', 'to have broken off all ties', etc.) or homonyms (Mr Woolf might take the guise of a wolf), it is no surprise to find that linguistic capacities of all kinds are secretly at work in the creation of dreams.

Unlike animals, the symbolic capacities of human beings, their capability to transmit their accumulated experiences and knowledge from one generation to the next, and their mnemonic capacities to store sequences of past experiences in the form of schemas or of dispositions makes them less dependent on immediate situations. They can free themselves from the diktats of the present by reflecting on past events or by planning or fantasising about events to come. They can even invent events which have never happened, as a way of dealing with the problems which preoccupy them, in the form of games, lies told to someone else, creative acts, daydreams or dreams.

The dream therefore is simply one form of expression among others, made possible by human mnemonic capacities and the symbolic capacity to imagine things which are not there or which do not exist. The dream is merely the prolongation, in sleep, of a symbolic activity which is at work in the waking state. As Norbert Elias wrote, human beings are by nature endowed with a 'greatly extended human capacity to evoke, by means of a sound-pattern memory, images of objects or events that are not present when the evocation takes place. The sounds can evoke such an image irrespective of whether or not the topic of communication represented by it occurs here and now.'[7]

In an attempt to distinguish the human species in relation to other animal species, and to reflect on human life in the context of its onto-genetic development, David Foulkes maintains that the dream is a symbolic production beyond the capacity of other animals, one which manifests itself only very gradually through early childhood, as the child begins to develop symbolic capacities. The capacity to dream is not therefore an innate capacity, in place from birth. Studies in child psychology situate between fifteen and eighteen months the moment where 'children begin to imagine or represent things in their minds in such a way that signs and symbols are now in use' and where 'symbolic play and language now become possible'.[8] The beginnings of oneiric activity could logically date from the same period, but studies show that the capacity to dream develops only very gradually.

The reason behind this is the fact that linguistic skills develop extremely slowly, and in the early stages the child has difficulty in expressing verbally the pre-verbal experience he or she has already mastered in practical terms. As Stern emphasises, specific episodes of life often 'fall through the linguistic sieve and cannot be referenced verbally until the child is very advanced in language, and sometimes never.'[9] Cultural inequalities can even be deeply divisive in such cases. But with the acquisition of an increasingly complex language, children can not only express their preverbal experiences but also distort the reality of their experiences:

With its emergence, infants become estranged from direct contact with their own personal experience. Language forces a space between interpersonal experience as lived and as represented . . . Finally, with the advent of language and symbolic thinking, children now have the tools to distort and transcend reality. They can create expectations contrary to past experiences. They can elaborate a wish contrary to present fact. They can represent someone or something in terms of symbolically associated attributes (for example, bad experiences with the mother) that in reality were never experienced all together at any one time but that can be pulled together from isolated episodes into a symbolic representation (the 'bad mother' or 'incompetent me').[10]

There is therefore a paradox in the acquisition of linguistic capacities, for, 'while language vastly extends our grasp on reality, it can also provide the mechanism for the distortion of reality as experienced.'[11] It is this paradox which potentially gives rise to imagination, the lie, self-reflection, anticipatory planning, daydreaming and dreams.

Foulkes develops his exploration of the dreams of children and adolescents by focusing on two studies: a longitudinal one (the same children were studied between the ages of three and five, then between five and seven, then again between seven and nine; others were studied between nine and eleven, then between eleven and thirteen and between thirteen and fifteen) and a transversal one (comparing children of different ages). He points out first of all that very young children have not yet acquired the capacity to symbolise or, in other words, mentally to represent absent realities or realities which do not actually exist as such: 'Infants can manipulate information currently available in the environment, but they cannot manipulate information without concurrent environmental support. In effect, they can "think" of dolly when it's there but not when it's not. How then, could they not only conjure up a picture of dolly but also make up a story about dolly while sleeping?'[12]

Dreaming is directly linked to our symbolic capacity to think in images, in waking life and while asleep, rather than simply to our perceptive skills. Seeing something in a dream is essentially a matter of thinking in images. Foulkes refers to studies which prove that people who went blind before the age of five were unable to think visually either in waking life or in dreams, but that people who went blind after the age of five continued to think in a visual form in both their waking life and their dreams.[13] This simple result would tend to prove that, once an autonomous system of internal visualisation is in place, the dreamer no longer needs to rely on their visual perceptive capacities in order to see things in their dreams.

Between the ages of three and six, the most common response of children when they are woken up during the period of paradoxical sleep implies they were not dreaming, and Foulkes suggests 'that preschoolers generally (that is, not just in their dreaming alone) have difficulty in mentally imagining an active self or any kind of movement or ongoing interaction.'[14] The images they see in dreams are often confined to fixed images; they are not themselves present in the dream and nor do they feel emotions in relation to the images. It is only between five and nine years of age that their dreams begin to resemble those of adults. The process of transformation comes about in the following way: initially descriptions of dreams get progressively longer but not necessarily more frequent; they include social interactions and movements, with the result that the dream shifts from being a static image to become an animated one, and the dreamer still does not feature in the dream; at a later stage dreams become more frequent, have a more complex narrative and feature the dreamer himself, who experiences emotions and thoughts in response to the events in the dream.

To sum up the work undertaken by Foulkes, it would seem that no dreams occur before the age of three; that between three and five there are relatively rare dreams, made up of isolated events, with static images and no participation of dreamers themselves in the dream; between five and seven dreams are slightly more frequent and include simple sequences of events and animated images, but still no participation of the dreamer; and finally, between the ages of seven to nine, dreams become relatively frequent, with a more complex narrative, animated images and the presence of the dreamer in the dream.[15]

The tendency not to dream and the relative sparsity of dreams between the ages of three and five are linked to what child psychologists have called 'childhood amnesia' – in other words, the incapacity to remember episodes from the first years of life. The initial incapacity and then the weak capacity to visualise mentally events experienced in early childhood make it difficult to remember or reuse them in a more or less modified state in the form of daydreams or dreams.[16] Whatever children know before the age of five is 'learned by body' (Bourdieu), in a practical or procedural manner (Dornes), but not necessarily in the form of episodes which can be memorised and therefore recalled subsequently. Likewise, animals are capable of acquiring habits but not of remembering what they have done in the past. They have internalised schemas of action, which can, as in the case of dressage for example, be the product of a deliberate inculcation, but they are completely in the situation which is currently unfolding around them, locked into the present. In the case of the human species, children gradually learn to visualise things in their minds and are capable of being both present and not present, of carrying out a task while thinking about something else altogether, of preparing for what will happen next or thinking about what has already happened and of dreaming.

Patricia A. Kilroe, an American linguist, put forward the idea that verbal thought could be 'the source from which all dream imagery is generated'.[17] According to her, 'the linguistic system is important to both dream content and dream formation.'[18] The dream can first of all include verbal utterances in which the dreamer speaks with other characters in the dream or is spoken to; he writes, reads, hears his thoughts or those of others, etc. The images which make up the dream can then be derived from linguistic tropes such as plays on words (e.g. a fox representing Mrs Fox)[19] or metaphoric expressions (e.g. seeing lightning in the dream can represent a romantic encounter). The dream can also be indirectly dependent on language when it frees itself from the present moment and calls on elements from the past or looks ahead to moments to come (which implies a mastery of the symbolic that only the acquisition of language makes possible). And, finally, the dream account refers to the non-observable mental states of the dreamer or of other characters in the dream, generally expressed by the use of verbs referring to mental experiences: 'I'm worried', 'I'm wondering', 'I want', 'I realise', etc., expressing states of mind which, without language, could not be expressed.[20]

Dream images therefore are as much to do with our linguistic capacities and our capacity to symbolise reality, in particular that constructed through language acquisition, as with our actual perceptive capacities. The ability to construct sequences of action in the form of images requires at the very least being able mentally to manipulate, without perceptive aid, images which symbolise reality.

Visualisation

One of the key characteristics of the dream, which it shares moreover with the many daydreaming moments that punctuate our days, is that, before being – potentially – a verbal account, it is a flow of images, sounds, sensations and emotions experienced by the dreamer. At the time of the dream, the dreamer is generally convinced that the dream experience is a real one. The dream is therefore structurally comparable to a film in which the dreamer is the principal actor and the visual dimension is a central part of the oneiric experience. As Scherner had already pointed out in 1861: 'The imagination speaks through visible impressions.'[21] This central property was reiterated by Freud, who wrote that 'dreams transform thoughts into visual images'[22] and that one of the difficulties in recounting a dream is precisely because it involves 'transforming thoughts into visual images'.[23] Oneiric dramatisation consists in a 'transformation of one thought in the scene . . . (its "dramatization")'.[24]

At the end of the 1980s, the American neuropsychiatrist John Allan Hobson confirmed the results established on an empirical basis in 1903 by the French physiologist and psychologist Henri-Étienne Beaunis to the effect that, in sensory terms, dreams are composed first and foremost of images, then of auditory and tactile sensations, and almost never of olfactory or gustatory sensations.[25] Other researchers added the kinesthetic dimension to this list (the feeling of falling, of flying, of not being able to move forward, of a sensation of heaviness in the legs or the body, etc.).[26] And, of course, all of these involve the accompanying emotions experienced by the dreamers.

At the same time, the need for thoughts to take a figurative form acts as a powerful constraint which has profound effects on the way they are expressed. The expressive intentions of the dreamer need to take a 'pictorial and concrete' form.[27] Out of 150 personal dreams noted and studied by Maurice Halbwachs, only around 10 per cent included words which were 'really uttered or heard':

> In the others, everything seemed indeed to be reduced to visual images, thoughts, emotional states. In the dream it is in fact very often extremely difficult to draw a distinction between what is actually said or heard by ourselves or by other people in the dream and what is simply thought, as though we found ourselves in the presence of people incapable of speech to whom we attributed speeches, questions, responses, repartee, none of which are actually articulated or given any voice.[28]

Yet why should the dreamer need to make his characters speak, since they are so intimately known to him or her, and given that he, or she, is at the same time both narrator and listener? Addressing only him- or herself, the dreamer is not obliged to respect the linguistic and, in particular, narrative conventions which ordinarily enable others to understand what we are saying.

Halbwachs also senses very pertinently that dream images function more as symbols or representative forms than as detailed images without any very powerful significance: 'We could conclude that there is indeed, behind the image glimpsed in the dream, a more or less general notion, and that the image itself, because it merely represents the notion, because it partly merges with it, bears closer resemblance to a simplified symbol than to a living painting.'[29] Since such images are the visual residue of a problem, they are in a sense visual schema. I dream not about X (person, place, object, etc.) but about what X represents for me, from a particular perspective.

Dramatisation-exaggeration

Another property of dreams, their tendency to dramatise and exaggerate, stems largely from their symbolic and visual nature. Faced with the need to convey a 'problem' in images, the dream uses symbolisation and metaphorisation, which tend to have a more marked effect on the mind than if the situation were being recounted verbally in the waking state. Dreaming of a gigantic wave which is about to engulf us, so as to convey the feeling of loss of control over existence, or dreaming of running but without making any headway, in order to convey the feeling of having failed in a project, gives the dream a dramatic dimension.

But, by dramatising a scene, the dream can also simply be faithfully depicting an emotion experienced in waking life. Marcel Foucault describes, for example, a child of six who dreamt he was being eaten by a lion. During the previous day, he had walked past a house where dogs were barking, and the little girl he was with had told him that the dogs might eat him. This idea frightened him very much, and that very night this fear was depicted in a scene in a dream. He had seen lions during a previous holiday and therefore replaced the dog by a lion, a much more imposing animal and indeed capable of eating him, in order to express the intensity of his fear and to make the oneiric situation match that described by the little girl.[30] Likewise, a banal incident which happened in the classroom (the pupils smiling at a slip of the tongue) led to a teacher having a dream which magnified the event and revealed his fear of not being able to exert his authority. That evening he dreamt that the pupils in his class were behaving so rowdily that he could not even start his lesson. The principal came into the classroom at the worst possible moment and observed the uproar without managing to calm the situation down.[31]

When, in 1876, F. W. Hildebrandt published a study on dreams, he noted that 'the dream gives a magnified image to the dreamer of his moral tendencies.'[32] Théodore Flournoy, for his part, describes the 'curious power of dramatisation'[33] in dreams. In the same way, the exaggeration of feelings is present when one of Freud's patients dreams of the death of her second nephew, because the death of her first nephew was associated, through contiguity, with meeting a man of whom she was fond.[34] Freud explained that the dream did not make her sad because, in her mind, the death of her second nephew was mentally associated with the chance of seeing the man she loved. But he disregarded the fact that the patient in question clearly stated that she preferred the first nephew (who had died some time previously). The absence of grief therefore also conveys, in a more pronounced and dramatised way, her feelings in relation to the second nephew. From the starting point of very real feelings, the dream condenses, caricatures and exaggerates.

Jacques Montangero also noticed the hyperbolic nature of dreams: 'Quite often we find in dreams details of events, objects and people. It could be said that the rhetorical figure of hyperbole is frequently used in the process of oneiric production.'[35] The Swiss psychologist and psychotherapist analyses one of his own dreams, in which he saw himself as 'a dwarf of the Roman army' leaving the action in a 'serious and gloomy' manner as a way of representing his feeling of being small, ridiculous, obsolete (from another age), since in real life he was confronted with the painful situation of having to stop practising psychotherapy for reasons outside his control.[36] The oneiric scenario visibly transposes in a very striking manner a feeling that words would struggle to describe as effectively.[37]

Since dreams depict situations, feelings and problems in an 'exaggerated manner', this confirms the hypothesis of an almost total absence of censorship and restraint. The dreamer does not need to make compromises with others and can let go, resort to caricature or go 'straight to the point' in a way that would not be possible in the context of their interactions in daily life. Forced to deal with a problem in a visual way, and with no need to disguise what they have to say with euphemisms, the dream uses eloquent images which present the situation in a dramatised manner. For example, Freud's patient who dreams of the death of her second nephew is not in the least bit concerned about her lack of compassion, since it is not a real death but simply an effective way of saying that she would like to re-encounter the man to whom she is attracted, while at the same time acknowledging her preference for her first nephew who did actually die.

Personal or universal symbolisation

Certain forms of symbolisation involve representing one 'thing' by the sign for 'something' else, the properties of which suggest those of the first thing. So, for example, if the scales are the symbol of justice and cannot be replaced by some other arbitrary sign (a coffee machine or a breadboard), it is because they represent the use of the scales to weigh both for and against. Likewise, if long objects can symbolise the erect phallus, or if any form of cavity symbolises the female genitalia, it is because of their structural properties. Some symbols are therefore based on analogies. Others are more conventional, so that, for example, a rose can symbolise love, the colour red can suggest revolutionary commitment, and the dove can be associated with peace. For a symbol to exist, the object or the sign for the object must be taken not at face value but for what it suggests, what it represents or with what it is historically associated. The ornithologist studying doves is not working on a symbol of peace any more than the botanist who is interested in roses is a specialist in love, and people who sell umbrellas or knives are not in the business of marketing phallic symbols.

Any object or any sign can therefore become a symbol of values, things, activities or actions. But the question still arises as to how we can know *for whom* these objects or these signs act as a symbol. For a symbol to be recognised as such, both those who have devised it and those who are on the receiving end of it need to share common experiences or knowledge. Symbols can be very widely used or have a very limited use (a couple or a group of friends could share symbols which are not recognised by people outside their micro-group), but, in all cases, they are based on mental habits of association that are susceptible to historical, cultural or social variation.

For example, Jeannette Mageo, an American anthropologist, demonstrated the significance of the presence of the car in dreams recounted by undergraduate students at Washington State University (thirty-five students, made up of eighteen male and seventeen female students, and 300 dream accounts, including 193 written by men and 107 by women). In forty-seven of the 300 dreams studied, the car was a key feature in the dream.[38] A practical object and a cultural theme of central importance in the United States, the car can thus symbolically express a social status, sexuality, the need for a sense of freedom, of autonomy, of adventure, of mobility, etc. All these themes feature in advertising, films, novels, etc., and the car becomes a way of expressing fundamental aspects of life such as the notion of choice or of direction (taking the right lane when on a motorway slip-road), the idea that old age is like the battered wreck of an old car, the idea that life is a journey, the idea whereby some people just keep going while others are left by the wayside, the idea of power and status associated with owning a large, fast and powerful car or of weakness associated with ownership of a small, slow and unreliable car, the idea of being in the dominant position or the active position when seated at the wheel of the car, or of being in a dominated and passive position when merely a passenger or being driven, etc. If American dreamers often see cars in their dreams, it is because these are for the most part widely shared symbols which aid communication between self and others and enable a condensed form of expression to be used in self-to-self communication.

Ever since people started to take an interest in dreams, commentators have constantly drawn attention to their symbolic dimension. But the question still remains as to the exact nature of the symbols involved. From 'dream books' to Freud, the temptation to compile lists or dictionaries of universally relevant oneiric symbols has been a considerable one. Depending on whether the unconscious is seen as the product of an archaic, innate and universally shared foundation or as that of an individual social history, psychoanalysis hopes to determine once and for all, for all dreamers from all societies and across all eras, the meaning of the symbols that feature in their dreams. Are dream symbols universally shared or personal? And, if symbols can be personal, how is it that symbols which are supposedly shared by groups, either large or small, may be shared only by a single individual?

From antiquity onwards, this question of the nature of symbols has been addressed by oneirocritics. Artemidorus of Daldis established a difference between 'theorematic dreams' and 'allegorical dreams', the former being those which 'came true in the way that it had been presented in sleep' and the latter 'those which signify one thing by means of another'.[39] Judging by some of his comments, Artemidorus tends to favour a method which can be adapted to each new case rather than to a fixed dictionary of universal symbols. He shows, for example, that the same kind of dream or the same elements within a dream can mean or symbolise very different things depending on the dreamer. A dreamer who is transformed into a bridge might see in this image his future role as ferryman, but another person dreaming of a bridge is expressing the fact that they feel they are being held in contempt and 'trampled underfoot', whereas others could use the image of a bridge where many people 'go over them' to symbolise their sense of being treated like prostitutes. In each case, the same elements do not represent the same things, and detailed knowledge of the dreamer's life is needed in order to know what they are referring to.[40] We therefore observe in Artemidorus the 'importance accorded to taking into account all the circumstance of the dream and the elements of the dream' and the 'importance of adapting the symbolic system to the place the interpreter is practising his art, one element possibly having one meaning in one place and another somewhere else, depending on local customs.'[41] Some of the advice of the most famous oneirocritic seems therefore to point both towards a psychology or a sociology on an individual scale and towards a sociology or an anthropology of cultures and customs associated with groups or peoples.

Among the European scholars of the nineteenth century, it is Antoine Charma who directly confronts the question of symbols in the dream. Charma declares that the dream speaks 'a language of its own' which rarely confines itself 'to simple and direct expression': 'It seeks out metaphor and allegory; it symbolises, dramatises everything. Does the notion of some kind of danger come into your mind? A lion immediately leaps forward to devour you! Does an awkward position make you fear you are falling out of your bed? An abyss suddenly appears into which you are falling!'[42]

The dream uses symbols, metaphors and allegories, and Charma is undoubtedly the first person to have clearly identified this aspect of oneiric language. But, to these remarks made in his capacity as a quasi-linguist of dream language, he also adds a mythical explanation, making it the language of primitive peoples and of children: 'This figurative, oriental style is the language spoken by men and the world still in their infancy; these disjointed, unconsidered, impetuous combinations represent the thinking we see in the infancy of nations and of individuals. . . . for the child, sleep means going back to a primitive state; for men, it means becoming a child again!'[43] This mixture of the mythical and the scientific inevitably ends up undermining his argument.

In his book *Das Leben des Traums* (The life of dreams), published in 1861, Karl Albert Scherner also claimed that psychic activity expressed itself in a symbolic language capable of being interpreted. He tends to make symbols into universal elements of language. He claims, for example, that 'in a universal manner' the imagination indicates the human body by a 'building made of walls' – in other words, by a 'house'.[44] Similarly, according to him the 'bright yellow bird' is 'a favourite dream of women and young girls who love children', and 'a happy frame of mind in a dream is conveyed by flowers which bend gently towards each other.'[45] He is one of the first people to refer to male sexual symbols (knives, pointed weapons, pipes, clarinets, etc.) and to their female equivalents (narrow courtyards, staircases) in the context of dreams: 'Sexual movement is symbolised in the form of replicas of the excited organ itself or by images and actions of the imagination which express the desire for sexual satisfaction.'[46] Freud found enough here to inspire his own 'sexualist' convictions, based on other grounds and in particular on his study of cases of hysteria. But what is interesting is that Scherner sees in this symbolisation of genital organs merely one type of symbolisation among others, whereas Freud tended (even if he sometimes denied it) to bring everything back to disguised sexuality.

Even if he understands that visual symbolism is a constraint specific to the dreamer which can in itself explain some of the strange qualities of the dream, Freud still clings to the hypothesis that censorship is at work whenever symbolism is present. The psyche will rely on symbolisation in order to get around the censorship: 'Thus symbolism is a second and independent factor in the distortion of dreams, alongside of the dream-censorship. It is plausible to suppose, however, that the dream-censorship finds it convenient to make use of symbolism, since it leads towards the same end – the strangeness and incomprehensibility of dreams.'[47] Yet symbols disguise nothing, since they function as summaries of experience which speak to the dreamer and, with rather extraordinarily minimal means, allow him or her to use the dream to consider the problems arising from his or her history and everyday life. The dreamer is in this sense like a mathematician manipulating mathematical symbols in order to work with a simplified language on the essential elements of problems.

Freud would, moreover, continue for a long period to hesitate and oscillate between two approaches: the interpretation of symbols in the context of the patient's history and an understanding of their inner world through the association of ideas *versus* an interpretation based on the search for universal symbols. Some of his followers encouraged him to adopt this second approach. So, for example, in 1909, the doctor, psychologist and psychoanalyst Wilhelm Stekel proposed assembling a collection of dreams with a view to studying the most frequently occurring symbols.[48] Like Freud, his aim was to produce a 'dictionary of dream symbols'. Similarly, Otto Rank, two of whose texts, including 'Dream and creative writing', were included by Freud in the 1914 edition of *The Interpretation of Dreams*, worked not on biographies but on an 'interpretation of the individual symbols . . . unfolded without the dreamer's free associations' which, along with 'thematically subdivided and numbered supplements', are 'brought to bear on the analysis'.[49] And Carl Gustav Jung also chose to focus on interpreting the collective unconscious, neglecting individual history a little too much in Freud's view: 'Jung attempted to give to the facts of analysis a fresh interpretation of an abstract, impersonal and non-historical character, and thus hoped to escape the need for recognising the importance of infantile sexuality and of the Œdipus complex, as well as the necessity for any analysis of childhood.'[50]

Freud did not reduce all symbols to universal symbols and showed himself to be much more cautious than Stekel, Rank or Jung: 'Some symbols are universally disseminated and can be met with in all dreamers belonging to a single linguistic or cultural group; there are others which occur only within the most restricted and individual limits, symbols constructed by an individual out of his own ideational material.'[51] He was also surrounded by scholars who were dubious about the viability of a project to compile a dictionary of symbols.[52] But, in a note added to *The Interpretation of Dreams* in 1925, he suggests that, if the analytical method 'cannot be applied unless we have access to the dreamer's associative material', it is nevertheless possible 'if, namely, the dreamer has employed symbolic elements in the content of the dream.'[53] And, in the same text, he adds that 'we may expect that the analysis of dreams will lead us to a knowledge of man's archaic heritage, of what is physically innate in him.'[54] Freud therefore acknowledges the existence of symbols which are universally effective and interpretable and which as a result obviate the need for knowledge of the dreamer's own experience: '[The symbols] allow us in certain circumstances to interpret a dream without questioning the dreamer, who indeed would in any case have nothing to tell us about the symbol.'[55]

Freud also tends to generalise his interpretations without always taking care to link the dream symbols to the dreamer's own experiences. For him, the emperor and the empress, the king and the queen, of necessity symbolise the parents (they 'really represent the dreamer's parents'),[56] all long objects can represent the male organ, and all boxes, chests, wardrobes or cavities symbolise the vagina.[57] The thoughts of a four-year-old child towards his mother are interpreted as a symbolic way for the child to think about reproduction (children grow in the mother just as trees grow in the ground [earth mother = mother] and the father is in the image of God in creating the world [father = God])[58] and 'a "large party" meant, as we already know, a secret'![59] We are sometimes not very far from the wildest frontiers of oneiromancy.

However, the study of specific dreams makes it clear that Freud was fully aware of the extremely personal nature of dream symbols, in the sense that these refer to particular experiences. The dreamer keeps in his dream only the elements that speak to him most pertinently. These act almost like personal symbols, which represent and condense many aspects of the dreamer's own experience. These '"nodal points" upon which a great number of the dream-thoughts converge'[60] are elements of the dream which we should seek to understand by looking firstly and most importantly at the dreamer's representations and associations before referring to any general or universal symbols.[61]

And even in cases where symbols are more widely shared (as in the case of policemen or -women, schoolmasters or -mistresses, kings or queens, who represent figures of authority or of power; or in that of major historical figures such as Hitler or Mussolini), it is preferable to know what such symbols represent in the mind of each dreamer: 'Let us point out at once that certain symbols are clearly personal and are based only on memories, impressions or judgments which are particular to the dreamer. Others are of such a general nature that anyone at all is capable of understanding them. But closer examination reveals that even the latter have been chosen because they correspond to something personal to the dreamer.'[62]

There are images or symbols which are shared collectively but which do not, however, symbolise the same experiences. The Eiffel Tower could be a symbol of social power for some, of personal ambition for others, a symbol of the fear of a terrorist attack, a phallic symbol or a symbol of love for those who enjoyed a romantic rendezvous there. It is the systematicity of interpretations which is a problem, as, for example, when Freud and the majority of psychoanalysts see kings and queens, emperors and empresses automatically as *analogons* of parents. By so doing they are assuming that all dreamers have had parents or parent substitutes representing figures of authority and that only parental figures – rather than those from a superior hierarchy for example – are capable of coming back to haunt dreamers. Only the associations of ideas made by dreamers are 'capable of encapsulating a generalised desire within individual circumstances and of allowing the dreamer's affective problem to be understood.'[63]

Oneiric symbols must therefore always be contextualised within the specific formulation which constitutes each individual dream and in the very fabric of the existence of the dreamer for whom a particular symbol can represent a very specific type of experience. As Allendy wrote: 'More often than not, the interpreter finds himself confronted with a symbolic language that is tailored to the dreamer. It is clear that, in such conditions, it is impossible to establish a sort of interpretation table, a symbolic dictionary similar to the "Dream books" used in popular superstitions and which can provide only the universal value of symbols.'[64] This does not in itself prevent the study of dreams experienced by dreamers who share certain elements of their existential situation (redundancy, accidents, imprisonment, illness, etc.) or the identification of trans-individual recurrences, but the exercise has its limits and needs to be looked at alongside more in-depth case studies to ensure that a purely artificial community has not been created.

And, in all cases, research must bid farewell to any possibility of creating a dictionary of universal symbols or metaphors. If he does not respect the principle of the use of context (oneiric, circumstantial and biographical) for symbols, the scholar can say what the dream makes him think of, on the basis of his own existential background, but this is not necessarily that of the dreamer. On the contrary, interpretation should look first at the various elements of the dream and the dreamer's own representation of them in order to begin to understand why they are present. For example, if the city of New York appears in a dream, questions should be asked about the role of that city in the dreamer's experience and whether, for that individual, it represents 'a huge pulsating city', 'a world artistic centre', 'a place where I was free and happy', etc.[65]

This need to be familiar with the dreamer's experience in order to interpret their dream correctly and to avoid overinterpretation was very clearly expressed by Erich Fromm:

Let us assume that someone has had a saddening experience in a certain city; when he hears the name of that city, he will easily connect the name with a mood of sadness, just as he would connect it with a mood of joy had his experience been a happy one. . . . As a result, we need associations of the dreamer in order to understand what the accidental symbol means. Had he not told us about the experience he had in the city of which he dreamed or about the connection between the person he dreams of and his experiences with this person, we could not possibly understand what these symbols mean.[66]

Metaphor

Conveying an anxiety as a monster or conveying it as a dinner that is difficult to digest – these are two metaphors.
(Paul Valéry, *Questions du rêve*, p. 94)

The use of metaphor emerges as a central element in oneiric creation. Patricia Kilroe refers, for example, to a dream 'in which the dreamer is standing in front of a woman who is trying to pull her sweater over her head.'[67] Questioned about her dream, the dreamer explained that a woman in her workplace was trying 'to pull the wool over her eyes' – in other words, to deceive her. Deception or trickery, which, all things considered, are rather abstract notions, find a vivid means of expression in the culturally based metaphor 'to pull the wool over someone's eyes'.

The visual constraint which imposes itself on thinking within the dream is what makes the metaphor such an important means of oneiric expression. It is as though the need for expression was making the most of all the visual expressions available to the dreamer in order to succeed in spite of the visual constraint. The omnipresence of metaphor, which is an indication of the strength of the visual constraint (the dreamer has no choice but to think in images), also proves that oneiric images are not completely independent of the culturally determined structures of verbal language, given that an extremely vivid verbal expression can be the framework used to express something in the dream.

The key role of metaphor in dreams has been emphasised by many scholars. Firstly, it was Gotthilf Heinrich Schubert who spoke of 'a metaphoric mode of expression used by the soul'[68] in dreams. Then it was Freud's turn to draw attention to the use made of metaphor in dreams, which he saw as resulting from a need to thwart the censorship. The act of speaking of something in an indirect way, in terms designed to distance it from reality, can, for him, be interpreted only as a form of disguise or misrepresentation. Nevertheless, the mere existence of a constraint of visual representation of thoughts is in itself enough to justify the dreamer's use of whichever means are most appropriate for this objective or for these conditions of expression. And this is even more pertinent given that what is to be explained in the form of concrete images often starts out as something rather abstract (e.g. a feeling or a series of feelings).

In one of his dreams,[69] Freud saw himself riding a horse in an awkward and timid manner. He encountered one of his colleagues, also on horse-back but sitting in a much more confident way, who made a disagreeable comment to him about his riding style. Following this, he began to find himself sitting more and more comfortably on the horse and observes that he feels quite at home 'up there'. At that time Freud was afflicted with a boil at the base of the scrotum and would have been incapable of riding a horse. The dream therefore placed him is a situation where he defied suffering and, in a sense, denied it in order to continue practising his activity, which is what he did in reality. But at the same time the dream refers to tensions between Freud and a colleague who had taken over one of his patients. Freud felt that this colleague 'liked to ride the high horse over me' since this had happened. And, moreover, 'one of my few patrons among the leading physicians in this city' had recently, in reference to the position Freud occupied in the establishment where he was practising, made the following remark to him: 'You struck me as being firmly in the saddle there.' In a very condensed and effective way, the scene with the horse enabled him to make reference at one and the same time to his problem of the painful boil and the courage it took to continue to exercise his profession eight or ten hours per day, to the tension with a colleague who was treating him disdainfully, and to a compliment made by a power-ful colleague on the legitimacy of his position in the establishment where he was working.

And, with reference to a patient's dream, Freud wrote with great clarity that 'this dream achieved its purpose by an extremely simple device: it took a figure of speech literally and gave an exact representation of its wording.'[70] Indeed, in this dream the patient dreamt that a servant girl was throwing animals, and notably a monkey, at her. Freud commented that 'monkey', like other animal names, is an insult and that the expression which gives rise to the dream is therefore that of 'hurling invectives' (*mit Schimpfworten um sich werfen*). The need to express ideas visually and in a condensed manner, and not the fear of censorship, is therefore what lies behind this kind of process. Jean Piaget cites for example a dream recounted by Herbert Silberer, one of Freud's followers, who, in his waking state, was working on a comparison of the notions of time expressed by Kant and Schopenhauer. Having fallen asleep before he was able to complete this comparison, 'he sees himself in a public office, trying to contact two officials at different counters, and missing one after the other.'[71] Piaget does not say if, on the day of the dream or in the preceding days, Silberer had experienced or heard of a similar situation in a public office, but it is highly likely that he borrowed the visual model for his dream from a similar recent situation.

The process used, perfectly described by Freud, is a *literalisation of metaphor*. It is a literary process which is to be found, for example, in Kafka when he uses a legal metaphor to talk about the internal *trial* which is playing out inside him and of 'the terrible trial which is ongoing' between his father and himself.[72] He does not say explicitly that what Joseph K is experiencing *resembles* a permanent trial or that his social and subjective life is *comparable* to a courtroom, but he relates a story of a trial, of legal proceedings, and of guilt in such a strange manner that the reader is forced to tell himself that he cannot possibly be describing a real court or a genuine trial. In the same way, since his family, and particularly his father, considers him as a parasite, in his novella *Metamorphosis*, he describes a character who is transformed into a hideous parasite and brings misfortune to the whole family. The process is so powerfully present in Kafka's work that it is almost as though he did indeed draw inspiration from the oneiric processes that the transcription of his dreams led him to discover.[73]

A fine example of the literalisation of metaphor is to be found in a dream analysed by the Swiss psychiatrist Ludwig Binswanger and discussed by Michel Foucault. A woman aged thirty-three, with severe depression, who suffers from frequent outbursts of anger and is sexually inhibited (she had undergone a sexual trauma at the age of five), had been undergoing psychotherapy for a year when she had the following dream: 'She is crossing the frontier, a customs agent makes her open her luggage: "I take out all my things, the official takes them one by one, finally I take out a silver goblet, wrapped in tissue paper; then he says, 'Why do you bring out the most important thing last?'"'[74] The dream metaphorically enacts the process of psychoanalytic treatment: it is the place where, in ordinary language, people 'open their suitcases for inspection' and 'pour their hearts out'.* And, like a customs post, it enables you to pass from one world (the one in which you are ill) to another (the one in which you are cured). At the time of the dream, the sexual trauma had not yet been established but was about to be uncovered. The silver goblet which the dreamer takes out of her luggage produces a feeling of anguish in her and turns out to be associated, through contiguity-metonymy, with her grandmother, who had a similar object in her house. And it was while in the grandmother's house that she experienced her traumatic experience. In the very room where the incident took place, there was a silver teapot wrapped in tissue paper. The dream therefore expresses in a condensed way, with the aid of a literalised metaphor and metonymy, that the scene to be put under scrutiny in the context of the therapy had taken place at her grandmother's house. Thanks to the associations made during treatment, the dream-work begins to reveal the trauma which will be fully reconstituted in the waking state with the help of the psychiatrist.

Alfred Adler also maintained, in 1933, that the dream proceeds '"parabolically", metaphorically, in similes, somewhat like poets when they wish to arouse feelings and emotions.' But he notes that this use of metaphors is very much present in the waking state: 'We can add that people completely devoid of poetic gifts use comparisons when they wish to make

---

* Translator's note: In French the expression used is '*vider son sac*' – literally, 'empty your bags'.

an impression, if only by employing such terms of abuse as "ass", "old woman", etc., and teachers do the same when they despair of explaining something in simple words.'[75] René Allendy too observed that certain dreams 'resemble certain expressions in ordinary language.' He gives as an example the 'dream of a young and poor man who pictured his aunt, from whom he would inherit, setting off on a long journey (death)' and the 'dream of the man who sees a pretty salesgirl helping him try on shoes which fit him perfectly (finding a perfect match).'[76] But he also noted the presence of scenes from films which certain dreamers used in order to express themselves (e.g., in a dream, we find scenes from *Mystery of the Wax Museum* by Michael Curtiz, a film known to the dreamer and which she recalls during association therapy), all of which further reinforces the notion that it is the constraint of a visual form of expression that is the determining factor rather than the metaphor in itself.[77]

The literalisation of the metaphor is also illustrated by Maurice Halbwachs. The sociologist dreams of B, who is swimming in the sea, and of a huge mass of water which suddenly began to swirl around him like a whirlpool. Then he remembers that B had told him he needed to 'to get back on his feet again' and had described feeling as though he had 'emerged from a whirlpool'.[78] And the sociologist provides a further example in *Les Cadres sociaux de la mémoire*:

'I had spent the morning correcting proofs. I dreamt that I was reading through my article with an idealist philosopher and that we were exchanging opinions. We discussed my point of view, we had fully understood it: our thoughts soared. And then, suddenly, we started to rise up, I do not know how, right up to a dormer window; we went through it, and we climbed up the slope of the roof, going higher and higher.' The idea of a thought elevating itself can only be an idea. If it is represented in this way, and if I took the image seriously, maybe it is because the feeling that I was in a defined place, at any rate in space, was in my thoughts at that time.[79]

In 1969, Montague Ullman published an article entitled 'Dreaming as metaphor in motion', in which he demonstrated the structuring role of the metaphor.[80] He cites the example of a dreamer who had the following dream when he took a short nap one Sunday afternoon: 'I was calling the weather bureau to ask if the hurricane was expected to hit the city that afternoon. As I was asking the question, I began to feel embarrassed and guilty. I awoke as I was trying to terminate the call.' The fact that the dreamer felt guilty about asking a weather bureau about the possibility of a hurricane is initially odd, since we cannot feel guilty about a phenomenon which is completely independent of our own actions. But the hurricane is not a hurricane. Instead it is the metaphorical image of a loss of temper. All becomes clear if we reset the dream in its context. The dreamer is an architect who has for a number of weeks been working under pressure to meet a deadline. He has worked on the project on four consecutive Sundays, cutting himself off from family life and leaving his wife to look after their four children and all the domestic tasks. On the fourth Sunday, his wife was showing increasing signs of becoming angry and approaching a crisis point, such as, for example, losing her temper with the children. He fell asleep at the beginning of the afternoon and had a dream. The dream naturally corresponds very closely to the domestic situation in which he finds himself and he uses the metaphor of the hurricane to convey his wife's outbursts of temper in a visual image. In his associations, the dreamer even says that, if a new hurricane were to occur in reality, its name would begin with the same initial as that of his wife's name. His feeling of guilt towards his wife expresses itself; weekend after weekend, the feeling had been growing in him that, whatever his professional commitments, nothing could justify abandoning his family and putting pressure on his wife.

As Thomas Morton French and Erika Fromm observed, the metaphors used by the dreamer are not simply easy or practical means of expressing oneself. They have something specific to say and have a definite purpose. By asking what (what area of activity, what context) or who (people close to the dreamer) the metaphor is associated with, or what transformation of the real situation it implies, we can start to understand the reasons behind its use. For example, by substituting the image of the house and of cement for that of the family, the dreamer studied by the authors can deal with his problem in a less emotional and less involved way, making it less painful for him.[81]

The same process of distancing oneself from events which cause pain or are disturbing can be seen in post-traumatic dreams. Ernest Hartmann, for example, cites the following dream: 'I am walking along the beach. I think someone is with me, maybe my friend K. Suddenly a huge wave thirty feet tall comes and sweeps us away. I am under water struggling to get to the surface when I wake up.'[82] The dreamer in question is a man who has recently escaped from a burning house in which a member of his family died. He lives several hundred miles from the ocean and had not been there for at least a year. The dream puts his emotions into a visual form and enables him to say: 'I am terrified. I am overwhelmed. I am vulnerable.' The emotions do not become any less real as a result, but instead they are ordered, contextualised, depicting in this case two people, only one of whom succeeds in the struggle to get back to the surface. It is therefore a scene, a situation with its share of emotions (surprise or amazement, fear, the sense of being overwhelmed, overcome, swallowed up), that is presented in the form of an image. The use of metaphorical images allows the subject to shift their position in relation to the initial traumatic event, which at first obsessively repeats itself in waking reveries and in dreams.

In a study involving forty-four people from all over the United States who had been writing down their dreams over a period of several years,

Hartmann and his team asked their participants to let them have twenty dreams, notably the last ten dreams before 11 September 2001 and the ten which followed the events of that day. The corpus of the study was therefore focused on 880 dream accounts. The results were clear. Out of the 440 dreams after 11 September, not a single one depicted planes crashing into tower blocks.[83] Hartmann did, however, come across two dreams about planes crashing into tower blocks three and eight months respectively after 11 September. In both cases, the dreamers were under severe personal stress at the time, one because of the break-up of a long-term relationship and the other after a heart attack followed by quadruple bypass coronary surgery.[84] It is therefore new traumatic situations which trigger appropriation of the images of towers being struck by planes as a way of expressing in metaphorical terms a feeling of being dumbstruck, of shock or of emotional collapse.

Metaphors are more than mere figures of speech. Like the analogical connections or the associations made through contiguity on which they are based, metaphors are omnipresent both in waking life and in dreams, even if their sheer profusion ends up making them almost invisible. More than thirty years before D. Hofstadter and E. Sanders produced their major study on analogy,[85] George Lakoff and Mark Johnson advanced the argument that 'metaphor is pervasive in everyday life, not just in language but in thought and action', and that 'our ordinary conceptual system, in terms of which we both think and act, is fundamentally metaphorical in nature.'[86] Since the dream is under a visual constraint, it therefore merely accentuates or intensifies the use of metaphors already present in waking thought. Lakoff went on to apply the study of metaphors to the specific case of dreams.[87] For him, metaphors 'play a generative role in dreaming',[88] and Freud did not emphasise their importance sufficiently.

The examples of dreams that Lakoff gives show that the metaphor is a structuring force, that it is a privileged form because of its power to visualise complex feelings and situations without, however, generating (in the strongest sense of the term) those dreams which plunge their roots into the dreamer's existential background. A man named Steve, for example, had a recurring dream that he had become blind in spite of having no health problems which could lead him to suspect or fear loss of sight.[89] He would wake up his wife during the night, shouting: 'I'm blind!' Steve is an extremely scrupulous and meticulous academic who is always afraid of not knowing enough. There is a metaphor in English which says that 'knowing is seeing'. With the expression 'I can't see', Steve is therefore expressing his fear of being ignorant. But there is another expression in English which says that masturbation makes you blind (in French, it is said to make you deaf). Steve feels he lacks power and influence. The recurring dreams about loss of sight started just before he took up an important administrative post at a time when he was worried he would not manage to achieve anything of significance. In men, difficulty in having sexual relations is often put down to impotence, and this term indicates lack of power. In Steve's case, the academic situation reflects the fact that he is in fact not sufficiently fertile to have children. Saying 'I am blind' or seeing himself blind in a dream is therefore saying at the same time 'I am ignorant', 'I am powerless (academically)' and 'I am impotent (sexually).' The metaphor of blindness, therefore, allows an English-speaking dreamer to express in a condensed form very different fears and regrets which relate to not being intellectually bright enough, not being able to have children, and not having enough power over others in an academic context. These different elements are visibly manifestations of wider dispositions regarding knowledge, both of oneself and of others, which need to be brought to light with the help of biographical interviews. But Lakoff is a linguist and confines his argument to the limits of the dream account (hence his tendency to see a generator where in fact it is simply a matter of giving shape to situations and problems external to the dream).

A second example examined by Lakoff is that of an American called Herb, who falls in love and moves in with his girlfriend. The relationship turns out to be a disaster. They are incapable of living together without fighting and decide, not without sadness, to separate. That night he dreamt that they were setting out on a trip, but a violent storm caused the Richmond–San Raphael Bridge in San Francisco Bay to collapse. The dream used the metaphor of 'emotional climate'. The internal emotions are compared to external climatic conditions so that an emotional storm, which provoked the split, becomes a real storm in the dream. Happiness is associated with daylight, depression with the darkness of night-time. The dream is therefore based on three metaphors: emotional conflict is a storm; love is a journey; and romantic relationships are the links between people in love just as a bridge links the two sides of the river and can sometimes collapse.[90]

The other cases studied by Lakoff[91] all demonstrate the central role of a range of metaphors. For example, there is the case of the lawyer who leads a hectic life, both professionally and in his free time, but who also sometimes falls ill through sheer exhaustion and suffers from depression, and who has recurring dreams in which he flies through the air, but in an unpleasant way. He flies too high or too fast, both of which terrify him. Deciding to take some time off, this man takes an extended trip to Paris, where he leads a calmer life, playing music and making a lot of friends among the people he meets. He then has a 'flying' dream in which he is flying particularly high and fast and is afraid of crashing. He manages to land on the shoulders of a friend, does a back flip and finally lands on his feet. The partial change of lifestyle led him, thanks to the support of friends, to believe that he could, literally in the dream and metaphorically in life, 'fall on his feet' in spite of the highly dangerous flight.

In another, more complicated case, a woman called Eileen dreamt of a mule which was undergoing surgery. Its head was cut open and a time-bomb was placed inside. Then the animal was stitched up and began to run around, turning into a beautiful, graceful horse. Eileen looked on in terror as the horse pranced gracefully about with a bomb in its head. In order to understand this dream, we need first of all to know that the mule is an animal which is considered to be stubborn, sterile and clumsy in comparison with a horse. Eileen is in love with a man she wants to marry, but this would be his second marriage, and she is aware that 'the biological clock is ticking' and that she will soon be unable to have any children with this man, a prospect she finds very upsetting. She is also determined to pursue her career and feels, here too, that time is passing by and she should not leave it too late. Consequently, the way she envisages her career conflicts with her plan to get married and her anxiety about the possibility of having a child. Eileen is, moreover, someone who is constantly worried and has had anxiety attacks and, for some years, has been taking medication to avoid such attacks. She was seeing a doctor about this at the time of the dream and, just before her dream, had suffered an anxiety attack over the conflict between her desire to get married and her desire to have a career. Eileen had gone into therapy four years before the dream because she had broken up with her previous husband. The therapy had restored her self-confidence, and she could once more envisage getting back into a calm relationship with the man she now wants to marry while still maintaining her professional ambitions. Eileen is also a former dancer who enjoys taking part in physical activities to keep her healthy and stable, and her good physical state makes her feel optimistic about the possibility of having children. What is Eileen 'saying' through this dream? That she was metaphorically a mule before the therapy (the head surgery = therapy) and that she was transformed into a graceful horse. But she conserves some of the characteristics of the mule in that she is stubborn about the idea of getting married and pursuing a career and also sterile, in that she may not be able to have children with her second husband. Since her therapy, any tensions have calmed down and she has not had any anxiety crises, but she is aware of the risk of a return of such crises, like a time-bomb ready to go off. The time-bomb symbolises both the biological and the professional clock, and the possibility of its exploding symbolises as much the suspended anxiety crisis as the risk of the destruction of her hopes of having children and of pursuing her career. With her good physical condition, her good relationship and her pursuit of her professional career, she is like a graceful horse, but a horse with a time-bomb in its head.

And we will finally mention one further dream interpreted by Lakoff. A woman dreamt that she was invited to the home of an old Jewish couple she knew, and they greeted her warmly. After a while, she went into the adjoining room with her younger sister and began to do a jigsaw puzzle. The jigsaw pieces were in the form of cups, saucers and kitchen utensils. Then she went into the kitchen with the elderly Jewish couple, and her sister went in the opposite direction and disappeared from the dream. In order to understand the dream, and even to understand that it is expressed through metaphor, we need to know the history of the dreamer and the elements of the existential situation which she is working out here. The dreamer is half-Catholic, half-Jewish. Her Jewish father had converted to Catholicism and she had been brought up in a Catholic household. She had an unhappy childhood, with parents who were distant and showed little warmth towards her. She felt that her parents had never really accepted her and had always had the impression that Jewish parents were more understanding and sympathetic than Catholic ones. The dreamer left the Catholic Church when she was an adolescent, but her younger sister had remained very much a Catholic. She was an active member of the Church, had married a Catholic, and her children were educated in Catholic schools. The dreamer is confused about her cultural identity. She had met a Jewish man and was thinking of getting married to him, thinking in a positive way about her own part-Jewish heritage. She was also unsure about what kind of relationship she could have with her sister. In the dream, the elderly Jewish couple symbolise alternative parents who would have been Jews and, in her mind, much more loving than her Catholic parents. She tries to assemble the pieces of the identity puzzle between herself and her sister (the fact that the pieces are in the form of kitchen utensils brings the situation back to a domestic context). By leaving the room to go back to the old Jewish couple, she is choosing the Jewish house (that of her future husband), while her sister disappears from the dream by choosing the Catholic house.

The visual metaphor can help to resolve a current and relatively short-lived problem, but it can also put into images a particularly recurrent schema of experience which is a key element of the dreamer's personality. In a case described by Jacques Montangero,[92] a young woman sees herself in a dream sitting on the pavement with crowds of people going past her. We can translate the scene verbally by saying that people 'go on their way' without looking at her, without paying any attention to her, and that she herself is 'left by the wayside'. Yet analysis reveals quite a strong dispositional trait in the dreamer, who has the impression that people either ignore her or despise her. This disposition was formed in early childhood and remained throughout adolescence on account of her having been 'neglected and sometimes ill-treated' by her family. Since then, she expects other people to behave in a way which is 'always hostile or cold'.

The use of metaphors in dreams shows at the same time the economy of means demonstrated by oneiric thought and the evocative power and the pertinence of the images it uses to express what needs to be expressed. In the depths of sleep, the dreamer still possesses a consciousness capable of incredible semiotic feats. And this will also be evident in the study of the phenomena of condensation.

Condensation

> Condensation is not only a procedure for masking from the eyes of
> the censor. It is the distinctive procedure of the dream, required by
> oneiric consciousness.
> (Maurice Merleau-Ponty, *Institution and Passivity*, p. 156)

Condensation is a phenomenon peculiar to the dream which consists in
creating people, places, objects, etc., which are a combination of several
people, of several places or of several objects. But this hybridisation, these
combinations or blends, which have no respect for temporal differences
(between the past and the present), spatial differences (between places
separated from each other) or physiological, psychological or sociological
differences (which mean that a person can have the face or the clothes of
another person or that he can become the father to someone who is actually his own father, etc.), do not, in spite of everything, occur purely by
chance. They indicate that, for the dreamer, the combined elements, or
the realities to which the elements refer, are associated by contiguity or are
related through analogy. Incomprehensible on a first reading, dreams with
multiple condensation processes are nevertheless rich with all the analogical links that continue to be woven, quite unconsciously, in waking life as
well as during sleep.

In 1814, the German physician and naturalist G. H. Schubert came
close to putting his finger on the phenomenon of condensation. With
forays along both the wrong track (the idea of an innate language, the
premonitory nature of the dream) and the right one (the idea of a dream
language, of a metaphorical mode of expression, of the law of association
of ideas, of a specific environment during the sleeping state), he spoke of a
'language composed of abbreviations and hieroglyphics':

> In the dream, and already in that delirious state which very often
> precedes sleep, the mind seems to speak an entirely different language
> from the one usually used. .... As long as the mind speaks this
> language, its ideas are subject to a different law of association than
> is ordinarily the case, and it is undeniable that this new association
> of ideas is set in place in a much more rapid, mysterious and fleeting
> manner than in the waking state where we think more by resorting
> to words. By using this language, by means of a few hieroglyphic
> images, strangely mixed together and coming either swiftly one after
> the other or jointly at the same time – and which can represent our
> thoughts in the space of a few moments – we are able to express more
> than we manage to put into words over the space of several hours.[93]

It was then the turn of Karl Albert Scherner, in 1861, to refer to combinations of images in the dream (he cites for example the case of a dream

in which a cluster of nuts in a tree is also a nest)[94] and points out that the dream does not respect the 'sequence of time'[95] – things from the distant childhood past and from the most recent present sometimes turning up in the same situation. But it was particularly Alfred Maury, in the same year, who turned his attention to the phenomena of condensation by highlighting the analogy which binds them together:

> On another occasion, fearing a small financial loss, I found myself, in a dream, at the mercy of adventures which sprang from this preoccupation. I encountered my creditor, who was looking sad and gloomy: he seemed to be trying to avoid me. . . . his face was transformed and I recognised him as one of my friends: You take me, he said, for your creditor, I know him and will speak to him. The truth is that the existence of a relationship between my two characters was possible, even probable; but it had never occurred to me; it was only in a dream that it came to mind.[96]

The condensation of creditor and friend is linked to the analogy between two people which he had not been consciously aware of in his waking state. The dream reveals, in a condensed form which is unfamiliar to the waking consciousness, analogies that also exist in waking life but which never appear explicitly:

> Dreams, like the ideas of a madman, are therefore after all less incoherent than they first seemed; it is merely that the links between ideas occur through associations which lack any rationality, by means of analogies which generally escape us on waking and which, moreover, we are even less likely to understand given that ideas have become images, and we are not accustomed to seeing images fused together like the different sections of the canvas of a moving panorama.[97]

Then it was Hervé de Saint-Denys who, in 1867, explained that dreams draw on a blend of images or, more precisely, a 'superimposition of images'[98] based on analogy. For example, in one dream, he sees a church in Brussels (familiar from engravings) and a road in France (a living memory) and speculates about 'the possible links which may have been formed through an association of ideas' between these two images: 'One idea having called forth another, the corresponding images appeared immediately, combining two different memories in the same picture. Let us see then, briefly at first, how the train of ideas in dreams works, how they are associated and combined.'[99] He also refers to 'bizarre complications, fantastic conceptions', and describes the process whereby two things or two people are brought together because they share a common abstract quality.[100] Analogies between people, objects, places, etc., underpin the processes of condensation which the author describes in terms of abstraction, of superimposition or of fusion of ideas or of images.[101] Finally, in

1891, Yves Delage described processes similar to those which Freud would call condensation. He argued that dreams can integrate both recent and very distant memories, and that distant memories are linked by a complex play of associations to the more recent memories. And, above all, 'the visions and the ideas of the dream' are for him the 'simple continuation of those from the waking state; but, instead of remaining distinct, they are superimposed upon each other and fuse and combine so as to form scenes which are often absurd where certain elements, borrowed from real life, can seem unrecognisable.'[102]

Freud therefore followed on from the empirically rooted arguments of these different authors. He wrote that the dream is the result of 'condensation on a large scale' and that dreams are 'brief, meagre and laconic in comparison with the range and depth of the dream-thoughts'.[103] In order for condensation to occur, 'there must be one or more common elements in all the components.'[104] Freud thus compares the work of the dream to the work of Francis Galton, cousin of Charles Darwin, who, using a composite method of photography, superimposed a series of photos of family members to form a generic image in order to show morphological resemblances. But this process of fusion is not confined to dreams. It simply occurs more often in dreams than in the forms of expression associated with waking life.

When Freud said that it was always possible to find 'still more thoughts concealed behind the dream' and that, 'strictly speaking, then, it is impossible to determine the amount of condensation',[105] he was absolutely correct but lacked theoretical clarity. For it is not the experiences or the situations experienced in the past, taken one by one, that lie behind the dream; rather, it is the schemas or the schemes which have gradually taken shape over the course of multiple experiences and which are summaries of them. Freud uses the term 'condensation' because the manifest content of the dream seems to compress a rich psychic material. But the psychic material in question is then taken up by the analyst, who asks the patient to say what the various different elements of the dream make him or her think about. The patient begins by saying what each element brings to mind, before pursuing other recollections through the association of ideas. As a result, what is being referred to by these different associations of ideas is potentially the sum of all the experiences which reflect the situation contained within the manifest dream. But these past experiences have taken shape and crystallised in the form of schemes, of 'relating to ...', of schemas of experience, which have been reactivated by a recent diurnal experience and which contribute to the formation of the dream in question. If the patient was encouraged to go on speaking, the result would undoubtedly be a far longer list of situations, people, places, etc., all evoking the situations, people and places of the dream.

A character in a dream can be a 'composite formation' bringing together the traits associated with different people in real life. We could therefore say that these are 'composite' people: 'I may build up a figure by giving it the features of two people; or I may give it the form of one person but think of it in the dream as having the name of another person; or I may have a visual image of one person, but put it in a situation which is appropriate to another.'[106] Yet these people, blended together or confused without any apparent logic, have equivalent properties in the experience of the dreamer, and it is because, for him or her, these people are analogous that he or she does not distinguish between them: 'Instead of saying "*A* has hostile feelings towards me and so has *B*," I make a composite figure out of *A* and *B* in the dream, or I imagine *A* carrying out an act of some other kind which is characteristic of *B*.'[107] For example, on the subject of the famous dream about the injection given to Irma, Freud wrote that 'Irma became the representative of all these other figures which had been sacrificed to the work of condensation, since I passed over to *her*, point by point, everything that reminded me of *them*.'[108] The other people in question were other patients and his own daughter. The dream condenses all the people who, from a given angle, bear a family resemblance. And elements which in waking life remain consciously separated are condensed, combined and brought together in the dream which retains traces of them in the finished product. The dream therefore, more than any other form of expression, reveals the ceaseless work of analogical association carried out by the brain, day and night.[109]

René Allendy stressed the fact that 'comparison, resemblance, are expressed in the dream through a condensation: the two terms are merged into a single unity, or else they are blended into a composite formation, or one of the two terms is actively implicated while the other is simply present.'[110] For example, 'in order to express . . . that two marriages are comparable, the dream can simply feature, as a single couple, the husband of one and the wife of the other',[111] or else, to establish the analogy of places in the eyes of the dreamer, the dream can move without any discontinuity from the streets of Paris to the streets of London.

In a dream examined by Jacques Montangero, condensation enables a very real fear to be expressed with very limited means. A man named Julien had the following dream: 'I am in the changing rooms of a gym. There are lots of clothes hanging on hooks, including a brown check jacket. I open the door at the back of the cloakroom and notice, with disappointment, that I do not know anyone in the room. What is more, it is a classroom and the people in it are studying a difficult language.'[112] The check jacket is one worn by his cousin Jean, with whom he usually goes to fitness classes, but he has noticed that Jean has become less enthusiastic lately and realises that he might find himself going to the sessions on his own. Moreover, Julien goes every week to a German class, where he feels slightly ill at ease because the other students know each other and make him feel a little left out. The reason for the brutal transformation of one lesson into the other is therefore extremely clear: the dreamer is expressing his fear of finding himself alone in the fitness sessions as well as in the language lessons, owing to the defection of his cousin whose presence is indicated by metonymy (Jean's jacket symbolises Jean). More broadly, the dream exposes Julien's difficulties in fitting in with groups of people he does not know, a broader disposition which is tied into his life history.

Inversions, opposites, contradictions

In certain cases, the dream-work, according to Freud, is supposed to confuse the meaning of the dream by saying the opposite of what is actually thought (unconsciously), and this is always in order to evade the control of an omnipresent censorship. Yet such an interpretation provokes a certain scepticism. For what could make the analyst read a situation in one way or another (the opposite of the preceding one), particularly when he has made the waking patient someone likely firmly to resist interpretations? Since the analyst can no longer rely on the patient, he or she finds themselves in sole charge of navigating the dream interpretation machinery ...

In his case study of Dora's hysteria, Freud said to her: 'You said to yourself: "This man is persecuting me; he wants to force his way into my room. My 'jewel-case' is in danger, and if anything happens it will be Father's fault." For that reason in the dream you chose a situation which expresses the opposite – a danger from which your father is saving you. In this part of the dream everything is turned into its opposite.'[113] And on the subject of a dream recounted by another female dreamer, in which she dived into a lake, Freud again interpreted things in reverse: 'Dreams like this one are birth dreams. Their interpretation is reached by reversing the event reported in the manifest dream; thus, instead of "diving into the water" we have "coming out of the water", i.e. being born.'[114]

Similarly, Freud sees, in dreams he describes as 'hypocritical', situations which are the opposite of what might have motivated them. Thus, dreaming of reconciliation with a friend with whom cordial relations ended long ago would inevitably need to be interpreted in the opposite sense: the dreamer detests that person, but the dream depicts a reconciliation because it would be unacceptable to dream about hatred.[115] Why not simply imagine that the breakdown of any friendship is likely to produce a sense of failure in terms of relationships and personal regrets about the break-up? Seeing a reconciliation in a dream will not prevent the dreamer, once awake, remaining resentful or angry towards this former friend.

Certain dreams which appear to be more directly comprehensible and do not seem incoherent, incongruous or absurd will, according to Freud, have been subjected to 'a far-reaching revision': 'they appear to have a meaning, but that meaning is as far removed as possible from their true significance.'[116] And, on the subject of a personal dream, he confirms that this would divert attention (whose?) by introducing (non-existent) affection in order to render acceptable the negative judgement made about a person (Mr R): 'My dream-thoughts had contained a slander against R;

and, in order that I might not notice this, what appeared in the dream was the opposite, a feeling of affection for him.'[117]

If the 'infernal machine' which constitutes the mechanism for circumventing the censorship is destroyed, this method of transformation by inversion which Freud sometimes proposed, and which leaves the reader somewhat baffled, must also be abandoned – in other words, the idea that the oneiric stage might sometimes, but not always, show the opposite of what the dreamer unconsciously thinks. For we do not understand why certain things dreamt about are dreamt as direct, literal symbolisations and why others are supposed to express the opposite of what they seem to be expressing: 'The way in which dreams treat the category of contraries and contradictories is highly remarkable. It is simply disregarded. . . . Dreams feel themselves at liberty, moreover, to represent any element by its wishful contrary; so that there is no way of deciding at a first glance whether any element that admits of a contrary is present in the dream-thoughts as a positive or as a negative.'[118] If this were really the case, if the dream could say one thing which means either what it says or the opposite of what it actually says, then nothing could any longer be said with any certainty about the meaning of dreams.

Freud goes some way to meeting his critics by raising all the objections that could be directed towards him, yet for all that fails to answer them:

> You will argue in support of this that in the first place one never knows whether a particular element of the dream is to be understood in its actual sense or as a symbol, since the things employed as symbols do not cease on that account to be themselves. If, however, one has no objective clue for deciding this, the interpretation must at that point be left to the arbitrary choice of the interpreter. Furthermore, as a result of the fact that in the dream-work contraries coalesce, it is always left undetermined whether a particular element is to be understood in a positive or negative sense – as itself or as its contrary. Here is a fresh opportunity for the interpreter to exercise an arbitrary choice. Thirdly, in consequence of the reversals of every kind of which dreams are so fond, it is open to the interpreter to carry out a reversal like this in connection with any passage in the dream he chooses.[119]

However, by dint of seeing invisible inversions or contradictions everywhere, the father of psychoanalysis is proposing a model of interpretation which ends up being difficult to apply. The infinite possibilities for the analyst to distort the dream in the direction he wishes can only cast the shadow of doubt over his whole interpretive approach.

In spite of the limitations of the psychoanalytical interpretation of dreams, with the benefits of a historical perspective, we can still acknowledge the significance of Freud's breakthrough (coming in the wake of scholars such as Maury or Hervé de Saint-Denys). Not only did he identify the phenomena of symbolisation, of condensation, of blending or of partial or complete metamorphosis in dreams, but he also understood how these worked (the associations through analogy or through contiguity which underlie them).

Thirty years before Freud, at the beginning of the 1870s, the young Gabriel Tarde confined himself, in his annotated dream journal, to pointing out the links between the events of the previous day and the scenes in the dream and noting the hybridisations ('perhaps . . . I made a mix, a composite . . . of the actual face of Mme de C. and the face of P. Poisson, one of my former and much loved teachers, whom someone reminded me of the day before yesterday';[120] or, again, 'often, I have seen the face of one of my friends in a dream and attributed to it the name of another'),[121] or the symbolic substitutions ('I thought . . . that my own body was made of wood gnawed by termites; very often, that one particular person was another person, that a particular house was another house . . . ; and, even more extraordinarily, . . . I found myself dreaming that one of my parents was the larva of an insect'),[122] without ever seeking to know what these meant. For him, as for many other scholars, the dream images were still merely the random product of 'the interplay of the fibres of the brain'.

12

Variations in Forms of Expression

Two major intellectual approaches are available to those seeking a satisfactory resolution of a problem. The first, which more often than not imposes itself spontaneously, involves focusing attention on the problem in question by isolating it from all other problems which, it is assumed, will be resolved in the same manner by others. The second, which entails a less straightforward approach and a more wide-ranging thought process, consists in constructing a wider theoretical framework within which the problem in question becomes *a particular case of the possible*, a local problem among others, which will prove easier to resolve because of its insertion into a larger structure.

The first strategy is that favoured by specialised researchers, who believe that it is by separating problems and isolating them that solutions can best be found. The second strategy is that preferred by researchers less drawn to specialisation, but who firmly believe in the virtues of conceptualisation and comparison as the best way to set out problems and to find more easily solutions to the puzzle that each one of them represents.

The second strategy is clearly that adopted by Freud: 'Any disquisition upon dreams which seeks to explain as many as possible of their observed characteristics from a particular point of view, and which at the same time defines the position occupied by dreams in a wider sphere of phenomena, deserves to be called a theory of dreams.'[1] In order to express in an extremely vivid way the idea that comparison alone permits us to approach dreams correctly, he explains in *The Interpretation of Dreams* that it is far easier to crack a nut by crushing it against another one: 'When in the course of a piece of scientific work we come upon a problem which is difficult to solve, it is often a good plan to take up a second problem along with the original one – just as it is easier to crack two nuts together than each separately.'[2] Unity is strength . . . But rather than the image of two nuts cracked one against the other, we should instead say that it is by putting together a number of nuts, and, more precisely, by finding the 'right grouping' into which all our various nuts can fit, that each nut can reveal its specificity and its true meaning.

Inspired perhaps by Freud, the mathematician Alexander Grothendieck also used the image of a nut to clarify his thinking process. Grothendieck introduced two different approaches to proving a mathematical theorem. He compared the problem to opening a nut either by using a hammer and chisel to crack it in order to reach the flesh or else by leaving it to soak in an emollient liquid which will soften the shell gradually, over a period of time, eventually enabling the flesh to be accessed simply by pressure of the hand.[3] If Grothendieck's suggestion appears not to bring in other problems in order to solve the problem in question, it is because his focus in on the context (represented by the glass filled with an emollient liquid) inside which the problem can more easily be solved. And it is this context which allows problems to be compared and to be seen as cases of the possible.

In the two preceding examples, it is essentially the broader problematisation of a specific case – in other words, the construction of a general theoretical framework – which enables the solution to be found, not only for the case in question but also for all similar, related or relatively analogous cases.[4] The spontaneous approach, which consists of going straight to the problem (with a hammer and chisel) in order to solve it, is however less efficient in the long run than the longer and more counter-intuitive approach of stepping back and taking a broader view. This is what we shall see in the case of dreams.

An expressive continuum

One of the researchers who applied just such an intellectual approach to forms of expression is Ignace Meyerson. He chose to adopt a very broad point of view on these questions rather than that of the specialist who focuses all his or her attention on a given problem, or even on a specific part of this problem. With his theory of classes of human expression (art, science, technology, religion, social institutions, etc.), Meyerson is one of those who have succeeded in formulating the problem with considerable vision. Whatever form human expression takes, whether material or symbolic, practical or aesthetic, human beings never cease to express (in the sense of 'coming out of themselves'), through their actions and their different languages, their identity as social beings. 'There is a need to externalise and to express. This need is continuous and manifests itself in almost continuous expressive activity.'[5] We might say that the human being is biologically programmed for psychic activity and that this activity takes different forms depending on the physiological and social conditions in which it takes place at different periods in life.

The human world is structured in the form of sub-universes, Meyerson explains, and to each of these there is a corresponding and specific 'class of expression': 'Each one has its own content, its subject matter, its technical conditions of production, its structural frameworks, its rules.'[6] Painting, music, literature or mathematics thus constitute so many specific classes of expression, and the resulting forms of expression do not readily translate from one class to another.[7] But we need to go beyond the context of the theory of classes of expression, which is in a sense an expressive version of the theory of the social division of labour, and integrate into our thinking both those forms of expression that include the most mundane gestures, words and activities of manual workers, farm labourers, artisans, shop-keepers, etc., who, in their ways of doing things, of making things and of speaking or in their very lifestyles *express* schemas of experience, and such mental forms of expression as dreams and daydreams, which do not con-stitute classes of expression in the Meyerson sense. We need therefore to extend Meyerson's viewpoint to all possible forms of symbolic expression, whether waking or otherwise. Such an extension, which would consider the dream as one *case of the possible* in the whole range of human forms of expression, is the only way to resolve the problem which the dream represents from the point of view of scientific analysis. For the solution to this problem paradoxically implies *stepping outside the dream* and seeking to understand it *in comparison* with other forms of expression.

Moreover, Meyerson himself thought of the dream in terms of a psychic and expressive continuity without, however, ignoring its specific character:

> What is generally, particularly since Scherner, Volkelt and Freud, called the 'symbolic activity' of the dream is not specific to dreams: the symbolic aspect of the dream strikes us more powerfully than that of waking thought because the symbols are less clear. . . . Careful analysis of the content and the form of the dream does not confirm the classic hypothesis of an 'automatic', 'inferior' functioning linked to the absence of a 'superior' control. Instead, we are forced to admit that there is in the dream the same complex psychic ensemble as during waking life. The nature of the unity of the self, of the unity of the individual, is no different, but the unification of the person (already variable during waking life) does not appear the same during waking and in dreaming, the tension and relaxation are not focused on the same areas, on the same objects.[8]

It seems to me that the dichotomous thinking favoured by certain researchers specialising in the study of dreams, which uncompromisingly opposes dream and rationality, oneiric thinking and logical thinking, the oneiric world and the real world, nocturnal consciousness and diurnal con-sciousness, thinking in the sleeping state and thinking in the waking state, emotion and reason, is fatal to understanding. Instead of setting dreams in opposition to everything other than dreams, and therefore tending to isolate them and lose any points of comparison, *it is preferable to resituate the dream in a continuum of forms of expression which are indissociable from types of social situations and from types of mental and cerebral states.*

In order successfully to formulate this general theory of forms of symbolic expression, we need to bring together certain contributions from sociology, linguistics, the neurosciences and cognitive psychology. The dream is a reality of consciousness which has its specific characteristics but which is not a continent cut off from the other continents of the consciousness.

This situation is particularly true in relation to neuroscientific research on sleep. As Ludwig Crespin notes,

> in research on dreams there is an extremely popular tendency to dramatise the unique nature of this mental activity by making it a conscious experience which functions in a way that has nothing in common with waking mental life, even when this takes the form of a daydream. And this tendency leads to dreams being associated with neurophysiological characteristics unique to a very specific state of sleep, REM [rapid eye movement] sleep or paradoxical sleep. ...[9]

In fact, it is more the hypothesis of a 'continuum between the cognitive activity of REM sleep, non-REM sleep, and the waking state' that 'scientifically robust results' support more firmly, in spite of the tendency, 'from the birth of psycho-physiological research on dreams', to dichotomous thinking about waking/sleeping, and to a 'fascination for the neurophysiological properties'[10] of paradoxical sleep, despite many proofs of the existence of oneiric activity in all the phases of sleep.

In addition, certain very specialised sectors of dream studies, particularly those focusing on the quantitative analysis of the contents of dream accounts, resist the idea of distancing themselves from their subject in order to gain a better understanding of it. Thus, Ernest Hartmann criticised a psychologist like G. William Domhoff for focusing only on the dream without situating it in a continuum of mental functioning. In fact, Domhoff felt that studying dreams was already difficult enough without also having to turn his attention to daydreams.[11] But what he sees as a problematic dispersion of focus is in fact the condition required for a genuine understanding of the nature and functioning of the dream.

Moreover, the philosophical tendency to define man by his intelligence, his reason and his capacity for logical reasoning (rather than by his emotions, his analogical capacities and his vague and approximate reasoning) contributes to making the dream an exception outside the domain of reason, whereas in fact it consistently reveals the thought processes that are continuously woven into the operations of ordinary thought, even those most rationally controlled. For example, René Allendy, in a comparison typical of a mythical approach, describes the oneiric process as 'a regressive, backward-looking mode of thought, probably close to the consciousness of animals or very primitive humans (young children, savages)'.[12] The dream 'exactly represents primitive thinking, free from any logic, scarcely separate from instinct', and marked by the 'predominance of the affective element'.[13] Yet the same writer acknowledges that, in waking life, coherence and logic imply 'an effort that is supreme and difficult to sustain, a state of consciousness which is fragile and almost exceptional, a tour de force which cannot be maintained indefinitely':

> In reality, as soon as all the best conditions are no longer available, intellectual effort becomes more difficult. Emotion, fatigue, illness, fever, intoxication through alcohol or drugs, etc., have the initial effect of hampering the task of mental synthesis and inducing a state of consciousness where the sequence of representations is no longer controlled by a pragmatic and utilitarian will; such a state, depending on its degree, goes under the name of daydreams, delirium, insanity. It represents the normal psychological state during sleep and therefore produces the representations of the dream on which we shall focus in this book, but it is important to establish the total similitude of character between the dream, the waking daydream, delirious ramblings, madness. We see the same mechanisms at work everywhere, and, if we find in the dream a certain meaning and some laws, these must also apply to similar states.[14]

The error consists in taking waking consciousness in its most deliberate, introspective and rational form as the standard measurement against which the dream is viewed and interpreted. Such an approach turns the dream into a symbolic production which is inevitably 'strange', 'incoherent', 'illogical' and 'atypical' produced by beings who are fundamentally conscious and rational. The logocentrism or the logicocentrism of researchers makes them see dreams only as a deviation, a deterioration or an exception (sometimes negative and sometimes positive in cases where quasi-premonitory capacities are attributed to them) in relation to waking consciousness. The error is further compounded by the fact that the forms of expression taken as the reference points for waking consciousness are the most abstract examples of this consciousness (mathematical calculations, conceptual thinking, logical reasoning, etc.).

Rather than dreams being studied from the perspective of a certain form of waking consciousness, they should instead be regarded as simply one form of human consciousness among others. Portraying them as something strange prevents them from being considered as an *expressive variation*. In reality, not everything revolves around the reflexive and intentional consciousness, which is by no means the focus of psychic activity. Reflexive and intentional consciousness is itself merely one form of expression of the human consciousness among others. Waking reflexive consciousness must therefore be shifted from its central position to allow the dream to be repositioned on an expressive continuum. Not only do daydreams play a significant part in everyday life, not only are there many moments where control is weakened, but the willpower of each individual in his or her daily life is constantly overwhelmed by all the routine functioning of mental activity on autopilot.

Situated on a continuum, the dream is simply one possible form of expression among others. It takes its place on a vast expressive continuum which, starting with the dream, also includes, among others, hypnagogic (immediately before falling asleep) and hypnopompic (immediately before waking)[15] images, daydreams, delirious ravings and hallucinations (caused by taking alcohol, drugs, as a result of sunstroke, dehydration, a high temperature or as the manifestation of mental disorders such as paranoiac or schizoid delirium),[16] remarks made under hypnosis, the 'free associations' used in psychoanalytic therapy, automatic writing, writing in a private diary, daydreams triggered by reading fiction or watching films, children's games, informal conversations between people close to each other, the different forms of artistic creation (literary, pictorial, etc.), schoolwork, legal forms of expression, calculations or solutions to scientific, technical, mathematical or logic problems, etc.

Depending on the form of expression, the activity in question is private or public, solitary or in a group, internalised or externalised, personal or at the request of someone else, adapted for oneself or for others (people or institutions), confined to a sleeping or a waking state, involuntary and uncontrolled or deliberate and controlled, informal or formal, purely mental or backed up by some kind of external support, belonging within an institutional framework or not, belonging within a very open or a highly codified institution, etc. Even though it occupies an extreme position within the range of expressive possibilities, oneiric expression is therefore close to all those forms that share common contextual properties: 'Thought during sleep is closely related to waking thought, especially in those spontaneous and informal forms which arise when we allow our minds to wander, when we recall or anticipate an event, or when we recount it to those close to us. In such cases, cognition is vivid, disjointed and condensed, three characteristics shared by dreams.'[17]

Among researchers working on dreams, the American psychiatrist Ernest Hartmann is one of the few people (along with the Swiss cognitive-psychologist Jacques Montangero and the American psychologist David Foulkes) to insist that dreams are part of a mental and expressive continuum and should not be treated separately. Mental activity in the waking state ranges from 'the most focused waking thought through relaxed somewhat looser thought to reverie and daydreaming which begin to resemble dreaming.'[18] Hartmann points out that, when dreams are compared to waking forms of thought or mental activity, they are generally compared with radically different types of thinking which are logical, formal, rational, reflexive, etc. Yet 'we should rather compare dreaming (how our minds function at night) with the totality of our waking experience (how our minds function in the daytime) which includes living and navigating in the perceptual world as well as in the world of daydreams, fantasy and imagination.'[19] When these less controlled forms of waking activity are observed, we find that they can be 'as visual and "dreamlike" and bizarre as dreaming'. Moreover, dreams can sometimes depict perfectly ordinary scenes.[20]

The question of dreams belongs therefore in the context of a *sociology of intra-individual variations in behaviour* and, more specifically, in *expressive behaviour*. In the same way that embedded cultural dispositions express themselves differently depending on the context (private or public, depending on the cultural domain in question, on the type of situation and the circumstances, etc.),[21] so expressive impulses do not express themselves in the same way, depending on whether the individual is awake or asleep or on the nature of the context (formal or informal, institutionally constrained or codified or not, etc.). The difference between the dream and hypnagogic images, daydreams, the experiments in automatic writing advocated by surrealism,[22] or the 'free associations' of the psychoanalyst is in terms of *degree* (*continuity theory*) rather than of nature (*discontinuity theory*), and the dream appears not to be such a radically specific type of thought and of expression.[23]

That the same individuals can use all or part of these forms of expression suggests that each of them is composed of a variable part and a relatively invariable part. Demonstrating that the dream is a *specific form of expression* and a *form of psychic activity* intrinsically linked to a *context of expression* is also a way of understanding what, for a given individual, *does not vary* from one type of activity or context to another and underlies all of these forms of expression – from dreams to play, from play to daydreams, from daydreams to reading, etc. For any given individual, at any particular moment of his or her history, the form of expression, the type of psychic activity and the nature of the context will vary, but the *schematic or dispositional foundation*, which can be heterogeneous, does not vary. It is the only *relatively invariant element* underpinning a triptych in *perpetual variation*.

For Freud himself, the dream was already essentially simply just one of many forms of psychic activity unified by a theory of the unconscious. 'The interpretation of dreams is the royal road to a knowledge of the unconscious activities of the mind',[24] but it is not the only one. Study of so-called Freudian slips as well as that of psychic disorders shows that the unconscious is present at all moments of existence, but that it 'acts' differently depending on the context of expression. It was after studying a range of psychic disorders, and particularly cases of hysteria, that Freud discovered the dream as an interpretable element which allowed access to patients' unconscious. The dream cannot therefore be considered to be radically different from all the many other forms of expression by the simple fact that it maintained a direct relationship with the unconscious. The latter manifests itself in spoken words, thoughts, perceptions and waking actions just as much as in dream images. What changes are the conditions of production of words, thoughts, perceptions and actions and, at the same time, the forms these take.

On close inspection, Freud quite literally transferred onto the dream the theory he had begun to formulate on the subject of cases of hysteria. The same relation between the latent content and the manifest content of the dream, on the one hand, and between repressed traumas from the past and the symptoms of hysteria, on the other, the same process of transference-transformation of the first to the second, the same importance attributed to the unconscious, the same determining role of 'psychosexual factors', and even 'infantilism'[25] as explanatory factors. Just as 'hysteria originates through the repression of an incompatible idea from a motive of defence',[26] the dream was to be understood as a compromise formation between unconscious thoughts and censorships. And, like the symptoms of hysteria, the dream is the fulfilment of an unsatisfied (sexual) wish.[27]

Consequently, for Freud, the dream becomes one type of symptom among others, indicative of repressed unconscious wishes:

> If dreams turned out to be constructed like symptoms, if their expla-
> nation required the same assumptions – the repression of impulses,
> substitutive formation, compromise-formation, the dividing of the
> conscious and the unconscious into various psychical systems – then
> psychoanalysis was no longer a subsidiary science in the field of
> psycho-pathology, it was rather the foundation for a new and deeper
> science of the mind which would be equally indispensable for the
> understanding of the normal.[28]

With the study of dreams, Freud therefore moves from psychopathology to the study of psychic activity in normal life. Stating that dreams and the symptoms of psychological disorders are two similar realities – that is to say, compromise formations between wishes and censorship – means opening psychoanalysis up to a much broader field, one which encompasses all aspects of psychic life, both normal and pathological.[29]

Freud was not therefore in any sense seeking to be simply a theorist of dreams. Describing the goal towards which he and his colleagues were working, he said: 'We want something that is sought for in all scientific work – to understand the phenomena, to establish a correlation between them and, in the latter end, if it is possible, to enlarge our power over them.'[30] He compares dreams to psychological disorders but also to literary creation,[31] just as he compares literary creation, games and daydreams. 'He compared', wrote Ellenberger, dreams, fantasies, neurotic symptoms, witticisms and artistic creations.'[32] By establishing connections between these different forms of psychic activity, he showed that he was on the way to constructing a general interpretive model which would make it possible to study a whole range of psychic manifestations, both from waking and from sleeping life and both normal and pathological. But, by suggesting that 'the laws governing the formation of dreams are the same as the laws governing the formation of myths and works of art (the myth being defined as an objective waking dream)',[33] Freud nevertheless failed to take into account the specificity of the social contexts of production of the different forms of expression (literary games for literary creation, the context of sleep for the dream, the tribal context for the myth, etc.).

It is therefore by comparing dreams to other narrative productions, intentional or unintentional, formal or informal (daydreams, oral accounts which are to a greater or lesser extent in an institutionalised context, or literary accounts), or to other forms of expression (such as games or hallucinations), that we can further our understanding of dreams, rather than by choosing to focus exclusively on them, as is the case of some of those specialising in dreams and sleep.

Forms of expression, forms of psychic activity and types of social context

Because, at an institutional level in research organisations and university departments, there are neuroscientists, linguists, psychologists, sociologists and, more generally, researchers in the social sciences, all of whom are conducting separate and broadly autonomous research, a distinction is usually made between cerebral problems and psychological or psychic problems, language-related, linguistic or symbolic problems, and social problems. However, it quickly becomes apparent that the variety of forms of psychic activities corresponds to a variety of forms of expression, and that this is in itself closely linked to the variety of types of social contexts.

And now that the brain sciences have made available significant findings in the field of cerebral activity, we should also point out that these forms of psychic activity, these forms of expression and these types of social context are linked to *types of cerebral activity*. The study of dreams makes it necessary to include in this triptych questions regarding the state of cerebral activity in so far as the brain does not function in exactly the same conditions in the waking state and during sleep.[34] The dream therefore raises questions about 'ordinary' or modified states of consciousness or, better still, about the permanent modification of states of consciousness.

What generally discourages sociologists from taking account of the specifically linguistic (or symbolic) and psychological dimensions of any social activity, let alone the neurobiological or neurophysiological dimensions, is the fact that, in each instance, they are dealing with very different linguistic practices and psychic activities. These range from the simplest to the most complex, from those which are most circumstantial and linked to immediate contexts of action to the most elaborate, encapsulated in the form of long written texts, from the most formally or morally controlled to the most free-ranging, all of which require a different set of analytical tools. In concrete terms, between the use of language and the psychic activity in the social context of an ordinary commercial transaction and the use of written language and of the corresponding psychic activity to create a literary work in the context of literary activity, or to craft a political speech in the context of the political arena, the function and structure of language and the associated mental activity, as well as the social context in which these different linguistic practices and psychic activities take place, differ considerably.

Knowing that researchers who, within the field of linguistics, focus on verbal interactions or conversations, ordinary examples of writing, political speeches, literary or scientific works, all generally inhabit separate communities and scarcely communicate with each other (there is, for example, no dialogue between researchers who analyse conversations and those who analyse speeches, between specialists of domestic writing or professionals and theorists of literature, etc.); and given that psychologists working on logical thought or on cognitive strategies in the resolution of mathematical problems and those working on paranoiac delusions or on dreams are just as unlikely to communicate;[35] and, furthermore, that researchers who work on institutions, organisations, on relatively institutionalised fields or the situations of interaction in daily life are generally separated by their aims, their methods and their concepts, it becomes all too easy to understand why a certain degree of hesitation accompanies any attempt to reunite or bring together the different types of aims and the different domains studied (linguistic, psychological and sociological).

But the complexity of problems should not undermine attempts, however modest, to resolve them. It is first of all by observing the great variety of types of linguistic practice, of forms of psychic activity and of different social contexts, and in interpreting their concomitant variations, that progress is possible. If language and psychic activities take very different forms, it is because they are associated with or belong to different types of practice or activities and because, as a result, they therefore fulfil heterogeneous social functions. Wittgenstein thus emphasised the 'countless language games', all of which he sees as a 'form of life', and cited as examples of language games 'giving orders and acting on them', 'cracking a joke; telling one' or 'requesting, thanking, cursing, greeting, praying', as well as 'reporting an event', 'presenting the results of an experiment in tables and diagrams', 'making up a story' and 'translating from one language into another'.[36] And each of these forms of expression has a corresponding mental activity.

A theoretician of language who was as much interested in the forms of verbal interaction in everyday life as in the forms of the novel, Mikhail Bakhtin formulated the problem in the following manner: 'All the diverse areas of human activity involve the use of language. Quite understandably, the nature and forms of this use are just as diverse as are the areas of human activity. This, of course, in a way disaffirms the national unity of language.'[37] And it is precisely because language games (or 'discursive genres'), types of psychic activity and forms of life ('areas of human activity' or 'spheres of human activity') are so closely linked that the linguistic sciences, the psychological sciences and the social sciences should strive to work together. But the glaring differences between the novel, the utterance taken from an ordinary conversation, the standardised command or the dream account have made it difficult to try to establish a general theory of the linguistic practices associated with forms of psychic life and with forms of social life.

The false 'free expression' of dreams and the varying levels of contextual constraints

In order to explain practices fully, we need to reconstruct, on the one hand, the elements of an incorporated past that could potentially be mobilised and, on the other hand, the characteristics of the contexts in which the practice occurs. However, one of the principles governing the variation of these different contexts lies in the greater or lesser degree of constraint or of coercion they impose on practices. There are contexts which impose very powerful constraints on actors and those which, within given limits, allow actors to give expression to their own dispositions. The general formula applied to practices – Dispositions ↔ Context of action → Practices – can therefore also be seen as a balance of power between dispositions and contexts, a balance which is not always equal.

Sometimes the context dictates exactly which aspects of the incorporated past will be actualised, and sometimes the context is sufficiently undefined, or more flexibly defined, to allow more scope for the interplay of dispositions.[38] The case of literary writing and legal writing, which can be seen alongside each other in the work of a writer-lawyer such as Kafka,[39] shows that legal writing is infinitely more codified and institutionally prepared, planned and scheduled than literary writing, which, free of expectations and potentially multiple in both structure and subject matter, leaves much more potential for invention. There is clearly a world of difference between writing for factual-reporting purposes and more creative types of writing.

Pierre Bourdieu referred to such variation in contexts (domains/fields

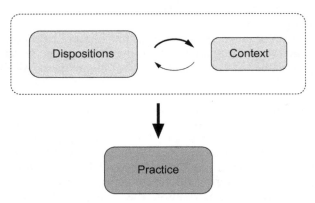

Figure 6 Dispositions under weak contextual constraints

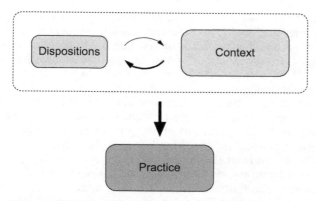

Figure 7 Dispositions under strong contextual constraints

of practice) when he distinguished 'between the areas that are apparently "freest" because given over in reality to the regulated improvisation of the habitus . . . and the areas most strictly regulated by customary norms and upheld by social sanctions.'[40] But the degree to which practices are governed by context is not just a matter of codification or of legal normalisation. The question of dreams allows us to distinguish within the expressive activity moments that are either more or less restrictive in terms of the external solicitations to which the individual responds or reacts.

The dream is the 'domain of perpetual creation',[41] according to an expression used by Halbwachs. The dreamer's body is in a stable state (and, during the period of paradoxical sleep, it even experiences a muscular atony) and any interaction with the external world is limited. In sleep, the brain is not required to direct any practical tasks, nor does it need to resolve any specific problems and can instead concentrate on the production of oneiric images. It is no longer at the mercy of the peremptory and even sometimes tyrannical demands of relationships with others which constantly structure, control and demand the attention of the individual in waking life, nor is it subject to the demands of a material or human entourage which would seek its attention and distract it away from the flow of thoughts. The brain has a sensory system in a permanent stage of vigilance, which pays attention only to the most unusual auditory, tactile, olfactory, visual events (such elements are either integrated into the dream in a somewhat adapted form, or they force the dreamer to wake up). The dreamer unintentionally produces a world of images to which he is the only recipient (self-to-self communication) without the obligation to exert any control over the structure or the content of what is seen, since he 'is speaking to himself' or 'telling stories' to himself and does not need to clarify or be careful in relation to any social norms which might be transgressed (sexual, hierarchical, legal, moral, etc.). The dream does not have to relate to any institutionalised or, still less, codified domain of practice, and the dreamer therefore has no objectivised history against which to 'situate' himself or refer to. Finally, dreamers do not always recount their dreams; they are not schooled in any institution (there is no school of dreams) and are not subject to any sanctions of a social, positive or negative nature.

In spite of its socially non-institutionalised nature, focusing on the dream does not, however, mean we are dealing with a 'mind which works without constraint',[42] and we cannot claim that the mental processes which occur during sleep 'liberate thought from restrictive rules',[43] that 'the dream reveals the operations of human consciousness in the process of, as it were, freewheeling',[44] or that 'thought flows freely'[45] or 'wanders freely'.[46] The dream is created in a context that is not without constraints or totally free from any demands, but, in this case, such demands and constraints are essentially internal. It is organised 1) by schemas and dispositions – products of the dreamer's social history – structuring the dreamer's personality; 2) by structuring elements of his or her existential situation; 3) by internal stimuli which, as the deferred effects of recent external demands (the recent events of waking life which have revived the dreamer's dispositions, along with elements of his or her existential situation), act as triggers for the dream images.[47]

The immediate present weighs less heavily on the dreamer's brain than on that of the waking individual. The dreamer is, consequently, focused less on the urgent matters of the present and better able to concentrate on those elements of the past (recent or more distant) which are most structuring. With the dream, it is less a matter of a 'compromise formation' (in Freud's sense of the term) in which the incorporated past of the individual is subjected to the sometimes restricting contexts of present life. The formula Dispositions $\leftrightarrow$ Context of action $\rightarrow$ Practices is thus, in the case of the dream, quite clearly weighted in favour of the incorporated past.

The daydream is, along with hypnographic and hypnopompic images, undoubtedly the waking form of expression closest to the dream in terms of the nature of the constraints imposed. Situations involving delirium or hallucinations are also quite similar in the sense that the person speaking (we are dealing with words, rather than images, in such cases) pays no attention to people around them. Then come, for example, analysis and its free associations, automatic writing, informal conversations with close contacts which can sometimes permit the expression of all sorts of fantasies, ideas, feelings, etc., in total confidence and without any consequences in real life. Literary creation is structured more by shared constraints (an objectivised history in the form of literary traditions, a literary education at school, literary criticism, literary meetings and events or literary interviews, writers in residence, literary grants, libraries and bookshops, literary prizes, etc.), but still much less so than writing associated with the law or with mathematics, etc., etc.

Bakhtin's observations on the more or less 'individual' nature of each utterance and, ultimately, of each 'speech genre' are particularly pertinent here. Every utterance, says Bakhtin, is 'individual and can therefore reflect the individuality of the speaker (or writer).'[48] But he differentiates between utterances depending on the degree to which they allow access to the individuality of the speakers. Certain fields of activity, such as law, the army or certain sectors of science, favour the most codified genres possible, which restrict the potential for individuals who speak or write to express 'personal' or 'unusual' things. Speakers are then effectively crushed by the codes, formulae, rules, hierarchised ritual exchanges, etc., promoted by the institutions within which they are working.

Other domains, such as the literary domain as it is structured historically in the form of a relatively autonomous universe, are, on the other hand, more open to the expression of individuality:

> But not all genres are equally conducive to reflecting the individuality of the speaker in the language of the utterance, that is, to an individual style. The most conducive genres are those of artistic literature: here the individual style enters directly into the very task of the utterance, and this is one of its main goals (but even within artistic literature various genres offer different possibilities for expressing individuality in language and various aspects of individuality). The least favourable conditions for reflecting individuality in language obtain in speech genres that require a standard form, for example, many kinds of business documents, military commands, verbal signals in industry, and so on. . . . In the vast majority of speech genres (except for literary-artistic ones), the individual style does not enter into the intent of the utterance, does not serve as its only goal, but is, as it were, an epiphenomenon of the utterance, one of its by-products.[49]

If Bakhtin was indeed focusing his attention largely on the literary question, his comments could equally apply to the subject of dreams or daydreams, which are forms of expression not directly solicited, and of course non-codified, and even more likely to reveal the 'individuality of the subject'. We might say, therefore, that *the interpretation of dreams is the most direct means of accessing the individuality of the dreaming subject*.

As David Foulkes said, 'We may believe that we think whatever we want, but our mental activity is under a great degree of control by where we are and who we are with.'[50] In the dream, we therefore think only what it is possible to think in the light of our own incorporated past, the state of our existential situation, the recent events of our life, and the particular context of sleep as a state of withdrawal from the normal flow of social interactions and as a distinct mode of functioning of our cerebral activity.

The dream between assimilation and accommodation

The dream is particularly indicative of the dreamer's dispositions in the sense that the impact of the immediate context is much less powerful than it is in most other forms of expression. The context does not force dispositions to shift, adapt, adjust to the logic of the current situation. Consequently, the problems to be faced, the existential knots and the emotional schemas underpinning them express themselves much more directly, even if they express themselves in a self-to-self communication with considerable economy of means (visual symbolisation, dramatisation, metaphorisation, condensation, etc.) and in a highly implicit way (hence the need to interrogate dreamers in order to reconstruct the implicit knowledge on which the dream sequences rest).

Piaget's concepts of assimilation and accommodation prove to be extremely pertinent when it comes to understanding the situation of the dream. For Piaget, assimilation is 'integration into previous structures . . . which may remain unaffected or else be modified to a greater or lesser degree by this very integration, but without any break of continuity with the former state – that is, without being destroyed and simply adapting themselves to the new situation.'[51] Conversely, accommodation refers to 'any modification produced on assimilation schemata by the influence of environment to which they are attached'. And if there can be no assimilation without accommodation, there can be no accommodation without assimilation: 'this is as much as to say that environment does not merely cause a series of prints or copies to be made which register themselves on the subject, but it also sets in motion active adjustments; which is why every time we speak of accommodation the phrase "accommodation of assimilation schemata" is to be understood.'[52] Such a dialectic shows the links of permanent interdependence which are established between the individual and the surrounding world of people, objects, animals and places, etc.

But just as I have indicated that the balance of power between dispositions and contexts could be tipped in favour of one or the other, so Piaget sees, for example, in the way children play with objects an 'almost pure assimilation'[53] (with very little accommodation), in the sense that the playing child subjects things to his own tendencies rather than adapting what he (or she) is to external constraints. 'In most cases, indeed, the doll only serves as an opportunity for the child to re-live symbolically her own life in order to assimilate more easily its various aspects as well as to resolve daily conflicts and realise unsatisfied desires. We can be sure that all the happenings, pleasant or unpleasant, in the child's life will have repercussions on her dolls.'[54]

Expression is always more or less restricted according to the nature of the context in which it takes place: we do not write scientific or legal texts in the same way that we would write an 'exquisite corpse' (a word-game introduced by the surrealists); we do not play with figurines or objects (stones, pieces of wood, string) in the same way we would in the course of a game of chess. From this point of view, the dream is indeed like a child's game, closer to 'pure assimilation' than to accommodation to a context. It is infinitely less externally constrained than the composition the schoolchild is expected to produce for the teacher or even the oral account given in front of an audience. And, like playing with dolls, the dream unfolds through a series of symbolic scenarios, the meaning of which it consciously grasps only rarely, rather than by more explicit explanations:

> But in many games we find symbols whose significance is not under-stood by the child himself. For instance, a child who has been made jealous by the birth of a younger brother and happens to be playing with two dolls of unequal size will make the smaller one go away on a journey, while the bigger ones stays with its mother. Assuming that the child is unaware that he is thinking of his younger brother and himself, we shall call a case of this kind secondary or unconscious symbolism.[55]

As a result, the dream reveals the process of underlying analogical rap-prochement, carried out unconsciously by the brain, in a much more direct manner than in any other form of expression. It is because of the 'primacy of assimilation' that 'in dreams there is a constant recurrence of symbolic thought analogous to that of children's play. They thus provide interest-ing indications as to the working of unconscious assimilations and the organization of the subject's affective schemas.'[56] The dreamer's schemas (affective or other) do not need to be transposed or translated in rigidly imposed gestures, actions and contexts, but instead they take the form of symbols and metaphors which act as models. Thus, the process of conden-sation identified by Freud demonstrates the analogical process at work: 'condensation, like generalization, involves giving a common meaning to a number of distinct objects, thus making it possible to give expression to a nest of affective schemas assimilating to one another various situations which are often widely separated in time.'[57]

What the child does in play, the child, and later the adult, continues to do in their dreams: 'children's dreams are as it were a continuation of symbolic play.'[58] For example, a two-year-old child reproduces a meal-time scene with her dolls during which she subjects the children/dolls to maternal authority. Or else a child, aged five years and eight months, who has fallen out with her father gets her revenge by making an imaginary character cut off her father's head. In this way, the problems of the child's relational and affective life are, if not 'dealt with', at least expressed in these games just as they are in dreams. In certain dreams 'a painful happening is recalled, but given a happy ending, as in the context of play.'[59] The same child who had one of her imaginary characters cut off her father's head, and who displays a marked preference for her mother and hostility towards her father, had, during the day, been very frightened by the doctor who had come to give her an injection. That night she dreamt of a doctor who killed a 'very small' man (on the subject of which she said to her father 'he had a fat tummy like you; he was just like you!'), projecting on the scene both her fear of the (dangerous) doctor and her desire to make her father disappear.[60] Dreams are therefore 'closely related to symbolic play'; they 'carry the subject far beyond the point his conscious would wish',[61] even if the waking consciousness of the player can lead to the game being an activity which is 'much more deliberately controlled' than the dream.

The dream, as opposed to literature

The dream or the daydream have sometimes been compared to literary creation.[62] This comparison, when not just a simple metaphorical parallel between dream and literature, is an extremely useful one in terms of what it reveals to us about the dream and its specific nature. Dreams have a natural life which has nothing in common with artistic activity even of the most vocational and personal sort. Indeed, the dreamer does not choose to dream or not to dream, and we cannot, as we might in the case of literature, even ask ourselves how the dreamer came to dream – whether by a process of identification or by training. The dream is not simply one of a range of expressive possibilities among others to which we may choose whether or not to subscribe. It is a human reality which inevitably applies to all human beings once they have acquired the capacity to use symbolic forms.

Neither are dreamers active 'agents' who would be capable of positioning themselves in relation to other dreamers (living or dead), who would dream with or against them, or who would put in place oneiric strategies and fight for a certain oneiric recognition. There is therefore no field of dreamers. The pressing necessity of the dream imposes itself onto everyone in the guise of the need to 'put to work' their schemas of experience – that is to say, to transpose into the oneiric context elements of what might be referred to as their existential situation. If the idea of 'expressive impulse' or of 'expressive interest' (Pierre Bourdieu) is important in the study of creators,[63] it is even more so when it comes to studying dreamers. The oneiric process is not a choice in its own right, but each dream is a product of the dreamer's need to *express something*.

The dream allows the dreamer *to work on elements of his or her existential situation*. It is a way for the individual to test out what is possible or to test the constraints of the real. And it is for this reason that it is impossible to grasp the exact nature of oneiric transpositions without knowledge of the dreamer's real life, past and present, and without piecing together the sociogenesis of what makes up his or her psychic structure and individual heritage of schemas or dispositions (for seeing, feeling and acting) – in short, without access to what only the sociological biography is able to provide.

Unlike literature, the dream is a transhistorical truth. If each particular dream is the product of a socially significant individual history, the oneiric process is not in itself in any way the product of history (this would imply that there would be societies with dreams and societies without dreams, just as there are societies with writing systems and a state and others with neither writing nor state) and has never been part of an established socio-historical configuration. It is not 'commissioned' by anyone, and nobody deliberately directs the form it takes; no particular institution maps it out or codifies it (there are no institutions of dreams where people could be trained to dream better or to find their own way of dreaming). In our societies, it is not even destined to be obligatorily shared and distributed, even if it might sometimes be recounted to an intimate circle (sufficiently intimate to be present when the dreamer awakes or to be the confidant of such a personal account). The dream is not assessed, judged or appreciated on a scale of values, and recounting it brings no obvious social advantage.

Continuing the comparison with literature, it might be said that the writer would need to have progressed historically from the status of a 'craftsman' (who, even when he is recognised as being highly competent, produces works according to the implicit or explicit expectations of the public and/or of a patron) to that of an 'artist', so that he would cease having to deal with demands, expectations, tastes and mental and behavioural habits of an external nature and, instead, be guided by his own emotions, questions or imagination. Someone who, on the basis of their own existential problems or doubts, could allow themselves to set out the lineaments of their own life, more or less transformed, to work in a literary context on their most personal obsessions or torments, to put forward their own point of view, to cultivate their distinctiveness and their originality, all those aspects which seem to us today to be 'natural' for an artist but which are nevertheless the products of history. The dream, however, is first and foremost 'self-expression'; and this status is not one the dreamer has had to fight hard to obtain. The dreamer is therefore the very image of the 'independent artist'.[64]

Without access to the dreamer's existential circumstances, the dream would remain a riddle, one for which a primitive oneirology, immediately regarding the dream as open to an infinite number of interpretations, could nevertheless cheerfully provide a commentary according to the particular interests of each commentator. A detailed knowledge of the dreamer's sociological biography is not therefore just an arbitrary decision about the method to adopt which would have no connection with the nature of the object studied. Because dreamers are placed in a situation where they can express their 'personality' and their problems, their dreams can be understood only through a careful study of their schemas of experience, their preoccupations and their dispositions. Taking as the starting point the dreamer's own horizon, what he or she perceives as problems to resolve, obstacles to surmount, difficulties or preoccupations which belong uniquely to them, in order to understand the transfiguration, in all its complexity, of that horizon and of these problems into dreams, is indeed the goal of a science of dreams as a science of oneiric creation.

Play and the dream

Freud compared literary creation, daydreams and childhood play.

> Should we not look for the first traces of imaginative activity as early as in childhood? The child's best-loved and most intense occupation is with his play or games. Might we not say that every child at play behaves like a creative writer, in that he creates a world of his own, or rather, rearranges the things of his world in a new way which pleases him? . . . The creative writer does the same as the child at play. He creates a world of phantasy which he takes very seriously – that is, which he invests with large amounts of emotion – while separating it sharply from reality.[65]

Freud gives the example of a game 'with a wooden reel' or of 'Gone-there' ('disappearance and return'). A child of one and half (his grandson) was playing with a wooden reel with string tied round it which he would throw into his cot, to the accompaniment of an 'O-o-o-o!' sound, before then pulling it back out with the string and calling out 'da!' ('there'). The game had a structure (disappearance–reappearance, far–near, not there–there) and could be described as a schema of 'throwing–bringing back/retrieving'. By expressing it in these terms, it is easy to understand that the child could, through this game, simulate in a symbolical way an analogous situation: the mother going away (absence) and the mother coming back (presence). The reel is the *analogon* of the mother, and the coming and going of the reel mimics the coming and going of the mother. The string can symbolise the link between the child and the mother; the mother is sufficiently attached to the child to come back even if she goes away; and the child knows that, by crying or screaming, he can make his mother come back to him (he holds her in the same way the string holds the reel). The game therefore symbolically repeats a traumatic situation (the disappearance or the going away of the mother) which is for him a way of appropriating and controlling symbolically what has been passively experienced: 'At the outset [to the experience of his mother going away] he was in a *passive* situation – he was overpowered by the experience; but, by repeating it, unpleasurable though it was, as a game, he took an *active* part.'[66] An 'impulse to work over in the mind some overpowering experience' allowed the child to become 'master of the situation';[67] each new repetition 'seems to strengthen the mastery they are in search of.'[68]

Out of a situation initially traumatic and unpleasant for him (the mother's absence), the child even manages to create a situation which brings him pleasure in the form of the game with the reel, through which he effectively controls both its going away (it is he who throws the reel) and its return (it is he who pulls on the string to bring it back). From a situation which is largely imposed on him (the mother goes away or stops breast feeding, and the child cannot do anything about it), or only partially controlled (crying can bring the mother back and the child then understands that, by crying, he can make his mother return; if she fails to respond to his cries at all, then he makes the practical deduction that crying serves no purpose), the child creates a situation totally in his control.

The game is therefore a sort of daydream which relies on physical props, in the same way that reading is a sort of daydream which relies on a textual support.[69] Freud wrote: 'the growing child, when he stops playing, gives up nothing but the link with real objects; instead of *playing*, he now *phantasises*. He builds castles in the air and creates what are called *day-dreams*.'[70] The *phantasie* (or fantasy) is simply the continuation, by other means, of childhood play. In both cases, it is an activity which takes place in a sort of relative isolation. The child creates his world; he plays by himself 'or forms a closed physical system with other children for the purposes of a game.'[71]

But if childhood play indeed bears some resemblance to dreams, it is also because of its capacity to metamorphose situations from ordinary life. The child projects onto the objects of his or her play, or onto the scenes played out with these objects, what the dreamer projects onto the dream images. Like the dream, childhood play is therefore based on analogies: 'A central characteristic of symbolic play is its "make-believe" nature. An object, such as a wooden block, is used to "make believe" it is a car, and the child plays cars with the block, driving it around the apartment to the accompaniment of a droning noise. In doing so, he abstracts the true property of the block and symbolises it as a car.'[72] From the age of one year or eighteen months, children can play (act out) behaviours symbolically without being completely conscious of what they are doing. They are using symbolism but not yet in a declarative form, whether explicit or reflexive. They play using different characters and act out an interactional understanding but would not yet be capable of verbally describing the type of behavioural schema they are enacting. The same is true of dreams where things get 'said' visually in the form of stories, of scenes, without the person who sees them knowing precisely what has been said. Knowledge is conveyed through the actions of symbolic play. It is a 'procedural-symbolic knowledge which is not declarative/explicit and in which a symbolic action therefore takes the place of a linguistic expression.'[73]

The psychoanalyst Melanie Klein, who has treated a great many children, used toys to enable children to express problems which could not be revealed in an explicit verbal form. She compares playing to dreaming:

The child expresses its phantasies, its wishes and its actual experiences in a symbolic way through play and games. In doing so, it makes use of the same archaic and phylogenetically acquired mode of expression, the same language, as it were, that we are familiar with in dreams; and we can only fully understand this language if we approach it in the way Freud has taught us to approach the language of dreams.[74]

But the adult should not for all that be reduced simply to a being of conscious verbal expression, since adults also express themselves just as much through non-verbal behaviours as through forms of verbal expression, and they also consciously use daydreams and uncontrolled dreams which are symbolic means of expression.[75]

Finally, dreams can be compared to childhood play insofar as they involve making up a story, but one whose fictional nature is forgotten. The dreamt story and the played-out story are stories in which both child and dreamer participate in an intense and very serious manner. With rare exceptions, the dreamer is plunged into the story which is unfolding inside his head as though it were real. He or she feels fear, anxiety or joy as though really experiencing the terrifying, harrowing or joyous events and can wake up sweating and with a beating heart. The sensations are so powerful that it is almost a case of autosuggestion.

Dreams and daydreams

In 1827, in his note on sleep, Théodore Jouffroy considered the proximity between dreams and daydreams: 'I believe', he wrote, 'that, if we were to closely study the mind during sleep, the great number and variety of facts that could be gathered would lead us to conclude that there is very little difference between this state and that of *daydreaming* and of building *castles in the air* during the waking state.'[76] And, in 1914, Paul Borel also emphasised their shared psychological properties: 'Loss of consciousness of surroundings, diminished voluntary awareness, increased automatism of the flow of representations; like sleep, daydreams can result from solitude, dreary external stimulation, music, boredom, all those matters which weary concentration.'[77] All those solitary interludes (time spent in transit, resting time, waiting time, etc.) are conducive to those moments, long or short, when individuals are no longer caught up the never-ending flow of external demands and are 'lost in their thoughts', an expression which perfectly describes this immersion in an internal world and the sense of being cut off from the surrounding world. They are, as it were, engrossed in this internal cinema and often emerge from their daydreams only when forced to do so because of some external intervention (someone speaks to them or taps them on the shoulder, a sudden noise jolts them out of their thoughts, etc.).

Freud refers to 'day residues', which he considers worthy of the same kind of interpretation as dreams themselves: 'Like dreams, they are wish-fulfilments; like dreams, they are based to a great extent on impressions of infantile experiences; like dreams, they benefit by a certain degree of relaxation of censorship.'[78] But, unlike his treatment of dreams, Freud never turned his attention to studying the daydreams which his patients could have told him about. The hypothesis of a fulfilment of a wish and of a return to childhood experiences is therefore, to say the least, subject to doubt.

In 1944, at the time when he was just embarking on his teaching career, the American sociologist Anselm L. Strauss began to conduct a study by asking his students to note down some daydreams.[79] In this study he showed that these imaginary scenarios which we mentally project in moments of inactivity, or which can accompany gestures carried out without the need of much conscious attention, can be divided into two main categories: *anticipatory daydreams*, in which actors construct little scenarios in which they try out or practise future situations, and *retrospective daydreams*, in which actors replay scenes they have experienced and which, sometimes, had displeased or upset them, imagining how things could have turned out differently. Preparation for experiences yet to come or the chance to go back over experiences already in place, these were what Strauss took away from this first foray into the domain of daydreams. What interested the sociologist was seeing how these moments of daydreaming were still linked to individuals' actions and that these were in their way an integral part of them. Far from being 'castles in the air' completely unconnected with real experience, such moments represented ways of continuing to allow the schemas of their personal experiences to go on working.[80] In order to obtain these first results, which in a sense fall within a pragmatic sociology of action,[81] only the manifest content of daydreams was considered, and no link was made between the daydreams in question and other elements drawn from the biography of daydreamers.

In the early 1990s, another sociologist, Delores F. Wunder, asked forty-one people with a disabled brother or sister about dreams and daydreams they may have had on the subject of their disabled siblings.[82] Both dreams and daydreams were anticipations of certain scenes of daily life with a disabled person, scenarios where the dreamer appeared as an impressive saviour, commanding respect for having come to the aid of a disabled person, scenes where the disabled person made a miraculous recovery or, in some cases, died, or scenes portraying a strong sense of guilt about being normal when the brother or sister is handicapped.[83]

In the daydreams studied by sociologists, people, places, objects and scenes seem much more *realistic* than in any dreams featured in scientific literature or those we might record ourselves. They are the direct extensions, revivals, reworkings or adaptations of real-life scenes experienced in a more or less recent past or of scenes yet to come. This does not mean, however, that dreams and daydreams have nothing in common. Dreams and daydreams are rooted in the dreamers' preoccupations and offer an opportunity to work on the problems they have to face in their lives, and both draw on an incorporated past. The differences between them stem largely from the different contexts of sleep and daydreaming. If, in both cases, these forms of expression imply some state of retreat or isolation in order to be able to be 'lost in thought', the context of sleep means that dreams are often less controlled and ultimately stranger or more incongruous than daydreams.

A proximity between daydreams and dreams has been observed in more experimental psychological research. In all phases of sleep, and not only in the paradoxical phases but also in 'a relaxed waking state',[84] similar forms of thinking are reserved: 'It quickly became clear . . . that this "physical" rest did not in any sense imply mental inactivity. In the absence of an explicit task, subjects almost immediately engaged in "spontaneous thoughts, including daydreaming, planning out the future, recalling memories, and so on".'[85] Not only are all dreams not peculiar or strange, with some even involving rather ordinary scenes from daily life,[86] but certain daydreams can be just as fantastical or strange, incoherent and improbable, as certain dreams.[87] Our thoughts 'when we are in the shower, on public transport or in a waiting room . . . share many of the characteristics of dreams, with their vividly visual nature, their incompleteness, their discontinuity.'[88] And, reinforcing still further the argument of a continuity rather than a radical difference between the two forms of mental expression, research has shown that some (between one-fifth and a quarter) daydreams are experienced with the same sense of reality as during dreams,[89] and that they are often similarly difficult to remember or as fleeting as dreams.

Summing up several decades of research on daydreams, Ludwig Crespin wrote:

> The difference between thinking occurring during sleep and that occurring during waking hours is far from being as clear-cut as might have been thought. In as much as we are able to put our trust in descriptions obtained on waking, the sleeper's thinking is not always hallucinatory and strange, and, conversely, when an individual loses rational control of his thoughts without actually falling asleep, he frequently experiences the hallucinatory episodes and strange mental content which almost turn his daydream into a waking dream. Moreover, and in contradiction to a persistent prejudice, the evanescence of dreams is clearly not a trait confined to night-time thinking: whether waking or sleeping, roaming thoughts are destined to be quickly forgotten, particularly when they lack perceptual sharpness. In such conditions, it is at the very least questionable to try to explain the dream, as well as the forgetting of the dream, on the basis of the neurocognitive mechanisms associated with paradoxical sleep, such as 'aminergic demodulation', and, more generally, by related mechanisms, including those of a neurophysiological nature . . . which are at work when we are dreaming and in moments when, although wide awake, we are absorbed in our daydreams, even to the extent where we can no longer distinguish between the real and the imaginary.[90]

Daydreams are also very close to so-called hypnagogic (in the phase of falling asleep) or hypnopompic (in the phase of waking up) images. But giving these images different names, and implying that these are very different states, always means running the risk of losing the common psychological and expressive theme which constantly runs through individual experience, from being awake to falling asleep, from falling asleep to sleep, from sleep to wakening, and from wakening to different states of wakefulness. Time spent in the state of wakefulness is not homogeneous but includes moments of voluntary concentration of consciousness on certain tasks, alone or in a group, and other moments which are more routine or somehow in suspense (without activity), sometimes allowing the activation of daydreams which are relatively autonomous and detached from the individual's external surroundings. And in times of rest or inactivity during the waking state, there is often a blend of perceptions of external events or elements, of thoughts and recollections triggered by that perception, and of more autonomous daydreams divorced from any connection with perceptible things of the world. These daydreams, which distract the individual's attention away from all attentive perception of the world, are often triggered or motivated by the preoccupations which play the role of internal stimuli, just as in dreams themselves.

If dreams are generally more disorganised and strange than daydreams, if the imaginary process is generally even less controlled by the dreamer than by the daydreamer,[91] there are nevertheless exceptions, and the blurring of frontiers proves that we are not dealing in this case with radically differentiated forms of expression which would be governed in a rigid way by specific neurophysiological or neurobiological conditions.

Psychoanalytic therapy: re-creating the conditions of the dream

With psychoanalytic therapy, which is a talking therapy, Freud made innovations on both a methodological and a therapeutic level. When these treatments first began, the father of psychoanalysis sat facing the patient, but later he began to sit in such a way as to be invisible to the patient, notably with a view to preventing his own unconscious attitudes from influencing him or her. 'I strongly advise positioning the patient on a couch, while you seat yourself behind him, out of his sight. . . . Since I like to give myself over to my own unconscious thoughts while I listen, I do not want the patient trying to interpret my expression, nor do I want to influence what he is telling me.'[92] In the same way, neutrality and a sympathetic attitude should be standard practice for the psychoanalyst so as to avoid the patient feeling they are being in any sense judged or directed. From the context of hypnosis which he had previously practised, Freud retained only the supine position of the patient, which allowed maximum relaxation: 'So I abandoned hypnosis, only retaining my practice of requiring the patient to lie upon a sofa while I sat behind him, seeing him, but not seen myself.'[93]

In the course of this treatment, the psychoanalyst asks patients to give a 'detailed account' of their illness, to talk about their lives, to reveal their dreams, all in no particular order. He puts considerable store, on the other hand, on 'free association', through which he attempts to break through both the formal and the moral censorship. This process involves avoiding any attempt to be coherent or concise, allowing thoughts, however far removed from the starting point, to flow freely, and not worrying about the moral correctness of what is said (allowing 'embarrassing or distressing'[94] thoughts to express themselves). For the patient, therefore, the process consists in telling the analyst anything that comes into his or her head during the session in relation to a dream they have had or to the initial associations they have begun to make. The historical origins of this technique stem from a time when Freud, having already abandoned hypnosis, was asked by a patient to listen to her without interrupting with questions. This is what he would say to his patients:

> One more thing before you start. What you tell me must differ in one respect from ordinary conversation. Ordinarily you rightly try to keep a connecting thread running through your remarks and you exclude any intrusive ideas that may occur to you and any side-issues, so as not to wander too far from the point. But in this case you must proceed differently. You will notice that as you relate things various thoughts will occur to you which you would like to put aside on the ground of certain criticisms and objections. You will be tempted to say to yourself that this or that is irrelevant here, or is quite unimportant, or nonsensical, so that there is no need to say it. You must never give in to these criticisms, but say it in spite of them – indeed, you must say it precisely because you feel an aversion to doing so. Later on you find out and learn to understand the reason for this injunction, which is really the only one you have to follow. So say whatever goes through your mind. Act as though, for instance, you were a traveller sitting next to the window of a railway carriage and describing to someone inside the carriage the changing views which you see outside. Finally, never forget that you have promised to be absolutely honest, and never leave anything out because, for some reason or other, it is unpleasant to tell it.[95]

When the patient is speaking about a dream he or she has had, free association on each element of the dream allows the different threads to be untangled, any condensed material to be analysed, and, in a certain sense, makes it possible to work backwards using the dream as a starting point, since the situations, people, objects, places, etc., which appeared in the dream are *analogons* of other situations, people, objects, places, etc., and by encouraging the dreamer to make such associations it becomes possible to identify these and to understand better what the dream is saying.

A patient lying down 'in a comfortable position on their back' on a bed or couch, who lets his thoughts and memories drift wherever their associations take them; a neutral and kindly psychoanalyst who remains out of the patient's sight and does not try to impose too much control over the exchanges; the treatment is a sort of 'conversation between two people equally awake, but one of whom is spared every muscular exertion and every distracting sensory impression which might divert his attention from his own mental activity'[96] . . . What Freud is essentially setting up is a situation of social exchange which is similar to the situation of the daydream or the dream. Awake but inactive, lying down and physically at rest, speaking to an unobtrusive person unseen by the patient, who authorises and even encourages them to say 'whatever comes into their head' without any structural or moral control, and who refrains from making any judgements, the patient is thus almost in the situation of dreaming or daydreaming. Freudian dream theory is therefore embodied in the quasi-oneiric mechanism of psychoanalytic therapy which places the patient in a situation where they can come as close as possible to that form of expression of their thought that is experienced during sleep.

It is not by chance that the American psychiatrist Ernest Hartmann found himself comparing dreams to psychotherapy. Both dreaming and expressing yourself in the context of therapy involve establishing connections between emotions or events in the confines of a 'safe place'. The context of sleep without any demands from other people, without movement, without noise or disturbance for the dreamer echoes the context of confidence and of letting go with a psychotherapist.[97]

Situating the dream in an expressive continuum not only avoids turning it into a completely inaccessible island, a total mystery which can only be interpreted thanks to special talents, but also points to an understanding that the world of waking consciousness is anything but homogeneous. Under the pen of many writers who oppose diurnal consciousness to nocturnal consciousness, thinking in a waking state and thinking during sleep, waking consciousness would fall in the realm of rational, logical, reflective thought, whereas sleeping consciousness would be seen as archaic, child-like, primitive, pre-logical, etc. Such a stance effectively revives the highly classical mythical differences against which anthropology has needed to strengthen its position in order to justify scientifically the differences between types of society or modes of thinking.[98]

Waking consciousness is not confined to moments of extreme concentration, of profound reflexivity and of maximum control of thought. And even such moments as these are underpinned by processes over which we have very little control. Understanding dreams means understanding a form of expression which has its specificities, but it also provides the tools for a better understanding of the complexity and variety of our psychic and expressive activity in the most ordinary moments of waking life.

13

Elements of Methodology for a Sociology of Dreams

> If a man could decide to note down all his dreams without
> distinction or precaution, faithfully and in detail, and with a
> commentary which would include everything he could himself
> explain about his dreams based on his life and his reading, he would
> be offering a great gift to humanity. But humanity being what it is
> today, it is probable that nobody will do so. It would already be no
> bad thing to try to do so for oneself and one's own edification.
> (Friedrich Hebbel, *Tagebücher*)

When, after all sorts of false trails and preconceptions, the researcher has finally succeeded in constructing the dream-object, it is then time for him or her to turn their attention to the various possible ways of accessing the different elements of information needed to interpret dreams as accurately as possible. The required methodology is simply the logical and practical next step for the researcher once that object has been constructed. Applying the usual sociological methods to dreams, as would normally be done with any other new object, would be to reverse the order of priorities – a case of the tail wagging the dog.

Starting with the most rigorous methodology possible – particularly when this is quantitative and gives the impression of perfectly representing the scientific ideal – and then applying it mechanically, whatever the object, is the surest way of missing out on the specificity of the object in question. Counting or measuring without knowing exactly what it is we are counting or measuring, asking questions without clear knowledge of what information is being sought and what methods would be most appropriate, would be to demonstrate a commendable positivist attitude which, while giving the impression that the rule of empirical proof is being respected, in fact only hinders the establishment of scientific knowledge worthy of that name.

Over the course of the following pages, we shall see at the same time the particular challenge posed by the collecting of dream accounts because of the fleeting and fragile nature of memories of dreams and the interest of the so-called free-associations method put in place by Freud, but also on account of the need for a more systematic approach to the dreamer's life in the context of his or her sociological biography. Finally, I will discuss how these approaches can be combined in conducting case studies and in determining the modalities of the interview methods to be used.

The fleeting nature of dreams and dream accounts

> All our dreams fly away at the cock-crow of reality.
> (Henri-Fréderic Amiel, *Journal intime*, 17 May 1878)

Evidence acquired by waking people in sleep laboratories tends to show that oneiric activity is a permanent activity of the sleeping consciousness. Whatever the period of sleep (slow-wave sleep – deep or light – or para-doxical sleep), when people are woken up, they are capable of providing relatively long and complex accounts of what they were dreaming about. But remembering dreams on waking is an extremely fragile matter. John Allan Hobson estimates that more than 95 per cent of psychic activity during sleep is forgotten on waking.[1] It is enough for the dreamer simply to be uninterested in their dreams or to be immediately caught up by the demands and needs of waking life for the delicate memories to fade and disappear.

Generally, it is an interest in dreams, sometimes maintained within a family context where children are encouraged to describe their dreams or adults share their dreams with their children, which predisposes people to recall their dreams more frequently on waking.[2] This interest is often more marked in girls than in boys, reflecting the feminine culture of intimacy.[3] It is also more common in people more inclined to introspection and psychology, as is the case of artists and people drawn to the arts and to culture in general, or to issues associated with psychology and human relations, and who, according to Ernest Hartmann, are characterised by having 'thin boundaries' between dream thinking and waking thinking, than in people whose professional lives incline them more to a culture of openness and objectivity and who maintain 'thick boundaries' between dreams and reality (legal or military professionals, salespeople, administrators and accountants, scientists, engineers or technicians, manual and agricultural workers, etc.).[4] Depending on their social and professional activity, indi-viduals will spend more or less time either wandering aimlessly, dreaming, giving way to imagination or to self-reflection or else responding to urgent situations, making decisions, calculating, resolving technical problems, giving or taking orders, etc. Professional commitments and the amount of time available immediately on waking can, depending on the case, either facilitate or act as major obstacles when it comes to remembering or describing dreams.

The degree of interest in dreams and the habit of taking notes on waking have a positive effect on dreamers' capacity to remember their dreams, and this has been observed by researchers in this field.[5] 'The fact that on waking we can recall the oneiric experiences of sleep', wrote Ludwig Crespin, 'indicates that these must have been accorded a certain amount of attention which allowed them to be stored in the short-term memory for subsequent cognitive investigation.'[6] Conversely, if the interest or the desire to note down the dream on waking is absent, the dreamer can be easily distracted from remembering their dreams by the immediate environment and find themselves caught up in other tasks. Freud noted for example that, 'After waking, moreover, the world of the senses presses forward and at once takes possession of the attention with a force which very few dream-images can resist.'[7]

The fleeting nature of dream memories can, however, also be associated with their complex, incongruous, incoherent or illogical nature. On waking, the dreamer returns to the context of waking thought, which means that the many oddities of the dream can be difficult to remember or to find expression in contexts that are fundamentally very different. Hobson notes that, 'Strümpell, writing in 1877, thought that dream images are weak on awakening and also, owing to their bizarreness, unintelligible. For these two reasons, they might therefore be swamped by the stronger, clearer sensations of waking.'[8] Jacques Montangero would also support this notion on the evidence of findings from cognitive psychology: 'The tendency to forget a dream which has been momentarily recalled on waking is reinforced by the unaccustomed nature of the oneiric sequence, which does not belong to a known "script" – a recognised sequence of events. Research in cognitive psychology on waking thought has shown that if a series of events does not form part of a script it is less firmly fixed in the memory.'[9] But Freud rejected explanations associated with difficulties in memorising complex and incongruous plots; he did not refer to the culturally and socially uneven interests of dreamers towards dreams and did not consider the preoccupation of the subject with the pressing imperatives of his or her surroundings as the central cause for the fleeting nature of the dream. Here, as elsewhere, the repression of the unconscious is seen as the prime cause of any failure to remember: 'the dream memories are forcibly crammed back down into the unconscious from which they have sprung; they are repressed.'[10]

We do not have any definitive knowledge of dreams beyond what dream accounts can bring us. In spite of advances in the neurosciences, nobody has so far had direct access to the dream. The conditions of production of these dream accounts have often been meticulously set out by scholars working on this question. However, in this area, Freud is conspicuous for his methodological negligence. Focusing his attention on the theoretical construction of his argument, he is not particularly attentive to the conditions of production of oneiric narrative material, even mistrusting written evidence and regarding it as of little use to ask patients 'to write down every dream immediately on waking';[11] nor does he pay much attention to the conditions in which material of biographical interest, or associated with the dream, should be collected. His patients recount their dreams orally in the context of their psychoanalytic therapy, and there can therefore be an interval of several days or even several weeks before the description of a dream is heard. The risks of reworking, or of 'secondary elaboration', to use Freud's own words, is therefore very high. Referring to the practice of 'deferred recording', Marcel Foucault wrote, in 1906, that this process 'is most often used by psychologists who are not concerned with scientific accuracy.'[12] Freud is of course one of those principally targeted by this criticism.

With Marcel Foucault, 'the psychology of dreams cannot be separated from questions relating to the method by which they are collected.'[13] Foucault's methodological remarks are an indication of an advanced scientific approach. He notes first of all that 'the concrete fact that the psychology of the dream must explain, the fact that provides it with the empirical elements of information, is not the dream itself but the memory of the dream': 'It is therefore the memory of the dream that needs to be considered, described, analysed, explained if we are to succeed in explaining the dream itself.'[14] But working on the dream account requires an awareness of the 'risk of losing some of its elements through forgetting' and of the 'work of transformation or of elaboration'[15] in the interval separating the dream itself and the dream account. He defends Alfred Maury's system of 'immediate recording', which involves waking the dreamer during his sleep and noting down any images recalled immediately: 'If we want to understand the dream and preserve it in the form in which it appeared to our consciousness on first waking,' Foucault wrote, 'it is essential to make a note of it immediately in writing. It is even necessary to take precautions to avoid any source of distraction, for example, before going to sleep, ensuring paper and a pencil or pen are within easy reach, or firmly resolving before falling asleep to make a subjective observation of the dream immediately on waking.'[16] When, as a professor of philosophy in Mâcon and then in Nevers, Marcel Foucault decided to collect the dream accounts of his pupils, he specifically asked them to write them down immediately on waking up, using paper and pencil already prepared, and then to complete them by adding contextual elements concerning the previous days and the day of the dream. The sooner after waking the dream was noted, the more evidence there was of 'discontinuous scenes which the waking mind tries to organise into an uninterrupted plot.'[17] Deferred transcription therefore favours the 'work of elaboration' and 'making sense' of 'discontinuous' and 'incoherent' scenes. It is as though the waking mind cannot tolerate the fragmentary structure of the visual account.

More recently in the history of scientific research on dreams, researchers came up with a hypothesis which was initially proposed by Edmond Goblot in 1896:[18] 'According to this argument, more recently formulated by the psychologist Calvin Hall and championed in France by the neuro-biologist Jean-Pol Tassin: "dreams could be shaped during the period of waking up" from information perceived in their physical surroundings at that time.'[19] The resulting argument indicates a radical scepticism as to the existence of a thought process during sleep. It would be simply a matter of hypnopompic images (at the time of waking). However, as Fabian Guénolé and Alain Nicolas have pointed out, in a perfectly argued article, such an argument does not stand up in the face of data concerning the process of waking up:

> If dreams were really of a hypnopompic nature, the type of awaken-ing, whether abrupt or more gradual, should have an influence on dream accounts: these should logically be more frequent and more detailed in the second case. This has been explored on numerous occasions, and it has been known for a considerable time now that abrupt awakenings – and not gradual ones – produce the most detailed reconstruction of oneiric content, in all sleep phases.[20]

Rather than concluding that dreams do not exist during sleep, attention should be given to the transition from the dream to the dream account and the way in which such accounts are formulated.

It might be suggested that the ordering of experience through realist narrative structures,[21] underpinned by the social contexts of expression associated with waking life and the constraints of communication with others, gradually reasserts its hold on awakening. David Foulkes, making a distinction between 'involuntary conscious experience' during sleep and the account of this experience, observes that the narrative, with its plots, appears as the most widespread form of expression but is acquired only gradually during childhood.[22] Narrative skills are therefore unequally developed in different age categories. But this turns out to be the case in different social groups as well.[23] These narrative skills depend largely on the educational level of the dreamers, with the result that children and less educated individuals generally provide dream accounts which are less detailed than others.[24]

Do we need to know the dreamers to understand their dreams?

André Breton wrote a letter to Freud in 1937 about a project for a book he was considering, a book of dream accounts which would be called *Trajectoire du rêve*. Freud's response was unequivocal: 'A collection of dreams without any detail about the associations these might have, without any information about the circumstances in which the dream took place – for me such a collection would be meaningless and I would struggle to imagine what it could mean for other people.'[25] No dream can be understood without reference to what is going on outside the dream. It is, moreover, as a consequence of this that in *The Interpretation of Dreams* Freud justified the impossibility of referring to dreams without knowledge of the dreamers: 'It will become plain in the course of the work itself why it is that none of the dreams already reported in the literature of the subject or collected from unknown sources could be of any use for my purposes. The only dreams open to my choice were my own and those of my patients undergoing psychoanalytical treatment.'[26]

Sociologists today might well give the same response as Freud on the matter of interpreting dreams. Charma displayed a certain degree of naivety when he expressed his hopes for a rigorous science based purely on written accounts of dreams: 'It would be highly desirable for scholars to collect their dreams and be prepared to publish them. It is only in multiplying observations of this nature that matter for serious scientific study can be made available to philosophers.'[27] For if the written objectivisation of dreams, fleeting objects par excellence, does indeed represent the first step in enabling them to be studied, it cannot advance very far without some knowledge of the dreamer.[28]

Even those most reticent about any foray outside the dream itself in the quest to understand dreams, whether literalist content analysts or neuroscientists inclined to think that the dream should only be linked to cerebral processes, invariably end up, at some point in their reasoning, admitting the legitimacy of the use of sources of information about the dreamer in order to interpret dreams or else make use of such information themselves. For example, John Allan Hobson might indeed claim that, in his work as a neuropsychiatrist, 'it is not necessary to resort to interpretation via the technique of free association to find dream meanings',[29] and that, 'by regarding the dream story as transparent', 'one can discern significant personal meaning without either free association or the interpretation of putative symbols.'[30] He admits, however, that 'The laboratory is too cumbersome, too expensive and too intimidating a setting', and that it is important to integrate 'the biographical tradition of psychoanalysis'.[31] Throw biography out through the door and it sneaks back in through the window.

For if the neurosciences can provide answers, for example, to the question of knowing why we can *see* in dreams, they are, on the other hand, unable to do so when it comes to the question of knowing *why we see what we see*: 'One could answer the first question by saying: "Because the visual system of my brain is activated in a manner formally similar to that of waking," while the second question has no secure answer given today's limited knowledge of the brain basis of motivation and memory.'[32] And it is precisely this second type of question that the human and social sciences are trying to answer.

When he cites his own dreams, Hobson certainly seems to have forgotten any reticence he might have had as to the notion of biography: 'That my brain, auto-activated during sleep, should cook up such a story is not hard either to accept or to explain, since all the psychological issues and conflicts that are manifest in the dream are enduring, important, and even deep concerns of mine.'[33] He assumes 'that the coherence of the story, which is eroded by the deficits of thinking specific to the REM dream state, derives from the dreamer's biographical experience'[34] and even adds that 'it will be important to verify biographical surmises in living subjects whose dreams are interpreted.'[35]

Yet the question of the exact contours of this 'non-dream state', of this knowledge of the dreamer, represents a genuine challenge for dream science.[36] Saying that 'giving meaning to oneiric content is insight into the experience of the person who has had that dream'[37] is a step in the right direction, but it gives no indication of what kind of 'experience' is involved and how to access it. Is it a matter of immediate experience, of past experience or of a mixture of both of these? And if the past is also involved, does this past exist only in the form of detailed memories, or is it also to be found in schemas, whether affective or of action or thought – in short, in the overall structures of feelings and behaviour? And how can it be reconstructed?

Scholars and researchers have definitively abandoned the hypothesis of a universally shared set of dream symbols, of a universal and archaic dream language or of a collective unconscious which would determine oneiric material. They have gradually rejected the idea that the dream is merely the response to internal or external stimuli during sleep and have understood that, when these stimuli produced effects in dreams, these were always caught up in oneiric processes that went beyond them. They have also learned to recognise the links between the dream and the events of the previous day or of the days preceding the dream (what Freud called day residues). But they have learned as well to detect the presence of oneiric structures or schemas which go back to the dreamer's own deeply rooted tendencies (enduring personality traits or the network of feelings linked to the dreamer's personal history).

It therefore emerges very clearly that understanding dreams requires, on the one hand, questioning the dreamer about their dream, or in any case collecting data to support understanding in relation to the different elements of the dream, and, on the other hand, asking the dreamer about the structuring elements of his or her past by means of sociological biography. This is what we shall gradually see, firstly with the method of associations and then with that of the sociological biography.

Access to the non-dream state: associations

Freud's acknowledgement in *The Interpretation of Dreams* of the oneiro-critical tradition represented by Artemidorus of Daldis was by no means intended as a provocation or a thumbing of the nose to science. Not only did Artemidorus consider that it was possible to interpret dreams, not only did he refuse to see all dreams simply as a means of predicting the future, but he also advocated the most detailed possible knowledge of the dreamer's situation.[38] Freud however prefers to concentrate any attention given to the non-dream state on the associations made in connection with the dream, and it would not occur to him to get involved in a biographical interview of any depth in order to understand the dreamer's most powerful dispositionalist tendencies, the state and the origins of his or her most pressing preoccupations at the time of the dream, or the triggering elements which gave rise to the dream.

David Foulkes was right to think that 'Using free association to try to place dreams within the context of the mind that actually dreamed them was a giant step forward both methodologically and conceptually.'[39] Associations make it possible to reconstitute all the presuppositions on which the different elements of the dream are based: 'My associations to the dream were bringing to light connections which were not visible in the dream itself.'[40]

The psychoanalytical technique of free association consists in going over each fragment of the dream in order to identify the 'background thoughts' to which it is linked. The psychoanalyst asks the dreamer with what they associate this particular element in their mind ('Does nothing else occur to you in connection with the jewel-case?'[41] Freud asks Dora, for example),[42] urging them 'not to give way to critical objections which sought to put certain associations on one side on the ground that they were not sufficiently important or that they were irrelevant or that they were altogether meaningless.'[43] Creating the right conditions for a series of associations in a sense means placing the dreamer in a daydreaming mode 'in such a way that the psychological tropisms which have brought together the elements of the dream can act again in the same manner.'[44]

The many instances of the unsaid or the implicit in dreams can be explained by the fact that the dreamer is speaking to themselves and consequently does not need to make what they see clear for anyone else. This means that the existential background of the dream must be reconstructed in order for the dream to be understood. And that implies therefore that it is up to the dreamer to supply the missing elements of the puzzle and not to the psychoanalyst to fill in the gaps or arbitrarily to decide the meaning of different fragments of the dream. Freud wrote that, unlike the Ancients, who wondered what thoughts might be provoked by each particular element of the dream, psychoanalysis seeks to identify what is associated with this element *in the dreamer's mind*: 'it imposes the task of interpretation upon the dreamer himself. It is not concerned with what occurs to the interpreter in connection with a particular element of the dream, but with what occurs to the dreamer.'[45] Freud can, however, be caught red-handed here in contradicting himself, for he sometimes imposes and even forcibly applies interpretations (for the most part of a sexual nature) onto dreams without any reference to the representations of dreamers who, moreover, supposedly repress certain aspects of their experience and resist the analyst's interpretation.

The same is true of someone who was for a time his disciple, Carl Gustav Jung. In a book which claims to be based on almost 400 dreams of a young Austrian physicist (Wolfgang Pauli, 1900–1958), Jung introduces the technique of association in a very convincing way.[46] In order to understand a dream, he explained, there is no alternative other than to 'adopt the method we would use in deciphering a fragmentary text or one containing unknown words: we examine the context.' And that context is provided by associations: 'The psychological context of dream-contents consists in the web of associations in which the dream is naturally embedded.' Jung rightly insists on the 'absolute rule', which is to assume 'that every dream, and every part of a dream, is unknown at the outset, and to attempt an interpretation only after carefully taking up the context.' Jung drew attention to the need to be particularly careful not to project onto the dream any interpretations which would not be linked to the psychological context of the dreamer. Nevertheless, he admits, the method he advocates 'seems to run directly counter to this basic principle of dream interpretation': 'It looks as if the dreams were being interpreted without the least regard for the context.' He justifies this twist of the rules by the fact that he is dealing with a long series of dreams, rather than with isolated dreams, and on the grounds that 'the series is the context which the dreamer himself supplies.' And yet, throughout his analysis, Jung imposes his conception of symbols in a particularly crude manner: in a hat, for example, he sees an allusion to 'a mandala'; the sea is meant to be the symbol of the collective unconscious 'because unfathomed depths lie concealed beneath its reflecting surface'; sheep make him (him, the psychoanalyst) think about allegories of the shepherd and his sheep in primitive Christianity, and so on.[47]

Beyond associations

> In order to determine the quantity of a trend discovered qualitatively
> in a dream, other aspects must be taken into account: repetition of
> this or similar themes in other dreams, associations of the dreamer,
> his behaviour in real life, or whatever else – like resistance to the
> analysis of such a trend – may help to get a better view of the
> intensity of desires and fears.
> (Erich Fromm, *The Forgotten Language*, p. 146)

In spite of everything, Freud does not rely exclusively on associations alone, fully aware moreover that these are merely the associations the psychoanalyst is able to obtain in a given relational context: 'We must, however, bear in mind that free association is not really free. The patient remains under the influence of the analytic situation even though he is not directing his mental activities onto a particular subject. We shall be justified in assuming that nothing will occur to him that has not some reference to that situation.'[48] The father of psychoanalysis has the methodological lucidity to see that the association is not as 'free' as all that, given that it depends on the context of the analysis, in the same way, it might be added, as the dream depends on the context of sleep.

As an innovative scholar, Freud experiments with numerous methodological routes which he does not necessarily express in theoretical terms and which he only rarely systematises. He often asks his patient to describe their illness, often has some idea about their more general history, and also observes their behaviour during the course of the psychoanalytic therapy. In the case of Dora, for example, Freud demonstrates that the person undergoing analysis 'speaks' as much through their behaviour as through what they say: 'Here, too, attention was directed beyond the patient's words to her conduct as a whole whenever Freud noted symptomatic acts in her – accidental or incidental behaviors in the course of the treatment. In this case history, Freud demonstrates in an exemplary manner how the psychoanalyst can use a set of symptomatic acts to supplement the dream report and the associations to it, producing seamless "circumstantial evidence".'[49] He is still attentive to the signs of transfer from patients onto himself, to their parapraxes or slips of the tongue.

But Freud can even, in certain cases, have recourse to indirect evidence to reconstitute the kinds of very early experiences which remain inaccessible to the dreamer's consciousness. With Dora, he 'also gathered anamnestic data produced by those close to her, information from Dora's entourage, particularly from her father.'[50] And, in order to understand his own dreams, Freud, who had a nanny from birth to the age of two and a half, asked his mother to describe her and to tell him exactly how she had behaved towards him. The logic behind such a request meant that he would sometimes gather evidence about the childhood of the dreamer from adults who had known him or her as a child.[51]

This multiplicity of methodological routes and of sources of information is not a problem in itself – quite the contrary in fact. Freud methodologically uses every possible means at his disposal by prioritising, through all possible avenues, the search for the truth. What is more problematic is the absence of thorough reflection on the majority of them, the absence too of any systematic approach in their application and the manifest lack of precision in the conditions in which evidence is gathered, which casts the shadow of doubt over any information collected.

Introducing Dora's case, he wrote:

> I will now describe the way in which I have overcome the *technical* difficulties of drawing up the report of this case history. The difficulties are very considerable when the physician has to conduct six or eight psychotherapeutic treatments of the sort in a day, and cannot make notes during the actual sitting with the patient for fear of shaking the patient's confidence and of disturbing his own view of the material under observation. . . . The case history itself was only committed to writing from memory, after the treatment was at an end,

but while my recollection of the case was still fresh and heightened by my interest in its publication. Thus the record is not absolutely – phonographically – exact, but it can claim to possess a high degree of trustworthiness. Nothing of any importance has been altered in it except in several places the order in which the explanations are given: and this has been done for the sake of presenting the case in a more connected form.[52]

Freud evidently took no notes during the treatment and saw numerous patients each day. In such conditions, when the sessions of the various patients could follow on from each other without any possibility of having time to think about what had been said, how could there be any guarantee that the material under scrutiny was not the product of a selective or distorting process on the part of the psychoanalyst? The precise recording of what is said (with notes being taken or, today, audio recordings) is nevertheless a fundamental condition of all attempts to achieve any kind of precise scientific objectivity. Freud does not deny the problem, but nor does he provide a very satisfactory response.[53]

Freud errs also through his sometimes unsystematic methods which put too much store on an undirected approach and make it difficult to interrogate the dreamer in any kind of depth: 'I now let the patient himself choose the subject of the day's work, and in that way I start out from whatever surface his unconscious happens to be presenting to his notice at the moment. But on this plan everything that has to do with the clearing-up of a particular symptom emerges piecemeal, woven into various contexts, and distributed over widely separated periods of time.'[54]

Since Freud's time, a great many psychoanalysts have advocated an undirected and unstructured approach on the part of the analyst as opposed to a more structured methodological (and therapeutic) one.[55] So, for example, certain psychoanalysts have expressed their opposition to any form of systematic questioning whatsoever, which is seen as an imposition inflicted on the patient. Advocating 'unfocused attention, the basic rule of psychoanalysis', as opposed to the idea, put forward by researchers such as Alan Roland and Thomas M. French, of an 'active attitude on the part of the analyst, who will ask the analysand questions in order to discover the facts, thoughts and emotions which he or she has in relation to the dream', they worry that this will undermine the complexity of the dream and that patients will be subjected to questioning.[56] But what these writers see as impositions, other researchers – psychoanalysts or sociologists – may see, quite to the contrary, as a means of helping and supporting (in both meanings of the word: something to lean on and also an encouragement) the individual undergoing analysis to put things into words. For of course it is a matter not of imposing interpretations onto interviewees or of steering them to a very specific place they may not necessarily wish to visit but, rather, of giving them the possibility of deciding which way is best for them.

Access to the non-dream state: the sociological biography

The American psychoanalyst Thomas M. French was rather critical of the tendency of psychoanalysts to make their patients' reactions conform to certain model life stories considered by Freud to be typical and even, in some cases, universal. This is the case, for example, with the Oedipus complex: 'But no individual is entirely typical. Instead of using Freud's account of the Oedipus complex as a Procrustean bed into which everything must fit we should try rather to find the actual memories which have shaped the patterns of this particular patient's behavior.'[57] Instead of assuming life scenarios or classic conflict situations, it is preferable instead to work on reconstructing the genuine and recurrent situations from the past which have shaped the patient's behaviour. This is precisely what sociological biography sets out to do.[58]

Sociological biography seeks first of all to reconstruct the successive or parallel socialising experiences – familial, professional, emotional, political, religious, sporting, etc. – that have gone into forming the individual interviewed and which have gradually accumulated in him or her in the forms of schemas or of dispositions to believe, see, feel, act. A certain mistrust of such a method in sociology stems from the fact that it is often seen as a way of isolating the individual, of locking them into a particular destiny, which will have been part of them right from the very beginning and which they will continue to unfurl throughout the course of a linear trajectory. A biography can, however, be the best way of reconstructing all the links which connect or have connected a given individual to other individuals, to groups or to institutions, and of reconstituting the tight network of internal (dispositional) and external (contextual) constraints which permanently weigh on his or her acts, feelings or thoughts. A means too of identifying links of interdependence and experiences in the chronological order of their effects.

In our societies, the family comes first in the order of experiences and generally forms the foundations for any subsequent experiences (educational or professional notably). But the family framework is not a specialised framework of socialisation. The child learns everything there: how to speak, moral codes, tastes in food or clothing and cultural preferences, relationships towards power, to the body, to money, to time, knowledge, etc. And, through it, society as a whole is reflected depending on the social, and particularly dispositional, properties of the parents and of all the other members of the familial constellation to which the child belongs. As Eric Fromm pointed out,

Psychoanalysis explains instinctual development in terms of the life experiences of the earliest childhood years: that is to say, in terms of a period when the human being scarcely has anything to do with 'society' but lives almost exclusively in the circle of his family. . . . Of course, the first critical influences on the growing child come from the family. But the family itself, all its typical internal emotional relationships and the educational ideals it embodies, are in turn conditioned by the social and class background of the family: in short, they are conditioned by the social structure in which it is rooted. ... The family is the medium through which the society or the social class stamps its specific structure on the child, and hence on the adult. *The family is the psychological agency of society.*[59]

And it would even be more accurate to say that the family is the *first* psychological agency of society and that it conditions the type of experiences that children can experience in the various other 'agencies' they will find themselves frequenting throughout their lives (school, workplace, political party, union, religious institution, cultural association, sports club, etc.).

The sociological biography also makes it possible to establish the different elements of the existential situation which the biographical journey has gradually helped to shape. In a twist on the words of Norbert Elias, it might be said that, in order to understand an individual, we need to know the most important wishes he or she hopes to fulfil and to be familiar with the problems with which that individual is confronted. But neither these wishes nor these problems are inscribed in the individual prior to any form of experience. They begin to take shape from the very earliest infancy as a result of coexistence with others and continue to develop and transform throughout that individual's existence.[60] Such an approach bears no resemblance to anecdotal, event-centred biography, which focuses only on the succession of events, and which has no ambition to throw light on the structures of action, on socialisation and behaviour, on sensibility or on personality.

The better acquainted we become with a dreamer's life, the more chance we have of understanding the links, the analogies between the characters in the dreams and real people, places or objects dreamt about and real places and objects, and, *in fine*, between situations or stories in dreams and those in real life. By carrying out biographical interviews, whether partial (on specific dimensions of the experience or in order to understand the sociogenesis of a specific problem or a particular disposition) or systematic, the sociologist is able to show that dreams, which appear only from the time when the dreamer acquires language, are structured by the dreamer's socially constituted schemas or dispositions, as well as by the elements of his or her existential situation.[61]

And rather than assuming that the dream is inevitably the fulfilment of an unsatisfied wish, the biographical interview enables comparisons to be made between what the dream says and what the dreamer experiences in waking life in order to discover whether the dream is *compensatory* (certain dreamers who are sexually frustrated in real life have numerous sexual dreams, while others who suppress their aggressivity in real life have very aggressive dreams;[62] still others can show themselves to be egoistic in dreams, whereas in life they are altruistic and easily taken advantage of),[63] *supportive* (dealing, in an analogical manner, with the same kinds of problems as those faced during waking life), *attenuating* (it dedramatises the real problem by dealing with similar situations which are less emotionally fraught) or *exaggerating* (it dramatises or accentuates the actual situations or problems). The more familiar the dreamer's life becomes, the easier it is to identify the links and distortions between the real situation and the situation in the dream.

Clarifications, associations, partial or systematic biographical accounts

> When a dream is interpreted we might say that it is fitted into a
> context in which it ceases to be puzzling.
> (Ludwig Wittgenstein, *Lectures and Conversations on Aesthetics,*
> *Psychology and Religious Belief*, p. 45)

The scientific point of view set out in this book makes it imperative, at least initially, to put in place *case studies* which make it possible to acquire, in the most favourable conditions, all the data needed to explore this issue in the most thorough way possible. As a result, I have gradually found myself turning to a type of interview previously untried in sociology – an interview which, using dream accounts written by dreamers as the starting point, can then progress to detailed explanations, associations and biographical questions in connection with the different elements of the dream.

In the standard sociological practice of the long biographical interview, as in the case of interviews focused on the description of practices, most of the questions are prepared in advance and are set out in interview grids, where biographical details and accounts of experiences in a variety of different fields can be recorded. Only requests for more spontaneous exemplification, information or follow-up – when the researcher feels that it is important to pursue the thread of the conversation further than planned – constitute any form of departure from the very well-charted territory of the interview grid. Yet the interview of the type clarification and detailed information/associations/biography, which focuses on specific dreams, is not based on a grid of questions prepared in advance and applied without variation from one interview to another. The approach is always the same, but the questions vary necessarily from one dreamer to the next or from one dream to another. The sociologist uses as a base a dream account supplied in advance by the dreamer and picks up every possible thread in order to link the different components of the dream to the dreamer's own experience.

The sociologist therefore takes as the starting point a dream account with which he or she is completely unfamiliar. The dream account is approached as though it were a text written in an unknown language. At first, the sociologist feels as though he or she will never succeed in working out what it is about. Then, gradually, through discussions, through clarification and detailed information and associations, the oneiric language becomes clearer and the code begins to emerge. But, for a long time, all this remains uncertain, and the work can prove to be particularly exhausting. Sessions of three or four hours, duly recorded and fully transcribed, can focus on just two or three long and complex dreams. Instead of getting the interviewee to talk about practices or tastes with a view to understanding them more clearly, the sociologist focuses on the accounts of *individual* dreams and sets out to re-create the conditions and the process that brought them into being. The interpretation does not aim to highlight a general relationship to a field of given behaviours but focuses on *unique* productions.

The situation of the interpreter becomes more comfortable as he or she gradually gets to know the dreamer better – their social background, their preoccupations, their interests and some of their most prominent dispositions, the people in their family, social and professional circles, the places they frequent, etc. – and as he or she becomes more accustomed to the style of dream that person tends to produce. Working on a series of dreams from the same person makes it possible to identify any recurrences more easily and provides a more reliable foundation for interpretation.[64] And when the dreamer is able to supply several dreams from one and the same night, these often turn out to be 'inspired by an identical emotional situation'[65] which therefore makes this situation easier to detect.

Chronologically, the procedure consists therefore in asking the dreamer to first note down a series of dreams by respecting the following protocol:

1. Take notes on the dream, if possible immediately on waking (the memory of the dream disappears very quickly as soon as the dreamer gets caught up in the concerns of waking life.
2. Do not try (too hard) to give structure or narrative to the dream if it turns out to be no more than just a series of scenes or of images without any obvious connections. Stay as close as possible to what you actually saw in the dream.
3. Do not alter embarrassing or shameful things. Prioritise the truth about the dream above any concern for decorum or morality.

In addition to the dream account:

4. Note down any general feelings associated with the dream: positive, neutral or negative.
5. Note down any elements linked to the day preceding the dream (events, situations, places, people, objects, etc.) which clearly reflect any elements of the dream.
6. Note down any major preoccupations, serious worries, great joys or any significant current tensions or anxieties (of the relevant 'period')

and especially those associated with the day of the dream or the preceding days.
7. For each element of the dream (places, objects, people, etc.), wherever possible, say what it reminds you of. For example, 'It's a house which looks like mine, but which, in some aspects, looks like some other house.' Or, 'To my mind, the object in question is an object which belongs to such and such a person and this person represents this or that for me.'

Once the dreamer has managed to write down a few dreams, he or she is interviewed and given a chance to discuss these dreams and the situations to which they relate in the dreamer's life. Each part of the dream is read by the sociologist, who systematically asks for details or for clarification on any points that a reader without knowledge of the dreamer's life could not understand spontaneously. For example, where there appears either a person with a particular first name or a particular place, the sociologist seeks to ascertain their status in the dreamer's real life and what experiences, positive or negative, they might be associated with. Scenes or situations are also subjected to questioning in order to determine what associations they may have. The sociologist asks, for example: What does that conjure up for you? What does that make you think of? Does it reflect a particular experience or a situation you have encountered, recently or in the past? Does it remind you of anything in particular? In this manner, the sociologist patiently gathers together all the feelings, all the images, all the memories, all the representations linked to each element of the dream. The dreamer's remarks can reveal associations of *contiguity* (e.g. a particular cap is associated with the grandfather who used to wear it, a swimming pool is associated with the wasps which often used to surround it or with a drowning accident which happened there, etc.). They can also indicate *analogies* (e.g. the boyfriend turns into the father in the course of the dream because they share certain traits; the fear of failure in a particular oneiric situation could refer to a fear of failure in a completely different situation in real life, etc.). Associations made by the dreamer in the context of the interview with the sociologist are not necessarily those which, strictly speaking, gave rise to the dream, but they nevertheless make it possible to identify which relatively coherent series of experiences (schemas) are associated with the different elements making up the dream.[66]

In terms of explanations and associations, the sociologist must at the same time focus on separating the different elements of the dream in order to determine of what they might be the representatives, symbols or *analogons*, and at the same time make sure he or she does not lose sight of the overriding narrative[67] or the overall impression of the situations in the dream. He, or she, must try to reformulate the particular situations of the dream in more general terms in order to help the dreamer understand in what way these might be linked to their own experiences. For example, the dreamer is attempting to do something, but is prevented from doing so; the dreamer feels good, but something gets in the way of that pleasure; or the dreamer wanted something which he or she does not get, but finds reasons to accept the situation and not see it as a failure, etc. That is why the sociologist must take into account the dominant emotion or feeling present in the dream and ask the dreamer about situations in real life when they might have experienced this type of feeling or emotion. Analogy is also often an emotional or affective analogy.

Moreover, whenever clarifications, detailed information or associations allow, the sociologist weaves together the biographical threads by getting dreamers to provide partial biographical accounts (about their families, their friends, the emotional relationships, their education, their work colleagues, their illness, etc.) in order to gain an understanding of what the people, places, objects, animals or activities featured in the dream represent for him or her. If the biographical accounts are insufficiently detailed, the sociologist sets aside one or more interview sessions, not for discussing dreams, but for reconstructing the dreamer's biography in a more systematic manner.[68]

The task of dream interpretation is ultimately similar to the work of palaeontologists who, on the basis of a few fossilised elements, try to reproduce the skeleton and sometimes even the complete body (with soft tissues) of a prehistoric animal or man. The possibility of reconstituting the complete animal or man in question relies on access to the knowledge capable of filling in the gaps left by all the missing parts. The same applies to the dream, which, in order to be understood, requires bringing together all the biographical, dispositional or circumstantial contexts within which the fragments of narratives slot into place and acquire meaning. The difference, however, lies in the fact that palaeontology studies physical evidence and can reconstruct the missing data by using objective comparisons based on the skeletons of numerous other cases or species, whereas the sociology of dreams studies mental evidence that can be understood only by questioning the dreamer on his or her past life and on the circumstances of their present life and by taking into account the problems with which the dreamer is faced.

Here we reach the limits of the admirable metaphor of the last fragment of a painting being completed by the painter-interpreter, which Wittgenstein uses to describe the task of interpretation. For this unfortunately gives the impression that the interpreter relies purely on his or her own imagination in order to fill in the blanks, whereas in reality he or she needs to engage with the dreamer in order to complete the picture:

It is as though we were presented with a bit of canvas on which were painted a hand and a part of a face and certain other shapes, arranged in a puzzling and incongruous manner. Suppose this bit is surrounded by considerable stretches of blank canvas, and that we now paint in forms – say an arm, a trunk, etc. – leading up to and fitting on to the shapes on the original bit; and that the result is that we say: 'Ah, now

I see why it is like that, how it all comes to be arranged in that way, and what these various bits are ...'[69]

In order to provide a provisional conclusion to these methodological observations, it should be stressed that, in the interpretation of dreams, it is particularly difficult to achieve perfect empirical exemplification of all the dreams studied. In reality, it is rare to be able to work on empirical corpuses which are sufficiently complete and detailed in *all* areas of the problem, as I have formulated it, to systematically allow a comprehensive or complete proof. The problems of recollection, of incomplete information linked to the conditions in which the dream was noted down (particularly relating to the pressing demands of the day about to begin), the state of mind or health of the dreamer at the time of the interview, can all affect the quality of information obtained.

But what the study of a single dream or a given research method may not achieve in a totally satisfactory way, the multiplicity of cases and of variety of research tools sometimes succeeds in achieving much more reliably. By demonstrating the relevance of partial analyses of different dreams from the same dreamer, or of dreams from different dreamers, we can, to my mind, arrive at a proof which is just as complete and satisfying. This is what the second volume of this research will set out to demonstrate.

Conclusion 1:
A Dream without any Function

Dreams were invented in order to avoid getting bored during sleep.
(Pierre Dac)

In the course of this book, I have deliberately left to one side a question which nevertheless continues to preoccupy the world of dream research. On the evidence of the many theorists of the dream, it would appear that no theory would be quite complete unless it stated what the *function* of the dream might be. The answer to the question 'What are dreams for?' would apparently need to be expressed in the singular (function rather than functions) in order to be totally persuasive and perhaps to satisfy the reader's need for certainty – and, even more so, that of the writers who compete for originality in the race to find new and sometimes surprising functions. My own conviction is that the dream has no unique function and that no amount of wondering what its purpose might be will help us understand it any better.

Freud prepared the way by explicitly proposing just such a function. Although dreams were essentially perceived by him to be the fulfilment of unsatisfied desires or wishes, he nevertheless suggested that the dream would have a permanent structuring aim, which would be to protect sleep. Dreams would therefore be, according to the still famous phrase, 'the GUARDIANS of sleep'.[1] In a letter to Fliess, written on 9 June 1899, he wrote: 'There is *one* wish that every dream is intended to fulfil, though it assumes various forms. That is the wish to sleep! You dream to avoid having to wake up, because you want to sleep.'[2] Freud himself referred to authors (Burdach, Novalis and Purkinje) who attribute to dreams a healing or calming effect on the wounds inflicted by daily life.[3]

The reader may indeed wonder about all those dreams which are terrifying, harrowing, disturbing or sad, or those which cause dreamers to start abruptly from their sleep in tears, drenched in sweat, choked by anxiety or fear. He or she may well doubt the relevance of this theory in relation to all those dreams which are anything but reassuring or restful. Yet Freud would still maintain that dreams had a unique and urgent function, insisting that, just as the purpose of the stomach is to digest food, the function of the dream is to protect sleep. The function of the dream is indeed to protect sleep, it is just that it does not always succeed in doing so:

> There is no difficulty in discovering the general function of dreaming. It serves the purpose of fending off, by a kind of soothing action, external or internal stimuli which would tend to rouse the sleeper, and thus of securing sleep against interruption. External stimuli are fended off by being given a new interpretation and by being woven into some harmless situation; internal stimuli, caused by instinctual demands, are given free play by the sleeper and allowed to find satisfaction in the formation of dreams, so long as the latent dream-thoughts submit to the control of the censorship. But if they threaten to break free and the meaning of the dream becomes too plain, the sleeper cuts short the dream and awakens in terror (dreams of this class are known as *anxiety-dreams*). A similar failure in the function of dreaming occurs if an external stimulus becomes too strong to be fended off (this is the class of *arousal-dreams*).[4]

As Ernest Hartman points out in a book called *The Nature and Functions of Dreaming*, a great many writers since Freud have put forward suggestions of their own about the function of dreams. Depending on which of these is consulted, the purpose of dreams is to help resolve conflicts, to make up for neglected aspects of personality, to develop the ego, to maintain and develop the self, to regulate mood, to adapt to stress or to reduce tension, to step back in time to an agreeable past, to get rid of useless or burdensome things (*'clear the software'*), and so on and so forth.[5]

The Finnish psychologist and neuroscientist Antti Revonsuo even proposed a function of the dream in the context of a model of evolutionary psychology. By doing so he takes the opposite position to all those who believe that the dream does not in itself have any natural function. The fact that the phenomenal content of dreams and the forms they take are not random but organised and selective leads this researcher to emphasise the fact that, during the dream, the brain constructs a complex model of the world in which certain types of elements are under-represented in comparison with waking life, whereas others are over-represented. And, rather than wondering which of the dreamer's social frameworks of experience and thought and which events or experiences in their life are responsible for selecting and over-representing these elements rather than any others, he proposes the hypothesis that the biological function of dreams is to simulate threatening events, and thus to rehearse threatening situations along with the means of avoiding them.

This function would make sense in relation to the original ancestors of the human species whose life was short and extremely dangerous. In such conditions, any behavioural advantage when faced with extremely dangerous events would increase the chance of survival and protect the reproduction of the species. A dream-production mechanism which selects threatening events from waking life and simulates them over and over again in different combinations would have been imperative to maintain or develop the skills required to avoid danger. For Revonsuo, the empirical data regarding the normative dream content, children's dreams, recurrent dreams, nightmares, post-traumatic dreams and the dreams of hunter-gatherers imply that our dream-production mechanisms are specialised in the simulation of threatening events. He therefore advances the hypothesis that the primary function of dreams is the simulation of danger.[6]

This explanatory leap taking us back to the origins of human life leads Revonsuo to reject any explanation more immediately linked to dreamers' conditions of life and types of experience. He sees the fact that children often dream about animals,[7] and about being attacked by animals, as additional proof in support of the evolutionary hypothesis of the biological function of dreams. Since, in his view, children are less preoccupied by their surroundings than adults (a comment which, in my view, makes no sense at all, given the quantity of research in child psychology, sociology and anthropology which has long demonstrated the determining role of socialising frameworks on the structure of children's behaviour and personality), they would be likely to dream about dangerous animals . . . as in the times of their ancestors. Revonsuo rejects as irrelevant any debate on the role of children's stories (and incidentally ignores the cuddly toys and other playthings which in our societies often take the form of animals) as a factor explaining this strong presence of animals in children's dreams. Nor does he wonder if the gradual disappearance of animals in dreams as children grow up might not simply be associated with their leaving behind the cultural world of childhood and entering a cultural and imaginary world where animals occupy a less important place.

Ernest Hartmann also claims to see a function in the fact that dreams incorporate highly traumatic events as a way of somehow defusing danger: 'As connections are made between the terrible recent event and other material, the emotion becomes less powerful and overwhelming and the trauma is gradually integrated into the rest of life.'[8] Nevertheless, not only does this kind of function apply only to situations which provoke a strong emotional impact on dreamers, but it is also not certain that it is confined only to dreams. Studies of people who have been victims or witnesses of terrorist attacks, accidents, natural catastrophes, fires, etc., would no doubt show that one way of 'coping' with the traumatic event consists in talking about it regularly with other people (spouse, friends, neighbours, doctors, psychologists, firemen, policemen, etc.) in order to share the anger, sadness or fear and to absorb, interpret and work out these issues. If ordinary conversation can have the same function of integration and de-emotionalisation, it must be that the dream has no unique role in this area. In this respect, the dream is only one aspect of the permanent effort we are obliged to make in order to face up to and resolve the problems

which confront us, but neither more nor less than the waking consciousness in terms of public action with others, those daydreaming moments
when we have time for uninterrupted consciousness, or those moments
devoted to personal writing, such as diaries, etc.

Yet why should dreams have only a single function, and should we
even wonder which function(s) it fulfils to be fully satisfactory from a
scientific point of view? Nothing could be less certain. A stubborn insistence on identifying the function of dreams is akin to trying to determine a
single function in language or in our mental representations. What is the
purpose of speaking? What is the purpose of thinking? Some might claim
that speaking serves 'to give orders' or 'to coordinate actions', while for
others speaking serves 'to express feelings', 'to put forward arguments',
'to remember certain things' or 'to predict or anticipate'... In fact, we
dream because we have the capacity to symbolise and because, as long
as the human organism continues to live, as long as the brain continues
to function, the work of representation and of expression can never stop.

Awake or asleep, active or at rest, under the influence of drink or drugs,
suffering from sunstroke or a very high temperature, or in perfect health
and in full possession of all their faculties, human beings never stop thinking, imagining, feeling and expressing themselves mentally or verbally.
'The brain continues its function during sleep the same as the heart and
lungs continue their functions during sleep',[9] wrote with great pertinence
Calvin S. Hall and Vernon J. Nordby. Thought is a permanent, continuous
process.[10] It is only the different forms it takes that vary, depending on the
cerebral, psychic, semiotic and social conditions in which it is expressed.

It could therefore be said that we dream because we live, and that we
live the life of a thinking, perceiving and feeling being, with death as the
only end. That was the view of Abbot Jérôme Richard in 1766: 'The mind
is perpetually occupied with images of some kind; its state of spirituality
does not allow it a single moment of inactivity; nor does it even have the
freedom to be otherwise – its essence is thought. Like fire which exists only
in movement, so it exists in continual activity.'[11] This insight[12] is borne out
by contemporary experimental research which shows that, even if some
people remember their dreams only rarely, it is highly likely that everybody dreams every night, in all the phases of sleep, and that only some of
them regularly, and spontaneously, remember their dreams on waking.[13]
Researchers experimented with waking sleepers up at various points in the
night, and the result obtained confirmed that on each occasion individuals
were able to recall the images and sensations they were in the process of
experiencing in their sleep.

And it is again to the metaphor of fire that Antoine Charma turned
in 1851 in order to express the same idea of the continuity of cognitive
activity from the waking state to sleep and from sleep to the waking state:
'Just as the smoldering brand which rekindles was holding in reserve some
hidden spark, so the man who recovers the full and complete exercise of
his faculties not only preserved them but, moreover, continued to exercise

them, although at a level undetectable to an external observer, in those moments of languor when they seem extinguished. Sleep is not death; waking is not therefore a resurrection.'[14] In the same vein, Paul Radestock defined the dream as the 'continuation of the activity of the mind during sleep'.[15]

To the question: 'Why do we dream?', we should therefore reply: 'We dream because we continue to live during sleep as linguistic beings capable of representation.' The brain continues its activity independently of our will, just as we breathe or digest our food without needing consciously to trigger these functions. As soon as there is capacity to represent the world mentally, the work of representation and of expression is under way, intentionally or not, awake or not. Sleep should be considered not as a ceasing of activity but as an activity in its own right. The cognitive neurosciences have enabled this notion, supported in the past by those researchers who had worked on dreams, to be proved beyond doubt: 'On the contrary, even in full darkness, it ceaselessly broadcasts global patterns of neural activity, causing what William James called "the stream of consciousness" – an uninterrupted flow of loosely connected thoughts, primarily shaped by our current goals and only occasionally seeking information in the senses).'[16] It is this diurnal-centrism, urging us to engage fully with the socialised world of waking activities, that leads us, erroneously, to think that sleep is passive and that only waking life is active, that time spent sleeping is a period of inactivity and waking time one of activity. Dreams are anything but passive. They are just one among others of the mind's forms of expression.

Dreams are the products of a capacity unique to the human species which enables them to represent things mentally and symbolically. They are generated by sleeping individuals who have no direct interaction with their surroundings or any means of intentionally or voluntarily controlling their representations. This form of thought or of human expression which arises from the human brain's need to pursue its activity regardless of the conditions in which it finds itself, and therefore also including during sleep, has no clearly determined or specialised function.[17]

Considered from this point of view, the function of 'guardian of sleep' proposed by Freud is something of a tautology. If we accept the fact that the dream is the form of thought which develops when people are asleep, then dreams and sleep are simply indissociable, without its being possible to say that the former's role is to preserve or protect the latter. Dreams do not make us sleep, but they are simply the type of mental activity that unfolds once we are sleeping. Likewise, claiming that the dream serves to enable the brain to stay active during periods of physical inactivity constituted by the sleeping state[18] is merely a way of turning the description of dreams into their function. Rather than *serving* to keep the brain active during sleep, they *are* the kind of mental process which takes place during sleep, given that cerebral activity does not stop when we are sleeping.

The great many examples of dreams published by researchers

demonstrate that dreams vary enormously in nature: we dream of stressful events to come (exams, plane travel, job interviews, etc.) or of anticipated or hoped-for events (romantic encounters, professional promotion, etc.), of past moments (which can include catastrophes or wars in the case of post-traumatic dreams, humiliating or embarrassing situations as well as sad or happy ones), of difficult situations (in a professional, familial, social, sentimental, sexual, political, religious, etc. context), of situations we wish for in our lives but which remain unfulfilled, and so on. There are as many types of dreams as there are subjects of reflection or of emotion, of questioning or of anxiety. And there are as many functions of dreams as there are functions of language. Making one form of language use or one type of dream a function would simply be an unwarranted generalisation. It would amount to going unjustifiably from recognising a certain process of functioning (it works *like that*) to the dubious attribution of a *function* (it works *because of that*).

We dream because, as long as we are alive, we have no choice but to continue to produce mental representations. Rather than trying to find answers to the question about why we dream, or what the function of dreams might be, it is therefore preferable to ask ourselves why we dream what we dream (rather than dreaming of something else) and why our dreams take specific forms (rather than any others). And, in order to answer these questions, we need to understand how the human mind functions, to be aware of the dreamer's incorporated past, to be familiar with his or her preoccupations and with the recent events he or she has experienced, and to understand the particular conditions – cerebral, psychic, semiotic and social – which prevail during sleep.

Conclusion 2:
Dreams, Will and Freedom

Dreams are the mind free-wheeling.
(Pierre Reverdy, *Le Livre de mon bord*)

In studying the dream, sociology continues Freud's work in its own way by showing that the social sciences still often attribute too much reflexive consciousness and will to individuals (with their stock of representations, tastes or preferences, values and conscious interests) than they have in reality. Freud said that 'the ego is not master in its own house'[1] and that psychic activity was not confined to intentional and voluntary conscious activity. Sociological dispositionalism does not assume that the dispositions and skills carried with individuals are consciously and voluntarily deployed and controlled or that those individuals are even aware of them. But the study of dreams has compelled researchers to become aware of the sheer scale of coherent psychic activity, albeit involuntary, operating within individuals. As a result of their many peculiarities, dream accounts oblige us to see the hidden process of unconscious analogical connections which is constantly at work. Conversely, in waking life, the descriptions of our practices, relatively coherent as they are, too often make us forget that process.

By comparing dream images to waking accounts framed in conventional linguistic formats and subject to the censorship imposed by institutions (we do not speak within the family in the same way we speak at school or at work), by circumstances (we do not speak at a celebratory meal in the same way as we speak at a funeral) and by our audience (we do not speak to a friend from outside the workplace in the same way we speak to our hierarchical superior), we first become aware of all the things that permanently weigh upon us in our waking social life and which have less resonance during sleep. We are so accustomed to adopting conventional linguistic formats,[2] adapted to the particular nature of the situations in which we find ourselves, that we no longer notice the constraints imposed on our forms of expression.

But taking the formal and the visible for the real in its totality, we end up forgetting what lies beneath appearances. Our involuntary psychic activity takes place during periods of sleep, but also in the waking state, in the numerous episodes when we are daydreaming, interrupted by interactions and external demands, and in all those moments when speech or behaviour are disturbed (hallucinations, delirium, slips of the tongue, parapraxes) as a result of fatigue, high temperature, mental illness, drug or alcohol use, etc.

It might be supposed that daydreams, temporary losses of self-control or even certain criminal acts which appear to have been committed by someone other than the self ('I was no longer myself') are no more than exceptional moments which do not deserve a high level of sociological attention. And yet, even active periods, periods of interaction and periods of waking reflection, which have all the characteristics of conscious and even sometimes rationally organised moments, are secretly connected to this same unintentional psychic activity which serves as the backdrop to individual gestures, words, decisions and reactions. Sociologists working exclusively on the waking state of publicly organised human behaviours neglect everything teeming just below the rational, public and official surface of things. Nevertheless, dreams, more than any other symbolic expression, reveal the practical, unintentional analogies which, structured by our past social experiences, constantly guide us and structure our relationships with the world and with other people. And the whole of sociology can ultimately be transformed by the inclusion of dreams in its theory of actors and of action.

We need therefore to ask ourselves what sociology might be were it to examine our waking lives with the same keen gaze as the one it is obliged to cast on the symbolic productions that are at work during periods of sleep. It would in particular be forced to take account of the depth and the opacity of that past experience which is a vital part of both our physical and linguistic acts, our actions and interactions, and of which, for the most part, we are only superficially aware. Yet our every gesture, each word we speak, carries within it the germ of all those past experiences which resonate in them. We see only the conscious or visible tip of all that is stirring within us, seeking expression and shaping our desires, our thoughts and our acts.

At each moment in our lives what 'we' do, say, think or feel is determined by the encounter between the series of relatively analogous past experiences (a series which varies in length depending on our age) and the constraints (limits, demands, questions, orders, obligations, sanctions, etc.) of the present context. And who exactly is this 'we' or this 'I', all too often perceived by us as a conscious and autonomous entity guiding by will and reason alone all these actions and gestures? The ordinary acts of social life are, to a much greater extent than we often realise, shaped by our socially constituted unconscious, permeated by culturally determined practical analogies.

Showing that the social world is still present in those moments where groups or institutions seem to be absent, where both personal and institutional interactions and demands are suspended, where will is weakened, where silence, darkness and a relaxing of muscular tone isolate the individual, largely cutting him or her off from their surroundings, is a way of proving that what the social world constrains individuals to experience in their waking lives, from the moment of birth onwards, continues to structure their mental representations during sleep. The era in which Maurice Halbwachs was reproached for his 'sociological imperialism' because he was targeting subjects initially regarded as the domain of 'individual psychology' is well and truly behind us, and it is time for sociology to pursue its research along the route mapped out by the author of *Les Cadres sociaux de la mémoire*.[3]

Sociology on the scale of groups and of institutions meant it was still possible to maintain the illusion of a fundamental and irreducible human freedom. When it studies biographical journeys, individual practices and representations, however, sociology already begins to shake the foundations of this myth of individual freedom. But when sociology on the individual scale probes deep into the most intimate heart of individual consciousness, all remaining illusions are completely shattered. As the surrealists wrote in 1924: 'the dream alone grants man all rights to freedom.'[4]

The myth of freedom has even led certain sociologists to make the dream into the last space of individual freedom. Jean Duvignaud, Françoise Duvignaud and Jean-Pierre Corbeau thus suggested that 'oneiric dramatizations ... would be just so many ways of choosing yourself amidst the warp and weft of a collective life and of overcoming its determinisms by a utopian vision.'[5] Failing to understand dreams, the authors envisage a deliberate and utopian escape from determinisms via dreams, a sort of oneiric liberation.[6] They raise the possibility that dreamers '"de-socialise" themselves through their dreams' and that certain dreams represent 'an attempt ... *magically* to modify social determinisms'.[7] Transforming an inability to understand a phenomenon into an indication of human freedom – this is what certain researchers end up doing. We understand from this how the reference to freedom is both an admission of failure to understand and a refuge of ignorance from where no scientific inquiry can be pursued.

The sociological interpretation of dreams demonstrates, on the contrary, that not a single strand of the various threads woven during our sleep exists independently from genuine social experiences and, as a result, from the multiple social determinisms that make us what we are. Freud was the first to be aware of this, with his close focus on the workings of the various processes which determine psychic activity and behaviour in individuals, largely outside their will or control. In his introductory lectures on psychoanalysis written in 1916–17, he argues boldly in favour of the idea of a psychic determinism: 'Once before I ventured to tell you that you nourish a deeply rooted faith in undetermined psychical events and in free will, but that this is quite unscientific and must yield to the demand of a determinism whose rule extends over mental life.'[8] This is the kind of remark that, if pronounced today, would provoke howls of protest from all those who love freedom, whether essayists, columnists or popular philosophers. Yet what Freud meant, and which is in fact anything but scandalous, was that nothing we think or do is the result of pure chance and that what has happened and will happen always comes with its conditions, motives and logic that can, with a sufficient amount of work, be revealed. Dreams do not represent 'the mind freewheeling' conjured up by the poet, or, if we are prepared to accept the metaphor, we must at least apply a literal interpretation to it and take 'the freewheeling' for what it is in reality, i.e. the result of a specific mechanism which is no less determined than any other.

Exposing determinisms does not mean anticipating or predicting what is going to happen; it is a way of demonstrating that what happens is neither spontaneous, nor voluntary, nor random, nor the result of some form or other of free will without any ties or roots. With far more sophisticated means than those available to the scholars in Freud's day, the cognitive neurosciences show that, if free will exists, it is an objectifiable equilibrium between internal and external, conscious and unconscious forces which are themselves the product of social determinations:

> Our actions can be thought out or not: there are reflexes or actions we carry out under the impetus of our unconscious emotions and others which we choose after genuine conscious deliberation – the latter seem to me to justify the term 'free' will. . . . If I have a difficult decision to take, I can consider all the alternatives for as long as is needed. Each of these alternatives is counterbalanced by my past knowledge, my preferences, consequences anticipated over others, the relative weight I attribute to them, etc. All of that is counterbalanced in this space of conscious work. In that case, I think it is right to talk about free will, even if someone who was able to gain access to all my synapses in advance could have predicted this decision.[9]

It is clear from these remarks made by the cognitive psychologist Stanislas Dehaene that the decision, even when it is thought out or carefully deliberated, is still no less socially determined: our past knowledge and experiences are socially differentiated, as are our preferences and our relations with others, and these deliberations, which are based on a large number of perceptions and unconscious thought processes, do not free us from determinisms.

What happens, both in the social and the physical sphere, on a macroscopic scale as well as a microscopic one, is not always predictable but is, nevertheless, still entirely determined by multiple forces. What makes sociology a particularly complex science, especially when it is working on an individual scale, is the fact that the individuals who are active in society at one and the same time carry within them a whole range of incorporated properties and are constantly subjected to variable forces which make different demands on these properties depending on the context within which they are acting.

Each of their unique behaviours is as unpredictable as the result of the throw of a pair of dice on a table. It is impossible to predict the numbers which will be thrown, and yet researchers know that the final result is totally physically determined. The numbers which will emerge – the dots which appear on the visible faces of the two dice – depend on the material from which the dice are made (plastic, metal, paper, cardboard, etc.), on their weight, on their size and on their degree of physical homogeneity (we know that loaded dice are designed in such a way that certain configurations are more likely than others), on the initial position of the dice in the hand, on the angle of the throw of the dice, on the strength of the thrower, the resistance of the air and the possible movements of air masses, on the nature of the surface onto which the dice fall, whether smooth or rough, and on which they will slide or roll, on the possible physical interactions between them in the hollow of the hand and even, once thrown, if they collide, etc. All of that is perfectly determined. We know it is. But what we do not know is how to make the necessary calculations so as to combine all the physical data and forces involved and to predict the numbers which will appear once the dice come to rest. If we imagine that, in addition to all that, each of the dice has a history of its own, and that the surroundings in which they suddenly find themselves also have their own history, we start to form an idea of the complexity of the task faced by researchers in the social sciences.

All those who resist the notion of the influence of social determinisms on individual behaviour have both an exclusively collective vision of the social and a simplistic and mechanistic image of determinism. They may very well observe that not *all* prisoners come from dominated groups in society, that not *all* members of Parliament come from the upper classes, that not *all* men are violent towards their partners, or that not *all* children from working-class backgrounds perform poorly at school, in order to provide support for their own interpretation: 'It's about individual responsibility', 'It's a matter of willpower and effort', etc. Roger Bastide already highlighted the suspicion expressed by psychoanalysts about the 'sociological theory of crime': 'If it is background that is responsible, we do not understand why, among individuals who belong to the same group, only some will become criminals and others not. It must therefore be that the individual make-up and the psychic structure of the person predominate over social factors.'[10] Determinism would therefore be the unequivocal explanation on the grounds of social background alone.

On the group scale, however, sociology can only advance arguments of probability. It does not say that all men beat their partners but that, in the current state of things, the probability that a woman will be beaten by a man is infinitely greater than the probability that a man will be beaten by a woman. And, when it focuses on the individual level, sociology does not confine itself to sweeping explanations based on background, class or group; rather, it tries to identify the combined effects of a great many social determinisms, both internal and external, those to be found internalised within dispositions as well as those which are to be found outside the individual (characteristics of the people, groups and institutions they frequent). It is these intersecting constraints which determine that individuals from the same group behave differently. Within the same family, the experiences of one or another member are never perfectly identical, the interactions or situations experienced never exactly the same, the positions within the configuration differing depending on whether the individual in question is a girl or boy, the oldest or the youngest, etc.

The anthropologist Ralph Linton said that 'Even identical environments, if such things are conceivable, will provide different individuals with different experiences and result in their developing different personalities. Even the best integrated society and culture provides the individuals who are reared in it with environments which are far from uniform.'[11] And Roger Bastide added that 'individuals participate not in the whole of civilisation but only in certain segments of it, depending on their place in society and on their sex, age, occupation, region, religion and, in a country of immigrants, ethnic group', the consequence of which is 'to substitute for general influences of civilisation the specific influences which have acted on the individual.'[12]

What is needed more than ever before is as much a sociology on a macro-sociological scale, the one Durkheim described as 'the science of institutions, of their genesis and of their functioning', as this sociology on the individual scale which reveals the traces of social life in the most intimate folds and recesses of psychic activity. The study of dreams in no sense involves stepping outside the social world, with its regularities, its constraints and its problems. It contributes to uncovering the processes through which individuals ceaselessly confront, by *expressing* them, the problems which are unique to them but which nevertheless come from outside.

The sociology of dreams, as a science of the social determinations at work in oneiric expression, therefore represents the ultimate attack on any illusions about the freedom or the will of the subject. By studying dreams, by showing that they are indissolubly linked to the social experiences of the dreamer, both past and present, my intention is to show that the social is to be found in the most intimate depths of individuals, even during those moments of sleep when they seem to be most completely cut off from ordinary social realities. Social logics continue to make their presence felt in the dreamer's psychic activity in the immediate absence of any institution, any group, any interaction or any external demands.

The sociological interpretation of dreams has taken on the task of toppling, over and over again, so endless does the task seem, all the opposition encountered by the social sciences, and in particular by sociology, to their claims of being able to reveal the social processes, and what we must indeed call the social determinisms, at work in the most personal of all human experiences.

Coda:
The Formula for
Interpreting Practices –
Implications and Challenges

The aim of a general formula for the interpretation of practices, what-ever form these may take, is to bring together the separate, and very often competing, avenues of scientific study concerning the social world. The competition between different programmes and between researchers makes it difficult to see the logical links which could unite them. Indeed, if competition can indeed be a driving force in the quest for knowledge, it can also end up partially blinding a great many of the competitors, whereas a broader and more distanced vision allows a far more effective resolution of the scientific problems that arise and a more balanced inter-pretation of human practices. We might say *that each competitor is wrong in failing to see to what extent the others are partially right.*

The general formula which is at the heart of this book allows us to consider individual or collective practices within the course of history at the intersection between the actors' incorporated pasts and the present context of their actions. The history of individuals, from their birth to their death, can thus be seen as the history of the interface (in itself an essential element in the transformation of both individuals and situations) between what the social world has made of them and what it constantly confronts them with.

The desire to understand why human beings do what they do, feel what they feel, think what they think, implies not only a detailed study of their *practices* (physical as well as symbolic) and the study of the incorporated *dispositions* or *schemas* they carry within them on the basis of their past experiences, but also the study of the *contexts* in which these practices were put into action and observed. It is impossible, for example, to understand the behaviour and the educational progress of a child without taking into account both the social dispositions, shaped notably within the family circle (relationship to knowledge and to language, relationship to authority, cultural dispositions, sense of competition or degree of asceticism, etc.), that he or she brings to the school context *and* the specific nature of the school context in question (the kind of knowledge taught, the nature of the relationship with knowledge which is inculcated there, the educational techniques and systems, the relationships of authority which are established between teachers and pupils, etc.). Similarly, on a more macro-sociological level, it is equally impossible to understand, for example, the cultural behaviour (cultural practices and preferences) of the members of a social class without investigating both the cultural dispositions they have inherited from their earliest familial experiences and their school experiences *and* the nature of the cultural context in question (the precise nature of the available cultural offer and its degree of diversity, the nature of the cultural hierarchies between the different cultural products, the characteristics of the cultural institutions, etc.).

The relationship between dispositions and context is a dialectical relationship that cannot be reduced to a simple relationship of cause and effect, which, more often than not and for chronological reasons, we imagine going from the past to the present, although also sometimes – from a pragmatist point of view – from the present to the past. The question of the 'direction of causality' between dispositions and context – in other words, the question which consists in asking if it is the past that determines what is perceived and interpreted of the present, as well as the manner in which it is perceived and interpreted, or else if it is more a case of the present (with its imperatives, its demands, its limitations and its constraints) determining which elements of the past can be reopened, mobilized, triggered, activated and, conversely, which elements should remain as dead letters, be suppressed or put on standby – is a question

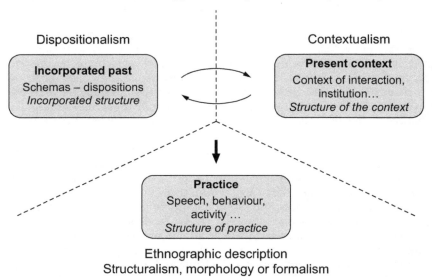

Figure 8 General formula for the interpretation of practices: dispositional-contextual genetic structuralism

of scant relevance. When all is said and done, the present context and dispositions *join forces* to generate practices – from the most routine to the most inventive or creative.

The only relevant question about the relationship between the incorporated past and the present context of action is to establish, on the one hand, the degree of constraint exercised by context on the actions of individuals and, on the other, the degree of strength or of power of their incorporated dispositions.

First of all, there are strong contexts and weak contexts, closed or rigid contexts and open or flexible contexts, contexts which are institutionalised and even codified (e.g. an official speech or a courtroom plea) and those which are less rigid, looser, or less highly institutionalised (e.g. a discussion between friends). The military institution is not the same as the friendship group, the family institution is not the same as the educational institution, the legal field is not the same as the literary one, the job interview is not the same as the informal chat in a café, the mathematical demonstration is not the same as the dream or the daydream, etc.

Furthermore, incorporated dispositions are not equally constituted, and their strength depends on the amount of reinforcement to which they have been subject: dispositions which have the advantage of being established at a very early age and in a systematic and enduring way are infinitely stronger and more active than dispositions developed at a later stage, on a more occasional basis and over a shorter period of time. It is for this reason that the incorporated cultural dispositions of children from the upper classes with access to extensive cultural capital are infinitely stronger and more effective than the cultural dispositions of children from the working or middle classes who learn to establish them less systematically, in a less enduring way, and/or at a later stage (essentially as a result of the socialising influence of school).

Depending on the degree of constraint or of coercion imposed by the context, dispositions may be called upon almost constantly, suppressed or allowed 'freer' expression. And depending on how solidly constituted and consolidated they are and on how powerful they are, dispositions can be mobilised or activated to a greater or lesser degree by the different contexts in which they are needed. They can also be more or less difficult to suppress or to leave dormant in certain contexts. More than unequivocal links of causality, it is the dynamic balance of the forces at work between dispositions and contexts which 'decides' what it is possible for individuals to do or to say.

Incorporated past and context have, moreover, a history which demands the *sociogenetic* study of these realities. Schemas or dispositions incorporated by individuals are the *product of the history* of their associations, whether from an early age or later, whether systematic or not, long or short, with differentiated contexts of socialisation (family institution, educational institution, professional settings, religious, cultural, political, sporting, etc., institutions). Schemas or dispositions are like the *summaries*

(Piaget) of independent sequences of relatively similar social experiences which individuals have found themselves experiencing throughout the course of their lives (very short ones in the case of newborns, much longer ones for the oldest adults).

The present context of action of the formula, with its specific properties, is also the *product of a history* of varying length: the history of the institution, the group, the world, the specialisation, etc., which confers on them their relevant properties and their specificity at a given moment in time. For example, the educational institution is by no means something written in stone but has continued to evolve from the days of the Jesuit schools set up under the 'Ancien Régime' to the present time and, similarly, the nature of the issues and the power struggles between the trends or the main areas of scientific research have varied considerably during the course of its history. The present context can therefore be considered from two different perspectives: 1) from the perspective of the effects of socialisation it produces on individuals (reinforcement or minor modification of schemas or dispositions already incorporated, or the setting in place of new schemas or dispositions); 2) from the perspective of the immediate effects of the process of triggering or putting on hold, of activation or of suppression, of those schemas or dispositions already incorporated by individuals.

The different elements of the formula need to be seen as a series of *structures* or *forms*, which may be incorporated, contextual or specific to particular practices themselves or to the products of these. Determining the nature of these structures represents a first scientific goal, which consists in trying to identify the *structure of experiences incorporated* in the form of schemas or dispositions, the *structure of contexts of action* (structure of the interaction, structure of the group, the institution, the world, speciality or field, etc.) and the *structure of observed practices* (structure of behaviour, structure of the narrative or speech, structure of the activity, etc.). But each of these scientific goals (knowledge of the incorporated structures, knowledge of the contextual structures and knowledge of the structure of practices) is sometimes considered by researchers as an end in itself, and this contributes to separating and isolating elements of the formula which are in fact inextricably linked.

The general formula for the interpretation of practices seems to me to form a logical whole, and, except on an exploratory basis or for practical reasons (limited time available for research or deficiencies in the empirical material available), it seems to me problematic to sever the dynamic links between the different components. As a result, therefore, I have set out, in the context of the formula, the possible interpretive variations or reductions:

1. when only the context is taken into account in order to interpret practices (*contextualism*);
2. when only the incorporated past is taken into account in order to interpret practices (*dispositionalism*);

3. when the focus is exclusively on practices in order to understand them ('simple' ethnographic description purportedly conveying the essence of what there is to know about the practices; linguistic, semiological or anthropological *structuralism, formalism* or *morphology*, the goal of which is simply to show the structure of practices without trying to relate them to other structures).

The formula for the interpretation of practices, to my mind, makes it possible to examine sociological problems better. But, with so much competition and specialisation in the scientific field, we may find ourselves wondering what chance there is for such an approach to succeed. By clarifying the scientific issues of the integrative approach which governs this formula, we can scarcely hope to convince the majority of competitors in this arena, and especially those who are too deeply committed to a particular point of view to be able to accept abdicating the claim to universality of their own interpretative model; rather, it is up to those who, having freshly arrived in the scientific field, can make a calm and considered assessment of such theoretical integration.

Apart from the effects of competition within the scientific field, another major obstacle to such an interpretive ambition comes in the form of a radical relativism and constructivism which is based on the premise that there cannot be any genuine progress in the human and social sciences. According to this point of view, there can be no accumulation of knowledge, it would be impossible or pointless to compare the relatively heuristic power of any competing scientific programs, and there would be no possibility of sharing the results of research. Any detailed consideration of all such ideas makes it clear that the notion of any kind of scientific progress or any synthetic integration of the various programmes proposing only one particular viewpoint would be eliminated, judged as naively scientistic (or 'naturalistic') and considered doomed to failure from the outset.

However, even a minimal knowledge of the history of science enables us to understand that the scientific efforts achieved by researchers as diverse as Darwin, Marx, Freud, Einstein, Durkheim or Bourdieu have involved synthesising, in an original way, areas of scientific knowledge and evidence which are often sparse and sometimes contradictory. By this same reasoning, the aim of the human and social sciences, *as elsewhere*, would be to bridge the divide between what are judged to be conflicting approaches (e.g. the way physics addresses the infinitely large and the infinitely small, the general theory of relativity and quantum mechanics or the fact that, in mathematics, algebra or arithmetic and geometry were long considered as separate approaches until researchers discovered ways of linking them) and to integrate different disciplinary or sub-disciplinary contributions.

The authors of *Reproduction in Education, Society and Culture* outlined their theory of the reproduction of the inegalitarian social system by citing the three principal sources (Marx, Durkheim and Weber) to whom they were jointly referring, even though these were considered (and, for many, still continue to be regarded) as totally antagonistic. Bourdieu's theory of fields and habitus would quite simply not exist had their author believed that each 'theory' or each 'scientific programme' should exist independently of all the others, had he believed that the comparison, confrontation or linking of scientific programmes from the past made no sense (each bringing 'its own truth' which bears no relation to the 'truths' of other similar programs), had he not flown in the face of the implicit taboos of his time ('when you are a Marxist, you cannot be a Weberian: when you are a Weberian, you cannot be Durkheimian, etc.') and synthesised the unsynthesisable.

This pervading scientific relativism, which disparages all scientific ambition within the human and social sciences and implies that the best that can be done in scientific terms is simply either to stay as close as possible to empirical material, without any real attempt to interpret the 'facts', or else to resort to provocation or rhetorical brilliance, also rests implicitly on a very sparse knowledge of the exact nature of the physical and life sciences. As historically dominant models which represent the very embodiments of science, these are generally considered to be scientific models which are unattainable by researchers in the human and social sciences. Yet, if we resist the temptation to idealise them, these sciences are not after all so very different from the human and social sciences. In the course of their history they have come up against comparable obstacles[1] and are rarely in a position to be able to devise tests of falsifiability capable of completely invalidating any elements of rival theories. Here, as in the human and social sciences, certain theories turn out, over the course of a lengthy process, to be more relevant than others (from the point of view of their internal coherence as well as of their capacity to fit with an ever-increasing body of facts). Nor is there anything in the historic character of the human and social sciences, often singled out on the grounds of their narrow focus and their obvious limitations (how, it may be asked, can anyone hope to make a science of a reality which is by nature changeable, too complex, not definable in terms of a finite series of variables and does not lend itself to being modelled?), which does not find an equivalent in the fields of the physical and life sciences.

To take just two examples from among the most glaring, the theory of evolution or geology do not deal with ahistorical realities but are, on the contrary, sciences of history which have never ceased to study the effects of 'deep' time on the realities they are studying.[2] The mythologisation of the experimental and obsessively empirical nature of the physical and life sciences, which could radically distinguish them from the human and social sciences where experiments are not possible and which can be speculative, tends to obscure the fact that all these sciences are not equally experimental,[3] that they willingly accept the most speculative research while awaiting empirical confirmation, and that they have never simply deduced theories capable of explaining specific facts directly from the immediate observation or perception of reality. Quite to the contrary, the most powerful theories have often been counter-intuitive in relation to what might seem to be the most firmly established empirical evidence (e.g. there is nothing more counter-intuitive than quantum mechanics, which nevertheless led to technological achievements as diverse as the transistor, the laser, the computer, GPS, MRI, the mobile phone, the microwave oven or the atomic clock). The physical and life sciences have always combined maximum theoretical risk taking (think for example of quantum physics or the more recent, and even more controversial, string theory) *and* the need to confront reality directly. Physics in particular would never have seen the remarkable advances in knowledge with which we are familiar had it not dared to formulate ambitious, synthesised or integrative theoretical programmes, which have often only much later led to sophisticated experimental validation (e.g. the theory of general relativity, quantum mechanics, or the Higgs boson theory).

Without denying the differences between the physical and life sciences on the one side and the human and social sciences on the other, it is nevertheless clear that nothing should discourage researchers in the human and social science in their scientific ambitions. Apart from powerful yet perfectly surmountable social obstacles, *a priori* there is no *epistemological* barrier to prevent them formulating, for example, synthesised theories or integrative models.

Notes

Introduction

1 G. A. Fine and L. Fischer Leighton, 'Nocturnal omissions: steps toward a sociology of dreams', *Symbolic Interaction*, 16/2 (1993): 95–104.

2 In spite of the importance of this work in the history of human sciences, we should point out, along with Lydia Marinelli and Andreas Mayer, that the first edition of *The Interpretation of Dreams* (dated 1900 but published in 1899) had a print run of 600 copies and the second edition, eight years later, one of 1,050. Marinelli and Mayer, *Dreaming by the Book: Freud's Interpretation of Dreams and the History of the Psychoanalytic Movement*. New York: Other Press, 2003, p. 42.

Chapter 1 Advances in the Science of Dreams

1 J. Roubaud, *Jacques Roubaud: rencontre avec Jean-François Puff*. Paris: Argol, 2008, p. 59.

2 E. Fromm, *Greatness and Limitations of Freud's Thought*. London: Jonathan Cape, 1980, p. 11.

3 J. Carroy and J. Lancel (eds), *Clés des songes et sciences des rêves: de l'Antiquité à Freud*. Paris: Les Belles Lettres, 2016.

4 J. Le Goff, 'Dreams in culture and collective psychology', in Le Goff, *Time, Work and Culture in the Middle Ages*. Chicago: University of Chicago Press, 1982, pp. 202–4. Gradually 'saints replaced the ancient elites of the dream: kings (Pharaoh, Nebuchadnezzar) and chieftains or heroes (Scipio, Aeneas)', and 'simple clerics – preceding common laymen – were favoured with significant dreams', writes Le Goff.

5 'Social prejudices' mean that, during the whole period of the High Middle Ages, 'saints, of course, alongside kings, monks and clerics', are more likely to be credited with 'authentic dreams, of divine origin, than simple men, illiterate people, laymen, *rustici* and, especially, women' (J.-C. Schmitt, 'Le sujet et ses rêves', in Schmitt, *Le Corps, les rites, les rêves, le temps: essais d'anthropologie médiévale*. Paris: Gallimard, 2001, p. 299).

6 Ibid., pp. 303–4.
7 A. Timotin, 'Techniques d'interprétation dans les clés des songes byzantines', in J. Carroy and J. Lancel (eds), *Clés des songes et sciences des rêves: de l'Antiquité à Freud*. Paris: Les Belles Lettres, 2016, pp. 46–60.
8 J.-C. Schmitt, 'Les clés des songes au Moyen Âge', ibid., pp. 61–71.
9 Schmitt, 'Le sujet et ses rêves', p. 308.
10 Oneirocriticism is the art of interpreting dreams, and an oneirocritic is someone who practises this art.
11 J. Richard, *La Théorie des songes*. Paris: Frères Estienne, 1766, p. 16.
12 Ibid., p. 4.
13 Ibid., p. 40.
14 J. Carroy, *Nuits savantes: une histoire des rêves (1800–1945)*. Paris: EHESS, 2012. Expressions such as 'nocturnal thoughts' or 'nocturnal visions', which I will sometimes use in this book, are merely practical shortcuts. It goes without saying that the dream is associated with sleep but not specifically with the night. It can occur just as easily during a siesta or in the course of longer periods of sleep during the day.
15 For example, Léon d'Hervey de Saint-Denys began to note his dreams in a special book at the age of thirteen. Twenty-two notebooks filled with coloured illustrations represent a series of 1,946 nights, or the equivalent of more than five years. See d'Hervey de Saint-Denys, *Dreams and How to Guide Them*. London: Duckworth, 1982, p. 19.
16 Jacques-Louis Moreau, or Moreau de la Sarthe (1771–1826), was a French doctor and anatomist who, in 1820, was the author of the section on dreams in the *Dictionnaire encyclopédique des sciences médicales* (ed. A. Dechambre, L. Lereboullet, and L. Hahn, Paris: Masson, 1876). Gotthilf Heinrich von Schubert (1780–1860) was a German physician and naturalist, author of *Die Symbolik des Traumes* (Bamberg: Kunz, 1814). Théodore Jouffroy (1796–1842) was a French philosopher and politician, author of 'Du sommeil' (1827), published in *Mélanges philosophiques* (Paris: Paulin, 1833). Antoine Charma (1801–1869) was a French philosopher, archaeologist and palaeographer, author of *Du sommeil* (Paris: Hachette, 1851). Alfred Maury (1817–1892) was a French archaeologist, historian, librarian, and professor at the Collège de France, who published *Le Sommeil et les rêves: études psycho- logiques sur ces phénomènes et les divers états qui s'y rattachent* (Paris: Didier, [1861] 1865). Léon d'Hervey de Saint-Denys (1822–1892) was a sinologist and professor at the Collège de France who wrote *Dreams and How to Guide them* (first published 1867). Karl Albert Scherner (1825–1889) was a German philosopher and psychologist, author of *Das Leben des Traums* (The life of dreams; Berlin: H. Schindler, 1861). Finally, Joseph Delbœuf (1831–1896) was a Belgian mathematician, philosopher and psychologist, author of *Le Sommeil et les rêves considérés principalement dans leurs rapports avec les théories de la certitude et de la mémoire* (Paris: Félix Alcan, 1885).
17 S. Freud, *The Interpretation of Dreams*, in *The Standard Edition of the Complete Psychological Works*, Vols IV and V. London: Hogarth Press, 1953; and *On Dreams* (1901), in *The Standard Edition*, Vol. V.
18 H. F. Ellenberger, *The Discovery of the Unconscious: The History and Evolution of Dynamic Psychiatry*. London: Fontana, 1994.
19 The original German title of Freud's work. It has been translated into English under the titles *Interpreting Dreams* and *The Interpretation of Dreams*.

20 L. Binswanger and M. Foucault, *Dream and Existence*. Seattle: Review of Existential Psychology and Psychiatry, 1986, p. 34.

21 Not only did Freud share with Artemidorus of Daldis the idea of giving meaning to dreams but, as Andreas Mayer points out ('La *Traumdeutung*, clé des songes du vingtième siècle? Freud, Artémidore et les avatars de la symbolique onirique', in Carroy and Lancel (eds), *Clés des songes et sciences des rêves*, p. 162), they agreed on two points: on the one hand, both break the dream down into separate elements in order to interpret it and, on the other, both take into account the individuality of the dreamer.

22 Many arguments against the Freudian model are summed up in G. W. Domhoff, 'Why did empirical dream researchers reject Freud? A critique of historical claims by Mark Solms', *Dreaming*, 14/1 (2004): 3–17.

23 For a general introduction to these issues, see F. Parot, *L'homme qui rêve*. Paris: Presses universitaires de France, 1995.

24 E. Schrödinger, *Nature and the Greeks and Science and Humanism*. Cambridge: Cambridge University Press, 1996, p. 109.

25 Ibid., p. 111.

26 The fascinating story of this success can be followed in S. Singh, *Fermat's Last Theorem*. London: Fourth Estate, 1998.

27 A. Grothendieck, 'Allons-nous continuer la récherche scientifique?', lecture given at CERN, Geneva, 27 January 1972, https://archive.org/stream/Allons-nousContinuerLaRechercheScientifique/Grothendieck_ARS_djvu.txt.

28 M. Halbwachs, *La Psychologie collective*. Paris: Champs classiques, 2015, p. 158.

29 N. Elias, *Essays 1: On the Sociology of Knowledge and the Sciences*. Dublin: University College Dublin Press, 2009, p. 202.

30 Carroy, *Nuits savantes*.

31 D. Holt, *Eventful Responsibility: Fifty years of Dreaming Remembered*. Oxford: Validthod Press, 1999.

32 The American website DreamBank, edited by the psychologists Adam Schneider and G. Willian Domhoff, gives access to around 22,000 dream reports spanning a period from 1897 to the present.

33 See C. Meyer (ed.), *Le Livre noir de la psychanalyse: vivre, penser et aller mieux sans Freud*. Paris: Arènes, 2005.

34 P.-H. Castel, 'Introduction', *L'Interprétation du rêve de Freud*. Paris: Presses universitaires de France, 1998.

35 We can only agree with Didier Anzieu when he writes about the theory of the dream set out in *The Interpretation of Dreams* and *On Dreams*: 'No psychoanalyst has ever challenged it and no researchers from other related disciplines (sociology, ethnology, psychiatry, neuropsychology, experimental and cognitive psychology) have, over the course of almost a century, successfully proposed a new conception of the dream' ('Table d'hôte', in S. Freud, *Sur le rêve*. Paris: Gallimard, 1988, p. 37). But, unmatched among general theories, it was nevertheless the subject of a great deal of criticism, some of which was entirely fair, yet without prompting many psychoanalysts in return to respond by proposing a reform or a reworking of the model.

36 We shall see examples of this notably in the work of the American psychoanalyst Thomas M. French, the American psychiatrist Ernest Hartmann and the Swiss cognitive psychologist Jacques Montangero.

37 Elias, *Essays 1: On the Sociology of Knowledge and the Sciences*, p. 50.

38 S. Freud, *Introductory Lectures on Psychoanalysis*, in *The Standard Edition of the Complete Psychological Works*, Vol. XV. London: Hogarth Press, 1963, p. 27.
39 Ibid., p. 97.
40 S. Freud, *The Origins of Psychoanalysis: Letters to Wilhelm Fliess, Drafts and Notes: 1887–1904*. London: Imago, 1954, p. 279.
41 N. Elias, *The Symbol Theory*. Dublin: University College Dublin Press, 2011, p. 16.
42 Ellenberger, *The Discovery of the Unconscious*.
43 M. Perrin, *Les Practiciens du rêve: un exemple de chamanisme*. Paris: Presses universitaires de France, 2011.
44 J. du Bouchet, 'Artémidore, homme de science', in Carroy and Lancel (eds), *Clés des songes et sciences des rêves*, p. 45.
45 Jacqueline Carroy and Juliette Lancel wrote, for example, that 'the focus shifted or transferred, over the course of Western history, from prophetic dreams to natural dreams', and that 'it is dreams – as internal phenomena (physiological and/or psychological) sowing turmoil in both soul and body – that provoke interest from the eighteenth century onwards' ('Introduction', in *Clés des songes et sciences des rêves*, p. 11). Such remarks are historically pertinent. But in the perspective of establishing a science of dreams, which is certainly not their objective, it would be more epistemologically 'realistic' to write that dreams were *discovered* to be *simply* 'natural' or 'human' and sent neither by God nor by the Devil.
46 See below, 'Limitations of environmentalist approaches: the ecology of dreams' (pp. 41–4).
47 The historian Jacqueline Carroy, for example, can reply to a question following one of her lectures on the history of scholarly conceptions of dreams by remarking that 'we know' that, the more one gets used to writing down dreams on waking, the easier it becomes to recall them. This implies a belief in the existence of certain genuine, established facts that can be relied on.
48 This is the case for Claude-Jean Cognasse des Jardins in his medical thesis *Essais sur les songes* (Montpellier, Martel Aîné, 1801, p. 5). And it is also the case for Léon d'Hervey de Saint-Denys, who, in 1867, drew attention to the courageous effort made by Hippocrates to step outside the confines of thinking in his time (*Les Rêves et les moyens de les diriger*, Paris: FB, 2015, pp. 30–1). NB: Translator's note: While an English translation of this book is available (*Dreams and How to Guide Them*), and will be referred to, certain sections from the original are not included, as is the case here.
49 V. Barras, 'Le rêve des médicines antiques', in Carroy and Lancel (eds), *Clés des songes et sciences des rêves*, p. 31.
50 K. A. Scherner, *La Vie du rêve*. Paris: Théétète, 2003, p. 10.
51 See Marc Géraud's preface, ibid., p. 5.
52 Scherner, *La Vie du rêve*, p. 9.
53 'The life of the soul becomes a foreboding of the outer limits, the dawn of the being longing for the furthest reaches of the extent and the limits of its life within the cosmos', writes Scherner (ibid., p. 28). Or again: 'All consciousness, all daytime thought, contains a light, a spiritual light' (ibid., p. 31). Or when he declares that the 'sensory dream . . . is well known to imitate plants' (ibid., p. 33), or when he refers to 'the ability of feelings' which 'stirs in the glimmers of life' (ibid., p. 70). Or when he launches into a long tirade on the

life of the soul: 'thus the soul reveals itself in the cosmic flow of the culture of humanity which unites everything, as in the monadic circles of individual personal evolution; and therefore in the movements of the harsh radiance of the waking mind as in the creative and interwoven whisperings of the dream – everywhere, the soul weaves life stitch by stitch, from stitches into lines and into circles, from circles into spirals, etc.' (ibid., p. 50).

54 A. Schütz, 'Symbol, reality and society', in Schütz, *Collected Papers 1: The Problem of Social Reality*. The Hague: Martinus Nijhoff, 1982, p. 232.

55 Ibid., p. 230.

56 It was the need for this kind of strategy that drew the philosopher Karl Albert Scherner to become a dream psychologist. By taking a scientific approach, he was, for example, able to demonstrate the symbolic nature of the components of dreams and the effect of the loss of control of consciousness during sleep.

57 Schütz, 'Symbol, reality and society', p. 243.

58 J.-C. Passeron, *Sociological Reasoning: A Non-Popperian Space of Argumentation*. Oxford: Bardwell Press, 2013, p. 293.

59 Maury, *Le Sommeil et les rêves*, p. 11.

60 F. Dastur, 'Preface', in L. Binswanger, *Rêve et existence*. Paris: Vrin, 2012, p. 31.

61 By introducing a false confrontation between the supposed passivity of the dreamer and the active character of the waking individual ('The Dreaming man – to use a distinction I have drawn elsewhere – "is" "life-function; waking, he creates "life history"', Binswanger and Foucault, *Dream and Existence*, p. 102). Binswanger certainly contributes to the enduring confusion about the nature of the activity of dreaming. We are permanently made and making, structured and structuring, produced and producers. In the dream, we are as much acting as acted, in the same way as in waking life we are as much acted as acting.

62 Dastur, 'Préface', p. 23.

63 'What we cannot reach flying we must reach limping. . . . The Book tells us it is no sin to limp' (the last lines of 'Die beiden Gulden', a version by Rückert of one of the Maqâmât of al-Hariri). S. Freud, *Beyond the Pleasure Principle* (1920), in *The Standard Edition of the Complete Psychological Works*, Vol. XVIII. London: Hogarth Press, 1955, p. 64.

64 Oneiromancy is a form of divination based on dreams.

65 S. Freud and E. Bleuler, *Lettres, 1904–1937*. Paris: Gallimard, 2016, p. 176. The same theme was taken up by the psychoanalysts Thomas Morton French and Erika Fromm: 'From the beginning, Freud insisted over and over that dreams are not nonsense' (*Dream Interpretation: A New Approach*. New York: Basic Books, 1964, p. 164).

66 Carroy, *Nuits savantes*, p. 263. This was, for example, the case of Gabriel Tarde, who thought that, 'in dreams, everything is merely the result of spontaneous combinations that the play of the fibres in the brain ceaselessly creates within us' (*Sur le sommeil: ou plutôt sur les rêves*. Lausanne, BHMS, 2009, p. 79). The same idea recurs in the work of Henri Bergson (Carroy, *Nuits savantes*, p. 168).

67 d'Hervey de Saint-Denys, *Les Rêves et les moyens de les diriger*, p. 80 (this section is not included in the English translation of the book). The author observed that the prize-winning paper was the work of a scholar who was

under an 'obligation to accommodate his subject within the demands of a framework furnished in advance'.
68 Y. Delage, *Le Rêve: étude psychologique, philosophique et littéraire*. Paris: Presses universitaires de France, 1924, pp. 574–5.
69 J. Montangero, *40 questions et réponses sur les rêves*. Paris: Odile Jacob, 2013, p. 101. The psychoanalyst Tobie Nathan made the same observation when he said that, for a majority of neuroscientists, 'the dream does not contain any message, does not merit any interpretation', and that, for this reason, 'it is simply a matter of describing the different ways in which it manifests itself' (*La Nouvelle Interprétation des rêves*. Paris: Odile Jacob, 2013, p. 21). It would, however, be more prudent to say that these researchers are focusing on the neurobiological or neurophysiological properties of the different phases of sleep and on the conditions in which dreams occur and almost totally neglect the question of the meaning dream accounts might have.
70 See my critical analysis in Lahire, *Franz Kafka: éléments pour une théorie de la création littéraire*. Paris: La Découverte, 2010, pp. 588–99.
71 In spite of the fact that Freud, on numerous occasions, affirmed the resolutely scientific nature of his work, Jean-Bertrand Pontalis said in 1966 that what Freud was proposing is an 'interpretation of dreams' and not a 'science of dreams', thus implicitly demonstrating his belief that an interpretation cannot be of a scientific nature (radio broadcast with Georges Charbonnier, 'Sciences et techniques, le rêve', *Les matinées de France Culture*, 30 December 1966).
72 Nathan, *La Nouvelle Interpretation des rêves*, p. 216.
73 J. A. Hobson, *The Dreaming Brain*. New York: Basic Books, 1988, p. 53.
74 In a German documentary entitled *Le Mystère des rêves lucides* (2013), the American neuropsychiatrist John Allan Hobson declared: 'We cannot study the content of dreams in a scientific manner because it amounts to literature. As a scientist, I am not concerned with literature. I am simply trying to understand where dreams come from. Certainly they do not stem from desires. Desires are expressed in dreams, but they are not the origin of them. The dream is the result of the activation of the brain. We should therefore be investigating why the brain is activated' (www.les-docus.com/le-mystere-des-reves-lucides/).
75 'The dream is an enigmatic phenomenon which will always contain deep within itself a mysterious core' (M. Hebbrecht, 'Les interpretations des rêves: de Freud à Bion', *Cahiers de psychologie clinique*, no. 42 (2014), p. 42).
76 M. Schröter, 'Bleuler et la psychanalyse: proximité et autonomie', in Freud and Bleuler, *Lettres, 1904–1937*, p. 272.
77 Freud and Bleuler, *Lettres, 1904–1937*, p. 61.
78 Ibid., pp. 123 and 128.
79 Schröter, 'Bleuler et la psychanalyse: proximité et autonomie', p. 252.
80 French and Fromm, *Dream Interpretation: A New Approach*, p. 19.
81 T. M. French, 'The art and science of psychoanalysis', *Journal of the American Psychoanalytic Association*, 6 (1958), p. 207.
82 French and Fromm, *Dream Interpretation: A New Approach*, p. 15.
83 Quoted in Schröter, 'Bleuler and la psychanalyse: proximité et autonomie', pp. 256–7.
84 Ibid.
85 I am using the term 'reductionisms' to refer either to the reduction of one complexity to a single factor or a single dimension (e.g. bringing all dreams

back to a sexual origin) or to the reduction of one level of reality to another level of reality (e.g. explaining social issues through biological ones).

86 Freud and Bleuler, *Lettres, 1904–1937*, p. 126.

87 Ibid., pp. 256–7.

88 See, in particular, attempts to theorise this programme, in Lahire, *Franz Kafka: éléments pour une théorie de la création littéraire*, and *Monde pluriel: penser l'unité des sciences sociales* (Paris: Seuil, 2012). A psychoanalytical interpretation of dreams makes sense only as the partial fulfilment of a much broader programme of research focusing on a theory of sexuality, the unconscious and censorship.

89 Elias, *The Symbol Theory*, pp. 33–4.

90 Since the publication of Lahire, *L'Homme pluriel* (1998). See *The Plural Actor*. Cambridge: Polity, 2011.

Chapter 2 The Dream

1 M. Halbwachs, 'Individual psychology and collective psychology', *American Sociological Review*, 3/5 (1938), pp. 616–17.

2 Ibid.

3 E. Aserinsky and N. Kleitman, 'Regularly occurring periods of eye motility and concomitant phenomena during sleep', *Science*, 118 (1953).

4 M. Jouvet, *The Paradox of Sleep: The Story of Dreaming*. Cambridge, MA: MIT Press, 1999.

5 W. Dement and N. Kleitman, 'The relation of eye movements during sleep to dream activity: an objective method for the study of dreaming', *Journal of Experimental Psychology*, 53 (1957).

6 D. Foulkes, *Children's Dreaming and the Development of Consciousness*. Cambridge, MA: Harvard University Press, 1999, pp. 123–4. And it is impossible not to agree with Ludwig Crespin on the problematic effects of the desire for a neurobiological-psychological coupling: 'It is difficult not to conclude that the fascination for paradoxical sleep, alongside popular misconceptions concerning the nature of the oneiric experience, have acted as a sort of "epistemological obstacle" . . . to the recognition of oneiric mental activity during the entire sleeping period – and still today hinders the acknowledgement of a form of oneiric experience in the waking state' (Crespin, 'Redécouvrir la conscience par le rêve: le débat entre théories cognitives et non cognitives de la conscience à l'épreuve de la recherche sur le rêve', PhD thesis, Université Blaise Pascal, Clermont-Ferrand, 2016, p. 59).

7 At least since the publication in the early 1960s of David Foulkes's 'Dream reports from different stages of sleep', *Journal of Abnormal and Social Psychology*, 65/1 (1962): 14–25. For a more recent synthetic approach to these questions, see M. Solms, 'Dreaming and REM sleep are controlled by different brain mechanisms', *Behavioural and Brain Sciences*, 23 (2000): 843–50; T. A. Nielsen, 'A review of mentation in REM and NREM sleep: "covert" REM sleep as a possible reconciliation of two opposing models', *Behavioral and Brain Sciences*, 23 (2000): 851–66; and A. Revonsuo, 'The interpretation of dreams: an evolutionary hypothesis of the function of dreaming', *Behavioral and Brain Sciences*, 23 (2000): 877–901. For further reading on these issues, see J. Montangero, *Comprendre ses rêves pour mieux se connaître*. Paris: Odile

Jacob, 2007, and *40 questions et réponses sur les rêves*. Paris: Odile Jacob, 2013.

8 M. Jouvet, *Le Sommeil, la conscience et l'éveil*. Paris: Odile Jacob, 2016, p. 15.
9 M. Jouvet, *Le Grenier des rêves: essai d'onirologie diachronique*. Paris: Odile Jacob, 1997, p. 17.
10 Ibid., p. 46.
11 Ibid., p. 97.
12 M. Jouvet, *De la science et des rêves: mémoires d'un onirologue*. Paris: Odile Jacob, 2013, p. 107.
13 E. Hartmann, *The Nature and Functions of Dreaming*. New York: Oxford University Press, 2011.
14 Jouvet, *The Paradox of Sleep*, p. 62.
15 F. Parot, 'De la neurophysiologie du sommeil paradoxal à la neurophysiologie du rêve', *Sociétés & Représentations*, no. 23 (2007): 195–212.
16 A. Hobson, *The Dreaming Brain*. New York: Basic Books, 1988, p. 3.
17 Ibid., p. 16.
18 Ibid., p. 266.
19 Ibid., p. 227.
20 Ibid., p. 213.
21 The neuroscience researcher Perrine Ruby indicated, during a conference, the possibility advanced by certain researchers of being able to predict, according to the nature of cerebral activity, if someone is in the process of dreaming about objects or about people. But we are still a long way from a time when it would genuinely be possible to 'see' the content of dreams.

When we can indeed see that, the researcher remarks, what will we do with it? We do not after all know where this information comes from. Only the dreamer knows that this hippopotamus is the hippopotamus that used to be in his or her classroom at secondary school, that this man, seen from behind, looks like his or her maths teacher and that this was the staircase in the shopping centre when they were children. . . . We strongly suspect that it is the elements of information grouped together which are important and that it is that which leads you to be surprised or shocked when you wake up each morning. It is then that you become aware that there are certain elements which shouldn't really go together at all. All that to say that, in order to do something with a dream, you practically have to know the person's entire life. (Ruby, 'À la source des rêves', Cycle: 'La science des rêves', *Cité des sciences et de l'industrie*, 15 March 2016)

22 Magnetic resonance imaging.
23 All stages of sleep involve the 'deactivation of the dorsolateral prefrontal cortex. The relation of this with executive cognitive functions – which control the process of thought and actions – is known' (Montangero, *40 questions et réponses sur les rêves*, p. 143).
24 Ibid., p. 154.
25 See below, 'Self-to-self communication: internal language, formal and implicit relaxation' (pp. 194–203).
26 He resolved such questions according to the knowledge available in his time. But the tremendous progress made in this area did not fundamentally change

things. He wrote to Fliess, for example, in a letter dated 22 September 1898: 'I am not at all in the least in disagreement with you, and have no desire at all to leave the psychology hanging in the air with no organic basis. But, beyond a feeling of conviction, I have nothing, either theoretical or therapeutic, to work on, and so must behave as if I were confronted by psychological factors only' (Freud, *The Origins of Psychoanalysis: Letters to Wilhelm Fliess, Drafts and Notes: 1887–1904*. London: Imago, 1954, p. 264).

27 J. Le Goff, 'Dreams in culture and collective psychology', in Le Goff, *Time, Work and Culture in the Middle Ages*. Chicago: University of Chicago Press, 1982, pp. 201–4. Initially published in 1971 in the journal *Scolies*, this introduces part of Le Goff's work on dreams conducted in the context of a course delivered at the École Normale Supérieure. See P. Burke, 'The cultural history of dreams', *in Varieties of Cultural History*. Cambridge: Polity, 1997, pp. 23–42; J.-C. Schmitt, 'Le sujet et ses rêves', in Schmitt, *Le Corps, les rites, les rêves, le temps: essais d'anthropologie médiévale*. Paris: Gallimard, 2001, pp. 303–4; J.-C. Schmitt, 'Récits et images de rêves au Moyen Âge', *Ethnologie française*, 33/4 (2003): 553–63; and G. Besson and J.-C. Schmitt (eds), *Rêver de soi: les songes autobiographiques au Moyen Âge*. Toulouse: Anacharsis, 2017.

28 C. Beradt, *The Third Reich of Dreams: The Nightmares of a Nation, 1933–1939*. Wellingborough: Aquarian Press, 1985.

29 See in particular B. Tedlock, 'The new anthropology of dreaming', *Dreaming*, 1/2 (1991): 161–78; M. Perrin, *Les Practiciens du rêve: un exemple de chamanisme*. Paris: Presses universitaires de France, 2011; S. Poirier, 'La mise en œuvre sociale du rêve: un exemple australien', *Anthropologie et Sociétés*, 18/2 (1994): 105–19; G. Charuty, 'Destins anthropologiques du rêve', *Terrain*, no. 26 (1996): 5–18. See also below, 'Limitations of environmentalist approaches: the ecology of dreams', pp. 41–4.

30 E. Durkheim, *Durkheim's Philosophy Lectures: Notes from the Lycée de Sens Course, 1883–1884*. Cambridge: Cambridge University Press, 2014.

31 M. Halbwachs, 'Dreams and memory images' and 'Language and memory', in Halbwachs, *On Collective Memory*. Chicago: University of Chicago Press, [1925] 1992, pp. 41–2 and pp. 43–5 (because the English translation does not include all the material from the original, it will sometimes be necessary to cite the French text: *Les Cadres sociaux de la mémoire*. Paris, Albin Michel, [1952] 1976, pp. 1–39 and pp. 40–82); 'Le rêve et le langage inconscient dans le sommeil', *Journal de psychologie normale et pathologique*, 33 (1946): 11–64.

32 J. Carroy, *Nuits savantes: une histoire des rêves (1800–1945)*. Paris: EHESS, 2012, p. 397.

33 R. Bastide, *Le Rêve, la transe et la folie*. Paris, Seuil, 2003, p. 27.

34 Ibid., p. 44.

35 Ibid., p. 47. The expression 'social contexts of the imagination' is undoubtedly an implicit reference to the work of Maurice Halbwachs on the social contexts of memory. Bastide nevertheless caricatures Halbwachs's position on dreams by saying that he turns them into a subject for both cerebral physiology and individual psychology.

36 R. Bastide, *Sociologie et psychanalyse*. Paris: Presses universitaires de France, 1950.

37 J. Duvignaud, F. Duvignaud and J.-P. Corbeau, *La Banque des rêves: essais*

d'anthropologie du rêveur contemporain. Paris: Payot, 1979. All the citations are taken from this work.

38 See chapter 11, The Oneiric Processes (pp. 218–47).

39 See Conclusion 2: Dream, Will and Freedom (pp. 298–304).

40 M. W. Calkins, 'Statistics of dreams', *American Journal of Psychology*, 5/3 (1893): 311–43.

41 C. S. Hall, 'What people dream about', *Scientific American*, 184 (1951): 60–3; *The Meaning of Dreams: Their Symbolism and Their Sexual Implications*. Lexington, KY: Iconoclassic Books, [1966] 2012.

42 The study focuses on 1,368 dreams of a paedophile named Norman between September 1963 and February 1967 (the dreamer was then thirty years old). A. P. Bell and C. S. Hall, *The Personality of a Child Molester: An Analysis of Dreams*. Chicago: Aldine, 1971.

43 Thirty-seven of Franz Kafka's dreams were studied. C. S. Hall and R. E. Lind, *Dreams, Life, and Literature: A Study of Franz Kafka*. Chapel Hill: University of North Carolina Press, 1970.

44 G. A. Fine and L. Fischer Leighton, 'Nocturnal omissions: steps toward a sociology of dreams', *Symbolic Interaction*, 16/2 (1993): 95–104; H.-G. Vester, 'Sex, sacredness and structure: contributions to the sociology of dreams', *Symbolic Interaction*, 16/2 (1993): 105–16; D. F. Wunder, 'Dreams as empirical data: siblings' dreams and fantasies about their disabled sisters and brothers', *Symbolic Interaction*, 16/2 (1993): 117–27; and R. Wagner-Pacifici and H. J. Bershady, 'Portents or confessions: authoritative readings of a dream text', *Symbolic Interaction*, 16/2 (1993): 129–43.

45 We can cite the more recent article by Barbara Vann and Neil Alperstein in the same interactionist vein: 'Dream sharing as social interaction', *Dreaming*, 10/2 (2000): 111–19. A questionnaire used on 241 people (undergraduate students at a private art college) asked the subjects if they had ever described their dreams to anyone, and, if so, to whom, to what purpose and in what social contexts, as well as whether there were types of dreams they would not describe and people with whom they would not share their dreams.

46 J. F. Hovden, 'Return of the repressed: the social structure of dreams: contribution to a social oneirology', in Hovden and K. Knapskog (eds), *Hunting High and Low*. Oslo: Scandinavian Academic Press, 2012, pp. 137–57.

47 Ibid., p. 144.

48 This is an important issue for the American anthropologist Barbara Tedlock. See Tedlock, 'The new anthropology of dreaming'. And, in an ethnomethodological vein, the sociologist Richard A. Hilbert supports the idea that situations or interactions in which context dreams are recounted (only by writing, in a familial context, between friends, in the group or tribe for certain societies, in the presence of a psychoanalyst or a sociological or anthropological investigator) can be the object of a sociological analysis. See Hilbert, 'The anomalous foundations of dream telling: objective solipsism and the problem of meaning', *Human Studies*, 33/1 (2010): 41–64.

49 What the anthropologist Sylvie Poirier calls 'local dream theories' (Poirier, 'La mise en œuvre sociale du rêve: un exemple australien', p. 105).

50 See, as examples, B. Kilborne, 'Moroccan dream interpretation and culturally constituted defense mechanisms', *Ethos*, 9/4 (1981): 294–313; or, more recently, C. Stewart, *Dreaming and Historical Consciousness in Island Greece*. Chicago: University of Chicago Press, 2017.

51 For example, Pascale Absi and Oliver Douville write, on the subject of
   Bolivian prostitutes, that 'anthropology does not make it possible to seize the
   particular resonance of the dream in the personal trajectory of each dreamer'
   ('Batailles nocturnes dans les maisons closes: l'univers onirique des prostituées de Bolivie', *Revue du MAUSS*, no. 37 (2011), p. 324).
52 In Great Britain, the anthropologist Edward B. Tylor sees animism (the
   first stage, according to him, of human religion) as based on the experience of dreaming (see *Primitive Culture: Researches into the Development
   of Mythology, Philosophy, Religion, Art and Custom*. London: John
   Murray, 1871). His ideas were discussed in 1912 by Émile Durkheim in
   The Elementary Forms of Religious Life (Oxford: Oxford University Press,
   2001). In 1922 Lucien Lévy-Bruhl also devoted an entire chapter to the
   representations and usages made of dreams in 'primitive societies' (see *The
   Notebooks on Primitive Mentality*. New York: Harper & Row, [1922] 1975).
   The precocity of anthropology in this domain and the considerable number
   of anthropological studies on the question over the course of the first half
   of the nineteenth century explains the fact that, in 1961, the American
   anthropologist Roy G. d'Andrade could propose an extremely rich synthesis of research on dream in anthropology (see D'Andrade, 'Anthropological
   studies of dreams', in F. L. K. Hsu (ed.), *Psychological Anthropology:
   Approaches to Culture and Personality*. Homewood, IL: Dorsey Press, 1961,
   pp. 296–332).
53 E. E. Bourguignon, 'Dreams and dream interpretation in Haiti', *American
   Anthropologist*, 56/2, Pt 1 (1954): 262–8.
54 D. Eggan, 'The manifest content of dreams: a challenge to social science',
   American Anthropologist, 54/4 (1952): 469–85.
55 G. Devereux, *Reality and Dream: Psychotherapy of a Plains Indian*. New
   York: New York University Press, 1969.
56 D. D. Schneider and S. Lauriston, *The Dream Life of a Primitive People:
   The Dreams of the Yir Yoront of Australia*. Washington, DC: American
   Anthropological Association, 1969.
57 We will refer here to just a handful of cases of anthropological research
   or studies: Tedlock, 'The new anthropology of dreaming'; B. Tedlock
   (ed.), *Dreaming: Anthropological and Psychological Interpretations*. Santa
   Fe: School of American Research Press, 1992; Perrin, *Les Practiciens du
   rêve: un exemple de chamanisme*; Poirier, 'La mise en œuvre sociale du rêve:
   un exemple australien'; D. Price-Williams, 'Cultural perspectives on dreams
   and consciousness', *Anthropology of Consciousness*, 5/3 (1994): 13–16; D.
   Price-Williams and L. Nakashima-Degarrod, 'Dreaming as interaction',
   Anthropology of Consciousness, 7/2 (1996): 16–23.
58 Fine and Fischer Leighton, 'Nocturnal omissions: steps towards a sociology
   of dreams', p. 95.
59 Referring to the 'reflection' of reality in dreams or to the question of relationships (of causality) between 'the dream' and 'society' (C. S. Hall and V. J.
   Nordby, *The Individual and His Dreams*. New York: New American Library,
   1972, p. 151), or saying that 'the dream translates the problems posed by
   society' (Bastide, *Le Rêve, la transe et la folie*, p. 69), are attempts to link
   abstract entities which are artificially separated and are doomed to failure.
   This dualist thought process is the equivalent of the childhood disease of
   human and social sciences.

60 Wagner-Pacifici and Bershady, 'Portents or confessions: authoritative readings of a dream text'.
61 Yet the authors do not seem fundamentally interested in knowing whether the dream was indeed a confession in disguise. Their knowledge of the area seems superficial, and the reader has the impression this is simply a sociological commentary on information obtained from the press. As a result, the sociologists can refer to rival interpretations (that of the dreamer and that of the police or the judges) without giving us the means to understand the reasons behind such a dream and the motives of such a story.
62 Schmitt, 'Le sujet et ses rêves', p. 310.
63 M. Schredl, 'Dream content analysis: basic principles', *International Journal of Dream Research*, 3/1 (2010), p. 65.
64 J.-C. Passeron and J. Revel, 'Penser par cas: raisonner à partir de singularités', in Passeron and Revel, *Penser par cas*. Paris: EHESS, 2005, pp. 9–44.
65 G. W. Domhoff, 'Dreams are embodied simulations that dramatize conceptions and concerns: the continuity hypothesis in empirical, theoretical, and historical context', *International Journal of Dream Research*, 4/2 (2011): 50–62.
66 Calkins, 'Statistics of dreams'. Moreover, in 1899, the great Italian psychologist and psychiatrist Sante de Sanctis published a book based on the dreams of 165 men and 55 women: *I sogni: studi clinici e psicologici di un alienista*.
67 Calkins, 'Statistics of dreams', p. 333.
68 Ibid.
69 C. S. Hall and R. L. Van de Castle, *The Content Analysis of Dreams*. New York: Appleton-Century-Crofts, 1966.
70 Hall and Nordby, *The Individual and His Dreams*, p. 9.
71 Hartmann, *The Nature and Functions of Dreaming*; R.-L. Punamäki, K. J. Ali, K. H. Ismahil, and J. Nuutinen, 'Trauma, dreaming and psychological distress among Kurdish children', *Dreaming*, 15/3 (2005): 178–94.
72 Beradt, *The Third Reich of Dreams*.
73 Wunder, 'Dreams as empirical data: siblings' dreams and fantasies about their disabled sisters and brothers'.
74 Absi and Douville, 'Batailles nocturnes dans les maisons closes: l'univers onirique des prostituées de Bolivie'.
75 D. Erlacher and M. Schredl, 'Dreams reflecting waking sport activities: a comparison of sport and psychology students', *International Journal of Sport Psychology*, 35 (2004): 301–8.
76 M. Schredl and D. Erlacher, 'Relation between waking sport activities, reading, and dream content in sport students and psychology students', *Journal of Psychology: Interdisciplinary and Applied*, 142/3 (2008): 267–75.
77 L. Vogelsang, S. Anold, J. Schormann, S. Wübbelmann, and M. Schredl, 'The continuity between waking-life musical activities and music dreams', *Dreaming*, 26/2 (2016): 132–41.
78 I. Arnulf, *Une fenêtre sur les rêves: neurologie et pathologies du sommeil*. Paris: Odile Jacob, 2014, pp. 192–4. Out of a total of 2,324 first-year medical students at the Université Pierre et Marie Curie, only 230 would be accepted for the second year. On the evening after the final exam they were asked what they had dreamt of during the preceding night, but also if they had dreamt of the final exam during their first term, and, if so, what the dreams were about. The ten highest graded students in the year had all dreamt about being late

for the exam or of handing in blank sheets of paper, and, 'the more students had dreamt about the final exam, even with similarly problematic scenarios, the better they performed' (ibid., p. 194).

79 A. Aron, 'The nightmare of Central American refugees', in D. Barrett (ed.), *Trauma and Dreams*. Cambridge, MA: Harvard University Press, 2001, pp. 140–7.

80 Punamäki et al., 'Trauma, dreaming, and psychological distress among Kurdish children'.

81 K. Valli, A. Revonsuo, O. Pälkäs, and R.-L. Punamäki, 'The effect of trauma on dream content: a field study of Palestinian children', *Dreaming*, 16/2 (2006): 63–87.

82 M. Schredl and F. Hofmann, 'Continuity between waking activities and dream activities', *Consciousness and Cognition*, 12/2 (2003): 298–308.

83 See, notably, Hall, *The Meaning of Dreams*; Hall and Nordby, *The Individual and His Dreams*; and G. W. Domhoff, 'The misinterpretation of dreams', a criticism of the new translation by Ritchie Robertson of Freud's *The Interpretation of Dreams* (Oxford University Press, 1999), in *American Scientist*, 88/2 (2000): 175–8.

84 G. W. Domhoff and A. Schneider, 'Studying dream content using the archive and search engine on DreamBank.net', *Consciousness and Cognition*, 17/4 (2008), p. 1238.

85 M. Halbwachs, in Halbwachs, *Les Cadres sociaux de la mémoire*. Paris: Albin Michel, [1925] 1976, p. 42.

86 Hall, *The Meaning of Dreams*, p. 29.

87 J. Malinowski and C. L. Horton, 'Evidence for the preferential incorporation of emotional waking-life experiences into dreams', *Dreaming*, 24/1 (2014): 18–31.

88 Hall, *The Meaning of Dreams*, p. 245. These facts, which were brought to our attention in the 1960s by Hall, continue to be confirmed by more recent research. There is evidence, for example, that the dreams of music students often focus on difficulties around musical performances. The context of learning and of musical performance is used as a situational model where a performance is assessed, resulting in success or failure. Dreamers dream they are unfamiliar with the piece they have to play, that they have forgotten their instruments, etc. See Vogelsang et al., 'The continuity between waking-life musical activities and music dreams'.

89 B. Kilborne, 'Pattern, structure, and style in anthropological studies of dreams', *Ethos*, 9/2 (1981), p. 166.

90 For example, having demonstrated, on the basis of retrospective statements about memories of dreams, that music students dream more often about music than other students, the authors of one study announce their intention of continuing to verify the hypothesis by working on dream diaries instead. See Vogelsang et al., 'The continuity between waking-life musical activities and music dreams'. This is the result of a science which is precise and rigorous but lacks any kind of theoretical context of any significance. With the continuity hypothesis, we are often not far from the most basic form of theoretical elaboration in which evidence which only touches on a minute and superficial part of a much wider and deeper problem is verified with impeccable meticulousness and attention.

91 Hall, *The Meaning of Dreams*, p. 89.

92 C. S. Hall, 'The two provinces of dreams', *Dreaming*, 1/1 (1991), p. 93.
93 Montangero, *40 questions et réponses sur les rêves*, p. 75.
94 'Content analysis is an attempt to use carefully defined categories and quantitative methods to extract meaning from a "text," whether it be a newspaper article, transcribed conversation, short story, or dream report' (G. W. Domhoff, 'New directions in the study of dream content using the Hall and Van de Castle coding system', *Dreaming*, 9/2–3 (1999), p. 116).
95 See D. Barrett, *Trauma and Dreams*. Cambridge, MA: Harvard University Press, 2001; D. Hollan, 'The influence of culture on the experience and interpretation of disturbing dreams', *Culture, Medicine and Psychiatry*, 33/2 (2009): 313–22; and Punamäki et al., 'Trauma, dreaming, and psychological distress among Kurdish children'.
96 Hall and Lind, *Dreams, Life, and Literature*, p. 16. In 1966 Bell and Hall came up with the same principle in their studies of the dreams of a paedophile: 'The basic assumption of such an analysis is that incidence is a direct measure of the importance of that element in the life of the dreamer. If he dreams frequently of his mother, as Norman did, it is inferred that the mother plays an important role in his life. This may be called the *continuity* hypothesis because it assumes there is continuity between dreams and waking life' (*The Personality of a Child Molester*, p. 117).
97 Ibid., p. 119.
98 Ibid., pp. 72–3.
99 Hall and Nordby, *The Individual and His Dreams*, p. 63.
100 G. W. Domhoff, 'Content analysis explained: if we don't "interpret" dreams, what do we do?', https://dreams.ucsc.edu/Info/content_analysis.html.
101 R. Barthes, 'The two criticisms', in *Critical Essays*. Evanston, IL: Northwestern University Press, 1972, pp. 249–54. And, in both cases, one ends up doing precisely what one forbids oneself to do. Like Barthes, who in his commentary on Kafka's *Metamorphosis* reintroduced biographical elements considered to be irrelevant, analysts of dream content use biographical data about dreamers when they can access it in order to interpret their dreams. See Hall, *The Meaning of Dreams*, p. 74.
102 In his writings on dreams, Paul Valéry contrasts his approach, which focuses on 'the potential and intrinsic nature of the phenomenon', to that of 'Freud and Co.', which is interested in 'its meaning, its relation to the subject's history – which doesn't concern me at all' (*Cahiers Paul Valéry*, 3: *Questions du rêve*. Paris, Gallimard, NRF, 1979, p. 81). However, the meaning cannot be reached without an analysis of the conditions within which the oneiric expression takes place and of the cognitive mechanisms specific to dreaming (which Freud had begun to do in analysing the modalities of 'the dreamwork'). Far from clashing, the two approaches are complementary. Yet if the study of dreams is reduced to what Valéry has to say, when he states that 'it's a mistake to approach dreams on the basis of the *significant*', then all sense of what happens in the dream would be lost.
103 Burke, 'The cultural history of dreams', pp. 33–4.
104 Ibid., p. 35.
105 D. Hofstadter and E. Sander, *Surfaces and Essences: Analogy as the Fuel and Fire of Thinking*. New York: Basic Books, 2013, pp. 106–7.
106 See below, 'Oneiric schemas and the incorporated past' (pp. 117–21).
107 See the criticism of the splitting up of the content of dreams into units such

as places, objects, people, etc., directed at Hall and Van de Castle by Michel Zlotowicz in *Les Cauchemars de l'enfant* (Paris: Presses universitaires de France, 1978), pp. 15–16. Similarly, Max Reinert, having conducted a statistical analysis of 212 accounts of adolescent nightmares, recognises that his method of 'analysing the distribution of vocabulary in utterances emphasises the places, objects and people in their denomination or physical description and not in terms of their function, not of their position as agents', and that 'the sequential aspect of the passage of time . . . is neglected', with the result that 'aspects of the décor, of the staging, end up playing a predominant role in relation to the drama itself, in its unfolding' ('Les "mondes lexicaux" et leur "logique" à travers l'analyse statistique d'un corpus de récits de cauchemars', *Langage et société*, no. 66 (1993), p. 27).

108 This is precisely what Freud succeeded in doing in his time. He began to enjoy the success of this approach to hysteria, on which he initially worked with the Viennese doctor and physiologist Joseph Breuer, before applying it to dreams. S. Freud, *An Autobiographical Study* (1925), in *The Standard Edition of the Complete Psychological Works*, Vol. XX. London: Hogarth Press, 1959.

109 Lucretius, *On the Nature of Things*. Indianapolis: Hackett, 2001, p. 126.

110 Artemidorus, *The Interpretation of Dreams: Oneirocritica*. Park Ridge, NJ: Noyes Press, 1975.

111 In preparing the ground for his *The Interpretation of Dreams*, Freud cites numerous writers who, in different ways, had put forward this hypothesis of the continuity between waking life and dreams. For example, Peter Willers Jessen wrote in 1855: 'The content of a dream is invariably determined more or less by the individual personality of the dreamer, by his age, sex, class, standard of education and habitual way of living, and by the events and experiences of his whole previous life'; Alfred Maury also observed in 1861 that 'We dream of what we have seen, desired, or done', and P. Haffner, in 1887, stated that 'dreams carry on waking life' and that there is almost always 'a thread which connects a dream with the experiences of the previous day'. See Freud, *The Interpretation of Dreams*, in *The Standard Edition of the Complete Psychological Works*, Vols IV and V. London: Hogarth Press, 1953, Vol. IV, p. 8. The same theme reappears in the 1930s, referred to in the writings of the French sociologist Roger Bastide, who says that he had always thought 'that there was continuity, rather than a complete split, between the preoccupations of the previous day and those of the sleeping individual, that the "social" was always hidden in what one might have thought to be purely subjective' (*Le Rêve, la transe et la folie*, pp. 23–4).

112 See below, 'Dream and outside the dream' (pp. 170–6), and chapter 13, Elements of Methodology for a Sociology of Dreams (pp. 274–91).

113 Hall and Nordby, *The Individual and His Dreams*, p. 161.

114 See, among others, A. Maury, *Le Sommeil et les rêves: études psychologiques sur ces phénomènes et les divers états qui s'y rattachent* (Paris: Didier, [1861] 1865); Freud, *The Interpretation of Dreams*; Freud, *On Dreams*, in *The Standard Edition of the Complete Psychological Works*, Vol. V. London: Hogarth Press, 1953; M. Foucault, *Le Rêve: études et observations*. Paris: Félix Alcan, 1906; Y. Delage, *Le Rêve: étude psychologique, philosophique et littéraire*. Paris: Presses universitaires de France, 1924; G. Lakoff, 'How metaphor structures dreams: the theory of conceptual metaphor applied to dream analysis', *Dreaming*, 3/2 (1993): 77–98; and J. Montangero, *Rêve et*

cognition. Brussels: Mardaga, 1999, and 'Dreams are narrative simulations of autobiographical episodes, not stories or scripts: a review', *Dreaming*, 22/3 (2012): 157–72.

115 For example, a diary which blows away can be a metaphor for memory lapses (Montangero, *Comprendre ses rêves pour mieux se connaître*, p. 50) or the collapse of bridge can symbolise the break-up of a romantic relationship (Lakoff, 'How metaphor structures dreams: the theory of conceptual metaphor applied to dream analysis', pp. 92–3.

116 B. Lahire, *Monde pluriel: penser l'unité des sciences sociales.* Paris: Seuil, 2012. See also figure 1: General formula for interpreting practice, p. 63.

117 See chapter 4, The Incorporated Past and the Unconscious (pp. 101–26), chapter 7, The Existential Situation and Dreams (pp. 166–79) and chapter 13, Elements of Methodology for a Sociology of Dreams (pp. 274–91).

118 See chapter 8, Triggering Events (pp. 180–90).

119 See below, 'Self-to-self communication: internal language, formal and implicit relaxation' (pp. 194–203).

120 See chapter 9, The Context of Sleep (pp. 191–203), chapter 10, The Fundamental Forms of Psychic Life (pp. 204–17) and chapter 11, The Oneiric Processes (pp. 218–47).

121 B. Lahire, *The Plural Actor.* Cambridge, Polity, 2011.

122 B. Lahire, *Portraits sociologiques: dispositions et variations individuelles.* Paris: Nathan, 2002.

123 Lahire, *Franz Kafka: éléments pour une théorie de la création littéraire.*

124 B. Lahire, 'Postface: Freud, Elias et la science de l'homme', in N. Elias, *Au-delà de Freud: les rapports entre sociologie et psychologie.* Paris: La Découverte, 2010, pp. 187–214, and *Monde pluriel*, pp. 264–79.

125 B. Lahire, *Culture écrite et inégalités scolaires: sociologie de l' 'échec scolaire' à l'école primaire*, Lyon: Presses universitaires de Lyon, 1993.

126 Lahire, *The Plural Actor*, p. 244.

127 B. Lahire, 'De la réflexivité quotidienne: journal personnel, autobiographie et autres écrits narratifs', *Sociologie et Société*, 40/2 (2008): 163–77.

128 Lahire, *Franz Kafka: éléments pour une théorie de la création littéraire.*

129 See chapter 12, Variations in Forms of Expression (pp. 248–73).

130 Halbwachs, 'Dreams and memory images', p. 42.

131 Ibid.

132 M. Halbwachs, 'Le Langage et la mémoire', p. 39.

133 Ibid., p. 53.

134 Ibid., p. 59.

135 Ibid., p. 59. See also, on this last point, G. Steiner, 'The historicity of dreams (two questions to Freud)', *Salmagundi*, no. 61 (1983): 6–21.

136 It proves to be more complex when applied in a dynamic perspective. It is, for example, clear that what is meant by the context of action can be seen, from another viewpoint, as a context of socialisation: the dispositions and abilities are simply the effects of incorporated socialisation produced by the relatively long-term frequentation, of an intense and systematic nature, of a range of social contexts.

137 T. M. French, *Psychoanalytic Interpretations.* Chicago: Quadrangle Books, 1970, p. 47.

138 R. Allendy, *Rêves expliqués.* Paris: Gallimard, 1938, p. 187. French is also close to an interpretive equilibrium when he says that dreams are the

product of two elements: 1) the personality of the dreamer as a relatively permanent constellation of reaction patterns and 2) the specific situation to which he or she needs to respond. See French, *Integration of Behavior*, Vol. 2: *The Integrative Process in Dreams*. Chicago: University of Chicago Press, 1954.

139 G. Bléandonu, *What Do Children Dream?* London: Free Association Books, 2006, pp. 69–70.

140 See figure 2: Incorporated past and contexts relevant to the study of dreams (p. 67) and figure 3: The process of dream production (p. 69). These schemas will gradually become clearer through the course of various chapters focusing on different elements and on the links between them. I felt it might be useful, however, to draw attention to them at this stage so as to give the reader an overall picture of the processes at work.

141 Referring to the 'focal problem', which is that of the dreamer at the moment of the dream, French and Fromm note that 'Every focal conflict is a reaction to some event or emotional situation of the preceding day which served as a "precipitating stimulus"' (*Dream Interpretation: A New Approach*. New York: Basic Books, 1964, p. 206).

142 Freud referred to the dependence of the dream upon 'stimuli which force their way upon perception during the state of sleep' (*On Dreams*, p. 633).

143 See chapter 12, Variations in Forms of Expression (pp. 248–73). The problem is not confined to dream studies or, more generally, to the social sciences. For example, in the case of physics, Albert Einstein, when drawing up the equation $E = mc^2$, forced people to think about the relations of interdependence that exist between dimensions often seen by preceding physicians as separate. With this formula, mass, energy and the speed of light can be seen to be closely linked. Energy was not, moreover, considered at the beginning of the nineteenth century as a general property of matter, but people thought in terms of specific forces, of forces unrelated to each other (wind power, the power of lightning striking a tree, the force of the falling tree, etc.). The existence of a global and unifying energy behind all these forces had not yet been discovered. And it goes without saying that nobody suspected the existence of a relationship between mass and energy, and even less between these and the speed of light.

144 We know that this aspect of writing down dreams is not a methodological detail. Writers, and sometimes Freud himself, do not always distinguish what comes from them and what comes from the dreamer and, in cases where it does indeed come from the dreamer, fail to give details of the particular conditions in which this information has been obtained. See, for example, J. Carroy, 'Observer, raconter ou ressusciter les rêves ? "Maury guillotiné" en question', *Communications*, no. 84 (2009): 137–49.

145 Allendy, *Rêves expliqués*, p. 7.

146 E. Fromm, *The Forgotten Language: An Introduction to the Understanding of Dreams, Fairy Tales and Myths*. London: Victor Gollancz, 1952, p. 14.

147 For this reason, it is not possible to agree with Norbert Elias when he refers to the 'realistic' character of certain images manipulated in the waking state of 'fantasy-images such as those of daydreams or night-dreams, which appear to be symptoms of drive-control rather than means of orientation to and control of the world in which one lives' (N. Elias, *The Symbol Theory*. Dublin: University College Dublin Press, 2011, p. 96). Seeing only 'fantasies' that are

'connections of experiences that one never has in reality, or only when asleep', he wrongly opposes 'private fantasies' and 'public or social fantasies' (ibid., p. 92), implying that the first would not be 'social'.

Chapter 3 Psychoanalysis and the Social Sciences

1 In philosophy, Jean-Paul Sartre (1905–1980) defined existentialism by placing it at the intersection between Marxism and psychoanalysis and even described his approach as existential psychoanalysis. One of the central issues of this thinking was to combine the respective contributions of Marxism, in its general ambition of relating speeches and actions to their class determinations, and psychoanalysis as an opportunity to probe into the singularity of people's lives and their individual journeys – for example, through the study of early intra-familial relationships.
2 S. Freud, *Group Psychology and the Analysis of the Ego*, in *The Standard Edition of the Complete Psychological Works*, Vol. XVIII. London: Hogarth Press, 1955, p. 69.
3 M. Bonaparte, A. Freud, and E. Kriss, 'Introduction', in S. Freud, *The Origins of Psychoanalysis: Letters to Wilhelm Fliess, Drafts and Notes 1887–1902*. London: Imago, 1954, p. 35.
4 Erich Fromm also noted that the Oedipus complex, in which 'the sexual impulses of the male infant, which are directed to his mother as the first and most important female "love-object", cause him to regard his father as a rival' (*The Crisis of Psychoanalysis: Essays on Freud, Marx and Social Psychology*. London: Penguin, 1970, pp. 139–40), wrongly led Freud 'to base the whole development of mankind on the mechanism of father hatred and the resultant reactions' (ibid., p. 162).
5 R. Bastide, *Sociologie et psychanalyse*. Paris: Presses universitaires de France, 1950, p. vii. The innatism and the ahistoric nature of some of Freud's theories on the unconscious, on drives, on the Oedipus complex, etc., are also singled out and criticised by Norbert Elias, in *Au-delà de Freud: les rapports entre sociologie et psychologie*. Paris: La Découverte, 2010.
6 M. Bakhtin, *Le Freudianisme*. Lausanne: L'Âge d'homme, 1980, p. 68. The English version of this text is published under the name of one of Bakhtin's close friends: V. N. Voloshinov, *Freudianism: A Critical Sketch*. Bloomington: Indiana University Press, 1987, p. 91.
7 Fromm, *The Crisis of Psychoanalysis*, pp. 159–60.
8 S. Freud, *An Outline of Psychoanalysis*, in *The Standard Edition of the Complete Psychological Works*, Vol. XXIII. London: Hogarth Press, 1964, p. 633. This Freudian inheritance of the 'archaic roots' lingered on in the works of certain of his disciples. Thus, René Allendy wrote that the unconscious is made up of 'latent memories', of 'obscure desires', of 'primordial tendencies' and of 'ethnic, innate knowledge' (*Les Rêves et leur interprétaion psychoanalytique*. Paris: Félix Alcan, 1926, p. 109).
9 Bastide, *Sociologie et psychanalyse*, p. v.
10 H. F. Ellenberger, *The Discovery of the Unconscious: The History and Evolution of Dynamic Psychiatry*. London: Fontana, 1994, p. 492.
11 J. Laplanche and J.-B. Pontalis, *The Language of Psychoanalysis*. London: Karnac Books, 2006, p. 12.

12 Freud nevertheless sometimes sought to maintain a balance between present determinants and those of the past.

13 'The relations of an individual to his parents and to his brothers and sisters, to the object of his love and to his physician – in fact all the relations which have hitherto been the chief subject of psychoanalytic research – may claim to be considered as social phenomena', declared Freud, defining with precision the theoretical and thematic limits of psychoanalysis. *Group Psychology and the Analysis of the Ego*, p. 69.

14 S. Freud, *Fragment of an Analysis of a Case of Hysteria* (1905), in *The Standard Edition of the Complete Psychological Works*, Vol. VII. London: Hogarth Press, 1975, p. 71.

15 Ibid, p. 87.

16 S. Freud, *The Interpretation of Dreams*, in *The Standard Edition of the Complete Psychological Works*, Vols IV and V. London: Hogarth Press, 1953, Vol. IV, p. 218.

17 J. Piaget, *Play, Dreams and Imitation in Childhood*. London: Routledge, [1978] 1999, p. 207.

18 S. Freud, *An Autobiographical Study* (1925), in *The Standard Edition of the Complete Psychological Works*, Vol. XX. London: Hogarth Press, 1959, p. 33.

19 Ibid., p. 76. Methodologically, Freud effectively dealt only with early child-hood recalled and reconstructed by his patients: 'Psychoanalysis, unlike any other psychological theory of the twentieth century, attributed to the very early years a decisive significance in terms of the subsequent development of the psyche. Its theories on this age were largely based on the analysis of adult patients and on what these people were able to describe about their child-hoods' (M. Dornes, *Psychanalyse et psychologie du premier âge*. Paris: Presses universitaires de France, 2002, p. xi).

20 Freud, *The Interpretation of Dreams*, Vol. IV, p. 191.

21 See below, 'A critique of the event-focused approach' (pp. 121–6).

22 As Luc Magnenat claims in *Freud*. Paris: Le Cavalier bleu, 2006, p. 94.

23 E. Fromm, *Greatness and Limitations of Freud's Thought*. London: Jonathan Cape, 1980, pp. 63–4.

24 Ibid., p. 66.

25 E. Fromm, *The Forgotten Language: An Introduction to the Understanding of Dreams, Fairytales and Myths*. London: Victor Gollancz, 1952, p. 84.

26 Freud, *The Interpretation of Dreams*, Vol. IV, p. 15.

27 S. Freud, *Introductory Lectures on Psychoanalysis*, in *The Standard Edition of the Complete Psychological Works*, Vol. XV. London: Hogarth Press, 1963, p. 210.

28 Ibid., p. 211.

29 Ibid., p. 213.

30 Freud, *The Interpretation of Dreams*, Vol. V, p. 553.

31 R. Allendy, *Rêves expliqués*. Paris: Gallimard, 1938, p. 207.

32 Ibid., p. 218. The author also claims that 'Dreams about the foetal state are more frequent than dreams about birth itself' (ibid., p. 207).

33 J.-M. Quinodoz, *Reading Freud: A Chronological Exploration of Freud's Writing*. London: Routledge, 2005, p. 94. A psychoanalyst and experimen-tal psychologist such as Martin Dornes, who, unlike Freud, worked on the subject of babies, refuses to associate the curiosity shown by new-born babies with *libido sexualis*. For him, Freud turns this curiosity into a 'sublimation

and modification' of 'sexual curiosity', whereas it in fact represents a very early independent autonomy in the baby. See Dornes, *Psychanalyse et psychologie du premier âge*, p. 28.

34 J. Breuer and S. Freud, 'Preface to the first edition' of *Studies on Hysteria* (1895), in *The Standard Edition of the Complete Psychological Works*, Vol. II. London: Hogarth Press, 1955, p. xxix.

35 Freud, *Fragment of an Analysis of a Case of Hysteria*, pp. 7–8.

36 Freud, *An Autobiographical Study*, pp. 23–4.

37 S. Freud and E. Bleuler, *Lettres, 1904–1937*. Paris: Gallimard, 2016, p. 193.

38 'The assertion that all dreams require a sexual interpretation, against which critics rage so incessantly, occurs nowhere in *The Interpretation of Dreams*. It is not to be found in any of the numerous editions of this book and is in obvious contradiction to other views expressed in it' [1991] (Freud, *The Interpretation of Dreams*, Vol. V, p. 397). And twenty-five years later he was still maintaining his position: 'On the other hand, I have never maintained the assertion which has so often been ascribed to me, that dream-interpretation shows that all dreams have a sexual content or are derived from sexual motive forces. It is easy to see that hunger, thirst or the need to excrete can produce dreams of satisfaction just as well as any repressed sexual or egoistic impulse' (*An Autobiographical Study*, p. 46).

39 L. Marinelli and A. Mayer, *Dreaming by the Book: Freud's Interpretation of Dreams and the History of Psychoanalytical Movement*. New York: Other Press, 2003, p. 78.

40 Ibid.

41 Ibid., p. 49.

42 S. Freud, *Beyond the Pleasure Principle* (1920), in *The Standard Edition of the Complete Psychological Works*, Vol. XVIII. London: Hogarth Press, 1955.

43 Freud, *The Interpretation of Dreams*, Vol. V, p. 188.

44 Ibid., p. 276.

45 Ibid., p. 356.

46 Ibid., p. 354.

47 Ibid., p. 399.

48 Ibid., p. 410.

49 Freud, *On Dreams*, p. 682.

50 Ibid., p. 683.

51 See, for example, J. Carroy, *Nuits savantes: une histoire des rêves (1800–1945)*. Paris: EHESS, 2012, p. 331.

52 As Scherner, a source of inspiration for Freud, puts it: 'All the terrors of the day, all the moving scenes of life, forgotten long ago, are revived. Scenes of shame, of wounded honour, of astonishment, of indignation, of deep anxiety, of tumultuous and turbulent joy, ghost stories once heard, loved ones now dead and everything which was ever a source of emotion and of dramatic upheaval in life, all of that rises up, comes together, condenses in storms of the mind, and pours its terrible and exciting power into the vision of the trembling soul' (*La Vie du rêve*. Paris: Théétète, [1861] 2003, p. 44).

53 M. Schröter, 'Bleuler et la psychanalyse: proximité et autonomie', in S. Freud and E. Bleuler, *Lettres: 1904–1937*. Paris: Gallimard, 2016, p. 248.

54 Y. Delage, *Le Rêve: étude psychologique, philosophique et littéraire*. Paris: Presses universitaires de France, 1924, p. 533.

55 A. Adler, *Social Interest: Adler's Key to the Meaning of Life.* Oxford: Oneworld, [1933] 2009, pp. 196 and 185.
56 Fromm, *The Forgotten Language*, p. 87.
57 Fromm, *Greatness and Limitations of Freud's Thought*, p. 27.
58 Ibid., p. 29.
59 Fromm, *The Forgotten Language*, p. 174.
60 Ibid.
61 Fromm, *Greatness and Limitations of Freud's Thought*, p. 26.
62 G. Róheim, *The Gates of the Dream.* New York: International Universities Press, 1952, p. 18.
63 Allendy, *Rêves expliqués.*
64 R. Allendy, *Les Rêves et leur interprétation psychanalytique.* Paris, Félix Alcan, 1926, p. 81.
65 N. Elias, *What is Sociology?* Dublin: University College Dublin Press, 1978, p. 131.
66 Ibid., 130.
67 See also N. Elias, 'Sociology and psychiatry' (1969–72), in S. H. Foulkes and G. S. Prince (eds), *Psychiatry in a Changing Society.* Abingdon: Routledge, 2013, pp. 117–44.
68 B. Lahire, *This is Not Just a Painting: An inquiry into Art, Domination, Magic and the Sacred.* Cambridge: Polity, 2019, pp. 22–247.
69 In a chapter entitled 'Orientational Metaphors', George Lakoff and Mark Johnson take the example of the opposition between high and low which structures many opposites: happiness/sadness, conscious/unconscious, health/sickness, life/death, heaven/hell, dominator/dominated, good/bad, rational/emotional. See *Metaphors We Live By.* Chicago: University of Chicago Press, [1980] 2008, pp. 14–21.
70 See A. R. Radcliffe-Brown, *Structure and Function in Primitive Society.* London: Cohen & West, 1961, p. 68; and J. Bowlby, *A Secure Base: Clinical Applications of Attachment Theory.* London: Routledge, 2005.
71 See, for example, Freud, *Introductory Lectures on Psychoanalysis*, p. 153.
72 P. Bourdieu, *Sociology in Question.* London, Sage, 1993, p. 47.
73 Freud, *The Interpretation of Dreams*, Vol. IV, pp. 250–5.
74 Ibid., pp. 285–9.
75 Ibid., Vol. V, p. 355.
76 Ibid., p. 410.
77 The American anthropologist Jeannette Mageo analyses a case of a dream which is structured around the model of climbing and the failure to climb. It concerns the case of Dylan, an undergraduate student at Washington State University, who is part of the sample of students studied (114 students: 995 dream accounts, including 400 written by men and 595 by women). The main structural line of the dream lies in the expression to '"climb to the top" (of a hill)', which is a metaphor representing success, as in the expression 'climb the career ladder' or 'achieve social advancement', and is associated with both educational success and, more broadly, success in life. Mageo, 'Dreaming and its discontents: U.S. cultural models in the theater of dreams', *Ethos*, 41/4 (2013): 387–410.
78 A. Charma, *Du sommeil.* Paris: Hachette, 1851, p. 50.
79 Ibid., pp. 97–8.
80 Adler, *Social Interest*, p. 193.

81 Freud, *The Interpretation of* Dreams, Vol. V, p. 393.
82 A. Adler, *The Neurotic Constitution*. London: Kegan Paul, 1921, p. 160.
83 Lahire, *This is Not Just a Painting: An inquiry into Art, Domination, Magic and the Sacred*.
84 Adler, *The Neurotic Constitution*, p. 169.
85 Ibid., p. 162.
86 Ibid., p. 163.
87 Ibid., p. 170.
88 Ibid., p. 171.
89 Ibid.
90 His study revealed 'the frequent occurrence of stories of megalomania in the course of daydreaming in the waking state; in these states, which recent studies have found to be of considerable importance in normal and pathological psychology and which are observable in the majority of individuals, we found a high number of ambitious ideas that constitute delusions of grandeur, ideas of wealth and glory, philanthropic ideas, of social reform, ideas of superiority both intellectually and in terms of invention, romantic dreams, dreams of a fulfilled life and of adventures, ideas of power, of domination, ideas which express in a variety of ways the constructive, but usually unintentional, work of the creative imagination' (P. Borel, 'Les idées de grandeur dans le rêve', *Journal de psychologie normale et pathologique*, no. 5 (1914): 400–12).
91 J. Duvignaud, F. Duvignaud and J.-P. Corbeau, *La Banque des rêves: essai d'anthropologie du rêveur contemporain*. Paris: Payot, 1979, p. 97.
92 Ibid., p. 96.
93 Ibid., p. 101.
94 Ibid., p. 104.
95 Ibid.
96 Allendy, *Rêves expliqués*, pp. 163–4.
97 Ibid., pp. 186–7.
98 M. Halbwachs, 'Le rêve et le langage inconscient dans le sommeil', *Journal de psychologie normale et pathologique*, 33 (1946), p. 27.
99 Freud, *The Interpretation of Dreams*, Vol. IV, pp. 106–18. Maurice Halbwachs himself writes about this dream, pointing out the competition and the rivalries that structure the relations between the different protagonists of the oneiric scene: 'But what interests us is not so much the explanation provided by the author so much as certain elements of information we find there which are uncontestably true. These concern the group which included Irma, Otto, Dr M…, Freud himself, with the rivalries which were rife there, the opinions each one has of the others (Dr M…, the most revered personality in their circle; Otto and other colleagues, who are unfamiliar with hysteria, and whom Freud looks down on, etc.)' ('Le langage et la mémoire', in Halbwachs, *Les Cadres sociaux de la mémoire*. Paris: Albin Michel, [1925] 1976, pp. 41–2).
100 Freud, *The Interpretation of Dreams*, Vol. IV, p. 118.
101 J. F. Hovden, Return of the repressed: the social structure of dreams: contribution to a social oneirology', in Hovden and K. Knapskog (eds), *Hunting High and Low*. Oslo: Scandinavian Academic Press, 2012, pp. 137–57.
102 These facts confirm the social dimension that Freud chose to ignore in dreams about flying.
103 M. Leibovici, 'Les fables politiques de Charlotte Beradt', in C. Beradt, *Rêver sous le IIIe Reich*. Paris: Payot, 2004, pp. 7–41.

104 C. Beradt, *The Third Reich of Dreams: The Nightmares of a Nation, 1933–1939.* Wellingborough: Aquarian Press, 1985, p. 5.

105 Ibid., pp. 15–16:

> Their background is clearly visible, and what lies on their surface lies also at their root. There is no façade to conceal associations and no outside person need provide the link between dream image and reality – this the dreamer himself does. Dreams of this nature also employ imagery, but it is an imagery whose symbols need no interpretation and whose allegories need no explanation; at best, one may decipher its code. These dreams adopt forms and guises which are no more complicated than the ones used in caricature or political satire, and the masks they assume are just as transparent as those worn at carnivals.

106 See the afterword by Reinhart Koselleck, in the French edition: Beradt, *Rêver sous le IIIe Reich*, pp. 173–90. Also the concluding essay by Bruno Bettelheim in the English version of the book.

107 Ibid., pp. 90–1.

108 F. Gantheret, 'Postface', in Beradt, *Rêver sous le IIIe Reich*, p. 209.

109 François Gantheret suggests something of this when, in order to defend an interpretation in terms of 'childhood sexuality', he writes that elements of the waking state used 'serve at the same time as support, mask and alibi to figures previously repressed' (ibid., p. 233).

110 Gary Alan Fine and Laura Fischer Leighton write that, in a dream about a dentist who had drilled a hole in two teeth, the sociologist cannot ignore the fact that this is indeed a dentist rather than any other kind of professional. Instead of concluding without any further information that teeth represent women and the hole pierced indicated a sexual act, he will start by acknowledging the situation described between a dentist and a patient ('Nocturnal omissions: steps toward a sociology of dreams', *Symbolic Interaction*, 16/2 (1993), p. 100). See also John L. Caughey, *Imaginary Social Words: A Cultural Approach* (Lincoln: University of Nebraska Press, 1984), who reminds us not to neglect the fact that, even if it is not realistic, the dream depicts the real social world, with a social environment and social relationships between more or less recognisable people.

111 Unless specifically mentioned, all the extracts are from J. A. Hobson, *The Dreaming Brain*. New York, Basic Books, 1988, pp. 220–2.

112 Ibid., p. 233.

Chapter 4 Incorporated Past and the Unconscious

1 See figure 2: Incorporated past and contexts relevant to the study of dreams (p. 67) and figure 3: The process of dream production (p. 69).

2 T. M. French and E. Fromm, *Dream Interpretation: A New Approach*. New York: Basic Books, 1964, p. 115.

3 R. Linton, *The Cultural Background of Personality*. London, Routledge, 1999, p. 55.

4 See chapter 6, Formal Censorship, Moral Censorship: The Double Relaxation (pp. 142–65).

5 'Transference phenomena emerging during the treatment serve to confirm this necessity for the repressed conflict to be re-enacted in the relationship with the analyst. In fact it was the ever-increasing consideration demanded by these phenomena and the technical problems they gave rise to which led Freud to complete his theoretical model of the cure by introducing transference repetition and working-through, alongside recollection, as major stages of the therapeutic process' (J. Laplanche and J.-B. Pontalis, *The Language of Psychoanalysis*. London: Karnac Books, 1988, p. 79).

6 J. Piaget, *The Origins of Intelligence in Children*. London: Routledge, 1953, p. 253.

7 H. Bergson, *Matter and Memory*. London: Swan Sonnenschein, 1911, p. 195.

8 D. Hume, *A Treatise on Human Nature*, Vol. 1: *Texts*. Oxford: Oxford University Press, 2007, p. 72.

9 See figure 4a: The comparative processes involved in the fabrication of dreams, memories and practice (p. 104).

10 The optimism surrounding the therapeutic effects of heightened awareness leads René Allendy to comment: 'As the patient gradually acquires, through analysis, a clear understanding of his deep-rooted tendencies, he becomes able to dominate them' (*Rêves expliqués*. Paris: Gallimard, 1938, p. 193).

11 The fact that psychoanalysis has accustomed us to associate 'compulsion' and 'disorders' contributes to preventing us from seeing that 'compulsion' is everywhere, both in the most ordinary normal acts and in pathological acts. These are pathological repetitions, those which are problematic for the individuals affected, which are seen as such and are treated as compulsive repetitions. Yet there is nothing less compulsive than our most ordinary ways of speaking, thinking or acting. Jean Laplanche and Jean-Baptiste Pontalis point out that, 'in French, the words *compulsion, compulsional*, have the same Latin origin (*compellere*) as *compulsive*: that which pushes, constrains' (*The Language of Psychoanalysis*, p. 85). And a disposition is precisely what *pushes* or *constrains* us to see, feel and act in a certain way.

12 S. Freud, 'Further recommendations in the technique of psychoanalysis: remembering, repeating and working through', in *The Standard Edition of the Complete Psychological Works*, Vol. XII. London: Hogarth Press, 1958, p. 153.

13 Ibid., p. 149.

14 M. Dornes, *Psychanalyse et psychologie du premier âge*. Paris: Presses universitaires de France, 2002, p. 325.

15 J. Delbœuf, *Le Sommeil et les rêves, considérés principalement dans leurs rapports avec les théories de la certitude et de la mémoire*. Paris: Félix Alcan, 1885.

16 Ibid. (emphasis added).

17 Ibid.

18 S. Freud, *Beyond the Pleasure Principle* (1920), in *The Standard Edition of the Complete Psychologial Works*, Vol. XVIII. London: Hogarth Press, 1955, p. 22.

19 Ibid., p. 36.

20 Ibid., p. 37.

21 Ibid., p. 38.

22 Ibid., p. 62.

23 The term 'Bayesian' comes from the name of the British mathematician Thomas Bayes (1702–1761), known for his work on probability.

24 Stanislas Dehaene, from a course given at the Collège de France, 21 February 2012.
25 Ibid.
26 S. Dehaene, *Consciousness and the Brain: Deciphering How the Brain Codes Our Thoughts*. New York: Penguin, 2014, p. 63.
27 Ibid., p. 86.
28 Ibid., p. 167.
29 Ibid., p. 63.
30 Ibid., p. 84.
31 Ibid., p. 196.
32 Hume, *A Treatise on Human Nature*.
33 Ibid., p. 92.
34 'To use the elevator in an apartment building that one has never been in before, does not one tacitly depend on the analogy with countless elevators that one has used before? . . . And when, after you've stepped out of the elevator and are just setting foot in the sixth-floor apartment, you see a big dog coming towards you, how do you deal with this situation if not on the basis of your prior experience with dogs, particularly large dogs?' (D. Hofstadter and E. Sander, *Surfaces and Essences: Analogy as the Fuel and Fire of Thinking*. New York: Basic Books, 2013, p. 23). In the case of objects or technical devices, the embedded schemas are indissociable from objective regularities. If I am capable of adapting to all sorts of new lifts, new washbasins, new doors, new computers, it is because, in reality, lifts, washbasins, doors or computers are relatively standardised.
35 Hume, *A Treatise on Human Nature*, p. 100.
36 See figure 5: The formation of schemas of experience (p. 116).
37 Laplanche and Pontalis, *The Language of Psychoanalysis*, p. 227.
38 It is perhaps to be regretted that authors from different disciplines (sociology, anthropology, experimental psychology, psychoanalysis, neuroscience) should have contributed by their disparate vocabulary (introjection, interiorisation, internalisation, assimilation, incorporation, subjectivation, subjective appropriation, mentalisation) to masking the real shared processes on which they were seeking to throw light. See notably, for psychoanalysis and psychology, J.-P. Tassin and S. Tisseron, *100 mots du rêve*. Paris: Presses universitaires de France, 2014, p. 28.
39 Dornes, *Psychanalyse et psychologie du premier âge*, p. 49. Note that the 'fantasy' in the psychoanalytical meaning of the term refers to an imaginary scenario.
40 Ibid., pp. 38–9.
41 Ibid., pp. 55–6.
42 Ibid., pp. 69–70.
43 Ibid., p. 56.
44 D. N. Stern, *The Interpersonal World of the Infant: A View from Psychoanalysis and Developmental Psychology*. New York: Karnac Books, 1998, p. 74.
45 Ibid., p. 95.
46 Dornes, *Psychanalyse et psychologie du premier âge*, p. 292.
47 Stern, *The Interpersonal World of the Infant*, p. 113.
48 J. Piaget, *Play, Dreams and Imitation in Childhood*. London: Routledge, [1978] 1999, p. 189.
49 Ibid., p. 176.

50 Ibid., pp. 188–9.
51 Ibid., p. 189.
52 H. Delacroix, 'Sur la structure logique du rêve', *Revue de métaphysique et de morale* (1904): 921–34.
53 Ibid., p. 929.
54 Ibid., pp. 232–3.
55 Hofstadter and Sander, *Surfaces and Essences*, p. 113.
56 Ibid., p. 115.
57 Ibid., p. 114.
58 P. Valéry, *Cahiers Paul Valéry*, 3: *Questions du rêve*. Paris: Gallimard, 1979, p. 63.
59 Ibid., p. 112.
60 G. Dumézil, *Mythe et épopée*, 3 vols. Paris: Gallimard, [1968–73] 1995.
61 C. Lévi-Strauss, *Structural Anthropology*. London: Hachette, [1958] 2008.
62 E. Panofsky, *Gothic Architecture and Scholasticism*. New York: New American Library, 1976.
63 J. Montangero, *40 questions et réponses sur les rêves*. Paris: Odile Jacob, 2013, p. 117.
64 Ibid., p. 172.
65 C. S. Hall and V. J. Nordby, *The Individual and His Dreams*. New York: New American Library, 1972, p. 17.
66 Ibid., p. 80.
67 Ibid., p. 94. Unfortunately, the authors juxtapose this sound scientific intuition with 1) the idea that dream accounts can be studied without necessarily needing any precise biographical data on the dreamers; and 2) the idea that the wishes and fears of dreams can be traced to prenatal experiences and racial history . . . (ibid., p. 146).
68 S. Freud and J. Breuer, *Studies in Hysteria* (1893–5), in *The Standard Edition of the Complete Psychological Works*, Vol. II. London: Hogarth Press, 1964, p. 6.
69 Ibid., p. 3.
70 Ibid., p. 4.
71 S. Freud, *An Autobiographical Study* (1925), in *The Standard Edition of the Complete Psychological Works*, Vol. XX. London: Hogarth Press, 1959, p. 20.
72 S. Freud, *An Outline of Psychoanalysis*, in *The Standard Edition of the Complete Psychological Works*, Vol. XXIII. London: Hogarth Press, 1964, p. 187.
73 S. Freud, *Group Psychology and the Analysis of the Ego*, in *The Standard Edition of the Complete Psychological Works*, Vol. XVIII. London: Hogarth Press, 1995, p. 69.
74 Dornes, *Psychanalyse et psychologie du premier âge*, p. 71.
75 J.-D. Nasio, *L'Inconscient, c'est la répétition*. Paris: Payot, 2012, pp. 67–8.
76 S. Freud, *The Interpretation of Dreams*, in *The Standard Edition of the Complete Psychological Works*, Vols IV and V. London: Hogarth Press, 1953, Vol. IV, p. 137.
77 P. Gay, *Freud: A Life for Our Time*. New York: W. W. Norton, 1998, p. xvi.
78 Ibid., p. 13.
79 Ibid., p. 14.
80 Ibid., p. 21.
81 Freud, *The Interpretation of Dreams*, Vol. IV, p. 192.

82 Ibid., p. 193.
83 Ibid., p. 197.

Chapter 5 Unconscious and Involuntary Consciousness

1 B. Lahire, 'Logiques pratiques: le "faire" et le "dire sur le faire"', *Recherche et Formation*, no. 27 (1998): 15–28.

2 This credulity on the part of the dreamer has been observed by many researchers, beginning with Freud himself, who wrote that, 'in dreams ..., we appear not to think but to experience; that is to say, we attach belief to the hallucinations' (*The Interpretation of Dreams*, in *The Standard Edition of the Complete Psychological Works*, Vols IV and V. London: Hogarth Press, 1953, Vol. IV, p. 50). Following him, authors as different as Marcel Foucault, Yves Delage, Calvin S. Hall and Vernon J. Nordby, John Allan Hobson or Jacques Montangero have made the same point. Montangero wrote, for example: 'the credulity of the dreamer in the face of his mental images is boundless: he is terrified by the danger depicted, filled with shame in certain situations and takes for real the most bizarre people, places, objects or events' (*Rêve et cognition*, Brussels: Mardaga, p. 9).

3 J. A. Hobson, *The Dreaming Brain*. New York: Basic Books, 1988, p. 5.

4 J. Montangero, *40 questions et réponses sur les rêves*. Paris: Odile Jacob, p. 23.

5 Freud, *The Interpretation of Dreams*, Vol. IV, p. 51.

6 Y. Delage, *Le Rêve: étude psychologique, philosophique et littéraire*. Paris: Presses universitaires de France, 1924, p. 668.

7 S. Freud, *An Outline of Psychoanalysis*, in *The Standard Edition of the Complete Psychological Works*, Vol. XXIII. London: Hogarth Press, 1964, p. 166.

8 S. Dehaene, *Consciousness and the Brain: Deciphering How the Brain Codes Our Thoughts*. New York: Penguin, 2014, p. 51.

9 E. Durkheim, *Durkheim's Philosophy Lectures: Notes from the Lycée de Sens Course, 1883–1884*. Cambridge: Cambridge University Press, 2014, p. 130.

10 A. Maury, *Le Sommeil et les rêves: études psychologiques sur ces phénomènes et les divers états qui s'y rattachent*. Paris: Didier, [1861] 1865, p. 96.

11 S. Freud and J. Breuer, *Studies in Hysteria* (1893–5), in *The Standard Edition of the Complete Psychological Works*, Vol. II. London: Hogarth Press, 1964, p. 223. In a letter to Fliess on 28 August 1898, Freud mentions Theodor Lipps (1851–1914), professor of psychology in Munich. In his book *Grundtatsachen des Seelenlebens* (1883), Lipps describes how 'unconscious processes lie at the bottom of all conscious ones and accompany them.' Freud refers to this extract in his own text (*The Origins of Psychoanalysis: Letters to Wilhelm Fliess, Drafts and Notes 1887–1902*. London: Imago, 1954, pp. 260–1).

12 S. Dehaene, *Consciousness and the Brain: Deciphering How the Brain Codes Our Thoughts*, p. 47.

13 Jacqueline Carroy observes that, in his *Journal*, Maine de Biran presents a day-to-day individual psychology which confuses and renders more complex the theoretical psychology that he supports: 'Day by day, the philosopher complains he is tossed about at the mercy of climatic and corporal vagaries, of distracted and somnambulist states of all sorts which prevent him from exercising his will and from thinking. He sees himself very often as scarcely

having self at all' ('Les réveils de Gabriel Tarde: science des rêves et autofictions', in Tarde, *Sur le sommeil: ou plutôt sur les rêves*. Lausanne: BHMS, 2009, pp. 13–14).

14 A. Adler, *Social Interest: Adler's Key to the Meaning of Life*. Oxford, Oneworld, [1933] 2009, p. 189.

15 L. Wittgenstein, *Tractacus Logico-Philosophicus*. Abingdon: Routledge, 2014, p. 22.

16 S. Freud, Some elementary lessons in psychoanalysis, in *The Standard Edition of the Complete Psychological Works*, Vol. XXIII. London: Hogarth Press, 1964, p. 283.

17 This is the view of a philosopher such as Norman Malcolm, for whom consciousness and sleep are two incompatible elements: 'If a person is in *any* state of consciousness it logically follows that he is not sound asleep' ('Dreaming and skepticism', *Philosophical Review*, 65/1 (1956), p. 21).

18 S. Dehaene and L. Naccache, 'Towards a cognitive neuroscience of consciousness: basic evidence and a workspace framework', *Cognition*, 79/1–2 (2001): 1–37.

19 'The criterion that we have identified in order to define what we mean by "to be conscious of something" is that of conscious "reportability". According to this criterion, being conscious of a mental representation means being able to report, to yourself or to other people, using language or in a non-verbal way, the content of this representation'; 'everything of which we are conscious can be reported and everything we report is conscious' (L. Naccache, *Le Nouvel Inconscient: Freud, le Christophe Colomb des neurosciences*. Paris: Odile Jacob, 2009, p. 229).

20 D. J. De Gracia, 'Paradigms of consciousness during sleep', Center for Molecular Medicine and Genetics, Wayne State University, Detroit, http://florence.ghibellini.free.fr/revelucidea/dondega.html.

21 See Dehaene, *Consciousness and the Brain: Deciphering How the Brain Codes Our Thoughts*, p. 126. Maury was already making the distinction between 'the voluntary intelligent act, resulting from a relatively prolonged thought process', and the 'intelligent but involuntary act, such as that which occurs in the dream, such as that which seems also to happen sometimes, in a waking state, as a result of habit' (*Le Sommeil et les rêves*, p. 97).

22 'Yet without going beyond the limits of basic school psychology, what exactly is this intermediary between the self and the non-self and how can we understand it?' wonders Gabriel Tarde, in an attempt to think about the dream without straying outside the context of Maine de Biran's thinking (Tarde, *Sur le sommeil: ou plutôt sur les rêves*. Lausanne: BHMS, 2009, p. 74).

23 B. Spinoza, *Ethics*. Ware: Wordsworth, [1677] 2001, pp. 75–6.

24 Naccache, *Le Nouvel Inconscient*, pp. 18–21

25 Ibid., pp. 277–8. But, long before experimental studies in the laboratory, Théodore Jouffroy described this kind of situation in his article on sleep 'Du sommeil' (*Mélanges philosophiques*. Paris: Paulin, [1827] 1833, pp. 318–43). Jouffroy said that acquiring the habit of hearing noises which at first are intriguing, strange, etc., means that the mind becomes accustomed to them and scarcely pays any attention to them. Curiosity and fear are not aroused, and, at the same time, the mind switches its attention away from such noises. This fact explains that sleep can be interrupted when surrounding sounds are unusual, but that it continues uninterrupted when the sleeper

is accustomed to them. Jouffroy takes the example of someone sleeping next to a sick person who is not woken up by the customary surrounding noises but who, on the other hand, can be woken by the slightest sound made by the suffering individual. According to him, even during sleep, the spirit 'keeps watch'.

26 H. F. Ellenberger, *The Discovery of the Unconscious: The History and Evolution of Dynamic Psychiatry*. London: Fontana, 1994, p. 312.

27 P. Nicole, *Traité de la grâce générale*, Vol. 1. Cologne: J. Fouillou, 1715, Second Part, first section.

28 S. Freud, *An Autobiographical Study* (1925), in *The Standard Edition of the Complete Psychological Works*, Vol. XX. London: Hogarth Press, 1959, p. 31.

29 Lionel Naccache makes the connection between this image of the primitive or primitive unconscious and the 'colonising European democracies'. Consciousness is noble, whereas the unconscious represents the colonised people or savages:

> The idea of absence of conscious control over the unconscious also corroborates the notion of a powerful barrier between the two mental spheres: 'you do not associate with the unconscious', you do not argue with it, since in any case it is outside of our control. No communication is possible with it. The third-class travellers crammed in the bowels of an ocean liner have nothing to do with the gentlemen in first class strolling about on the deck. This analogy between scientific speeches and the dominant social ideology shared by high Victorian society or by that of the Hapsburg Empire is not simply a didactic metaphor but one which imposes itself spontaneously onto a reading of the works of these European thinkers. (*Le Nouvel Inconscient*, pp. 185–6)

30 D. Foulkes, *Children's Dreaming and the Development of Consciousness*. Cambridge, MA: Harvard University Press, 1999, p. 124.

31 S. Laberge, *Exploring the World of Lucid Dreaming*. New York: Ballantine Books, 1991. Michel Jouvet (*The Paradox of Sleep: The Story of Dreaming*, Cambridge, MA: MIT Press, p. 78) estimates that there are only 1 to 2 per cent of 'lucid dreams' in which dreamers know that they are dreaming and can partly control their dream. Given the small percentage of so-called lucid dreams, it might be wondered whether 'lucid dreamers' are actually referring to images from dreams that persist (even for a very short period of time) when they wake up and become aware of the fact that they are dreaming. Studies have shown that 'the lucid dream seemed to occur during a transition phase between sleep and waking. This explains the fact that the lucid dream is rare and generally quite rapid. At the moment of the lucid dream there seems to be a reactivation of the prefrontal dorsolateral cortex, well known for the role this zone plays in the planning and control of action' (P. Ruby, 'Contrôler ses rêves, c'est possible . . . mais difficile: mode d'emploi', *Atlantico*, 13 February 2015, www.atlantico.fr/decryptage/controler-reves-c-est-possible-mais-diffi cile-mode-emploi-perrine-ruby-2003021.html#s0TtL57lJTWaWqEL.99).

32 S. Freud, *The History of the Psychoanalytic Movement*, in *The Standard Edition of the Complete Psychological Works*, Vol. XIV. London: Hogarth Press, 1957, p. 16.

33 Before Freudian theory gained ground, with its first and second topic, Joseph Breuer had already warned readers about the risks potentially incurred by the use 'metaphorically of spatial relations, as in the term subconsciousness', since there is the danger that the metaphor gets forgotten and instead the words are used as though they were a real object:

> Thus when we speak of ideas which are found in the region of clear consciousness and of unconscious ones which never enter the full light of self-consciousness, we almost inevitably form pictures of a tree with its trunk in daylight and its roots in darkness, or of a building with its dark underground cellars. If, however, we constantly bear in mind that all such spatial relations are metaphorical and do not allow ourselves to be misled into supposing that these relations are literally present in the brain, we may nevertheless speak of a consciousness and a subconsciousness. But only on this condition. (Breuer, 'Theoretical', in Freud and Breuer, *Studies on Hysteria* (1895), in *The Standard Edition of the Complete Psychological Works*, Vol. II. London: Hogarth Press, 1955, p. 228)

34 P. Bourdieu, *Outline of a Theory of Practice*. Cambridge: Cambridge University Press, 2013, pp. 78–9.
35 M. Dornes, *Psychanalyse et psychologie du premier âge*. Paris: Presses universitaires de France, 2002, p. 301.
36 Ibid., pp. 307–8.
37 Ibid., p. 307.
38 Ibid., pp. 324–5. Dornes makes a useful distinction on this point between two forms of procedural knowledge according to whether the knowledge in question has been procedural from the outset or has become so through practice. On the one hand, there is 'a knowledge which started out being declaratory/explicit/conscious (like a change of gear) and which subsequently became unconscious as it became automatised (secondary procedural knowledge)' and, on the other, a knowledge 'which has never been declaratory and which is from the beginning implicit/procedural/unconscious' (ibid, pp. 309–10).
39 Ibid., p. 313.
40 For an example of practical deduction around the subject of 'domestic', day-to-day writing in girls and boys, may I refer to B. Lahire, 'Masculin-féminin: l'écriture domestique', in D. Fabre (ed.), *Par écrit: ethnologie des écritures quotidiennes*. Paris: Maison des Sciences de l'Homme, 1997, pp. 145–61.
41 Dornes, *Psychanalyse et psychologie du premier âge*, p. 313.
42 Ibid., p. 315.
43 Ibid., p. 322.
44 Freud, *An Autobiographical Study*, p. 29.
45 See S. Freud, *The Ego and the Id* (1923), in *The Standard Edition of the Complete Psychological Works*, Vol. XIX. London: Hogarth Press, 1961. See also J.-M. Quinodoz, *Reading Freud: A Chronological Exploration of Freud's Writing*. London: Routledge, 2005, p. 205; and H. F. Ellenberger, *The Discovery of the Unconscious*, p. 519.
46 H. F. Ellenberger, *The Discovery of the Unconscious*.

Chapter 6 Formal Censorship, Moral Censorship

1 S. Freud, *An Outline of Psychoanalysis*, in *The Standard Edition of the Complete Psychological Works*, Vol. XXIII. London: Hogarth Press, 1964, p. 206:

> Throughout later life [the super-ego] represents the influence of a person's childhood, of the care and education given him by his parents and of his dependence on them – a childhood which is prolonged so greatly in human beings by a family life in common. And in all this it is not only the personal qualities of these parents that is making itself felt, but also everything that had a determining effect on them themselves, the tastes and standards of the social class in which they lived and the innate dispositions and traditions of the race from which they sprang.

2 M. Bakhtin, *Le Freudianisme*; an English version of the citation is in V. N. Volosinov, *Freudianism: A Marxist Critique*. New York: Academic Press, 1976, p. 70.
3 S. Freud, *Introductory Lectures on Psychoanalysis*, in *The Standard Edition of the Complete Psychological Works*, Vol. XV. London: Hogarth Press, 1963, p. 136.
4 Ibid., p. 139.
5 S. Freud, *On Dreams*, in *The Standard Edition of the Complete Psychological Works*, Vol. V. London: Hogarth Press, 1953, p. 627.
6 S. Freud, *The Interpretation of Dreams*, in *The Standard Edition of the Complete Psychological Works*, Vols IV and V. London: Hogarth Press, 1953, Vol. V, p. 526.
7 Freud, *Introductory Lectures on Psychoanalysis*, p. 87.
8 S. Freud, *Dream Psychology: Psychoanalysis for Beginners*. New York: James A. McCann, 1921, pp. 65–6.
9 Freud, *Introductory Lectures on Psychoanalysis*, p. 126.
10 Ibid., p. 142.
11 S. Freud, *The Origins of Psychoanalysis: Letters to Wilhelm Fliess, Drafts and Notes: 1887–1904*. London: Imago, 1954, p. 240.
12 Moreover, he uses the same example again in *The Interpretation of Dreams* (Vol. V, p. 529): 'This censorship acts exactly like the censorship of newspapers at the Russian frontier, which allows foreign journals to fall into the hands of the readers whom it is its business to protect only after a quantity of passages have been blacked out.'
13 Freud, *The Origins of Psychoanalysis: Letters to Wilhelm Fliess*, p. 437.
14 S. Zweig, *The World of Yesterday*. London: Cassell, 1943, pp. 65–6.
15 Ibid., p. 67.
16 Freud, *Introductory Lectures on Psychoanalysis*, p. 149.
17 Freud, *Dream Psychology: Psychoanalysis for Beginners*, p. 39.
18 Freud, *The Interpretation of Dreams*, Vol. IV, p. 160.
19 Ibid., p. 308.
20 Freud, *On Dreams*, p. 676.
21 Ibid., p. 679.
22 A. Charma, *Du sommeil*. Paris: Hachette, 1851, p. 20.

23 K. A. Scherner, *La Vie du rêve*. Paris: Théetète, 2003, pp. 22–3.
24 A. Maury, *Le Sommeil et les rêves: études psychologiques sur ces phénomènes et les divers états qui s'y rattachent*. Paris: Didier, [1861] 1865, p. 5.
25 Ibid., pp. 90–2.
26 See chapter 9, The Context of Sleep (pp. 191–203), and chapter 11, The Oneiric Processes (pp. 218–247).
27 M. Foucault, *Le Rêve: études et observations*. Paris: Félix Alcan, p. 181.
28 Ibid., p. 204.
29 Y. Delage, *Le Rêve: étude psychologique, philosophique et littéraire*. Paris: Presses universitaires de France, 1924, p. 569.
30 Freud, *Dream Psychology: Psychoanalysis for Beginners*, p. 65. We find the same fluctuation between the omnipresent censorship and a weakened censorship in his *The Interpretation of Dreams*, Vol. V, pp. 525–6.
31 Ibid., p. 72.
32 Ibid., p. 66.
33 J. Scott, *Domination and the Arts of Resistance: Hidden Transcripts*. New Haven, CT: Yale University Press, 1990.
34 P. Bourdieu, *Language and Symbolic Power*. Cambridge: Polity, 1991.
35 Scott, *Domination and the Arts of Resistance*, p. 18.
36 Scott borrows his analysis of back (behind the scenes) and front (on stage) zones from Goffman. Goffman says that behind the scenes all forms of transgression (physical, linguistic, clothing, etc.) are permitted in comparison with the norms which structure behaviour and attitudes on the stage (*Presentation of Self in Everyday Life*, London: Penguin, 1959, chapter 1, 'Performances', pp. 28–82).
37 Ibid., p. ix.
38 Scott, *Domination and the Arts of Resistance*, p. 8 (emphases added).
39 Ibid., p. xii.
40 Bourdieu, *Language and Symbolic Power*, p. 85.
41 P. Encrevé, 'Labov, linguistique, sociolinguistique', in W. Labov, *Sociolinguistique*. Paris: Minuit, 1976, p. 21 (NB this is the forword to the French edition of Labov's *Sociolinguistic Patterns*). I have myself used this model to show that 'cultural consumption' was more inclined to tend towards more commercial and less demanding offers than was consumption taking place in 'private' on account of the weakening of legitimate cultural norms and the effects of legitimacy. The perfect illustration of this is in the case of films watched, depending on whether they are seen in a cinema or on television: those consumers who have a high level of cultural capital still watch commercial films on the television and tend to go for more 'difficult' works when they go out to the cinema. See B. Lahire, *La Culture des individus: dissonances culturelles et distinction de soi*. Paris: La Découverte, 2004, chapter 16, 'Tensions et relâchements, en public et en privé', pp. 612–36.
42 Bourdieu, *Language and Symbolic Power*, p. 71.
43 Scott, *Domination and the Arts of Resistance*, p. 3.
44 P. Bourdieu, *Sociology in Question*. London, Thousand Oaks, CA: Sage, 1995, p. 90. The analysis is pertinent in almost every 'detail': as is clearly demonstrated by the case of someone dreaming (in a daydream or during sleep), all contexts of symbolic production are not fields.
45 See below, 'Self-to-self communication: internal language, formal and implicit relaxation' (pp. 194–203).

Notes to pp. 151–157

46 P. Bourdieu, 'Censorship and the imposition of form', in *Language and Symbolic Power*, p. 269.
47 Ibid.
48 Ibid.
49 This is also the case with the historian Peter Burke ('The cultural history of dreams', in Burke, *Varieties of Cultural History*. Cambridge: Polity, 1997, pp. 23–42). While he proposes to set out a history of forms of repression rather than acting as though censorship was a natural and universal form essentially dealing with matters of a sexual nature ('An attractive hypothesis, impossible to verify, is that in the early modern period, repression was more concerned with political and religious temptations and less with sexual ones than is the case today'; ibid., p. 42), he makes no attempt at all to challenge the Freudian idea of the dream as the product of a distortion of latent thoughts as a means of escaping censorship.
50 Freud, *The Interpretation of Dreams*, Vol. IV, pp. 141–2.
51 Ibid., p. 142.
52 See chapter 9, The Context of Sleep (pp. 191–203).
53 See M. Solms and O. Turnbull, *The Brain and the Inner World: An Introduction to the Neuroscience of Subjective Experience*. New York: Other Press/Karnac Books, 2002, p. 215.
54 M. Halbwachs. *Les Cadres sociaux de la mémoire*. Paris: Alban Michel, p. 57.
55 Ibid., p. 59.
56 M. Bakhtin, *Speech Genres and Other Late Essays*. Austin: University of Texas Press, 2010, pp. 97–8.
57 Freud, *The Interpretation of Dreams*, Vol. IV, p. 266.
58 Ibid., pp. 152–4.
59 Ibid., pp. 155–7.
60 Ibid., Vol. V, p. 606. Ludwig Wittgenstein brings up this paradox in his critical notes on Freud: 'Freud very commonly gives what we might call a sexual interpretation. But it is interesting that among all the reports of dreams which he gives, there is not a single example of a straightforward sexual dream. Yet these are common as rain' (*Lectures and Conversations on Aesthetics, Psychology and Religious Belief*. Berkeley: University of California Press, 2007, p. 47).
61 Freud, *The Interpretation of Dreams*, Vol. V, p. 369.
62 Scherner, *La Vie du rêve*, p. 71.
63 C. S. Hall and V. J. Nordby, *The Individual and His Dreams*. New York: New American Library, 1972, pp. 13–14.
64 Ibid., p. 147.
65 Ibid., pp. 20–1.
66 Ibid., p. 28.
67 Ibid., pp. 148 and 163.
68 Jacques Montangero cites the case of a thirty-year-old dreamer who dreams that her ex-partner tells her that he wants to leave. She tries to slap him and to pull his hair but without success. When she wakes up, she recalls the breakup and her feeling of impotent rage. The oneiric staging, more direct and less controlled, allows this feeling to be made concrete, even though in real life she would not have resorted to anything other than verbal explanations. Montangero, *40 questions et réponses sur les rêves*. Paris: Odile Jacob, 2013, p. 160.

69 R. Allendy, *Rêves expliqués*. Paris: Gallimard, 1938, p. 125.
70 Ibid., pp. 84–5.
71 J. Montangero, *Comprendre ses rêves pour mieux se connaitre*. Paris: Odile Jacob, pp. 43–4.
72 See below, 'Self-to-self communication: internal language, formal and implicit relaxation' (pp. 000–00).
73 L. d'Hervey de Saint-Denys, *Les Rêves et les moyens de les diriger*. Paris: FB, [1867] 2015, p. 38 (some sections from the French version are not included in the English translation, *Dreams and How to Guide Them*, London: Duckworth, 1982).
74 Ibid., pp. 38–9.
75 Yves Delage, *Le Rêve: étude psychologique, philosophique et littéraire*, p. 574.
76 Ibid., pp. 575–6.
77 E. Fromm, *The Forgotten Language: An Introduction to the Understanding of Dreams, Fairy Tales and Myths*. London: Victor Gollancz, 1952, p. 34.
78 Ibid., p. 48.
79 Ibid., p. 42.
80 E. Hartmann, *The Nature and Functions of Dreaming*. New York: Oxford University Press, 2011.
81 S. Freud, *Fragment of an Analysis of a Case of Hysteria* (1905), in *The Standard Edition of the Complete Psychological Works*, Vol. VII. London: Hogarth Press, 1975, p. 68. He also writes that 'it is entirely correct' that the dream can represent 'an intention, a warning, a reflection, a preparation, an attempt at solving a problem, etc.' (*Introductory Lectures on Psychoanalysis*, p. 222).
82 S. Freud, *Some General Remarks on Hysterical Attacks*, in *The Standard Edition of the Complete Psychological Works*, Vol. IX. London: Hogarth Press, 1959, p. 229.
83 Freud, *The Interpretation of Dreams*, Vol. IV, pp. 145–6.
84 Ibid., Vol. V, p. 558.
85 Ibid., Vol. IV, p. 151.
86 S. Freud, *Beyond the Pleasure Principle*, in *The Standard Edition of the Complete Psychological Works*, Vol. XVIII. London: Hogarth Press, 1955, pp. 7–64.
87 Wittgenstein, *Lectures and Conversations on Aesthetics, Psychology and Religious Belief*, pp. 47–8.
88 Freud himself refers to dreams of anticipation: 'During the night before a journey we not infrequently dream of having arrived at our destination: so too, before a visit to the theatre or a party, a dream will often anticipate the pleasure that lies ahead – out of impatience, as it were' (*On Dreams*, pp. 645–6).
89 Notes for the 1907 conference/lecture entitled 'À quoi servent les rêves?' (private archives), cited in M. Cifali, 'La Belle au Bois-Dormant en terre romande', *Le Coq-héron*, no. 218 (2014): 30–7.
90 Foucault, *Le Rêve: études et observations*, pp. 173 and 175.
91 Ibid., p. 187.
92 Ibid., p. 197.
93 Freud, *The Origins of Psychoanalysis: Letters to Wilhelm Fliess*, p. 201.
94 In a letter to Fliess on 19 February 1899, Freud wrote: 'My last generalization holds good and seems inclined to spread to an unpredictable extent. It is

not only dreams that are fulfilments of wishes, but hysterical attacks as well' (ibid., p. 277).

Chapter 7 The Existential Situation and Dreams

1 See above, figure 3: The process of dream production (p. 69).
2 'We can see here how difficult it is to elucidate – as a biographer, for example, tries to do – the problems individuals encounter in their lives, no matter how incomparable an individual's personality or achievements may be, unless one has mastered the craft of the sociologist' (N. Elias, *Mozart: Portrait of a Genius*. Cambridge: Polity, 1993, p. 14).
3 P. Bourdieu, *The Weight of the World: Social Suffering in Contemporary Society*. Cambridge: Polity, 1999; C. Dejours, *Souffrance en France: la banalisation de l'injustice sociale*. Paris: Seuil, 1998; E. Renault, *Social Suffering: Sociology, Psychology and Politics*. Lanham, MD: Rowman & Littlefield, 2017.
4 See M. Heidegger, *Being and Time*. London: HarperCollins, 2008.
5 It is in fact quite surprising that terms such as 'existence' or 'existential issues', which should refer to concrete aspects of the everyday life of individuals in society, seem now to be used in reference to purely philosophical questions relating to being in the world, the meaning of life or death. The social sciences should therefore reappropriate these questions which have been taken over by metaphysics, phenomenology or existentialism.
6 Translator's note: The French expression used by Lahire is 'problématique existentielle'. I have chosen to translate this phrase, which relates to all the problems, cares and preoccupations faced by an individual, as the 'existential situation'.
7 B. Lahire, *Franz Kafka: éléments pour une théorie de la création littéraire*. Paris: La Découverte, 2010, pp. 77–87.
8 I use the expression 'existential knots' here with reference to Wittgenstein's expression 'the knots in our thinking'. According to him, the philosopher's task should consist in treating the problems of thought by untying the 'knots in our thinking' (Wittgenstein, *Philosophical Remarks*. Oxford: Blackwell, 1975, p. 52).
9 C. S. Hall and R. E. Lind, *Dreams, Life, and Literature: A Study of Franz Kafka*. Chapel Hill: University of North Carolina Press, 1970.
10 T. M. French, *Psychoanalytic Interpretations*. Chicago: Quadrangle Books, 1970; and T. M. French and E. Fromm, *Dream Interpretation: A New Approach*. New York: Basic Books, 1964.
11 T. M. French and R. M. Whitman, 'A focal conflict view', in M. Kramer, R. M. Whitman, B. J. Baldridge and P. H. Ornstein (eds), *Dream Psychology and the New Biology of Dreaming*. Springfield, IL: Charles C. Thomas, 1969, pp. 65–71.
12 R. Bastide, *Le Rêve, la transe et la folie*. Paris: Seuil, 2003, p. 69.
13 This central fact can be verified in a vast corpus of dreams. This applies to dream accounts in the English language (the German dreams have been withdrawn for the sake of linguistic homogeneity) which can be found on the website www.dreambank.net. The chosen corpus is thus composed of 21,697 dream accounts from individuals who were mostly American and aged

between seven and seventy-four years old (63 per cent of these accounts are from female and 36.8 per cent from male dreamers) between 1897 and the 2000s. The constant presence of the dreamer in these dreams is evident from research carried out on the most frequent terms used. The most frequent word is 'I' (95.8 per cent), followed by 'my' (67.7 per cent), with 'me' appearing in sixth position (56.2 per cent). And, when the most frequent two-word sequences are looked at, the results show, in order, 'I go' (30.6 per cent), 'I see' (26.2 per cent), 'I think' (23 per cent), 'Me, I …' (22.2 per cent), 'I have' (20.8 per cent), 'then I' (19.9 per cent), 'I don't' (19.1 per cent), 'I say' (19.1 per cent), 'I watch' (14.2 per cent) and 'when I' (14.1 per cent).

14 S. Freud, *The Interpretation of Dreams*, in *The Standard Edition of the Complete Psychological Works*, Vols IV and V. London: Hogarth Press, 1953, Vol. IV, p. 322.
15 J. Montangero, *Comprendre ses rêves pour mieux se connaître*. Paris: Odile Jacob, 2007, p. 169.
16 See above, 'Limitations of environmentalist approaches: the ecology of dreams' (pp. 44–54).
17 S. Seked and H. Abramovitch, 'Pregnant dreaming: search for a typology of a proposed dream genre', *Social Science and Medicine*, 34/12 (1992), p. 1410.
18 I. Arnulf, *Une fenêtre sur les rêves: neurologie et pathologies du sommeil*. Paris: Odile Jacob, 2014, p. 27.
19 C. S. Hall and V. J. Nordby, *The Individual and His Dreams*. New York: New American Library, 1972, p. 34.
20 C. S. Hall and R. L. Van de Castle, *The Content Analysis of Dreams*. New York: Appleton-Century-Crofts, 1966.
21 K. Valli, T. Strandholm, L. Sillanmäki and A. Revonsuo, 'Dreams are more negative than real life: implications for the function of dreaming', *Cognition and Emotion*, 22/5 (2008): 833–61.
22 The fact is already crucial in itself, but we can also wonder about the other dreams that appeared to be more positive, a more detailed analysis of which might perhaps reveal some more problematic aspects.
23 L. Wittgenstein, *Lectures and Conversations on Aesthetics, Psychology and Religious Belief*. Berkeley: University of California Press, 2007, pp. 50–1.
24 E. Fromm, *The Forgotten Language: An Introduction to the Understanding of Dreams, Fairy Tales and Myths*. London: Victor Gollancz, 1952, p. 166.
25 Artemidorus, *The Interpretation of Dreams: Oneirocritica*. Park Ridge, NJ: Noyes Press, 1975, p. 14.
26 Ibid., p. 17.
27 Ibid., p. 23.
28 Ibid., pp. 21–2.
29 Ibid., p. 209.
30 Schmitt, 'Les clés des songes au Moyen Âge', p. 65.
31 Ibid., p. 66.
32 Ibid, p. 69.
33 J. Richard, *La Théorie des songes*. Paris: Frères Estienne, 1766, p. 32.
34 Ibid., pp. 36–7.
35 Ibid., p. 80.
36 Ibid., p. 40.
37 K. A. Scherner, *La Vie du rêve*. Paris: Théétète, [1861] 2003, p. 120.
38 Ibid., p. 121.

39 S. Freud, *On Dreams* (1901), in *The Standard Edition of the Complete Psychological Works*, Vol. V. London: Hogarth Press, 1953, p. 656.

40 In doing so, he was simply following in the footsteps of Léon d'Hervey de Saint-Denys, who had already relativised the role of both external and internal stimuli (sound, odour, physical contact and physical sensation) by stressing the importance of the 'customary occupations and preoccupations' of the dreamer (*Dreams and How to Guide Them*. London: Duckworth, 1982, p. 24). He thus distinguishes the two phenomena which unite in the dream: '1. The natural and spontaneous unfolding of a continuous chain of memories; and 2. The sudden intervention of an idea from outside the chain due to some accidental physical cause' (ibid., p. 39).

41 S. Freud, *An Autobiographical Study* (1925), in *The Standard Edition of the Complete Psychological Works*, Vol. XX. London: Hogarth Press, 1959, pp. 44.

42 A. Adler, *Social Interest: Adler's Key to the Meaning of Life*. Oxford: Oneworld, [1933] 2009, p. 190.

43 A. Adler, *The Neurotic Constitution*. London: Kegan Paul, 1921, p. 53.

44 L. Marinelli and A. Mayer, *Dreaming by the Book: Freud's 'The Interpretation of Dreams' and the History of the Psychoanalytical Movement*. New York: Other Press, 2003, p. 106.

45 Ibid., p. 185.

46 M. Halbwachs, 'Le rêve et le langage inconsciente dans le sommeil', *Journal de psychologie normale et pathologique*, 33 (1946), p. 44.

47 Ibid., p. 49.

48 Ibid., p. 60.

49 E. Hartmann, 'Outline for a theory on the nature and functions of dreaming', *Dreaming*, 6/2 (1996), p. 153.

50 Ibid., pp. 155–6.

51 Ibid., p. 158.

52 Hartmann refers to the case of one of his patients, the mother of two young children who has been dominated for a long period by an obsessive emotional anxiety, namely feelings of guilt about not being a good enough mother. Criticised by her parents from a very early age, she has always had the impression she was not doing things well enough and never came up to expectations. After leaving the parental home and getting married, she started to feel much better. But becoming a mother rekindled her anxiety. She started having dreams and nightmares, all on the same theme, which a long period of therapy was able to record: she dreamt that her children were lost and she was unable to find them, that her son was alone and a big cat was killing him, that her children were being swept away by the tide and drowned, etc. (ibid., p. 158).

53 See below, 'Psychoanalytic therapy: re-creating the conditions of the dream' (pp. 271–331).

54 See below, 'Clarifications, associations, partial or systematic biographical accounts' (pp. 287–91).

55 This kind of reasoning has led some psychologists and psychoanalysts from the Palo Alto school (notably Gregory Bateson, Jay Haley, Don Jackson and John Weakland) to introduce family therapies described as 'systemic' on the grounds that, if one member of a family has a problem, it is more often than not the result of the relationships that have developed between all the

members of the group. In order to treat the patient, it is therefore necessary to try to modify the nature of the relationships he or she maintains with each member of the family.

56 F. Fanon, *Black Skin, White Masks*. London: Pluto Press, 1986, p. 99.
57 Ibid.
58 Ibid., p. 100.

Chapter 8 Triggering Events

1 See above, figure 1: General formula for interpreting practice (p. 63) and figure 3: The process of dream production (p. 69).
2 S. Freud, *The Interpretation of Dreams*, in *The Standard Edition of the Complete Psychological Works*, Vols IV and V. London: Hogarth Press, 1953, Vol. IV, p. 322.
3 K. A. Scherner, *La Vie du rêve*. Paris: Théétète, [1861] 2003, p. 113.
4 A. Maury, *Le Sommeil et les rêves: études psychologiques sur ces phénomènes et les divers états qui s'y rattachent*. Paris: Didier, [1861] 1865, p. 33.
5 M. Jouvet, 'Mémoire et "cerveau dédoublé" au cours du rêve à propos de 2,525 souvenirs de rêve', *L'Année du Praticien*, 29/1 (1979): 27–32, and *The Paradox of Sleep: The Story of Dreaming*. Cambridge, MA: MIT Press, 1999, pp. 67–8.
6 E. Hartmann, 'The day residue: time distribution of waking events', *Psychophysiology*, 5/2 (1968), p. 222.
7 A. W. Epstein, 'The waking event-dream interval', *American Journal of Psychiatry*, 142/1 (1985), pp. 123–4.
8 T. A. Nielsen and R. A. Powell, 'The day-residue and dream-lag effects: a literature review and limited replication of two temporal effects in dream formation', *Dreaming*, 2/2 (1992): 67–77. The same type of proportion is established by C. J. G. Marquardt, R. A. Bonato and R. F. Hoffmann in 'An empirical investigation into the day-residue and dream-lag effects', *Dreaming*, 6/1 (1996): 57–65. The subjects were seventeen women and eleven men (average age = 20.6) who took part in the study during a first-year introduction to psychology course. The twenty-eight participants recorded a total of 208 dreams over a period of two weeks and reported an average of 7.43 dreams each, with a range of between two and fourteen, and a total of 270 day residues. The results confirm the effect of the day residue, as well as the ratio of around 2:1 between residues of the day itself and of the two preceding days.
9 S. Freud, *Introductory Lectures on Psychoanalysis*, in *The Standard Edition of the Complete Psychological Works*, Vol. XV. London: Hogarth Press, 1963, p. 212.
10 Freud, *The Interpretation of Dreams*, Vol. IV, p. 166.
11 Ibid., p. 174.
12 Ibid.
13 R. Allendy, *Rêves expliqués*. Paris: Gallimard, 1938, pp. 12–13.
14 Freud speculated as to whether all the 'thoughts' associated with the dream were related to the formation of the dream or simply arose in the course of analysis (*The Interpretation of Dreams*, Vol. IV, p. 280). The answer must be that these associated thoughts would not take their current form unless they had contributed to making the dreamer what he or she is. They must

therefore be linked with the origin of the dream, along with other sequences of thought which analysis was not in a position to reveal fully.

15 Among the huge amount of literature on the subject, see notably Hartmann, 'The day residue: time distribution of waking events', p. 222; Epstein, 'The waking event-dream interval', pp. 123–4; Nielsen and Powell, 'The day-residue and dream-lag effects: a literature review and limited replication of two temporal effects in dream formation'; J. Harlow and S. Roll, 'Frequency of day residue in dreams of young adults', *Perceptual and Motor Skills*, 74/3 (1992): 832–4; R. A. Powell, J. S. Cheung, T. A. Nielsen, and T. M. Cervenka, 'Temporal delays in incorporation of events into dreams', *Perceptual and Motor Skills*, 81/1 (1995): 95–104; Marquardt, Bonato and Hoffmann, 'An empirical investigation into the day-residue and dream-lag effects'; M. Jouvet, *Le Grenier des rêves: essai d'onirologie diachronique*. Paris: Odile Jacob, 1997; Jouvet, *The Paradox of Sleep*; M. Blagrove et al., 'Assessing the dream-lag effect for REM and NREM stage 2 dreams', *PLoS ONE*, 6/10 (2011), http://dx.doi.org/10.1371/journal.pone.0026708; M. Blagrove et al., 'A replication of the 5–7 day dream-lag effect with comparison of dreams to future events as control for baseline matching', *Consciousness and Cognition*, 20 (2011): 384–91; and M. Jouvet, *De la science et des rêves: mémoires d'un onirologue*. Paris: Odile Jacob, 2013.
16 See chapter 10, The Fundamental Forms of Psychic Life (pp. 204–17).
17 F. Roussy et al., 'Does early-night REM dream content reliably reflect pre-sleep state of mind?', *Dreaming*, 6/2 (1996): 121–30.
18 Jouvet, *Le Grenier des rêves*, p. 47.
19 Jouvet, *De la science et des rêves*, p. 248.
20 Ibid., p. 285.
21 Jouvet, *Le Grenier des rêves*, p. 189.
22 Jouvet, *De la science et des rêves*, pp. 284–5.
23 K. Macduffie and G. A. Mashour, 'Dreams and the temporality of conscious-ness', *American Journal of Psychology*, 123/2 (2010), p. 190.
24 Ibid., p. 195.
25 J. Richard, *La Théorie des songes*. Paris: Frères Estienne, 1766, p. 58.
26 J. Carroy, *Nuits savantes: une histoire des rêves (1800–1945)*. Paris: EHESS, 2012, p. 27.
27 Ibid., p. 88.
28 Ibid.
29 S. Freud, *The Interpretation of Dreams*, Vol. IV, p. 41. Very recent research takes a similar focus but on a more solid experimental basis. It proves, for example, that certain smells, when they are clearly associated with particular images during the day, can produce such images when sleepers are given them to smell, without their knowledge, during the night. See M. Schredl, L. Hoffmann, J. U. Sommer and B. A. Stuck, 'Olfactory stimulation during sleep can reactivate odor-associated images', *Chemosensory Perception*, 7/3 (2014): 140–6.
30 S. Freud, *On Dreams* (1901), in *The Standard Edition of the Complete Psychological Works*, Vol. V. London: Hogarth Press, 1953, p. 680.
31 'It would only remain to investigate the laws according to which the organic stimuli turn into dream images' (Freud, *The Interpretation of Dreams*, Vol. IV, p. 35).
32 Freud, *Introductory Lectures on Psychoanalysis*, p. 96.

33 More recent research has demonstrated that, in the waking state, as in sleep, 'the organism learns not to respond to a stimulus to which it is "indifferent", in other words one which promises neither danger nor pleasure':

> The brain has learned not to jeopardise the defence mechanisms that use a lot of energy (being alert, running away or attacking) in response to repeated 'neutral stimuli': it is Pavlov's 'internal inhibition' (or 'superliminal inhibition'), in the course of which the brain is no longer in a state of anxiety, therefore is no longer aroused and therefore goes back to sleep, in a state which means 'I'm no longer worried about anything and I am not expending any more energy.' This phenomenon can also be referred to as 'habituation to the waking response'. It allows us, for example, to sleep peacefully, even if we live next to a station or an airport. Results from experiments obtained through acoustic stimulation of cats during sleep show that, on the first day, the stimulation has to be repeated thirteen times before the sound no longer wakes them up; on the fourth day, three times is sufficient. There is therefore a learning process, and even 'a negative learning process', since the cat learns not to respond to a signal that is of no interest to it. On the other hand, if the acoustic stimulation is combined with electric shocks, causing some pain in the paw, the cat wakes up each time, since the acoustic stimulus has become a signal of pain. (Jouvet, *De la science et des rêves*, pp. 89–90)

34 Freud turned to the observations and experiments of Jessen, Meïer, Henning, Hofflauer, Gregory, Maury and Hildebrandt (*The Interpretation of Dreams*, Vol. IV, pp. 24–7). C. S. Hall also recounts an experiment which consisted in placing a candle in the dreamer's hand: on one occasion he dreamt he was playing golf and on another that he was lifting a bar in a gymnasium (see *The Meaning of Dreams: Their Symbolism and Their Sexual Implications*. Lexington, KY: Iconoclassic Books, [1966] 2012, pp. 6–7).
35 M. Géraud, 'Préface', in K. A. Scherner, *La Vie du rêve*, p. 6.
36 L. d'Hervey de Saint-Denys, *Les Rêves et les moyens de les diriger*. Paris: FB, 2015, p. 81.
37 See notably J. A. Hobson, *The Dreaming Brain*. New York: Basic Books, 1988; and J. Montangero, *Rêve et cognition*. Brussels: Mardaga, 1999.

Chapter 9 The Context of Sleep

1 See above, figure 3: The process of dream production (p. 69).
2 M. Halbwachs, 'Le rêve et les images-souvenirs', in Halbwachs, *Les Cadres sociaux de la mémoire*. Paris: Albin Michel, [1925] 1976, pp. 16–17.
3 S. Freud, *The Interpretation of Dreams*, in *The Standard Edition of the Complete Psychological Works*, Vols IV and V. London: Hogarth Press, 1953, Vol. IV, p. 6.
4 See above, 'Can the social be absorbed into the cerebral?' (pp. 31–6).
5 'Access to the internally activated brain-mind by input from the outside world has to be excluded in order for sleep – and the illusions of dreaming to be maintained' (J. A. Hobson, *The Dreaming Brain*. New York: Basic Books, 1988, p. 206.

6 J. Montangero, *40 questions et réponses sur les rêves*. Paris: Odile Jacob, 2013, pp. 35, 49 and 90–1.
7 Hobson, *The Dreaming Brain*, p. 230.
8 Ibid., p. 229.
9 Ibid., p. 217.
10 T. Jouffroy, 'Du sommeil', in *Mélanges philosophiques*. Paris: Paulin, [1827] 1833, p. 257.
11 Ibid., p. 358.
12 K. A. Scherner, *La Vie du rêve*. Paris: Théétète, [1861] 2003, pp. 22, 27, 38, 51, 55 and 82.
13 S. Freud, *Project for Scientific Psychology* (unfinished manuscript), in *The Standard Edition of the Complete Psychological Works*, Vol. I. London: Hogarth Press, 1966, p. 337.
14 I. Meyerson, 'Problèmes d'histoire psychologique des œuvres: spécificités, variation, expérience' (1948), in *Écrits 1920–1983: pour une psychologie historique*. Paris: Presses universitaires de France, 1987, p. 197.
15 Ibid., p. 198.
16 R. Allendy, *Les Rêves et leur interprétation psychanalytique*. Paris: Félix Alcan, 1926, p. 6.
17 A. Charma, *Du sommeil*. Paris: Hachette, 1851, pp. 22–3.
18 Ibid., p. 22.
19 The metaphor was used by the German Heinrich Spitta in 1878 to describe the force of attraction of the exterior world in the waking state, as opposed to that of sleep. It is cited by Joseph Delbœuf in *Le Sommeil et les rêves, considérés principalement dans leurs rapports avec les théories de la certitude et de la mémoire*. Paris: Félix Alcan, 1885.
20 'The dream reveals certain conscious functions of the Self which, because of withdrawal from the external world, are put to the task of self-observation; in fact, during sleep, the perceptive functions of the Self, deprived of external stimuli, turn their attention to internal psychic activity' (J. Rallo Romero, M.-T. Ruiz de Bascones, and C. Zamora de Pellicer, 'Les rêves comme unité et continuité de la vie psychique', *Revue française de psychanalyse*, 38/5–6 (1974), p. 917.
21 Charma, *Du sommeil*, p. 39.
22 L. d'Hervey de Saint-Denys, *Les Rêves et les moyens de les diriger*. Paris: FB, 2015, p. 61. The author is basing his comments largely on the ideas of doctor and philosopher Pierre Cabanis in *Rapports du physique et du moral de l'homme*. Geneva: Slatkine, [1802] 1980.
23 Freud, *The Interpretation of Dreams*, Vol. IV, p. 136.
24 M. Halbwachs, 'Le rêve et les images-souvenirs', p. 17.
25 M. Bakhtin, *Speech Genres and Other Late Essays*. Austin: University of Texas Press, 2010, pp. 95–6.
26 Montangero, *40 questions et réponses sur les rêves*, p. 131.
27 B. Bernstein, *Class, Codes and Control: Theoretical Studies towards a Sociology of Language*. London: Routledge, 2003, p. 100.
28 Ibid., p. 114.
29 Ibid., p. 196.
30 Ibid., p. 114.
31 Ibid., pp. 144 and 196.
32 See chapter 11, The Oneiric Processes (pp. 218–47).

33 Montangero, *40 questions et réponses sur les rêves*, pp. 89, 106, 111.
34 T. M. French and E. Fromm, *Dream Interpretation: A New Approach*. New York: Basic Books, 1964, p. 87.
35 Ibid., p. 162.
36 Freud, *The Interpretation of Dreams*, Vol. V, p. 437.
37 B. Tarde, *Sur le sommeil: ou plutôt sur les rêves*. Lausanne: BHMS, 2009, p. 78.
38 Bakhtin, *Esthétique de la création verbale*. Paris: Gallimard, 1984, p. 109.
39 Ibid.
40 Ibid., p. 89.
41 The dreamer can be compared to the little boy described by French and Fromm: 'For example, when a little boy tries to tell a story that he has seen in a movie, he tells the incidents in the story in whatever order they may occur to him. He does not realize that, in order for the hearer to understand each incident, he must usually have some idea of what has happened before' (*Dream Interpretation: A New Approach*, p. 160).
42 See B. Lahire, 'Les pratiques langagières orales en situation scolaire des enfants de milieux populaires', *Revue Internationale de Pédagogie*, 37/4 (1991): 401–13; 'L'inégalité devant la culture écrite scolaire: le cas de l'"expression écrite" à l'école primaire', *Sociétés contemporaines*, no. 11 (1992): 171–91; and *Culture écrite et inégalités scolaires: sociologie de l'"échec scolaire" à l'école primaire*. Lyon: Presses universitaires de Lyon, 1993.
43 As an example of this, here is the oral account of a nine-year-old child, the son of an unemployed construction worker and a housewife, who is in his third year of primary school, having already had to repeat one year:

> I . . . I go and eat. Then I, then afterwards my mum she . . . she goes for a walk. She goes for a walk, she goes for a walk, and I go outside for a walk. Once, once, a . . . loads of times in fact! I go round a bit, I go round my cousin's. Then I, then we . . . then we chat, we were chatting, they were chatting and all that. Then, er . . . my cousin, you know er . . . he's like the same size as me. Then we're chatting, we're chatting. Then . . . then er . . . we played a bit in the bedroom. Then er . . . F . . . er . . . he's called F. Then he said er: 'Go on . . . go back to yer mum.' Then er my, my mum she said to me er: 'Why don't yer go an play wiv F?' Then I said like 'No, I don't wanna play anymore.' Then she said to me: 'Well come on then, we're going home.' Then we went home, I saw the time, it was ten o'clock. Then we . . . then I went to sleep, my mum said: 'Go to sleep!' (Extract taken from empirical material from my PhD thesis, 1990)

44 It is not by chance that Jan Philipp Reemtsma, in his afterword to Adorno's *Dream Notes* (Cambridge, Polity, 2007, p. 87), refers to the situation 'of young children telling jokes and stories about their experiences, and . . . what a mess they make of it.' The author describes it as 'a mass of details' and 'unformed material'.
45 J. Vendryes, *Language: A Linguistic Introduction to History*. London: Routledge, 1996, p. 148.
46 Freud, *On Dreams*, p. 639.
47 S. Freud, *New Introductory Lectures on Psychoanalysis*, in *The Standard*

Edition of the Complete Psychological Works, Vol. XXII. London: Hogarth Press, 1981, p. 12.
48 Richard, *La Théorie des songes*, p. 120.
49 J. Montangero, *Rêve et cognition*. Brussels: Mardaga, 1999, p. 120.
50 'Stream of consciousness' is not exclusively verbal, according to William James, but is also made up of 'visual images'. See also S. M. Kosslyn, *Image and Brain: The Resolution of the Imagery Debate*. Cambridge, MA: MIT Press, 1996.
51 See below, 'Visualisation' (pp. 223–4).
52 L. S. Vygotsky, *Thought and Language*. Cambridge, MA: MIT Press, 1986, p. 182.
53 Ibid., p. 225.
54 Ibid., p. 243.
55 Ibid., p. 253.
56 M. Halbwachs, 'Le rêve et le langage inconscient dans le sommeil', *Journal de psychologie normale et pathologique*, 33 (1946), p. 26. Halbwachs forgets to mention here the dreamer's incorporated past, which also intervenes between the events of waking life and the dream.
57 Ibid., p. 13.
58 Ibid., p. 27.
59 Ibid., p. 36.
60 D. Cohn, *Transparent Minds: Narrative Modes for Presenting Consciousness in Fiction*. Princeton, NJ: Princeton University Press, 1978, p. 93.
61 Ibid., p. 96.
62 M. Tournier, *Friday or the Other Island*. London: Penguin, 1984, p. 48.
63 See below, 'Personal or universal symbolism' (pp. 226–32).

Chapter 10 The Fundamental Forms of Psychic Life

1 See figure 3: The process of dream production (p. 69).
2 D. Hofstadter and E. Sander, *Surfaces and Essences: Analogy as the Fuel and Fire of Thinking*. New York: Basic Books, 2013, p. 20.
3 Ibid., p. 3.
4 D. Stern, *The Interpersonal World of the Infant: A View from Psychoanalysis and Developmental Psychology*. New York: Karnac Books, 1998; M. Dornes, *Psychanalyse et psychologie du premier âge*. Paris: Presses universitaires de France, 2002.
5 Hofstadter and Sander, *Surfaces and Essences*, p. 35.
6 R. Allendy, *Les Rêves et leur interprétation psychanalytique*. Paris: Félix Alcan, 1926, p. 29.
7 E. Hartmann, *The Nature and Functions of Dreaming*. New York: Oxford University Press.
8 This is the argument advanced by Hobson, who fails to see that these changes and combinations have their own logic and coherence. They indicate either profound analogies between people, places, situations, etc., or associations between places and people, people and objects, objects or people who are associated with the same period, etc. Hobson does not believe that the reasons for all this are to be sought at the point of intersection between what the dreamer is seeking to express and the conditions in which he or

she expresses them (*The Dreaming Brain*. New York: Basic Books, 1988, p. 258).

9 Jacques Montangero wrote that, 'when one signifier stands in for another or blends with it in an unexpected way, we frequently observe the existence of a link between the two signifiers in the form of an association to the same class' (*Rêve et cognition*. Brussels: Mardaga, 1999, p. 200). But it should be pointed out that the association of different elements to one same class is based on analogical relationships.

10 M. Foucault, *Le Rêve: études et observations*. Paris: Félix Alcan, 1906, pp. 193–4. In other personal dreams, the author demonstrates the same fear of the headteacher, indicating that this is a case of a recurring relational schema, which no doubt includes a series of analogous situations.

11 G. Lakoff, 'How metaphor structures dreams: the theory of conceptual metaphor applied to dream analysis', *Dreaming*, 3/2 (1993), p. 94.

12 C. S. Hall and V. J. Nordby, *The Individual and His Dreams*. New York: New American Library, 1972, p. 69.

13 E. Fromm, *The Forgotten Language: An Introduction to the Understanding of Dreams, Fairy Tales and Myths*. London: Victor Gollancz, 1952, p. 70.

14 Allendy, *Les Rêves et leur interprétations psychanalytique*, pp. 26–7.

15 M. Halbwachs, 'Le rêve et les images-souvenirs', in Halbwachs, *Les Cadres sociaux de la mémoire*. Paris: Albin Michel, [1925] 1976, p. 17.

16 M. Halbwachs, 'Le langage et la mémoire', ibid., p. 43.

17 J. M. Quinodoz, *Reading Freud: A Chronological Exploration of Freud's Writings*. London: Routledge, 2005, pp. 67–8.

18 S. Freud, *An Autobiographical Study* (1925), in *The Standard Edition of the Complete Psychological Works*, Vol. XX. London: Hogarth Press, 1959, p. 42.

19 Erich Fromm rightly emphasises the infantilisation of the patient in psychoanalytic therapy:

> The entire constellation of the silent, allegedly unknown analyst who is not even supposed to answer a question, and his position of sitting behind the analysand (turning around and having a full look at the analyst is practically taboo), actually results during the hour in the analysand's feeling like a little child. Where else is a grown-up person in such a position of complete passivity? All prerogatives are the analyst's and the analysand is obliged to utter his most intimate thoughts and feelings towards the phantom; this in terms not of a voluntary act but of a moral obligation that he accepts once he has agreed to be an analytic patient. From Freud's standpoint this infantilization of the analysand was all to the good since the main intention was to discover or reconstruct his early childhood. (*Greatness and Limitations of Freud's Thought*. London: Jonathan Cape, 1980, p. 40)

20 S. Freud, *Fragment of an Analysis of a Case of Hysteria* (1905), in *The Standard Edition of the Complete Psychological Works*, Vol. VII. London: Hogarth Press, 1975, p. 118.

21 Ibid., p. 116.

22 S. Freud, *The Interpretation of Dreams*, in *The Standard Edition of the*

Complete Psychological Works, Vols IV and V. London: Hogarth Press, 1953, Vol. IV, p. 175.

23 E. Durkheim, *Durkheim's Philosophy Lectures: Notes from the Lycée de Sens Course, 1883–1884*. Cambridge: Cambridge University Press, 2004, p. 120. Associations through analogy and through contiguity, which we find in Aristotle's writing, but which were more clearly formulated by David Hume, are also at the heart of Saussure's linguistic thinking on syntagmatic and paradigmatic relationships, further developed by Roman Jakobson in his linguistic reflections on aphasia: 'one topic may lead to another either through their similarity or through their contiguity' ('Two aspects of language and two types of aphasic disturbances', in Jakobson, *On Language*. Cambridge MA: Harvard University Press, 1990, p. 129). Gilles Deleuze refers to these two types of association in an extremely clear and condensed presentation in lesson 70 of 20 November 1984 on 'cinema/thought' (transcription: Mathilde Lequin); available at www2.univ-paris8.fr/deleuze/article.php3?id_article=368.

24 K. A. Scherner, *La Vie du rêve*. Paris: Théétète, [1861] 2003, p. 127.

25 Ibid., p. 132.

26 In his writings on the dream, Paul Valéry approaches this question by outlining the hypothesis that the dream can substitute objects, places or people for other objects, places or people belonging to the same 'category' or 'logical class'. But since he refuses to associate dreams with the dreamer's history, Valéry fails to grasp the profoundly social nature of these categories or classes, which can be referred to as 'experience related' or 'existential' rather than 'logical'. See *Cahiers Paul Valéry, 3: Questions du rêve*. Paris: Gallimard, 1979, pp. 97 and 112.

27 J. Montangero, *40 questions et réponses sur les rêves*. Paris: Odile Jacob, 2013, p. 50.

28 Ibid., p. 51.

29 Ibid.

30 J. Laplanche and J.-B. Pontalis, *The Language of Psychoanalysis*. London: Karnac Books, 2006, p. 169.

31 S. Freud, *New Introductory Lectures on Psychoanalysis*, in *The Standard Edition of the Complete Psychological Works*, Vol. XXII. London: Hogarth Press, 1981, p. 11.

32 Freud, *The Interpretation of Dreams*, Vol. IV, pp. 319–20.

33 Freud, *Introductory Lectures on Psychoanalysis*, in *The Standard Edition of the Complete Psychological Works*, Vol. XV. London: Hogarth Press, 1963, pp. 119–20.

34 R. Allendy, *Rêves expliqués*. Paris: Gallimard, 1938, pp. 155–6.

35 Ibid., p. 58.

36 T. M. French, *Psychoanalytical Interpretations*. Chicago: Quadrangle Books, 1970, p. 256. See also D. Hollan, 'The influence of culture on the experience and interpretation of disturbing dreams', *Culture, Medicine and Psychiatry*, 33/2 (2009): 313–22; and R.-L. Punamäki, K. J. Ali, K. H. Ismahil and J. Nuutinen, 'Trauma, dreaming and psychological distress among Kurdish children', *Dreaming*, 15/3 (2005): 178–94.

Chapter 11 The Oneiric Processes

1 S. Freud, *Introductory Lectures on Psychoanalysis*, in *The Standard Edition of the Complete Psychological Works*, Vol. XV. London: Hogarth Press, 1963, p. 217.

2 S. Freud, *On Dreams* (1901), in *The Standard Edition of the Complete Psychological Works*, Vol. V. London: Hogarth Press, 1953, p. 642.

3 The problem raised by the Freudian model is accentuated by Jürgen Habermas when he claims that, with psychoanalysis, the patient learns how to read 'his own texts, which he himself has mutilated and distorted, and in translating symbols from a mode of expression deformed as a private language into the mode of expression of public communication' (*Knowledge and Human Interests*. Cambridge: Polity, 1987, p. 228). It is indeed a transition from a private language to a public communication which must be implemented in order for the dream to be understood by dreamers themselves. For, on waking, the dreamer no longer understands what he, or she, has produced. But to refer to pre-existing texts which would be mutilated makes no sense whatsoever.

4 S. Freud, *The Interpretation of Dreams*, in *The Standard Edition of the Complete Psychological Works*, Vols IV and V. London: Hogarth Press, 1953, Vol. IV, p. 122.

5 J. Bouveresse, *Le Mythe de l'intériorité: expérience, signification et langage privé chez Wittgenstein*. Paris: Minuit, 1987.

6 See the summary of the structural properties of the dream in Sophie Schwartz, 'Matière à rêver: exploration statistique et neuropsychologique des phénomènes oniriques au travers des textes et des images de rêves', thesis, University of Lausanne, 1999, pp. 195–310. However, setting out to link these different cognitive processes directly with cerebral mechanisms in seeking to draw comparisons between the quirks of the dream and neuropsychological syndromes prevents an understanding of what they mean in the experience of the dreamer and, by the same token, fails to grasp the underlying logic which governs all these apparent incongruities.

7 N. Elias, *The Symbol Theory*. Dublin: University College Dublin Press, 2011, p. 80.

8 D. N. Stern, *The Interpersonal World of the Infant: A View from Psychoanalysis and Developmental Psychology*. New York: Karnac Books, 1998, p. 163.

9 Ibid., p. 177.

10 Ibid., p. 182.

11 Ibid., p. 226.

12 D. Foulkes, *Children's Dreaming and the Development of Consciousness*. Cambridge, MA: Harvard University Press, 1999, p. 11.

13 Ibid., p. 15.

14 Ibid., p. 65.

15 Ibid., pp. 74–5.

16 Ibid., pp 145–6.

17 P. A. Kilroe, 'Verbal aspects of dreaming: a preliminary classification', *Dreaming*, 11/3 (2001), p. 107.

18 Ibid., p. 108.

19 See, on this point, P. A. Kilroe, 'The dream pun: what is a play on words without words?', *Dreaming*, 10/4 (2000): 193–209.
20 Kilroe, Verbal aspects of dreaming: a preliminary classification', p. 109.
21 K. A. Scherner, *La Vie du rêve*. Paris: Théétète, [1861] 2003, p. 95.
22 Freud, *The Interpretation of Dreams*, Vol. IV, p. 49.
23 Freud, *Introductory Lectures on Psychoanalysis*, p. 175.
24 S. Freud, *Dream Psychology: Psychoanalysis for Beginners*. New York: James A. McCann, 1921, p. 32.
25 J. A. Hobson, *The Dreaming Brain*. New York: Basic Books, 1988, pp. 73–4.
26 Michel Jouvet (*The Paradox of Sleep: The Story of Dreaming*. Cambridge, MA: MIT Press, 1999, p. 71) pointed out the predominance of 'visual dreams containing movement'. And, while reaffirming that 'the visual mode dominates representations in dreams' (*40 questions et réponses sur les rêves*. Paris: Odile Jacob, 2013, p. 22), Jacques Montangero also emphasises the kinesthetic dimension (*Rêve et cognition*. Brussels: Mardaga, 1999, p. 384).
27 Freud, *The Interpretation of Dreams*, Vol. V, p. 339.
28 M. Halbwachs, 'Le rêve et le langage inconsciente dans le sommeil', *Journal de psychologie normale et pathologique*, 33 (1946), p. 35.
29 M. Halbwachs. 'Le langage et la mémoire', in Halbwachs, *Les Cadres sociaux de la mémoire*. Paris: Albin Michel, [1925] 1976, p. 43.
30 M. Foucault, *Le Rêve: études et observations*. Paris: Félix Alcan, 1906, p. 188.
31 Ibid., p. 195.
32 See H. F. Ellenberger, *The Discovery of the Unconscious: The History and Evolution of Dynamic Psychiatry*. London: Fontana, 1994, p. 309.
33 T. Flournoy, 'Genèse de quelques prétendus messages sprirites', *Revue philosophique de la France et de l'étranger*, 47 (1899): 144–58; quoted by M. Cifali in 'La Belle au Bois-Dormant en terre romande', *Le Coq-héron*, no. 218 (2014), p. 32.
34 Freud, *The Interpretation of Dreams*, Vol. IV, p. 248. See above, 'What does the censorship do?' (pp. 155–9).
35 J. Montangero, *Comprendre ses rêves pour mieux se connaitre*. Paris: Odile Jacob, 2007, p. 122.
36 Ibid., p 13.
37 The work of G. William Domhoff is also based on the notion that dreams dramatise elements of the dreamer's cognitive make-up and that they are like theatrical productions. See in particular 'Dreaming as embodied simulation: a widower's dreams of his deceased wife', *Dreaming*, 25/3 (2015): 232–56. This theory is demonstrated by a quantitative analysis of emotions, social interactions, unhappy and happy events in a series of 143 dream accounts provided over a twenty-two-year period by a widower and on the subject of his deceased wife.
38 J. Mageo, 'Figurative dream analysis and U.S. traveling identities', *Ethos*, 34/4 (2006): 456–87.
39 Artemidorus, *The Interpretation of Dreams: Oneirocritica*. Park Ridge, NJ: Noyes Press, 1975, p. 15.
40 Ibid., p. 212.
41 J. Du Bouchet, 'Artémidore, homme de science', in J. Carroy and J. Lancel (eds), *Clés des songes et sciences des rêves: de l'Antiquité à Freud*. Paris: Les Belles Lettres, 2016, p. 41.

42 A. Charma, *Du sommeil*. Paris: Hachette, 1851, p. 50.
43 Ibid., p. 52.
44 Scherner, *La Vie du rêve*, p. 104.
45 Ibid., p. 34.
46 Ibid., p. 166.
47 Freud, *Introductory Lectures on Psychoanalysis*, p. 168.
48 L. Marinelli and A. Mayer, *Dreaming by the Book: Freud's Interpretation of Dreams and the History of the Psychoanalytic Movement*. New York: Other Press, 2003, p. 62.
49 Ibid., pp. 83–4.
50 S. Freud, *An Autobiographical Study* (1925), in *The Standard Edition of the Complete Psychological Works*, Vol. XX. London: Hogarth Press, 1959, pp. 52–3.
51 Freud, *On Dreams*, p. 684.
52 In a letter dated 26 March 1910, Eugen Bleuler wrote to Freud: 'Steckel's "Glossary of Dreams" seems to me premature; *vita est multiplex*' (S. Freud and E. Bleuler, *Lettres, 1904–1937*. Paris: Gallimard, 2016, p. 84).
53 Freud, *The Interpretation of Dreams*, Vol. IV, p. 241.
54 Ibid., Vol. V, p. 549.
55 Freud, *Introductory Lectures on Psychoanalysis*, p. 151.
56 Freud, *The Interpretation of Dreams*, Vol. V, p. 353.
57 Ibid., p. 354.
58 S. Freud, 'Associations of a four-year-old child', in *The Standard Edition of the Complete Psychological Works*, Vol. XVIII. London: Hogarth Press, 1955, p. 266.
59 Freud, *The Interpretation of Dreams*, Vol. IV, p. 288.
60 Ibid., p. 283.
61 Ibid., Vol. V, pp. 359–60.
62 R. Allendy, *Rêves expliqués*. Paris: Gallimard, 1938, p. 132.
63 Ibid., p. 55.
64 R. Allendy, *Les Rêves et leur interprétation psychanalytique*. Paris: Félix Alcan, 1926, p. 95.
65 Montangero, *Comprendre ses rêves pour mieux se connaitre*, p. 90.
66 E. Fromm, *Greatness and Limitations of Freud's Thought*. London: Jonathan Cape, 1980, pp. 89–90.
67 Kilroe, 'Verbal aspects of dreaming: a preliminary classification', p. 110.
68 G. H. Schubert, *La Symbolique des rêves* [Die Symbolik des Traumes]. Paris: Albin Michel, [1814] 1982, p. 64.
69 Freud, *The Interpretation of Dreams*, Vol. IV, pp. 229–30.
70 Ibid., p. 415.
71 J. Piaget, *Play, Dreams and Imitation in Childhood*. London: Routledge, [1978] 1999.
72 B. Lahire, *Franz Kafka: éléments pour une théorie de la création littéraire*. Paris: La Découverte, 2010.
73 'Their transcription must certainly represent a source of inspiration for him: an instrument of writing, a method of working out his literary objectives' (F. Guattari, *Soixante-cinq rêves de Franz Kafka*. Paris: Lignes, 2007, p. 11).
74 M. Foucault, 'Introduction', in L. Binswanger and Foucault, *Dream and Existence*. Seattle: Review of Existential Psychology and Psychiatry, 1986, p. 58.

75 A. Adler, *Social Interest: Adler's Key to the Meaning of Life*. Oxford: Oneworld, [1933] 2009, p. 190.
76 Allendy, *Rêves expliqués*, p. 99.
77 Michel Jouvet provides a personal example of a dream which demonstrates a process involving literalisation of a homonymy rather than a metaphor. His older brother died in 1981, aged seventy, and that very night he had a dream 'representing a severed hand'. He told his mother about the dream, and she reminded him that, when he first started to speak, around the age of two, for some unknown reason he called his brother 'Hand'. The dream about the severed hand therefore says, by means of a visual process, that his brother ('Hand') is dead ('cutting off' being a reference to 'killing'; we also refer to the 'Reaper' to represent death). Jouvet, *De la science et des rêves: mémoires d'un onirologue*. Paris: Odile Jacob, 2013, p. 252.
78 Halbwachs, 'Le rêve et le langage inconscient dans le sommeil', p. 18.
79 Halbwachs, 'Le langage et la mémoire', p. 46.
80 M. Ullman, 'Dreaming as metaphor in motion', *Archives of General Psychiatry*, 21 (1969): 696–703.
81 T. M. French and E. Fromm, *Dream Interpretation: A New Approach*. New York: Basic Books, 1964, pp. 63–7.
82 E. Hartmann, *The Nature and Functions of Dreaming*. New York: Oxford University Press, p. 7.
83 Ibid., pp. 17–19.
84 Ibid., pp. 24–5.
85 D. Hofstadter and E. Sander, *Surfaces and Essences: Analogy as the Fuel and Fire of Thinking*. New York: Basic Books, 2013.
86 G. Lakoff and M. Johnson, *Metaphors We Live By*. Chicago: University of Chicago Press, [1980] 2008, p. 3. See also J. L. Singer, 'Experimental studies of ongoing conscious experience', in *Ciba Foundation Symposium* 174: *Experimental and Theoretical Studies of Consciousness*. New York: Wiley, 1993, pp. 100–22.
87 Lakoff's work was inspired in particular by Montague Ullman, 'Dreaming as metaphor in motion', and John S. Antrobus, 'The dream as metaphor: an information-processing and learning model', *Journal of Mental Imagery*, 2 (1977): 327–38.
88 G. Lakoff, 'How metaphor structures dreams: the theory of conceptual metaphor applied to dream analysis', *Dreaming*, 3/2 (1993), p. 77.
89 Ibid., pp. 89–90.
90 Ibid., pp. 92–3.
91 Ibid., pp. 93–7.
92 Montangero, *Comprendre ses rêves pour mieux se connaitre*, p. 115.
93 Schubert, *La Symbolique des rêves*, p. 61.
94 Scherner, *La Vie du rêve*, p. 128.
95 Ibid., p. 42.
96 A. Maury, *Le Sommeil et les rêves: études psychologiques sur ces phénomènes et les divers états qui s'y rattachent*. Paris: Didier, [1861] 1865, p. 94.
97 Ibid., p. 117.
98 L. d'Hervey de Saint-Denys, *Dreams and How to Guide Them*. London: Duckworth, 1982, p. 33.
99 Ibid.
100 Ibid., p. 34.

101 Ibid., p. 137.
102 Y. Delage, 'Essai sur la théorie du rêve', *Revue scientifique*, 48 (1891–2), p. 47.
103 Freud, *The Interpretation of Dreams*, Vol. IV, p. 279.
104 Freud, *On Dreams*, p. 649.
105 Freud, *The Interpretation of Dreams*, Vol. IV, p. 279.
106 Freud, *On Dreams*, p. 651.
107 Freud, *The Interpretation of Dreams*, Vol. IV, p. 321.
108 Ibid., p. 293.
109 Introducing the psychoanalytical model of dream interpretation in the course of a conference given in 1909 at the Royal Society of Medicine of Budapest, Sandor Ferenczi spoke of the 'rules of the art of dream interpretation' of 'composite images', which consisted in asking the dreamer to associate each element of the dream to the memories that it brought to mind and then to identify 'on what basis of a common element or similarity the welding together has taken place'. See Ferenczi, 'The psychological analysis of dreams', *American Journal of Psychology*, 21/2 (1910): 309–28.
110 Allendy, *Rêves expliqués*, p. 87.
111 Ibid., p. 51.
112 Montangero, *Comprendre ses rêves pour mieux se connaître*, p. 47.
113 S. Freud, *Fragment of an Analysis of a Case of Hysteria* (1905), in *The Standard Edition of the Complete Psychological Works*, Vol. VII. London: Hogarth Press, 1975, p. 69.
114 Freud, *The Interpretation of Dreams*, Vol. V, p. 400.
115 Ibid., pp. 476–7.
116 Ibid., p. 490.
117 Ibid., Vol. IV, p. 141.
118 Ibid., p. 318.
119 Freud, *Introductory Lectures on Psychoanalysis*, p. 228.
120 G. Tarde, *Sur le sommeil: ou plutôt sur les rêves*. Lausanne: BHMS, 2009, pp. 59–60.
121 Ibid., p. 71.
122 Ibid., p. 96.

Chapter 12 Variations in Forms of Expression

1 S. Freud, *The Interpretation of Dreams*, in *The Standard Edition of the Complete Psychological Works*, Vols IV and V. London: Hogarth Press, 1953, Vol. IV, p. 75.
2 Ibid., pp. 135–6.
3 A. Grothendieck, *Récoltes et semailles: réflexions et témoignages sur un passé de mathématicien*. Montpellier: Université des Sciences et Techniques du Languedoc, 1985, pp. 552–3.
4 Hofstadter and Sander (*Surfaces and Essences: Analogy as the Fuel and Fire of Thinking*. New York: Basic Books, 2013, pp. 486) observe the same approach in Albert Einstein. What seems at first glance to be only 'bold leaps of an idiosyncratic intuition' turn out in the end, in the case of a physicist such as Einstein, to be a way to 'unify two concepts that . . . were clearly distinct' in such a way that 'this apparent distinction had to be dropped in favor of a single, more extended concept.'

5 I. Meyerson, *Les Fonctions psychologiques et les œuvres*. Paris: Albin Michel, 1995, p. 75.
6 I. Meyerson, 'Discontinuités et cheminements autonomes dans l'histoire de l'esprit' (1948), in *Écrits 1920–1983: pour une psychologie historique*. Paris: Presses universitaires de France, 1987, p. 61.
7 I. Meyerson, 'Problèmes d'histoire psychologique des œuvres: spécificités, variation, expérience' (1948), ibid., p. 82.
8 I. Meyerson, 'Remarques pour une théorie du rêve: observations sur le cauchemar' (1953), ibid., p. 206.
9 L. Crespin, 'Redécouvrir la conscience par le rêve: le débat entre théories cognitives et non cognitives de la conscience à l'épreuve de la recherche sur le rêve', PhD thesis, Université Blaise Pascal, Clermont-Ferrand, 2016, p. 48.
10 Ibid., p. 51.
11 E. Hartmann, *The Nature and Functions of Dreaming*. New York: Oxford University Press, 2011, pp. 84–5.
12 R. Allendy, *Les Rêves et leur interprétation psychanalytique*. Paris: Félix Alcan, 1926, p. 3. es
13 Ibid., p. 4.
14 Ibid., pp. 2–3.
15 The hypnopompic state is also a state of intermediate consciousness between that of waking and that of sleep but which occurs during the phase of waking up.
16 Alfred Maury as early as 1861 drew parallels between dreams during hallucination and those associated with mental illness. These, he declared, are 'different forms of delirium'. Maury, *Le Sommeil et les rêves: études psychologiques sur ces phénomènes et les divers états qui s'y rattachent*. Paris: Didier, [1861] 1865, p. 342.
17 J. Montangero, *40 questions et réponses sur les rêves*. Paris: Odile Jacob, 2013, p. 181.
18 E. Hartmann, 'Outline for a theory on the nature and functions of dreaming', *Dreaming*, 6/2 (1996), p. 153. Hartmann writes that these similarities have been demonstrated 'by studies of daydreaming and mental activity under relaxed isolated conditions by Foulkes and Fleisher (1975), . . . and Reinsel et al. (1992), among others' (ibid.).
19 Ibid., pp. 162–3.
20 Hartmann, *The Nature and Functions of Dreaming*, p. 34.
21 B. Lahire, *La Culture des individus: dissonances culturelles et distinction de soi*. Paris: La Découverte, 2004.
22 In his 'Manifesto of Surrealism' (1924; www.tcf.ua.edu/Classes/Jbutler/T340/SurManifesto/ManifestoOfSurrealism.htm), André Breton defined surrealism by its absence of moral or aesthetic control and linked it to 'the omnipotence of the dream, . . . the disinterested play of thought'. For him, automatic writing is a form of writing in which neither consciousness nor the will can intervene.
23 In 1872, *The Expression of the Emotions in Man and Animals* established a systematic parallelism between animals and man. In it, Darwin presented a comparative evolutionist ethology which broadly suggested a continuity between animal and human kingdoms, the differences here too appearing to be of degree and not of nature.
24 Freud, *The Interpretation of Dreams*, Vol. V, p. 608.

25 S. Freud, 'Preface to the second edition' of S. Freud and J. Breuer, *Studies on Hysteria* (1895), in *The Standard Edition of the Complete Psychological Works*, Vol. II. London: Hogarth Press, 1955, p. xxxi.
26 S. Freud, *The Psychotherapy of Hysteria*, in S. Freud and J. Breuer, *Studies in Hysteria*, p. 285.
27 S. Freud, *Fragment of an Analysis of a Case of Hysteria* (1905), in *The Standard Edition of the Complete Psychological Works*, Vol. VII. London: Hogarth Press, 1975, p. 67.
28 S. Freud, *An Autobiographical Study* (1925), in *The Standard Edition of the Complete Psychological Works*, Vol. XX. London: Hogarth Press, 1959, p. 47.
29 If Freud was turning from the pathological towards the normal, others were using his theory about dreams to examine forms of pathology other than hysteria. This was the case, for example, for Eugen Bleuler with schizophrenia: 'The principle contribution of "Freudian mechanisms" in Bleuler's research consisted in the possibility of interpreting the meanings of delirious manifestations and other symptoms of schizophrenia in a manner similar to that of oneiric formations' (M. Schröter, 'Bleuler et la psychanalyse: proximité et autonomie', in S. Freud and E. Bleuler, *Lettres: 1904–1937*. Paris: Gallimard, 2016, p. 243).
30 S. Freud, *Introductory Lectures on Psychoanalysis*, in *The Standard Edition of the Complete Psychological Works*, Vol. XV. London: Hogarth Press, 1963, p. 100.
31 'I was able to show from a short story by W. Jensen called *Gradiva*, which has no particular merit in itself, that invented dreams can be interpreted in the same way as real ones and that the unconscious mechanisms familiar to us in the "dream-work" are thus also operative in the processes of imaginative writing' (Freud, *An Autobiographical Study*, p. 65).
32 H. F. Ellenberger, *The Discovery of the Unconscious: The History and Evolution of Dynamic Psychiatry*. London: Fontana, 1994, p. 447.
33 M. Bakhtin, *Le Freudianisme*. Lausanne: L'Âge d'homme, 1980, p. 49.
34 Once the question of the neurobiological and neurophysiological conditions in which dreams occur has been raised, the next step is to examine the neurobiological and neurophysiological conditions in which the different moments of waking life are played out.
35 We could thus set Jean Piaget, who essentially worked on 'thought controlled by individual will and the principles of logic' (J. Montangero, *Rêve et cognition*. Brussels: Mardaga, 1999, p. 55) against Sigmund Freud, who worked on hysteria, paranoia, oral or written slips, dreams, etc.
36 L. Wittgenstein, *Philosophical Investigations*. Chichester: Wiley-Blackwell, 2009, p. 15 (no. 23).
37 M. Bakhtin, *Speech Genres and Other Late Essays*. Austin: University of Texas Press, 2010, p. 60.
38 See figure 6: Dispositions under weak contextual constraints (p. 258), and figure 7: Dispositions under strong contextual constraints (p. 259).
39 B. Lahire, *Franz Kafka: éléments pour une théorie de la création littéraire*. Paris: La Découverte, 2010.
40 P. Bourdieu, *Outline for a Theory of Practice*. Cambridge: Cambridge University Press, 1977, p. 21.
41 M. Halbwachs, *La Psychologie collective*. Paris: Champs classiques, 2015, p. 165.

42 Montangero, *40 questions et réponses sur les rêves*, p. 12.
43 J. Montangero, *Comprendre ses rêves pour mieux se connaître*. Paris: Odile Jacob, 2007, p. 25.
44 Montangero, *Rêve et cognition*, p. 38.
45 Montangero, *Comprendre ses rêves pour mieux se connaître*, p. 28.
46 Montangero, *Rêve et cognition*, p. 13.
47 See figure 3: The process of dream creation (p. 000).
48 M. Bakhtin, *Speech Genres and Other Late Essays*, p. 63.
49 Ibid.
50 D. Foulkes, *Children's Dreaming and the Development of Consciousness*. Cambridge, MA: Harvard University Press, 1999, p. 124.
51 J. Piaget, *Biology and Knowledge: An Essay on the Relations between Organic Regulations and Cognitive Processes*. Edinburgh: Edinburgh University Press, 1971, p. 4.
52 Ibid., p. 8.
53 J. Piaget, *Play, Dreams and Imitation in Childhood*. London: Routledge, [1978] 1999, p. 86.
54 Ibid., p. 107.
55 Ibid., p. 171.
56 Ibid., p. 209.
57 Ibid., p. 210.
58 Ibid., p. 176.
59 Ibid., p. 180.
60 Ibid., p. 178.
61 Ibid., p. 182.
62 Among all the texts which establish a parallel between certain forms of literature and dreams – for example, the work of Kafka, regularly considered as one of the 'masters of oneiric literature' (M. Robert, *Les Puits de Babel*. Paris: Grasset, 1987) – we are familiar with Freud's famous comments about daydreams and literary creation ('Creative writers and day-dreaming', in *The Standard Edition of the Complete Psychological Works*, Vol. IX. London: Hogarth Press, 1968, pp. 143–53).
63 Lahire, *Franz Kafka: éléments pour une théorie de la création littéraire*.
64 N. Elias, *Mozart: Portrait of a Genius*. Cambridge: Polity, 1993.
65 Freud, 'Creative writers and day-dreaming', p. 145.
66 S. Freud, *Beyond the Pleasure Principle*, in *The Standard Edition of the Complete Psychological Works*, Vol. XVIII. London: Hogarth Press, 1955, p. 16.
67 Ibid., p. 17.
68 Ibid., p. 35.
69 See the notion of a 'sociology of literary experience', which reflects a 'sociology of daydreams', which I formulated in *The Plural Actor*. Cambridge, Polity, 2011, p. 96.
70 Freud, 'Creative writers and day-dreaming', p. 422.
71 Ibid.
72 M. Dornes, *Psychanalyse et psychologie du premier âge*. Paris: Presses universitaires de France, 2002, p. 78.
73 Ibid., p. 318.
74 M. Klein, *The Psychoanalysis of Children*. London: Virago, 1989, p. 7.
75 It is this conflict which is referred to in Gérard Bléandonu's introduction to

Melanie Klein's work. The latter therefore discovered that children express through their play activities and behaviour that adults communicate in words (Bléandonu, *What Do Children Dream?* London: Free Association Books, 2006, p. 14).

76 T. Jouffroy, 'Du sommeil', in *Mélanges philosophiques*. Paris: Paulin, [1827] 1833, p. 223.
77 P. Borel, 'Les idées de grandeur dans le rêve', *Journal de psychologie normale et pathologique*, no. 5 (1914), pp. 401–2.
78 Freud, *The Interpretation of Dreams*, Vol. V, p. 492.
79 A. L. Strauss, *Continual Permutations of Action*. New York: Aldine de Gruyter, 1993.
80 I have suggested that reading literary texts triggers daydreams which make it possible to return to, to prolong, to support or to prepare an action. Far from being a passive activity disconnected from courses of action, reading is very much part of the action (B. Lahire, 'Literary experience: reading, daydreams and parapraxes', in *The Plural Actor*, p. 96).
81 Strauss did not deny the fact that daydreams could be 'idle, playful, or merely expressive' but 'was focusing on their relation to action' (*Continual Permutations of Action*, p. 6).
82 'Dreams as empirical data: siblings' dreams and fantasies about their disabled sisters and brothers', *Symbolic Interaction*, 16/2 (1993): 117–27.
83 Ibid.
84 Crespin, 'Redécouvrir la conscience par le rêve', p. 55.
85 Ibid., p. 56.
86 F. Snyder, 'The phenomenology of dreaming', in L. Madow and L. Snow (eds), *The Psychodynamic Implications of the Physiological Studies on Dreams*. Springfield, IL: Charles C. Thomas, 1970, pp. 124–51; D. Foulkes, *Dreaming: A Cognitive-Psychological Analysis*. London: Routledge, 1985; and G. W. Domhoff, 'Refocusing the neurocognitive approach to dreams: a critique of the Hobson versus Solms debate', *Dreaming*, 15/1 (2005): 3–20.
87 R. Reinsel et al., 'Bizarreness in dreams and waking fantasy', in J. S. Antrobus and M. Bertini (eds), *The Neuropsychology of Sleep and Dreaming*. Hillsdale, NJ: Erlbaum, pp. 157–84.
88 Montangero, *40 questions et réponses sur les rêves*, p. 131.
89 D. Foulkes and E. Scott, 'An above zero waking baseline for the incidence of momentarily hallucinatory mentation', *Sleep Research*, 2 (1973): 108, and D. Foulkes and S. Fleisher, 'Mental activity in relaxed wakefulness', *Journal of Abnormal Psychology*, 84/1 (1975): 66–75.
90 Crespin, 'Redécouvrir la conscience par le rêve', pp. 78–9.
91 S. Starker, 'Daydreaming styles and nocturnal dreaming', *Journal of Abnormal Psychology*, 83/1 (1974): 52–5.
92 S. Freud, *Papers on Technique*, in *The Standard Edition of the Complete Psychological Works*, Vol. XII. London: Hogarth Press, 1958, p. 134.
93 Freud, *An Autobiographical Study*, p. 28.
94 S. Freud, *Psycho-analytic Procedure*, in *The Standard Edition of the Complete Psychological Works*, Vol. VII. London: Hogarth Press, 1975, p. 251.
95 Freud, *Papers on Technique*, pp. 134–5.
96 Freud, *Psycho-analytic Procedure*, p. 250.
97 Hartmann, *The Nature and Functions of Dreaming*, p. 118.

98 J. Goody, *The Domestication of the Savage Mind*. Cambridge: Cambridge University Press, 1977.

Chapter 13 Elements of Methodology for a Sociology of Dreams

1 J. A. Hobson, *The Dreaming Brain*. New York: Basic Books, 1988.
2 J. Bachner, P. Raffetseder, B. Walz and M. Schredl, 'The effects of dream socialization in childhood on dream recall frequency and the attitude towards dreams in adulthood: a retrospective study', *International Journal of Dream Research*, 5 (2012): 102–7.
3 This feminine culture of intimacy may be seen, for example, in the experience of keeping a private journal, twice as likely in women as in men. The 2008 survey on the cultural practices of French people showed that 10 per cent of women aged over fifteen had kept a personal diary over the last twelve months, as opposed to only 5 per cent of men. O. Donnat, *Les Pratiques culturelles des Français à l'ère numérique: enquête 2008*. Paris: La Découverte, 2009, p. 201. See also B. Lahire, 'De la réflexivité quotidienne: journal personnel, autobiographie et autres écrits narratifs', *Sociologie et Société*, 40/2 (2008): 163–77.
4 E. Hartmann, *The Nature and Functions of Dreaming*. New York: Oxford University Press, 2011, pp. 95–6. The 2008 survey showed that executives and the more highly intellectualised professions (15 per cent) were seven times more likely to keep a private diary than agricultural workers (2 per cent) and five times more than manual labourers (5 per cent). Donnat, *Les Pratiques culturelles des Français à l'ère numérique*, p. 201.
5 The neuroscience researcher Perrine Ruby confirms that keeping a dream notebook each morning has positive effects on the ability to remember dreams: 'We know that this increases the frequency of remembering dreams, even if we do not know why' (D. Mascret, 'Comment le cerveau se souvient-il de certains rêves?', *Le Figaro*, 9 April 2015, http://sante.lefigaro.fr/actualite/2015/04/09/23607-comment-cerveau-se-souvient-il-certains-reves.
6 L. Crespin, 'Redécouvrir la conscience par le rêve: le débat entre théories cognitives et non cognitives de la conscience à l'épreuve de la recherche sur le rêve', PhD thesis, Université Blaise Pascal, Clermont-Ferrand, 2016, p. 34.
7 S. Freud, *The Interpretation of Dreams*, in *The Standard Edition of the Complete Psychological Works*, Vols IV and V. London: Hogarth Press, 1953, Vol. IV, p. 45.
8 Hobson, *The Dreaming Brain*, p. 47.
9 J. Montangero, *40 questions et réponses sur les rêves*. Paris: Odile Jacob, 2013, p. 31.
10 Hobson, *The Dreaming Brain*, p. 47.
11 S. Freud, *Papers on Technique*, in *The Standard Edition of the Complete Psychological Works*, Vol. XII. London: Hogarth Press, 1958, p. 95.
12 M. Foucault, *Le Rêve: études et observations*. Paris: Félix Alcan, 1906, pp. 19–20.
13 J. Carroy, *Nuits savantes: une histoire des rêves (1800–1945)*. Paris: EHESS, 2012, p. 282.
14 Foucault, *Le Rêve: études et observations*, p. 6.
15 Ibid.

16 Ibid., p. 12.
17 Ibid., p. 40.
18 E. Goblot, 'Le souvenir des rêves', *Revue philosophique de la France et de l'étranger*, 42 (1896): 288–90.
19 Crespin, 'Redécouvrir la conscience par le rêve', p. 95.
20 F. Guénolé and A. Nicolas, 'Le rêve est un état hypnique de la conscience: pour en finir avec l'hypothèse de Goblot et ses avatars contemporains', *Neurophysiologie clinique*, 40 (2010), p. 196.
21 J. S. Bruner, *Culture et modes de pensée: l'esprit humain dans ses œuvres*. Paris: Retz, 2000, and *Pourquoi nous racontons-nous des histoires?* Paris: Pocket, 2005.
22 D. Foulkes, *Children's Dreaming and the Development of Consciousness*. Cambridge, MA: Harvard University Press, 1999, p. 150.
23 M. Stubbs, *Language, Schools and Classrooms*. Abingdon: Routledge, 2012; and B. Bernstein, *Class, Codes and Control: Theoretical Studies towards a Sociology of Language*. London: Routledge, 2003.
24 C. S. Hall and V. J. Nordby, *The Individual and His Dreams*. New York: New American Library, 1972, p. 13.
25 Letter of 8 December 1937, photographically reproduced by Breton in *Trajectoire de rêve* (Paris: GLM, 1938); translated and with a commentary by Jean-Louis Houdebine in *Promesse*, no. 32, April 1972.
26 Freud, *The Interpretation of Dreams*, Vol. IV, p. xxiii.
27 A. Charma, *Du sommeil*. Paris: Hachette, 1851, p. 79.
28 Gérard Bléandonu wrote that 'some progress was made [in the study of dreams] when some reporters reported observations of their own children or children with whose family situation and lives they were very familiar' (*What do Children Dream?* London: Free Association Books, 2006, p. 7).
29 Hobson, *The Dreaming Brain*, p. 219.
30 Ibid., p. 222.
31 Ibid., p. 228.
32 Ibid., p. 231.
33 Ibid., p. 234.
34 Ibid., p. 271.
35 Ibid., p. 281.
36 Don Kuiken states very clearly that 'Freud's method of dream interpretation makes explicit that textual material beyond the dream report *per se* is required for dream interpretation' but points out that 'the boundaries of the additional relevant textual material are not very clear' ('Interpretation in *The Interpretation of Dreams*', *Dreaming*, 4/1 (1994): 85–8).
37 J. Montangero, *Comprendre ses rêves pour mieux se connaître*. Paris: Odile Jacob, 2007, p. 74.
38 See above, 'Dream and outside the dream' (pp. 170–5).
39 D. Foulkes, 'The *Interpretation of Dreams* and the scientific study of dreaming', *Dreaming*, 4/1 (1994), p. 84.
40 S. Freud, *On Dreams* (1901), in *The Standard Edition of the Complete Psychological Works*, Vol. V. London: Hogarth Press, 1953, p. 638.
41 S. Freud, *Fragment of an analysis of a Case of Hysteria*, in *The Standard Edition of the Complete Psychological Works*, Vol. VII. London: Hogarth Press, 1975, p. 61.
42 Freud, *The Interpretation of Dreams*, Vol. IV, pp. 103–4.

43 S. Freud, *An Autobiographical Study* (1925), in *The Standard Edition of the Complete Psychological Works*, Vol. XX. London: Hogarth Press, 1959, p. 40.
44 R. Allendy, *Les Rêves et leur interprétation psychanalytique*. Paris: Félix Alcan, 1926, p. 96.
45 Freud, *The Interpretation of Dreams*, Vol. IV, p. 98.
46 C. G. Jung, *Psychology and Alchemy*. Abingdon: Routledge, 2010.
47 Ibid., pp. 44–58.
48 Freud, *An Autobiographical Study*, pp. 40–1.
49 L. Marinelli and A. Mayer, *Dreaming by the Book: Freud's Interpretation of Dreams and the History of the Psychoanalytical Movement*. New York: Other Press, 2003, pp. 44–5.
50 S. Pons-Nicolas, 'Préface: Dora "la suçoteuse"', in S. Freud, *Dora: Fragment d'une analyse d'hystérie*. Paris: Payot & Rivages, 2010, pp. 12–13.
51 Freud, *The Interpretation of Dreams*, Vol. IV, pp. 247–8.
52 Freud, *Fragment of an Analysis of a Case of Hysteria*, pp. 9–10.
53 We may judge the session length of the Freudian treatment (a little less than an hour) both too short to give the patient time to expand on all the associations that come to mind on the different elements of the dream and too long to be remembered (without notes or recording) and worked on with all the precision and accuracy necessary. But, at the opposite end of the scale, what about the sessions of less than ten minutes advocated by a psychoanalyst such as Jacques Lacan? Any sociologist using the long (several hours) and repeated interview (the individual is seen several times during the course of the research) cannot fail to have grave doubts about a practice that limits the time available for the patient to speak to such an extent. But while the objectives of sociologists and psychoanalysts are not exactly the same, it is by no means certain that the scientific demand for objectivity, precision, rigour or tightly focused work on material obtained in the most advantageous conditions from the interviewee should not serve as a model on a therapeutic level.
54 Freud, *Fragment of an Analysis of a Case of Hysteria*, p. 6.
55 Like that of Thomas M. French and Erika Fromm, for example (*Dream Interpretation: A New Approach*. New York: Basic Books, 1964). Or like that of Alan Roland ('The context and unique function of dreams in psychoanalytic therapy: clinical approach', *International Journal of Psycho-Analysis*, 52 (1971): 431–9).
56 J. Rallo Romero, M.-T. Ruiz de Bascones, and C. Zamora de Pellicer, 'Les rêves comme unité et continuité de la vie psychique', *Revue française de psychanalyse*, 38/5–6 (1974), pp. 943–4.
57 T. M. French, *Psychoanalytic Therapy*. New York: Quadrangle Books, 1970, p. 238.
58 B. Lahire, *Portraits sociologiques: dispositions et variations individuelles*. Paris: Nathan, 2002, and *Franz Kafka: éléments pour une théorie de la création littéraire*. Paris: La Découverte, 2010.
59 E. Fromm, *The Crisis of Psychoanalysis: Essays on Freud, Marx and Social Psychology*. London: Penguin, 1970, p. 142.
60 The original reference is as follows: 'To understand a person, one needs to know the primordial wishes he or she longs to fulfil. . . . But they (the wishes) are not embedded in advance of all experience. They evolve from early childhood in life with other people' (N. Elias, *Mozart: Portrait of a Genius*. Cambridge: Polity, 1993, p. 7).

61 Jacques Montangero provides evidence for the fact that, in his experience of analysing dreams, the dream is linked to the experiences and problems of the dreamer: 'The many extended interviews I have held with volunteers or patients about their dreams demonstrated, around nine times out of ten, that certain elements of their dream originated from an autobiographical episode, a desired objective or a preoccupation' (*40 questions et réponses sur les rêves*, p. 159).
62 Hall and Nordby, *The Individual and His Dreams*, p. 103.
63 Montangero, *Comprendre ses rêves pour mieux se connaître*, p. 114.
64 Recognising the same wish in dreams from the same period, Gabriel Tarde wrote: 'An impatience to have news of the person in question has been my chief desire for some time now, and it is not surprising that this expresses itself in my dreams. But what I admire is the multiplicity of expressions this takes and how everything serves to demonstrate it' (*Sur le sommeil: ou plutôt sur les rêves*. Lausanne: BHMS, 2009, p. 59).
65 R. Allendy, *Rêves expliqués*. Paris: Gallimard, 1938, p 179. The author adds that, 'sometimes even, a dream is not fully comprehensible unless seen alongside another dream from the same night' (ibid., p. 183).
66 This is in essence what Jean Piaget was saying when he observed that the 'free associations' do not necessarily reveal the associations which gave rise to the dream, but they can nevertheless reveal the patient's 'complexes' (*Play, Dreams and Imitation in Childhood*. London: Routledge, [1978] 1999, p. 190). It is for this reason that the list of associations is potentially infinite and that, simply by extending the discussion, a great many more associations will emerge – in other words, analogous situations which can be both linked to and part of schemas of experience.
67 René Allendy spoke about the importance for the analyst of 'first of all finding the broad outline of the dream, its fundamental tendency' (*Rêves expliqués*, p. 170).
68 In the 1930s, a method called 'psychobiography' was introduced at the New York Psychoanalytic Institute under the direction of Abram Kardiner.

This comes close to life history but seeks to take into account those levels of experience of which the subject is not conscious, those forms of personal experience which fail to make sense to him or her. Rather than simply focusing on the subject's own presentation of him- or herself, it works through interaction with the researcher: the method encourages free associations, draws on oneiric material, practises dream analysis and uses psychological tests, especially the Rorschach test. This method was introduced by Cora du Bois in the years 1937–1939. (A. Raulin, *Les Traces psychiques de la domination: essai sur Kardiner*. Lormont: Le Bord de l'eau, 2016, p. 54)

In *The Mark of Oppression: A Psychosocial Study of the American Negro* (New York: W. W. Norton, 1951), Abram Kardiner and Lionel Lovesey wrote psychobiographies which extend to roughly ten pages in length. These include reference to social class, gender, age range, skin colour, family origins and existential situation (health-related, emotional, familial, professional, etc.), as well as to attitudes or behaviours (resentment, apathy, depression, fear of success, mistrust towards women, sexual impotence, self-esteem, etc.).

Current sociology, particularly when working on the individual scale, would benefit from taking inspiration from such attempts to move beyond the accepted routine methodological standards.

69 L. Wittgenstein, *Lectures and Conversations on Aesthetics, Psychology and Religious Belief*. Berkeley: University of California Press, 2007, pp. 45–6.

Conclusion 1

1 S. Freud, *The Interpretation of Dreams*, in *The Standard Edition of the Complete Psychological Works*, Vols IV and V. London: Hogarth Press, 1953, Vol. IV, p. 233.

2 S. Freud, *The Origins of Psychoanalysis: Letters to Wilhelm Fliess, Drafts and Notes: 1887–1904*. London: Imago, 1954, p. 283.

3 Freud, *The Interpretation of Dreams*, Vol. IV, pp. 82–3.

4 S. Freud, *An Autobiographical Study* (1925), in *The Standard Edition of the Complete Psychological Works*, Vol. XX. London: Hogarth Press, 1959, p. 45.

5 E. Hartmann, *The Nature and Functions of Dreaming*. New York: Oxford University Press, 2011, p. 108. See also C. S. Hall and V. J. Nordby, *The Individual and His Dreams*. New York: New American Library, 1972, p. 10. Michel Jouvet ('Le sommeil paradoxal: est-il le gardien de l'individuation psychologique ?', *Revue Canadienne de Psychologie*, 45/2 (1991): 148–68) added to this list the notion that the dream – which he does not distinguish from paradoxical sleep – could be the guardian of psychological individuation (in the sense of maintaining psychological heredity).

6 A. Revonsuo, 'The reinterpretation of dreams: an evolutionary hypothesis of the function of dreaming', *Behavioral and Brain Sciences*, 23 (2000), p. 898.

7 G. W. Domhoff ('The misinterpretation of dreams', *American Scientist*, 88/2 (2000): 175–8) points out that, in the USA, the percentage of characters in the form of animals declines from 40 to 50 per cent in young children to 4 to 6 per cent in adults.

8 E. Hartmann, 'Outline for a theory on the nature and functions of dreaming', *Dreaming*, 6/2 (1996), p. 166. René Allendy (*Rêves expliqués*. Paris: Gallimard, 1938, p. 36) already believed that dreams can de-dramatise the problematic situations of waking life by taking away the emotional burden attached to the problem: 'In this overturning of reality, the dream can take on a paradoxical, comical or absurd appearance. All these cases involve diminishing a fear by playing with the terrible object or ridiculing a daunting situation, or, conversely, of dignifying a reprehensible element, in order to retrieve your equilibrium and your place in an upside down world.'

9 Hall and Nordby, *The Individual and His Dreams*, p. 162.

10 This is what Durkheim was already pointing out in his philosophy course at the Lycée de Sens in 1883–4: 'Even when the activity of the mind is suspended, it continues to connect ideas unconsciously. In dreams, for example, ... during sleep ...' (*Durkheim's Philosophy Lectures: Notes from the Lycée de Sens Course, 1883–1884*. Cambridge: Cambridge University Press, 2004, p. 119).

11 J. Richard, *La Théorie des songes*. Paris: Frères Estienne, 1766, p. 57.

12 We find the same idea expressed in the work of Léon d'Hervey de Saint-Denys, based on his personal experience closely focused on oneiric activity: 'I

gradually arrived at the conviction that there can be no sleep without dreams, any more than there can be waking consciousness without thoughts' (*Dreams and How to Guide them*. London: Duckworth, 1982, p. 20). The scholar turns to the metaphor of fire and of the circulation of the blood to emphasise the continual activity of thought: 'thought never ceases entirely, just as the blood never ceases to course in our veins' (ibid., p. 24).

13 E. Hartmann, *The Nature and Functions of Dreaming*, pp. 95–6.
14 A. Charma, *Du sommeil*. Paris: Hachette, 1851, p. 29. In 1827, Théodore Jouffroy also asserted that the mind is never completely at rest. It simply changes its form of expression when it goes from waking situations, where the concentration and attention are sometimes very intensely required, to sleep, during which it abandons itself to the association of images: 'This is in fact its way of resting; it has no other. What fatigues it is not activity: activity is its essence, for the absence of activity would not be rest, but death; what fatigues it is directing its activity, the concentration of its faculties on one subject' ('Du sommeil', in *Mélanges philosophiques*. Paris: Paulin, [1827] 1833, p. 341).
15 P. Radestock, *Schalf und Traum: eine physiologisch-psychologische Untersuchung*. Leipzig, 1879, cited by Joseph Delbœuf, *Le Sommeil et les rêves, considérés principalement dans leurs rapports avec les théories de la certitude et de la mémoire*. Paris: Félix Alcan, 1885.
16 S. Dehaene, *Consciousness and the Brain: Deciphering How the Brain Codes Our Thoughts*. New York: Penguin, 2014, p. 14. Dehaene clarifies this point: 'Whatever the neurological explanation, sleep is clearly a period of boiling unconscious activity that supports much memory consolidation and insight' (ibid., p. 85).
17 This view is shared by David Foulkes, who maintains that 'we are in error when we ask for, propose, or accept grandiose theories of the function of dreaming' (*Children's Dreaming and the Development of Consciousness*. Cambridge, MA: Harvard University Press, 1999, p. 140). See also G. W. Domhoff, 'Dreams have psychological meaning and cultural uses, but no known adaptive function', www2.ucsc.edu/dreams/Library/purpose.html.
18 J. Montangero, *Rêve et cognition*. Brussels: Mardaga, 1999, p. 234.

Conclusion 2

1 S. Freud, *A Difficulty in the Path of Psychoanalysis*, in S. Freud, *The Standard Edition of the Complete Psychological Works*, Vol. XVII. London: Hogarth Press, 1975, p. 142.
2 It should be pointed out here that the light forms of informal conversation are no less conventional that the highly regulated forms of communication in the context of school or the legal system, for example.
3 T. Hirsch, 'Présentation: psychologie collective et sociologie', in M. Halbwachs, *La Psychologie collective*. Paris: Champs classiques, 2015, pp. 7–42.
4 J.-A. Boiffard, P. Éluard and R. Vitrac, 'Préface', *La Révolution surréaliste*, no. 1 (1924), p. 1.
5 J. Duvignaud, F. Duvignaud and J.-P. Corbeau, *La Banque des rêves: essai d'anthropologie du rêveur contemporain*. Paris: Payot, 1979, p. 19.
6 'Perhaps, trapped as we are in the economic and social universe, we try through dreams to complete a constantly incomplete life. Perhaps this game

frees us from the determinisms in which power and ideologies confine us' (ibid., p. 259). Not only are determinisms not decided by 'power and ideologies', but oneiric activity in no way liberates us from determinisms. It is merely the continuation and the transposition of these.

7 Ibid., pp. 28–9 (emphasis added).

8 S. Freud, *Introductory Lectures on Psychoanalysis*, in *The Standard Edition of the Complete Psychological Works*, Vol. XV. London: Hogarth Press, 1963, p. 106.

9 S. Dehaene, 'Une science de la conscience: entretien', *Études*, no. 12 (2015), p. 49.

10 R. Bastide, *Sociologie et psychanalyse*. Paris: Presses universitaires de France, 1950, p. 59.

11 R. Linton, *The Cultural Background of Personality*. London: Routledge, 1999, p. 95.

12 Bastide, *Sociologie et psychanalyse*, p. 127.

Coda

1 This quickly becomes apparent when we read the reply, simultaneously firm, astute and detailed, made by Henri Poincaré (in *The Value of Science: Essential Writings of Henri Poincaré*. New York: Modern Library, 2001) in response to the scientific scepticism and the epistemological nominalism of a contemporary philosopher (Édouard Le Roy). If the physical and life sciences have swept aside these radically conventionalist and intuitionist visions, there are unfortunately still plenty of 'Le Roys' at the heart of the human and social sciences.

2 S. J. Gould, *Time's Arrow, Time's Cycle*. Cambridge, MA: Harvard University Press, 1987.

3 If the physical, cosmic and life sciences are subject to the constraints of empirical verification, they are not always in a position to be able to construct experimental situations in the laboratory (think, for example, of cosmology or climatology) but can 'simply' observe phenomena (or their traces), which are as unique or remarkable as social or historical facts.

References and Bibliography

Absi, Pascale, 'La vie rêvée d'une anthropologue . . . au lit avec Yuli', *Chimères*, no. 86 (2015): 45–54.

Absi, Pascale, and Douville, Olivier, 'Batailles nocturnes dans les maisons closes: l'univers onirique des prostituées de Bolivie', *Revue du MAUSS*, no. 37 (2011): 323–46.

Adler, Alfred, *The Neurotic Constitution*. London: Kegan Paul, 1921.

Adler Alfred, *Social Interest: Adler's Key to the Meaning of Life*. Oxford: Oneworld, [1933] 2009.

Allendy, René, *Les Rêves et leur interprétation psychanalytique*. Paris: Félix Alcan, 1926.

Allendy, René, *Rêves expliqués*. Paris: Gallimard, 1938.

Antrobus, John S., 'The dream as metaphor: an information-processing and learning model', *Journal of Mental Imagery*, 2 (1977): 327–38.

Anzieu, Didier, 'Table d'hôte', in S. Freud, *Sur le rêve*. Paris: Gallimard, 1988, pp. 9–37.

Arnulf, Isabelle, *Une fenêtre sur les rêves: neurologie et pathologies du sommeil*. Paris: Odile Jacob, 2014.

Aron, Adriane, 'The nightmare of Central American refugees', in D. Barrett (ed.), *Trauma and Dreams*. Cambridge, MA: Harvard University Press, 2001, pp. 140–7.

Artemidorus, *The Interpretation of Dreams: Oneirocritica*. Park Ridge, NJ: Noyes Press,.

Aserinsky, Eugene, and Kleitman, Nathaniel, 'Regularly occurring periods of eye motility and concomitant phenomena during sleep', *Science*, 118 (1953): 273–4.

Bachner, Joachim, Rafetseder Peter, Walz, Benedikt, and Schredl, Michael, 'The effects of dream socialization in childhood on dream recall frequency and the attitude towards dreams in adulthood: a retrospective study', *International Journal of Dream Research*, 5 (2012): 102–7.

Bakhtin, Mikhaïl, *Esthétique de la création verbale*. Paris: Gallimard, 1984; part trans. in *Speech Genres and Other Late Essays*. Austin: University of Texas Press, 2010.

Bakhtin, Mikhaïl, *Esthétique de théorie du roman*. Paris: Gallimard, 1978.

Bakhtin, Mikhaïl, *Freudianisme*. Lausanne: L'Âge d'homme, 1980.

Barras, Vincent, 'Le rêve des médicines antiques', in J. Carroy and J. Lancel (eds),

Clés des songes et sciences des rêves: de l'Antiquité à Freud. Paris: Les Belles Lettres, 2016.

Barrett, Deirdre (ed.), *Trauma and Dreams*. Cambridge, MA: Harvard University Press, 2001.

Barthes, Roland, 'The two criticisms', in *Critical Essays*. Evanston, IL: Northwestern University Press, 1972, pp. 249–54.

Bastide, Roger, *Le Rêve, la transe et la folie*. Paris: Seuil, 2003.

Bastide, Roger, *Sociologie et psychanalyse*. Paris: Presses universitaires de France, 1950.

Bauer-Motti, Fanny, 'Les Rêves et leur interprétation: systèmes interprétatifs culturels et interprétation psychanalytique', PhD thesis, Strasbourg University, 2015.

Bell, Alan P., and Hall, Calvin S., *The Personality of a Child Molester: An Analysis of Dreams*. Chicago: Aldine, 1971.

Beradt, Charlotte, *The Third Reich of Dreams: The Nightmares of a Nation, 1933–1939*. Wellingborough: Aquarian Press, [1966] 1985.

Bergson, Henri, *Matter and Memory*. London: Swan Sonnenschein, 1911.

Bernstein, Basil, *Class, Codes and Control: Theoretical Studies towards a Sociology of Language*. London: Routledge, 2003.

Besson, Gisèle, and Schmitt, Jean-Claude (eds), *Rêver de soi: les songes autobiographiques au Moyen Âge*. Toulouse: Anacharsis, 2017.

Binswanger, Ludwig, *Rêve et existence*. Paris: Vrin, 2012.

Binswanger, Ludwig, and Foucault, Michel, *Dream and Existence*. Seattle: Review of Existential Psychology and Psychiatry, 1986.

Blagrove Mark, et al., 'A replication of the 5–7 day dream-lag effect with comparison of dreams to future events as control for baseline matching', *Consciousness and Cognition*, 20 (2011): 384–91.

Blagrove, Mark, et al., 'Assessing the dream-lag effect for REM and NREM stage 2 dreams', *PLoS ONE*, 6/10 (2011), http://dx.doi.org/10.1371/journal.pone.0026708.

Bléandonu, Gérard, *What Do Children Dream?* London: Free Association Books, 2006.

Boiffard, Jacques-André, Éluard, Paul, and Vitrac, Roger, 'Préface', *La Révolution surréaliste*, no. 1 (1924): 1–2.

Bonaparte, Marie, Freud, Anna, and Kris, Ernst, 'Introduction', in S. Freud, *The Origins of Psychoanalysis: Letters to Wilhelm Fliess, Drafts and Notes 1887–1902*. London: Imago, 1954.

Borel, Paul, 'Les idées de grandeur dans le rêve', *Journal de psychologie normale et pathologique*, no. 5 (1914): 400–12.

Bourdieu, Pierre, 'Censorship and the imposition of form', in *Language and Symbolic Power*. Cambridge: Polity, 1991, pp. 137–60.

Bourdieu, Pierre, *Habitus and Field*, Vol. 2 of *General Sociology: Lectures at the Collège de France, 1982–83*, trans. Peter Collier. Cambridge: Polity, 2019.

Bourdieu, Pierre, *Outline of a Theory of Practice*. Cambridge: Cambridge University Press, 2013.

Bourdieu, Pierre, *Classification Struggles*, Vol. 1 of *General Sociology: Lectures at the Collège de France, 1981–82*. Cambridge: Polity, 2019.

Bourdieu, Pierre, *Sociology in Question*. Thousand Oaks, CA: Sage, 1995.

Bourdieu, Pierre (ed.), *The Weight of the World: Social Suffering in Contemporary Society*. Cambridge: Polity, 1999.

Bourguignon, Erika E., 'Dreams and dream interpretation in Haiti', *American Anthropologist*, 56/2, Pt 1 (1954): 262–8.

Bouveresse, Jacques, *Le Mythe de l'intériorité: expérience, signification et langage privé chez Wittgenstein*. Paris: Minuit, 1987.

Bowlby, John, *A Secure Base: Clinical Applications of Attachment Theory*. London: Routledge, 2005.

Breton, André, 'Manifesto of Surrealism', 1924, www.tcf.ua.edu/Classes/Jbutler/T340/SurManifesto/ManifestoOfSurrealism.htm.

Breton, André, *Trajectoire du rêve*. Paris: GLM, 1938.

Bruner, Jérôme S., *Culture et modes de pensée: l'esprit humain dans ses œuvres*. Paris: Retz, 2000.

Bruner, Jérôme S., *Le Développement de l'enfant: savoir faire, savoir dire*. 3rd edn, Paris: Presses universitaires de France, 1991.

Bruner, Jérôme S., *Pourquoi nous racontons-nous des histoires?* Paris: Pocket, 2005.

Bulkeley, Kelly, and Domhoff, G. William, 'Detecting meaning in dream reports: an extension of a word search approach', *Dreaming*, 20/2 (2010): 77–95.

Burke, Peter, 'The cultural history of dreams', in *Varieties of Cultural History*. Cambridge: Polity, 1997, pp. 23–42.

Cabanis, Pierre, *Rapports du physique et du moral de l'homme*. Geneva: Slatkine, [1802] 1980.

Calkins, Mary Whiton, 'Statistics of dreams', *American Journal of Psychology*, 5/3 (1893) 311–43.

Carroy, Jacqueline, *Nuits savantes: une histoire des rêves (1800–1945)*. Paris: EHESS, 2012.

Carroy, Jacqueline, 'Observer, raconter ou ressusciter les rêves ? "Maury guillotiné" en question', *Communications*, no. 84 (2009): 137–49.

Carroy, Jacqueline, 'Les Réveils de Gabriel Tarde: science des rêves et autofictions', in G. Tarde, *Sur le sommeil: ou plutôt sur les rêves*. Lausanne: BHMS, 2009, pp. 1–44.

Carroy, Jacqueline, and Lancel, Juliette (eds), *Clés des songes et sciences des rêves: de l'Antiquité à Freud*. Paris: Les Belles Lettres, 2016.

Cartwright, Rosalind, 'Review of Freud's *The Interpretation of Dreams*', *Dreaming*, 4/1 (1994): 74–6.

Castel, Pierre-Henri, 'Introduction', in *L'Interprétation du rêve de Freud*. Paris: Presses universitaires de France, 1998.

Caughey, John L., *Imaginary Social Words: A Cultural Approach*. Lincoln: University of Nebraska Press, 1984.

Charbonnier, Georges, Bourguignon, André, Pontalis, Jean-Bertrand, and Belaval, Yvon, 'Sciences et techniques, le rêve', *Les matinées de France Culture*, 30 December 1966.

Charma, Antoine, *Du sommeil*. Paris: Hachette, 1851.

Charuty, Giordana, 'Destins anthropologiques du rêve', *Terrain*, no. 26 (1996): 5–18.

Cifali, Mireille, 'La Belle au Bois-Dormant en terre romande', *Le Coq-héron*, no. 218 (2014): 30–7.

Cognasse des Jardins, Claude-Jean, *Essai sur les songes*. Montpellier: Imprimerie Jean Martel Aîné, 1801.

Cohn, Dorrit, *Transparent Minds: Narrative Modes for Presenting Consciousness in Fiction*. Princeton, NJ: Princeton University Press, 1978.

Colin, Patrick, 'Entre interprétation et explicitation: le rêve chez Medard BOSS', *Cahiers de Gestalt-thérapie*, no. 102 (2001): 169–76.

Crespin, Ludwig, 'Redécouvrir la conscience par le rêve: le débat entre théories cognitives et non cognitives de la conscience à l'épreuve de la recherche sur le rêve', PhD thesis, Université Blaise Pascal, Clermont-Ferrand, 2016.

D'Andrade, Roy G., 'Anthropological studies of dreams', in F. L. K. Hsu (ed.), *Psychological Anthropology: Approaches to Culture and Personality*. Homewood, IL: Dorsey Press, 1961, pp. 296–332.

Darwin, Charles, *The Expression of the Emotions in Man and Animals*. London: Penguin [1872], 2009.

Dastur, Françoise, 'Preface', in L. Binswanger, *Rêve et existence*. Paris: Vrin, 2012, pp. 9–31.

De Gracia, Donald J.,'Paradigms of consciousness during sleep', Center for Molecular Medicine and Genetics, Wayne State University, Detroit, http://flor ence.ghibellini.free.fr/revelucidea/dondega.html.

Dehaene, Stanislas, *Consciousness and the Brain: Deciphering How the Brain Codes Our Thoughts*. New York: Penguin, 2014.

Dehaene, Stanislas, 'Une science de la conscience: entretien', *Études*, no. 12 (2015): 41–52.

Dehaene, Stanislas, and Naccache, Lionel, 'Towards a cognitive neuroscience of consciousness: basic evidence and a workspace framework', *Cognition*, 79/1–2 (2001): 1–37.

Dejours, Christophe, *Souffrance en France: la banalisation de l'injustice sociale*. Paris: Seuil, 1998.

Delacroix, Henri, 'Sur la structure logique du rêve', *Revue de métaphysique et de morale* (1904): 921–34.

Delage, Yves, 'Essai sur la théorie du rêve', *Revue scientifique*, 48 (1891–2): 40–8.

Delage, Yves, *Le Rêve: étude psychologique, philosophique et littéraire*. Paris: Presses universitaires de France, 1924.

Delbœuf, Joseph, *Le Sommeil et les rêves, considérés principalement dans leurs rapports avec les théories de la certitude et de la mémoire*. Paris: Félix Alcan, 1885.

Dement, William, and Kleitman, Nathaniel, 'The relation of eye movements during sleep to dream activity: an objective method for the study of dreaming', *Journal of Experimental Psychology*, 53 (1957): 339–46.

Devereux, Georges, *Reality and Dream: Psychotherapy of a Plains Indian*. New York: New York University Press, 1969.

Diatkine, René, 'Rêve, illusion et connaissance', *Revue française de psychanalyse*, 38/5–6 (1974): 779–820.

Domhoff, G. William, 'Content analysis explained: if we don't "interpret" dreams, what do we do?', https://dreams.ucsc.edu/Info/content_analysis.html.

Domhoff, G. William, 'Dreaming as embodied simulation: a widower's dreams of his deceased wife', *Dreaming*, 25/3 (2015): 232–56.

Domhoff, G. William, 'Dreams are embodied simulations that dramatize conceptions and concerns: the continuity hypothesis in empirical, theoretical, and historical context', *International Journal of Dream Research*, 4/2 (2011): 50–62.

Domhoff, G. William, 'Dreams have psychological meaning and cultural uses, but no known adaptive function', n.d., www2.ucsc.edu/dreams/Library/purpose. html.

Domhoff, G. William, *Finding Meaning in Dreams: A Quantitative Approach*. New York: Plenum Press, 1996.

Domhoff, G. William, 'The misinterpretation of dreams', *American* Scientist, 88/2 (2000): 175–8 [review of Freud's *The Interpretation of Dreams*].

Domhoff, G. William, 'New directions in the study of dream content using the Hall and Van de Castle coding system', *Dreaming*, 9/2–3 (1999): 115–37.

Domhoff, G. William, 'Refocusing the neurocognitive approach to dreams: a critique of the Hobson versus Solms debate', *Dreaming*, 15/1 (2005): 3–20.

Domhoff, G. William, 'Why did empirical dream researchers reject Freud? A critique of historical claims by Mark Solms', *Dreaming*, 14/1 (2004): 3–17.

Domhoff, G. William, and Schneider, Adam, 'Studying dream content using the archive and search engine on DreamBank.net', *Consciousness and Cognition*, 17/4 (2008): 1238–47.

Donnat, Olivier, *Les Pratiques culturelles des Français à l'ère numérique: enquête 2008*. Paris: La Découverte, 2009.

Dornes, Martin, *Psychanalyse et psychologie du premier âge*. Paris: Presses universitaires de France, 2002.

du Bouchet, Julien, 'Artémidore, homme de science', in J. Carroy and J. Lancel (eds), *Clés des songes et sciences des rêves: de l'Antiquité à Freud*. Paris: Les Belles Lettres, 2016.

Dumézil, Georges, *Mythe et épopée*, 3 vols. Paris: Gallimard, [1968–73] 1995.

Durkheim, Émile, *Durkheim's Philosophy Lectures: Notes from the Lycée de Sens Course, 1883–1884*. Cambridge: Cambridge University Press, 2014.

Durkheim, Émile, *The Elementary Forms of Religious Life*. Oxford: Oxford University Press, 2001.

Duvignaud, Jean, Duvignaud, Françoise, and Corbeau, Jean-Pierre, *La Banque des rêves: essai d'anthropologie du rêveur contemporain*. Paris: Payot, 1979.

Eggan, Dorothy, 'The manifest content of dreams: a challenge to social science', *American Anthropologist*, 54/4 (1952): 469–85.

Eggan, Dorothy, 'The significance of dreams for anthropological research', *American Anthropologist*, 51/2 (1949): 177–98.

Elias, Norbert, *Au-delà de Freud: les rapports entre sociologie et psychologie*. Paris: La Découverte, 2010.

Elias, Norbert, *Essays 1: On the Sociology of Knowledge and the Sciences*. Dublin: University College Dublin Press, 2009.

Elias, Norbert, *Mozart: Portrait of a Genius*. Cambridge: Polity, 1993.

Elias, Norbert, 'Sociology and psychiatry' (1969–72), in S. H. Foulkes and G. S. Prince (eds), *Psychiatry in a Changing Society*. Abingdon: Routledge, 2013, pp. 117–44.

Elias, Norbert, *The Symbol Theory*. Dublin: University College Dublin Press, 2011.

Elias, Norbert, *What is Sociology?* Dublin: University College Dublin Press, 1978.

Ellenberger, Henri F., *The Discovery of the Unconscious: The History and Evolution of Dynamic Psychiatry*. London: Fontana, 1994.

Encrevé, Pierre, 'Labov, linguistique, sociolinguistique', in W. Labov, *Sociolinguistique*. Paris: Minuit, 1976, pp. 9–35.

Epstein, Ari W., 'The waking event-dream interval', *American Journal of Psychiatry*, 142/1 (1985): 123–4.

Erlacher, Daniel, and Schredl, Michael, 'Dreams reflecting waking sport activities: a comparison of sport and psychology students', *International Journal of Sport Psychology*, 35 (2004): 301–8.

Fanon, Frantz, *Black Skin, White Masks*. London: Pluto Press, 1986.

Ferenczi, Sandor, 'The psychological analysis of dreams', *American Journal of Psychology*, 21/2 (1910): 309–28.

Fine, Gary Alan, and Fischer Leighton, Laura, 'Nocturnal omissions: steps toward a sociology of dreams', *Symbolic Interaction*, 16/2 (1993): 95–104.

Flournoy, Théodore, *Des Indes à la planète Mars: étude sur un cas de somnambulisme avec glossolalie*. Paris: Seuil, [1900] 1983.

Foucault, Marcel, *Le Rêve: études et observations*. Paris: Félix Alcan, 1906.

Foucault, Michel, 'Introduction' to L. Binswanger, *Dream and Existence*. Seattle: Review of Existential Psychology and Psychiatry, 1986.

Foulkes, David, *Children's Dreaming and the Development of Consciousness*. Cambridge, MA: Harvard University Press, 1999.

Foulkes, David, 'Dream reports from different stages of sleep', *Journal of Abnormal and Social Psychology*, 65/1 (1962): 14–25.

Foulkes, David, *Dreaming: A Cognitive-Psychological Analysis*. London: Routledge, 1985.

Foulkes, David, 'The *Interpretation of Dreams* and the scientific study of dreaming', *Dreaming*, 4/1 (1994): 82–5.

Foulkes, David, and Fleisher, Stephan, 'Mental activity in relaxed wakefulness', *Journal of Abnormal Psychology*, 84/1 (1975): 66–75.

Foulkes, David, and Scott, E., 'An above zero waking baseline for the incidence of momentarily hallucinatory mentation', *Sleep Research*, 2 (1973): 108.

French, Thomas Morton, 'The art and science of psychoanalysis', *Journal of the American Psychoanalytic Association*, 6 (1958): 197–214.

French, Thomas Morton, *Integration of Behavior*, Vol. 2: *The Integrative Process in Dreams*. Chicago: University of Chicago Press, 1954.

French, Thomas Morton, *Psychoanalytic Interpretations*. Chicago: Quadrangle Books, 1970.

French, Thomas Morton, and Fromm, Erika, *Dream Interpretation: A New Approach*. New York: Basic Books, 1964.

French, Thomas Morton, and Whitman, Roy M., 'A focal conflict view', in M. Kramer, R. M. Whitman, B. J. Baldridge, and P. H. Ornstein (eds), *Dream Psychology and the New Biology of Dreaming*. Springfield, IL: Charles C. Thomas, 1969, pp. 65–71.

Freud, Sigmund, *A Difficulty in the Path of Psychoanalysis*, in *The Standard Edition of the Complete Psychological Works*, Vol. XVII. London : Hogarth Press, 1975.

Freud, Sigmund, *A General Introduction to Psychoanalysis*. Ware: Wordsworth, 2012.

Freud, Sigmund, *An Autobiographical Study* (1925), in *The Standard Edition of the Complete Psychological Works*, Vol. XX. London: Hogarth Press, 1959.

Freud, Sigmund, *An Outline of Psychoanalysis* in *The Standard Edition of the Complete Psychological Works*, Vol. XXIII. London: Hogarth Press, 1964.

Freud, Sigmund, 'Associations of a four-year-old child', in *The Standard Edition of the Complete Psychological Works*, Vol. XVIII. London: Hogarth Press, 1955.

Freud, Sigmund, *Beyond the Pleasure Principle* (1920), in *The Standard Edition of the Complete Psychological Works*, Vol. XVIII. London: Hogarth Press, 1955.

Freud Sigmund, *Correspondance, 1873–1939*. Paris: Gallimard, 1979.

Freud, Sigmund, 'Creative writers and day-dreaming' (1908) in *The Standard Edition of the Complete Psychological Works*, Vol. IX. London: Hogarth Press, 1968.

Freud, Sigmund, *Dora: An Analysis of a Case of Hysteria*. New York: Simon & Schuster, 1997.

Freud, Sigmund, *Dream Psychology: Psychoanalysis for Beginners*. New York: James A. McCann, 1921.

Freud, Sigmund, *The Ego and the Id* (1923), in *The Standard Edition of the Complete Psychological Works*, Vol. XIX. London: Hogarth Press, 1961.

Freud, Sigmund, *Fragment of an Analysis of a Case of Hysteria* (1905), in *The Standard Edition of the Complete Psychological Works*, Vol. VII. London: Hogarth Press, 1975.

Freud, Sigmund, 'Further recommendations in the technique of psychoanalysis: remembering, repeating and working through', in *The Standard Edition of the Complete Psychological Works*, Vol. XII. London: Hogarth Press, 1958.

Freud, Sigmund, *Group Psychology and the Analysis of the Ego* (1921), in *The Standard Edition of the Complete Psychological Works*, Vol. XVIII. London: Hogarth Press, 1955.

Freud, Sigmund, *The History of the Psychoanalytic Movement*, in *The Standard Edition of the Complete Psychological Works*, Vol. XIV. London: Hogarth Press, 1957.

Freud, Sigmund, *The Interpretation of Dreams*, in *The Standard Edition of the Complete Psychological Works*, Vols IV and V. London: Hogarth Press, 1953.

Freud, Sigmund, *Introductory Lectures on Psychoanalysis*, in *The Standard Edition of the Complete Works*, Vol. XV. London: Hogarth Press, 1963.

Freud, Sigmund, *On Dreams* (1901), in *The Standard Edition of the Complete Psychological Works*, Vol. V. London: Hogarth Press, 1953.

Freud, Sigmund, *The Origins of Psychoanalysis: Letters to Wilhelm Fliess, Drafts and Notes: 1887–1904*. London: Imago, 1954.

Freud Sigmund, *Papers on Technique*, in *The Standard Edition of the Complete Psychological Works*, Vol. XII. London: Hogarth Press, 1958.

Freud, Sigmund, *Project for Scientific Psychology* (unfinished manuscript), in *The Standard Edition of the Complete Psychological Works*, Vol. I. London: Hogarth Press, 1966.

Freud, Sigmund, *Psycho-analytic Procedure*, in *The Standard Edition of the Complete Psychological Works*, Vol. VII. London: Hogarth Press, 1975.

Freud, Sigmund, *Some General Remarks on Hysterical Attacks*, in *The Standard Edition of the Complete Psychological Works*, Vol. IX. London: Hogarth Press, 1959.

Freud, Sigmund, *Studies on Hysteria* (1895), in *The Standard Edition of the Complete Psychological Works*, Vol. II. London: Hogarth Press, 1955.

Freud, Sigmund, and Bleuler, Eugen, *Lettres, 1904–1937*. Paris: Gallimard, 2016.

Freud, Sigmund, and Breuer, Joseph, *Studies on Hysteria*, in *The Standard Edition of the Complete Psychological Works*, Vol. II. London: Hogarth Press, 1955.

Fromm, Erich, *The Crisis of Psychoanalysis: Essays on Freud, Marx and Social Psychology*. London: Penguin, 1970.

Fromm, Erich, *The Forgotten Language: An Introduction to the Understanding of Dreams, Fairy Tales and Myths*. London: Victor Gollancz, 1952.

Fromm, Erich, *Greatness and Limitations of Freud's Thought*. London: Jonathan Cape, 1980.

Gantheret, François, 'Postface', in C. Beradt, *Rêver sous le IIIe Reich*. Paris: Payot, 2004, pp. 191–238.

Gay, Peter, *Freud: A Life for Our Time*. New York: W. W. Norton, 1998.

de la Genardière, Claude, 'D'un rêveur à l'autre', *Le Coq-héron*, no. 189 (2007): 113–21.

Glose, Bernard, 'Rêves, cauchemars et processus de pensée', *Journal de pédiatrie et de puériculture*, 5/5 (1992) : 283–7.

Goblot, Edmond, 'Le souvenir des rêves', *Revue philosophique de la France et de l'étranger*, 42 (1896): 288–90.

Goffman, Erving, *The Presentation of Self in Everyday Life*. London: Penguin, 1959.

Goodenough, D. R., et al., 'A comparison of "dreamers" and "nondreamers": eye movements, electroencephalograms, and the recall of dreams', *Journal of Abnormal and Social Psychology*, 59/3 (1959): 295–302.

Goody, Jack, *The Domestication of the Savage Mind*. Cambridge: Cambridge University Press, 1977.

Gould, Stephen Jay, *Time's Arrow, Time's Cycle*. Cambridge, MA: Harvard University Press, 1987.

Grothendieck, Alexandre, 'Allons-nous continuer la recherche scientifique?', lecture given at CERN, Geneva, 27 January 1972, https://archive.org/stream/Allons-nou sContinuerLaRechercheScientifique/Grothendieck_ARS_djvu.txt.

Grothendieck, Alexandre, *Récoltes et semailles: réflexions et témoignage sur un passé de mathématicien*. Montpellier: Université des Sciences et Techniques du Languedoc, 1985.

Guattari, Félix, *Soixante-cinq rêves de Franz Kafka*. Paris: Lignes, 2007.

Guénolé, Fabian, and Nicolas, Alain, 'Le rêve est un état hypnique de la conscience: pour en finir avec l'hypothèse de Goblot et ses avatars contemporains', *Neurophysiologie clinique*, 40 (2010): 193–9.

Habermas, Jürgen, *Knowledge and Human Interests*. Cambridge: Polity, 1987.

Halbwachs, Maurice, 'Dreams and memory images' and 'Language and memory', in *On Collective Memory*. Chicago: University of Chicago Press, [1925] 1992.

Halbwachs, Maurice, 'Individual psychology and collective psychology', *American Sociological Review*, 3/5 (1938): 615–23.

Halbwachs, Maurice, *La Psychologie collective*. Paris: Champs classiques, 2015; part trans. in *On Collective Memory*. New York : Harper & Row, 1980.

Halbwachs, Maurice, 'Le rêve et le langage inconscient dans le sommeil', *Journal de psychologie normale et pathologique*, 33 (1946): 11–64.

Halbwachs, Maurice, 'Le rêve et les images-souvenirs' et 'Le langage et la mémoire', in M. Halbwachs, *Les Cadres sociaux de la mémoire*. Paris: Albin Michel, [1925] 1976, pp. 1–39, 40–82.

Hall, Calvin S., *The Meaning of Dreams: Their Symbolism and Their Sexual Implications*. Lexington, KY: Iconoclassic Books, [1966] 2012.

Hall, Calvin S., 'The two provinces of dreams', *Dreaming*, 1/1 (1991): 91–3.

Hall, Calvin S., 'What people dream about', *Scientific American*, 184/5 (1951): 60–3.

Hall, Calvin S., and Lind, Richard E., *Dreams, Life, and Literature: A Study of Franz Kafka*. Chapel Hill: University of North California Press, 1970.

Hall, Calvin S., and Nordby, Vernon J., *The Individual and His Dreams*. New York: New American Library, 1972.

Hall, Calvin S., and Van de Castle, Robert L., *The Content Analysis of Dreams*. New York: Appleton-Century-Crofts, 1966.

Hall, Edward T., *The Dance of Life: The Other Dimension of Time*. New York: Doubleday, 1983.

Halton, Eugene, 'The reality of dreaming', *Theory, Culture & Society*, 9 (1992): 119–39.

Harlow, John, and Roll, Samuel, 'Frequency of day residue in dreams of young adults', *Perceptual and Motor Skills*, 74/3 (1992): 832–4.

Hartmann, Ernest, 'The day residue: time distribution of waking events', *Psychophysiology*, 5/2 (1968): 222.

Hartmann, Ernest, *The Nature and Functions of Dreaming*. New York: Oxford University Press, 2011.

Hartmann, Ernest, 'Outline for a theory on the nature and functions of dreaming', *Dreaming*, 6/2 (1996): 147–70.

Hartmann, Ernest, Kunzendorf, Robert, Rosen, Rachel, and Gazells, Grace Nancy, 'Contextualizing images in dreams and daydreams', *Dreaming*, 11/2 (2001): 97–104.

Hebbrecht, Marc, 'Les interprétations des rêves: de Freud à Bion', *Cahiers de psychologie clinique*, no. 42 (2014): 27–43.

Heidegger, Martin, *Being and Time*. London: HarperCollins, 2008.

Hennevin, Elizabeth, 'Le rêve vu par les neurosciences', *Champ psychosomatique*, no. 31 (2003): 69–79.

d'Hervey de Saint-Denys, Léon, *Dreams and How to Guide Them*. London: Duckworth, 1982; part translation of *Les Rêves et les moyens de les diriger*. Paris: FB, [1867] 2015.

Hilbert, Richard A., 'The anomalous foundations of dream telling: objective solipsism and the problem of meaning', *Human Studies*, 33/1 (2010): 41–64.

Hirsch, Thomas, 'Présentation: psychologie collective et sociologie', in M. Halbwachs, *La Psychologie collective*. Paris: Champs classiques, 2015, pp. 7–42.

Hobson, John Allan, *The Dreaming Brain*. New York: Basic Books, 1988.

Hobson, John Allan, 'The ghost of Sigmund Freud haunts Mark Solms's dream theory', *Behavioral and Brain Sciences*, 23 (2000): 951–2.

Hofstadter, Douglas, and Sander, Emmanuel, *Surfaces and Essences: Analogy as the Fuel and Fire of Thinking*. New York, Basic Books, 2013.

Hollan, Douglas, 'The influence of culture on the experience and interpretation of disturbing dreams', *Culture, Medicine and Psychiatry*, 33/2 (2009): 313–22.

Holt, David, *Eventful Responsibility: Fifty Years of Dreaming Remembered*. Oxford: Validthod Press, 1999.

Hovden, Jan Frederik, 'Return of the repressed: the social structure of dreams: contribution to a social oneirology', in J. F. Hovden and K. Knapskog (eds), *Hunting High and Low*. Oslo: Scandinavian Academic Press, 2012, pp. 137–57.

Hume, David, *An Enquiry Concerning Human Understanding*. Oxford: Oxford University Press, [1748] 2007.

Jakobson, Roman, 'Two aspects of language and two types of aphasic disturbances', in R. Jakobson, *On Language*. Cambridge MA: Harvard University Press, 1990.

Jouffroy, Théodore, 'Du sommeil', in *Mélanges philosophiques*. Paris: Paulin, [1827] 1833, pp. 318–43.

Joulain, Patrick, 'Rêve et neurosciences', *Cahiers jungiens de psychanalyse*, no. 138 (2013): 111–27.

Jouvet, Michel, *De la science et des rêves: mémoires d'un onirologue*. Paris: Odile Jacob, 2013.

Jouvet, Michel, *Le Grenier des rêves: essai d'onirologie diachronique*. Paris: Odile Jacob, 1997.

Jouvet, Michel, 'Mémoire et "cerveau dédoublé" au cours du rêve à propos de 2,525 souvenirs de rêve', *L'Année du Praticien*, 29/1 (1979): 27–32.

Jouvet, Michel, *The Paradox of Sleep: The Story of Dreaming*. Cambridge, MA: MIT Press, 1999.

Jouvet, Michel, *Le Sommeil, la conscience et l'éveil*. Paris: Odile Jacob, 2016.

Jouvet, Michel, 'Le sommeil paradoxal: est-il le gardien de l'individuation psychologique ?', *Revue Canadienne de Psychologie*, 45/2 (1991): 148–68.

Jung, Carl Gustav, *Psychology and Alchemy*. Abingdon: Routledge, 2010.

Kahn, David, et al., 'Dreaming and waking consciousness: a character recognition study', *Journal of Sleep Research*, 9 (2000): 317–25.

Kahn, David, et al., 'Emotion and cognition: feeling and character identification in dreaming', *Consciousness and Cognition*, 11/1 (2002): 34–50.

Kaivola-Bregenhøj, Annikki, 'Rêver: étude de folkloristique contemporaine', *Ethnologie française*, 33/2 (2003): 243–9.

Kardiner, Abram, and Lovesey, Lionel, *The Mark of Oppression: A Psychosocial Study of the American Negro*. New York: W. W. Norton, 1951.

Kilborne, Benjamin, 'Moroccan dream interpretation and culturally constituted defense mechanisms', *Ethos*, 9/4 (1981): 294–313.

Kilborne, Benjamin, 'Pattern, structure, and style in anthropological studies of dreams', *Ethos*, 9/2 (1981): 165–85.

Kilroe, Patricia A., 'The dream as text, the dream as narrative', *Dreaming*, 10/3 (2000): 125–37.

Kilroe, Patricia A., 'The dream pun: what is a play on words without words?', *Dreaming*, 10/4 (2000): 193–209.

Kilroe, Patricia A., 'Reflections on the study of dream speech', *Dreaming*, 24/1 (2016): 1–16.

Kilroe, Patricia A., 'Verbal aspects of dreaming: a preliminary classification', *Dreaming*, 11/3 (2001): 105–13.

Klein, Melanie, *The Psychoanalysis of Children*. London: Virago, 1989.

Kosslyn, Stephen M., *Image and Brain: The Resolution of the Imagery Debate*. Cambridge, MA: MIT Press, 1996.

Kuiken, Don, 'Interpretation in *The Interpretation of Dreams*', *Dreaming*, 4/1 (1994): 85–8.

Kunzendorf, Robert G., Hartmann, Ernest, Cohen, Rachel, and Cutler, Jennifer, 'Bizarreness of the dreams and daydreams reported by individuals with thin and thick boundaries', *Dreaming*, 7/4 (1997): 265–71.

Laberge, Stephen, *Exploring the World of Lucid Dreaming*. New York: Ballantine Books, 1991.

Lahire, Bernard, *La Culture des individus: dissonances culturelles et distinction de soi*. Paris: La Découverte, 2004.

Lahire, Bernard, *Culture écrite et inégalités scolaires: sociologie de l'échec scolaire' à l'école primaire*, Lyon: Presses universitaires de Lyon, 1993.

Lahire, Bernard, 'De la réflexivité quotidienne: journal personnel, autobiographie et autres écrits narratifs', *Sociologie et Société*, 40/2 (2008): 163–77 [special edn: 'L'archive personnelle des enquêtés, une source sociologique?'].

Lahire, Bernard, *L'Esprit sociologique*. Paris: La Découverte, 2005.

Lahire, Bernard, *Franz Kafka: éléments pour une théorie de la création littéraire*. Paris: La Découverte, 2010.

Lahire, Bernard, 'L'inégalité devant la culture écrite scolaire: le cas de l'"expression écrite" à l'école primaire', *Sociétés contemporaines*, no. 11 (1992): 171–91.

Lahire, Bernard, 'Logiques pratiques: le "faire" et le "dire sur le faire"', *Recherche et Formation*, no. 27 (1998): 15–28.

Lahire, Bernard, 'Masculin-féminin: l'écriture domestique', in D. Fabre (ed.), *Par écrit: ethnologie des écritures quotidiennes*. Paris: Maison des Sciences de l'Homme, 1997, pp. 145–61.

Lahire, Bernard, *Monde pluriel: penser l'unité des sciences sociales*. Paris: Seuil, 2012.

Lahire, Bernard, *The Plural Actor*. Cambridge: Polity, 2011.

Lahire, Bernard, *Portraits sociologiques: dispositions et variations individuelles*. Paris: Nathan, 2002.

Lahire, Bernard, 'Postface: Freud, Elias et la science de l'homme', in N. Elias, *Au-delà de Freud: les rapports entre sociologie et psychologie*. Paris: La Découverte, 2010, pp. 187–214.

Lahire, Bernard, 'Les pratiques langagières orales en situation scolaire des enfants de milieux populaires', *Revue Internationale de Pédagogie*, 37/4 (1991): 401–13.

Lahire, Bernard, *La Raison scolaire: école et pratiques d'écriture, entre savoir et pouvoir*. Rennes: Presses universitaires de Rennes, 2008.

Lahire, Bernard, *This is Not Just a Painting: An Inquiry into Art, Domination, Magic and the Sacred*. Cambridge: Polity, 2019.

Lakoff, George, 'How metaphor structures dreams: the theory of conceptual metaphor applied to dream analysis', *Dreaming*, 3/2 (1993): 77–98.

Lakoff, George, and Johnson, Mark, *Metaphors We Live By*. Chicago: University of Chicago Press, [1980] 2008.

Laplanche, Jean, *La Révolution copernicienne inachevée, 1967–1992*. Paris: Presses universitaires de France, 2008.

Laplanche, Jean, and Pontalis, Jean-Baptiste, *The Language of Psychoanalysis*. London: Karnac Books, 2006.

Le Goff, Jacques, 'Dreams in culture and collective psychology', in Le Goff, *Time, Work and Culture in the Middle Ages*. Chicago: University of Chicago Press, 1982.

Leavitt, John, 'L'analyse des rêves', *Gradhiva*, no. 2 (2005): 109–24.

Leibovici, Martine, 'Les fables politiques de Charlotte Beradt', in C. Beradt, *Rêver sous le IIIe Reich*. Paris: Payot, 2004, pp. 7–41.

Le Vine, Sarah, 'The dreams of young Gusii women: a content analysis', *Ethnology*, 21/1 (1982): 63–77.

Lévi-Strauss, Claude, *Structural Anthropology*. London: Hachette, [1958] 2008.

Lévy-Bruhl, Lucien, *The Notebooks on Primitive Mentality*. New York: Harper & Row, [1922] 1975.

Linton, Ralph, *The Cultural Background of Personality*. London: Routledge, 1999.

Lucretius, *On The Nature of Things*. Indianapolis: Hackett, 2001.

Macduffie, Katherine, and Mashour, George A., 'Dreams and the temporality of consciousness', *American Journal of Psychology*, 123/2 (2010): 189–97.

MacKenzie, Norman Ian, *Dreams and Dreaming*. New York: Vanguard, [1965] 1982.

Mageo, Jeannette, 'Dreaming and its discontents: U.S. cultural models in the theater of dreams', *Ethos*, 41/4 (2013): 387–410.

Mageo, Jeannette, 'Figurative dream analysis and U.S. traveling identities', *Ethos*, 34/4 (2006): 456–87.

Magnenat, Luc, *Freud*. Paris: Le Cavalier bleu, 2006.

Malcolm, Norman, 'Dreaming and skepticism', *Philosophical Review*, 65/1 (1956): 14–37.

Malinowski, Josie, and Horton, Caroline L., 'Evidence for the preferential incorporation of emotional waking-life experiences into dreams', *Dreaming*, 24/1 (2014): 18–31.

Marinelli, Lydia, and Mayer, Andreas, *Dreaming by the Book: Freud's Interpretation of Dreams and the History of the Psychoanalytic Movement*. New York: Other Press, 2003.

Marquardt, Clinton J. G., Bonato, Richard A., and Hoffmann, Robert F., 'An empirical investigation into the day-residue and dream-lag effects', *Dreaming*, 6/1 (1996): 57–65.

Mascret, Damien, 'Comment le cerveau se souvient-il de certains rêves?', *Le Figaro*, 9 April 2015, http://sante.lefigaro.fr/actualite/2015/04/09/23607-comment-cerveau-se-souvient-il-certains-reves.

Maury, Alfred, *Le Sommeil et les rêves: études psychologiques sur ces phénomènes et les divers états qui s'y rattachent*. Paris: Didier, [1861] 1865.

Mayer, Andreas, 'La *Traumdeutung*, clé des songes du vingtième siècle? Freud, Artémidore et les avatars de la symbolique onirique', in J. Carroy and J. Lancel (eds), *Clés des songes et sciences des rêves: de l'Antiquité à Freud*. Paris: Les Belles Lettres, 2016.

Merleau-Ponty, Maurice, *Institution and Passivity: Course Notes from the Collège de France (1954–1955)*. Evanston, IL: Northwestern University Press, 2010.

Meyer, Catherine (ed.), *Le Livre noir de la psychanalyse: vivre, penser et aller mieux sans Freud*. Paris: Arènes, 2005.

Meyerson, Ignace, 'Discontinuités et cheminements autonomes dans l'histoire de l'esprit' (1948), in *Écrits 1920–1983: pour une psychologie historique*. Paris: Presses universitaires de France, 1987, pp. 53–65.

Meyerson, Ignace, *Les Fonctions psychologiques et les œuvres*. Paris: Albin Michel, 1995.

Meyerson, Ignace, 'Problèmes d'histoire psychologique des œuvres: spécificités, variation, expérience' (1948), in *Écrits 1920–1983: pour une psychologie historique*. Paris: Presses universitaires de France, 1987, pp. 81–91.

Meyerson, Ignace, 'Remarques pour une théorie du rêve: observations sur le cauchemar' (1953), in *Écrits 1920–1983: pour une psychologie historique*. Paris: Presses universitaires de France, 1987, pp. 195–207.

Montangero, Jacques, *Comprendre ses rêves pour mieux se connaître*. Paris: Odile Jacob, 2007.

Montangero, Jacques, 'Dreams are narrative simulations of autobiographical episodes, not stories or scripts: a review', *Dreaming*, 22/3 (2012): 157–72.

Montangero, Jacques, *40 questions et réponses sur les rêves*. Paris: Odile Jacob, 2013.

Montangero, Jacques, *Rêve et cognition*. Brussels: Mardaga, 1999.

Movallali, Kéramat, 'Travail du rêve et neurophysiologie du sommeil', *Chimères*, no. 86 (2015): 115–26.

Le Mystère des rêves lucides, ZDF, 2013, www.les-docus.com/le-mystere-des-reves-lucides/ [documentary].

Naccache, Lionel, *Le Nouvel Inconscient: Freud, le Christophe Colomb des neurosciences*. Paris: Odile Jacob, 2009.

Nasio, Juan-David, *L'Inconscient, c'est la répétition*. Paris: Payot, 2012.

Nathan, Tobie, *La Nouvelle Interprétation des rêves*. Paris: Odile Jacob, 2013.

Nelson, Julius, 'A study of dreams', *American Journal of Psychology*, 1/2 (1888): 330–2.

Nicole, Pierre, *Traité de la grâce générale*, Vol. 1. Cologne: J. Fouillou, 1715.

Nielsen, Tore A., 'A review of mentation in REM and NREM sleep: "covert" REM sleep as a possible reconciliation of two opposing models', *Behavioral and Brain Sciences*, 23 (2000): 851–66.

Nielsen, Tore A., and Powell, Russell A., 'The day-residue and dream-lag effects: a literature review and limited replication of two temporal effects in dream formation', *Dreaming*, 2/2 (1992): 67–77.

Palombo, Stanley R., 'The dream and the memory cycle', *International Review of Psycho-Analysis*, 3/1 (1976): 65–83.

Panofsky, Erwin, *Gothic Architecture and Scholasticism*. New York: New American Library, 1976.

Parot, Françoise, 'De la neurophysiologie du sommeil paradoxal à la neuro-physiologie du rêve', *Sociétés & Représentations*, no. 23 (2007): 195–212.

Parot, Françoise, *L'Homme qui rêve*. Paris: Presses universitaires de France, 1995.

Passeron, Jean-Claude, *Sociological Reasoning: A Non-Popperian Space of Argumentation*. Oxford: Bardwell Press, 2013.

Passeron, Jean-Claude, and Revel, Jacques, 'Penser par cas: raisonner à partir de singularités', in Passeron and Revel, *Penser par cas*. Paris: EHESS, 2005, pp. 9–44.

Perrin, Michel, *Les Praticiens du rêve: un exemple de chamanisme*. Paris: Presses universitaires de France, 2011.

Peters, Larry G., 'The role of dreams in the life of a mentally retarded individual', *Ethos*, 11/1–2 (1983): 49–65.

Piaget, Jean, *Biology and Knowledge: An Essay on the Relations between Organic Regulations and Cognitive Processes*. Edinburgh: Edinburgh University Press, 1971.

Piaget, Jean, *The Language and Thought of the Child*. London: Routledge, 2002.

Piaget, Jean, *The Origins of Intelligence in Children*. London: Routledge, 1953.

Piaget, Jean, *Play, Dreams and Imitation in Childhood*. London: Routledge, [1978] 1999.

Poincaré, Henri, *The Value of Science: Essential Writings of Henri Poincaré*. New York: Modern Library, 2001.

Poirier, Sylvie, 'La mise en œuvre sociale du rêve: un exemple australien', *Anthropologie et Sociétés*, 18/2 (1994): 105–19.

Pollock, George H., 'Foreword', in Thomas M. French, *Psychoanalytic Interpretations*. Chicago: Quadrangle Books, 1970, pp. vii–xi.

Pons-Nicolas, Sylvie, 'Préface: Dora "la suçoteuse"', in S. Freud, *Dora: Fragment d'une analyse d'hystérie*. Paris: Payot & Rivages, 2010, pp. 7–39.

Powell, Russell A., Cheung, Jennifer S., Nielsen, Tore A., and Cervenka, Thomas M., 'Temporal delays in incorporation of events into dreams', *Perceptual and Motor Skills*, 81/1 (1995): 95–104.

Price-Williams, Douglass, 'Cultural perspectives on dreams and consciousness', *Anthropology of Consciousness*, 5/3 (1994): 13–16.

Price-Williams, Douglass, and Nakashima-Degarrod, Lydia, 'Dreaming as interaction', *Anthropology of Consciousness*, 7/2 (1996): 16–23.

Punamäki, Raija-Leena, Ali, Karzan Jelal, Ismahil, Kamaran Hassan, and Nuutinen, Johanna, 'Trauma, dreaming and psychological distress among Kurdish children', *Dreaming*, 15/3 (2005): 178–94.

Quinodoz, Jean-Michel, *Reading Freud: A Chronological Exploration of Freud's Writing*. London: Routledge, 2005.

Radcliffe-Brown, Alfred, *Structure and Function in Primitive Society*. London: Cohen & West, 1961.

Radestock, Paul, *Schlaf und Traum: eine physiologisch-psychologische Untersuchung*. Leipzig: 1879.

Rallo Romero, José, Ruiz de Bascones, Maria-Teresa, and Zamora de Pellicer, Carolina, 'Les rêves comme unité et continuité de la vie psychique', *Revue française de psychanalyse*, 38/5–6 (1974): 839–962.

Raulin, Anne, *Les Traces psychiques de la domination: essai sur Kardiner*. Lormont: Le Bord de l'eau, 2016

Reemtsma, Jan Philipp, 'Afterword', in T. W. Adorno, *Dream Notes*. Cambridge: Polity, 2007.

Reinert, Max, 'Les "mondes lexicaux" et leur "logique" à travers l'analyse statistique d'un corpus de récits de cauchemars', *Langage et société*, no. 66 (1993): 5–39.

Reinsel, R., et al., 'Bizarreness in dreams and waking fantasy', in J. S. Antrobus and M. Bertini (eds), *The Neuropsychology of Sleep and Dreaming*. Hillsdale, NJ: Erlbaum, pp. 157–84.

Renault, Emmanuel, *Social Suffering: Sociology, Psychology and Politics*. Lanham, MD: Rowman & Littlefield, 2017.

Reverdy, Pierre, *Le Livre de mon bord*. Paris: Mercure de France, 1948.

Revonsuo, Antti, 'The reinterpretation of dreams: an evolutionary hypothesis of the function of dreaming', *Behavioral and Brain Sciences*, 23 (2000): 877–901.

Richard, Jérôme, *La Théorie des songes*. Paris: Frères Estienne, 1766.

Robert, Marthe, *Les Puits de Babel*. Paris: Grasset, 1987.

Róheim, Géza, *The Gates of the Dream*. New York: International Universities Press, 1952.

Roland, Alan, 'The context and unique function of dreams in psychoanalytic therapy: clinical approach', *International Journal of Psycho-Analysis*, 52 (1971): 431–9.

Roubaud, Jacques, *Jacques Roubaud: rencontre avec Jean-François Puff*. Paris: Argol, 2008.

Roussy, Francine, et al., 'Does early-night REM dream content reliably reflect pre-sleep state of mind?', *Dreaming*, 6/2 (1996): 121–30.

Ruby, Perrine, 'À la source des rêves', Cycle: 'La science des rêves', *Cité des sciences et de l'industrie*, 15 March 2016, www.cite-sciences.fr/fr/ressources/conferences-en-ligne/saison-2015-2016/cycle-la-science-des-reves/.

Ruby, Perrine, 'Contrôler ses rêves, c'est possible . . . mais difficile: mode d'emploi', *Atlantico*, 13 February 2015, www.atlantico.fr/decryptage/controler-reves-c-est-possible-mais-difficile-mode-emploi-perrine-ruby-2003021.html#s0TtL57lJTWaWqEL.99.

Sahel, Claude, 'Charlotte Beradt, *Rêver sous le IIIe Reich*', *Che vuoi?*, no. 19 (2003): 261–8.

Scherner, Karl Albert, *La Vie du rêve* [Das Leben des Traumes]. Paris: Théétète, [1861] 2003.

Schmitt, Jean-Claude, 'Les clés des songes au Moyen Âge', in J. Carroy and J. Lancel (eds), *Clés des songes et sciences des rêves: de l'Antiquité à Freud*. Paris: Les Belles Lettres, 2016, pp. 61–71.

Schmitt, Jean-Claude, 'Récits et images de rêves au Moyen Âge', *Ethnologie française*, 33/4 (2003): 553–63.

Schmitt, Jean-Claude, 'Le sujet et ses rêves', in Schmitt, *Le Corps, les rites, les rêves, le temps: essais d'anthropologie médiévale*. Paris: Gallimard, 2001.

Schneider, David D., and Lauriston, Sharp, *The Dream Life of a Primitive People: The Dreams of the Yir Yoront of Australia*. Washington, DC: American Anthropological Association, 1969.

Schorske, Carl E., 'Politique et parricide dans "L'interprétation des rêves" de Freud', *Annales: Économies, Sociétés, Civilisations*, 28/2 (1973): 309–28.

Schredl, Michael, 'Dream content analysis: basic principles', *International Journal of Dream Research*, 3/1 (2010): 65–73.

Schredl, Michael, 'Dream recall frequency in a representative German sample', *Perceptual and Motor Skills*, 106 (2008): 699–702.

Schredl, Michael, and Erlacher, Daniel, 'Relation between waking sport activities, reading, and dream content in sport students and psychology students', *Journal of Psychology: Interdisciplinary and Applied*, 142/3 (2008): 267–75.

Schredl, Michael, and Hofmann, Friedrich, 'Continuity between waking activities and dream activities', *Consciousness and Cognition*, 12/2 (2003): 298–308.

Schredl, Michael, Hoffmann, Leonie, Sommer, J. Ulrich, and Stuck, Boris A., 'Olfactory stimulation during sleep can reactivate odor-associated images', *Chemosensory Perception*, 7/3 (2014): 140–6.

Schrödinger, Erwin, *Nature and the Greeks and Science and Humanism*. Cambridge: Cambridge University Press, 1996.

Schröter, Michael, 'Bleuler et la psychanalyse: proximité et autonomie', in S. Freud and E. Bleuler, *Lettres: 1904–1937*. Paris: Gallimard, 2016, pp. 215–73.

Schubert, Carla C., and Punamäki, Raija-Leena, 'Posttraumatic nightmares of traumatized refugees: dream work integrating cultural values', *Dreaming*, 26/1 (2016): 10–28.

Schubert, Gotthilf Heinrich von, *La Symbolique des rêves* [Die Symbolik des Traumes]. Paris: Albin Michel, [1814] 1982.

Schütz, Alfred, 'Symbol, reality and society', in A. Schütz, *Collected Papers 1: The Problem of Social Reality*. The Hague: Martinus Nijhoff, 1982.

Schwartz, Sophie, 'Matière à rêver: exploration statistique et neuropsychologique des phénomènes oniriques au travers des textes et des images de rêves', thesis, University of Lausanne, 1999.

Scott, James, *Domination and the Arts of Resistance: Hidden Transcripts*. New Haven, CT: Yale University Press, 1990.

Sebag, Lucien, 'Analyse des rêves d'une Indienne guayaki', *Les Temps modernes*, 217 (1964): 2181–237; trans. in *Journal of Ethnographic Theory*, 7/2 (2017), www.journals.uchicago.edu/doi/10.14318/hau7.2.043.

Seked, Susan, and Abramovitch, Henry, 'Pregnant dreaming: search for a typology of a proposed dream genre', *Social Science & Medicine*, 34/12 (1992): 1405–11.

Singer, Jerome L., 'Experimental studies of ongoing conscious experience', in *Ciba Foundation Symposium* 174: *Experimental and Theoretical Studies of Consciousness*. New York: Wiley, 1993, pp. 100–22.

Singh, Simon, *Fermat's Last Theorem*. London: Fourth Estate, 1998.

Snyder, F., 'The phenomenology of dreaming', in L. Madow and L. Snow (eds), *The Psychodynamic Implications of the Physiological Studies on Dreams*. Springfield, IL: Charles C. Thomas, 1970, pp. 124–51.

Solms, Mark, 'Dreaming and REM sleep are controlled by different brain mechanisms', *Behavioral and Brain Sciences*, 23 (2000): 843–50.

Solms, Mark, and Turnbull, Oliver H., *The Brain and the Inner World: An Introduction to the Neuroscience of Subjective Experience*. New York: Other Press/Karnac Books, 2002.

Spinoza, Baruch, *Ethics*. Ware: Wordsworth, [1677] 2001, pp. 75–6.

Starker, Steven, 'Daydreaming styles and nocturnal dreaming', *Journal of Abnormal Psychology*, 83/1 (1974): 52–5.

Steiner, George, 'The historicity of dreams (two questions to Freud)', *Salmagundi*, no. 61 (1983): 6–21.

Stern, Daniel N., *The Interpersonal World of the Infant: A View from Psychoanalysis and Developmental Psychology*. New York: Karnac Books, 1998.

Stewart, Charles, *Dreaming and Historical Consciousness in Island Greece*. Chicago: University of Chicago Press, 2017.

Strauch, Inge, and Meier, Barbara, *In Search of Dreams: Results of Experimental Dream Research*. Albany: State University of New York Press, 1966.

Strauss, Anselm L., *Continual Permutations of Action*. New York: Aldine de Gruyter, 1993.

Stubbs, Michael, *Language, Schools and Classrooms*. Abingdon: Routledge, 2012.

Takahara, Madoka, Nittono, Hiroshi, and Hori, Tadao, 'Effect of voluntary attention on auditory processing during REM sleep', *Sleep*, 29/7 (2006): 975–82.

Tarde, Gabriel, *Sur le sommeil: ou plutôt sur les rêves*. Lausanne: BHMS, 2009.

Tassin, Jean-Pol, 'Le sommeil, la mémoire et le rêve', *Spirale*, no. 34 (2005): 31–9.

Tassin, Jean-Pol, and Tisseron, Serge, *100 mots du rêve*. Paris: Presses universitaires de France, 2014.

Tedlock, Barbara (ed.), *Dreaming: Anthropological and Psychological Interpretations*. Santa Fe: School of American Research Press, 1992.

Tedlock, Barbara, 'The new anthropology of dreaming', *Dreaming*, 1/2 (1991): 161–78.

Timotin, Andrei, 'Techniques d'interprétation dans les clés des songes byzantines', in J. Carroy and J. Lancel (eds), *Clés des songes et sciences des rêves: de l'Antiquité à Freud*. Paris: Les Belles Lettres, 2016, pp. 47–60.

Tournier, Michel, *Friday or the Other Island*. London: Penguin, 1984.

Tylor, Edward Burnett, *Primitive Culture: Researches into the Development of Mythology, Philosophy, Religion, Art and Custom*. London: John Murray, 1871.

Ullman, Montague, 'Do we need a sociology of dreams?', *Dream Appreciation Newsletter*, 4/2 (1999): 1–2.

Ullman, Montague, 'Dreaming as metaphor in motion', *Archives of General Psychiatry*, 21 (1969): 696–703.

Valentino, Nicola, 'Rêves des détenus de la prison spéciale de Palmi', *Chimères*, no. 86 (2015): 193–206.

Valéry, Paul, *Cahiers Paul Valéry*, 3: *Questions du rêve*. Paris: Gallimard, 1979.

Valli, Katja, Revonsuo, Antti, Pälkäs, Outi, and Punamäki, Raija-Leena, 'The effect of trauma on dream content: a field study of Palestinian children', *Dreaming*, 16/2 (2006): 63–87.

Valli, Katja, Strandholm, Thea, Sillanmäki, Lauri, and Revonsuo, Antti, 'Dreams are more negative than real life: implications for the function of dreaming', *Cognition and Emotion*, 22/5 (2008): 833–61.

Van de Castle, Robert L., 'A brief perspective on Calvin Hall: commentary on Hall's paper', *Dreaming*, 1/1 (1991): 99–102.

Vann, Barbara, and Alperstein, Neil, 'Dream sharing as social interaction', *Dreaming*, 10/2 (2000): 111–19.

Vendryes, Joseph, *Language: A Linguistic Introduction to History*. London: Routledge, 1996.

Vester, Heinz-Günter, 'Sex, sacredness and structure: contributions to the sociology of dreams', *Symbolic Interaction*, 16/2 (1993): 105–16.

Vogelsang, Lukas, Anold, Sena, Schormann, Jannik, Wübbelmann, Silja, and Schredl, Michael, 'The continuity between waking-life musical activities and music dreams', *Dreaming*, 26/2 (2016): 132–41.

Volosinov, V. N., *Freudianism: A Marxist Critique*. New York: Academic Press, 1976.

Vygotsky, Lev Semenovitch, *Thought and Language*. Cambridge, MA: MIT Press, 1986.

Wagner-Pacifici, Robin, and Bershady, Harold J., 'Portents or confessions: authoritative readings of a dream text, *Symbolic Interaction*, 16/2 (1993): 129–43.

Whitmer, Benjamin, *Pike*. Oakland, CA: PM Press, 2010.

Wittgenstein, Ludwig, *Lectures and Conversations on Aesthetics, Psychology and Religious Belief*. Berkeley: University of California Press, 2007.

Wittgenstein, Ludwig, *Philosophical Investigations*. Chichester: Wiley-Blackwell, 2009.

Wittgenstein, Ludwig, *Philosophical Remarks*. Oxford: Blackwell, 1975.

Wittgenstein, Ludwig, *Tractatus Logico-Philosophicus*. Abingdon: Routledge, 2014.

Wolf, Christa, *Ce qui reste*. Aix-en-Provence: Alinéa, 1990.

Wunder, Delores F., 'Dreams as empirical data: siblings' dreams and fantasies about their disabled sisters and brothers', *Symbolic Interaction*, 16/2 (1993): 117–27.

Zlotowicz, Michel, *Les Cauchemars de l'enfant*. Paris: Presses universitaires de France, 1978.

Zweig, Stefan, *The World of Yesterday*. London: Cassell, 1943.

Index

through analogy and contiguity
204, 214–17, 218, 237, 247
see also analogy; free association
Australia, Yir Yoront people 43
authority figures
conflicts with 120
dreams of 52–3, 230, 231
autobiographical nature of dreams 58
autobiographies 60
automatic writing 253, 260
avant-garde literature, inner language
in 202

babies
internalisation of regularities of
experience 113–15
and the unconscious 139–40
Bakhtin, Mikhail 195, 198
on censorship 143, 154–5
on forms of expression 257–8, 260–1
La Banque des rêves (Duvignaud et al.)
38–40
Barras, Vincent 17
Barthes, Roland 52
Bastide, Roger 38, 72, 74, 168, 302, 303
Bayesian (statistician) brain, and the
incorporated past 108–11, 114
Beaunis, Henri-Étienne 223
belief in the reality of the dream 128–9
Bell, Alan P. 40, 51
Beradt, Charlotte, study of dreams
under the Third Reich 37, 96–8
Bergson, Henri 30, 103
Berkeley, George 110
Bernstein, Basil 196
Bershady, Harold J. 43–4
Beyond the Pleasure Principle (Freud)
22, 84, 162
Binswanger, Ludwig 21, 234
biographical accounts of dreams
285–91
biography
knowing dreamers and
understanding their dreams
279–80
sociological 59, 60, 285–7

biological function of dreams 293–4
biologism in Freud 27, 73–6
Bleuler, Eugen 11, 22, 24–5, 27–8, 83,
85
Bonaparte, Marie 73–4
Borel, Paul 94, 268
boundaries between dreams and
realities 275
Bourdieu, Pierre 41, 90, 137, 219, 222,
264, 309
on contextual constraints 258–9
Habitus and Field 129
on moral and structural censorship
148, 149–52
Bourguignon, Erika E. 42, 43
the brain 8, 9, 35–6
and analogy in dreams 208
the Bayesian (statistician) brain
108–11, 114
cerebral activity and social context
256
cerebral constraints in sleep 192–3
and consciousness 134–5
deactivation of the frontal cortex 36
and the function of dreams 295,
296
interpreting practices 64
in sleep 259
and triggering events 187
and understanding dreams 279
see also neuroscience
Breton, André 278
Breuer, Joseph 11, 76, 82, 121, 130
Burke, Peter 36–7, 52–3, 72

Cabanis, Pierre Jean Georges 159
Calkins, Mary Whiton 40, 45–6
care, and the existential situation 166
cars in dreams 226–7
cause, non-consciousness of 133
censorship 4, 10, 13, 27, 67, 71, 141,
142–65
and analogy in dreams 209, 217
camouflage techniques in dreams
147–8
and the existential situation 175

Crespin, Ludwig 251, 270, 276
  aminergic demodulation 270
cultural beliefs about dreams 17, 18
cultural context of dreams 16
cultural history of dreams 37
cultural structuring of dreams 43
current circumstances 68
Curtiz, Michael, *Mystery of the Wax
  Museum* 235

Dac, Pierre 292
Darwin, Charles 243, 309
day residues
  in Freud 75, 76–7, 175, 181, 268–9,
    280
  triggering events 181–2, 183–7
daydreams 3, 60, 117–18, 221, 295,
    299
  analogy in 207
  and censorship 149, 152–3
  and children's games 267, 268
  and consciousness 132, 136
  as a form of expression 250, 251,
    252, 253, 254, 268–71
  and inner language 202
  and literature 264
  and sleep 193
  and triggering events 187
de Gracia, Donald J. 132
deferred effects, of triggering events
    187–8
Dehaene, Stanislas 109–10, 130, 132,
    301
Delacroix, Henri 117–18, 129
Delage, Yves 23, 85
  on censorship in dreams 159–60
  on condensation 243
  on repression in waking life 146–7
Delboeuf, Joseph 9, 106–7, 128–9
deliriums 3
Descartes, René 135, 188
  Treatise of Man 8
determinism 4, 300–1, 302–4
Devereux, Georges 43, 72
diaries 47, 60, 253, 295
  of waking life 184

disabled people, dreams of 269
discontinuity theory 254
displacement 10
  and analogy in dreams 209, 216–17
  and censorship 143, 145
  and Freud's wish-fulfilment 164
  and the unconscious 135
dispositionalist-conceptualist theory
    28–9, 57–61, 308–11
  and Freudian psychoanalysis 76, 77
  incorporated dispositions of the
    dreamer 4, 59, 60
  three major elements of 59–60
dispositions 3
  and censorship 151
  and conscious awareness 131
  and contextual constraints 258–9
  and the existential situation 167
  and forms of expression 254, 260,
    261–2, 264
  and the incorporated past 4, 101–2,
    104, 106, 107, 110–17, 120–1
  interpreting practices 305, 306,
    307–8
  and practical analogy 205–6
  in the process of dream production
    69
  and sociological biographies 285, 286
  and triggering events 180, 181–2
  see also incorporated past
diurnal life
  and analogies in dreams 209
  dreams linked to 27, 40, 59–60, 172
  and the lucidity of the dreamer 160
  see also day residues
Domhoff, G. William 45, 46, 48, 50,
    52, 72
  on the expressive continuum 251
domination
  censorship in relations of 148–9,
    149–52, 156
  dreams of 87, 88–100
  symbols in dreams 227, 230
Dornes, Martin 113–14, 122, 123
  on repression and the unconscious
    138–9